ADVANCED PRAISE FOR
FINANCE FOR NORMAL PEOPLE

editor of the *Journal of Wealth Management* and author of *Goals-Based Wealth Management*

"*Finance for Normal People* is a tour de force. Literally covering the field of Behavioral Finance from A to Z, this is a user friendly book that should be read and on the shelf of every serious financial advisor/manager and all serious investors." —**Harold Evensky**, Chairman at Evensky & Katz and Professor of Practice, Department of Personal Financial Planning, Texas Tech University

"A pioneer of behavioral finance, professor Statman is offering us a wonderful book which explores how people actually make financial decisions, what are the salient features of financial markets, and how people could improve their financial decision making." —**Gur Huberman**, Robert G. Kirby Professor of Behavioral Finance, Graduate School of Business, Columbia University

FINANCE FOR NORMAL PEOPLE

How Investors and Markets Behave

Meir Statman

Oxford University Press is a department of the University of Oxford. It furthers
the University's objective of excellence in research, scholarship, and education
by publishing worldwide. Oxford is a registered trade mark of Oxford University
Press in the UK and certain other countries.

Published in the United States of America by Oxford University Press
198 Madison Avenue, New York, NY 10016, United States of America.

Library of Congress Cataloging-in-Publication Data
Names: Statman, Meir, author.
Title: Finance for normal people : how investors and markets behave / Meir Statman.
Description: New York City : Oxford University Press, 2017.
Identifiers: LCCN 2016041676 | ISBN 9780190626471 (hardback)
Subjects: LCSH: Finance, Personal. | BISAC: BUSINESS & ECONOMICS / Budgeting. |
PSYCHOLOGY / Applied Psychology.
Classification: LCC HG179 .S8117 2017 | DDC 332.024—dc23
LC record available at https://lccn.loc.gov/2016041676

9 8 7 6 5 4 3 2 1

Printed by Edwards Brothers Malloy, United States of America

To Navah

CONTENTS

Finance for Normal People

Introduction: What is Behavioral Finance?

You are contemplating a gift to your beloved and wonder whether it should be a red rose or $10, the price of the rose. You are a rational man who knows a bit of finance, so here's your thinking: A rose has no utilitarian benefits—she cannot eat or drink it. And a rose is a waste. She'll toss it out after a few days, when the petals drop off.

Now, $10 is not a rose by any other name. Your beloved can put the $10 in her savings account, where it would grow to pay for nursing home expenses when she's old. And if she wants to spend the $10 now, what do you know of her preferences, or "utility function," as economists call it? Perhaps a bottle of vinegar would maximize her utility function?

We—normal people—know that this kind of thinking might be rational, but it is pretty stupid. Following this script would surely not make you *her* beloved. Normal people know that roses have no utilitarian benefits, but they have a lot of expressive and emotional benefits. A rose says, "I love you." A rose says, "I'm a thoughtful man—you'll do well to marry me." Imagine yourself instead at her doorstep on Valentine's Day, holding a $10 bill as your gift.

Well, you say, this is a nice story, but what does it have to do with finance? I say it has much relevance because stocks, bonds, and all other financial products and services are like roses, watches, cars, and restaurant meals—all providing utilitarian, expressive, and emotional benefits. We miss many insights into our financial behavior and the behavior of financial markets when we think of financial products and services as providing only utilitarian benefits.

Behavioral finance is finance for normal people, like you and me. Normal people are not irrational. Indeed, we are mostly intelligent and usually "normal-smart." We do not go out of our way to be ignorant, and we do not go out of our way to commit cognitive and emotional errors. Instead, we do so on our way to seeking and getting the utilitarian, expressive, and emotional benefits we want. Sometimes, however, we are "normal-foolish," misled by cognitive errors such as hindsight and overconfidence, and emotional errors such as exaggerated fear and unrealistic hope.

This book is about behavioral finance—finance for normal people and with normal people. It is about what we—normal consumers, savers, investors, and managers—want as we make financial choices, what we know, think, and feel about financial choices, how we behave, and how our behavior affects financial markets and is reflected in them.

This book is also about the transformation from a normal-ignorant stage to one of being normal-knowledgeable, learning the lessons of behavioral finance and applying them to reduce ignorance, gain knowledge, and increase the ratio of smart to foolish behavior on our way to seeking and getting what we want.

Behavioral finance presented here is a second-generation behavioral finance. The first generation, starting in the early 1980s, largely accepted standard finance's notion of people's wants as "rational" wants—restricted to the utilitarian benefits of high returns and low risk. That first generation commonly described people as "irrational"—succumbing to cognitive and emotional errors and misled on their way to their rational wants.

The second generation describes people as normal. It begins by acknowledging that the full range of people's normal wants and their benefits—utilitarian, expressive, and emotional—distinguishes normal wants from errors, and offers guidance on using shortcuts and avoiding errors on the way to satisfying normal wants. People's normal wants, even more than their cognitive and emotional shortcuts and errors, underlie answers to important questions of finance, including saving and spending, portfolio construction, asset pricing, and market efficiency. These topics are presented in this book.

We want more from our investments than the utilitarian benefits of wealth. We want the expressive and emotional benefits of hope for riches and freedom from the fear of poverty, nurturing our children and families, being true to our values, gaining high social status, playing games and winning, and more.

The expressive and emotional benefits of playing investment games and winning attract billionaire investment professionals, just as they attract amateur day traders and the rest of us. Listen to John Paulson of the

Paulson & Co. hedge fund, known for the billions he made on mortgage-backed securities in the 2008–2009 financial crisis. Paulson, like many of his peers, does not intend to retire anytime soon, even although his wealth vastly exceeds what he can spend in many lifetimes. "I'm still relatively young, you know, being 56," he said. "If you look at [George] Soros—he's 81, I think. [Warren] Buffett, he's 81. How old is [Carl] Icahn?"

Paulson is clear about investing as a game and candid about his wants for the expressive and emotional benefits of playing and winning. "Some people like playing chess, some like backgammon. This is like a game, and playing games is fun." And, he adds, "It's more fun when you win."[1]

We often hear that behavioral finance is nothing more than a collection of stories about irrational people misled by cognitive and emotional errors, that it lacks the unified structure of standard finance. Yet today's standard finance is no longer unified, because wide cracks have opened between its theory and the evidence. This book offers behavioral finance as a unified structure that incorporates parts of standard finance, replaces others, and includes bridges between theory, evidence, and practice.

Standard finance is built on five foundation blocks:

1. People are rational
2. People construct portfolios as described by mean-variance portfolio theory, whereby people's portfolio wants include only high expected returns and low risk
3. People save and spend as described by the standard life-cycle theory, whereby people find it easy to find and follow the right way to save and spend
4. Expected returns of investments are accounted for by standard asset pricing theory, whereby differences in expected returns are determined only by differences in risk
5. Markets are efficient, in the sense that prices equal values in them and in the sense that they are hard to beat

Behavioral finance offers an alternative foundation block for each of the five foundation blocks of standard finance, incorporating knowledge about people's wants and their cognitive and emotional shortcuts and errors. According to behavioral finance,

1. People are normal
2. People construct portfolios as described by behavioral portfolio theory, whereby people's portfolio wants extend beyond high expected returns and low risk, such as for social responsibility and social status

3. People save and spend as described by behavioral life-cycle theory, whereby impediments, such as weak self-control, make it difficult to find and follow the right way to save and spend
4. Expected returns of investments are accounted for by behavioral asset pricing theory, whereby differences in expected returns are determined by more than differences in risk, such as by levels of social responsibility and social status
5. Markets are not efficient in the sense that prices equal values in them, but they are efficient in the sense that they are hard to beat

Standard finance, also known as modern finance or modern portfolio theory, dates back to the late 1950s and early 1960s. Merton Miller and Franco Modigliani, who went on to win Nobel Prizes in economics, described investors as rational in 1961.[2] Eugene Fama, who also won a Nobel, described efficient markets in 1965.[3] In 1952[4] Harry Markowitz, another Nobelist, prescribed the initial form of mean-variance portfolios to investors who care only about portfolios' expected returns and risk, and in 1959[5] he prescribed these portfolios in a more detailed form. William Sharpe, still another Nobel winner, adopted Markowitz's *prescription* of mean-variance portfolios as if it were a *description* of actual investor choices, and in 1964 introduced the capital asset pricing theory (CAPM).[6] According to that theory, differences in expected returns are determined only by differences in risk.

Standard finance was preceded by what we might call *proto-behavioral finance* and followed, beginning in the early 1980s, by behavioral finance. Proto-behavioral finance was the "obese" era of finance. It acknowledged normal wants for utilitarian, expressive, and emotional benefits, and described normal behavior guided by cognitive and emotional shortcuts and derailed by cognitive and emotional errors. But proto-behavioral finance was essentially unstructured and unfit, often going straight from anecdotes to general conclusions.

Standard finance ruled in the "anorexic" era of finance. Proponents of standard finance were busy excluding questions from the domain of finance rather than answering them. Hersh Shefrin and I, early proponents of behavioral finance, argued in a 1984 article that investors' wants and cognitive and emotional shortcuts and errors affect their preferences for particular stocks.[7] Merton Miller, a founder of standard finance, responded in a 1986 article:

[S]tocks are usually more than just the abstract "bundles of return" of our economic models. Behind each holding may be a story of family business, family quarrels, legacies received, divorce settlements, and a host of other considerations almost totally irrelevant to our theories of portfolio selection. That we abstract from all these stories in building our models, is not because the stories are uninteresting but because they may be too interesting and thereby distract us from the pervasive market forces that should be our principal concern.[8]

Yet questions about the effects of family business, family quarrels, legacies, and divorce settlements are questions of finance. Underlying these questions are wants for utilitarian, expressive, and emotional benefits, instincts for taking cognitive and emotional shortcuts, and pitfalls of cognitive and emotional errors. We might splurge our parents' bequest money but feel compelled to preserve for our children money they labeled as a legacy. We might be reluctant to sell stocks and spend their proceeds, yet ready to spend dividends. Moreover, pervasive market forces are powered by our behavior. We cannot hope to understand these forces unless we understand that behavior.

Behavioral finance is still under construction today, as we strive for a "muscular and fit" finance. The concept describes the wants, shortcuts, and errors that affect the behavior of normal people and are reflected in financial markets. Behavioral finance includes explorations into our wants for expressive and emotional benefits of investments, beyond the utilitarian benefits of high profits, the shortcuts we employ and cognitive and emotional errors we commit on our way to our wants, how we construct our portfolios, why some investments tend to yield higher returns than others, and whether we can hope to beat the market. And behavioral finance includes lessons for people who strive to transform themselves from ignorant to knowledgeable and increase the ratio of smart to foolish behavior.

PART ONE

Behavioral People Are Normal People

CHAPTER 1

Normal People

The brains of "rational" people, as economists have portrayed them, are never full; they are immune to cognitive and emotional errors and able to process huge amounts of information quickly and correctly. The brains of normal people, however, are often full, like the brain of the student in the Far Side cartoon, by Gary Larson, who raises his hand and asks, "Mr. Osborne, may I be excused? My brain is full."

Merton Miller and Franco Modigliani described rational investors in their 1961 article about dividends.[1] Rational investors, they wrote, are investors who "always prefer more wealth to less and are indifferent as to whether a given increment to their wealth takes the form of cash payments or an increase in the market value of their holdings of shares." This is a good beginning of a description of the rational investors of standard finance.

The rational people of standard finance can be described more comprehensively as people who are immune to the entire range of making cognitive and emotional errors. Moreover, rational people separate their roles as investors from their roles as consumers. As investors, rational people care only about utilitarian benefits, mainly high returns and low risk. As consumers, rational people also care about expressive and emotional benefits.

Rational investors "always prefer more wealth to less." They are never willing to sacrifice the utilitarian benefits of high wealth for lower wealth accompanied by expressive and emotional benefits such as those of social responsibility or social status. And rational investors "are indifferent as to whether a given increment to their wealth takes the form of cash payments or an increase in the market value of their holdings of shares" (p. 412). They never commit "framing" errors that make a dollar of cash dividends seem larger than a dollar increase in the market value of their shares.

Rational people are also immune to cognitive and emotional errors beyond framing errors. Rational people never commit cognitive errors such as "hindsight" errors, which mislead them into concluding that they can see the future in foresight as clearly as they see the past in hindsight, and "confirmation" errors, which mislead them into looking for evidence confirming their views and overlooking disconfirming evidence. And rational people never commit emotional errors such as exaggerated fear and unrealistic hope.

Think of a rational person whose $50,000 wealth consists of 100 shares of company stock whose current share price is $500. She is immune to framing errors that make a dollar of company-paid cash dividends seem larger than a dollar increase in the market value of her shares. She is indifferent to whether she receives a 3 percent company-paid cash dividend, amounting to $1,500, or doesn't receive a dividend. This indifference is because, in the absence of taxes and transaction costs, the value of the shares can be expected to drop by 3 percent to $48,500 once the dividend has been paid, leaving her with the same $50,000 of wealth she would have had if the company did not pay a dividend.

Normal people, however, are not always indifferent to having wealth in the form of capital or equal wealth composed of capital and dividend. Framing wealth into distinct mental accounts, "buckets" of capital and "buckets" of dividends, helps normal people control their spending when self-control is too weak to withstand spending temptations. Normal people do so by following the rule "spend dividends, but don't dip into capital." Rational people have no use for such a rule, because they are immune to framing errors, knowing that an increment to their wealth in the form of dividends is identical to an increment in their wealth in the form of capital, and because perfect self-control protects them from spending temptations.

COGNITIVE AND EMOTIONAL SHORTCUTS AND ERRORS

Which restaurant should we choose for dinner tonight? We care about a range of benefits and costs when we choose a restaurant, including its meal price—high, medium, or low—its meal quality—say, one, three, or five stars—and its distance away—say, one, two, or six miles.

Rational people's brains are never "full." They are able to rank all restaurants by benefits and costs quickly and accurately, and choose the best.

But ranking all restaurants by the three sets of benefits and costs is complicated, and the brains of normal people are often full. We begin with a cognitive shortcut that simplifies the problem, for instance, by deleting consideration of stars and limiting distance to one mile and the price to medium. We might add an emotional shortcut, making Italian cuisine more appealing tonight than French or Japanese. We dine that evening at a good restaurant, even if not the best, a medium-priced Italian restaurant one mile away.

Good shortcuts take us close to the best choices, solutions, and answers. An Italian restaurant one and a half miles away might have been the best choice if we had not limited our search to restaurants within a mile. But the choice of an Italian restaurant one mile away comes close enough to our best choice.

Cognitive and emotional shortcuts turn into errors when they take us far from our best choices. Emotional shortcuts stirred by the fragrance of fresh cookies might induce us to buy a house they were baked in, while we ignore a shaky foundation and leaky roof. Cognitive shortcuts that simplify choices induce us to buy 100 shares when a stockbroker offers a choice of 100 or 200 shares, when we would have chosen to buy no shares if it were among the presented choices.

SYSTEM 1 AND SYSTEM 2

Intuition, reflected in cognitive and emotional shortcuts, leads us well in most of life. But reflection leads us better when intuition misleads. Psychologists Keith Stanovich and Richard West and Nobel Laureate psychologist Daniel Kahneman described two systems in our minds, System 1 and System 2.[2] System 1 is the intuitive "blink" system, automatic, fast, and effortless, whereas System 2 is the reflective "think" system, controlled, slow, and effortful.

We might begin with a System 1 intuitive claim or hypothesis, such as the claim that stocks of companies paying generous dividends yield higher returns than stocks of companies paying no dividends. But we subject that claim to the reflective System 2, examining the claim by the tools of science—logic and empirical evidence—in a controlled, slow, and effortful process (see Box 1.1).

Use of System 2 is easier when we have time to engage it, and it is most beneficial when the consequences of poor choices by System 1 are substantial. Choosing the fish entrée by our System 1 gut is a good cognitive and emotional shortcut when a waiter hovers over us and our tablemates are impatient. So is recoiling by System 1 instinct from a tossed rubber snake. But choosing to buy a house without use of System 2 thinking is an error, and so is a choice to forgo diversification in our portfolios.

Reflect on a question from the Cognitive Reflection Test (CRT).[3] "If it takes 5 machines 5 minutes to make 5 widgets, how long would it take 100 machines to make 100 widgets?" The intuitive answer, processed by System 1, is 100 minutes, but the reflective answer, processed by System 2, is 5 minutes.[4]

Rational people use the reflective System 2 whenever the intuitive System 1 misleads, whereas normal people regularly forgo reflection once they have found an answer by System 1. Yet normal people vary, standing at points along the range from ignorant to knowledgeable. Knowledgeable people have learned, imperfectly and with much effort, to use System 2 when System 1 misleads.

THREE KINDS OF KNOWLEDGE

We can divide knowledge in the context of finance into three kinds: financial-facts knowledge, human-behavior knowledge, and information knowledge. Financial-facts knowledge includes facts about financial markets; stocks, bonds, and other investments; and the benefits of diversification, the drawbacks of investment fees, and the difficulty of beating the market.

Human-behavior knowledge is about our wants, the cognitive and emotional shortcuts we take, and the errors we make. Human-behavior knowledge includes knowledge of wants such as for riches, social status, and adherence to values. It also includes knowledge of cognitive shortcuts and errors such as in framing, hindsight, and confirmation, and emotional shortcuts and errors such as in hope, fear, pride, and regret.

Information knowledge consists of three groups: exclusively available, narrowly available, and widely available information. We know exclusively available information also as private or inside information, and we know widely available information also as public information.

Exclusively available information is that available to one person, such as a company chief executive officer (CEO). Narrowly available information includes information available to two, three, or a few dozen executives of a company, analysts, or readers of publications geared to industry or technology specialists. Exclusively and narrowly available information includes corporate earnings before they are announced and become widely available, planned but unannounced future actions of the Federal Reserve Bank, and information of the kind possessed by skilled financial analysts, money managers, and people who are able to combine widely available information with narrowly available information into clear "mosaics" of information. I will use the metaphor of mosaics again in later chapters.

Widely available information is available to everyone. It includes information published prominently in major newspapers like *The Wall Street Journal* and *The New York Times*, widely read websites such as Bloomberg, and widely watched television programs on finance, such as broadcast by CNBC. Widely available information is *available* to everyone, but it does not imply that everyone actually knows that information.

There is no sharp line separating narrowly available information from widely available information. We can make finer gradations of information availability, distinguishing very narrowly available information, such as available only to company insiders, from information that is not as narrowly available, such as is also available to some analysts. And we can distinguish widely available information, such as in the business section of *The New York Times*, from very widely available information, such as on the front page of *The New York Times*.

FROM IGNORANT TO KNOWLEDGEABLE

Teachers of economics and finance guide students in the search and application of financial-facts, human-behavior, and information knowledge. They guide students to ignore "sunk costs" that have already been incurred and cannot be salvaged, even when cognitive and emotional errors prod them otherwise, and they apply sunk-cost lessons in life beyond investments. Professors of economics are likely to leave disappointing movies earlier than professors of biology or the humanities; the former acknowledge that it is best to ignore sunk time spent watching the early part of a bad movie, as that time cannot be salvaged, and not sink additional time that is salvageable only by leaving the theater.[5]

Experience can also be a good teacher. People learn the diversification benefits of international stocks in their portfolios.[6] The proportion of such stocks increase over the years in the portfolios of both older and younger people. Moreover, educated people possessing financial-facts knowledge allocate more of their portfolios to international stocks than do less-educated people.

Ignorant people have not learned to proceed beyond the intuitive System 1 even when it misleads. Moreover, these people often mistrust financial-facts knowledge. A survey asked economic experts and average Americans whether they agree with statements such as "it is hard to predict stock prices." Answers reveal that 100 percent of economic experts agreed, whereas only 55 percent of average Americans did. The mistrust of average Americans in financial-facts knowledge is evident in the finding that the proportion of those Americans who agreed that it is hard to predict stock prices declined from 55 percent to 42 percent when they were told that economic experts agreed with the statement.[7]

In fact, there is much evidence that it is difficult to forecast stock prices, qualifying that difficulty as a financial fact. Neither amateur investors nor writers of investment newsletters and Wall Street strategists are good at predicting stock prices. Indeed, predictions of above-average returns were generally followed by below-average returns, and predictions of below-average returns were generally followed by above-average returns.[8]

Still, while System 2 generally points us toward better answers than System 1, it does not always deliver us to sure and correct answers. Approximately 39 percent of economic experts agreed that CEOs are over-paid, but most other experts disagreed or were unsure. Approximately 95 percent of economic experts agreed that the North American Free Trade Agreement (NAFTA) increased economic welfare, but a few experts disagreed or were unsure. And the proportion of economic experts who agreed that the benefits of the US 2009 stimulus exceeded its costs was only slightly higher than the proportion of those who disagreed or were unsure.

We pay in money, time, and exertion, both physical and mental, when we transform ourselves from ignorant into knowledgeable in any activity, whether it concerns medicine, driving, or investments. And we pay in money, time, and exertion when we substitute the reflective System 2 for the intuitive System 1. Transformation is worthwhile when benefits exceed costs. It is generally worthwhile for Americans to pay the cost of transformation into knowledgeable drivers staying on the right side of the road. But it is not generally worthwhile for them to pay the cost of transformation into knowledgeable drivers keeping to the left side of the road, as in Great Britain, Australia, and South Africa. Still, it is worthwhile for Americans, Britons, Australians, and South Africans to transform themselves from ignorant into knowledgeable investors.

I was among the students transformed from ignorant to knowledgeable about dividends by Miller and Modigliani's article, "Dividend Policy, Growth, and the Valuation of Shares." I came to the article as ignorant, confusing frame and substance in the belief that dollars received in the form of company-paid dividends are different in substance, not only in frame, from dollars received from the sale of shares of stocks. Specifically, I thought that the two are different because dollars from company-paid dividends tend to be stable from year to year and therefore less risky than dollars from the sale of shares of stocks whose prices can fluctuate greatly day by day. Miller and Modigliani's exposition transformed me.

Approximately 59 percent of mortgage borrowers committed refinancing errors—52 percent chose mortgages with less than the best interest rates, 17 percent waited too long to refinance, and 10 percent committed both errors. Knowledgeable borrowers made smaller errors, refinancing at rates closer to optimal rates and waiting less time after mortgage rates were optimal. Moreover, borrowers transformed themselves from ignorant to knowledgeable as they learned from their refinancing errors, committing smaller errors on their second refinancing than on their first.[9]

Still, financial-facts knowledge is widely deficient. The Financial Industry Regulatory Authority (FINRA) found that only 37 percent of people have high financial literacy, meaning they could answer correctly 4 or more questions on a 5-question financial literacy quiz.[10] We constantly need to learn and check ourselves about what we know.

CONCLUSION

We use the term "rational" in everyday language as equivalent to "normal-smart." Financial economists, however, use the term more narrowly in their writings and models. Rational people want only utilitarian benefits from investments, mostly in the form of wealth, whereas normal people also want expressive and emotional benefits, such as from social responsibility and social status. Rational people are either immune to cognitive and emotional errors or able to overcome them easily. Normal people, however, are susceptible to cognitive and emotional errors, and not always able to overcome them.

Shortcuts are the intuitive "blink" System 1 in our normal minds, leading to good choices in most of life. But shortcuts turn into errors when they mislead us into poor choices. System 2, the reflective "think" system in our minds, leads to better choices when System 1 misleads. Still, we are not doomed to ignorance or to being misled by System 1. We can learn and transform ourselves from normal-ignorant to normal-knowledgeable. We have learned by System 2 that the earth is round, even though System 1 tells us that it is flat, and we can learn by System 2 that predicting stock prices is difficult, even if System 1 tells us that it is easy.

CHAPTER 2

Wants for Utilitarian, Expressive, and Emotional Benefits

We want three kinds of benefits—utilitarian, expressive, and emotional (see Box 2.1)—from all products and services, including financial products and services.[1] Utilitarian benefits are the answer to the question "what does something do for me and my pocketbook?" The utilitarian benefits of a car are in ferrying us from one place to another, and the utilitarian benefits of investments are in increasing our wealth.

Expressive benefits convey to us and to others our values, tastes, and social status. They answer the question "what does something say about me to others and myself?" An environmentally friendly Prius hybrid, like an environmental mutual fund, expresses environmental responsibility, whereas a stately Bentley, like a hedge fund, expresses high social status.

Emotional benefits are the answer to the question "how does something make me feel?" A Prius and socially responsible mutual funds make us feel virtuous, whereas a Bentley and hedge funds make us feel proud.

Diamonds are largely devoid of utilitarian benefits but they are laden with expressive and emotional benefits. People are more willing to pay premiums upward of 18 percent for a diamond that is a half-carat than for one that is slightly smaller and between 5 percent and 10 percent for a 1-carat diamond than for one that is slightly smaller. This preference is because prospective grooms convey their emotions and express their desirability as mates by the size of the diamond engagement rings they offer.[2]

The utilitarian benefits of two investments are identical when they yield an identical return, but the satisfaction they yield, reflecting expressive and emotional benefits, varies by the paths of that identical return. Investors

are most satisfied when the value of their investments falls at first and then
recovers, and they are least satisfied when the value of their investments follows the opposite path. This preference is true whether the identical return of
the two investments is positive or negative. Moreover, investor satisfaction
influences risk preferences, return beliefs, and ultimately trading decisions.[3]

Our wants include the utilitarian, expressive, and emotional benefits of
riches and protection from poverty, nurturing our children and families,
demonstrating competence, playing games and winning, staying true to our
values, enjoying the comfort of familiarity and the passion of patriotism,
gaining high social status, promoting fairness, paying no taxes, and more.

We face trade-offs among our wants, such as between the utilitarian
benefits of great wealth and the expressive and emotional benefits of
adherence to values. Trade-offs are evident in experiments in which some
people were induced to think that time is money by highlighting hourly
wages and their utilitarian benefits, whereas other people were not induced
to think so. People induced to think that time is money derived fewer emotional benefits from listening to pleasurable music than those not induced
to think so. They exhibited less patience and experienced less enjoyment.[4]

We also face conflicts between our wants and the wants of others. These
include conflicts between the wants for utilitarian, expressive, and emotional
benefits received by corporate managers and their shareholders, money
managers and their investors, and financial advisers and their clients.

WE WANT RICHES AND PROTECTION FROM POVERTY

Riches bring utilitarian, expressive, and emotional benefits, and so does
protection from poverty. An ad for an Internet brokerage firm in the stock-
market boom of the late 1990s illustrates our want for riches. "Someone's

going to win the lottery," it said, "just not you." It urged investors to trade stocks instead.[5]

An ad for an insurance company in the 2008 financial crisis illustrates our want for protection from poverty. "And you'll get guaranteed income. For life," says a financial adviser to a client. "Guaranteed," says the client. "I like the sound of that."[6]

Hope for riches urges us to invest our entire portfolio in stocks and lottery tickets. The Dickenson Report, part of the deliberations leading to the 1934 Securities Act, said, "It must always be recognized that the average man has an inherent instinct for gambling in some form or other. It has been recognized as a social evil, always inveighed against since early times. No method of combating it has ever been completely successful."[7]

Fear of poverty urges us to invest our entire portfolio in government bonds and hold tightly to Social Security. When President Franklin Roosevelt introduced Social Security he said the following:

> We can never insure one hundred percent of the population against one hundred percent of the hazards and vicissitudes of life, but we have tried to frame a law which will give some measure of protection to the average citizen and to his family against the loss of a job and against poverty ridden old age.[8]

We balance our two wants by dividing our money into layers of portfolio pyramids, some devoted to hope for riches and others to freedom from the fear of poverty. We place bonds and annuities paying guaranteed income in layers at the bottom of the pyramid, designed to free us from the fear of poverty, while we place stocks and lottery tickets in layers closer to the top of the pyramid, designed to give us hope of riches.

WE WANT TO NURTURE OUR CHILDREN AND FAMILIES

Parents have always invested in their children. A 1929 bank advertisement shows a father in an armchair with two little children playing with a toy train at his feet. "Invest today for their tomorrow," it says. "Good securities are among the surest and the least troublesome income producers you can possibly leave to your dependents."[9]

A more recent advertisement by a mutual fund company shows a father holding a sleeping child on his shoulder below a stock-market ticker tape showing the word "priorities" among tickers of stocks whose prices move up and down. It says, "Over times, our financial investments provide us opportunities to enjoy what we treasure most."[10]

Parents are especially concerned about investments in their children's education and helping them start households. A survey of employees of academic institutions found that 86 percent believe that it is important to provide for children's education, and 85 percent consider helping children start households. But only 60 percent consider it important to provide a bequest. Parents who plan to leave bequests to children spend less than those who do not plan to leave them, and they accumulate more savings.[11]

Parents want children to be financially independent when they turn into adults. Children want it as well. "I [began to think of myself as an adult] maybe when I was like 20," said one young woman. "And really, like, got out of my parents' house and started, like, living, I mean working to pay the bills."[12]

Yet financial independence is not easy to reach. Large numbers of American middle-class and upper-class sons and daughters receive financial assistance from their parents well into their 30s.[13] Financial contributions from parents to children between the ages of 18 and 34 average $2,200 per year, and many young adults receive financial support even when they are employed. One woman had $50,000 of debt when she graduated from college but found no more than a part-time job. Her parents pay $1,300 each month for a Manhattan apartment she shares with her fiancé. "I am really lucky to have their support," she said. "I know friends [whose] parents cut them off when they graduate and they flounder really hard for a while."[14]

WE WANT TO PLAY GAMES AND WIN

Trading can bring the utilitarian benefits of great wealth, but many are drawn to it by the expressive and emotional benefits of playing and winning. The caption of an ad by an online brokerage company says, "Trying to make money is only half the fun. No . . . that's pretty much it."[15] But the picture below the caption is all about fun, showing traders frolicking in a trading room.

Peter Millman, a day trader, spoke about the emotional benefits of trading and its addictive nature in a *New Yorker* magazine interview posted on YouTube: "I love what I do, and this is the job of my dreams. . . . The thing about really big days is that you could lose it all the next day. Is it adrenalin? Is it a drug? Is it addicting? Absolutely. . . . I mean, even if we go on vacation it's so hard to really get away. You're constantly looking. What am I missing? What's on CNBC? It's very addictive. Once you're in it's tough to get out. And if you get out you want to get back in."[16]

Motif Investing offers collections of investments with common themes—Pet Passion, Fighting Fat, or Rest in Peace—a collection of stocks of hospice and funeral-service companies. "The core Motif customers are likely to remain people who invest at least partly for the fun of it," wrote Bloomberg reporter Ben Steverman. He described an investor who tried Wealthfront, an online adviser that creates buy-and-hold diversified portfolios, but he "kind of got bored." With Motif, he said, "you get to buy things you actually care about." That investor doubled his small investment in the Bear China motif by correctly timing the Chinese stock market's collapse. But he put half his portfolio in the Solar Stock motif, which lost 33 percent.[17]

Traders prefer lottery-like stocks whose return distributions are skewed toward high returns, satisfying wants for the utilitarian, expressive, and emotional benefits of playing and winning. Stocks of over-the-counter companies are lottery-like stocks, and traders overpay for them as gamblers overpay for lottery tickets. Stocks of over-the-counter companies yielded a negative 40 percent average return, not much different from the average negative return of lottery tickets.[18]

We see the emotional benefits of playing and winning in functional magnetic resonance imaging (fMRI) studies of the brain. Reaction in the anterior insula portion of the brain was stronger when people considered asymmetric gambles than when they considered symmetric gambles with equal expected value and variance. Reaction in the nucleus accumbens (NAcc) portion of the brain was stronger when people considered positively skewed gambles—skewed toward high returns—than when they considered negatively skewed gambles—skewed toward low returns. Positively skewed gambles elicited more positive arousal and negatively skewed gambles elicited more negative arousal than symmetric gambles with equal expected value and variance. Differences in NAcc activity and arousal were reflected in differences in preferences for skewed gambles.[19]

WE WANT TO DEMONSTRATE OUR COMPETENCE

Isn't it silly to waste time solving a Sunday crossword puzzle? After all, you can find the solution to the puzzle in the same newspaper next Sunday. And isn't it silly to waste time and money in solving stock puzzles when evidence indicates that trading based on amateur stock solutions is more likely to bring losses than gains? Time and money devoted to solving puzzles imposes utilitarian costs, but some people derive expressive and emotional benefits from solving puzzles, as they demonstrate their competence to others and to themselves.

Consider a deck of twenty well-shuffled down-facing cards. You know that ten are black and ten are red. You win if you draw a red card. Now consider a second deck of twenty well-shuffled down-facing cards. You know that all twenty are either black or red. You win if you draw a red card. Which deck do you prefer to draw a card from?

Considerations of probabilities indicate that you would be indifferent about whether to draw a card from the first deck or the second. The probability of drawing a red card from the first deck is 50 percent and so is the probability from the second. Yet most of us are averse to drawing a card from the second all-black or all-red deck. We know this aversion as "ambiguity aversion."

Ambiguity aversion might arise from the expressive and emotional benefits we gain by demonstrating our competence to others and to ourselves. Psychologists Chip Heath and Amos Tversky wrote that the consequences of bets include not only monetary payoffs but also "psychic payoffs of satisfaction or embarrassment . . . from self-evaluation or from an evaluation by others."[20]

In one experiment they offered people a choice between two bets.

1. A stock is selected at random from *The Wall Street Journal*. You guess whether it will go up or down tomorrow. If you're right you win $5.
2. A stock is selected at random from *The Wall Street Journal*. You guess whether it went up or down yesterday. If you're right you win $5.

Two-thirds of people preferred the first bet, most likely because it does not place them at competence disadvantage relative to the experimenter, as neither they nor the experimenter knows the correct answer. The second bet, however, places them at a competence disadvantage relative to the experimenter, as the experimenter most likely knows the correct answer. This result is consistent with the finding that people prefer to guess the outcome of a die roll, sex of a child, or winner of a soccer game before the event rather than after. Guessing before the event is satisfactory if right and less uncomfortable if wrong.

Further evidence about the importance of demonstrating competence comes from its influence on trading frequency. Male investors and investors with larger portfolios or more education perceive themselves as competent, whereas female investors and investors with smaller portfolios or less education perceive themselves as less competent. Investors who perceive themselves as more competent demonstrate their competence by trading more frequently.[21]

WE WANT TO STAY TRUE TO OUR VALUES

An ad by a fund company specializing in socially responsible mutual funds highlighted the utilitarian, expressive, and emotional benefits of socially responsible investing and the trade-offs among them. A woman says, "Truth be told, I'm as financially ambitious as I'm socially conscious." The fund company answers, "We hear you. You want to do good. You also want to do well. That's why we manage . . . with our disciplined process for finding stocks with strong growth potential and avoiding those at risk from unethical business practices."[22]

A young investor illustrated his want for combing the benefits of doing good with those of doing well. He said, "I've made the decision to shift my investments to socially responsible vehicles, but I haven't yet made the actual shift. I brought it up with my father, who was in the financial services business, and with my financial adviser and my attorney, and the response from all three originally was that I am likely to generate lower returns. . . . In the past year, however, I did some research on my own, and I learned [that] . . . socially responsible investments did not earn lower returns. . . ."[23]

The conflicts between wants are starkly evident in the cases of Cerberus and Freedom Works. A gunman murdered twenty children and six adults at the Sandy Hook school in Newtown, Connecticut, in December 2012, a horrible carnage that increased the expressive and emotional stigma put on gun manufacturers. Cerberus, a private equity firm, owned Freedom Works, the manufacturer of AR-15, the rifle used by the Newtown gunman. The carnage and Cerberus's want for doing good prompted its decision on the day following the massacre to sell Freedom Works even though it had not identified any potential buyer.[24]

Cerberus tried to sell Freedom Works by auction but found no buyers at a price satisfying Cerberus investors not willing to sacrifice utilitarian benefits of doing well for the expressive and emotional benefits of doing good. Instead, Cerberus placed Freedom Works in a new entity, Remington Outdoors, allowing Cerberus investors who want the expressive and emotional benefits of doing good, such as public pension funds, to divest themselves of Remington Outdoors shares while allowing Cerberus investors who want to do well to keep their shares.[25]

Values vary, directing wants for particular utilitarian, expressive, and emotional benefits. The Ave Maria mutual funds and their investors follow the precepts of Catholicism, excluding shares of companies associated with contraception or abortion. The Amana mutual funds and their investors follow the precepts of Islam, excluding companies that pay interest or receive it. Yet other mutual funds and their investors exclude weapon manufacturers and companies that pollute the environment.

Changes in circumstances affect trade-offs between utilitarian, expressive, and emotional benefits. Circumstances changed in the 2008 financial crisis, when the market values of many houses sank "underwater," below their mortgage balances. Many homeowners had no choice but default, having no means to continue paying their mortgage amounts. Other homeowners had the means to continue paying, but some of them chose to cease paying in a "strategic default." Strategic defaults carry utilitarian benefits, as homeowners shed the financial burdens of their mortgages. But strategic defaults also impose expressive and emotional costs on homeowners who want to conform to values and social norms that frown on such defaults.

The financial crisis relaxed social norms against strategic defaults and reduced their expressive and emotional costs. Homeowners surrounded by other homeowners who defaulted strategically became more inclined to default. The financial crisis also weakened enforcement of social norms. Peers of defaulting homeowners could not distinguish easily strategic defaulters from defaulters lacking financial means, and were therefore reluctant to punish defaulting homeowners.[26]

WE WANT HIGH SOCIAL STATUS

Private banking brings utilitarian benefits in solutions to complex financial problems and expressive and emotional benefits in high social status. A bank ad shows a person in a chauffeured Rolls Royce and a caption that says, "Once you've earned exclusive service, there's no turning back."[27]

Status seeking can underlie ethical consumption, beyond adherence to values. One reader emphasized the quest for ethical consumption in a letter to the editor of *The Economist*: "Ethically minded consumers can best save the planet by avoiding meat, the process of which, such as providing food for livestock, uses energy and resources." But another reader emphasized the quest for high social status: "An important element motivating acolytes of the ethical-food movement is snob appeal. Now even something as prosaic as grocery shopping can display someone's financial and educational status."[28]

Movies are status investments, delivering expressive and emotional benefits and hope for utilitarian ones. Media Society, headed by Wade

Bradley, solicits wealthy people to invest a minimum of $150,000 in a slate of independent films. Investors share in the utilitarian benefits of profits, if any, and enjoy expressive and emotional benefits in patron trips to the Sundance Film Festival, Oscar parties, and visits to film sets. One investor, an executive at an engineering firm, visited the set of *Big Stone Gap* and met its stars. "That was absolutely a mind-blowing event to have somebody of Whoopi Goldberg's caliber thank us for helping make the film a reality."[29]

Paintings join movies in providing expressive and emotional benefits. Indeed, paintings and other collectibles are commonly described as "emotional assets," paying "emotional dividends." Collectibles provide low utilitarian price appreciation on average, especially when their high transaction costs are accounted for. But some people accept great expressive and emotional benefits as adequate compensation for meager utilitarian benefits.[30]

Investments in Silicon Valley start-ups combine high risk with high social status. Nancy Hua of Apptimize amassed about $2 million in seed investments from wealthy sources known as angel investors. She had to turn down other angel investors who wanted to join. "Seed investing is the status symbol of Silicon Valley," said Sam Altman, president of a start-up accelerator. "Most people don't want Ferraris, they want a winning seed investment."[31]

Angel Labs is a company arranging workshops for investors interested in angel investing. "For many of these investors, they want to be part of the process, to feel the pleasure of creating something new," said Recep Bildik, private market director at the Turkish Borsa Istanbul, which hosted a seventy-person event organized by Angel Labs. "That may be more valuable than the return they're expecting."[32]

Managers derive expressive and emotional benefits from high social status when they work for companies that enjoy public admiration. Boards of directors of such companies extract utilitarian concessions from managers in the form of lower pay. Total compensation is lower on average for CEOs heading companies ranked among America's most admired in *Fortune*'s surveys.[33]

WE WANT FAIRNESS

"Okay, kids, here's today's magic stock—we get big incentives on this one so get on the phones—we got a lot of stock to move," said a man in a commercial by an investment company protesting the unfair practices of investment companies of the type employing that man. "Tell your customers it's red hot ... just don't mention the fundamentals—they stink. . . . Let's put some lipstick on this pig. Get to work, people."[34]

We want fairness but differ about what we consider fair. Fairness can be regarded as a claim to rights, including the right to freedom from coercion and the right to equal power. The right to freedom from coercion is violated, for example, when thieves steal our property or when we are coerced to refrain from trading with willing traders, whether they possess inside information or not. The right to equal power is violated, for example, when income inequality is high, as when CEOs of corporations are paid many multiples of the wages of their employees, or when one trader has access to inside information but another does not.[35]

People disagree about rankings of fairness rights by ideology and self-interest. Consider the following vignette and question about the fairness of insider trading: Paul Bond is a lawyer at the Brown & Long law firm. Standing outside his office at Brown & Long, he overheard John Grand, another lawyer at the firm, talking with an associate about his work on a proposed purchase of the Pillow company by the Down company for $120 per share. Paul Bond had no role in the work on the proposed purchase of Pillow, and Brown & Long represented only Down, not Pillow. Paul Bond bought 1,000 shares of Pillow for $70 per share. Please rate Paul's behavior as

A. completely fair or acceptable
B. unfair or very unfair

Paul Bond in this vignette corresponds to James O'Hagan, who was found guilty by the US Supreme Court of insider trading. Justice Ruth Bader Ginsburg addressed fairness in the Court's decision as she stressed that "[a]n investor's informational disadvantage vis-à-vis a misappropriator with material, nonpublic information stems from contrivance, not luck; it is a disadvantage that cannot be overcome with research or skill."[36]

Justice Ginsburg combined two notions of fairness in her argument. First, insider trading is unfair because inside information is misappropriated—stolen—violating the right to freedom from coercion. Second, insider trading is unfair because insiders have power, in the form of an informational advantage that "cannot be overcome with research or skill," violating the right to equal power.

Notions of fairness vary by culture. Only 5 percent of professionals in the United States and the Netherlands judged Bond's behavior completely fair or acceptable, followed by Australia and Israel, where 16 percent similarly judged Bond's behavior. The numbers of professionals who judged Bond's behavior completely fair or acceptable in Tunisia, Italy, India, and Turkey were much higher. Knowledge of the law and perhaps lawyer identity inhibits insider trading. Insiders with law degrees earn lower returns when they buy stocks than insiders without such degrees. And insiders with law degrees trade less following Securities and Exchange Commission (SEC) enforcement activity.[37]

CEOs and other corporate executives are paid much more than typical employees, contributing to income inequality, but is their high pay unfair? One study sought to dispel the perception that CEOs' pay is unfair. It noted that CEOs are paid for performance and penalized for poor performance.[38] Another study, however, found that executives' stock and stock-option grants, salaries, and bonuses are rigid and resistant to reductions.[39]

Public perception of unfair executive compensation influences its level and structure. The negativity of press reports on CEO pay varied significantly during 1992–2008, and stock options were its most contentious part. Companies reduced option grants and increased less contentious types of pay such as salary after negative press reports, although overall pay did not change.[40] Some CEOs, aware of the perception that their high pay is unfair, work for a $1 annual salary. Yet the $1 salary is likely a ruse to deflect public outrage. CEOs with $1 salaries are paid as much as other CEOs, making up visible lost salary by less visible stock-based compensation and other benefits.[41]

WE WANT TO PAY NO TAXES

"[A tax shelter] is a deal done by very smart people who are pretending to be rather stupid," said tax lawyer David Hariton. "The really rich people figure out how to dodge taxes anyway," said President George W. Bush. And comedian Dave Barry summed it all up: "We'll try to cooperate fully with the IRS, because, as citizens, we feel a strong patriotic duty not to go to jail."[42]

Low taxes deliver utilitarian benefits—people who send less to the IRS keep more for themselves. But tax-saving strategies deliver expressive and emotional benefits in addition to utilitarian ones. We express ourselves as high-income investors, with social status as high as our tax brackets. We want to be smart while pretending to be stupid: this device is what it takes to avoid taxes. Indeed, people would sooner move to a country where they would save $4,000 in taxes than to one where they could save $5,000 in the cost of food.[43]

Circumstances changed when customer-owned companies whose shares are not traded on stock markets were converted into public companies whose shares are traded. The conversions introduced many to stock markets and highlighted wealth, increasing the desire to shield it from taxation by left-of-center parties. A 10 percent increase in stock-market participation was followed by a 1.4 percent to 3.2 percent increase in right-of-center vote share.[44]

Tax-minded top executives avoided payments by realizing capital gains before the tax hikes set by the American Taxpayer Relief Act of 2012 and the Health Care and Education Reconciliation Act of 2010. They avoided nearly $741 million in personal taxes and helped shareholders avoid nearly $700 million in taxes.[45] Tax avoidance increases utilitarian benefits, as people keep more of their earnings, but tax avoidance can also reduce utilitarian benefits. Companies that engage in tax avoidance pay higher interest rates on bank loans. Such companies also suffer more stringent loan terms.[46]

Some Americans use Swiss bank accounts to hide substantial amounts from the US taxman. Several banks loaded funds onto clients' untraceable debit cards. At other banks, clients who wanted to transfer cash used code phrases such as "can you download some tunes for us?" One bank allowed a client to convert Swiss francs into gold, which was then stored in a relative's safe-deposit box.[47]

Not all readers of an article about these tax practices were outraged. One wrote, "Tax cheating? I don't think so. I would rather say asset

---

Box 2.2 A LIST OF COMMON WANTS

We want riches and protection from poverty
We want to nurture our children and families
We want to play games and win
We want to enjoy familiarity and exhibit patriotism
We want to demonstrate our competence
We want to stay true to our values
We want high social status
We want fairness
We want to pay no taxes

protection." Another reader protested, "Are you really apologizing for those who evaded the tax man?" And yet another reader flashed anger in his retort: "Really, I love how we just accept that 47 percent of the population that pays ZERO tax gets a vote on much of MY paycheck I owe to keep them up."

See Box 2.2 for a list of common wants.

OUR WANTS VARY

We vary in our wants by personality traits such as conscientiousness, values such as protecting the environment, religion such as Islam, circumstances such as wealth, and culture, Asian-Americans or European-Americans, upper class or lower class.

Wants vary by social class. Upper-class men derive expressive and emotional benefits from do-it-yourself projects as an expression of their abilities as craftsmen and a therapeutic escape from knowledge work. Lower-class men derive expressive and emotional benefits from do-it-yourself projects as an expression of their identities as family handymen, distinct from the identities of their female partners.[48]

Wants vary by identities, such as professional identities. In an experiment, employees of a large international bank were asked to toss a coin 10 times and report the results online. Each winning toss could be worth $20. Employees were more dishonest when their professional identities as bankers were made prominent by asking questions about their professional work in the pre-experiment survey.[49]

Wants vary by culture. One woman joined a Web discussion about cultural differences between Asian-American and European-American families. Her boyfriend and his parents are Asian-Americans and she is European-American. She would never think of giving money to her parents unless they needed it. He would never think of accepting money from his parents unless he needed it.[50]

All people want the benefits of high social status, but status symbols vary by culture across countries. Status symbols among Chinese businesspeople include fancy cars and properties abroad. Rich young men in the Persian Gulf display high social status by owning lions, cheetahs, and other big cats. And Japanese executives earn high social status with a desk at a window with a nice view.[51]

Wants for high social status compelled Chinese investors to take much risk. Developed provinces in China experienced more income growth and accompanying growth in inequality than those in still undeveloped provinces between 1998 and 2009. Fiercer status competition in developed provinces led to greater demand for local stocks so as not to lag behind neighbors in status competitions.[52]

Wants vary by political leanings. Companies with Democratic culture are less likely to be the subject of environmental, labor, or civil rights–related litigation, consistent with core Democratic Party values of equal opportunity, humanitarianism, and protection of the environment. Companies with Republican culture are less likely to be the subject of litigation related to securities fraud and violation of intellectual property rights, consistent with core Republican Party values of self-reliance that support business, property rights, market discipline, and limited government regulation.[53]

And wants vary by religion. Default rates on Islamic loans are less than half the rates on conventional loans. Defaults on Islamic loans are especially low during Ramadan and where the share of votes for religious-political parties is high. This finding suggests that values rooted in religion play roles in loan defaults.[54]

All of an Indonesian bank's late-paying credit card customers receive a basic reminder to repay their debt one day after they miss a payment due date. In an experiment, some customers also received a text message that quotes an Islamic religious text stating that "non-repayment of debts by someone who is able to repay is an injustice." This message increased the share of customers meeting their minimum payments by nearly 20 percent. By contrast, a simple reminder or an Islamic quotation that is unrelated to debt repayment had no effect. Moreover, customers responded more strongly to moral appeals than to substantial financial incentives: receiving the religious message increases repayments by more than offering a cash rebate equivalent to 50 percent of the minimum repayment.[55]

OUR WANTS AS INVESTORS AND CONSUMERS

Rational investors are different from normal investors, whether ignorant or knowledgeable, in their willingness to separate their roles as investors from their roles as consumers. As investors they care only about wealth production. As consumers they care about all benefits of wealth consumption: utilitarian, expressive, and emotional. Standard finance focuses on production of wealth and its utilitarian benefits. It leaves exploration of the expressive and emotional benefits of wealth consumption to other disciplines, such as marketing and consumer behavior.

Separation of production of wealth from its consumption is possible at times, and so is separation of utilitarian costs and benefits from expressive and emotional ones. Sanford I. "Sandy" Weill produced much wealth as chief executive and chairman of Citigroup, enjoying its substantial utilitarian benefits and most likely its expressive and emotional benefits as well. More recently, Sandy Weill and Joan Weill, his wife, offered to trade the utilitarian benefits of $20 million of their wealth for the expressive and emotional benefits of attaching their name to a college—turning Paul Smith's College into Joan Weill–Paul Smith's College. The trade was scuttled, however, when a judge ruled that the college's name cannot be changed.[56]

More often, though, it is impossible to separate production of wealth from its consumption, and it is impossible to separate utilitarian costs and benefits from expressive and emotional ones. Absence of separation exposes trade-offs among utilitarian, expressive, and emotional benefits, evident in the exchange between Charlie Munger, vice chairman of Berkshire Hathaway, and Bill Ackman, who heads Pershing Square Capital Management, a hedge-fund sponsor.

Munger accused Ackman of trading the expressive and emotional benefits of morality for the utilitarian benefits of profits, describing Ackman's large holdings of Valeant shares as "deeply immoral." Valeant, a pharmaceutical company, has been accused of buying the rights to drugs with expired patents and boosting their prices substantially. Ackman shot back, describing Coca-Cola, one of the largest holdings in the Berkshire Hathaway portfolio, as a company that "has probably done more to create obesity and diabetes on a global basis than any other company in the world."[57]

One reader of the article about the spat between Munger and Ackman wrote in a online comment to the article, "If Ackman is so moral, he should care about all the scientists that were laid off because of this Allergan-activists-Valeant saga. So spare me the lesson, Mr. Ackman." Another wrote, "Morality is in the eye of the beholder I guess. Munger is a long-time proponent (and heavy financial supporter) of the abortion industry." And yet another urged separation of utilitarian from expressive and emotional benefits, and promotion of exclusive pursuit of utilitarian benefits. He wrote, "Hedge funds are about making money. Period."

Houses combine investment and consumption. When our houses gain value we highlight them as investments, but we accept them as consumption when they lose value. And houses combine utilitarian benefits with expressive and emotional ones. Houses offer utilitarian benefits in giving us a roof over our heads, expressive benefits in displays of social status and taste, and emotional benefits in pride of ownership. Nonresident foreign home buyers crowd out local residents in highly desirable areas of Paris, especially in boom times, and those nonresidents overpay for the houses they buy and realize lower capital gains when reselling, suggesting that they are willing to sacrifice utilitarian benefits for expressive and emotional ones.[58]

Financially sophisticated people, as measured by schooling and work experience, are less likely to make financial mistakes when buying and owning a home. They are less likely to pay too high a mortgage rate and more likely to refinance when it is financially advantageous to do so. But financially sophisticated people are also more willing to sacrifice utilitarian benefits for expressive and emotional ones. They are more likely to overpay for houses they buy and less likely to commit strategic default when significantly underwater in their mortgages.[59]

Art, like houses, combines investment and consumption and utilitarian benefits with expressive and emotional ones. We highlight paintings as investments when they gain value, but accept them as consumption when they lose value, continuing to enjoy their expressive and emotional "dividends." Lottery tickets, slot machines, and other gambles also combine investment and consumption and utilitarian benefits with expressive and emotional ones. We congratulate ourselves for making a wise investment when we win, enjoying utilitarian benefits, and when we lose we say, "We had great fun," focusing our attention on expressive and emotional benefits.

OUR WANTS AND ERRORS

People do well when they satisfy their wants for utilitarian, expressive, and emotional benefits while avoiding cognitive and emotional errors. A distinction between wants and errors is not always clear, but it can be clarified.

Consider lottery tickets. People might be enticed into buying lottery tickets by cognitive errors, exaggerating the odds of winning. Suppose, however, that we provide information about the true odds of winning. If people stop buying lottery tickets, we can conclude that cognitive errors enticed them into buying them. But people might continue to buy the tickets because they want the expressive and emotional benefits of hope and the miniscule chance of the utilitarian benefits of the prize money. They might deny to others and even to themselves that their odds of winning are indeed as low as truth indicates.

Thrills and sensations, whether in fast driving or heavy trading, illustrate further the difference between wants and errors. We can divide sensation seekers into two groups, knowledgeable sensation seekers and ignorant ones. Ignorant sensation seekers are blind to errors caused by overconfidence in their abilities as drivers or traders. They want thrills and sensations but are ignorant of their price. Knowledgeable sensation seekers, however, acknowledge their overconfidence. They want thrills and sensations and are willing to pay their price.

Frequent traders in Finland tend to be fast drivers, accumulating many speeding tickets. Some of them are ignorant sensation seekers, as overconfident in their trading abilities as in their abilities to negotiate hairpin turns at ferocious speeds. Yet others are knowledgeable sensation seekers, free of overconfidence. They know the high price of heavy trading and fast driving and are willing to pay it.

Frequent traders are more likely to sacrifice returns than augment them by their trading. Their average returns lag behind those of infrequent traders, and the average returns of infrequent traders lag behind average returns of investors who abstain from trading. Peter Millman, the day trader quoted earlier, is not likely to be surprised to find that he is sacrificing utilitarian returns for these expressive and emotional benefits. But not all traders are equally knowledgeable and not all are willing to admit to themselves, let alone to others, that they are motivated to trade by the desire for expressive and emotional benefits.

Behavior that satisfies wants can be intertwined with cognitive or emotional errors, but not always. Consider a person with debt balances on two credit cards. The debt on the first is large and its interest rate is high, whereas the debt on the second is small and its interest rate is low. Now suppose that the person has cash sufficient to fully extinguish the small debt on the low-interest card but not sufficient to fully extinguish the large debt on the high-interest card. Wants for utilitarian benefits direct that person to reduce the debt balance on the high-interest card. Indeed, we might regard a decision to extinguish the debt on the low-interest card as a cognitive or emotional error. Yet it is not, because sacrificing short-term utilitarian benefits by extinguishing the debt of the low-interest card might enhance long-term utilitarian benefits. The expressive and emotional benefits of the small victory that comes with fully extinguishing the small low-interest debt balance might encourage a person to persevere in extinguishing the large high-interest debt.

One experiment examined the small-victories strategy by breaking down an unpleasant task into its component parts. It turned out that people completed the overall task faster when the parts were arranged from smallest to largest, providing the expressive and emotional benefits of small victories, than when arranged from largest to smallest.[60]

OUR WANTS AND SHOULDS

Rational people are free of conflicts between wants and "shoulds," whereas normal investors are not. The voice of wants says, "I want to eat this tasty hamburger now," but the voice of shoulds says, "You should choose the healthy salad instead." Wants are visceral, whereas shoulds are reasoned. Wants' benefits are in the present, whereas shoulds' benefits are usually in the future. Wants focus our attention on expressive and emotional benefits, whereas shoulds usually focus it on utilitarian ones. Investment advice is full of shoulds: save more, spend less, diversify, buy and hold.

Eating large amounts of unhealthy but tasty food is a want, prompted by the visceral System 1, whereas eating moderate amounts of healthy but less tasty food is a should, prompted by the reflective System 2. Hunger, part of the visceral System 1, is crucial for survival, as it prompts us to eat. Yet hunger prompts us to eat large amounts of unhealthy food when the reflective System 2 is not engaged. Hungry people choose unhealthy food when asked what they prefer to eat now. They even choose unhealthy food when asked what they prefer to eat next week.[61] Wants for large amounts of unhealthy but tasty food are evident in increasing obesity rates.

Information can influence use of System 2, nudging people away from their wants to their shoulds. Calorie information on Starbucks' menus decreased average calories per meal by 6 percent.[62] Yet nudges and the use of System 2 are not all good when wants are more enjoyable than shoulds. Calorie information can diminish the enjoyment of eating large amounts of unhealthy food.

Moreover, attempts to nudge people toward consuming small amounts of healthy food are not always successful. Indeed, such attempts often backfire. Information portraying food items as healthy leads people to infer that they are not tasty. Conversely, food items portrayed as unhealthy are perceived as tasty and are enjoyed more than food items portrayed as healthy.[63] People are more likely to underestimate the caloric content of main dishes and choose higher-calorie side dishes, drinks, or desserts when fast-food restaurants claim to serve healthy food than when they make no such claim.[64]

CONFLICTS AND TRADE-OFFS OF UTILITARIAN, EXPRESSIVE, AND EMOTIONAL BENEFITS WITHIN A PERSON

The utilitarian benefits of renting houses often exceed those of owning them, but homeowners enjoy expressive and emotional benefits, including pride of ownership and freedom from landlords. A 1996 survey of a sample of Swiss found that 83 percent of them prefer to own their homes rather than rent them. Yet only one-third of the Swiss own their homes, whereas two-thirds of Americans do. Much of the difference between the rates of home ownership is explained by differences in utilitarian benefits. Homeowners in Switzerland, but not in the United States, pay income tax on the virtual rent they derive from living in houses they own, and renters in Switzerland are better protected from landlords than in the United States.[65]

Socially responsible investors commonly shun companies producing guns along with companies in the tobacco, alcohol, gambling, military, and nuclear industries. Yet evidence shows that stocks of shunned companies earn higher returns, even when adjusted for risk, than stocks of accepted companies. Shares of Smith & Wesson, a gun manufacturer, increased nearly 400 percent from 2010 to 2015. They reached their highest price on Monday, December 7, 2015, the day after President Obama's call for stronger gun control following the massacre of 14 people in San Bernardino by Syed Rizwan Farook and Tashfeen Malik, a married couple who pledged allegiance to the Islamic State.[66]

Trade-offs associated with social responsibility are also evident in the effects of employer social responsibility on wages that workers demand. In a 2016 study, workers were recruited for short-term jobs. Some received information about the employer's high social responsibility, whereas others did not. Prospective workers submitted 44 percent lower wage bids for the same job after learning about the employer's high social responsibility. This result suggests that workers value the expressive and emotional benefits of purpose and meaning at work, and are willing to trade utilitarian benefits for the expressive and emotional benefits of working for a socially responsible employer. High-performing workers in the study were especially willing to trade utilitarian benefits for expressive and emotional ones.[67]

CONFLICTS AND TRADE-OFFS OF UTILITARIAN, EXPRESSIVE, AND EMOTIONAL BENEFITS AMONG PEOPLE

Investors are principals who hire agents, including corporate managers, money managers, analysts, and financial advisers, to satisfy their wants for utilitarian, expressive, and emotional benefits. The wants of agents, however, can conflict with those of their principals, tempting them to satisfy their own wants rather than those of their clients. We know these as conflicts of interest, or principal-agent conflicts.

We see conflicts between the wants of corporate managers and shareholders in choices centered on mergers, acquisitions, and takeovers. Takeovers frequently force target-company CEOs to retire early, pitting CEOs who want the utilitarian, expressive, and emotional benefits of keeping their CEO posts against shareholders who want the utilitarian benefits of high share prices.

Young CEOs benefit greatly by keeping their CEO posts, but benefits are smaller when they near sixty-five, the normal retirement age. Managers of companies considering takeovers exploit the wants of target-company CEOs. The likelihood of takeover offers increases sharply when target CEOs are at the threshold of age sixty-five. The increase appears at that threshold, with no gradual increase earlier. Moreover, takeover premiums—the difference between prices offered for shares and current prices—are lower when CEOs of target companies are older than sixty-five, and the returns of stocks of such target companies when takeover bids are announced are also lower.[68]

Managers in countries of the British Commonwealth are candidates for honors, such as knighthoods and damehoods, recognizing charitable work. Honors bestow expressive and emotional benefits of high social status on managers, but honors might detract from the utilitarian benefits of shareholders if they divert managers' time and corporate resources from the task of increasing stock prices. Knighthoods and damehoods in New Zealand were abolished in April 2000 but reinstated in August 2009. Availability of honors diverted managers' time and corporate resources from the task of increasing stock prices.[69]

Money managers satisfy the wants of their investors for utilitarian benefits when they deliver high investment returns, and analysts satisfy them when they deliver incisive analysis and accurate forecasts that facilitate high investment returns. Financial advisers satisfy the wants of their investors for utilitarian, expressive, and emotional benefits by delivering good advice and helping in its application. Brokers satisfy the wants of their investors when they buy for them securities at low prices and sell their securities at high prices.

Money managers, analysts, financial advisers, and brokers satisfy their wants for utilitarian, expressive, and emotional benefits in high compensation and pride in jobs well done. At times, however, conflicts arise between the wants of investors and those of money managers, analysts, financial advisers, and brokers. Money managers who lose their jobs lose current benefits and imperil future benefits. Career concerns lead mutual fund managers to herd—trade together—in stocks upgraded by analysts and herd out of downgraded stocks. This approach is especially true for downgrades, and among money managers with greater career concerns because holding losing stocks poses greater reputational and litigation risks.[70]

CONCLUSION

Ask investors what they want from their investments and they are likely to say that all they want is to make money. But what is the money for? Standard finance rarely answers this question, considering the question and its answer beyond its domain. But this question and its answer are central in the domain of behavioral finance. Money is for satisfying many wants, some common to all of us and some varying among us. A survey of investors found that almost all say that money is for satisfying wants of financial security, but satisfying wants of helping children become successful and educating them is not far behind. Further down the list are wants for helping the less fortunate, wants for money as barometers of success, and wants for high social status.[71]

The first generation of behavioral finance work, starting in the early 1980s, focused on people's shortcuts and errors as they made choices. A typical first-generation behavioral finance study found that trading diminishes wealth more often than enhances it and attributed eagerness to trade to cognitive errors. Some investors' eagerness to trade might well be properly attributed to cognitive errors, but that same eagerness among other investors might be due to wants for the expressive and emotional benefits of playing the trading game and winning. The second generation of behavioral finance accepts people's wants and distinguishes wants from errors, thereby providing a truer portrait of normal people.

CHAPTER 3

Cognitive Shortcuts and Errors

Cognitive shortcuts are part of the intuitive "blink" System 1 in our minds, leading to good choices in most of life. But shortcuts turn into errors when they mislead us into poor choices. System 2, the reflective "think" system in our minds, leads to better choices when System 1 misleads. People with knowledge of human behavior and financial facts employ cognitive shortcuts correctly, whereas people lacking such knowledge commit cognitive errors as they employ them incorrectly. We know cognitive shortcuts also as cognitive rules of thumb and as cognitive heuristics.

There is no uniform list of cognitive shortcuts and associated errors, and not all cognitive shortcuts and associated errors on lists are distinct from one another. Moreover, cognitive errors on many lists are tainted by hindsight errors. Action is faulted as a "jumping to conclusions" cognitive error once we know, in hindsight, that refraining from action would have brought a better outcome, whereas refraining from action is faulted as a "status quo" cognitive error once we know, in equal hindsight, that action would have brought a better outcome. I describe here cognitive shortcuts and associated errors most relevant in the context of finance, including framing, hindsight, confirmation, anchoring and adjustment, representativeness, availability, and confidence.

FRAMING

A commercial for running shoes illustrates framing shortcuts and errors. Two barefoot men are bantering as they walk in an African savanna. Suddenly, they spot a growling lion. "Do you think you're faster than a lion," asks one as he watches the other put on his running shoes. "No," says the man, "but I'm faster than you." And with that he runs away. Next we see the lion closing in on the barefoot man, who lags behind.[1]

The man in running shoes possesses human-behavior and "race facts" knowledge. He uses a good framing shortcut, whereas the barefoot man commits a framing error. The man in running shoes frames the race correctly as between him and the barefoot man, whereas the barefoot man frames the race in error as between each of them and the lion.

Think of trading stocks, bonds, and other investments as a trading race. Traders who commit framing errors frame the trading race as between them and the market, as the barefoot man frames his race as against the lion. Where is the economy going, ask "barefoot traders," and what are the prospects of this company?

Traders possessing human-behavior and financial-facts knowledge frame trading correctly as against traders on the other side of the trades— the likely buyers of what they sell and likely sellers of what they buy. This is the frame of "traders in running shoes" who ask, do my computers help me outrun other traders as my running shoes help me outrun barefoot men, or are the computers of high-frequency traders on the other side of my trades much faster than mine? Do I know more about the prospects of this company than company insiders who might be on the other side of my trade, wearing "running shoes" of exclusively or narrowly available information, whereas I wear "heavy boots" of widely available information? Traders committing framing errors fail to understand that trading is a race against other traders. It is no wonder that such traders predominate among losers.

The US Leading Economic Index (LEI) illustrates the race between slow traders and the fast ones. The LEI, aimed at predicting the future direction of the economy, is composed of components such as building permits and manufacturers' orders. The Conference Board, a research association, compiles the LEI and makes its composition available to all. Anyone can calculate the LEI precisely once its last component has been made public, twenty-four hours before the LEI's official release. Good LEI news is generally followed by increases in stock prices on the day of the official release and bad news is generally followed by decreases that day.

Traders who frame the trading race correctly are the fast traders. They calculate the LEI from its components and act twenty-four hours before its official release, buying stocks when the LEI news is good and selling when it is bad. Traders who commit framing errors are the slow traders. They trade twenty-four hours later, after the LEI's release. Fast traders earn an extra 8 percentage points of annual returns as they win their trading race against their slow rivals.[2]

Frames in Mental Accounting

We commonly frame monies into distinctly labeled mental accounts and treat them accordingly. Mental accounts resemble checking accounts, and money in mental accounts resembles money in checking accounts. Mental accounts help us keep track of our money and direct it to where we want it to go. We make sure that there are sufficient balances in each of our mental accounts, just as we make sure that we have sufficient balances in each of our checking accounts, so that checks we sign at an appliance store or send to a credit card company do not bounce.

Sometimes we fail at mental accounting, as when we fail to account for exceptional expenses. Purchases fall along a continuum from ordinary to exceptional, and many of the largest expenses, such as for electronic gadgets, gifts, and celebrations, are the most exceptional. People are generally adept at budgeting for ordinary expenses but tend to underestimate spending on exceptional purchases overall and overspend on each individual exceptional purchase. This miscalculation is probably because we frame exceptional expenses too narrowly, regarding each as unique and consequently underestimating its sum.[3]

Mental accounting is common to all, from Hollywood movie stars to rural people in China's regions of Gansu and Inner Mongolia. Gene Hackman, star of the film *The French Connection,* tells of a visit to the home of Dustin Hoffman, star of the film *The Graduate.* Hoffman asked to borrow some money for food, and Hackman agreed to lend it. Next, Hackman entered Hoffman's kitchen only to find glass jars on a ledge, one labeled rent, another entertainment, and so on. All the jars had money in them except the one labeled food, which was empty. "You have money," protested Hackman. "I cannot take money for food from the other jars," explained Hoffman.[4]

Jars labeled "gasoline" might be uncommon on kitchen ledges but we regularly keep mental accounts with gasoline labels in our minds. The prices of low-octane and high-octane gasoline fell in tandem in the second half of 2008 as the financial crisis raged and the Great Recession deepened. Consumers cut back on spending wherever they could, replacing eating out with meals at home and expensive cuts of beef with cheaper ones. Yet consumers did not replace high-octane gasoline with low-octane gasoline. Instead they did the opposite, replacing low-octane gasoline with high-octane gasoline. It is as if the money consumers kept in mental accounts labeled gasoline could not be transferred into mental accounts labeled food to be spent on better cuts of beef. Similarly, people who received vouchers for drinks spent 25 percent more on drinks than those who received vouchers for the entire meal.[5]

We regularly distinguish income earned with much effort, such as salaries, from unearned income obtained with little effort, such as gifts. We tend to place earned income in one mental account and unearned income in another, and we spend unearned income more easily than earned income. The expression "easy come, easy go" is common across languages: "как нажито, так ипрожито" in Russian, "lai de rong yi, qu de kuai" in Chinese, "lo que llega fácil, fácil se va" in Spanish, and "bekelalu yemta, bekalau yehedal" in Amharic, spoken in Ethiopia. That distinction is evident among rural people in China and Tanzania who spend earned income on staple foods and education, while spending unearned income on clothing, alcohol, tobacco, and non-staple foods.[6]

The source of money also affects willingness to take risk. In one set of experiments Koreans were divided into two groups of hard earners and windfall receivers, and so were Britons. People in the hard-earner groups received an amount of money for completing work requiring physical effort—peeling twenty-five potatoes or making nine envelopes within thirty minutes. People in the windfall-receiver groups received the same amount of money as a gift, with no work requirement. Subsequently, people in the hard-earner groups made less risky and more patient choices than people in the windfall-receiver groups.[7]

Frames in the Winner's Curse

Framing errors also underlie the "winner's curse," whereby winners of auctions pay too much for what they buy, such as oil wells. Think of many bidders who estimate the value of an oil well yet to be drilled. Each estimate combines the yet unknown $100 million true value of the well with an error that makes the estimate too high or too low. The cursed winner is the one whose estimation error is too high by the most, perhaps paying $200 million.

Bidders who frame auctions correctly are aware of the winner's curse. They know that their estimate of the value of an oil well is likely to include both its true value and an error that might inflate the well's estimated value beyond its true worth. Therefore, they scale back their bids below their estimates. Bidders who frame the auction incorrectly commit a framing error, failing to scale back their bids and very likely being cursed with overpayment when their bids turn out to be the winning ones.

A choice to submit a high auction bid, however, is not always an error. Indeed, bidding choices illustrate the difference between wants and errors. Oil wells are not likely to yield bidders expressive and emotional benefits, and their utilitarian benefits are probably the same among bid-ders. Therefore, bids that exceed the utilitarian benefits of oil wells very likely reflect errors. But particular houses, paintings, and antique cars very likely yield expressive and emotional benefits that vary among bidders. A high bid for a particular house, painting, or antique car might reflect wants for these benefits, rather than errors.

Frames in the Money Illusion

Framing shortcuts also turn into framing errors in the money illusion, whereby we use nominal units of money in place of "real"—inflation-adjusted—units of money. A 2 percent nominal pay raise when inflation is at 3 percent is a 1 percent real pay cut, whereas a 1 percent nominal pay raise when inflation is at zero is a 1 percent real pay raise. Yet we often perceive the first as better than the second because we frame pay cuts and raises in nominal money units in which a 2 percent raise is better than a 1 percent raise, rather than in real money units in which a 1 percent cut is worse than a 1 percent raise.

In an episode of *All in the Family*, a 1970s situation comedy, Archie Bunker gleefully tells Edith, his wife, Gloria, his daughter, and Michael, his son-in-law, of a labor settlement in a time of high inflation.

EDITH: Archie, did you get a good raise?
ARCHIE: Edith, a three-year contract with 15 percent.
MICHAEL: Arch, what about the cost of living escalator clause?
ARCHIE: The hell with the escalator, we're on firm ground with 15 per-
cent. Now don't make me mad!

When Archie and Edith leave Michael speaks to Gloria:

MICHAEL: I did not want to spoil his happy moment but he is not any
better now than before. . . .
Remember reading in the paper the cost of living went up 12 percent last year? Next year it is going up another 8 percent. That's 20 per-cent. Archie thinks that he's 15 percent ahead, but he's already 5 per-cent behind.[8]

Still, money illusion can be beneficial in maintaining expressive and emo-tional benefits when real pay cuts diminish utilitarian benefits. This is one reason for the preference of central banks for moderate inflation, such as an annual 2 percent, over zero inflation. A nominal 1 percent raise when inflation is 2 percent implies a 1 percent real pay cut, but it is misperceived by money illusion as a 1 percent pay raise.

Money illusion also makes cuts in real pay by currency devaluations easier to bear than cuts in nominal pay. Consider the case in which the drachma is Greece's currency, as it formerly was, and the current exchange rate is 2 drachmas to the euro. Think of an employee earning an annual 100,000 drachmas, equal to 50,000 euros. A drachma devaluation from 2 to the euro to 4 leads over time to a 50 percent cut in the employee's real pay, from 50,000 euros to 25,000 euros. The employee is not likely to complain vociferously, however, since his nominal pay remains at 100,000 drachmas.

Now consider the case in which the euro is Greece's currency and the employee earns an annual 50,000 euros. Cutting her real pay by 50 percent requires cutting her nominal pay to 25,000 euros, very likely leading to vociferous complaints, street demonstrations, and social and political upheaval.

Holding periods for houses are long, allowing for substantial inflation to accumulate and facilitating money illusion. Danish researchers simplified an experiment by specifying the accumulated inflation over each holding period, eliminating possible errors in computing it.[9]

In one scenario, "Maria bought a house for 2,000,000 Danish Krone (DKK). Some years later she sold it. In the period she owned the house, inflation was 31 percent (i.e., over the entire period, prices in society increased by 31 percent). Maria received 2,515,200 DKK for the house (i.e., 25.8 percent more than she paid for it)." The researchers asked people to rate on a scale from 1 to 15 the advantageousness of the purchase and sale of the house.

Responses to this scenario and others like it revealed that 17 percent of people were free of money illusion: their evaluations of advantageousness were unaffected by the nominal money frame, but the evaluation of 60 percent of people was consistently affected by money illusion, failing to conclude that the purchase and sale of the house were not advantageous because Maria lost when gains and losses are calculated in real money. Moreover, people with high scores on the CRT were less susceptible to money illusion, consistent with the observation that people with high CRT scores tend to pause after finding answers by the intuitive System 1 and engage the reflective System 2 before reaching their conclusions.

People are compelled to overcome money illusion when gaps between nominal money units and real ones grow big and have major life consequences. Inflation in Israel increased to 111 percent in 1979 and 445 percent in 1984. Israelis responded by pricing everything in American dollars, from houses to cars and many less costly items. Yet in the process of overcoming one money illusion, Israelis succumbed to another, albeit smaller, money illusion as they overlooked inflation in the United States. That inflation was at 11.3 percent in 1979 and 4.3 percent in 1984.

HINDSIGHT

Good hindsight shortcuts lead us to repeat actions that brought good outcomes and avoid actions that brought bad ones. We did favors for friends and they subsequently returned them. We learned that reciprocated favors are the likely outcomes of doing favors. Hindsight shortcuts can turn into hindsight errors, however, where randomness and luck are prominent, loosening associations between past events and future events and between actions and outcomes.

Fast driving when luck is good gets us faster to our destination, but fast driving when luck is bad gets us a speeding ticket or worse. Hindsight errors can mislead lucky drivers into thinking that fast driving always gets them to their destinations more quickly, and mislead unlucky drivers into thinking that fast driving always gets them a speeding ticket. Hindsight errors also mislead lucky traders into thinking that fast trading always gets them to their profit destinations more quickly and mislead unlucky traders into thinking that fast trading always inflicts losses.

Psychologist Baruch Fischhoff, who introduced us to hindsight shortcuts and errors, wrote, "In hindsight, people consistently exaggerate what could have been anticipated in foresight. . . . People believe that others should have been able to anticipate events much better than was actually the case. They even misremember their own predictions so as to exaggerate in hindsight what they knew in foresight."[10]

Fischhoff tells of his first experiment on hindsight, when President Nixon was about to leave for his historic trip to China. Fischhoff asked people to assess the probabilities of various outcomes of the trip. Would Nixon meet Chairman Mao? Would Nixon announce that the trip was a success? After the visit, he asked the same people for the probabilities they had assigned to outcomes before the visit. Fischhoff found that people recalled assigning higher probabilities to actual outcomes than the probabilities they originally assigned.

One manifestation of hindsight errors is an underestimation of the volatility of stock prices. People free of these errors increase their estimates of volatility when they observe unexpectedly high or low returns, but people misled by hindsight errors fail to be surprised and consequently fail to understand that such returns were unexpected. Instead, they think that they knew it all along. In one experiment, hindsight errors led students to underestimate the volatility of stock prices and hindsight errors detracted from the performance of investment bankers. The performance of bankers with high propensity for hindsight errors was, as one might expect, worse than the performance of bankers with a lower propensity for them.[11]

Apple Shares in Foresight and Hindsight

You could have bought a share of Apple for approximately $14 on April 1, 2003, and sold it for more than $610 by July 31, 2012. Indeed, the 2003 price was approximately $7 if we take into account a 2005 split in which 1 Apple share was replaced with 2. A dollar invested in Apple shares on April 1, 2003, would have grown to $88.39 by July 31, 2012, an astounding 61.64 percent annualized return. A dollar invested in the S&P 500 Index during that time would have grown only to $1.96, a 7.49 percent annualized return. On August 20, 2012, *The Wall Street Journal* wrote, "Apple Now Biggest-Ever U.S. Company." The total values of all Apple shares was not only higher than the total value of the shares of any other American company at the time, but also higher than the record value of the shares of Microsoft in December 1999.[12]

Some investors saw Apple's stock astounding returns in foresight, or at least glimpsed it. One investor counted the accomplishments of Steve Jobs, Apple's CEO, in an April 16, 2003, post on Yahoo's message board: "OS X, iPod, iLife, iMac, PB, Pixar, Mac, Apple II, etc. That is his track record. For my money I think he is the best on planet." But another investor wrote on the same day, "Jobs doesn't have a clue . . . time to gracefully retire and let someone else try to do something with this messed up company." Another wrote, "Thanks to [Jobs's] 'leadership' AAPL [Apple] is in the toilet. But boy has he got 'charisma.' Hahahahahahaha!!!!"[13]

The price of Apple shares reached a peak exceeding $700 by September 2012 but fell below $460 by the end of January 2013. Comments on Apple's message board that month show that hindsight remained much clearer than foresight. One investor wrote on September 10, 2012, that Apple's share price is "not going to drop that much . . . but may give back a few points . . . I've been loading up big time simply because anybody with any sense knows Apple will easily hit $800 come this January . . . and I'll be laughing all the way to the bank as usual." But another investor displayed foresight, writing on September 12, 2012, "How much more do you folks want? Find me another chart in the history of stock markets that has a similar chart and DIDN'T crash. It doesn't exist."

Did investors really know in foresight, on April 1, 2003, that Apple's share would do so very well, compounding a single dollar into more than $88 by July 31, 2012? Did they know in foresight that shares of Terra Nitrogen would do even better, compounding a single dollar into more than $99 during the same period, and that shares of Monster Beverage would do better still, compounding a single dollar into more than $243?

We can see the manifestation of hindsight errors when we consider the price that an Apple share would have fetched on April 1, 2003, if investors, as a whole, had perfect foresight. That price would have been approximately $315, higher than the actual $7 price by a multiple of 45. From then on, the price of a share of Apple would have compounded at the S&P 500 Index's annualized 7.49 percent return, reaching the actual $610 price by July 31, 2012. The fact that Apple's share price on April 1, 2003, was approximately $7 rather than $315 implies that we have known Apple's good fortune in hindsight, on July 31, 2012, but not in foresight, when it mattered, on April 1, 2003.

CONFIRMATION

Confirmation errors mislead the proverbial dog that believes that his bark makes UPS trucks go away. The dog can test his belief by seeking disconfirming evidence. How about not barking next time when the UPS truck is in the driveway? If the truck stays in the driveway, that would be confirming evidence, but if the truck leaves, that would be disconfirming evidence.

Confirmation errors abound in investment behavior. Investors who believe they can pick winning stocks are regularly oblivious to their losing records, recording wins as evidence confirming their stock-picking skills but neglecting to record losses as disconfirming evidence. Some investors go further, realizing gains and considering them as confirming evidence of their stock-picking abilities but, by refraining from realizing losses and considering unrealized losses as no losses at all, never confronting losses as disconfirming evidence.

Confirmation errors mislead investors to choices that degrade returns while they expect their choices to bolster returns. Investors interacting in the virtual community of the largest message board in South Korea committed confirmation errors when they processed board information, overlooking or assigning little weight to disconfirming facts and opinions.

Investors who committed greater confirmation errors expected higher returns, traded more frequently, but realized lower returns.[14]

Confirmation errors underlie some managers' decisions to acquire other companies when evidence indicates that most such acquisitions add no value to acquiring companies. Many actually subtract value. In one set of experiments, undergraduate business students and business managers saw three case studies placing them in merger and acquisition decision-making capacities. The cases described the activities of the companies and the potential motivations for mergers and acquisitions. People could use hyperlinks to reach pages labeled Competition and Market Share, Financials, Integration Issues, Legal and Regulatory Considerations, Operating Synergies, Acquiring Company Information, Target Company Information, Tax Ramifications, and Proceed to Final Decision. Clicking on each information link brought another page containing information on the relevant topic.[15]

The experiments revealed that managers seek merger and acquisition information differently from how students do and evaluate information differently. Managers reviewed fewer pages of information than students and were less likely to change their minds after seeing new information. This difference was not because managers are quicker at digesting information than students, since managers did not even review certain information.

Confirmation errors are also evident in assessment of the usefulness of trading rules. One such rule is based on the Bearish Sentiment Index, compiled from stock-market recommendations of writers of investment newsletters. The Bearish Sentiment Index is the ratio of the number of writers of investment newsletters who are bearish, expecting stock-market declines, to the number of writers expressing an opinion, bullish or bearish, about the stock market's future direction. A contrarian use of the Bearish Sentiment Index calls for buying stocks when bearish sentiment is high and selling when it is low.

A proper test of the hypothesis that the Bearish Sentiment Index predicts stock-market increases and decreases places observations into four boxes, depicted in Figure 3-1. The first includes "positive hits"—predictions of stock-market increases followed by realized increases. The second includes "negative hits"—predictions of declines followed by realized decreases. The third includes "false positives"—predictions of increases followed by realized decreases, and the fourth includes "false negatives"—predictions of decreases followed by realized increases. We commit confirmation errors when we assign much weight to the confirming evidence in the boxes of positive and negative hits, while assigning little weight to the disconfirming evidence in the boxes of the false positives and negatives.

Realization / Prediction	Stock Prices Increased	Stock Prices Declined
Stock prices will Increase	Positive Hits	False Positives
Stock price will decline	False Negatives	Negative Hits

Figure 3-1 Predictions of changes in stock prices and their realizations.

It turned out that the sum of positive and negative hits of the Bearish Sentiment Index was approximately equal to the sum of false positives and negatives, indicating no reliable association between the Bearish Sentiment Index and subsequent stock-market increases or decreases. The persistent belief in the usefulness of the Bearish Sentiment Index is very likely rooted in confirmation errors of users who focus on confirming cases and overlook disconfirming ones.[16]

Confirmation errors can lead to immensely sad consequences. Presumptions of guilt lead to convictions of innocent people. Investigators first conclude, on the basis of beliefs or some confirming evidence, that suspects are guilty. Next, they subject suspects to accusatory interrogations. Last, they pressure suspects to confess guilt. People who stated their beliefs of guilt or innocence early in the review of a mock police file were disposed to seek confirming evidence and interpret ambiguous evidence as further confirming it.[17]

We are often driven into confirmation errors by motivated reasoning that alleviates cognitive dissonance. This is the discomfort we feel when confronted with beliefs or facts that disconfirm our own views. People who live in a house on a bluff overlooking the ocean are tempted to assign little weight to evidence that the ocean poses erosion danger to their house. It is much more pleasurable to believe that no danger accompanies the ocean's soothing sounds at night and the beautiful sights in the morning.

Motivated reasoning is distinct from reasoning in the absence of motivation, evident in functional neuroimaging of thirty people, all committed supporters of John Kerry, the Democratic candidate in the 2004 presidential election, or George W. Bush, the Republican candidate. People engaged in reasoning tasks involving assessment of information unfavorable to their own candidate and information unfavorable to the other. Motivated reasoning inclined Kerry supporters to assign little weight to unfavorable information about their candidate, and inclined Bush supporters to assign little weight to unfavorable information about their candidate. Motivated reasoning was associated with activations of the ventromedial prefrontal cortex, anterior cingulate cortex, posterior cingulate cortex, insular cortex, and lateral orbital cortex in the brain.[18]

ANCHORING AND ADJUSTMENT

We begin the process of estimating the value of a house for sale by finding the average price of houses sold recently in the same neighborhood. We use that average price as an anchor and adjust our value estimate up or down to account for the fact that this house has four bedrooms, whereas the average house has only three, and the fact that this house is situated on a less desirable street than the average house.

We see the workings of anchoring and adjustment shortcuts and errors in a measurement experiment. Do you think that the runway of the Hong Kong Kai Tak Airport is longer or shorter than 7.3 kilometers? Now what is your estimate of the price of a brand-new air-conditioned double-decker bus? Sixty students at the Chinese University of Hong Kong were asked this question. Sixty other students were asked the same runway and bus questions, but the 7.3 kilometers in the runway question were replaced by 7,300 meters. A 7.3-kilometer runway is as long as a 7,300-meter runway, and approximately two-thirds of students in each group answered correctly that the Kai Tak runway is shorter than 7.3 kilometers or 7,300 meters.[19]

I do not know the price of a double-decker bus and you probably do not know it, either. Indeed, the question was chosen because few know the price. But if we are not misled by anchoring and adjustment errors as we form our estimates, we will find that that the average estimated price of a double-decker bus in the 7,300-meters group is approximately the same as the average estimated price in the 7.3 kilometers group. Yet it turned out that the average estimated price was much higher in the 7,300-meters group than in the 7.3-kilometers group. Evidently, people in the 7,300-meters groups were misled by anchoring and adjustment errors, as the group members remained anchored to the irrelevant 7,300 number and failed to adjust sufficiently away from it. People in the 7.3-kilometers groups were equally misled by anchoring and adjustment errors, as they remained anchored to the irrelevant 7.3 number and again failed to adjust sufficiently away from it.

We gain additional insights into anchoring and adjustment shortcuts and errors by contemplating the answer to a question posed by psychologists Amos Tversky and Daniel Kahneman. What is your 5-second estimate of the product of $1 \cdot 2 \cdot 3 \cdot 4 \cdot 5 \cdot 6 \cdot 7 \cdot 8$? We very likely start our way to an estimate by multiplying 1 by 2, getting 2, then multiplying 2 by 3, getting 6, then multiplying 6 by 4, getting 24. With our 5 seconds running out we jump to an estimate, perhaps 500 or even 1,000. But we probably do not jump far enough to come close to 40,320, the correct answer. It is as if we were anchored to the last number we got in our multiplication by a short chain restricting sufficient adjustment. Tversky and Kahneman found that the average estimate was 512.[20]

Now consider a 5-second estimate of the product of $8 \cdot 7 \cdot 6 \cdot 5 \cdot 4 \cdot 3 \cdot 2 \cdot 1$. We are already at 56 when we multiply 8 by 7 and at more than 300 when we multiply 56 by 6. We are anchored to a higher number when we jump to an estimate in this form of the question than in the earlier one. Tversky and Kahneman found that the average estimate in this form of the question was 2,250, still much lower than the correct 40,320 answer but much higher than the average 512 estimate in the first form.

My coauthor Roger Clarke and I encountered our susceptibility to anchoring and adjustment errors when we studied the Dow Jones Industrial Average (DJIA). The DJIA was introduced in 1896 at a level of 41 and reached 9,181 by the end of 1998. The DJIA, like the Standard & Poor's (S&P) 500 Index and almost all indexes, is a capital index—it does not include dividends paid to the shareholders of the companies in the index and the compounding of reinvested dividends over time. Now think of a DJIA in which dividends are reinvested and compounded over time. What is your 5-second estimate of the level of this compounding DJIA at the end of 1998? The correct answer is 652,230.[21]

When Clarke and I first explored the compounding DJIA not long after the end of 1998 we were sure that we had made some mistake in our calculation. Doing the calculation in our minds, we started with 9,181, the level of the DJIA at the end of 1998, and multiplied it by a large number, perhaps 20, knowing that compounding works quickly and forcefully. But the number we chose was much too small. We were anchored to the 9,181 DJIA level by a short chain and failed to adjust sufficiently by multiplying it by more than 70.

Anchoring and adjustment errors are evident in many financial settings. Expert consensus economic forecasts from Money Market Services are anchored to data from previous months and the errors are substantial.[22] Stock traders use the 52-week high—the highest price during the previous 52 weeks—as an anchor and reference point against which they evaluate the potential impact of news. When good news pushes a stock's price near its 52-week high, traders are reluctant to bid the price higher even if the news warrants it. And when bad news presses a stock's price near its 52-week low price, traders are unwilling to sell at prices that are as low as the news implies.[23] Similarly, the odds of stock downgrades by analysts when share prices approach the 52-week high are 32.7 percent higher than the odds of downgrades at other times.[24]

Predictions of long-term returns are anchored by recent returns. Predictions by Scandinavian students in one experiment were anchored to recent returns by shorter chains than predictions by Scandinavian financial professionals, but even anchoring and adjustment errors by professionals were substantial. Moreover, professionals were not conscious of their susceptibility to anchoring and adjustment errors.[25] Similarly, Bidz.com online bidders are anchored to posted "buy now" prices. They submit higher bids on items with high "buy now" prices than on identical items with low "buy now" prices.[26]

Anchoring and adjustment errors also deter us from buying insurance policies with high deductibles.[27] The price of an insurance policy with no deductible is a natural anchor for evaluating policies with deductibles. Think of an insurance policy with no deductible on a Mercedes S-600, costing $2,000 per year. A policy with a $500 deductible seems overpriced at $1,900 if we are anchored to $2,000 and expect the policy with the $500 deductible to cost $1,500. Our $2,000 anchor prevents us from adjusting our calculation to note that there is only a small probability that we would have an accident during the year and have to pay the $500 deductible.

Anchoring and adjustment errors underlie our continuing surprises at encountering the supposedly rare "black swan" events described by Nassim Taleb.[28] In the 1980s we were anchored to an image of Japan as a giant looming over a US weakling, and in the 1990s, following the collapse of the Soviet Union, we were anchored to an image of the United States as an invulnerable superpower. In the early 2000s we were anchored to increasing prices of houses bought with cheap mortgages. We found that house prices can go down and bring down giant financial institutions such as Fannie Mae, Freddie Mac, Bear Stearns, and Lehman Brothers.

REPRESENTATIVENESS

The shortcuts and errors of representativeness resemble those of the "duck test." Representativeness information inclines us to conclude that if a thing looks like a duck, swims like a duck, and quacks like a duck, then it is probably a duck. But base-rate information might indicate that such a conclusion is unwarranted because there are many kinds of fowl that look like a duck, swim like it, and quack like it, but are not ducks.

Consider a call from a telemarketer interrupting your dinner with an offer of a free trip. Would you listen to the entire pitch or would you quickly put down the phone? As we make our decision to listen or quit, we properly take into account two pieces of information. First is representativeness information—how representative is this particular telemarketer of the group of telemarketers who were worth listening to? Second is base-rate information—the proportion of the many telemarketers who have interrupted our dinners yet were worth listening to. We put down the phone because base-rate information tells us that few sales pitches are worth listening to, even though the voice of this particular telemarketer is pleasant.

Amos Tversky and Daniel Kahneman illustrated representativeness shortcuts and errors with a description of Steve, a very shy and withdrawn man, invariably helpful but with little interest in people or the world of reality. People using representativeness shortcuts assess the probability that Steve is a farmer, salesman, or librarian by the degree to which Steve is representative of a farmer, salesman, or librarian. Most conclude that the probability that Steve is a librarian is higher than the probability that he is a farmer or salesman because Steve is more representative of a librarian stereotype than a farmer or salesman stereotype. This conclusion would have been warranted if the base rate of librarians—their proportion in the population—had been equal to or higher than the base rates of farmers and salesmen. But this conclusion is not warranted if the base rate of librarians is much lower than the base rates of other occupations. The low base rate of librarians implies that we should estimate the probability that Steve is a librarian as lower than we would have estimated if the base rate of librarians had been high.[29]

Entrepreneur Elizabeth Holmes is a real-life analog of Steve. Holmes established a company, Theranos, offering a technology whereby a wide range of laboratory tests can be performed on a tiny sample of blood from a finger prick, eliminating the need for intravenous blood draws. The company raised more than $400 million in venture capital, and Holmes's personal stake amounted to $4.5 billion. Subsequently, doubts were raised about the effectiveness of the technology and the viability of the company. Financial journalist James Stewart described the elements of representativeness information.

"Like Bill Gates, Steve Jobs and Mark Zuckerberg, Ms. Holmes dropped out of college. Like Steve Jobs, she wears a uniform of black turtlenecks, suggesting she has loftier things to think about than what to wear. . . . Like Mr. Jobs, she's picky about her diet. . . . And like Google's co-founders, Larry Page and Sergey Brin (Don't Be Evil), and Mark Zuckerberg (Connect the World), her mission is lofty. As she has repeatedly said, Ms. Holmes envisions a world brought about through improved health care in which 'no one ever has to say goodbye too soon.' Theranos also had a slogan: "One tiny drop changes everything."[30] But investors in Holmes's Theranos might have neglected to examine base-rate information, the ratio of the number of ventures that fail to the number of ventures that succeed as much as those of Bill Gates, Steve Jobs, Mark Zuckerberg, Larry Page, and Sergey Brin.

Consumer Reports recommends cars, dishwashers, and computers on the basis of rigorous and unbiased tests and surveys of the experiences of thousands of users. These tests and surveys form part of base-rate information. Such information might well lead us to conclude that dishwashers ranked at the top, say, by Whirlpool, are of high quality. Imagine, however, that you bought the recommended Whirlpool dishwasher and were disappointed, as it failed to clean dishes and was prone to breaking down. This is representativeness information. You commit a representativeness error if you conclude that all Whirlpool dishwashers are faulty. It is more likely that your particular dishwasher is a fluke, and it makes sense to replace it with another from Whirlpool.

Consider the influence of representativeness information and base-rate information in assessing health risk. Base-rate information reflects the prevalence of a disease in the population, whereas representativeness information reflects the symptoms of a disease in a person. It turns out that a person is likely to underestimate his or her health risk when the base rate of the disease in the population is high but representativeness information indicates that his or her health risk is low. Conversely, a person is likely to overestimate his or her health risk when the base rate of the disease in the population is low but representativeness information indicates the health risk to be high.[31]

We also see the influence of representativeness information and base-rate information in assessing financial risk, such as the risk of financial fraud associated with data breaches. Base-rate information reflects the prevalence of breaches in the population, whereas representativeness information reflects whether a consumer was personally affected by a breach. A remarkably large proportion of consumers who were directly affected by a 2012 data breach in the South Carolina Department of Revenue acquired fraud protection immediately afterward. In contrast, the response of consumers who were not directly exposed to the breach, but who were exposed to news about it, was negligible. Even among consumers directly exposed to the data breach, the incremental effect of additional news about the breach was small.[32]

Representativeness errors are also reflected in misperceptions of chance that mislead us into seeing patterns in random sequences because we expect outcomes in random sequences to represent randomness, not only in long sequences but also in short ones. We regard the coin flipping sequence H-T-H-T-T-H as more likely to appear than H-H-H-T-T-T because it seems more representative of randomness. Yet the two sequences have an equal chance of appearing. Two prominent examples of patterns we are misled to see are "hot hand" patterns, in which we expect continuations of sequences, and "gambler's fallacy" patterns, in which we expect reversal of sequences.

Lottery players shy away from numbers that have recently been drawn, consistent with gambler's fallacy, and toward numbers that have been drawn several weeks in a row, consistent with the hot-hand fallacy.[33] Lottery players spread their four or six numbers relatively evenly across the possible range, preferring numbers in the center of the lottery form, avoiding the edges, and tending to choose numbers that are readily available in their memory. Players favor personally relevant numbers and form number combinations with an eye for symmetry and aesthetics. "Altogether," wrote Rogier Potter Van Loon and his coauthors, "our results suggest that number preferences in lotteries are especially driven by joy seeking, attention, and misunderstanding of randomness."[34]

Amateur investors tend to extrapolate recent investment returns as if the process of generating returns conformed to hot hand at times and cold hand at other times. They expect high future returns following high past returns, extrapolating high future returns from high past returns. And they expect low future returns following low past returns, extrapolating low future returns from low past returns.

Gallup surveys asked investors a pair of questions each month: "What was the overall percentage rate of return you got on your portfolio in the PAST twelve months?" and "What overall rate of return do you expect to get on your portfolio in the NEXT twelve months?" It turns out, as depicted in Figure 3-2, that investors, on average, extrapolated past portfolio returns into future returns.[35]

Representativeness errors are evident among traders who estimate variation of series of stock prices that they observe in graphs. These errors mislead traders to infer variation from representativeness information— maximum and minimum prices in the series—assigning little weight to other prices that serve as base-rate information alongside the maximum and minimum prices. Traders infer higher variation in a series in which maximum and minimum prices are more extreme even where, in fact, the distributions of series are identical in mean, variance, and other distribution parameters. Moreover, experience does not diminish the effects of representativeness. Indeed, representativeness errors are more pronounced among traders who are more educated, employed full time, trade more frequently, have had longer trading experience, and trade a wider range of securities.[36]

Misperceptions caused by representativeness errors can lead to unfair decisions as judges try to make them fair. Gambler's fallacy inclines judges to deny asylum after long sequences of asylum grants and grant asylum after long sequences of asylum denials. The same is true for loan officers and baseball umpires.[37]

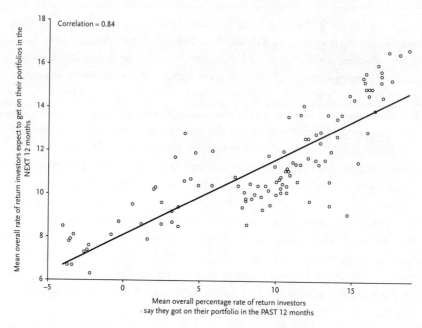

Figure 3-2 Investors extrapolate past portfolio into future portfolio returns, expecting high returns following high returns and low returns following low returns (June 1998–December 2007).

Technical analysis of stocks and other investments involves a search for patterns in series of past prices that predict future prices. The series of Berkshire-Hathaway daily stock *prices* in Figure 3-3a does not seem representative of randomness. Instead, it seems representative of a declining pattern that might lead technical analysts to recommend buying or selling shares. But a series of Berkshire-Hathaway daily stock *returns* derived from these Berkshire-Hathaway's stock prices, presented in Figure 3-3b, shows a pattern representative of randomness.

An early study found that popular technical analysis trading rules, such as moving average rules, generated extra returns during a period ending in 1986.[38] But a subsequent study of the post-1986 period found no evidence of extra returns, suggesting that the extra returns found in the earlier study are likely an example of representativeness errors where patterns are spotted in random sequences.[39] This suggestion is bolstered by the further finding that the absence of extra returns is evident immediately after 1986, indicating that this is not a case in which patterns existed before 1986 but were eliminated subsequently by arbitrage as traders exploited them for extra returns.

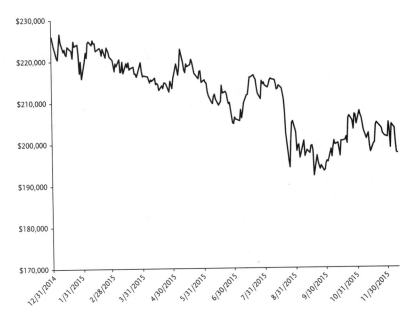

Figure 3-3a Daily *prices* of Berkshire-Hathaway shares are representative of a pattern.

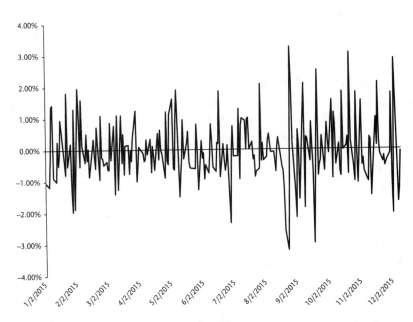

Figure 3-3b Daily *returns* of Berkshire-Hathaway shares are representative of randomness.

Representativeness errors when one is forming expectations promote increased trading. This increase is especially true among traders who perceive trading as a game of skill. Investors misled by representativeness change their expectations abruptly because stock returns are volatile, supplying reasons for trades that hamper returns.[40]

Traders at the Draft King and Fan Duel fantasy sports sites perceive trading as a game of skill. They choose players with the best chances to win and are rewarded when these players win. Many traders on fantasy sports sites become addicted, losing large amounts of money. "For Addicts, Fantasy Sites Can Lead to Ruinous Path," said a *New York Times* article. Josh Adams owed $30,000 to friends and family when he finally quit fantasy sports. 'Gambling counselors say they could more easily help people like Mr. Adams if fantasy companies did not portray their games as involving mostly skill. That alone is a risk for addiction,' said Keith Whyte, executive director of the National Council on Problem Gambling."[41]

AVAILABILITY

We use availability shortcuts when we assess the probability that our airplane would arrive on time by retrieving from our minds the proportion of our flights that have arrived on time, yet *aware* that the proportion among all flights is likely different. We commit availability errors when we assess that probability by our flight experience, yet *unaware* that the proportion among all flights is likely different. We also commit availability errors when our retrieval process is biased, as when friends who beat the market share their stories with us but friends who lag the market do not. And we commit availability errors when our search processes are ineffective, as when we fail to search the performance records of all funds, not only those readily available in our minds.

Availability shortcuts and errors stem from what Daniel Kahneman described as the belief that "what you see is all there is."[42] Attention is a scarce resource. We conserve attention by gravitating toward easily available information, especially information that is vivid. We commonly fail to ask whether this information is all there is, let alone search for additional information.

Availability shortcuts and errors are evident in political arenas. Between October 1996 and November 2000, the conservative Fox News Channel was introduced to the cable programming of 20 percent of US towns. Availability of the Fox News Channel in these towns induced an extra 3 to 8 percent Republican vote.[43]

Amateur investors are frequently buyers of attention-grabbing stocks, such as those in the news, those experiencing extreme trading volume, and those with extreme one-day returns. Attention-driven buying stems from the difficulty of searching among the thousands of stocks investors can buy. Investors do not face similar difficulty when selling because they sell only the much smaller number of stocks they already own.[44]

Workplaces are a setting for trading motivated by availability errors. Workers' stock purchases are similar to those of coworkers because workers make them available to fellow workers. Yet stocks purchased under stronger coworker purchase activity do not yield higher returns. Moreover, social interactions limit diversification, increasing risk with no increase in expected returns.[45]

Round numbers are more easily available to one's mind than odd numbers, prompting availability errors. Traders who submit "limit" orders to buy shares specify the highest price they are willing to pay, whether an odd number such as $99.78 or a round number such as $100. Similarly, traders who submit limit orders to sell shares specify the lowest price they are willing to accept. There is a pronounced clustering of limit orders at round prices. The most frequent limit order prices are multiples of 100, followed by multiples of 50, and multiples of 10. Amateur traders are especially prone to clustering limit orders at round prices, and such traders earn low returns.[46] Availability errors also bestow an advantage on companies whose names are at the beginning of the alphabet. Stocks of such companies draw more traders, especially amateur traders.[47]

Three groups of investors in one experiment reviewed two successful funds of a fictional Allen Funds group and were asked whether they were willing to invest in a new Allen fund. The information presented to the first group said that Allen has exactly two funds, the information presented to the second said that Allen has thirty funds, and the information presented to the third said nothing about Allen's number of funds. Mention of thirty funds alerted investors to the possibility of availability errors, but investors failed to consider that possibility when nothing was said about the number of Allen funds. Indeed, answers did not differ when nothing was said about the number of funds and when the number of funds was said to be two.[48]

Mutual funds with high returns attract investors only if the stocks in these funds were recently featured in the media. Yet availability through the media does not help investors gain better returns. Instead, availability errors amplify the tendency of investors to flock to mutual funds containing stocks with recently featured high past returns. Mutual fund managers exploit availability errors by purchasing such stocks at times close to the dates when they report the contents of their funds, a strategy most prevalent among poorly performing mutual funds.[49]

CONFIDENCE

Confidence is of three types, classified by psychologists Don Moore and Paul Healy: estimation, placement, and precision.[50] Confidence shortcuts and errors correspond to these three types. We commit *overestimation errors* if we expect a 12 percent portfolio return when objective assessment indicates that its expected return is 8 percent. We commit *underestimation errors* if we expect a 6 percent portfolio return. We commit *overplacement errors* if we expect our portfolio return to place us among the top 10 percent of investors, when objective assessment places us among the bottom 40 percent. We commit *underplacement errors* if we expect our return to place us among the bottom 30 percent. We commit *overprecision errors* if we believe that there is a 90 percent probability that our portfolio return will fall between 10 percent and 14 percent when objective assessment indicates that there is a 90 percent probability that it will fall between a negative 10 percent return and a 26 percent return. We commit *underprecision errors* if we believe that there is a 90 percent probability that our portfolio return will fall between a negative 20 percent return and a 36 percent return.

Overconfidence can be useful. People who commit overplacement errors enjoy higher status than modest people who underplace themselves or place themselves objectively.[51] Moreover, people who commit overplacement errors maintain their high status even when their overplacement errors are revealed.[52]

Overestimation, overplacement, and overprecision are not different manifestations of one underlying type. Instead, wrote Moore and Healy, they are conceptually and empirically distinct. They noted further that *underconfidence* is common, even if not as common as overconfidence, and identified circumstances in which people are likely to display overconfidence or underconfidence.[53]

Underestimation errors are likely when we are contemplating *easy* tasks, whereas *overestimation errors* are likely when we are contemplating *difficult* tasks. Underestimation and overestimation errors occur because any estimate includes an error component. This component makes it likely that we underestimate performance on easy tests but overestimate performance on difficult tests. After all, we cannot overestimate our A grade on an easy test but we can overestimate our C grade on a difficult test, estimating it as a B grade.[54] Investors who perceive investing as a *difficult* task are likely to *overestimate* their future returns.

Overplacement errors are likely when we are contemplating *easy* tasks, whereas *underplacement errors* are likely when we are contemplating *difficult* ones. Driving is an easy task, prompting overplacement. A frequently cited study reported that 93 percent of American drivers and 69 percent of Swedish drivers commit overplacement errors, placing themselves, on average, above average.[55] Juggling and unicycle riding, unlike driving, are difficult tasks. A more recent and less frequently cited study found that people on average place themselves *below* average at juggling and unicycle riding.[56] Investors who perceive investing as a *difficult* task are likely to *underplace* themselves relative to other investors.

Another frequently cited article reported that people tend to *overplace* themselves in the likelihood of positive events, such as owning their own homes. And people tend to *underplace* themselves in the likelihood of negative events, such as attempting suicide.[57] A more recent and less frequently cited study found, however, that our tendency to *overplace* ourselves as likely to own a home and *underplace* ourselves as likely to attempt suicide is due mostly to the feature of commonness—common or rare—rather than the feature of valence—positive or negative. We commit overplacement when contemplating common events, such as owning our own homes or living past the age of seventy, but we commit underplacement when contemplating rare events, such as suicide or living past the age of a hundred, whether these events are positive or negative.[58] Investors who perceive above-average future returns as a *common* event are likely to *overplace* themselves relative to other investors.

Overprecision errors are usually demonstrated in experiments in which people are asked to specify 90 percent confidence intervals around some numerical estimate, such as the weight of a Boeing 747 airplane or the length of the Nile River. Confidence intervals that include the true weight, length, or other numerical estimates occur as rarely as 30 percent of the time, rather than 90 percent.

Overprecision errors afflict even professionals. Substantial overprecision errors are evident in forecasts of stock-market returns by financial executives. In the absence of these errors, 80 percent of realized stock-market returns are within the executives' 80 percent confidence intervals. But realized returns are within 80 percent confidence intervals only 33 percent of the time. Greater overprecision errors in forecasts of stock-market returns are associated with greater overprecision errors in executives' forecasts of their companies' projects and with higher corporate investment.[59]

Moreover, managers who have issued accurate forecasts in the past tend to become overconfident in the precision of their future forecasts. Specifically, managers who have predicted earnings accurately in the previous four quarters are less accurate in their subsequent earnings predictions. Investors and analysts seem aware of managers' overprecision, reacting less strongly to their later forecasts.[60]

Managers' overestimation of future performance increases their propensity to engage in reporting fraud. Overestimating managers are more likely to engage in earnings management where they "borrow" from future earnings to boost current ones. They also overestimate future earnings available to cover borrowed earnings. When earnings turn out to be lower than estimated they choose to engage in even greater earnings management rather than come clean.[61] And CEOs who commit overplacement errors are overly eager to acquire companies, reducing the returns of their shareholders while increasing their own status.[62]

One criticism of overprecision experiments is that their questions bear little resemblance to questions in daily life. We do not consider a 90 percent confidence interval around travel time when we leave for a lunch meeting. Instead, if punctuality is important, we leave early. More generally, we consider the costs of erring on each side such as arriving too early or too late, and our uncertainty, such as about travel time. Still, experiments accounting for costs and uncertainty found that people commit overprecision errors even when they know the relevant costs and uncertainty. Overprecision often brings bad consequences, as when we arrive late to important meetings, miss planes, or bounce checks.[63]

Examination of a large group of British investors confirmed that the three kinds of overconfidence—overestimation, overplacement, and overprecision—are distinct.[64] There was a substantial propensity for overprecision errors. More than 8 out of 10 investors were overprecise in estimates of stock-market returns, and a similar proportion was overprecise in estimates of their own portfolio returns. Yet there was no general propensity for making overplacement errors. Fewer than half of investors expected their risk-adjusted portfolio returns to exceed those of the market. And there was no general propensity for overestimation, although a minority of investors greatly overestimated their returns. Whereas only slightly more than half of investors overestimated their portfolio returns, the mean overestimation was 4.3 percentage points, pulled up by that minority.

We find further evidence of underestimation, overestimation, underplacement, and overplacement in a Gallup survey of American investors. Compare expectations of returns in June 1998, in the stock-market boom, to expectations in June 2002, in the bust that followed. A reasonable expectation of stock-market return during the twelve months following June 1998 is 8.8 percent, the sum of the 5.3 percent Treasury-bill yield that month and a 3.5 percent "equity premium," the extra expected return from risky stocks over the returns of practically risk-free Treasury bills. We can describe estimates above 8.8 percent as overestimates and those below 8.8 percent as underestimates.

The Gallup survey asked people for their expectations of stock-market returns during the following 12 months and tabulated expectations by ranges: 4 percent or lower, 5–9 percent, 10–14 percent, and so on up to 30 percent or higher. Figure 3-4a shows the distribution of expectations of returns for the 12 months following June 1998. The mean expectation of stock-market returns was 15.2 percent, and the median was 12.0 percent. The higher level of the mean than the median indicates that very high expectations of returns were prevalent among a minority of investors.

Consider expectations of stock-market returns in the 5–9 percent range as representing reasonable ones, as they include the 8.8 percent reasonable expectation. The return expectations of approximately 21 percent of investors fell within that range. About 3 percent of investors underestimated returns as 4 percent or lower, whereas about 76 percent overestimated returns as 10 percent or higher. We see, then, a strong tendency to overestimate returns.

A reasonable expectation of stock returns during the 12 months following June 2002 is 5.7 percent, composed of a 2.2 percent Treasury-bill rate and a 3.5 percent equity premium, placing it also in the 5–9 percent range. The return expectations of approximately 40 percent of investors fell within that range. The mean expectation of stock-market returns during the 12 months following June 2002 was 10.3 percent, and the median was 6.0 percent. The higher level of the mean than the median indicates that very high expectations of returns were prevalent among a minority of investors, as they were in June 1998. Figure 3-4b shows the distribution of expectations of returns for the twelve months following June 2002. Overestimation of stock-market returns in June 2002 was somewhat more prevalent than underestimation, but much less than in June 1998. Approximately 28 percent of investors underestimated returns as 4 percent or lower, and approximately 32 percent overestimated returns as 10 percent or higher. Lower expectations of future returns in 2002 than in 1998 correspond to lower overestimation.

Comparison between answers to a pair of Gallup questions sheds further light on overplacement and underplacement. One question, discussed earlier, asked people for their expectations of stock-market returns during the following twelve months. Another asked people for their expectations

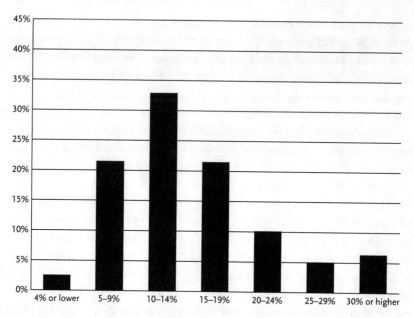

Figure 3-4a Stock market returns expected by investors in June 1998 during the following twelve months

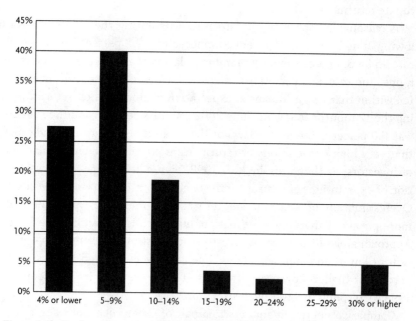

Figure 3-4b Stock market returns expected by investors in June 2002 during the following twelve months.

of the returns of their *own portfolios* during the same following twelve months. Figure 3-5a shows six-month moving means of both expectations. Overplacement is more prevalent than underplacement. Mean expectations of returns of people's own portfolios consistently exceed mean expectations of returns of the stock market. We note that reasonable expectations, free of overplacement and underplacement, are likely to place people's mean expectations of the returns of their own portfolios *below* their mean expectations of stock-market returns, as people's own portfolios are likely to also include bonds whose expected returns are lower than those of stocks.

Comparison of six-month moving averages of medians rather than means, presented in Figure 3-5b, shows overplacement as well, but gaps between medians of expectations of returns of one's own portfolios and the stock market are narrower than gaps between means. This finding indicates that a particular group of investors has an especially high propensity for overplacement, not equally shared by all.

Other evidence is consistent with the observation that propensity for overestimation and overplacement errors is concentrated among particular groups, such as active traders. A poll at the Fidelity Traders Summit

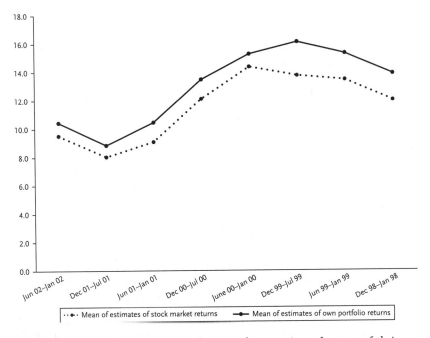

Figure 3-5a Six-month moving mean of investors' expectations of returns of their own portfolios and the stock market.

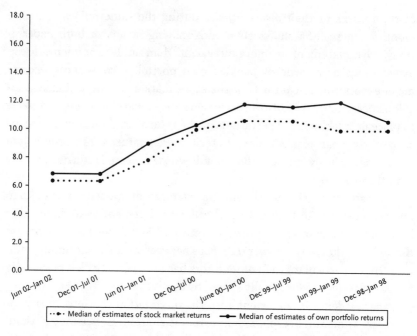

Figure 3-5b Six-month moving median of investors' expectations of returns of their own portfolios and the stock market.

revealed that 62 percent of active traders expected to beat the market and 29 percent expected to match it, leaving only a handful who expected to lag the market.[65]

People often overestimate their control, stumbling into an "illusion of control." Terror attacks are becoming more frequent around the globe, shattering people's sense of control. Experience in Israel, a country that experienced frequent terror attacks, indicates that concern about terrorism increases people's desire for control and leads to avoidant behavior. The extent of avoidance depends on perceptions of control over the odds of becoming a terror victim. People who perceive low control exhibit avoidant behavior, changing their preferences and patterns of consumption accordingly.[66]

Overestimation of control reflected in illusion of control can possibly enhance performance in settings where people have some control, but not in settings where they have no control. Studies showing that overestimation of control degrades performance are typically conducted in settings where people have no control, making it impossible to underestimate it. The task of professional traders in one study was to raise an investment index as much as possible by pressing keys on a keyboard. Traders were told that changes in the index are partly random but three keys, Z, X, and C, have a special effect. In truth, any sense of control was illusory because movements in the index were entirely random. Some traders overestimated their control while others did not, yet no traders could have *underestimated* their control, because the setting of the experiment precluded *any* control.[67]

Some evidence indicates that overestimation of control can enhance performance in settings where people have some control, such as in a game of golf or a memory test. Golfers who were told they are receiving a lucky ball scored better than players who were told nothing, and students who were allowed to keep a lucky charm with them did better on a memory test than students whose lucky charms were kept in another room.[68]

Overestimation of control can also increase savings rates and wealth accumulation. People who agree with statements such as "I have little control over the things that happen to me," and "there is really no way I can solve some of the problems I have" are people who have an external locus of control. People with an internal locus of control are likely to agree with statements such as "what happens to me in the future mostly depends on me," and "I can do just about anything I really set my mind to do." People with an internal sense of control save more and accumulate more pension wealth than people with an external locus of control.[69]

CONCLUSION

Cognitive errors are commonly placed at the center of behavioral finance. Indeed, a disposition to commit cognitive errors underlies the common description of people as irrational. Cognitive shortcuts, however, are more frequent than cognitive errors and more important. These shortcuts lead us right almost all the time, even if on occasion they turn into errors. Knowledge of cognitive shortcuts and errors helps us use shortcuts while avoiding errors.

Overconfidence errors are regularly listed as the most common and pernicious cognitive errors. Mention of average drivers who place themselves above average commonly leads to an assertion that average investors place themselves above average. Yet most evidence indicates that average investors actually do not place themselves above average.

The most common and pernicious cognitive errors in the context of finance are framing, hindsight, and confirmation. Framing errors mislead investors into framing trading as a jog in the park, rather than a race against possibly better runners in finance. Hindsight errors mislead investors into thinking that future stock-market booms and crashes can be seen as clearly as past ones. And confirmation errors mislead investors into seeking and assigning much weight to confirming evidence, while overlooking disconfirming evidence. See Box 3.1 for a summary of cognitive shortcuts and errors.

Box 3.1 COGNITIVE SHORTCUTS AND ERRORS

Framing shortcuts and errors—We use framing shortcuts when we simplify complex problems and substitute solutions to the simplified problems for solutions to the complex problems. We use framing shortcuts well when the solutions to the simplified problems are close to the solutions to the complex problems. We commit cognitive errors when the solutions to the simplified problems are far from the solutions to the complex problems.

Hindsight shortcuts and errors—We use hindsight shortcuts when we predict future events from past events, and when we predict outcomes of actions. We use hindsight shortcuts well when we can reliably predict future events from past events and when we can reliably predict outcomes of actions. We commit hindsight errors when we believe, erroneously, that we can reliably predict future events from past events, and when we believe, erroneously, that we can predict reliably outcomes of actions.

Confirmation shortcuts and errors—We use confirmation shortcuts when we examine evidence to confirm or disconfirm claims or beliefs. We use confirmation shortcuts well when we search for disconfirming evidence as vigorously as we search for evidence confirming them, and assign equal weight to disconfirming and confirming evidence. We commit confirmation errors when we search for confirming evidence while overlooking disconfirming evidence, and when we assign lower weight to disconfirming evidence than to confirming evidence.

Anchoring and adjustment shortcuts and errors—We use anchoring and adjustment shortcuts when we estimate prices, distances, weights, and other numerical values. We use anchoring and adjustment shortcuts well when we begin with proper anchors and adjust from them properly. We commit anchoring and adjustment errors when we begin with faulty anchors and adjust from them improperly.

Representativeness shortcuts and errors—We use representativeness shortcuts when we assess the probability of events by their similarity or representativeness to other events. We use representativeness shortcuts well when we consider both representativeness information and base-rate information. We commit representativeness errors when

---

(continued)

Box 3.1 (Continued)

we assign too much weight to representativeness information and too little to base-rate information.

Availability shortcuts and errors—We use availability shortcuts when we assess the probability of events by information that is readily available in our minds. We use availability shortcuts well when all the information is available in our minds, or when we are aware that not all the information is available in our minds. We commit availability errors when not all the information is available in our minds, or we are not aware of its absence.

Confidence shortcuts and errors—Confidence shortcuts and errors are of three types— *estimation shortcuts and errors, placement shortcuts and errors,* and *precision shortcuts and errors.* We use confidence shortcuts well in estimation, placement, and precision when we assess them objectively and place objective confidence in them. We commit overconfidence errors when we place too much confidence in them, and we commit underconfidence errors when we place too little confidence in them.

CHAPTER 4

Emotional Shortcuts and Errors

We often speak about emotions in finance as if they were shorthand for emotional errors. We are advised to set emotions aside when we are making financial choices, and use reason alone. But this advice is neither feasible nor smart, for two reasons. First, we cannot set emotions aside. Second, emotional shortcuts help more than emotional errors harm. Emotional shortcuts complement reason, and the interaction between emotional shortcuts and reason is beneficial, often critically so.

Emotional shortcuts, like cognitive shortcuts, are part of the intuitive "blink" System 1 in our minds, leading to good choices in most of life. But shortcuts turn into errors when they mislead us into poor choices. System 2, the reflective "think" system in our minds, leads to better choices when System 1 misleads. People with knowledge of human behavior and financial facts use emotional shortcuts correctly, whereas people lacking such knowledge commit emotional errors, because they use them incorrectly.

Fear acts as an emotional shortcut that turns into an error when fear is absent or when it is exaggerated. Fear guides us rightly when it prompts us to retreat from a knife-wielding stranger bearing an angry face, and when it prevents us from buying houses likely to be repossessed in foreclosures. But fear guides us wrongly when it prompts us to retreat from a knife-wielding friend who chops vegetables, and when it compels us to sell all our stocks in a financial crisis.

A case in point: SM was a patient with focal bilateral amygdala lesions that blocked fear. Attempts to induce fear into SM included live snakes and spiders, a tour of a haunted house, and emotionally evocative films, yet SM was never afraid. Absence of fear was also evident in three months of observation of SM's real-life experiences, and a life history replete with traumatic events, including emotional errors such as approaching a drugged-out man who pulled a knife and threatened to kill her.[1]

Neuroscientist Antonio Damasio described Somatic-Marker as the mechanism whereby emotional shortcuts prompt reasonable choices. He tells the story of one of his patients, a man with ventromedial prefrontal brain damage that blocked emotions. Lack of emotional response prevented the man from making a simple choice between two dates for an appointment. Instead he went on to list reasons for and against each date, from previous engagements to weather, until the choice was made for him.[2]

In April 1838 Charles Darwin famously listed pro and con reasons for marrying. On the pro side were "constant companion" and "charms of music and female chit-chat." On the con side were "means limited," and "terrible loss of time." Yet emotion overcame the list. "The day of days!" is how he described the day in November 1838 when Emma Wedgwood accepted his marriage proposal.[3]

The interaction between cognition and emotion makes it difficult to attribute shortcuts, errors, and choices to one or the other. Reason tells us that flying is safer than driving long distances, yet some choose to drive. The choice can be attributed to cognition, where images of crashed airplanes are more readily available to mind than images of crashed cars, or to emotion, whereby airplane crashes evoke greater fear, or to a combination of both.

EMOTION, MOOD, AND AFFECT

Emotion, mood, and affect (see Box 4.1) are regularly commingled, but they are distinct by intensity, duration, focus, and valence—positive or negative. Fear was a very intense negative emotion felt in early 2009 as we focused on stock markets that cut retirement savings by half for some and threatened to cut much more. Fear abated into a less intense but longer-lasting negative mood that has persisted even as the stock market recovered. The emotion of fear and its mood have subsequently faded into a much less intense but longer-lasting negative affect of stock markets.

Psychologist Paul Ekman classically listed seven emotions whose physiological effects are evident in facial expressions: Fear, anger, sadness, disgust, surprise, happiness, and contentment[4] Yet there is no generally accepted list of emotions. Other lists also include hope, pride, regret, shame, guilt, and self-control.

Box 4.1 EMOTION, MOOD, AND AFFECT

Emotion is very intense, with a short duration and clear focus.

Mood is muted emotion, less intense than emotion, but longer lasting.

Affect is the faint whisper of emotion or mood, stripped down to valence, positive or negative.

The appraisal-tendency framework (ATF), popular in psychology, distinguishes *cognitive appraisals* from *appraisal tendencies*.[5] Each emotion is defined by a specific pattern of cognitive appraisals. We experience anger if we appraise a car accident as being caused by other people, such as bad drivers. But we experience sadness if we appraise it as being controlled by factors beyond human control, such as bad weather. Six cognitive dimensions of appraisals underlie emotions: pleasantness, anticipated effort, certainty, attentional activity, responsibility—our own responsibility or responsibility of others—and control, our own control or control by others or situations.[6]

People experience anger after being cut off in traffic by bad drivers. Appraisal tendencies activated by this anger shape future perceptions and behavior. Appraisal tendencies lead angry people to take more risk in future activities even if these are unrelated to driving, such as taking more investment risk.

HOPE AND FEAR

Fear is a negative emotion arising in response to danger, whereas hope is a positive one in anticipation of reward. Cognitive appraisal notes that fear is unpleasant and hope is pleasant, but the two are similar in that control is in the hands of others, whether other people or situations. We fear the danger of an airplane crash but cannot control the outcome. We hope to win the lottery but cannot control the outcome. Exuberance is extreme hope, as in the famed case of "irrational exuberance."

We enhance hope by contemplating all the things we would buy if we won the lottery and we alleviate fear by recoiling, as we do from a snake, or by attaching ourselves to other people, such as parents. Fearful people who cannot attach themselves to others do so instead to branded products, as toddlers who attach themselves to security blankets. Consumers who experience fear in the presence of branded products feel greater emotional attachment to these brands than do consumers who experience other emotions in the presence of those goods.[7]

Stock-market declines induce fear. Days of substantial stock-market declines are also days of substantial increases in hospital admissions, especially for fear-related conditions of anxiety and panic disorder.[8] High stock returns are associated with better mental health, whereas high volatility of returns is associated with poorer mental health.[9] Fear induced by earthquakes increases the probability that people assign to stock-market crashes.[10]

Fear increases risk aversion even among financial professionals, leading to high risk aversion in financial busts and low risk aversion in financial booms. In an experiment, financial professionals asked to read a story about a financial bust became more fearful than those asked to read a story about a financial boom, and fear led them to reduce risky investments.[11]

Fearful investors fly to safety, switching from risky investments into safe ones. The Chicago Board Options Exchange volatility index (VIX) is a risk gauge also known as the fear index. It measures expectations of future risk by expectations of future volatility of stock returns. Flight-to-safety episodes coincide with increases in the VIX, bearish consumer sentiment, and bond returns that exceed stock returns.[12] A financial planner described clients who asked her to sell all their stocks in 2008 and 2009, after the stock-market crash, yet reversed themselves and asked her to buy stocks in 2014, after the stock market recovered. "It's an emotional reaction," she said. "[The years] 2008 and 2009 were like being in the fetal position." Now in 2014 "everyone wants to buy."[13]

Fearful investors expect low returns with high risk, whereas hopeful investors expect high returns with low risk. Brokerage records and matching monthly surveys show that high past returns are associated with increased return expectations combined with decreased risk perceptions and risk aversion.[14] A Gallup survey of investors asked, "Do you think that now is a good time to invest in the financial markets?" Figure 4-1 shows that high recent returns are followed by high percentages of investors who think that now is a good time to invest. For example, 78 percent of investors answered "yes" in the exuberant days of February 2000, after major stock gains. Yet only 41 percent answered so in the fearful days of March 2003, after major stock losses. Gallup also asked investors if they believe that the market is overvalued or undervalued. Figure 4-2 shows that months when large proportions of investors believed that the stock market is *overvalued* were also months when they thought that now is a *good time to invest* in the financial markets. These beliefs are consistent with the operation of the

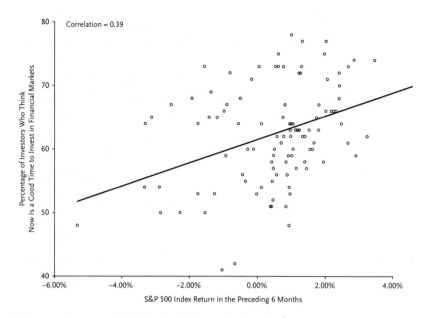

Figure 4-1 Investors think that times following high stock returns are good times to invest in financial markets (June 1998–December 2007).

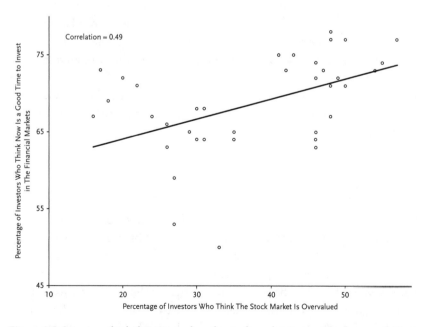

Figure 4-2 Investors think that times when the stock market is overvalued are good times to invest in financial markets (June 1998–July 2002).

intuitive System 1, but not with the operation of the reflective System 2, in which a belief that the stock market is overvalued is accompanied by a belief that now is not a good time to invest.

Links between fear and risk aversion have been uncovered in many experiments. Consider the Cash-Out experiment, lasting 25 rounds. You begin with $10 in a stock whose price can go up or down in each round. After the current price of the stock is displayed, you can choose to play the next round or cash out by selling the stock at the current price. If you choose to cash out at the start of the game, you keep your $10. If you play one or more rounds, you keep whatever the price of the stock is at the end of the last round you play. How many rounds would you play?

Video clips showing scenes from two horror movies, *The Sixth Sense* and *The Ring,* induced fear into one group of people playing the Cash-Out game. People in a control group saw scenes from two benign documentaries about Benjamin Franklin and Vincent van Gogh. Fear led to early sell-off of the stock. The emotion is also contagious. Fearful people sold especially early when they believed that their fear is shared by others.[15]

People in another experiment saw a clip from *Hostel*, another horror movie, showing a man tortured in a dark basement. Increased risk aversion was evident among people who watched the clip, but not among those who reported enjoying horror movies. The experiment complements surveys among clients of an Italian bank conducted in 2007, before the financial crisis, and in mid-2009, when the financial crisis was vivid. Risk aversion was measured qualitatively by asking clients about their willingness to take risk, and quantitatively by asking them to specify the sure amount that would persuade them to forgo a 50-50 chance to win 5,000 euros. Both measures indicated higher risk aversion in the crisis period than in the pre-crisis period, and these measures are consistent with actual changes in the portfolios of the bank's clients.[16]

GREED, AMBITION, AND STATUS SEEKING

Greed is commonly positioned at the opposite end of the spectrum from fear, but greed is best seen as a reflection of ambition and status seeking heightened by fear and hope. We fear being outpaced by the social status of our competitors and hope to outpace them instead. The status order in society is never stable, because lower-status neighbors can outpace us by investing in business ventures that turn out to be successful, or by picking handfuls of stocks that multiply manyfold. People holding $1 billion do not fear an absence of food and shelter, but they fear being outpaced in social status by neighbors who had $800 million yesterday but might have $2 billion tomorrow. We describe ourselves as ambitious as we strive to add to our wealth and increase our social status. Yet we describe as greedy our neighbors who do the same.

Corporate CEOs likely to have more wealth than necessary for several lifetimes of spending but they do not always perceive their social status as sufficiently high. Status competition in the marriage market leads unmarried male CEOs to take more risk than married ones. The investment policies of unmarried male CEOs are more aggressive, and the volatility of the returns of their company stocks is higher than those of married male CEOs. The effect is weaker for older male CEOs, who are not as keen on status competition in the marriage market.[17]

People vary in their status seeking. Levels of status seeking can be measured by levels of agreement with statements such as "I would really like an important job in which people look up to me," "I like talking to people who are important," and "I like to be admired for my achievements." People strongly disposed toward status seeking focus on achieving gains, whereas weakly disposed people focus on avoiding losses.[18]

Status order is especially unstable in periods of exuberance, as in the late 1990s, when people could see neighbors overtaking them by investing in the right dot-com stock. People seem greedy as they buy stocks held by their status competitors so as to "keep up with the Joneses," or concentrate their portfolios in fewer stocks, hoping that high returns would help them "move ahead of the Joneses," but it is status seeking, not greed, that animates them.

HAPPINESS, SADNESS, AND DISGUST

Happiness comes with gains and enjoyment, sadness with losses and helplessness, and disgust with proximity to distasteful objects or ideas. Happiness encourages us toward actions that bring further gains and enjoyment, sadness prods us to pause and contemplate actions that would stem losses and helplessness, and disgust prompts us to expel repellent objects and keep our distance from abhorrent ideas.

Happiness and sadness affect appraisal tendencies. Sadness promotes the desire for immediate gratification and increased spending. Sadness was induced into one group by a clip from the movie *The Champ*, portraying the death of a boy's mentor. People in a control group watched a neutral clip from a *National Geographic* special, portraying fish at the Great Barrier Reef. Sadness brought "myopic misery," increasing impatience and focus on obtaining money immediately.[19] Sadness among mutual fund managers following the death of a parent was associated with a 3-percentage-point decline in their funds' returns. Sadness induced greater impatience, higher risk aversion, and increased sensitivity to losses.[20]

Happiness, however, promotes delayed gratification and increased savings. Happiness was induced in one group of people by a montage of stand-up comedy bits from Robin Williams's *Live on Broadway*. A control group watched neutral images of landscapes and wildlife. People in the happy group were more willing to delay gratification than people in the control one.[21]

Disgust was induced into one group of people by a video clip from *Trainspotting*, portraying a man using a filthy toilet. People in the control group saw a neutral clip from the *National Geographic* special. All people were given closed boxes, told that they contained office supplies, and asked to shake them to establish a sense of ownership. People who were induced to feel disgust were ready to dispose of their boxes, willing to sell them at prices lower than those set by people who watched the neutral clip.[22]

ANGER

Anger, like fear, is a negative and unpleasant emotion arising in response to threats or dangers. Yet whereas fearful and anxious people perceive control as being in the hands of others, angry people perceive control to be in their own. Lack of control discourages fearful and anxious people from taking risk, prompting them to act as pessimists do, whereas a sense of control encourages angry people to take risk, prompting them to act as optimists do. People disposed toward anger agree with statements such as "I am an impulsive person," "I get angry when I have to wait because of others' mistakes," and "when I am frustrated, I feel like hitting someone." People disposed toward anger are more willing to invest in stocks than those not so disposed. They also prefer medium- and long-term investments, and believe that they can forecast stock-market trends. People disposed toward anxiety agree with statements such as "I feel blue," "I worry too much over something that really doesn't matter," and "I take disappointments so keenly that I can't put them out of my mind." They prefer interest-bearing accounts, and do not believe that they can forecast stock-market trends.[23]

Anger can occasionally counter cognitive errors, attenuating the tendency to commit confirmation errors. Angry people who read an article about a controversial social issue were more likely to consider disconfirming information than sad people who read the same article.[24] But anger can mislead into poor choices, as it induces underestimation of the likelihood of losses and other bad outcomes. Angry people have a higher than average likelihood to divorce, suffer more cardiovascular disease, and face problems at work, while rating themselves less likely to experience these problems.[25]

The Balloon Analog Risk task offers insights about the usefulness of anger. People click on pumps that inflate balloons on a computer screen. Each pump of the balloon without an explosion adds money into an account. But the money in the account associated with that balloon is lost if the balloon explodes. The objective is to get the most money. People tend to be overly cautious in the balloon task, avoiding explosions but collecting relatively little. Angry people, however, inflate balloons further, bearing the risk of balloon explosions but collecting more money overall.[26]

Anger can be beneficial in negotiations. Negotiators expressing anger convey toughness, which can evoke fear among counterparts and lead to greater concessions. A film director said, "I use [anger] as an excuse to say what I've been wanting to say and it comes out in such a volcanic way that no one can argue with that. Just, boom, I'm over the edge and everything comes out."[27] But anger in negotiations can backfire, leading counterparts to escalate conflicts, act in retaliation, or walk away from the negotiation table, because they infer that angry negotiators are particularly selfish.[28]

Walking away from profitable deals imposes costs now but yields possible benefits later, as it teaches fairness. Imagine that I am holding $1,000 in cash, facing you and a person behind a curtain. You will never know the identity of the person behind the curtain, and he or she will never know your identity. I ask the person behind the curtain to make an offer for the division of the $1,000 between the two of you, perhaps $500 for each of you or perhaps $10 for you and $990 for him or her. But the offer is an ultimatum, not open to counteroffer or negotiation. This is the "ultimatum game."

If you accept the offer, I will divide the money as offered. But if you reject the offer, I'll keep the $1,000 and neither of you will receive anything. Suppose that the person behind the curtain offered you $10. Do you accept? Anger prompted by a sense of unfairness leads many to turn down offers of $200 and even more. We pay now as we deprive ourselves of the utilitarian benefits of $200 but we enjoy now the emotional benefits of self-righteousness. And we may benefit later as turning down unfair offers teaches others to be fair.

The anger of credit card holders at the unfairness of their card companies culminated in the Credit Card Accountability, Responsibility and Disclosure (CARD) Act of 2009. For several decades beforehand, the balance of power favored credit card companies over cardholders, affording the firms much leeway to impose sizable fees and major increases in interest rates even when cardholders missed no payments. Consumer advocacy groups have regularly pressed for limits on the powers of credit card companies, to no avail. Anger boiled over in 2009, during the financial crisis, facilitating enactment of the CARD Act.[29]

Anger against the investment establishment was on display in 2015, directed at high-frequency traders. Their trades take place in milliseconds, powered by high-speed computing and fiber-optic connections. Michael Lewis's book *Flash Boys* crystallized the anger of investors who perceive themselves as losing while high-frequency traders gain. He described high-frequency trading as computerized scalping that allows traders with the fastest computers and best fiber-optic connections to gain at the expense of other investors.[30]

REGRET AND PRIDE

Regret is a "cognitive emotion," a negative and unpleasant one we experience when we can easily imagine a different choice that would have brought a better outcome. People mention regret as the most frequent negative emotion they experience.[31] We kick ourselves for buying a laptop computer for $1,199 when we see an ad offering it for $999 a few days later. Pride is at the opposite end of the emotional spectrum from regret. We fill with pride for buying the laptop at $1,199, before its price increases to $1,399. Regret and pride come when we exercise control and carry responsibility. We exercise our choice to buy a laptop now or later and we bear responsibility for the timing.

Regret is painful, whereas pride is pleasurable, but both are useful parts of System 1, warning us against behavior likely to inflict regret and encouraging us to toward behavior likely to generate pride. Yet engagement of System 2 is necessary when System 1 misleads us into overlooking randomness and luck in the relation between choice and outcome.

"The cat, having sat upon a hot stove lid, will not sit upon a hot stove lid again," said Mark Twain, "but he won't sit upon a cold stove lid, either." We need not kick ourselves with regret when choices that were reasonable in foresight are followed by sad outcomes, and we should not stroke ourselves with pride when choices that were unreasonable in foresight are followed by happy outcomes.

Regret aversion and pride seeking affect financial choices, such as the choice to buy a stock or sell it. Investors who sell stocks at a loss very likely regret buying them. Repurchasing these stocks weeks or months later at higher prices adds to the pain of regret, as opening old wounds adds to physical pain. Repurchasing stocks whose prices declined subsequent to an earlier sale, however, brings the joy of pride, as we congratulate ourselves for selling in time. Investors prefer to repurchase stocks they previously sold at a gain rather than stocks they previously sold at a loss, and they prefer to repurchase stocks whose prices declined subsequent to an earlier sale rather than stocks whose prices increased. These preferences, however, do not add to investors' returns.[32]

The entrepreneur Joe Green helped Mark Zuckerberg create "Facemash," a short-lived web application that asked users to rate the attractiveness of Harvard women. Later, Green turned down Zuckerberg's offer of a position at Facebook, on the advice of Green's father, a professor who said, "I don't think you should do any more of these Zuckerberg projects." Green soothes his regret by recalling choices that were followed by happy outcomes. "Every once in a while you can have a moment of bitterness," he said, "but in general I have been so blessed with what I have been able to do."[33]

Another former Zuckerberg colleague, Ali Fedotowsky, soothes her regret by insisting that her choice to leave was reasonable. Fedotowsky left a marketing position at Facebook and millions in unvested stock options to find love on *The Bachelorette*, a reality television show. Her eighteen-month engagement to Roberto Martinez ended before Facebook went public, but she expresses no regrets. "Would I change anything if I could go back and keep my job at Facebook instead of doing *The Bachelorette*? Absolutely not. I don't regret one decision."[34]

Regret is associated with responsibility, as responsibility for choices opens the door to regret if choices turn out poorly. I am not burdened by responsibility for choosing to turn down an early Facebook job or quit such a job early, as I have neither been offered a Facebook job nor quit one. You are probably not burdened by that responsibility, either. We might be disappointed not to have had the choice to be employed by Facebook in its early days, but we do not feel regret for forgoing such an absent choice. Yet Joe Green and Ali Fedotowsky had Facebook choices and bear responsibility for outcomes.

Responsibility for choices can escalate commitment to them, as people try to minimize regret. People who choose to wait for a bus keep on waiting, trying to minimize the regret they would feel if they left, and anticipating the extra regret they would feel if the bus arrived soon after they had left.[35]

We alleviate regret by keeping ourselves ignorant of the outcomes of choices we have considered but did not make.[36] We also alleviate regret by shifting responsibility. Joe Green can alleviate some of his regret by shifting responsibility and blame to his father. Some people are experts at shifting responsibility, assuming responsibility when choices turn out well and shirking it when choices turn out badly. This shift underlies the brokers' lament: When a stock goes up, investors say *they* bought the stock. And when it goes down they say *their broker* sold them the stock.

Regret over past choices is painful, but it is anticipation of future regret that affects today's choices. We contemplate the regret we will feel in the future if choices we made today turned out badly. For instance, a study found that people who anticipate regret following unsafe sex reduce their reported subsequent risky sexual behavior.[37]

SELF-CONTROL

Self-control centers on the interaction between the hot emotion of System 1 and the cool cognition of System 2. Self-control can be insufficient, excessive, or just right. Self-control is insufficient when hot emotion urging immediate gratification overcomes cool cognition urging delayed gratification. Self-control is excessive when hot emotion urging delayed gratification overcomes cool cognition urging immediate gratification.

Excessive self-control is as prevalent as insufficient self-control.[38] Too much self-control is evident in the tendency to spend less today than our ideal level of spending. Excessive self-control drives tightwads to extremes beyond frugality. The prospect of spending money inflicts emotional pain on tightwads even as cognition encourages them to spend. The interplay between emotion and cognition is evident in functional MRIs of people who see a product followed by its price and then are asked to decide whether to buy it or not. In an experiment, seeing the price caused greater activation in the brain's insula among people who decided not to buy the product than among people who decided to buy (the insula being the region associated with painful sensations such as social exclusion and disgusting odors.)[39]

Psychologist Walter Mischel and his coauthors described the interaction between emotion and cognition in the Cognitive-Affective Processing System and explored it in famous marshmallow experiments of the 1960s and 1970s. They presented four-year-olds with a marshmallow, telling them that they could eat it at any time or wait and eat two marshmallows when the experimenter returned. They found that children who were able to wait longer did so by cognitive strategies such as covering their eyes, singing songs, or imagining that they faced a cotton ball rather than a tasty marshmallow. In subsequent work they found that those who exhibited stronger self-control as four-year-olds by waiting for the second marshmallow matured into adults more successful at relationships, work, and handling stress than children who were quick to eat the single marshmallow.[40]

We resist the temptation of chocolate by buying it in small quantities, and we resist the temptation of chocolate cake by pushing it away. Pushing temptations away is effective in bolstering self-control and so is pulling goals closer. This push-and-pull is evident in an experiment in which people faced temptation-related activities, such as watching a movie, and goal-related activities, such as exercising at the gym. People were asked to push a lever away from them or pull it toward them when presented with a temptation or a goal. People were quicker to push the lever away from them when faced with a temptation and quicker to pull the lever toward them when faced with a goal.[41]

The self-control battle waged in the brain is illuminated in other studies of functional MRIs.[42] The brains of twenty-six of the original participants in the marshmallow experiments were scanned as they watched pictures of happy faces, analogs of marshmallows, and fearful faces, asking them to suppress their positive reactions to happy faces. The prefrontal cortex, a brain area associated with intelligence and self-control, was highly active among those who exhibited strong self-control as four-year-olds, whereas the ventral striatum, a brain area linked to addiction, was highly active among those who exhibited weak self-control as four-year-olds, as if the cool cognitive system of those with weak self-control were hijacked by the hot emotional system.

Nature, reflected in our genes, affects our mastery of self-control. Each of us is born with the capacity for self-control, just as we are born with capacity for language, but some of us are born with greater capacity than others, and some of us are born with personalities that facilitate it better than others. Saving requires self-control. A study of twins revealed that genetics account for approximately one-third of differences in saving behavior. The study also revealed that parents do not have long-term effects on their children's saving behavior beyond the genetic endowment they provide. The effect of parents on their children's saving behavior is strongest when children are in their twenties but disappears by middle age.[43]

The MAOA gene, one part of our genetic endowment, encodes monoamine oxidase A (MAOA), an enzyme that affects neurotransmitters such as serotonin, dopamine, and epinephrine in parts of the brain. Some forms of MAOA are associated with impulsive and addictive behavior. These forms of the gene are also associated with the accumulation of credit card debt, reflecting deficient self-control.[44] Heroin addicts are more likely than non-addicts to choose smaller immediate awards over delayed larger ones, and their degree of impatience corresponds to a measure of impulsiveness.[45]

Conscientiousness, closely related to self-control, is one of the Big Five personality traits described by personality psychologists. The other traits are extraversion, openness, agreeableness, and neuroticism. Conscientious people are likely to say that they do not buy things on impulse, spend too much money, or buy things they don't really need. Conscientiousness is the personality trait most closely related to academic achievement, job performance, marital stability, and longevity. Conscientious people accumulate more wealth than less conscientious people, even after accounting for differences in income, education, and cognitive ability.[46]

MOOD

Mood is muted emotion, less intense than emotion, but longer lasting. Fear of unemployment is less intense than fear of an impending automobile accident but the former can last for months and years, qualifying as mood. Fear of unemployment damages workers' mental health, especially those whose mental health is already precarious.[47]

Seasons, weather, and sunshine influence mood, as evident by sun lamps used to chase away winter blues. A study found that good weather in New York City was associated with high stock returns.[48] The same was found in twenty-six countries. People are generally happier on sunny days than on cloudy ones, as sunshine induce good moods, focusing them on good news, whereas clouds induces bad mood, focusing investors on bad news.[49] Cloudy days in the city of a stock market, relative to seasonal norms, are associated with low stock returns on that market. Cloudy days also increase perceived overpricing in both individual stocks and an index of stocks and increase the selling propensities of institutions.[50] Weather affects art prices as well. High daylight duration during art auction dates has been associated with high prices.[51]

Daylight affects circadian rhythms and associated moods. Mood associated with Seasonal Affective Disorder (SAD), also known as winter blues, is similar to the emotions of sadness and depression, but less intense. SAD increases risk aversion in financial decisions. SAD sufferers have a stronger preference for safe choices during the winter than those without SAD, but their preferences do not differ from those of non-SAD sufferers during the summer.[52]

Latitudes determine hours of daylight in winter—people in Sweden who live at 59°N latitude enjoy fewer hours of daylight than people in Japan who live at 36°N latitude. Seasonal variations in stock returns among countries are consistent with variations in risk aversion associated with SAD.[53]

The SAD phenomenon and its associated increase in risk aversion are also evident in seasonal variation in flows into and out of mutual funds.

Flows out of risky mutual fund categories and into safe categories increase in the fall, when daylight is diminishing, and flows out of safe categories into risky ones increase when it becomes more abundant.[54]

Not all the evidence points to a strong association between mood and markets, however. Local weather, length of day, daylight savings, and lunar phase influence Finnish investors as they choose to buy or sell stocks, but only little of the day-to-day variation in trading is explained by mood variables.[55]

Divorce is distressing and affects mood. It also affects investment decisions. Investors earn lower returns on their trades in the three-year period surrounding their divorces than other investors and lower than their own returns in other years, but effects varied by gender. Trades of both men and women yield lower returns during the immediate period surrounding divorce. Women's trading abilities recover after two years to pre-divorce levels, while those of men continue to be significantly lower.[56]

Mood affects loan officers' decisions. A study used three mood proxies: outcomes of key sporting events such as the Super Bowl, outcomes of the *American Idol* competitions, and days around major holidays. Positive mood events were associated with a 4.5 percent higher loan approval, and negative ones had an opposite effect of smaller magnitude. The effect was stronger among applicants of marginal quality, in which loan officers had more discretion. The extra loans approved on positive-mood days experienced higher defaults.[57]

Mood also affects the volume of real estate loans. The volume of these loans in the period preceding the 2008 financial crisis grew fastest in banks with the most optimistic CEOs, and such banks had lower stock returns during the 2008 financial crisis. There is no evidence that CEOs made loans while aware of the impending crisis.[58]

Optimism and pessimism can be described as moods. Optimism is associated with the emotions of hope and happiness, and pessimism with the emotions of fear and sadness, but optimism and pessimism are not as intense as hope, happiness, fear, or sadness. Sentiment in the context of investments often corresponds to mood. Bearish sentiment corresponds to a pessimistic mood and bullish sentiment to an optimistic one. Major terrorist attacks induce pessimism, affecting analysts' earnings forecasts. Analysts located near major terrorist attacks issued more pessimistic forecasts than analysts who are farther away.[59]

Propensities for optimism and pessimism are rooted in our genetics. The OXTR gene codes for the receptor for oxytocin, a hormone that contributes to positive mood and social bonding. People who have one or two copies of the OXTR gene with an "A" (adenine) allele at a particular location tend to be less optimistic than those with two copies of the "G" (guanine) allele. The A-allele is also associated with high levels of depressive symptoms.[60]

Optimism can plainly be useful. A study measured optimism by the difference between people's subjective estimates of how long they would live and objective estimates derived from statistical tables. It found that optimists work harder, anticipate longer age-adjusted work careers, and are more likely to remarry if divorced.[61] Another study measured optimism by weather, sports, and politics. Economic recessions are weaker, expansions are stronger, and economic recovery is faster in US states where people are optimistic.[62]

People prescribe more optimism for someone implementing decisions but prescribe accuracy to someone deliberating decisions. This tendency indicates that people advise optimism selectively, when it can affect performance. Experiments reveal that people believe optimism improved outcomes when a person's actions had large, rather than small, influence over performance. It turns out that optimism improved persistence but did not improve performance by much. People overestimated the association between optimism and performance even when their focus was not on optimism exclusively.[63]

Optimism enhances our life today as we contemplate an enjoyable future, but optimism has downsides. Optimism can lead to excessive debt loads. Optimistic Finns not only accumulated more debt than pessimists but were also burdened by excessive debt loads. Moreover, optimists were less attentive to forecast errors than their pessimistic fellows.[64]

A downside of optimism is also evident among people at risk for Huntington's disease (HD), a hereditary degenerative disease that limits life span. Genetic testing is perfectly predictive of HD and carries little economic cost. Yet few among those at HD risk choose to undergo pre-symptomatic testing. People with confirmed HD adjust their financial choices in ways consistent with their diagnosis, but untested people express optimistic beliefs about their health and make financial decisions, such as about retirement, as if they were not at risk for HD.[65]

Estimates of costs and profits are, on average, optimistic. Cost overruns in military hardware development projects are notorious. In a study conducted in the early 1960s, average cost overruns were 70 percent for fighter planes, 200 percent for bombers, 20 percent for cargo ships and tankers, and 390 percent for missiles.[66] More recent estimates indicate average cost overruns of 45 percent for rails, 34 percent for bridges and tunnels, and 20 percent for roads.[67]

Optimistic estimates in military hardware and public works projects may be unique because of their particular organizational pressures. Yet optimistic estimates are also common in the private sector, where cost overruns cut into profits. The average cost overrun in one pharmaceutical company was 125 percent in development of new drugs, 70 percent in drugs compounded from existing drugs, and 51 percent in alternate dosage forms of existing drugs. Similar cost overruns were evident in the projects of another pharmaceutical company, 266 percent for projects requiring large or medium technological advances and 82 percent for projects requiring only small technological advances.[68]

Business strategist Dan Lovallo and psychologist Daniel Kahneman attributed the prevalence of underestimation of costs and overestimation of profits to organizational pressures and optimism reflected in the planning fallacy.[69] Anchoring errors are one part of the planning fallacy. Managers usually put in contingency funds to cover cost overruns, yet they regularly fail to put in enough contingency funds, because they are anchored to original cost estimates and fail to adjust sufficiently for the likelihood of problems, delays, and expansions of projects. Framing errors are another part of the planning fallacy, misleading managers into framing projects as dependent entirely on their own company's abilities and plans and excluding the potential abilities and actions of competitors.

Organizational pressures affecting private-sector projects are not much different from organizational pressures affecting public-sector ones. Competition for time and money within companies is intense, as people jockey to champion their own projects. Estimates of costs and profits are critical weapons in these battles, again leading people to underestimate costs and overestimate profits.

Lovallo and Kahneman noted that optimism has two faces leading to two consequences, bad and good. The bad is selection of losing projects. The good is motivation of project champions and their teams to work hard on completing projects at promised low costs and high profits. They suggested supplementing the "inside view," which tends to focus on a company's own capabilities, experiences, and expectations, with an "outside view" consisting of statistical analysis of similar projects completed earlier in their companies or other ones. Inside view corresponds to analysis of representativeness information about the features of this particular project. Outside view corresponds to analysis of base-rate information about the rate of success of similar projects.

Lovallo and Kahneman further noted that the good consequences of optimism can be obtained without the bad consequences. Indeed, backup plans can harm the pursuit of goals. The mere act of thinking through backup plans can reduce the drive toward goals and the efforts devoted to reaching them.[70] Project review committees can select projects that promise to be profitable, on the basis of their own estimates of costs and profits, properly adjusting upward cost estimates provided by project champions and adjusting downward profit estimates. The committee's estimates need not be shared with project champions, however, setting for them the ambitious targets they have committed to, and prodding champions and their teams to work hard on making projects profitable even if short of target.

AFFECT

Affect is the faint whisper of emotion or mood, stripped down to valence, positive or negative. Psychologist Robert Zajonc, an early proponent of the importance of affect in choices, wrote, "We do not just see a house: We see a handsome house, an ugly house, or a pretentious house.... We sometimes delude ourselves that we proceed in a rational manner and weigh all the pros and cons of the various alternatives. But this is rarely the case. Quite often 'I decided in favor of X' is no more than 'I liked X.' We buy the cars we 'like,' choose the jobs and houses we find 'attractive,' and then justify these choices by various reasons."[71]

The importance of affect in choices is evident in our numbness to statistics, yet sensitivity to images that bring tears to our eyes. "Image of Drowned Syrian, Aylan Kurdi, 3, Brings Migrant Crisis Into Focus" was the headline in *The New York Times*. "Once again," it said, "it is not the sheer size of the catastrophe—millions upon millions forced by war and desperation to leave their homes—but a single tragedy that has clarified the moment. It was 3-year-old Aylan, his round cheek pressed to the sand as if he were sleeping, except for the waves lapping his face."[72]

People leaving a psychological experiment had the opportunity to contribute up to $5 of their earnings from the experiment to the Save the Children organization. Those asked to donate money to feed Rokia, a seven-year-old African girl, contributed more than twice the amount contributed by those asked to donate impersonally to the same organization working to save millions of Africans from hunger. People in a third group were asked to donate to Rokia but were also shown the statistics given to the second group about the millions in need. Coupling Rokia's story with the statistical realities reduced contributions.[73]

Investments, like houses, cars, and people, exude affect, good or bad, beautiful or ugly, admired or spurned. Affect can distort information and influence beliefs. Positive affect of risky investments increases people's confidence in their ability to evaluate them. People update beliefs in a way that is consistent with the self-preservation motive of maintaining a positive emotional state and avoiding cognitive dissonance. Self-preservation induces confirmation errors that deter incorporating news that contradicts past choices, and contributes to the formation of incorrect beliefs.[74]

The emotional benefits of positive affect are evident among Singaporean Chinese. The number 8 is considered lucky in Chinese culture and its affect is positive, whereas the number 4 is considered unlucky and its affect is negative. Singaporean Chinese are averse to apartments on floors with numbers ending in 4. Such apartments sell at 1.1 percent below average price, whereas apartments on floors with numbers ending in 8 sell at above average price. Yet residents of lucky-numbered homes enjoy no special utilitarian benefits. They are no less likely to be involved in car accidents than residents of unlucky-numbered homes, suggesting that choices and prices are founded on the emotional rather than on utilitarian benefits.[75]

Companies listed on the Chinese Shanghai and Shenzhen stock market are identified by a numerical code, the equivalent of the ticker symbol common in American markets. Lucky and unlucky numbers affect prices in Chinese initial public offerings. Newly listed shares with codes that included at least one lucky digit and no unlucky digit traded at a premium when offered, but the premium dissipated within three years.[76]

The meaning assigned to the numbers 8 and 4 illustrates the often blurry boundary between wants and errors. People might be committing an emotional error when they pay more for an apartment on the 8th floor, since it offers no greater utilitarian benefits than an apartment on the 4th floor. Or they might be committing no emotional error. Instead they pay more for an apartment on the 8th floor because it yields the emotional benefits of conformity to culture, whereas an apartment on the 4th floor imposes emotional costs of deviation from culture. In that, culturally based preference for an apartment on the 8th floor is no different from culturally based preference for art or music.

The preference for the number 8 is very likely rooted in wants more than in errors. But the preference for Class A shares is likely rooted in errors more than in wants. All know that A grades on exams are superior to B grades. But not all know that Class B shares are superior to Class A shares because they have all the benefits of Class A shares in addition to greater voting rights. Each Class A share has one vote, whereas each Class B share has five or 10 votes. Yet investors are willing to pay more for Class A shares than for Class B shares although the returns of Class A shares are lower than those of Class B.[77]

Affect led South African borrowers in one experiment to pay higher interest rates when advertised loans displayed attractive female bank loan officers.[78] Elsewhere, on Internet sites, loan applicants post the interest rates they are willing to pay, as well as their credit scores, employment history, homeownership, and other financial information. They also post photographs. Beautiful applicants were more likely to get loans and pay lower interest rates than less attractive applicants with the same financial information. Moreover, beautiful borrowers were less likely to repay their loans than less attractive ones.[79]

Stocks of admired companies are like beautiful loan applicants, basking in the glow of positive affect. Stocks of spurned companies are like unattractive loan applicants, wilting in the dark of negative affect. We embrace stocks of admired companies, expecting high returns with low risk, while we keep our distance from stocks of spurned companies, expecting low returns with high risk. Evidence, however, indicates that affect misleads investors into forgoing stock returns. On average, stocks of admired companies delivered lower returns than stocks of spurned companies.[80]

CONCLUSION

Emotions, mood, and affect have by now assumed behavioral-finance roles that are as important as the role of cognition. Acceptance of the importance of these roles, however, is relatively recent. Early work in behavioral finance centered on cognition, particularly cognitive errors. The reluctance to incorporate emotions into behavioral finance earlier reflected the prevalent view at the time, that emotions are convoluted, whereas cognition is straightforward. The resistance also reflected the view that emotions necessarily imply emotional errors, rather than combinations of emotional shortcuts that guide us rightly most of the time, and emotional errors that guide us wrongly sometimes. This view is reflected in the still common advice to set emotions aside when we are making financial choices.

To be sure, the role of emotions, mood, and affect in financial choices was not ignored entirely in the early days of behavioral finance. The role of regret, a cognitive emotion, was emphasized, and so was the role of self-control, combining emotion with cognition.

Still, focus in the early days remained squarely on cognition. Psychologist Paul Slovic and his coauthors noted the emotion of fear in the title of their article, "Facts versus Fears: Understanding Perceived Risk," in the 1982 volume *Judgment under Uncertainty: Heuristics and Biases*.[81] But the article itself attributed misperceptions of risk to cognition rather than to emotion. Specifically, it attributed misperceptions to the cognitive errors of availability and overconfidence.

But when Paul Slovic and his coauthors discussed these and similar findings in the 2002 volume *Heuristics and Biases: The Psychology of Intuitive Judgment,* they attributed misperceptions to affect. The title of their chapter is "The Affect Heuristic."[82] Daniel Kahneman and Shane Frederick wrote in the same volume, "It has become evident that the affect heuristic (Slovic el al.) should replace anchoring on the list of major general-purpose heuristics. In hindsight, the failure to identify this heuristic earlier reflects the narrowly cognitive focus that characterized psychology for some decades."[83] Emotions critically matter in behavior and in behavioral finance.

CHAPTER 5

Correcting Cognitive and Emotional Errors

Human-behavior and financial-facts knowledge are correcting tools. Investors can acquire such knowledge formally, as in investment classes, or informally, as by investment media and experience. Amateur investors in Indian stocks, for example, have been found to correct themselves by investment experience. Experienced investors have profited more by trading less than inexperienced ones and holding more diversified portfolios.[1]

Financial experts gain their expertise over time by acquiring human-behavior and financial-facts knowledge and using the reflective System 2 to process it. Expertise allows eventual reliance on the intuitive System 1, bypassing System 2, in predictable environments such as meteorology or chess, where quick and precise feedback readily corrects cognitive and emotional errors. Meteorologists learn to assess correctly the likelihood of precipitation by extensive training and feedback, and chess masters choose quickly from 50,000 to 100,000 chess patterns.

Yet expertise requires explicit use of the reflective System 2 in less predictable environments where quick and precise feedback is scarce. Psychologists Daniel Kahneman and Gary Klein noted that financial professionals, like psychotherapists and intelligence officers, know much about particular companies, patients, and international conflicts, and they may receive quick and precise feedback about short-term outcomes. But the feedback they receive about long-term outcomes is delayed, sparse, and ambiguous, promoting confidence in choices without promoting quality of choices.[2]

It makes little sense to turn all people into experts in medicine, investments, or home appliances, but it makes much sense for nonexperts to correct their cognitive and emotional errors by following experts' advice. Appliance experts at *Consumer Reports* recommend the best washers, dryers, and refrigerators. Investment experts recommend portfolio diversification, and medical experts recommend low-cost store-brand drugs rather than high-cost national brands.

Store-brand drugs are generic, costing less than national brands although generally equal in quality. Pharmacists buy national-brand drugs less often than average consumers. People lacking college education are especially likely to buy national brands. Health-care professionals—including nurses and doctors—are more likely to buy store brands than are lawyers, who have the equivalent amount of education but not equal pharmaceutical expertise.[3]

Passive investment strategies deliver to individual investors higher returns on average than active investment strategies. Twice as many finance professors invest passively, such as in index funds that deliver market-matching returns, rather than actively, such as in mutual funds that promise market-beating returns.[4] Most individual investors, however, choose active strategies.

Financial advisers can guide investors well, providing human-behavior and financial-facts information and correcting cognitive and emotional errors.[5] Advisers can point out the cognitive errors of availability and hindsight when mutual fund advertisements are about to steer clients into funds with high recent returns but unlikely high future returns. They can point out the emotional errors of exaggerated fear when these errors threaten to steer clients into selling all their stocks after stock-market crashes.

Evidence indicates that financial advisers improved the financial behavior and well-being of both working and retired people, although improvements were smaller among retired people.[6] Advised Dutch investors reduced risk by diversifying their portfolios more widely than non-advised investors.[7] They also benefitted from reduced trading activity and increased risk-adjusted stock returns.[8]

Investors who purchase mutual fund shares through advisers tend to avoid taxable distributions more than investors who buy shares directly. The difference is especially pronounced for distributions that have large tax consequences. Furthermore, the difference is larger in December but only when investors face large capital losses, indicating that financial advisers guide investors to realize losses.[9]

Financial advice increases the likelihood that homeowners will keep their homes and receive mortgage loan modifications. Moreover, counseled borrowers who receive loan modifications are less likely to default subsequently than borrowers who are not counseled. Homeowners who receive counseling in the early stages of default are more likely to receive loan modifications and keep their homes than those who receive counseling only when seriously delinquent.[10]

Financial advisers are especially effective at improving the financial behavior of their clients when they educate them with "just in time" human-behavior and financial-facts knowledge.[11] The benefits of just-in-time financial information are evident in the $35 billion market for overdraft fees in checking accounts in which just-in-time information was conveyed inadvertently by surveys. People who answered overdraft-related questions incurred fewer overdraft fees in the survey month, very likely because the questions conveyed useful financial information. People avoided overdrafts by making fewer debit transactions and by cancelling automatic recurring withdrawals.[12]

The effects of just-in-time information about overdrafts, however, do not always last. A large Turkish bank tested short-message-service direct marketing promotions to 108,000 existing holders of checking accounts that impose 60 percent interest rates on overdrafts. Offering a large discount from the high interest rate charged for overdrafts *reduced* overdraft usage, very likely because it highlighted the high interest rate even when discounted. In contrast, messages mentioning overdraft availability without mentioning interest rates *increased* usage. Neither change persisted long after messages stopped.[13]

CORRECTING BY PROMPTING USE OF SYSTEM 2

We vary in susceptibility to cognitive and emotional errors and resulting investment errors. Some of this variation is rooted in our genetics. Genetic factors explain up to 50 percent of the variation in susceptibility to investment errors, such as the reluctance to realize losses, the propensity to select investments with high recent returns, and the preference for familiar investments. These genetic factors also influence non-investment choices—people disposed toward familiar options as they choose stocks are disposed toward familiarity in other domains.[14]

High intelligence diminishes susceptibility to cognitive and emotional errors. High-IQ Finnish investors were found less likely to own categories of funds that charge high fees—including balanced funds, actively managed funds, and funds marketed through retail networks. Moreover, high-IQ investors preferred the lowest-fee funds within each fund category.[15]

Intelligence prompts us to use the reflective System 2, but the tendency to use System 2 is more closely related to disposition for reflection than to intelligence. Intelligent people are better able to use System 2 to correct overconfidence and hindsight errors than less intelligent ones, but they are no better able to correct anchoring errors or overcome the resistance to realizing losses.[16]

More reflective people are better able to use System 2, yet blind spots hamper even reflective people. We are better at identifying blind spots in others than in ourselves. Blind spots are exacerbated by our tendency to trust our own introspections about judgment and behavior more than we trust perceptions by others.[17]

We can correct many cognitive and emotional errors by full engagement of System 2. Correcting framing errors is one example. Some MBA students were asked to list their objectives for summer internships. Students used System 1, framing the question narrowly and listing seven objectives on average, such as "improves my attractiveness for full-time job offers" and "helps me develop my leadership skills." Next, the objectives listed by all students were combined into a master list, and students were prompted to use System 2 to frame the question broadly and asked to note their objectives once more after reviewing the twenty-nine objectives in the master list. This time students listed fifteen objectives on average, implying that engaging System 2 prompted students to add eight objectives they considered important but were not prompted by System 1.[18]

Proper framing can correct anchoring errors. Recall the airport runway and double-decker bus experiment described in Chapter 3, "Cognitive Shortcuts and Errors," whereby estimates of a price of a double-decker bus were anchored to information about the length of an airport runway. People estimated the price of a double-decker bus as higher when they were told that the length of the runway is 7,300 meters than when told that it is 7.3 kilometers.

The length of the runway is the "anchor" in this experiment, and the price of a double-decker bus is the "target." Anchors affect estimates of targets by highlighting features shared by the anchor and the target, and obscuring features of the target that differ from those of the anchor. Transportation is highlighted as a feature shared by runways and buses. But while the shared transportation feature is highlighted, features that are not shared by airport runways and buses are obscured. For example, *air* transportation is a feature of runways, whereas *ground* transportation is a feature of buses.[19] Proper framing highlights differences between the features of anchor and target, making the length of runway less prominent in the evaluation of the price of a bus and weakening the chain that links the length of the runway to the estimate of the price of the bus.

Proper framing also corrects anchoring errors when it makes us consider many anchors rather than one. Plausible anchors for the price of a double-decker bus, such as the price of a single-decker bus, exert greater influence on estimates than implausible ones, such as the length of a runway. People facing multiple anchors evaluate the plausibility of each anchor relative to the others. People facing the length of a runway as one anchor for the price of a double-decker bus and the price of a single-decker bus as another anchor choose the price of a single-decker bus as an anchor because it is more plausible.[20]

Framing and mental accounting can bolster self-control, but they can be costly. People with insufficient self-control succumb to excessive indulgence. Some bolster self-control by combining savings accounts yielding low interest rates with credit card balances at high interest rates. Approximately 20 percent of British households co-hold an average £6,500 of revolving consumer credit alongside £8,000 of savings accounts. Co-holding is not caused by ignorance. Co-holders are typically more financially literate, with above-average income and education.[21]

Prospective hindsight is a System 2 method that corrects hindsight errors.[22] An investor considering concentrating her portfolio in the biotechnology sector might be guided to ask that question: Imagine that we are a decade from now; why did biotechnology stocks yield lower returns than other stocks? Such a question elicits potential causes for failure that do not come to mind easily when we are using System 1.

Properly calibrated 80 percent confidence intervals of future S&P 500 Index returns contain the realized return in 80 percent of forecasts. Yet 80 percent confidence intervals by corporate chief financial officers manifest overprecision errors, containing the true return only 33 percent of the time. Two methods correct overprecision errors. One splits the question into parts, asking for 10 percent and 50 percent confidence intervals before asking for those at 80 percent confidence levels. This question prompts people to use System 2 and acknowledge that an 80 percent confidence interval must be wider than a 10 percent or 50 percent confidence interval. Another method asks people to estimate confidence intervals first for 1 month in the future and then 2 months in the future before asking them to estimate confidence intervals for 3 months in the future. This question makes time explicit, highlighting the uncertainty of estimates and leading people to better calibrated confidence intervals, knowing that 3-month confidence intervals are likely wider than those of 2-month intervals and those for 2 months are likely wider than those of 1 month.[23]

The general "wisdom of crowds," method, even wisdom of crowds within oneself, can also correct overprecision errors. What is your best guess for the S&P 500 Index level four years from now? Now assume that you are wrong. What is your next guess? It turns out that the average of two guesses is generally more accurate than either guess. Wisdom of crowds is more accurate than wisdom of crowds within. An average of the guesses of two people is generally more accurate than an average of two guesses of one person.[24]

We commit representativeness errors when we believe in the "law of small numbers," a tongue-in-cheek offshoot on the robust "law of large numbers." The latter is an important law of statistics. It teaches us, for example, that the percentage of heads in a sequence of coin flips is likely to be closer to 50 percent when we flip a coin a large number of times, such as 30, than when we flip it a small number of times, such as 6. One manifestation of belief in the law of small numbers is that six years of beating the market are interpreted as representative of a skillful mutual fund manager as much as 30 years of beating the market.

Insensitivity to predictability exacerbates representativeness errors. Variation in the quality of meals at a restaurant tends to be small, whereas variation in the performance of a mutual fund tends to be large. We can predict quite accurately the quality of future meals at a restaurant by the quality of six past meals, but we cannot predict nearly as accurately the future performance of a mutual fund by performance in six past years.

Consider judging the probability that a particular mutual fund manager would generate returns exceeding benchmark returns, such as the returns of an index fund with similar characteristics. Analysis free of representativeness errors guides us to examine both representativeness information about the returns of this particular fund relative to its benchmark, and base-rate information about the returns of all funds relative to their benchmarks. Judging a fund by its representativeness information alone, we might be tempted to conclude that a manager who beat the benchmark six years in a row provides clear evidence of skill at generating returns exceeding benchmark returns. After all, the chance of six heads in six flips of a coin is only one in sixty-four. But once we note that base-rate information indicates that few mutual fund managers beat their benchmarks consistently over years and know that this fund manager is one among hundreds or thousands of fund managers in the population of funds, we understand that it is as likely that there would be lucky fund managers who beat their benchmarks six times in a row as there are lucky coin flippers who flip six heads in a row.

Yet investors, even professional institutional investors, continue to neglect base-rate information. Institutional investors prefer active money management, promising to beat the market, over passive money management, promising to match it, as with index funds. In particular, institutional investors trust their judgment about the application of representativeness information in identifying skilled money managers, evaluating their performance and choosing to retain or terminate them. Stated reasons for preferring active management include whether a handful of skilled active managers can be identified and combined to generate market-beating returns. In contrast, stated reasons are only vaguely associated with base-rate information about the performance of the average manager.[25]

Economist Alan Marcus corrected representativeness errors by considering both representativeness information and base-rate information as he assessed the performance of Peter Lynch, who managed Fidelity's Magellan fund during the 13 years from 1977 to 1989. Representativeness information includes the observation that Lynch beat the S&P 500 Index in 11 of the 13 years. Base-rate information includes the observation that if 500 coin flippers flip 13 coins each, the winner will on average flip 11.63 heads.[26]

Psychologist Peter Wason was among the first to examine confirmation shortcuts and errors. He noted that correcting confirmation errors requires "a willingness to attempt to falsify hypotheses and thus to test those intuitive ideas which so often carry the feeling of certitude."[27] Wason explored confirmation errors by presenting to people the faces of four cards marked

D   F   7   5

Assume that each card has a letter on one side and a number on the other. Which card or cards should you turn over to find if they satisfy the rule "If a card has a D on one side, then it has a 7 on its other side"? The correct answer calls for turning over the card with the letter D on one side to see if it confirms the rule by having the number 7 on the other. But the correct answer also calls for turning over the card with the number 5 on one side to see if it disconfirms the rule by having the letter D on its other side.

Most people choose to turn over the card with the letter D on one side, searching for confirming evidence. Some choose to turn over the card with the letter F on one side or the one with the number 7. These choices can offer neither confirming nor disconfirming evidence because there is nothing in the statement relating to what is on the other side of cards with the letter F, and there is nothing in it indicating that cards with letters other than D on one side cannot have the number 7 on the other. But few choose to turn over the card with the number 5, which can offer disconfirming evidence by having the letter D on the other side.

Proper framing, such as by the box of positive and negative hits and false positives and negatives or by concrete and familiar settings, helps correct confirmation errors. The frame of Wason's question is abstract and unfamiliar. Consider a concrete and familiar analog to Wason's cards in four cards marked

Beer   Diet Coke   23 Years Old   19 Years Old

Which card or cards would you turn over to find if they satisfy the rule "if a person drinks beer, then that person is 21 or older"? The correct answer calls for turning over the Beer card, providing confirming evidence if its other side shows that the person is 21 or older, and the 19 Years Old card, providing disconfirming evidence if its other side says beer. Few fail to correct confirmation errors in this frame.

More than abstraction and unfamiliarity make the frame of D, F, 7, 5 more prone to confirmation errors than the frame of Beer, Diet Coke, 23 Years Old, 19 Years Old. Evolutionary psychologist Leda Cosmides argued that the second frame activates a "cheater detector" module embedded into our brains by evolution. That module is proficient at detection of cheaters on social contracts.[28] Psychologists Gerd Gigerenzer and Klaus Hug provided evidence consistent with Cosmides' argument in an experiment in which people were given the social contract rule "if an employee gets a pension, then that employee must have worked for the firm for at least 10 years." People faced 4 cards:

Pension   No Pension   Worked 12 Years   Worked 8 Years

Some people were told that they are the employer in the story, whereas others were told that they are the employee. Those told that they are the employer were better at detecting cases where the employee cheated, receiving a pension despite having worked only 8 years, whereas those told that they are the employee were better at detecting cases in which the employer cheated, providing no pension to an employee who worked for 12 years.[29]

Double-blind tests of candidate drugs in the pharmaceutical arena counter confirmation errors. These are tests in which some patients receive the candidate drug, whereas others receive placebos, and in which both physicians and patients are blind to whether the administered drug is the candidate drug. Health improvements in patients who receive the candidate drug are confirming evidence of its effectiveness, but equal health improvement in patients who receive the placebo are disconfirming evidence, casting doubt on the candidate drug's effectiveness.

Still, double-blind tests are not always feasible. Consider a university admissions committee admitting only candidates who meet the selection criteria.[30] A comprehensive examination of the hypothesis that the selection criteria are valid calls for looking at confirming evidence—the eventual success of admitted candidates—and also disconfirming evidence—the eventual success of those not admitted. Yet information about the fate of non-admitted candidates is difficult to collect. Moreover, a truly fair examination of the latter requires admission of such candidates despite failure to meet the selection criteria, so as to ascertain the candidates' eventual success under conditions identical to those of candidates admitted because they have met the selection criteria. It might be that examination of disconfirming evidence would reveal that the eventual success of candidates admitted despite failure to meet the selection criteria turn out to be greater than the eventual success of candidates admitted because they have met the selection criteria. Admission of candidates who failed to meet the selection criteria might, however, impose costs on a university, including the cost of lower reputation for quality.

Quantitative models are powerful correcting methods. Michael Lewis's book, *Moneyball*, describes the application of such models to evaluating professional baseball players whereby intuitive evaluations are biased by cognitive errors. Recruiters and team managers commonly commit availability and representativeness errors by overweighting players' easily available recent performance and perceived similarity to other players.[31]

Quantitative models and algorithms regularly outperform human judgment. A linear model for selecting applicants to a graduate program is one example. The model combines student performance with other features, such as grade point average, Graduate Record Examination scores, quality of undergraduate university attended, and strength of recommendation letters, and specifies the weight of each feature for the best forecast of the performance of future students. An investment model may be based on the inputs of profitability, financial stability, susceptibility to bankruptcy, and margin of safety. The model simplifies the investment selection process and helps avoid cognitive errors that might degrade the selection process.[32] Yet people regularly prefer human judgment over quantitative models and algorithms, and lose confidence in algorithmic forecasters faster than they lose confidence in human forecasters after seeing them make the same mistake.[33]

Correction of the "endowment effect" illustrates the use of System 2 to counter emotional errors, specifically the emotional error of regret. We do that by reducing our sensitivity to the pain of regret by "thinking like a trader." Consider receiving a coffee mug as a gift that is yours to keep. How much would you be willing to pay for such a mug if you were to buy one? And how much would you ask for the mug if you were to sell it? If you are like most people you are likely willing to pay a lower amount, say $6, for the mug if you are to buy it than the amount, say $10, you ask for the mug you own if you are to sell it. We know this tendency as the endowment effect. It is as if the act of being endowed with an item enhanced the item's worth in the eyes of a person who owns it. But what rationale underlies the endowment effect?

The usual rationale offered for the effect is loss aversion[34] —specifically, giving up an item we own involves a loss, a loss absent when we are considering acquiring that same item. Loss aversion implies that we are willing to give up an item we own only at a price that compensates us for the item and also for its loss. We might think of the $10 we ask for the mug as composed of $6 compensation for the mug itself and $4 as compensation for its loss.

Yet the emotional benefits of pride and especially the emotional costs of regret are likely prominent among rationales underlying the endowment effect. Think of receiving a $20 bill as a gift that is yours to keep. How many $10 bills would it take to induce you to sell your $20 bill? And how many $10 bills are you willing to pay for a $20 bill? No endowment effect is likely in this case.

Uncertainty about the market value of an item differentiates the mug case from the $20 case. So does willingness to bear the emotional cost of regret when finding, in hindsight, that you sold an item for less than its market value. You might believe that the market value of the mug is $8 but you are likely unsure about it. What if you sell the mug for $8 only to find, too late, that its market value is $10? You would suffer the emotional costs of regret. It is true that you would enjoy the emotional benefits of pride if it turns out that the market value of the mug you sold for $8 is only $6. But the emotional costs of regret are greater than the emotional benefits of pride at equal dollar amounts. A $10 price asked for a mug likely worth $8 compensates for the possible emotional costs of regret at finding, in hindsight, that the mug is worth more than $8.

Now think of a lottery ticket you received as a gift and is yours to keep. Would you be willing to exchange it for another lottery ticket? There is no uncertainty about the odds of winning—they are the same for both tickets. But there is great uncertainty as to whether the original ticket or the exchanged one would win the lottery, and great responsibility for a decision to exchange the ticket. Imagine the emotional cost of regret if you have chosen to exchange your ticket only to find that your original ticket won the lottery. Fewer than half of people agreed to exchange a lottery ticket they received as a gift for another lottery ticket. In contrast, more than nine in ten agreed to exchange a pen they have received as a gift for another pen.[35]

The endowment effect can be corrected by encouraging "thinking like a trader," ready to bear the emotional costs of regret. Professional traders might possess an innate ability to regulate their emotions or have learned to regulate them. Psychologist Peter Sokol-Hessnera and his coauthors wrote, "It is possible that professionals and amateurs are fundamentally different people from the start, but it is also possible that professionals have learned not just facts about investments, but strategies for addressing the normal emotional responses that might prevent amateurs from making the same decisions, given the same information. Indeed, professional sports card dealers, condominium investors (rather than owners), and experienced cab drivers show less apparent response to loss than less experienced agents."[36]

CORRECTING BY INCENTIVES

Incentives can improve choices by reducing the cost of good choices and increasing the cost of poor ones. Tax deferrals and employer matching reduce the cost of retirement savings, and penalties increase the cost of early withdrawals. Incentives can also correct cognitive and emotional errors.

Emotions such as the love of children can bolster insufficient self-control and counter the pull of immediate gratification that tempts us to dip into mental accounts for our children's education for vacation spending. So can mental accounts created by placing money into envelopes with photographs of our children. Low-income workers in India rarely have bank accounts. They subsist in a cash economy and save little of their weekly wages even though they would like to save, especially for their children. One experiment arranged for a group of such workers to receive portions of their weekly cash wages in envelopes labeled savings. Some workers received their savings-labeled wages in a single envelope, whereas others received it split into two envelopes. Some had photographs of their children affixed to the envelopes, whereas others did not. People saved more when they received the savings-labeled wages in two envelopes, representing two mental accounts, and saved even more when photographs of their children were affixed to the envelopes.[37]

Love of projected older selves can also bolster insufficient self-control. People who saw computer pictures of their faces as they would look when old were more likely to choose future monetary rewards over immediate ones.[38] Prompts encouraging consumers to consider the future outcomes of their present decisions were also effective among people with insufficient self-control.[39]

"Commitment devices" offer incentives that bolster self-control. These devices include placing savings in accounts that prevent premature withdrawals,[40] imposing deadlines with penalties to deter procrastination on coursework,[41] and placing money in accounts that would be forfeited if the commitments are not fulfilled.[42] In one experiment, smokers who wanted to quit were divided into two groups. Money was deposited in accounts of people of the first group, to be used six months later if urine tests showed they were free of nicotine. Otherwise, the money would go to charity. People who were offered that incentive were more likely to quit smoking during the six months than people in the second group who were offered no incentive. Moreover, such people were likely to stay off smoking after twelve months.[43]

SticKK.com is a website that offers such accounts. Commitments of SticKK users include losing weight, cleaning a living space, learning Japanese, waking up on time, and using absolutely no drugs (cocaine, opiates, or alcohol). Users commit an amount of money that would go to a group they abhor if they fail to fulfill their commitments. The National Rifle Association is a common choice among liberals advocating gun control. Referees verify that commitments have indeed been fulfilled before money is returned to users.

One satisfied user wrote, "I have lost over fifty pounds to date with my Stickk.com contract. I've lost weight before, but I have never been as motivated as I have been with Stickk." Another wrote, "As a student studying economics, I have been taught over and over that people are rational and forward-looking, but anyone who has procrastinated knows that isn't the case. This past semester, with papers to read and exams approaching, a friend and I decided that we need to start studying more. A professor had told us about stickK.com, so we gave it a try, 'stickKing' each other to go to the library 10 hours each week for six weeks. When we accomplished that goal, we increased it to 15 hours a week. When classes ended and it came time to study for final exams, I increased it again to 50 hours a week. As a poor graduate student, I knew that I couldn't afford not to study! We both ended up achieving our goals, not having to pay a cent, and, most importantly, making it through the semester. Now that I am teaching courses, I make sure to let my students know that stickK.com really works (even if its efficacy undermines traditional economic theory)."

"Temptation bundling" also offers incentives that bolster self-control. They bundle wants such as reading the *Hunger Games* with shoulds such as going to the gym. One experiment placed people in a temptation bundling group that received access to iPods containing four audio novels of their choice. But they could listen only when exercising at the gym. Other people were placed in a group that received access to four audio novels of their choice, loaded onto their personal iPod and available at any time. But they were encouraged to follow a rule whereby they would listen only while exercising. Yet other people were placed in a group that received a gift certificate whose value is approximately equal to the cost of borrowing four audio novels. It turned out that people in the first group were most likely to exercise at the gym, followed by people in the second group and people in the third.[44]

Some investments serve as temptation bundles. Prize-linked savings (PLS) accounts are a prominent example, bundling the want of winning a lottery with the should of saving. Holders of PLS accounts receive little or no interest on their accounts. Instead, they are entered into lotteries that pay lucky winners more than they could have received as interest. Consumers in Nebraska who were offered PLS accounts directed gambling money into savings.[45]

Whereas people with insufficient self-control are overly eager to indulge, people with excessive self-control are excessively reluctant to do so. They benefit from commitment devices that counter excessive self-control. In one experiment women were offered a choice between a spa package valued at $80, or $85 in cash. Most chose the spa package, explaining that they were afraid that excessive self-control would drive them to spend the cash on utilitarian products such as groceries if they did not commit themselves to the indulgence of the spa.[46]

Incentives are not always effective in correcting cognitive and emotional errors. Indeed, incentives can backfire in sports and test taking, reducing performance by increasing anxiety and heightening tendencies to replace reliable formulas with idiosyncratic ones in attempts to improve performance. The effects of accountability in this context are similar to those of incentives. Accountability improves performance where effort improves performance, but it is not effective alone in correcting cognitive and emotional errors.[47]

The double edge of incentives is evident in loan officers' choices. Large incentives promote greater screening effort and more profitable lending decisions, but the effect of incentives is limited when compensation cannot be clawed back if loans go sour. Moreover, incentives distort the assessment of credit risk, even among trained professionals with many years of experience.[48]

Incentives encouraging poor advice can induce poor advice even when incentives are removed. In one experiment, financial advisers had information about three investments. The inferior investment was designed to appeal only to risk-seeking investors. Half of advisers recommended that investment to clients when offered a bonus for recommending it. In contrast, only 4 percent of advisers who were not offered a bonus recommended it. Moreover, the effect of the bonus persisted after it was removed. Advisers who were offered a bonus for recommending the inferior investment were almost six times more likely to recommend it after the bonus was removed than advisers who were never offered the bonus. Advisers who were offered a bonus were even more likely to choose the inferior investment for themselves. The behavior of such advisers is consistent with wants for the expressive and emotional benefits of a positive self-image of being incorruptible. Maintaining such image induces advisers to offer consistent advice, even if it reduces their own utilitarian benefits.[49]

READINESS FOR CORRECTION

Correction requires a readiness for correction. Financial advisers can correct the cognitive and emotional errors of investors and guide them well only if investors are ready to be guided. In a series of studies, Swiss investors who needed financial advice most were least likely to seek it.[50] And German investors who needed financial advice most were least likely to obtain it. Moreover, the 5 percent of German investors who did obtain advice hardly followed it.[51] Having financial information did not help Dutch investors make good retirement-savings choices. This finding was true even when information was made easy to understand, disseminated by appropriate media, and adapted to people's circumstances.[52] Evidently, mere availability of good financial advice is a necessary but not a sufficient condition for acquiring human-behavior and financial-facts knowledge and correcting cognitive and emotional errors.

Fatigue and distraction hamper choice readiness because they hamper activation of System 2. Fatigued people find it difficult to perform tasks requiring self-control and distracted people are more likely to succumb to temptation. Poverty hampers activation of System 2 because scarcity distracts attention from important future needs, directing it to today's pressing needs. This distraction results in over-borrowing that increases the difficulty of climbing out of poverty.[53]

Visceral influences such as hunger also hamper choice readiness. The sad caricature of justice as "what the judge ate for breakfast" can be true, even among experienced judges. In a study, the percentage of favorable rulings dropped gradually from approximately 65 percent to nearly zero before food breaks and returned abruptly to approximately 65 percent after breaks.[54]

It is thus good to postpone choices when depleted, fatigued, angry, aroused, hungry, or distracted. Yet we are not always aware of our lack of readiness and we often resist correction when it conflicts with our wants.

Evidence-based medicine and evidence-based investing are useful correcting methods. They augment or replace physicians' and investors' System 1 intuition and unsystematic evidence with System 2 reflection and systematic evidence. Yet many physicians resist correction by evidence-based medicine in prescribing medical treatments, and many investors, even professional ones, resist evidence-based investing.

Some resistance to evidence-based medicine and investing stems from differences in equally valid evidence-based studies that differ in conclusions. Other resistance, however, stems from challenges that evidence-based medicine and investing pose to the autonomy of physicians and investment professionals, their incomes, and their status. An article on the website of the government's Agency for Healthcare Research and Quality said, "Physicians and other providers could accept the goals of payers and patients in principle. However, achieving these goals required changes in physician behavior and redistribution of income. Cutting costs, for example, requires reducing the income of physicians, hospitals, and other providers as well as changing the way medicine is practiced."[55] As Upton Sinclair famously noted, "It is difficult to get a man to understand something, when his salary depends on his not understanding it."

One physician expressed his opposition to evidence-based medicine on the AngryOrthopod.com website. "Forever," he noted, "medical practitioners have enjoyed the latitude that allows them to treat patients on an individual basis. This is otherwise known as the practice of medicine. . . . Evidence Based Medicine may be just another way to remove a physician's (sorry, 'health care provider's') autonomy. This trend has marched on for years, castrating us bit by bit."[56]

Banks, hotels, health clubs, mutual fund companies, and credit card companies can help correct the cognitive and emotional errors of their customers. Yet many of these firms choose to exploit their customers' errors, such as by hiding information or shrouding it.

Knowledgeable people free of cognitive and emotional errors infer that hidden or shrouded prices are likely high prices. Thus providers of products and services choose to reveal information in markets in which all people are knowledgeable. Providers might choose to hide or shroud information in markets in which not all people are knowledgeable, thereby exploiting the errors of their less knowledgeable customers rather than correcting them.[57]

Think of hotel owners who provide rooms at $80, a price lower than their $100 cost, but also provide add-ons at prices much higher than their costs, knowing that purchases of add-ons gives them an overall profit. Ignorant guests buy add-ons such as meals, phone use, and minibar goodies, whereas knowledgeable guests avoid these costs by eating outside the hotel, using cell phones, and staying away from the minibar. In essence, hotel owners exploit ignorant guests by selling them add-ons at prices that greatly exceed costs, whereas knowledgeable guests exploit hotel owners by renting rooms at less than their costs.

Exploiting by shrouding is evident in the context of the 1968 landmark Truth in Lending Act (TILA). TILA requires lenders to disclose all relevant loan terms, but it emphasizes the annual percentage interest rate (APR). This requirement is an attempt to counter pre-TILA lender practices, whereby lenders marketed "low monthly payments" and either shrouded interest rates or presented alternatively defined rates that are lower than the APR. For example, a $1,000 loan to be paid in 12 monthly installments of $88.33 totaling $1,060 was advertised as a 6 percent loan. The APR of this loan is closer to 11 percent, as all payments except one are made before the end of the 12-month period. Many lenders, however, continue to exploit borrowers' propensity for underestimation despite threats of litigation and fines. People with high propensity for underestimating APR pay approximately 4 percentage points more of APR than people with low propensity for underestimating APR.[58]

Mexico's privatized social security system offers another shrouding example. Mexico privatized its social security system in 1997, with individual private accounts managed by approved fund management companies. Between ten and twenty-one well-known fund management companies have competed in the market since the system's inception. Yet high fees persisted.

During the 2004 through 2006 period, the average up-front fee on contributions paid by workers was 24 percent and the average annual fee paid on assets under management was more than 0.26 percent. Halfway through the period, the government introduced a fee index to increase transparency and sensitivity to fees. The index combined upfront fees and annual fees by a particular formula. The government advertised the index to workers as the fee measure they should consider when choosing fund managers.

People paid little attention to fees before the fee index was introduced, but were strongly guided by the index in selecting funds afterward. Fund management companies, however, did not respond by lowering fees. Instead, they shrouded them to minimize the index. This response erased gains to people as a whole, and shifted them from high-income people who pierced the shrouds placed by fund management companies and calculated the true fees to low-income people who did not.[59]

Sellers of lottery tickets exploit buyers' representativeness errors reflected in beliefs in the hot-hand and gambler's fallacies. Lottery buyers tend to avoid tickets whose numbers are similar to those of previously winning tickets, in accordance with the gambler's fallacy. At the same time, buyers tend to prefer tickets from sellers of previously winning tickets, in accordance with the hot-hand fallacy. Sellers increase their profits by exploiting the belief in both fallacies.[60]

Some mutual fund companies are adept at exploiting availability errors. The availability shortcut directs our attention to easily available information, shrouding information that is not as readily available. Such mutual fund companies exploit availability errors by advertising their best performing funds. Morningstar classifies the top 10 percent of funds into the 5-star group, but the proportion of 5-star funds among advertised funds is much higher than 10 percent.[61]

Conflicts of interest induce some advisers to misguide investors rather than guide them well. In an experiment, trained auditors met financial advisers, presented their portfolios, and asked for advice. Some portfolios reflected investment errors in line with the financial interests of the advisers. Other portfolios reflected good investment strategies yet counter to the interests of advisers.

In the first case—chasing fund returns—the auditor holds a portfolio in which 30 percent is invested in an exchange traded fund consisting of stocks of companies in a single industry that performed well in the previous year. He expresses an interest in identifying more industries that had done well recently. In this case, the incentives of the adviser and of the client are not aligned: the adviser benefits from the bias of the client since it allows him to churn the portfolio more often and generate more fees, whereas the client would profit from a better diversified portfolio. In the second case—employer stocks—an auditor holds 30 percent of his portfolio in the company stock of his employer. Thus, incentives of the adviser and of the client are aligned: it is in the best interest of the adviser to reduce or eliminate the client's bias since holding company stock also reduces the adviser's ability to generate fees. In the third scenario, the auditor holds a diversified, low-fee portfolio consisting of index funds and bonds.

It turned out that advisers failed to correct the errors of investors and often reinforced errors that conformed to their interests. Advisers encouraged choice of investments with high recent returns and pushed for high-cost active mutual funds even when auditors presented to them well-diversified, low-cost index portfolios.[62]

In another experiment demonstrating the effects of conflicts of interest, financial advisers in the Indian insurance market recommended inferior products paying high commissions rather than superior products paying lower commissions. Advisers were especially likely to offer inferior products to consumers with little financial knowledge. Moreover, mandating disclosure of commissions made advisers less likely to recommend products mandating disclosure.[63]

A survey of Canadian financial advisers revealed that they induce their clients to take more risk, thereby raising expected returns. There is limited evidence of customization, however; advisers direct clients into portfolios independent of investors' risk preferences and life-cycle stages. Advisers' own portfolios are good predictors of portfolios they recommend to clients. This one-size-fits-all advice is not cheap. Clients pay an average of more than 2.7 percent in fees each year, giving up most or all of the expected returns gained by taking higher risk.[64]

Some accusations of misguiding borrowers during the housing boom of the 2000s turn out to be true, evident in steering borrowers toward predatory loans. Brokers and real estate professionals steered home buyers to lenders that offered loans at high interest rates. Such borrowers were charged 0.40- to 0.60-percentage-point higher interest rates than those not steered, yet were 2 percentage points less likely to default compared to similar borrowers who were not steered. This result suggests that steered borrowers received inferior loans relative to their qualifications.[65]

Managers of some health clubs exploit unrealistic optimism and insufficient self-control, promoting contracts that provide unlimited visits for a monthly fee. It turns out that the monthly contracts work better for health clubs than for their members. Club members who chose the monthly contracts visited their clubs less than five times each month on average, in effect paying a fee exceeding $17 per visit. They would have saved money by paying the $10 per-visit fee.[66]

Managers of some credit card companies, like managers of some health clubs, design their offerings to exploit cognitive and emotional errors, including unrealistic optimism and insufficient self-control. Card issuers targeted less-educated customers with low introductory interest rates but high late and over-limit fees. In contrast, cards with mileage programs, which are offered mainly to the most-educated consumers, rely much less on late and over-limit fees.[67]

Many practices of credit card companies have been prohibited by the CARD Act of 2009. The Card Act reduced overall borrowing costs by an annualized 1.6 percent of average daily balances, with a decline of more than 5.3 percent for consumers with low credit scores. There were no offsetting increases in interest charges or reductions in the amount of credit. Taken together, the CARD Act saved consumers $11.9 billion a year.[68]

The CARD Act provides further evidence that information alone is not always an effective correction tool. The CARD Act requires credit card companies to present dual payoff information in account statements in addition to the specific amount that pays the balance in full. The dual payoff information specifies the number of years of payments when customers are paying the balance in minimum monthly payments, and the monthly payments when they are paying the balance in three years. Yet many consumers who were given dual payoff information chose *lower* monthly payments than those given the specific amount that pays the balance in full, and were *less* likely to pay the full balance.[69] Similarly, informing people that colleagues save 15 percent of their incomes can motivate them to save more than the 5 percent they save now, but it can also *demotivate* them from saving even 5 percent, knowing that there is no way for them to catch up to their colleagues.[70]

CORRECTING, NUDGING, AND MANDATING

Cognitive and emotional errors mislead people on the way to satisfying their wants. We *correct*—debias—cognitive and emotional errors when we *point* people toward their wants. *Wants,* however, are different from *shoulds.* Wants draw us to an engaging novel, whereas shoulds guide us to a textbook. We *nudge* when we *press* people toward their shoulds. And we *mandate* when we *shove* people toward their shoulds. Mandates are paternalistic, as they do not allow people to resist by opting out, and nudges are "libertarian-paternalistic," as they allow people to resist by opting out. Corrections are libertarian when people ask for them and libertarian-paternalistic or paternalistic when people do not.

We see the distinctions between correcting, nudging, and mandating functions in retirement savings. Psychologist Craig McKenzie and behavioral finance analyst Michael Liersch found that anchoring errors in the intuitive System 1 mislead people into underestimating exponential growth of savings, likely underestimating the effects of compounding and the potential growth of money saved when they are young. Consequently, System 1 misleads people who want adequate old-age income into inadequate savings when young and inadequate spending when old.[71] A $1,000 savings account grows exponentially to $10,286 at 6 percent annual growth rate during 40 years, yet people commonly underestimate its growth as closer to $3,400, as if the account grew linearly. Handing people calculators is not an adequate System 2 correcting method, because many people plug in the wrong math.

Good shortcuts are a useful System 2 correcting method. The "rule of 72" is a cognitive shortcut we use to estimate the number of years it would take an amount to double when it grows exponentially. It involves dividing 72 by the annual rate of growth, such as 6 percent, yielding an estimate of 12 years. Precise calculation shows that it actually takes 11 years and 11 months for an amount to double at a 6 percent annual growth rate, but a one-month difference is small, qualifying the rule of 72 as a good cognitive shortcut. Both 12 years and 11 years and 11 months are considerably shorter than 16 years and 8 months, the estimate made as if the amount grew linearly.

People using the rule of 72 can estimate that $1,000 would grow into $2,000 in 12 years, $4,000 in 24 years, and $8,000 in 36 years. Their estimate of growth at the end of 40 years would be $9,920 if they calculate the last four years linearly, short of the correct $10,286 but not by far. Indeed, evidence indicates that the rule of 72 is quite effective in reducing errors in estimation of exponential growth.[72]

We correct when we point people to their wants, whether for greater savings or lesser ones. People who know exponential growth might choose to save more when they are young, motivated by wants for ample spending when they are old. Or they might choose to save *less* when young, motivated by wants for ample spending when young, knowing that smaller savings would grow exponentially to amounts large enough to satisfy their wants for adequate but less than ample spending when old.

McKenzie and Liersch, however, did not aim at correcting—pointing people to their wants. Instead, they aimed at nudging people to the should of greater savings. That should might reflect the wants of a person's old self for ample old-age spending, silenced by the wants of that person's young self for ample current spending. Or it might reflect a should that policy makers consider wise even if neither a person's young self nor his old self want it. McKenzie and Liersch started with the premise that people do not save enough for retirement and therefore should be nudged to greater savings. Indeed, they were concerned that their correcting method might point people to lesser savings and relieved to find that it nudged people to greater savings.

Mandating goes a step beyond nudging by shoving people into their shoulds. Social Security shoves people into saving, mandating contributions made during working years and payments made in retirement. Americans can refuse to be nudged into defined-contribution retirement savings plans, because such plans are voluntary, but they cannot refuse to be shoved into Social Security, because it is mandatory.

The Food and Drug Administration (FDA) does not nudge physicians and patients away from drugs it considers unsafe or ineffective; it shoves physicians and patients away from them by mandating that such drugs not be prescribed. One proposal has called for an "FDA for financial innovation." Specifically, companies inventing new financial products would be forbidden to sell them until they are examined by a government agency similar to the FDA and found to be safe and effective.[73]

CONCLUSION

We are susceptible to cognitive and emotional errors, yet can correct them by human-behavior and financial-facts knowledge. This knowledge transforms us from normal-ignorant to normal-knowledgeable, and transforms our choices from normal-foolish to normal-smart.

The first step to transformation is awareness of our cognitive and emotional shortcuts and errors. The second is use of the reflective System 2 when the intuitive System 1 misleads us. Consider, for example, the common criticism of authorities for failing to foresee terrorist acts because they "failed to connect the dots." Awareness of hindsight shortcuts and errors helps us comprehend and accept that connecting dots in hindsight is easier than in foresight, when it would have helped foil terrorist acts.

Similar awareness helps us comprehend and accept that foreseeing the next stock-market boom or crash is easier in hindsight than in foresight.

Human-behavior knowledge about hindsight shortcuts and errors is most effective when combined with financial-facts knowledge about the record of market-timing investors who try to buy stocks before booms and sell them before crashes. A System 2 method that compels us to examine all evidence about market timing, both confirming and disconfirming, can tell whether market timers are indeed successful.

It is unfortunate that some financial actors exploit our cognitive and emotional errors, rather than help correct them. They include mutual fund companies that exploit availability errors by making their best-performing funds available to memory by advertising. We tend to overlook the small print of "past performance does not guarantee future results" in the ads. Rules based on human-behavior and financial-facts knowledge help correct these errors as well.

CHAPTER 6

Experienced Happiness, Life Evaluation, and Choices

Expected-Utility Theory and Prospect Theory

Think of Margaret and Ann. Margaret's wealth decreased from $4 million to $3 million yesterday, while Ann's wealth increased from $1 million to $1.5 million. Who experiences greater happiness today? And who reports higher life evaluation?

Daniel Kahneman and fellow Nobelist Angus Deaton distinguished between two concepts of happiness, "experienced happiness" and "life-evaluation."[1] Experienced happiness is also called "emotional well-being" and "hedonic well-being." Kahneman and Deaton assessed experienced happiness by answers to questions about yesterday's experiences, such as yesterday's enjoyment, affection, sadness, or anger. They assessed life evaluation by Cantril's Self-Anchoring Scale, whereby people place themselves on a ladder whose rungs go from the bottom, "worst possible life," to the top, "best possible life." Kahneman and Deaton found that life evaluation rises steadily with income, but experienced happiness does not rise beyond an annual income of approximately $75,000.

We can think of experienced happiness as "fleeting happiness," and life evaluation as "sustained happiness." People with annual incomes much below $75,000 report lower experienced happiness than people with annual incomes closer to $75,000. They report less happiness yesterday—less enjoyment, less frequent smiling. and less laughter, and they report more misery yesterday—more worry and greater sadness. Indeed, people with incomes much below $75,000 might be deprived of experienced happiness most days. Worry about losing a job if their car breaks down might deprive them of experienced happiness one day, and calls from debt collectors might deprive them of experienced happiness the following day.

People whose annual incomes exceed $75,000 by much do not report greater experienced happiness than people whose annual incomes exceed $75,000 by only little. They do not report more enjoyment yesterday or less worry. Both groups have the means to rent a car if theirs breaks down, and neither gets calls from debt collectors. But both groups can be deprived of experienced happiness during some days by a disappointing bonus, misbehaving children, or a breakup of a relationship.

Yet people whose annual incomes exceed $100,000 report substantially higher life evaluation than people whose annual income is $75,000, and people whose annual income is $200,000 report substantially higher life evaluation than people whose annual income is $100,000. Life evaluation reflects all the benefits of wealth, including the utilitarian benefits of consumption of goods and services, and the expressive and emotional benefits of high social status and pride. Indeed, in the absence of expressive and emotional benefits of wealth it is hard to explain why people whose wealth exceeds what they can reasonably consume in several lifetimes continue to strive for even greater wealth.

The experienced happiness of Ann is likely greater than Margaret's because Ann gained $500,000 of wealth yesterday while Margaret lost $1 million of wealth. Ann is more likely than Margaret to report happiness, enjoyment, and frequent smiling and laughter today, and less likely to report worry and sadness. But the life evaluation of Margaret is likely greater than Ann's because Margaret's wealth is $3 million, exceeding Ann's $1.5 million.

LEVELS OF WEALTH AND GAINS AND LOSSES OF WEALTH

Expected-utility theory and prospect theory are two theories that assess happiness and predict choices. Expected-utility theory was introduced by mathematician Daniel Bernoulli,[2] and prospect theory was introduced by psychologists Daniel Kahneman and Amos Tversky.[3] Expected-utility theory is associated with standard finance, whereas prospect theory is associated with behavioral finance, yet neither is comprehensive. A comprehensive theory that assesses happiness and predicts choices combines expected-utility theory and prospect theory and goes beyond them.

Utility in expected-utility theory is *wealth utility*, shorthand for life evaluation or sustained happiness derived from wealth. One prediction of

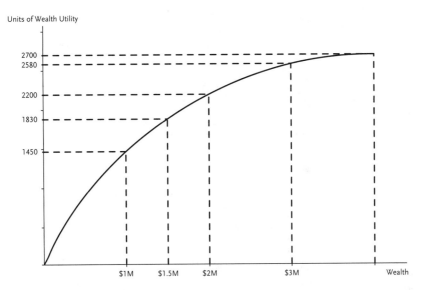

Figure 6-1 Wealth and wealth utility in expected-utility theory: wealth utility is life evaluation or sustained happiness derived from levels of wealth.

expected-utility theory, depicted in Figure 6-1, is that sustained happiness from wealth is high when wealth is high, placing the wealthy higher on the life-evaluation ladder. Indeed, this prediction conforms to the first part of economists Merton Miller and Franco Modigliani's definition of rational investors as ones who prefer more wealth to less.[4]

Expected-utility theory predicts that Margaret's life evaluation is higher than Ann's because Margaret's $3 million wealth confers 2,580 units of wealth utility, whereas Ann's $1.5 million confers a mere 1,830 units. (Note that the scale of wealth utility here is arbitrary. We could have replaced 2,580 with 25,800 or any other number. Only the ratios of wealth utility relative to one another matter.)

Wealth utility increases more slowly than wealth. For example, the first million dollars adds 1,450 units of wealth utility to the zero units of wealth utility of $0, but the second million adds only 750 units of wealth utility, totaling 2,200, and the third million adds even less, 380 units, totaling 2,580. The association between wealth and wealth utility varies among people. An addition to wealth, from $2 million to $3 million, adds 380 units of wealth utility to one person, but it might add only 360 units to another person.

Utility in prospect theory is *gain-loss utility*, shorthand for experienced happiness, or fleeting happiness derived from gains and losses of wealth relative to a reference point. Levels of wealth yesterday, such as Margaret's $4 million and Ann's $1 million, are likely reference points. Prospect theory

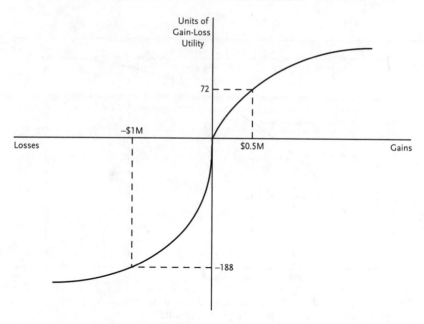

Figure 6-2 Gains and losses and gain-loss utility in prospect theory: gain-loss utility is experienced happiness, or fleeting happiness derived from gains and losses of wealth.

predicts that Ann's experienced happiness today exceeds Margaret's because Ann gained $500,000 yesterday, relative to her $1 million reference point, a gain of 72 units of gain-loss utility, depicted in Figure 6-2, whereas Margaret lost $1 million yesterday relative to her $4 million reference point, a loss of 188 units. (The scale of gain-loss utility, like that of wealth utility, is arbitrary. We could have replaced 72 with 720 or any other number. Only the ratios of gain-loss utility relative to one another matter.) The association between gains and losses and gain-loss utility, like the association between wealth and wealth utility, varies among people. A gain of $500,000 adds 72 units of gain-loss utility to one person, but it might add 76 units to another person.

Expected-utility theory predicts that people are not confused by the frame of wealth, consistent with the second part of Miller and Modigliani's definition of rational investors, whereas prospect theory predicts that people are regularly confused. A frame that comes easily to the minds of Elizabeth and Ann is prospect theory's frame of gains and losses relative to yesterday's wealth as the reference point—Ann gained $500,000, whereas Margaret lost $1 million. A friend of Elizabeth might cheer her up, however, by suggesting that she edit her frame within prospect theory, setting her reference point at the $2 million she had last year, highlighting the gain from $2 million to $3 million and obscuring the loss from $4 million to $3 million. That friend might also direct Elizabeth's attention from prospect theory's gains and losses of wealth to expected-utility theory's levels of wealth, highlighting the fact that Margaret's $3 million of wealth exceeds Ann's $1.5 million.

Both expected-utility theory and prospect theory offer predictions about choices. Expected-utility theory predicts that people's choices reflect a preference for high wealth over low wealth, and prospect theory predicts that people's choices reflect a preference for high gains over low gains or losses. Both theories also predict that choices reflect risk aversion, but definitions of risk by the two theories differ, which I now discuss.

VARIANCE AVERSION AND LOSS AVERSION

Expected-utility theory predicts that all choices correspond to risk aversion and never to risk seeking, when risk is measured by the variance of returns. Risk aversion in expected-utility theory is better described as *variance aversion* and risk seeking is better described as *variance seeking*.

Prospect theory also predicts that all choices correspond to risk aversion, but risk aversion in prospect theory can be *variance aversion, loss*

Expected-Utility Theory and Prospect Theory	
Expected-Utility Theory (EUT)	Prospect Theory (PT)
1. Utility is wealth utility	1. Utility is gain-loss utility
2. Wealth utility is sustained happiness, or life evaluation	2. Gain-loss utility is fleeting happiness, or experienced happiness
3. Wealth utility is determined by total wealth	3. Gain-loss utility is determined by gains and losses relative to a reference point
4. Choices are made by considering the effects of outcomes on total wealth	4. Choices are made by considering the effects of outcomes on gains and losses
5. Perceptions of total wealth are not affected by framing	5. Perceptions of gains and losses are affected by framing
6. People's choices always conform to risk aversion, where risk aversion is variance aversion	6. People's choices always conform to risk aversion, where risk aversion is variance aversion, loss aversion, or shortfall aversion
7. People's choices always conform to variance aversion, never to variance seeking	7. People's choices sometimes conform to variance seeking, when variance seeking reflects shortfall aversion
8. People estimate objectively probabilities of outcomes	8. People estimate subjectively probabilities of outcomes, replacing objective probabilities by "probability weights"
9. Emotions play no role in choices	9. Emotions play roles in choices, especially hope, fear, pride, and regret

aversion, or *shortfall aversion.* Some prospect theory choices conform to variance aversion, consistent with expected-utility theory, whereas other choices conform to variance seeking, consistent with shortfall aversion in prospect theory, but inconsistent with expected-utility theory.

CHOICES WHEN ALL OUTCOMES ARE IN THE DOMAIN OF GAINS

People are likely to choose a sure $10,000 over a 50-50 gamble for $20,000 or $0. This choice is consistent with variance aversion in expected-utility theory because the $10,000 expected value of the gamble equals the sure $10,000—the mean of $20,000 and $0—while the variance of the possible outcomes of the gamble exceeds the zero variance of the sure $10,000.

We can describe expected-utility theory choices more precisely in the frame of total wealth, depicted in Figure 6-3, as the theory predicts that this is how people frame their choices, explicitly or, more likely, implicitly.

Suppose that current wealth is $20,000, yielding 220 units of wealth utility. The sure $10,000 brings total wealth to $30,000, yielding 258 units

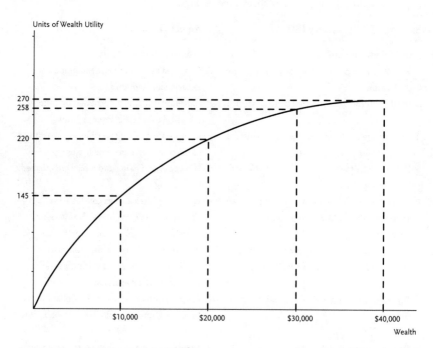

Figure 6-3 Choices by expected-utility theory when gamble outcomes cannot reduce total wealth.

of wealth utility. The gamble offers a 50-50 chance to leave total wealth at its current $20,000, yielding 220 units of wealth utility, or bring it to $40,000, yielding 270 units. The mean of 220 and 270 units of wealth utility associated with the gamble is 245 units, a number lower than the 258 units derived from $30,000 of total wealth. Therefore, expected utility theory predicts that people would choose the sure $10,000.

The choice of the sure $10,000 is also consistent with variance aversion in prospect theory for people whose reference point is $0, depicted in Figure 6-4.

Both the sure amount and the possible outcomes of the gamble are in the domain of gains, as neither can result in a loss relative to the $0 reference point. The sure $10,000 gain yields 110 units of gain-loss utility. A $20,000 gain in the 50-50 gamble yields 137 units and a $0 gain yields zero units. The mean of the gamble's 137 units and zero units of gain-loss utility is 68.5 units, a number lower than the 110 units yielded by the sure $10,000. Therefore, prospect theory predicts that people would choose the sure $10,000.

People whose choices conform to expected-utility theory might choose a 50-50 gamble for $80,000 or $0 over a sure $10,000 if their variance aversion is not high. The sure $10,000 would bring total wealth to a sure $30,000, the sum of the $20,000 current wealth and the additional $10,000. The gamble would bring total wealth to $100,000 or leave it at $20,000. The

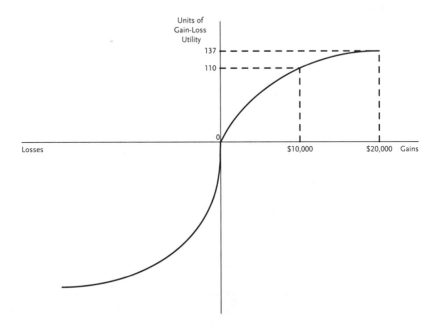

Figure 6-4 Choices by prospect theory when outcomes are all in the domain of gains.

variance of the possible outcomes of total wealth if the gamble is chosen exceeds the zero variance of the sure $30,000 if the sure $10,000 is chosen. But the $60,000 expected wealth if the gamble is chosen, the sum of the current $20,000 and the $40,000 expected value, if the gamble is chosen, exceeds the sure $30,000, if the sure $10,000 is chosen. The difference between wealth utility derived from $60,000 and that derived from $30,000 might overcome variance aversion and lead some to choose the gamble.

This choice, too, is consistent with variance aversion in prospect theory for people whose reference point is $0 and their variance aversion is not high, because the $40,000 expected value of the gamble is 4 times the sure $10,000, and both the sure amount and the possible outcomes of the gamble are in the domain of gains.

LOSS AVERSION

Now consider a choice between a sure $0 and a 50-50 gamble for a $20,000 gain or a $5,000 loss. We can describe the expected-utility theory choice in the frame of total wealth, depicted in Figure 6-5. Current wealth is $20,000, yielding 220 units of wealth utility. The sure $0 leaves total wealth unchanged

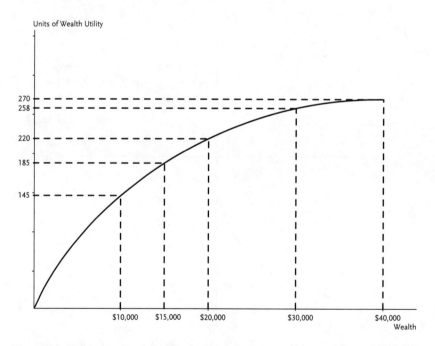

Figure 6-5 Choices by expected utility theory when some outcomes can reduce total wealth.

at $20,000, yielding the same 220 units. The gamble offers a 50-50 chance to reduce total wealth to $15,000, yielding 185 units of wealth utility, or increase it to $40,000, yielding 270 units. The mean of 185 units and 270 units of wealth utility associated with the gamble is 227.5 units, a number higher than the 220 units of utility associated with the sure amount. Therefore, expected-utility theory predicts that people would choose the gamble.

Loss aversion, however, might incline against this gamble people whose choices conform to prospect theory. This resistance is because the possible outcomes of the gamble span the domains of both gains and losses, and the pain of losses looms larger than the pleasure of gains of equal magnitude. Loss aversion is reflected in a prospect-theory function that declines by more in the domain of losses than it increases in the domain of gains in the range close to the reference point.

The sure $0 yields zero units of gain-loss utility, depicted in Figure 6-6. A $20,000 gain in the 50-50 gamble yields 137 units of gain-loss utility, but a $5,000 loss yields a loss of 150 units of gain-loss utility. The mean of the gamble's units of gain-loss utility is a negative 6.5 units of gain-loss utility, a number lower than the zero units yielded by the sure amount. Therefore, prospect theory predicts that people would reject the gamble and choose the sure $0.

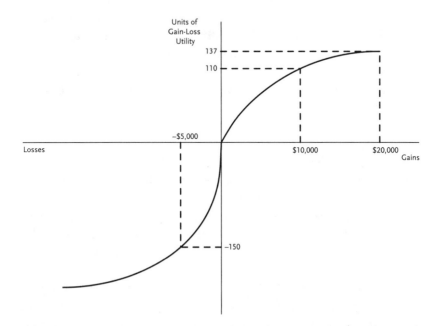

Figure 6-6 Choices by prospect theory when some outcomes are in the domain of losses.

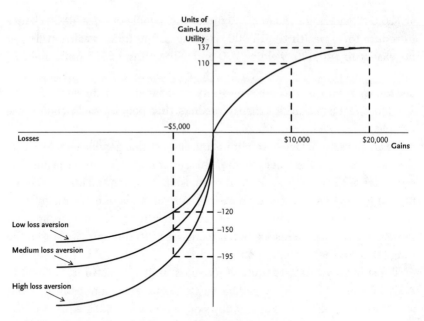

Figure 6-7 Choices of people who vary in loss aversion.

People vary in loss aversion and variations affect choices. Consider three people represented in Figure 6-7, one presented earlier in Figure 6-6 whom we describe now as medium loss averse, and two more we describe as low loss averse and high loss averse. The medium-loss-averse person rejects the gamble because its mean gain-loss utility of 137 units and a negative 150 units is a negative 6.5 units. The high-loss-averse person rejects the gamble even more emphatically because its mean gain-loss utility of 137 units and a negative 195 units is a negative 29 units. The low-loss-averse person accepts the gamble, however, because its mean gain-loss utility of 137 units and a negative 120 units is 8.5 units, higher than the zero gain-loss utility associated with the sure $0.

Next, suppose that you are given an opportunity to replace your current investment portfolio with a new one. The new portfolio has a 50-50 chance for a 50 percent gain in your lifetime standard of living. Yet the new portfolio also has a 50-50 chance for an X percent loss in your lifetime standard of living. What is the maximum X percent loss in lifetime standard of living that you are willing to accept for a 50-50 chance to gain 50 percent in lifetime standard of living?

Loss aversion implies that people would offer less than 50 percent loss in lifetime standard of living for a 50-50 chance at a 50 percent gain. Indeed, American investors are, on average, willing to accept no more than

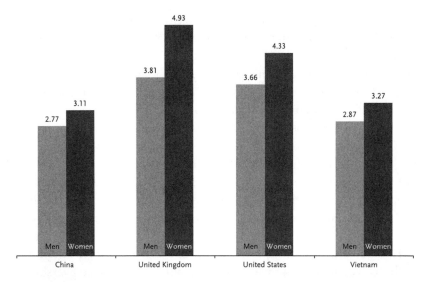

Figure 6-8 Loss aversion of men and women in China, United Kingdom, United States, and Vietnam.

Ratio of a 50 percent gain in lifetime standard of living to maximum percent loss in lifetime standard of living they are willing to accept a 50-50 chance for a gain or loss.

12.5 percent loss in lifetime standard of living for a 50-50 chance for a 50 percent gain. In other words, they are willing, on average, to accept a 50-50 chance for a potential loss or a gain only if the potential gain is at least 4 times as large as the potential loss.[5]

Loss aversion varies considerably by gender and age. Men are on average less loss averse than women, and the young are on average less loss averse than the old. Loss aversion also varies across countries. Figure 6-8 shows that people in China are on average less loss averse than people in the United States, and people in the United States are on average less loss averse than people in the United Kingdom.

SHORTFALL AVERSION

Shortfall aversion differs from loss aversion, although the two are often confused. The reference point in loss aversion is our current position. The current position is current wealth when we contemplate a 50-50 chance to win $20,000 or lose $5,000, and the current position is our current standard of living when we contemplate a 50-50 gamble for a 50 percent gain in our standard of living or a 20 percent loss. In contrast, the reference point in shortfall aversion is an *aspiration level* higher than our current position.

People gambling in a casino with a small amount of money who aspire to a large amount by morning do better with a bold bet that offers a chance, however small, to eliminate the shortfall from their aspiration than with timid bets that offer even smaller chances to eliminate it. They accept risk in the form of variance and in the form of potential loss to reduce risk in the form of shortfall from their aspiration.

Consider a choice between a sure $5,000 loss and a 50-50 gamble for a $15,000 loss or a $0 loss, as in Figure 6-9. The sure $5,000 loss implies a sure $5,000 shortfall from aspired wealth, equal to wealth before the loss, with no chance to eliminate that shortfall. A $5,000 loss reduces gain-loss utility by 150 units. The gamble, however, offers a 50-50 chance to eliminate the shortfall if the outcome of the gamble is a $0 loss, even though it also imposes a 50-50 chance for a $15,000 loss. The gain-loss utility of $0 loss is zero units, and the gain-loss utility of a $15,000 loss is 205 units.

The choice of the gamble is inconsistent with variance aversion in expected-utility theory. Expected wealth if the gamble is chosen is $12,500, lower by $7,500 than the current $20,000 wealth. Wealth if the sure loss is chosen is $15,000, lower by only $5,000 than the current $20,000 wealth. This difference gives the advantage to the choice of the sure loss over the choice of the gamble. Moreover, the variance of the possible wealth outcomes of the gamble is higher than the zero variance of the sure $15,000

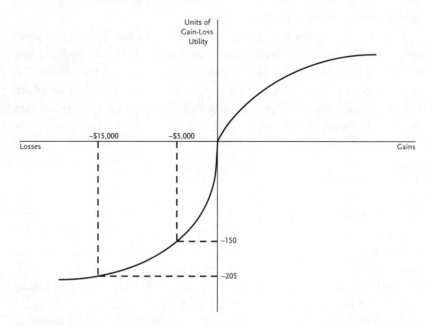

Figure 6-9 Shortfall aversion in prospect theory.

wealth. Both lower expected wealth and higher variance incline against the gamble people whose choices conform to expected-utility theory. But the choice of the gamble is consistent with shortfall aversion of people whose choices conform to prospect theory. The mean gain-loss utility of the gamble is a negative 102.5 units, the mean of a negative 205 units and zero units, still better than the loss of 150 units of gain-loss utility of the sure $5,000 loss.

One example of shortfall aversion is the tendency of racetrack bettors to bet on long shots towards the end of the day. Suppose that the reference point of bettors who have lost $5,000 in the morning is their wealth before the loss. They frame their afternoon choice as between a sure $5,000 shortfall if they leave the racetrack now and a long-shot gamble such as a 10 percent probability for eliminating the shortfall by winning $5,000 and a 90 percent probability of losing an additional $10,000, thereby increasing the shortfall to $15,000. Racetrack bettors who are very shortfall averse choose the gamble, whereas racetrack bettors who are not as shortfall averse choose to accept their $5,000 shortfall and leave for the day.

Marathon runners' shortfall aversion is evident in the bunching of finishing times at round numbers, such as 4 hours, that runners set as their finishing-time aspirations. A study of more than 9 million marathon finishing times uncovered such bunching, driven by increased effort near the finish line as runners strain to avoid shortfalls from their finishing-time aspirations.[6]

Car owners are also shortfall averse. A study explored the distance driven by cars in Singapore during a period when changes in government policies caused substantial variation in purchase prices. A $4,500 increase in the price of cars was associated with an 8.8 percentage point increase in distance driven. Drivers appear to strive to break even, avoiding shortfalls relative to the higher price.[7]

ASPIRATIONS AND SHORTFALL AVERSION

We buy lottery tickets, start new businesses, and immigrate to new countries for a chance to reach our aspirations. We are not risk seekers. Rather, risk is payment for a chance to reach our aspirations. Indeed, variance acceptance is the price of shortfall avoidance.

Many who bought houses in the boom years of 2006 and 2007 lost them to foreclosures in the years that followed. It is easy to characterize these home buyers as risk seekers, but aspirations for the utilitarian, expressive, and emotional benefits of middle-class lives in homes of their own drove them to buy, and risk in the form of variance was payment for avoiding the risk of falling short of their aspirations.

Members of upper social classes join members of lower ones in aspirations for the utilitarian, expressive, and emotional benefits of even higher social classes. Rajat Gupta was a member of the hundreds-of-millions-holding class who ran the consulting firm McKinsey from 1994 to 2003 and later served as a member of Goldman Sachs's board of directors. By now Gupta has completed a prison sentence for disclosing inside information to Raj Rajaratnam of the Galleon hedge fund, the sad outcome of risking his millions and freedom for a chance to reach the billionaire class. "My analysis of the situation is he's enamored with [Kohlberg, Kravis, and Roberts private equity firm] and I think he wants to be in that circle," said Rajaratnam in a telephone conversation played at his trial. "That's a billionaire circle, right? Goldman is like the hundreds-of-millions circle, right?"[8]

Gupta's aspirations are evident in his words before his fall. Speaking to university students, Gupta said, "When I look at myself, yeah, I am driven by money. And when I live in this society, you know, you do get fairly materialistic, so I look at that. I am disappointed. I am probably more materialistic today than I was before, and I think money is very seductive. . . . You have to watch out for it, because the more you have it, you get used to comforts, and you get used to, you know, big houses and vacation homes and going and doing whatever you want, and so it is very seductive. However much you say that you will not fall into the trap of it, you do fall into the trap of it."

Gupta aspired for the utilitarian, expressive, and emotional benefits of money that buys big houses and vacation homes. He aspired even more for the social status of a philanthropist, willing to exchange the utilitarian benefits of money for the expressive and emotional benefits of high social status. "He wanted to burnish his legacy as a philanthropist," wrote journalist Anita Raghavan, "and focused on charitable works tied to India, like the Indian School of Business, his pet cause. At the urging of Bill Clinton, he had already helped start the American India Foundation."[9]

Gupta is not alone in setting the wealth and incomes of others as reference points for his aspirations. One study explored life satisfaction, perception of incomes in reference groups, and intensity of income comparisons. Japanese people compare their incomes to those of friends, whereas Europeans compare theirs to those of colleagues. Japanese, moreover, compare their incomes to the incomes of their reference group more intensely than Europeans. Life satisfaction diminishes when income is low relative to perceived incomes of others, and life satisfaction diminishes further among those who are more intense in comparing their incomes to other people's.[10]

Another study tested the hypothesis that income inequality causes financial distress among low-income people who observe the large gaps between their incomes and the much higher incomes of others. The effect of income inequality was assessed by lottery prizes in very small Canadian neighborhoods. A C$1,000 increase in a lottery prize caused a 2.4 percent rise in subsequent bankruptcies among the close neighbors of these winners. Conspicuous consumption is a mechanism for this causal effect. Lottery prizes increased visible assets, such as houses, cars, and motorcycles, but not invisible assets, such as cash and pensions.[11]

The role of aspirations in risk taking is central in Nobel Laureate economist Milton Friedman and mathematician Leonard Savage's observations many decades ago. "Men will and do take great risks to distinguish themselves even when they know what the risks are." They quoted Adam Smith's observation of many decades before about "The presumptuous hope of success" that entices "so many adventurers into . . . hazardous trades. . . ."[12]

Friedman and Savage introduced a utility function whereby people derive utility from levels of wealth and are variance averse, as in expected-utility theory, except for a particular region of wealth where they are variance seeking—shortfall averse—as they seek to "distinguish themselves" by reaching their aspirations. Harry Markowitz modified this depiction, centering the region of wealth where people are variance seeking on their current wealth and arguing that people consider gains and losses relative to their current wealth as they make choices.[13] Daniel Kahneman and Amos Tversky built on the insights of Friedman and Savage and Markowitz in prospect theory, whereby utility is determined by gains and losses of wealth relative to reference wealth.[14] That reference wealth of people might be current wealth, but might also be their aspired wealth.

PROBABILITY WEIGHTS, ASPIRATIONS, AND EXPRESSIVE AND EMOTIONAL COSTS AND BENEFITS

Expected-utility theory predicts that people use objective probabilities of possible outcomes as they consider choices, whereas prospect theory predicts that people use subjective probabilities that can depart from objective probabilities. "Probability weights" are ratios of subjective probabilities to objective probabilities. Objective probability indicates a 1-in-1,000,000 chance to win the lottery, but a 100,000 probability weight overweighs this objective probability to a subjective probability to a 1-in-10 chance.

Probability weights equal 1, and subjective probabilities equal objective probabilities when we are free of making errors and consider only utilitarian costs and benefits. Probability weights depart from 1 even when we are free of making errors if we also consider aspirations and expressive and emotional costs and benefits, such as those of hope and fear.

In the movie *Dumb and Dumber,* a man who desperately aspires to attract a woman responds when she says that his chances are not good: "You mean, not good like 1 out of 100?" he asks. "I'd say more like 1 in a million," she answers. The man pauses as he ponders the odds and then says with a happy grin, "So you're telling me there's a chance! Yeah!" The man's aspiration and his hope for reaching it are reflected in a giant—and illusory—probability weight, perhaps 10,000, turning an objective probability of 1 in a million into a subjective probability of 1 in 100.

We can think of that man as one whose aspiration and hope to attract that woman set a prospect-theory reference point much higher than his current position. Aversion to shortfall from his aspiration and hope for reaching it prompt him to assign a much higher subjective probability to the outcome in which he attracts her than objective probability indicates.

Daniel Kahneman described a "fourfold pattern" in which probability weights reflect gaps between objective and subjective probabilities.[15] Think of a $20 lottery ticket that offers an objective 0.001 percent probability to win a $1 million prize. The expected payoff of the ticket is $10, the product of the 0.001 percent objective probability and the $1 million prize. The variance of the payoff of the ticket is high, as differences are great between the potential payoffs of $1 million and $0. Expected-utility theory predicts that we are unwilling to buy the ticket, because its $10 expected payoff is half its $20 price and the variance of wealth resulting from winning or losing is much higher than the zero variance of keeping our current wealth by forgoing the lottery (Figure 6–10).

Prospect theory's loss aversion in the absence of probability weights predicts even more strongly that we are unwilling to buy the ticket when we consider only utilitarian costs and benefits. Prospect theory's loss aversion implies that the $20 we lose if the ticket does not win looms large relative to the 0.001 percent probability of winning the $1 million prize. Yet prospect theory predicts that some are inclined to buy this ticket when they consider aspirations and emotional costs and benefits in addition to utilitarian costs and benefits.

A lottery ticket carries the emotional benefits of the hope of winning, thereby reaching high aspirations. Aspirations and hope of reaching them are reflected in probability weights that overweigh the objective probabilities of winning. Imagine that we desperately aspire to have $1 million but

Emotional benefits of hope of winning a large amount	Emotional costs of fear of losing a large amount
Question: Pay $20 for a ticket to a $1 million lottery?	Question: Pay $2,000 to insure a $1 million house?
Objective probability of winning = 0.001%	Objective probability of fire = 0.1%
Subjective probability of winning = 10%	Subjective probability of fire = 1%
Probability weight = 10,000	Probability weight = 10
Choice: We buy the lottery ticket	Choice: We buy insurance
Emotional costs of anticipated regret of foregoing a sure gain of a large amount	**Emotional benefits of hope of avoiding a sure loss of a large amount**
Question: Accept $700,000 as settlement or proceed to trial with a 95% probability of receiving $1 million?	Question: Pay $700,000 as settlement or proceed to trial with a 95% probability of paying $1 million?
Objective probability of receiving zero in trial = 5%	Objective probability of paying zero in trial = 5%
Subjective probability of receiving zero in trial = 40%	Subjective probability of paying zero in trial = 40%
Probability weight = 8	Probability weight = 8
Decision: We accept the settlement	Decision: We proceed to trial

Figure 6-10 Probability weights and choices.

have only $20. Aspirations and the emotional benefits of hope of winning a $1 million prize might imply a 10,000 probability weight, overweighing the objective 0.001 percent probability of winning into a 10 percent subjective probability. A 10 percent probability of winning $1 million might overcome aversion to a $20 loss, leading us to buy the ticket. As one lottery buyer said, "I've dug so many holes for myself over the years that, realistically, winning the lottery may be my only ticket out."

Now think of a $2,000 fire insurance policy for our $1 million home. The objective probability of the house burning down is 0.1 percent. We might be inclined against buying an insurance policy if we consider utilitarian costs and benefits alone. This inclination is because the $2,000 sure loss when we pay for the insurance policy looms large relative to the $1,000 expected loss—the product of a $1 million loss and its 0.1 percent objective probability. But the probability weight we assign to the objective 0.1 percent probability might be 10 when we also consider our aspiration to avoid shortfall from our current position, where we own a house or have the $1 million insurance payment to replace it, and the emotional cost of the fear if we do not have an insurance policy that will pay $1 million if the house burns down.

The 10 probability weight overweighs the 0.1 percent objective probability of the house burning down into a 1 percent subjective probability. The 1 percent subjective probability makes the expected loss if we do not buy a policy seem like $10,000 rather than $1,000, much more than the $2,000 price of the policy. This perception inclines us toward buying a policy.

Next consider a choice to accept a $700,000 payment before trial as settlement of a claim, or proceed to trial with a 95 percent objective probability of a favorable judgment awarding us $1 million, and a 5 percent objective probability of an unfavorable one awarding us nothing. Consideration of utilitarian costs and benefits alone might incline us to proceed to trial, as its $950,000 expected payment, the product of the 95 percent probability and the $1 million award, greatly exceeds the $700,000 settlement offer. Yet shortfall aversion from the offered $700,000 and the anticipated emotional cost of regret if the judgment is unfavorable can make the 5 percent objective probability of an unfavorable judgment seem like a 40 percent probability, implying a probability weight of 8. A 60 percent probability of a favorable judgment awarding us $1 million amounts to $600,000, less than the $700,000 settlement offer. This probability inclines us to accept the settlement offer.

Last, consider a choice to pay $700,000 before trial as settlement of a claim against us or proceed to trial with a 95 percent objective probability of an unfavorable judgment and a $1 million payment from us and a 5 percent objective probability of a favorable judgment and a zero payment from us. Consideration of utilitarian costs and benefits alone might incline us to avoid trial, as its $950,000 expected payment from us greatly exceeds the $700,000 settlement payment from us. Yet shortfall aversion and the emotional benefits of hope of avoiding a large loss if the trial concludes with a favorable judgment can make the objective 5 percent probability of a favorable judgment seem like a 40 percent probability, implying a probability weight of 8. A 60 percent probability of a $1 million payment from us amounts to $600,000, less than the $700,000 we would pay if we agreed to the settlement payment. This probability inclines us to reject the settlement payment and proceed to trial.

The effect of emotions on probability weights is evident in an experiment in which one group of students was asked to choose between a sure $50 in cash and a sure opportunity to meet and kiss their favorite movie star. Another group was asked to choose between a lottery offering a 1 percent chance to win $50 and a lottery offering a 1 percent chance of an opportunity to meet and kiss the star. A kiss may have a cash equivalent of less than $50, but a kiss is much more emotionally evocative than the cash. In the sure condition, 70 percent preferred cash over a kiss, but in the low-probability condition, 65 percent preferred a kiss over cash. Evidently, hope of kissing a star increased the probability weight beyond its 1 percent objective probability.

Another experiment examined the effect of fear on probability weights in a choice between paying $20 cash or a sure, short, painful, but not dangerous electric shock. In this sure condition, most students preferred to receive the shock than pay $20. In the 1 percent condition, however, fear induced students to offer an average $7 for avoiding a 1 percent chance of an electric shock, whereas they offered an average of only $1 for avoiding a 1 percent chance of a $20 payment.[16]

The effect of emotions on probability weights is also evident in answers to a survey question about probabilities of a catastrophic stock-market crash: "What do you think is the probability of a catastrophic stock market crash in the U.S., like that of October 28, 1929, or October 19, 1987, in the next six months, including the case that a crash occurred in the other countries and spreads to the U.S.? (An answer of 0 percent means that it cannot happen, an answer of 100 percent means it is sure to happen.)" Answers, likely motivated by fear, placed the probability of a crash at the 10 percent to 19 percent range, implying an enormous probability weight, given that catastrophic stock-market crashes like those of October 28, 1929, or October 19, 1987, occurred only twice in more than 100 years.[17]

CONCLUSION

Attempts to capture in a graph all the factors that underlie people's happiness—utility—and predict people's choices are bound to fail. These many factors simply cannot be captured in a single graph. This is true whether it is the graph of expected-utility theory or prospect theory. Both theories, however, capture important factors underlying people's happiness and choices.

Total wealth is the factor at the center of expected-utility theory. Wealth underlies sustained happiness—life evaluation. Greater wealth lets us climb higher on a ladder whose rungs go from the "worst possible life" to the "best possible life." Gains and losses of wealth are the factors at the center of prospect theory. Gains add fleeing happiness—experienced happiness—and losses subtract from it. Today's wealth gain increases experienced happiness, and today's wealth loss subtracts from it. Prospect theory also highlights the role of emotions in choices—hope, fear, pride, and regret.

Placing the two theories side by side highlights differences in notions of risk and risk aversion, whether variance aversion, loss aversion, or short-fall aversion, and the tensions among these notions. A portfolio composed entirely of safe Treasury bills is consistent with variance aversion and loss aversion among young people saving for retirement, since the variance of the daily returns of Treasury bills is low, and so are their probability and likely amount of losses. But such a portfolio is not consistent with shortfall aversion of these young people, as it leaves them short of their retirement-income goals.

CHAPTER 7

Behavioral Finance Puzzles

The Dividend Puzzle, the Disposition Puzzle, and
the Puzzles of Dollar-Cost Averaging and Time
Diversification

Descriptions of the financial choices and solutions to their puzzles combine "Wants for Utilitarian, Expressive, and Emotional Benefits" (Chapter 2), "Cognitive Shortcuts and Errors" (Chapters 3), "Emotional Shortcuts and Errors" (Chapter 4), tools for "Correcting Cognitive and Emotional Errors" (Chapter 5), and the implications of expected utility and prospect theories for "Experienced Happiness, Life Evaluation, and Choices" (Chapter 6). Combining these features now allows us to offer solutions to four important puzzles in finance: the dividend puzzle, the disposition puzzle, and the puzzles of dollar-cost averaging and time diversification.

The dividend puzzle is about the preference for spending dividends while refraining from selling stocks and spending their proceeds. The disposition puzzle is about the disposition to realize gains quickly but procrastinate in the realization of losses. The puzzles of dollar-cost averaging and time diversification are about their popularity among investors despite faults in the usual arguments that underlie them.

THE DIVIDEND PUZZLE

Merton Miller spoke at a conference at the University of Chicago in October 1985 when the Swedish Academy announced that it had awarded the Nobel Prize in Economics to Franco Modigliani, in part for the article on dividends he wrote with Miller.[1] Newspaper reporters from around the world called Miller early that morning, asking for a one-sentence description of this joint work. "Moving money from your left pocket to the right won't make you rich," said Miller with a chuckle. "Franco and I proved it rigorously!"

Why then do so many investors care if their money is in their left "dividends" pocket or their right "capital" pocket? This is what economist Fischer Black called the dividend puzzle. "Why do corporations pay dividends? Why do investors pay attention to dividends? . . . The harder we look at the dividend picture, the more it seems like a puzzle, with pieces that just don't fit together."[2]

The solution to the dividend puzzle combines wants for saving and spending; cognitive and emotional shortcuts and errors, including framing, mental accounting, hindsight, regret, and self-control; and tools for correcting them, including distinctions between capital and dividends, rules that regulate saving and spending, and insights from expected utility and prospect theories.[3]

WANTS FOR UTILITARIAN, EXPRESSIVE, AND EMOTIONAL BENEFITS

We want to save for tomorrow, yet we also want to spend it all today. Saving provides utilitarian, expressive, and emotional benefits, and so does spending, but the two wants conflict. Distinctions between capital and dividends help us balance our conflicting saving and spending wants and regulate them.

We derive utilitarian, expressive, and emotional benefits from today's spending on food, shelter, cars, movies, and vacations. We also derive expressive and emotional benefits *today* from today's savings, in security, pride, and high social status. Savers with more than $1 million possess high social status, qualifying as "accredited investors," members of an exclusive club with access to hedge funds and other "alternative" investments unavailable to people with less. And even savers with lesser holdings enjoy the emotional benefits of security and pride, knowing they can tap their savings to replace their cars, support their children, and never ask their children to support them.

Normal-ignorant investors frame the capital of a stock as a fruit tree and dividends as its fruit. In that frame, collecting dividends and spending them does not diminish the capital of the stock any more than picking fruits off a tree and consuming them diminishes its size. In the correct frame, however, we consider an alternative to consuming the fruits. Selling the fruits and buying other fruit trees with the proceeds would have grown our orchard. Similarly, reinvesting the dividends rather than spending them would have grown our capital.

Rational investors know the correct frame for dividends and capital. They know that $1,000 in "homemade" dividends from the sale of shares is identical in substance to $1,000 from a cashed dividend check, even if different in form, and they care only about their total wealth, not its form. If we set aside taxes and trading costs, a dollar in the form of dividends is different from a dollar in the form of the capital in shares of stock only in form, not in substance. This discrepancy is because payments of dividends do not affect the total wealth of investors. The price of shares of a company declines when a company pays dividends, but the wealth of shareholders does not decline, because the decline in the price of shares when a dividend is paid equals the cash added to shareholders' bank accounts as they deposit their dividend checks. Capital declines among investors who spend their dividends, but not among investors who reinvest their dividends rather than spend them.

Normal-knowledgeable investors know that $1,000 in homemade dividends from the sale of shares is identical in substance to $1,000 from a cashed dividend check, but they are not necessarily indifferent in their preference between the two. Normal-ignorant investors, however, regularly confuse form for substance, believing that $1,000 in homemade dividends from the sale of shares is different in substance from $1,000 of a cashed dividend check.

Miller and Modigliani noted confusion between form and substance in the minds of normal-ignorant investors. They wrote that the fact that company-paid dividends are different from homemade dividends in form but not in substance "is obvious, once you think of it." But, they added, "Obvious as the proposition may be, however, one finds few references to it in the extensive literature on the [dividend] problem."[4] Indeed, there would have been little news in Miller and Modigliani's article and little reason to publish it if all investors were rational or normal-knowledgeable.

You might wonder whether homemade dividends are different from company-paid dividends in substance, not only in form. There is indeed a difference in substance between the two, but it only deepens the dividend puzzle because taxes confer an advantage on homemade dividends, likely more than offsetting brokerage commissions paid when selling shares to create homemade dividends.

Consider the case in which the tax rate on dividends is 20 percent, equal to the tax rate on capital gains. The $40 current price of your shares is lower than the $100 price you paid when you bought them, such that you have a $60 unrealized loss per share. You create a $1,000 homemade dividend by selling 25 shares at $40 each. The 20 percent tax rebate that comes with realizing losses amounts to $12 per share, increasing your wealth by $300. In contrast, the 20 percent tax on $1,000 company-paid dividends reduces your wealth by $200.

Now consider the case in which the $125 current price of shares is higher than the $100 price you paid when you bought them, such that you realize a $25 gain per share when you sell them. You create a $1,000 homemade dividend by selling 8 shares at $125 each. The 20 percent tax that comes with realizing gains amounts to $5 per share, reducing your wealth by $40. In contrast, the 20 percent tax on $1,000 company-paid dividends reduces your wealth by $200.

SELF-CONTROL

Company-paid dividends have an advantage over homemade dividends because they facilitate exercise of self-control. Consider young investors who want to save for retirement yet are tempted to spend their money today on movies, vacations, and luxury cars. They can limit today's spending by exercising self-control, suppressing the urge to replace their battered old car with a new luxury model. Yet they know that their self-control is sometimes too weak to withstand the temptation of spending, and that in a moment of weakness they might sell shares of stock for that new luxury car.

Young investors bolster their self-control by setting separate mental accounts for income, including salary and dividends, and capital, including stocks. They add a rule—"spend income but don't dip into capital"—that permits spending salary and dividends from the income mental account but prohibits creating homemade dividends by selling stocks from the capital mental account and spending them. Adherence to this rule diminishes the likelihood that temptation coupled with self-control lapses would turn a 3 percent homemade dividend into a 30 percent homemade dividend that would deplete portfolios and imperil retirement prospects. Adherence to this rule also benefits older investors who draw money from their portfolios for retirement expenses and worry that self-control lapses would turn a 3 percent homemade dividend into a 30 percent homemade one that would deplete their retirement portfolios too fast.

Stocks paying no dividends and mutual funds with automatic reinvestment of dividends, interest, and capital gains are self-control tools for people who want to limit spending, but are concerned that spending temptations will overpower weak self-control if dividends, interest, and capital gains are paid.

In the absence of automatic reinvestment, mutual funds deposit "distributions"—dividends, interest, and realized capital gains—into money market funds, where they become commingled with regular income such as salary deposited directly, making them readily available for spending. Automatic reinvestment of distributions reduces the availability of dividends, interest, and realized capital gains, making it easier to resist spending temptations even when self-control lapses.

Con Ed, New York's supplier of gas and electricity, suspended its dividends in 1974 as its cash was depleted by soaring fuel prices in the wake of the Arab oil embargo. Shareholders attending Con Ed's shareholders' meeting described poignantly the hardships caused by the suspension. A woman said, "Who is going to pay my rent? I had a husband. Now Con Ed has to be my husband." A man said, "A lady came over to me a minute ago and she said to me, 'Please say a word for the senior citizens.' And she had tears in her eyes. And I really know what she means by that. She simply means that now she will get only one check a month, and that will be her Social Security, and she's not going to make it, because you have denied her that dividend." These Con Ed shareholders did not even contemplate creating homemade dividends by selling the shares, let alone spending them.[5]

Corporate chief financial officers consider maintaining dividends as important as funding profitable investments.[6] This goal was also true for Charles F. Luce, the chairman of the board of Con Ed. Speaking with a heavy heart at the Con Ed shareholders' meeting he said, "Investors buy Con Edison stock for assured income. . . . Most of our stockholders are women, many widowed. . . . When the dividend check doesn't come, there is a real hardship for many people."

Stock dividends illustrate further the power of mental accounts and their use for self-control. A company paying stock dividends pays no cash. Instead, it sends shareholders additional shares in proportion to the number they already own. A shareholder with four shares before a stock dividend is paid might now have eight.

Stock dividends make no sense to rational investors, because they are the equivalent of cutting a pizza into eight slices instead of four without increasing its size. Cutting pizzas or stocks one way or another changes their form without changing their substance. Merton Miller was fond of illustrating the futility of stock dividends, telling the story of the pizza delivery man who comes to Yogi Berra after a baseball game and says, "Yogi, how do you want this pizza cut, into quarters or eights?" "Cut it into eights," says Yogi. "I'm hungry tonight."[7]

Rational investors understand the pizza story as a joke, but the story is no joke to many normal investors who are happier when their companies pay stock dividends rather than no dividends at all. One shareholder at the Con Ed meeting asked why stock dividends were not paid "so at least the blow which was given to stockholders by the omission of the [cash] dividend would have been much less." Con Ed's chairman answered that stock dividends would not make shareholders better off, echoing the rational pizza logic. But stock dividends would have made many Con Ed shareholders better off by reducing expressive and emotional costs even if not increasing utilitarian benefits. Stock dividends are placed in the income mental account, like cash dividends, and therefore can be sold and their proceeds spent without transparent violation of the spend-income-but-don't-dip-into-capital rule.

HINDSIGHT, REGRET, AND PRIDE

Company-paid dividends have an advantage over homemade dividends because they are less likely to inflict regret. Compare John, who buys a laptop computer for $1,399 with dividends received today from shares of his stock, to Jane, who buys the same laptop today with $1,399 homemade dividends from the sale of shares of the same stock. Now suppose that the shares' price increased by 3 percent on the following day. Both Jane and John might commit hindsight errors, believing that they could have seen in foresight that the shares' price would increase by 3 percent on the following day, but Jane very likely suffers greater emotional costs of regret because she bears greater responsibility for choice.

This is the case because Jane can easily imagine a different choice that would have turned out better: for example, waiting another day before selling her shares. John, however, cannot imagine such a different choice as easily because the timing of the dividends was not in his hands. Moreover, Jane bears responsibility for her choice to create homemade dividends, whereas John bears no responsibility for the company's choice to pay dividends. It is true that responsibility for choice would let Jane enjoy pride if the shares' price falls by 3 percent on the following day rather than increases, but the decline in gain-loss utility that accompanies a 3 percent loss exceeds the increase in gain-loss utility that accompanies a 3 percent gain, consistent with loss aversion in prospect theory.

FRAMING IN PROSPECT AND EXPECTED-UTILITY THEORIES

Framing bestows another advantage on company-paid dividends in the context of prospect theory. "Suppose you are offered the following choice," wrote Fischer Black, describing the dividend puzzle. "You may have $2 today and a 50-50 chance of $54 or $50 tomorrow. Or you may have nothing today and a 50-50 chance of $56 or $52 tomorrow. Would you prefer one of these gambles to the other?"[8]

"Probably you would not," presumed Black, consistent with the definition of rational investors as indifferent to frames and conforming to the predictions of expected-utility theory. The two options are identical in the total wealth they can yield, so rational investors are indifferent between them. If you choose the stock that pays no cash dividends you have a 50-50 chance to end up with $52 or $56. If you choose the stock that pays dividends you have an identical 50-50 chance to end up with the identical $52 or $56. The $52 is composed of $50 of the stock itself plus the $2 dividend, and the $56 is composed of $54 of the stock itself and the $2 dividend. Why then are many investors not indifferent to dividends?

Some of the answer is in prospect theory, focusing on gains and losses of wealth rather than on total wealth. Consider a normal investor who bought Black's stock for $40. The outcome of Black's dividend-paying stock consists of a $2 dividend plus a 50-50 chance for a capital gain of either $10 or $14. Our investor frames dividends into one mental account and capital into another. Both mental accounts show gains, and our investor savors the two separately, like two individually wrapped gifts: a $2 dividend gift and a $10 or $14 capital-gain gift. According to prospect theory, the total gain-loss utility of our investor is greater than it would have been if the two gains were lumped together into one capital gain of either $12 or $16, as offered in Black's no-dividend stock.

As presented in Figure 7-1a, the prospect theory gain-loss utility of a $2 gain is 80 units. The gain-loss utility of $10, $12, $14, and $16 gains are, respectively, 287, 314, 337, and 357. The total gain-loss utility of a $2 dividend gain plus a 50-50 chance at a $10 or $14 capital gain is 392:

$$80 + \frac{1}{2}(287 + 337) = 392$$

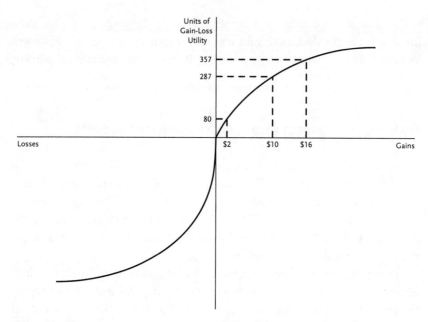

Figure 7-1a Comparing prospect theory gain-loss utility with dividends paid and not paid—the case where the price of the share increased

This is higher than the 335.5 total gain-loss utility of a 50-50 chance at a capital gain of $12 or $16.

$$\frac{1}{2}(314 + 357) = 335.5$$

(Recall that the units of gain-loss utility are arbitrary but their ratios are not. The ratio of a $10 gain to a $2 gain is 5, but the gain-loss utility associated with a $10 gain is 287 units, less than 5 times the 80 gain-loss utility associated with a $2 gain. Similarly, the increase in gain-loss utility that comes with an increase from $10 to $12 is 27 units, but the increase in gain-loss utility that comes with an increase from $12 to $14 is only 23 units. Note also that ratios of gain-loss utility presented here are not universal. The ratios can vary by the particular parameters of prospect-theory functions that can vary from person to person.)

Now suppose that our investor bought Black's stock for $70. Black's dividend-paying stock brings a $2 dividend plus a capital loss of either $16 or $20. Again, our investor frames dividends into one mental account and capital into another. The capital mental account shows a loss, but the dividend mental account shows a gain. There is no gain in Black's no-dividend stock when the single capital mental account shows a loss of either $14 or $18.

As presented in Figure 7-1b, the prospect theory gain-loss utility of a $2 dividend gain is 80 units. The gain-loss utility of $14, $16, $18, and $20 losses are, respectively, negative 546, 566, 584, and 599. The total gain-loss utility of a $2 dividend gain plus a 50-50 chance at a $16 or $20 capital loss is a negative 502.5:

$$80 - \frac{1}{2}(566 + 599) = -502.5$$

This is better than the negative 565 total gain-loss utility of a 50-50 chance at a capital loss of $14 or $18:

$$-\frac{1}{2}(546 + 584) = -565$$

Last, suppose that our investor bought Black's stock for $51. Black's dividend-paying stock brings a $2 dividend and a 50-50 chance at a $3 capital gain if the stock's price increases to $54, or a $1 capital loss if the stock's price decreases to $50. The non-dividend stock brings a 50-50 chance for a

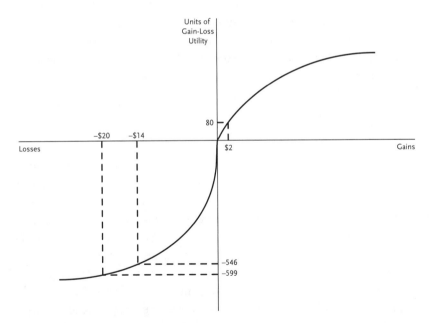

Figure 7-1b Comparing prospect theory gain-loss utility with dividends paid and not paid—the case where the price of the share declined.

$5 capital gain or a $1 capital gain. If it turns out that the price of the stock decreased to $50 and our investor is able to integrate mental accounts, he would prefer to integrate the dividend and capital loss into a $1 total gain, eliminating consideration of a loss. Otherwise, this is a case where he would prefer a non-dividend-paying stock.

THE DISPOSITION PUZZLE

Rational investors are quick to realize losses and slow to realize gains, because realized losses reduce tax bills, whereas realized gains add to them. Yet many normal investors are quick to realize gains and slow to realize losses, displaying a disposition to "sell winners too early and ride losers too long." Studies show the disposition effect among investors in the United States, Israel, Australia, Finland, Portugal, China, and many other countries.[9] It is also evident among professional investors. Professional stock traders who incur losses in morning trades attempt to recoup their losses in the afternoon by trading more aggressively.[10]

Why do investors display that disposition? This is the disposition puzzle. The solution to the puzzle combines wants for the emotional benefits of pride and avoidance of the emotional costs of regret, the roles of expected utility and prospect theories, the use of cognitive and emotional shortcuts and the pitfalls of their errors, including framing, mental accounting, hindsight, regret, and self-control, and the tools for correcting errors, including rules and systems that induce the realization of losses.[11]

Wants, Shortcuts, and Errors

Financial analyst Howard Snyder tried to teach investors "how to take a loss and like it" in 1957. Explaining that realizing losses adds utilitarian benefits by reducing taxes, he wrote, "There is no loss without collateral compensation" in the form of lower taxes. Snyder added, however, that investors are reluctant to realize losses because they want to get even, selling at a price no lower than what they paid. "Human nature being what it is we are loath to take a loss until we are forced into it. Too often we believe that by ignoring a loss we will someday glance at the asset to find it has not only recovered its original value but has shown some appreciation."[12]

Realizing losses imposes the emotional costs of regret, whereas realizing gains yields the emotional benefits of pride. Neural data from an experiment indicates that when people observe a positive return for a stock they declined to purchase, a regret signal appears in an area of the brain that is commonly active during reward processing. People are unwilling to repurchase stocks whose prices increased subsequent to sales, even though repurchases are optimal by the design of the experiment. The strength of the reluctance to repurchase is greater when the neural measures of regret are higher. People who exhibit great reluctance to repurchase also exhibit large disposition effects.[13]

LeRoy Gross, a stockbroker, had extensive experience with investors reluctant to realize losses, calling it the "getevenitis disease."[14] Many clients, he wrote in his stockbrokers' manual, "will not sell anything at a loss. They don't want to give up the hope of making money on a particular investment, or perhaps they want to get even before they get out. The getevenitis disease has probably wrought more destruction on investment portfolios than anything else. Rather than recovering to an original entry price, many investments plunge sickeningly to even deeper losses."

Reluctance to realize losses can increase cheating as people suffering the getevenitis disease attempt to get even. One experiment divided people into four groups and asked them to perform an effortful task. Possible outcomes were framed as gains for people in one pair of groups and as losses for people in the other pair. Performance on the task was monitored in one group of each pair but not the other. It turned out that the self-reported performance in the unmonitored groups was significantly higher than actual performance in the monitored condition—a clear indication of cheating. The level of cheating, however, was highest in the unmonitored group whose outcomes were framed as losses.[15]

Normal people frame a share of stock bought for $100 today into a mental account distinct from mental accounts containing the other investments in their portfolios. We can think of this mental account as a savings account we have just opened with a $100 deposit. We bought this share because in foresight we saw its price increasing to $140 tomorrow, so we might close our mental account at a gain by selling the share and realizing our $40 gain.

The utilitarian benefits of the $40 we hope to gain prod us to buy the share, but so do the emotional benefits of pride at our $40 gain. Yet we are aware of the utilitarian costs of a potential $40 loss and the emotional costs of the regret at such loss. We choose to buy the share for a combination of reasons. First, we might believe that the probability of a $40 gain is much higher than the probability of a $40 loss. Second, the option of realizing gains and refraining from realizing losses lets us enjoy the emotional benefits of pride while postponing or avoiding the emotional costs of regret. Third, we might derive expressive and emotional benefits from trading stocks as others derive such benefits from playing video games or golf. Last, we might be able to shift responsibility for choices to buy shares, claiming for ourselves responsibility and the emotional benefits of pride when choices yield gains, while shirking that responsibility and the emotional costs of regret when choices yield losses.

Consider the unfortunate case in which we find in hindsight that the share's price fell to $60 on the following day, imposing a $40 unrealized loss. Still, taxes confer utilitarian benefits on realizing losses, inducing rational investors to realize losses quickly. Imagine that the capital gains tax is at 20 percent. Realizing the $40 loss yields an $8 tax rebate. Taxes also impose utilitarian costs on realizing gains, inducing rational investors to postpone realizing gains. Realizing a $40 gain as the share price increases from $100 to $140 imposes an $8 tax.

Yet hindsight errors mislead normal investors into thinking that what is clear in hindsight was equally clear in foresight. We bought a share for $100 because we saw, in foresight, its price increasing to $140. But now, in hindsight, we remember all the warning signs displayed in plain sight on the day we bought our share. The government was about to increase corporate taxes. Cars produced by the company were about to be recalled. The CEO just announced that past earnings would be restated.

Responsibility for choices is crucial in the emotional costs of regret. We experience disappointment when a broker who bears responsibility for choosing stocks for us makes a choice that sustains losses. But we suffer regret when we ourselves bear responsibility for that choice. We bear responsibility when we choose to buy shares of stock whose price subsequently declined because we can easily imagine, in hindsight, choosing shares of another company's stock whose price subsequently increased. We procrastinate in the realization of losses because the emotional pain of regret when we realize a loss is searing. This is when we give up hope that we would close our mental account at a gain. As Gross wrote in his brokers' manual, "Investors are also reluctant to accept and realize losses because the very act of doing so proves that their first judgment was wrong. . . . Investors who accept losses can no longer prattle to their loved ones, Honey, it's only a paper loss. Just wait. It will come back."[16]

In one set of experiments, some people bore responsibility for choices, whereas others did not.[17] It turned out that the disposition effect occurred only among those who bore responsibility. Investors who delegate investment choices also delegate responsibility and blame for losses, thereby facilitating their realization.[18]

Gross suggested a framing cure for the reluctance to realize losses by using "transfer your assets" as "magic selling words." We transfer our assets by selling our General Motors shares, thereby realizing the losses we have incurred on them, and buying shares of Ford with the proceeds. The magic selling words divert our attention from the distasteful realization of losses as we close the General Motors mental account, toward the fresh opening of the attractive Ford mental account. Evidence indicates that transferring assets has a magical effect. Investors show no disposition effect on days when they engage in both selling and buying, closing one mental account and opening another.[19] Attractive uses of money to be made available by realizing losses, such as for reaching savings goals, also facilitate the realization of losses by highlighting the hopeful opening of new mental accounts while obscuring the painful closing of old ones.[20]

More losses are realized in December than in any other month, providing further illustration of the power of mental accounts and diversion of attention. There is nothing rational about the role that December plays in the realization of losses. Investors get no more tax benefits from realizing losses in December than in any other month. Indeed, rational investors increase their wealth most by realizing losses when they occur rather than wait until year-end. But December concentrates attention on taxes more than November does. What is labeled a loss in November is labeled a tax deduction in December. Experiments show that investors become more willing to realize losses when sensitized to the tax benefits of loss realization.[21]

"Harvest your losses" is another set of magic words facilitating realization of losses by obscuring the offensive smell of closing mental accounts at a loss. Harvesting losses brings to mind plucking ripe peaches while strolling in an orchard, rather than realizing rotten losses while bent over our portfolios. Stop-loss orders are another tool facilitating the realization of losses by pre-commitment and automatic action. An investor who buys a share of stock at $100 and places a stop-loss order at $60 does not face the painful choice of closing a mental account at a loss, because closing is made automatically when the price drops to $60.[22]

Framing can blur a purchase price as the reference point for gains and losses, muting the disposition effect when investors are not sure that they are realizing a loss.[23] Conversely, framing can highlight a purchase price as the reference point, bolstering the disposition effect. In February 2011 Betfair, a UK betting exchange, introduced a new "Cash-Out" display. A prominent yellow banner, placed centrally on the computer screen, now indicated the gains or losses that bettors would realize if they closed existing bets at current prices. Clicking on the display closes a bet and realizes its gain or loss.

Bettors could have recalled their bets' initial prices and calculated their gains and losses before the introduction of cash-out displays, and they exhibited a pronounced disposition effect during the period. The frequency of realizing gains was 68.1 percent higher than the frequency of realizing losses. But the display exacerbated the disposition effect, increasing by 4.2 percent the difference between the frequency of realizing gains and realizing losses.[24]

Economists Nicholas Barberis and Wei Xiong cast the emotional costs of regret and emotional benefits of pride in the language of "realization utility." The emotional benefits of pride when one is realizing gains is a positive realization utility and the emotional costs of regret when realizing losses is negative realization utility.[25] Functional MRI can trace these positive and negative realization utilities. Activity in an area of the brain known to encode the value of choices is especially high in people who are disposed to realize gains quickly and who procrastinate in the realization of losses. Activity also spikes in a brain area known to encode pleasure when people issue a command to realize gains.[26]

Framing in Expected-Utility and Prospect Theories

Consider an investor who bought a share of stock yesterday for $100 and finds that, unfortunately, it is selling at $60 today. Suppose there is a 50-50 chance that the share's price would increase by $40 tomorrow to its $100 purchase price or decline by a further $40 to $20. The capital gains tax rate is 20 percent. The investor must now choose whether to realize his $40 loss today by selling the share for $60, or hold it until tomorrow.

Expected-utility theory predicts that our investor would realize his loss today because his current wealth already reflects the $60 current price of the share. Realizing his loss would increase his wealth beyond his current wealth by a tax rebate of 20 percent of $40, amounting to $8. Prospect theory, however, predicts that our investor will procrastinate in realizing his loss. According to prospect theory, our investor frames his choice as between options A and B:

A. Sell the share today, thereby realizing a $40 loss.
B. Hold the share for another day, accepting a 50-50 chance of losing a further $40 for a total of an $80 loss, or getting even if the price of the share increases by $40 to equal its $100 purchase price, implying no loss.

Option A imposes on the investor a sure $40 shortfall from his $100 reference point if he has not made peace with his $40 loss by reducing his reference point to $60. A $40 shortfall corresponds to negative 140 units of gain-loss utility, depicted in Figure 7-2a.

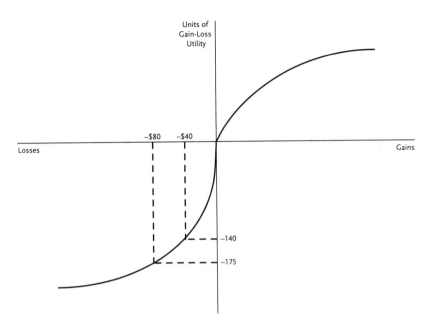

Figure 7-2a Gain-loss utility associated with options A and B.

Option B entails a 50-50 chance to lose $80, corresponding to negative 175 units of gain-loss utility, and an equal chance to lose $0, corresponding to zero units of gain-loss utility. The expected units of gain-loss utility associated with option B are negative 87.5, the mean of negative 175 and zero. This expectation makes option B better than option A, which is associated with negative 140 units. Indeed, the shape of prospect theory's function in the domain of losses implies that our investor would be inclined to hold the share for another day even if the odds of getting even were less than 50-50. If the odds of getting even become sufficiently low, however, our investor would be inclined to realize his $40 loss.

Prospect theory predicts not only a reluctance to realize losses but also an eagerness to realize gains. Consider a fortunate investor who bought a share of stock yesterday for $60 and finds that it is selling at $100 today. Suppose there is a 50-50 chance that the price of the share would increase by a further $40 to $140 tomorrow, or decline by $40 back to $60. Our investor must now choose whether to realize his $40 gain today or hold on to the share. According to prospect theory, our investor frames his choice as between options C and D:

C. Sell the share today, thereby realizing a $40 paper gain.

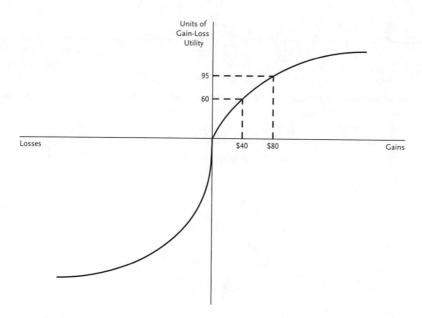

Figure 7-2b Gain-loss utility associated with options C and D.

D. Hold the share, accepting a 50-50 chance of getting even if the share price declines to its $60 purchase price tomorrow, or gaining an additional $40 for a total of $80 if the share prices increases to $140.

The shape of prospect theory's function in the domain of gains, depicted in Figure 7-2b, implies that our investor would be inclined to choose option C, realizing his $40 gain. Option D entails a 50-50 chance to gain $80, corresponding to 95 units of gain-loss utility, and an equal chance to gain $0, corresponding to zero units of gain-loss utility. The expected units of gain-loss utility associated with option D are 47.5, the mean of 95 and zero. This expectation makes option D inferior to option C, which is associated with 60 units of gain-loss utility.

Countering the Disposition Effect

Some studies relying entirely on prospect theory found it difficult to derive the disposition effect, while other studies relying entirely on the theory reached a more extreme prediction in which investors never realize their losses. Yet emphasis on the role of prospect theory in the disposition effect is misplaced. Comprehensive analysis of the disposition effect must also account for the roles of cognition, including framing and mental accounting, hindsight, and emotions including self-control, regret, and pride, and extending to fear, sadness, disgust, and anger. Moreover, comprehensive analysis must account for measures taken by knowledgeable investors to correct cognitive and emotional errors and counter the disposition effect.

"Contrary to the dictates of rationality," wrote Ira Glick, "traders are very much prone to let their losses ride. . . ."[27] Glick, an anthropologist who studied the behavior of professional traders, zeroed in on the control of losses as the major challenge facing traders and the role of self-control in meeting that challenge. Self-control involves an interaction between reason and emotion, and trade-offs between utilitarian benefits and expressive and emotional ones. Utilitarian benefits in the form of lower taxes urge traders to be quick in realizing losses, but expressive and emotional costs, especially the emotional costs of regret, retard loss realization. Losses become an occupational problem, wrote Glick, when traders lack the self-control necessary to realize them.

Putative rational investors are born with perfect self-control, whereas real-world normal-knowledgeable investors acquire imperfect self-control with difficulty. One trader described this difficulty. "When you're breaking in a new trader, the hardest thing to learn is to admit that you're wrong. It's a hard pill to swallow. You have to be man enough to admit to your peers that you're wrong and get out. Then you're alive and playing the game the next day."[28]

Mutual fund managers know the utilitarian benefits of realizing losses, and most have learned to muster the self-control necessary to do so, but a substantial fraction exhibit the disposition effect, preferring to realize gains rather than losses. Teams managing a fund are more susceptible to the disposition effect, especially when investors pull money from that fund.[29]

Rules are a self-control device facilitating the realization of losses. "I have a hard-and-fast rule that I never let my losses on a trade exceed ten percent," said one professional trader. "Say I buy a ten-dollar stock. As soon as it goes to nine dollars, I must sell it and take a loss. Some guys have a five percent rule. Some may have fifteen. I'm a ten man. . . . The traders who get wiped out hope against hope. . . . They're stubborn. They refuse to take losses. . . ."[30]

Professional traders set rules and control systems that track trades and force the realization of losses when traders' self-control fails. One rule and associated control system mandates that traders settle their trading positions at the end of each day, realizing gains on good days and losses on bad days. The ability of control systems to force traders to realize losses is, however, only as good the ability of those systems to prevent rogue traders from thwarting them. Major trading frauds combine traders' reluctance to realize losses with their ability to thwart control systems. Infamous traders Jerome Kerviel of Societe Generale and Kweku Adoboli of UBS knew their banks' control systems and how to hide losses by thwarting these systems. Reluctance to realize small losses led to larger bets in attempts to get even, recouping losses, leading instead to larger losses that were impossible to hide.

More commonly, however, rules and control systems lead professional traders to realize losses quickly. Analysis of the trades of professional currency traders revealed that this behavior is especially true later in the year, and among older and more experienced traders.[31] Similarly, analysis of the trades of mutual fund managers revealed that they are generally quick to realize losses.[32] The authors of both cited studies interpreted their evidence as contrary to the disposition effect, yet it is not. Instead, it is evidence that acquired self-control and effective rules and control systems help experienced professional investors overcome their reluctance to realize losses.

Economists Itzhak Ben-David and David Hirshleifer found that investors tend to realize large losses quickly, seemingly inconsistent with the disposition effect, and are slower at realizing small losses. Moreover, investors who do not realize losses tend to buy additional shares as their prices decline. Ben-David and Hirshleifer interpreted their findings as indicating that beliefs about future prices underlie the reluctance to realize small losses but not large ones. Investors might be realizing large losses quickly because they conclude that their expectations of price increases are wrong. They do not realize small losses, instead buying additional ones as prices decline, because they expect prices to increase soon. Beliefs about future prices have a role in the disposition effect, but they do not have the central role.[33]

Most investors eventually come to terms with their losses and realize them in a process that might take days, months, or years. Consider John, who bought shares of stock for $100 in expectation that their price would increase to $140 tomorrow, only to see the price plunge by 40 percent to $60. Reason prompts John to rethink his rationale for buying the shares and accept that it is likely wrong. The emotion of fear joins reason in highlighting the possibility that his loss might increase further beyond his ability to sustain it. Aversion to regret stands in the way of realizing the loss but self-control might overcome it. Self-control would be bolstered by rules such as mandating the realization of losses exceeding 10 percent, leading John to realize his loss that day.

Compare John to Paul, who bought shares for $100 with expectations identical to those of John but found a day later that their price declined by 2 percent to $98. If John is like a frog dropped into the boiling water of a 40 percent loss, Paul is like the frog dropped into lukewarm water of a 2 percent loss. Reason might not prompt Paul to rethink his rationale for buying the shares, because 2 percent stock price declines are common, likely to be reversed in the following days. Fear is not likely to arise, either, as the loss is small, and self-control might not overcome aversion to regret. Small gains interspersed among the losses in the following days and weeks might keep alive his hope of getting even when the price of shares increases back to $100. Indeed, losses in the days and weeks following the initial purchase can escalate Paul's commitment to his shares and disposition to hold on to them. He might "average-down," buying more shares as their price declines, quieting his cognitive dissonance and affirming the wisdom of his initial purchase.

As weeks and months pass, however, Paul's reason and emotions evolve. By now the price of shares might have declined from the initial $100 to $40, and reason indicates only a small likelihood of getting even. Paul's regret is most intense when he realizes his losses but awareness of unrealized losses injects continuous pain of regret, even if in smaller doses. That continuous pain and the corresponding continuous joy of pride injected by gains are evident in investors' reluctance to observe losses and eagerness to observe gains. Investors are less likely to log in to observe account balances on days of stock-market losses than on days of stock-market gains.[34]

Paul might eventually be induced to realize his losses by the attraction of another investment requiring the money tied up in the losing investment. He might be induced to realize his losses by the advice of a broker who counsels "transfer your assets" or "harvest your losses." And he might find it easier to realize his losses in December, when losses are framed as tax deductions. Paul might be further induced to realize his losses by fear, intensifying as his losses mount. Sadness might prompt him to change his circumstances by selling his shares, even if at a loss, and disgust might prompt him to expel the "rotten" shares, as one expels rotten food. Finally, anger might prompt him to decisive action, realizing his losses.

The Disposition Effect among Corporate Managers

Corporate managers are optimistic when they initiate investment projects as investors are optimistic when they buy new stocks. And they are just as susceptible to the disposition effect, disposed to "throw good money after bad" into losing projects rather than terminate them. Some of the reluctance is due to conflicts of interest between managers and their corporate bosses or between managers and shareholders, because termination of losing projects might lead to termination of the managers who lead them. Yet evidence about the reluctance to realize losses in the absence of conflicts of interest suggests that conflicts are not the only reason for the disposition effect among managers.

Standard finance calls on managers to adopt increasing their shareholders' wealth as their sole goal. Adherence to this goal directs managers to select all investment projects that offer positive net present value, continue projects that maintain positive net present value, and terminate projects that slide into negative net present value. But these actions are not always what managers do.

Estimates of future costs and profits are necessarily imprecise. Standard finance calls for no more than unbiased estimates, neither optimistic nor pessimistic. Pessimism yields underestimates of net present value by cost overestimates or profit underestimates. Project review committees misled by pessimistic estimates reject projects offering positive net present value, inhibiting increases in the value of a company and the wealth of its shareholders. Optimism yields overestimates of net present value by cost underestimates or profit overestimates. Project review committees misled by optimistic estimates select projects offering negative net present value, decreasing the value of a company and the wealth of its shareholders.

A project review committee at a company accepted a project promoted by its project "champion," who will serve as its leader if the project is accepted. The project offers an estimated $349,766 net present value. It requires a $100,000 investment today, consisting of the salary of the project leader and her team. This would be followed a year from now with a $500,000 investment in equipment that has no resale value. Thereafter, the project would yield profits estimated at $400,000 at the end of each of the following three years. The committee estimates the project's cost of capital, the discount rate for its costs and profits, at 10 percent.

$$349,766 = -100,000 - \frac{500,000}{(1+.10)} + \frac{400,000}{(1+.10)^2} + \frac{400,000}{(1+.10)^3} + \frac{400,000}{(1+.10)^4}$$

Now, a year later, the project is once more before the project review committee to decide whether to continue or terminate it. Committee members know that the $100,000 invested a year ago is "sunk cost" that cannot be recovered. New estimates indicate that equipment would cost $550,000 rather than $500,000 estimated a year ago, and profits in each of the following three years would be $200,000 rather than $400,000 estimated last year. The net present value of the project at this point, properly excluding the sunk $100,000, is a negative $52,630, calling for project termination if the committee's goal is to increase the market value of the company and with it increase the wealth of the company's shareholders.

$$-52,630 = -550,000 + \frac{200,000}{(1+.10)} + \frac{200,000}{(1+.10)^2} + \frac{200,000}{(1+.10)^3}$$

In practice, however, the project may be continued rather than terminated, as its project champion presses on, arguing that annual profits would be higher than the $200,000 estimate of the project review committee, and the project review committee acquiesces. Projects are often described as express trains slowing down at project review stations but never with the intention of stopping.[35]

Consider a report on the development of an eight-inch floppy disk drive. The project was initially seen as a positive net-present-value project by a company that had already established itself as a leader in disk drives. The company started the project in 1980, and supported it generously. The project was terminated in 1983, after severe time and cost overruns and long after disk drives made by competitors had been designed into computers that the company considered part of its market.[36] The vice president of finance later said, "I was controller then, [and] the vice president of finance and I presented an economic justification for eliminating this product in August 1982. . . . The vice president of the disk-drive division immediately championed the product and signed up for lower costs. He also argued the 'asset recovery' issue. I find that if any champion is willing to stick up for a project, then the financial analysis is rejected."

Failure to terminate projects with negative net present values detracts from the utilitarian benefits of shareholders, but it adds to the expressive and emotional benefits of project leaders and their teams who avoid the utilitarian, expressive, and emotional costs that accompany project termination. These include the utilitarian costs of loss of a bonus or a job, the expressive costs of loss of status, and the emotional costs of regret about choosing a project that, at least in hindsight, turns out to be a mistake. The difference between the utilitarian benefits of shareholders and the utilitarian, expressive, and emotional benefits of managers is evident in stock prices when projects known to have negative net present values are terminated. Increases in stock prices and corresponding shareholder wealth indicate shareholders' relief at finding that managers would no longer throw good money after bad so as to avoid their own utilitarian, expressive, and emotional costs by imposing utilitarian costs on their shareholders.

On December 7, 1981, the Lockheed Corporation announced that it had terminated its L-1011 Tristar jumbo jetliner project. Lockheed had started the Tristar project in 1968 in partnership with Rolls Royce, hoping to compete with Boeing, which had delivered its first 747 jumbo airplanes, and McDonnell-Douglas, which was beginning its DC-10 airplane project.

Lockheed's Tristar project was known as a negative net-present-value project for many years before its termination. Indeed, the project would have bankrupted the company if not for a federal government bailout.[37] The relief of shareholders is evident in Lockheed's 18 percent stock price increase on the day following the termination announcement.

Lockheed's Tristar case is not unique. Announcements of project terminations with known negative present values were greeted as good news, reflected in stock price jumps at termination announcements. In contrast, stock price jumps did not follow announcements of terminations of projects not known to have negative net present value before termination announcements were made. This is likely because the bad news that a project is a negative net value project countered the good news that it is being terminated.

Reluctance to terminate losing projects increases with responsibility for choosing them, entrapping managers into negative net present value projects. The role of responsibility is illustrated in an experiment in which people played the role of corporate executives making choices about the allocation of research and development funds to projects.[38] Choice materials described the Adams and Smith Company, a large company suffering declining profitability. People had descriptions of the company's two divisions, industrial products and consumer products, and ten years of sales and earnings data.

The degree of responsibility for choices varied. People in the high-personal-responsibility case chose one of the two divisions and invested $10 million in it, whereas people in the low-personal-responsibility case were told that a financial officer who preceded them had already chosen the division for investment. Later, people received a second part of the case, which included sales and profit information based on the 5-year period following the initial $10 million investment. One-half of people received information indicating that their chosen division was improving, whereas the other half received information indicating that their chosen division was deteriorating further. All people were told that they had an additional budget of $20 million to distribute between the two divisions.

There is a strong interaction between personal responsibility and choices. People allocated the highest amounts in the second part to the division they had chosen in the first part, when the initial choice had negative consequences and when people had high personal responsibility for that choice.

The pronounced reluctance to terminate projects in the presence of high personal responsibility is consistent with the desire to get even and a link between responsibility and regret. Managers who choose projects are responsible for their choices. The regret felt by such managers when they terminate projects before they get even by recovering sunk costs is greater than the regret felt by managers who terminate projects that have been chosen earlier by others.

Workout units can counter responsibility and commitment to losing projects. Loan officers responsible for the original loan decisions are likely to accept disadvantageous arrangements rather than admit that loans are bad and terminate them. In contrast, officers in the workout unit carry little responsibility for the original loan decisions and are more likely to act aggressively in pursuit of payment even when such pursuit might disclose that earlier loan decisions were faulty.

Top-level managers do not always confront the problem of entrapment in bad projects. Indeed, sometimes the project that needs termination is the overall strategy of top management. The reluctance to terminate overall strategy is evident in Major League Baseball. New baseball managers are likely to divest low-performing players.[39] That reluctance is also evident in CEOs' investment cycles. New CEOs terminate early in their tenures poorly performing investment projects that their predecessors initiated but were unwilling to terminate. Later in their tenure new CEOs initiate investment projects that they are later reluctant to terminate, despite poor performance. This behavior is true whether new CEOs replace CEOs who were fired for poor performance or CEOs who left for no performance-related reasons.[40]

THE PUZZLES OF DOLLAR-COST AVERAGING AND TIME DIVERSIFICATION

Investors with cash destined for stocks employ dollar-cost averaging by dividing their cash into segments and committing to convert each segment into stocks, according to a predetermined schedule. Investors with $120,000 in cash might employ dollar-cost averaging by committing to invest $10,000 in stocks on the 10th of each of the coming 12 months. The alternative to dollar-cost averaging is lump-sum investing, investing the entire $120,000 in stocks today. Both logic and simulations indicate that investors are more likely to increase their wealth with lump-sum investing than with dollar-cost averaging, yet the practice of dollar-cost averaging persists.[41,42] Why do investors engage in dollar-cost averaging? This is the dollar-cost-averaging puzzle.

Time diversification centers on the belief that the risk of stocks declines as the investment horizon increases. That belief, shared by amateur and professional investors alike, is often accompanied by graphs, such as Figure 7-3, showing that the probability of stock-market gains increases as their holding periods increase. Indeed, during 1926–2015 there were no 15- or 20-year periods with stock-market losses.[43] Yet, in truth, the risk of stocks does not decline as the investment horizon increases.[44] Why then

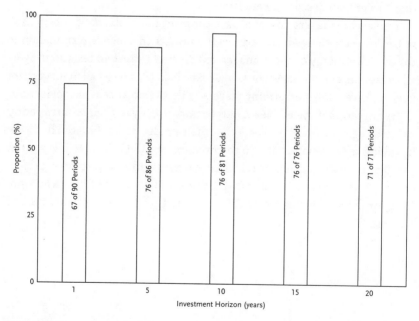

Figure 7-3 Proportion of stock-market periods with gains by time horizon (1926–2015).

does the time-diversification belief persist? This is the time-diversification puzzle.

Time diversification has much in common with dollar-cost averaging. Both are popular among investors yet puzzling to justify within the framework of standard finance. The solutions to the puzzles combine wants for utilitarian, expressive, and emotional benefits, the application of expected utility and prospect theories, the roles of cognitive and emotional shortcuts and errors, and tools for correcting errors.[45]

Framing and Expected-Utility and Prospect Theories in Dollar-Cost Averaging

Consider an investor with $2,000 in cash he has chosen to invest in stocks because stocks are likely to yield higher long-term wealth than cash, even though they also impose higher variance of wealth. This choice is consistent with expected-utility theory if the investor's variance aversion is not too high. Yet loss aversion, a feature of prospect theory, might deter our investor from buying stocks altogether if his aversion to potential short-term losses imposed by stocks during the coming day or week exceeds his desire for high expected long-term gains. Dollar-cost averaging overcomes loss aversion in a frame that highlights gains and obscures losses.

Our investor employs dollar-cost averaging by dividing his $2,000 cash into two segments of $1,000 each, depicted in Table 7-1, investing one segment in shares of a stock today and committing to invest the second segment in shares of that stock on a specific day next month. He buys 20 shares today at $50 per share. Imagine that the price of shares declined subsequently to $12.50 and he buys 80 shares next month.

Framed the rational way, as in standard finance, our investor started with $2,000 in cash and now, a month later, owns 100 shares worth $12.50 each for a total of $1,250, implying a $750 loss. Framed the normal way, as

Table 7-1 DOLLAR-COST AVERAGING

Period	Amount Invested	Price per Share	Number of Shares Bought
12	$1,000	50	20
	$1,000	12.5	80
Total	$2,000		100

Average cost of shares held at the end of the two periods: $2000/100 = $20
Average price at which shares were bought during the two periods: (50 + 12.5)/2 = $31.25

proponents of dollar-cost averaging do, our investor bought 100 shares at an average cost of $20 per share, while the average price per share on the two dates, $50 and $12.50, was $31.25, implying an $11.25 per-share gain. Indeed, framed the normal way, our investor sees gains in all circumstances except when stock prices never change.

The popularity of dollar-cost averaging can be traced back at least to the 1940s. That popularity has never waned, illustrated by the recent description of dollar-cost averaging as "a basic investment concept" by the American Association of Individual Investors. "Invest a fixed amount at equal intervals and continue to do so over a long period. The result is that more shares of a stock or mutual fund are purchased when prices are relatively low and less are purchased when prices are relatively high. This can result in lower average per-share cost over time."[46]

This relatively recent description of the merit of dollar-cost averaging is similar to Fred Weston's classic 1949 description: "In the usual exposition of the principle of dollar-cost averaging, its merit is urged on the basis of a relationship that holds without exception: at any point after a fluctuation in security prices the average cost of total shares held is less than the average price of the shares."[47]

Weston exposed the irrelevance of this fact to rational investors: "The crucial test is whether the shares held can at any time be sold at a gain. For this to be possible, average cost must be less than the current market price per share." Similarly, William Sharpe noted in his investment textbook that while it is mathematically interesting that the average cost per share paid by dollar-cost averaging investors is lower than the average price per share, it actually has no economic significance.[48] High volatility in stock prices causes large differences between the average cost per share and the average price per share, but dollar-cost averaging does not change uncertainty from vice to virtue. Yet the passage of time has done little to dampen enthusiasm for dollar-cost averaging.

Pride, Regret, and Fear in Dollar-Cost Averaging

Normal investors anticipate the emotional benefits of pride and emotional costs of regret when they make choices, knowing that the emotional costs of regret at losses exceed the emotional benefits of pride at gains of equal dollar amounts. Normal investors with $120,000 in cash might be inclined to keep it rather than buy stocks and suffer the emotional costs of regret that accompanies losses relative to the $120,000 cash reference point, if stock prices subsequently decline. Normal investors with $120,000 in stocks might be equally inclined to keep them rather than sell for cash and suffer the emotional costs of regret that accompanies opportunity losses relative to the $120,000 stock reference point, if stock prices subsequently increase.

Investors mitigate their anticipated emotional costs of regret when they convert only one part of their cash into shares of stock today. This way they can console themselves if share prices plunge during the coming month and even enjoy the emotional benefits of pride by the thought that they can now buy shares at lower prices with the other parts of their cash. Similarly, investors mitigate their anticipated emotional costs of regret when they convert only one part of their stocks into cash today. This way they can console themselves if share prices zoom during the coming month and even enjoy the emotional benefits of pride by the thought that they can now sell the remaining shares at higher prices.

Dollar-cost averaging is a "non-contingent" investment plan. The non-contingent nature of dollar-cost averaging is manifested in the strict rule set at the initiation of the plan to invest a particular amount in each subsequent period, not contingent on any subsequent information, such as changes in interest rates, economic growth, or stock prices.

Economist George Constantinides proved that non-contingent dollar-cost averaging is inferior in the eyes of rational investors to a plan contingent on information that arrives subsequent to the initiation of the plan. He added that in light of this proof it is ironic that proponents of dollar-cost averaging go to great lengths to emphasize that investors must have the courage to ignore new information as they follow their inferior non-contingent investment plan. Constantinides illustrated this emphasis by quoting from an investment textbook: "The important thing is to stick to your schedule—to buy, even though the price keeps falling, which, psychologically, is hard to do. . . . To engage in dollar-cost averaging you must have both the funds and the courage to continue buying in a declining market when prospects may seem bleak."[49] Yet normal investors find advantages in strict non-contingent rules because rules bolster self-control, counter fear, and mitigate regret.

Self-Control in Dollar-Cost Averaging

Suppose an investor starts her dollar-cost averaging stock-buying plan with the expectation that the probability of an increase in stock prices in the coming period equals the probability of a decrease. Once several decrease-periods occur, the investor finds it hard to refrain from revising her expectations by extrapolating past losses into higher probabilities of future losses. The stock-buying plan that was attractive by the old probabilities might no longer seem attractive, inclining her to abandon the plan. The strict rules of dollar-cost averaging combat self-control lapses, compelling her to stick to the stock-buying plan, "to buy, even though the price keeps falling, which, psychologically, is hard to do."

Periodic buying of stocks is a feature of 401(k) and similar retirement savings programs, in which money is automatically deducted from paychecks to buy stocks. Such periodic buying is different from dollar-cost averaging in that employees do not face a choice between investing in a lump sum or in installments, as in dollar-cost averaging. Nevertheless, 401(k) and similar retirement saving programs offer normal investors benefits similar to those of dollar-cost averaging programs. Investors frame themselves as winners because they buy shares at an average cost lower than the average price of shares over time. And automatic transfers from salary to retirement savings accounts preclude the effects of lapses of self-control.

REVERSE DOLLAR-COST AVERAGING

A prominent feature of dollar-cost averaging is that it is recommended with equal force to investors with cash who consider converting it into stocks and investors with stocks who consider converting them into cash. This feature is useful in countering the argument that the benefits of dollar-cost averaging are in risk reduction.

The risk of stocks, measured by the variance of returns or by the probability and amount of potential loss, is higher than that of cash. An investor with $2,000 in cash who converts his entire amount into stocks today bears more variance risk and loss risk tomorrow than when he follows dollar-cost averaging and converts only $1,000 into stocks today, keeping the other $1,000 in cash. This frame might support the argument that the benefits of dollar-cost averaging are in risk reduction. Consider, however, reverse dollar-cost averaging. An investor with $2,000 in stocks who converts her entire amount into cash today bears *less* variance risk and loss risk tomorrow than when she follows reverse dollar-cost averaging, converting only $1,000 into cash and keeping the other $1,000 in stocks.

Risk reduction cannot be the rationale for both dollar-cost averaging and reverse dollar-cost averaging. Imagine two investors, John and Jane, who are identical except that John has $2,000 in cash and Jane has $2,000 in stocks. John faces a choice between keeping his cash and converting it into stocks, while Jane faces the reverse choice. The choices facing John

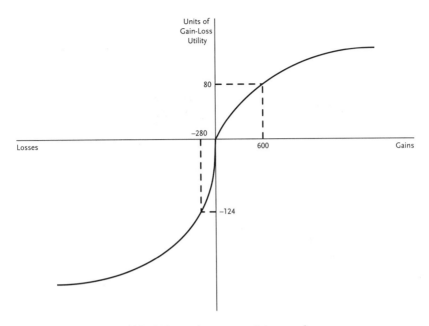

Figure 7-4a Choice to hold $2,000 in cash or convert it into stocks.

and Jane are identical when both are rational because Jane can convert her stocks into cash, placing her in a position identical to that of John. Therefore, their choices are predicted to be identical.

Frames and choices are different, however, when John and Jane are merely normal. Assume that the two agree that the return on cash is zero and that $2,000 in stocks will, with equal probabilities, either increase by $600 to $2,600 tomorrow or decrease by $280 to $1,720. How does John frame his choice? The reference point of John is $2,000 in cash, and he frames the choice as between holding his $2,000 of cash or converting it into stocks, as in Figure 7-4a

> Keep in cash: A sure gain of $0
> Convert cash into stocks: A 50-50 chance to gain $600 or lose $280

The expected units of gain-loss utility of John if he chooses to convert his $2,000 of cash into stocks is a negative 22, the mean of a gain of 80 utility units if he gains $600, and a loss of 124 utility units if he loses $280. These negative 22 units are less than the zero units of gain-loss utility if he chooses to keep his $2,000 in cash, inclining John to keep his $2,000 in cash. Dollar-cost averaging overcomes this inclination, inducing John to buy stocks.

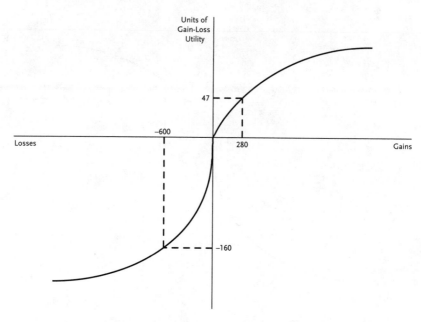

Figure 7-4b Choice to hold $2,000 in stocks or convert it into cash.

How does Jane frame her choice? The reference point of Jane is $2,000 in stocks, and she frames the choice as between holding her $2,000 of stocks or converting them into cash, as in Figure 7-4b:

> Convert stocks into cash: A 50-50 chance for an (opportunity) gain of $280 if the price of shares declines or an (opportunity) loss of $600 if the price of shares increases.
> Keep in stocks: A sure (opportunity) gain of $0.

The expected units of gain-loss utility of Jane if she chooses to convert her $2,000 of stocks into cash is a negative 56.5 units, the mean of a gain of 47 utility units if she gains $280, and a loss of 160 utility units if she loses $600. These negative 56.5 units are less than the zero units of gain-loss utility if she chooses to keep her $2,000 in stocks, inclining Jane to keep her $2,000 in stocks. Reverse dollar-cost averaging overcomes this inclination, inducing Jane to sell stocks.

Framing and Expected-Utility and Prospect Theories in Time Diversification

The time-diversification puzzle is related to the equity premium puzzle. Why are long-term investors reluctant to invest large proportions of their portfolios in stocks when the long-term expected returns from them are so much higher than those of Treasury bills? Economists Jeremy Siegel and Richard Thaler illustrated this equity premium puzzle with $1,000 in Treasury bills at the end of 1925 that compounded to a mere $12,720 by the end of 1995, whereas $1,000 in stocks compounded to $842,000.[50]

Siegel and Thaler offered several possible solutions to the equity premium puzzle but favored the "myopic loss aversion" solution of economist Shlomo Benartzi and Thaler.[51] Myopic loss aversion is rooted in prospect theory's loss aversion. The frequency of losses varies by the length of periods over which returns are observed. Losses are more frequent over short periods than over long periods. Investors who observe returns over short periods might exhibit myopic loss aversion—misled into the belief that losses are more likely over long periods than they truly are.

Benartzi and Thaler presented to people distributions of simulated 1-year and 30-year returns similar to those in Figure 7-5a and Figure

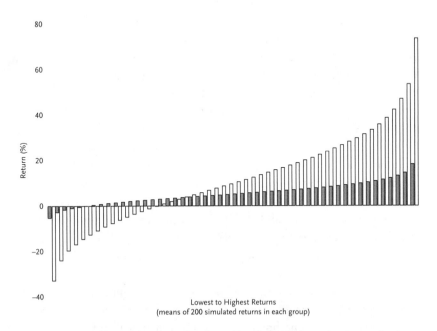

Figure 7-5a Distribution of returns of stocks and bonds during 1-year investment horizons. Bond returns in black and stock returns in white.

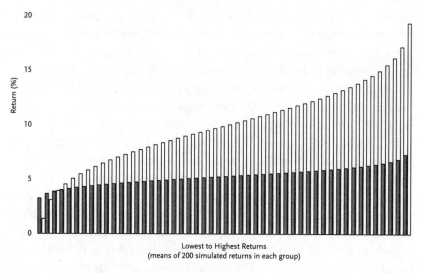

Return (%)

25

20

15

10

5

0

Lowest to Highest Returns
(means of 200 simulated returns in each group)

Figure 7-5b Distribution of returns of stocks and bonds during 30-year investment horizons.
Bond returns in black and stock returns in white.

7-5b. The figures are based on 10,000 random drawings of US stock and bond returns from a group of 1926–2014 returns. The first bar on the left in Figure 7-5a is the mean return of the lowest 200-bond 1-year returns. The bar next to it is the mean return of the lowest 200-stock 1-year returns, and so on. Similarly, the first bar on the left in Figure 7-5b is the mean return of the lowest 200 annualized 30-year bond returns, and so on.[52]

The difference in the allocation to stocks between those who saw the 1-year chart and those who saw the 30-year chart was enormous. The median allocation to stocks among those who saw the 1-year chart was 40 percent. The median allocation to stocks among those who saw the 30-year chart was 90 percent. Benartzi and Thaler argued that investors who saw the 1-year chart made the wrong choice because they were fooled by myopic loss aversion into thinking that the probability of losses over the long run is higher than it truly is.

More recent evidence indicates, however, that myopic loss aversion has little effect on investment choices. People invest as much in stocks when they see one-year or long-horizon historical return distributions, but they invest less in stocks when they see no historical return distributions. This behavior suggests that lack of knowledge of high historical stock returns rather than myopic loss aversion makes investors excessively pessimistic about future stock returns.[53] Indeed, it is less knowledgeable investors who are excessively pessimistic about future stock returns. Knowledgeable investors hold beliefs about future returns that are close to historical returns. That group includes people with high lifetime earnings, high education, high cognitive abilities, and defined contributions savings plans rather than defined benefits pension plans.[54]

Framing Errors in Time Diversification

Economist Paul Samuelson, a Nobel Prize winner, argued that the advocacy of time diversification is built on framing errors that mislead investors into an illusory happy ending, as if the probability of losses over the long run were zero. To understand the nature of these framing errors, consider an investor who invests $1,000 in a portfolio with a 50-50 chance to gain 20 percent or lose 10 percent each year. The investor has a 50 percent probability of losing money if her horizon is one year, but she has only a 25 percent probability of losing money if it is two years. If risk is framed as the *probability of losing money*, risk declines as the horizon increases, but if risk is framed as the *total amount of money that can be lost*, risk increases as the horizon increases. The investor might lose $100 after one year, but she

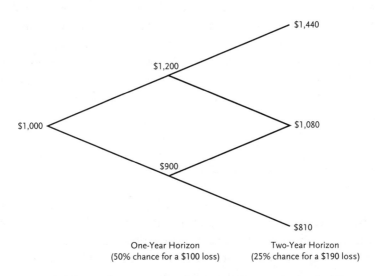

Figure 7-6 Probabilities of losing money and amounts of money that can be lost.

might lose more, $190, after two years. These probabilities and amounts of losses are laid out in Figure 7-6.

Samuelson noted that the effect of time on the *probability* of losses can be perfectly balanced by the effect of time on the *total amount of money that can be lost*. If so, risk neither increases nor decreases as the investment horizon increases. But what if investors do not assess correctly the probability of losses over the long run and overlook the total amount of money that can be lost?

Many proponents of time diversification assume, in error, that the probability of losses with stocks held over the long run is zero. Economists James Glassman and Kevin Hassett published their book *Dow 36,000* in September 1999, just before major stock losses in 2000–2002 pushed the Dow below 7,300. In August 2002 they wrote a column, "Dow 36,000 Revisited," in *The Wall Street Journal*. "Higher returns are normally correlated with higher risk," they wrote, "but work by Jeremy Siegel of the Wharton School and others ha[ve] found that if stocks are held over long periods, risk declines dramatically. Mr. Siegel looked at nearly 200 years, and found that during their worst 20-year period ever, stocks rose more than 20 percent."[55] And an investment professional wrote in the *Financial Analysts Journal*, "A positive return [on stocks] in the long run is near certainty. . . . There is no reason to expect a negative return on the broadest possible stock index. . . ."[56]

Yet there is reason to expect a negative return even on the broadest possible stock index in the very long run. The error of framing small probabilities as zero probabilities might be described as the illusory-happy-ending error. As Samuelson wrote, "When a 35-year-old lost 82 percent of his pension portfolio between 1929 and 1932, do you think that it was fore-ordained in heaven that it would come back and fructify to +400 percent by his retirement at 65? How did the 1913 Tsarist executives fare in their retirement years on the Left Bank of Paris?"[57] The illusory-happy-ending error that Samuelson pointed out stands in contrast to the myopic-loss-aversion error.

Regret and Self-Control in Time Diversification

Three years of losses can turn investors with 30-year horizons into investors with 3-year horizons—they want out. Investors become optimistic after increases in stock prices and pessimistic after decreases. The argument that time diversification reduces risk is as flawed as the argument that dollar-cost averaging reduces risk, but both are useful in bolstering self-control and mitigating fear and regret over losses.

Time diversification comes with stay-the-course rules, keeping alive hope of high future gains and countering the urge to sell all stocks, perhaps at the bottom of the market, when extrapolating three bad stock-market years into a world-is-coming-to-the-end conclusion. But there comes a time when even long-run stay-the-course investment horizons are reached and hope for gains is gone. This is when the option to extend time horizons is most valuable.

Time diversification is usually presented in a frame where investment time horizons are fixed, set when investments are made. But investors often describe time horizons in a flexible form—simply "the long run"—rather than in a fixed form—"30 years." A flexible form of time horizon does not alter wealth. The wealth of an investor with a $10,000 paper loss at the end of a 30-year horizon is no different from that of an investor with a $10,000 realized loss. But an investor with options on time can postpone the realization of paper losses, thereby avoiding closing a mental account at a loss and suffering the accompanying pain of regret.

The attraction of options on time is illustrated in investors' preference for "bond ladders." A bond ladder consists of individual bonds at staggered maturities. A ladder might consist of one bond maturing a year from now, another maturing in two years, and so on to the tenth bond, maturing in ten years. Investors typically replenish bond ladders so proceeds from a matured one-year bond are used to buy a ten-year bond and the composition of the ladder remains intact.

Many advocate bond ladders over bond mutual funds. One wrote that bond ladders "help investors preserve their capital and improve their return ... It also will help ward off potential losses that bond funds are likely to suffer as the Fed pushes interest rates higher."[58]

The perception of bond ladders as instruments that preserve capital, improve returns, and ward off potential losses better than bond mutual funds is puzzling to rational investors, since bond ladders are, in substance, homemade bond mutual funds. The values of both bond ladders and bond mutual funds decrease when interest rates increase. And the default risks of bond ladders very likely exceed those of bond mutual funds if the former are less diversified than bond mutual funds. The real benefits of bond ladders are in options on time.

Compare a just-established bond ladder to its equivalent bond mutual fund, containing the same bonds. Suppose that interest rates have increased. The values of the bonds have now decreased such that all the bonds in the bond ladder register losses. The net asset value of the bond mutual fund is equally lower. Yet ladder investors who are reluctant to realize their losses but want cash can choose among options. They can sell some bonds and realize losses, or they wait until the one-year bonds mature, avoiding the realization of losses. Mutual fund investors have no such choice among options. They are never sure that they would be able to avoid the realization of losses, regardless of how long they wait.

A financial commentator explained the time option advantage of individual bonds over bond mutual funds, noting that while prices of both individual bonds and bond funds fluctuate, "investors rarely pay attention" to the price fluctuations of individual bonds, and have "less to worry about." This behavior is because "if you sell before maturity, you'll get the current market price which, as with bond funds, could either be more or less than you originally paid. If you hold to maturity, however, you're guaranteed your principal back—something bond funds never do."[59]

Zero-coupon bonds are bought at prices lower than what they will yield at maturity, assuring the realization of gains if they are held to maturity. Their time options are reflected in their description as a safety net with the bounce of a trampoline.[60] You can realize gains if bond prices rise between now and maturity, or hold to maturity if bond prices fall before maturity, knowing that you would get the promised face value of the bonds at maturity.

CONCLUSION

The dividend puzzle is about investors' preference for company-paid dividends over "homemade" dividends created by selling shares. Errors underlie the dividend preference of some investors. They believe, in error, that company-paid dividends differ from homemade dividends in substance, not just in form. Such investors will cease their preference for company-paid dividends once their error has been corrected. Wants, however, underlie the preference of other investors, in particular, conflicts between wants for saving and spending, and rules that bolster self-control, which is necessary for their regulation. The rule of "spend income but don't dip into capital" is prominent among these rules.

The question that matters is not whether wants for regulating saving and spending are normal, but how we can satisfy them at the lowest cost. Dividend-capture funds satisfy wants for higher spending. The dividend yields of such funds are higher than regular dividend yields, satisfying investors who want to spend more than regular dividend yields, without explicit violation of the spend-income-but-don't-dip-into-capital rule. But dividend-capture funds are expensive, yielding lower total returns than other funds and imposing higher taxes. Lower-cost methods exist for satisfying wants for regulating saving and spending. They include, for example, managed payout mutual funds that send investors periodic payments of pre-specified percentages of the balances of the funds.

The disposition puzzle is about the disposition effect: investors' disposition to realize investment gains quickly but procrastinate in realizing investment losses. It is also about managers' disposition to throw good money after bad as they procrastinate in terminating losing projects.

Here, too, the question is not whether the disposition effect is normal, but how we can counter it at the lowest cost. Rules that mandate realizing losses once they have reached a predetermined percentage are one example. Corporate review committees that assess the progress of projects and decide whether to continue or terminate them, are another.

The dollar-cost averaging puzzle is about investors' reluctance to wholly invest an amount in stocks immediately, in a lump sum, and their preference for investing it in stocks gradually, over time, in the dollar-cost-averaging method. The time-diversification puzzle is about the persistence of the belief that the risk of stocks declines as the investment horizon increases.

Investors want the utilitarian, expressive, and emotional benefits of the high expected returns of stocks, but they also want to avoid the expressive costs of the image of being losers and the emotional costs of fear and regret over losses. They tend to procrastinate when advised to invest in stocks immediately, in a lump sum, but are willing to invest in stocks gradually through dollar-cost averaging.

Prescriptions of dollar-cost averaging and time diversification are like prescriptions of eyeglass choices. Eyeglasses are wrong when they distort the sight of people with perfect vision, but they are right when they improve the sight of people with poor vision. Eyeglasses correct the distortion in the sight of people with poor vision by introducing another distortion. It is a case of two wrongs that make a right.

Compare an adviser who counsels a client to convert cash into stocks in a lump sum to an adviser who counsels the client to use dollar-cost averaging. Lump-sum conversion from cash to stock might be optimal for rational investors, as no glasses are optimal for people with perfect vision. But such conversion is unappealing to normal investors with less than perfect investment vision who are deterred from action because they contemplate the regret that they would feel if the stock market were to crash as soon as their cash is converted into stocks. Dollar-cost averaging provides corrective "financial" glasses that lead investors to allocate portions of their wealth to stocks.

Myopic people can focus on short horizons but not on long ones. Their myopic loss aversion leads them to allocate too little to stocks. They need corrective financial eyeglasses that help them focus on long horizons. Hyperopic people can focus on long horizons but not on short ones. Their belief in an illusory happy ending leads them to allocate too much to stocks. They need corrective financial eyeglasses that help them focus on short horizons. Financial advisers in those cases are like optometrists. They prescribe financial eyeglasses that correct the investment vision of investors and lead them to prudent investment choices. Prudent financial advisers use dollar-cost averaging arguments when necessary to prod investors to switch from cash to stocks or from stocks to cash gradually, when investors are inclined not to switch at all. Prudent advisers use time-diversification arguments when necessary to restrain investors from switching from stocks to cash all at once, when a stock-market crash prods such investors to dump their stocks in haste.

PART TWO

Behavioral Finance in Portfolios, Life Cycles, Asset Prices, and Market Efficiency

CHAPTER 8
Behavioral Portfolios

Mean-variance portfolio theory, described by Harry Markowitz in 1952,[1] is the portfolio theory of standard finance, whereas behavioral portfolio theory, described in its initial form by Hersh Shefrin and Meir Statman in 1987 and 2000, is the portfolio theory of behavioral finance.[2]

Mean-variance portfolio theory prescribes portfolios on *mean-variance frontiers* to investors whose wants extend no further than the utilitarian benefits of high expected returns and low risk, measured by the variance of portfolio returns. We call it "textbook" mean-variance portfolio theory because it is the mean-variance portfolio theory as presented in typical investment textbooks.

Behavioral portfolio theory describes portfolios on *behavioral-wants frontiers* and prescribes them to investors whose wants extend beyond the utilitarian benefits of high expected returns and low risk, to expressive and emotional benefits such as those of demonstrating sincere social responsibility, high social status, hope for riches, and protection from poverty.

Markowitz noted that the benefits of diversified portfolios were known long before 1952. "What was lacking prior to 1952 was an adequate *theory* of investment that covered the effects of diversification when risks are correlated, distinguished between efficient and inefficient portfolios, and analyzed risk-return trade-offs on the portfolios as a whole."[3] Markowitz provided that in textbook mean-variance portfolio theory.

Later, beginning in 1959, Markowitz sketched what he calls "game-of-life" portfolios that incorporate wants beyond high expected returns and low risk, such as caring for children and families. This sketch bears affinity to behavioral portfolio theory.[4]

Mean-Variance Portfolios Theory (MVPT)	Behavioral Portfolio Theory (BPT)
1. Efficient portfolios are on the mean-variance frontier	1. Efficient portfolios are on the behavioral-wants frontier
2. Portfolios on the mean-variance frontier satisfy wants for utilitarian benefits (high expected returns and low risk)	2. Portfolios on the behavioral-wants frontier satisfy wants for utilitarian benefits, but also for expressive and emotional benefits (e.g., sincere social responsibility, high social status)
3. Investors consider portfolios as a whole	3. Investors consider portfolios as layered pyramids, in which each layer is a mental account or "bucket" associated with a want and goal
4. Investors measure risk by the variance of returns	4. Investors measure risk by the probability of shortfall from a goal, the amount of shortfall, or a combination of both
5. Investors have a single risk aversion in their portfolio as a whole	5. Investors have many risk aversions, one for each mental account
6. Investors are always risk averse, where risk is measured by the variance of returns	6. Investors are always risk averse, where risk is measured by the probability of shortfall from a goal, the amount of shortfall, or a combination of both. Risk aversion, as measured in BPT, can correspond to risk seeking, as measured in MVPT

Markowitz wrote that "the simulated family's enjoyment for the period would depend, for instance, on the size of the family, whether it lives in a large house or small apartment, or whether it now has to move because someone has a new job elsewhere. The approach required here is both "behavioral" and "rational." It should be behavioral in that it reflects plausible human choices. It should be rational, for example, in that the rational-decision-making family understands the consequences of high-interest-rate credit card debt."[5]

Textbook mean-variance portfolio theory begins with estimation of the parameters of investments—the expected return and standard deviation of the returns of each investment and the correlation between the returns of every pair of investments.

Next, investors place these parameters into a mean-variance optimizer that yields a mean-variance frontier, depicted in Figure 8-1. The frontier consists of portfolios with the highest expected return for each level of standard deviation.

Last, investors choose among portfolios on the mean-variance frontier the one, such as C in Figure 8.1, corresponding to the trade-off between their wants for high expected returns and their wants for low standard deviations.

Actual mean-variance portfolio practice differs from its textbook description, embodying features of behavioral portfolio theory. Here is an example. Investment consultants were asked to present an optimal portfolio to the board of a large US public pension fund. They started the optimization process by eliciting from the fund's managers estimates of the expected return and standard deviation of returns of each investment, and the correlation between the returns of each pair of investments—US stocks, international stocks, bonds, real estate, alternative investments, and so on. Next, they modified the estimates to make them more reasonable and consistent with more general estimates. Last, they identified a mean-variance efficient portfolio, marked

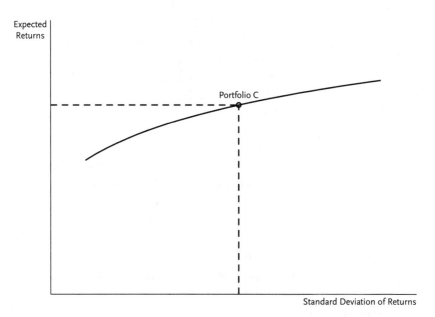

Figure 8-1 A mean-variance frontier and Portfolio C on the frontier.

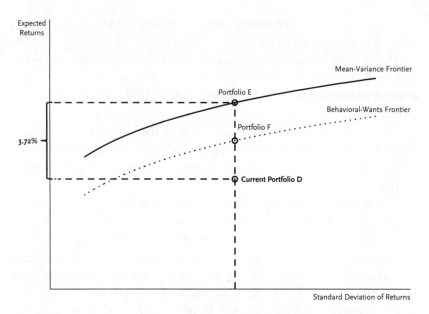

Figure 8-2 A mean-variance frontier and a behavioral-wants frontier.

E in Figure 8-2, with a standard deviation identical to that of the fund's current portfolio, D. The optimized mean-variance portfolio offered an extra 3.72 annual percentage points of expected return with the same standard deviation.

Yet the consultants did not proceed to recommend their optimized mean-variance portfolio to the board, because they expected the board to find it "unpalatable," prescribing allocations much different from current allocations in that pension fund and similar ones. For example, the pension fund allocated 33 percent of its portfolio to US stocks and 20 percent to international stocks, but the mean-variance optimized portfolio prescribed zero allocation to US stocks and 54 percent allocation to international stocks.

The consultants proceeded to place constraints on allocations in the mean-variance optimization process to make allocations palatable, such as a minimum allocation to US stocks and a maximum allocation to international stocks. They recommended portfolio F, whose combination of expected return and standard deviation is below the mean-variance frontier yet above the current portfolio D.

But why is portfolio E, which promises to deliver the highest expected return at no higher standard deviation, deemed unpalatable?

We find the answer in an analogy between investment portfolios and "food portfolios" we know as diets. In 1939, many years before he won a Nobel Prize, economist George Stigler considered 77 food items, from wheat flour to sirloin steaks and strawberry preserves, and found that the lowest-cost diet consists of only 5 food items. A moderately active man weighing 154 pounds would have satisfied all his nutritional needs for a year at an annual cost of $39.93. The diet consisted of 370 pounds of wheat flour, 57 cans of evaporated milk, 111 pounds of cabbage, 23 pounds of spinach, and 285 pounds of dried navy beans.[6]

Textbook mean-variance diners perceive foods as no more than bundles of nutrients. Benefits and costs other than the utilitarian benefits of nutrition and its cost do not matter, because all foods mix in the stomach, releasing identical nutrients whether from expensive steak or cheap hamburger. Similarly, textbook mean-variance investors perceive investments as no more than bundles of expected returns, their standard deviations, and their correlations. Features other than these do not matter, because all investments mix in the portfolio, whether shares of General Electric or General Motors.

Stigler's diet is on the *nutrition-cost frontier* of food, depicted in Figure 8-3. It provides the necessary nutrition at the lowest cost. Similarly, a portfolio on the mean-variance frontier of investments provides the necessary expected return at the lowest standard deviation of returns. But normal diners want more than diets on the nutrition-cost frontier of foods, and

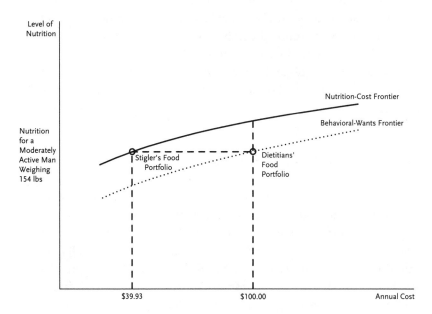

Figure 8-3 A nutrition-cost frontier and a behavioral-wants frontier.

normal investors want more than portfolios on the mean-variance frontier of investments.

Stigler compared his minimum-cost portfolio of foods to the portfolio of foods that dietitians described as providing the cheapest combination of foods that satisfy nutritional requirements. That food portfolio would have cost $100 in 1939, more than double the cost of Stigler's food portfolio, placing it below the nutrition-cost frontier of foods in Figure 8-3.

Why do diets proposed by dietitians as cheapest cost so much more than Stigler's diet? The answer, wrote Stigler, is that dietitians consider not only the utilitarian benefits of high nutrition and low cost but also the expressive and emotional benefits of palatability, variety, prestige, and culture. Primarily on such grounds, he noted, can we explain dietitians' recommendation to include meat and sugar in minimum-cost diets. The same is true for portfolio recommendations by investment consultants.

The dietitians' recommended food portfolio is on the *behavioral-wants frontier* in Figure 8-3, accounting for diners' wants for the full range of food benefits—utilitarian, expressive, and emotional. This recommendation is optimal even if these portfolios are below the *nutrition-cost frontier* of diners who want only the utilitarian benefits of food.

Similarly, investment portfolios on the behavioral-wants frontier are optimal for investors who want the full range of investment benefits: utilitarian, expressive, and emotional. The portfolio recommended by the consultants is on the behavioral-wants frontier of the managers of the pension fund, providing the utilitarian benefits of higher expected return than the current portfolio at the same standard deviation but also expressive and emotional benefits, including the benefits of conformity to the portfolio conventions of this pension fund and similar pension funds.

INVESTORS' WANTS AND THE BEHAVIORAL-WANTS FRONTIER

Portfolios are on the behavioral-wants frontier when they satisfy investors' wants for utilitarian, expressive, and emotional benefits, free of cognitive and emotional errors. Portfolios on behavioral-wants frontiers are regularly below mean-variance frontiers. Examples of portfolios on the behavioral-wants frontier include those that provide the expressive and emotional benefits of social responsibility, patriotism and familiarity, pride and avoidance of regret, and convention.

Wants for Social Responsibility

Exclusion of stocks of nuclear companies from portfolios by socially responsible investors is puzzling within mean-variance portfolio theory. Why not separate portfolio production from portfolio spending, constructing portfolios that include stocks of nuclear companies if they yield the greatest wealth at the desired level of risk, and then spend the extra wealth in contributions to antinuclear campaigns?

Separation of production of wealth from its spending goals makes no sense to socially responsible investors. Neither does separation of utilitarian benefits from expressive and emotional ones. Cheryl Smith of Trillium Asset Management, a company serving socially responsible investors, tells of an experience following a 1985 letter on social justice and the economy by the US Conference of Catholic Bishops. "The letter spoke very powerfully to participants about the need to be involved ethically in the economic life of the country, and they kept asking, 'Where does the archdiocese invest its money?' It turned out that the archdiocese's holdings included the stock of the company running the Rocky Flats Nuclear Arsenal, while its Peace and Justice Office was sending demonstrators to chain themselves to the arsenal's fence."[7]

Exclusion of stocks of nuclear companies from portfolios is not puzzling within behavioral portfolio theory. Such portfolios might well be on the behavioral-wants frontier, consistent with spending goals and their utilitarian, expressive, and emotional benefits. A survey by the Spectrem Group revealed that 37 percent of investors with a net worth of $1 million to $5 million consider social responsibility when they invest.[8]

One study compared optimized mean-variance portfolios constrained to include only socially responsible mutual funds to unconstrained optimized mean-variance portfolios including all mutual funds.[9] It found that the expected annual returns of constrained socially responsible portfolios fell below the unconstrained mean-variance frontier by more than 3 percentage points.[10] Yet wants for the utilitarian, expressive, and emotional benefits of social responsibility might place constrained socially responsible portfolios on the behavioral-wants frontier, as illustrated in Figure 8-4.

Wants for Patriotism and Familiarity

Patriotic foods yield expressive and emotional benefits, and so do patriotic investments. Frankfurters were turned into hot dogs when Americans fought Germans in World War I, and French fries were briefly

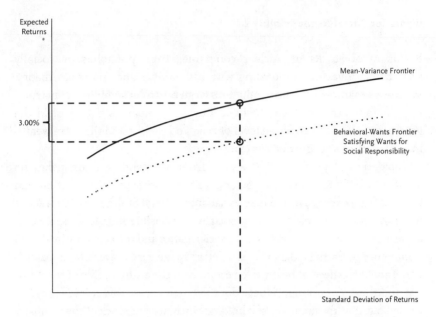

Figure 8-4 A mean-variance frontier and a behavioral-wants frontier satisfying wants for social responsibility.

turned into Freedom fries by Americans unhappy with the opposition of the French to the war in Iraq. Likewise, Liberty Bonds expressed patriotism in World War I, War Bonds expressed patriotism in World War II, and Patriot Bonds conveyed patriotism after the September 11, 2001, terrorist attacks.[11]

Patriotism is part of nationalism, distinct from globalism. Globalists, wrote Jonathan Haidt, a social psychologist, want a world free of patriotism, where, in the words of John Lennon, there are no countries, and the world is one. Nationalists, however, "see patriotism as a virtue; they think their country and its culture are unique and worth preserving. This is a real moral commitment, not a pose to cover up racist bigotry."[12]

Wants for patriotism promote "home bias," a preference for the investments of home countries. The term implies cognitive and emotional errors that mislead investors into bearing extra risk with no extra expected returns as they forgo the risk-reducing benefits of global diversification. But wants for patriotism likely underlie home bias. Investors in countries with high proportions of patriotic citizens invest larger proportions of their portfolios in stocks of their home countries than do investors in less patriotic countries. And American investors in patriotic US regions invest larger portions of their portfolios within their regions than do American investors in less patriotic regions.[13]

Home bias places portfolios below the mean-variance frontier. Home bias also places portfolios below the behavioral-wants frontier if it stems from errors. But home bias places portfolios on the behavioral-wants frontier if it stems from wants for the expressive and emotional benefits of patriotism.

Wants for familiarity join wants for patriotism in preference for home investments, as in preference for home foods. Indeed, familiar foods offer not only emotional benefits in fragrance and taste but also utilitarian benefits in caloric intake. Indians who migrate from their origin states to other Indian states derive 7 percent fewer calories than locals per rupee of food expenditures. Moreover, the gap in caloric intake between migrants and locals depends on the suitability of local foods for migrants and the intensity of migrants' preference for foods of their origin states.[14]

Wants for familiarity are evident in aversion to mutual fund managers with foreign-sounding names. Such managers suffer about 10 percent lower inflows into their funds. They also suffer lower inflows following good performance and higher outflows following bad performance. Inflows to funds with managers with Middle Eastern names declined following the September 11 terrorist attacks.[15]

The late 1990s were not only the time of the great dot-com bubble but also the time of a great divergence between the returns of US stocks and international stocks. The cumulative return of the S&P 500 Index of US stocks exceeded 151 percent during the five years ending in December 1997, whereas the cumulative return of the EAFE (Europe, Australasia, and Far East) Index of international stocks was less than 71 percent.

Many investors were misled to abandon global diversification in the late 1990s by the cognitive errors of representativeness and hindsight and by the emotional cost of regret. Representativeness errors led them to extrapolate from past returns and conclude that future returns of international stocks would continue to trail those of US stocks. Hindsight errors misled them into thinking that the relatively poor performance of international stocks was as clear in foresight as in hindsight. Regret compounded hindsight, inflicting frustration for not having switched from international stocks to US stocks years before.

Wants for familiarity are evident in a *Wall Street Journal* article subtitled "Drop Global-Investing Bunk."[16] It taunted proponents of global diversification, describing them as people who believe that "the 'sound' investor is defined as one who has moved a goodly chunk of his money out of the society he knows to countries with which he is unfamiliar. . . ."

Behavioral-wants frontiers vary from investor to investor by wants and trade-offs between utilitarian, expressive, and emotional benefits.

Portfolios with 20 percent allocation to international stocks might be on the behavioral-wants frontier of some investors, and portfolios with 60 percent allocation to international stocks might be on the behavioral-wants frontier of other investors.

Wants for Pride and Avoidance of Regret

Pride is an emotional benefit and regret is an emotional cost. Gains bestow the emotional benefits of pride and the expressive benefits of the image of a winner, whereas losses inflict the emotional cost of regret and the expressive costs of the image of a loser. Frames of covered calls highlight gains and obscure losses, magnifying pride and muting regret. Here is the sales pitch for covered calls scripted by LeRoy Gross in his manual for brokers:[17]

> JOE SALESMAN: You have told me that you have not been too pleased with the results of your stock market investments
>
> JOHN PROSPECT: That's right. I am dissatisfied with the return or lack of it on my stock portfolio.
>
> JOE SALESMAN: Starting tomorrow, how would you like to have three sources of profit every time you buy a common stock?
>
> JOHN PROSPECT: Three profit sources? What are they?
>
> JOE SALESMAN: First, you could collect a lot of dollars—maybe hundreds, sometimes thousands—for simply agreeing to sell your just-bought stock at a higher price than you paid. This agreement money is paid to you right away, on the very next business day— money that's yours to keep forever. Your second source of profit could be the cash dividends due you as the owner of the stock. The third source of profit would be in the increase in price of the shares from what you paid to the agreed selling price.

Think of buying a $30 share of stock and selling for $1 a call option on that stock with an exercise price of $40. You enjoy one gain as you receive $1 for the option, which is the "agreement money . . . that's yours to keep forever." You enjoy a second gain as you collect the $2 dividend on the stock, and a possible third gain as you collect the potential $10 increase in the price of the share from $30 to $40. The covered call's potential loss, however, is obscured. You lose $60 of potential profits if the share's price zooms beyond $40 to $100.

"Tracking-errors optimization" is a popular application of mean-variance analysis among money managers. In this application, returns are replaced by tracking errors—gains and losses relative to the returns of benchmark portfolios. Similarly, variance of returns is replaced by variance of tracking errors, and the mean-variance frontier of returns and their standard deviations is replaced by the mean-variance frontier of tracking errors and their standard deviations. Money managers choose their optimal tracking-errors portfolio on the mean-variance frontier of tracking errors—a portfolio with expected returns higher than those of the benchmark portfolio, implying high positive tracking errors, but with relatively low standard deviation of tracking errors.

Portfolios on the mean-variance frontier of tracking errors and their standard deviations fall below the mean-variance frontier of returns and their standard deviations.[18] But tracking-error optimization might lead to portfolios on the behavioral-wants frontier as it satisfies money managers' wants for avoiding the expressive costs of the image of a loser that comes with returns lower than their benchmark, the emotional costs of regret, and perhaps the utilitarian costs of losing clients.[19]

Wants for Adherence to Convention

Constraints on portfolio allocations are common in the construction of portfolios, whether mean-variance or behavioral. A constraint might prevent the allocation to US stocks from falling below 30 percent of the portfolio, or prevent the allocation to gold from exceeding 2 percent. Constraints can assure adherence to convention, making portfolios palatable. Recall the pension fund consultants who placed constraints on portfolio allocations derived from a mean-variance optimizer so as to adhere to the allocation conventions of this and similar funds.

Some argue that mean-variance portfolios optimized without constraints are unpalatable because imprecise estimates of investment parameters lead to unpalatable extreme allocations to stocks, bonds, gold, or other investments. Extreme allocations, however, are inherent in mean-variance efficient portfolios constructed with precise estimates.[20] A recommendation that investors accept optimized mean-variance portfolios, even if unpalatable, as their best portfolios has been rejected in the past, as illustrated in the pension fund example, and will be rejected in the future.

Indeed, Harry Markowitz, who introduced mean-variance portfolio theory and its optimizer, describes constraints as useful judgment tools in the construction of good portfolios rather than diversion from them.[21] Estimates of mean-variance parameters involve judgment. Even a purely historical approach to estimation involves judgment in the choice of the estimation period, whether the most recent decade or the last four decades, whether derived from monthly or annual returns. Moreover, investor wants, including wants for the expressive and emotional benefits of adherence to convention, extend beyond the utilitarian benefits of high expected returns and low variance of returns. Constraints on allocations are a sensible way to incorporate judgment and wants into portfolios.

REPLACING IGNORANCE WITH KNOWLEDGE AND CORRECTING COGNITIVE AND EMOTIONAL ERRORS

Good portfolio practice, whether mean-variance or behavioral, calls for improving investor behavior and portfolio performance by replacing ignorance with knowledge and correcting cognitive and emotional errors. The task is possible, evident in experience following the German reunification. East Germans acquired investment knowledge quickly and changed their financial behavior. They became as likely to invest in risky securities as West Germans, and more likely to use consumer debt, without signs of regret.[22]

Yet the task of replacing ignorance with knowledge is not easy. Many investors are not only ignorant of the damaging effect of high investment costs on their savings but also resistant to knowledge. A ruling of the Israeli Securities Authority sought to convey knowledge about investment costs by requiring portfolio managers to obtain their clients' consent, in writing, to receiving kickbacks from brokers executing clients' trades. A subsequent study revealed that sophisticated investors did not consent to kickbacks but most investors resisted knowledge about kickbacks or failed to act on it—about 89 percent of investors consented to kickbacks. The authors noted that this percentage is remarkably high, considering that not responding to the question about kickbacks was taken as not consenting to kickbacks. The portfolios of investors consenting to kickbacks underperformed in the year following their consent.[23]

The majority of people with low socioeconomic status have no stock investments. This lack is detrimental to wealth accumulation. Socioeconomic status may influence the process by which people learn. People with low socioeconomic status hold more pessimistic beliefs about stock returns than do people with higher socioeconomic status.[24]

Another example of the difficulty of replacing ignorance with knowledge involves misperceptions of benefits of portfolio diversification. Diversification reduces the volatility of portfolios, measured by the standard deviation of returns, while leaving expected returns unchanged. Yet many misperceive the benefits of diversification. People hampered by low financial literacy believe that diversification *increases* the volatility of portfolios. This misperception is because the returns of familiar securities, such as the stocks of Apple or IBM, seems more predictable than the returns of a portfolio, such as an S&P 500 portfolio, which is diversified among 500 mostly unfamiliar stocks. Moreover, people possessing *high* financial literacy believe that diversification *increases the expected returns* of portfolios, when in truth it leaves expected returns unchanged. Consequently, investors hampered by low financial literacy might fail to diversify because they misperceive diversification as adding risk rather than reducing it, and those possessing high financial literacy might choose risky diversified portfolios because they misperceive them as offering high returns.[25]

Errors relating to correlations are yet another example of the difficulty of replacing ignorance with knowledge. Elucidating the role of correlations in the benefits of diversification is an important part of Harry Markowitz's analytical contribution. Failure to consider correlations and misperceptions of their role in the benefits of diversification are errors that increase the risk of portfolios, imposing utilitarian costs without compensating with utilitarian, expressive, and emotional benefits. Consider the example in Table 8-1.

The expected return of a portfolio composed of two investments in equal proportions is the 8 percent mean of the expected returns of the two investments:

$$E(R_p) = \frac{1}{2} \times 6\% + \frac{1}{2} \times 10\% = 8\%$$

But the standard deviation of the returns of a portfolio composed of two investments in equal proportions is less than the 30 percent mean of the standard deviations of the returns of the two investments, unless the correlation between their returns is a perfect 1.0.

Table 8-1 THE ROLE OF CORRELATION IN THE STANDARD DEVIATION OF PORTFOLIO RETURNS

Investment	Expected return	Standard deviation
Investment 1	6 percent	20 percent
Investment 2	10 percent	40 percent
Correlation between returns of the two investments: 0.3		

$$\sigma_{(R_p)} = \sqrt{(1/2)^2 \times 20^2 + (1/2)^2 \times 40^2 + 2 \times (1/2)^2 \times 0.3 \times 20 \times 40} = 24.9\%$$

Failure to consider correlations in forming portfolios is common, pointing to investors' cognitive errors. One study presented to people expected returns, standard deviations, and correlations between the returns of three investments, A, B, and C, and asked them to form portfolios.[26] The correlation between the returns of A and B and between the returns of A and C was set at zero. The correlation between the returns of B and C, however, was set at zero for people in one group, 0.8 for another, and a negative 0.8 for a third group. The differences between the correlations provided to the three groups are very large, such that if people were to consider correlations they would have chosen very different portfolios. Yet no significant differences were found between the portfolios chosen by people in the three groups. In essence, people overlooked correlations as they constructed their portfolios.

Even professional investors who consider correlations regularly err, as they misperceive them and their role in the benefits of diversification. The 2008 global financial crisis exposed some of these misperceptions. An early 2009 cover of a journal for financial advisers asked, "Is Markowitz Wrong?" One financial adviser said, "The problem with diversification is correlation, or the tendency of correlations to peak in bear markets."[27]

The benefits of diversification indeed disappear when correlations between the returns of investments reach 1.0, but we tend to misperceive correlations of 0.9 as leaving little diversification benefits. In truth, 0.9 correlations and even 0.99 correlations provide substantial diversification benefits. Moreover, the benefits of diversification depend not only on the correlations between the returns of investments but also on their standard deviations. The benefits of diversification are low when correlations are high, but the benefits of diversification are *high* when standard deviations are high. Indeed, contrary to common perceptions, the benefits of diversification tended to be *higher* in bear than in bull markets. While correlations tended to be higher in bear markets than in bull markets, standard deviations also tended to be higher in such markets and the higher standard deviations in bear markets added to the benefits of diversification more than the higher correlations in bear markets subtracted from these benefits.[28]

By considering return gaps, we can replace ignorance with knowledge about the role of correlations in the benefits of diversification. These are gaps between the returns of pairs of investments such as US stocks and international stocks. Return gaps serve as better measures of the benefits of diversification than do correlations alone, because they account for the effects of both correlations and standard deviations. Moreover, these gaps provide an intuitive yet accurate measure of the benefits of diversification. Table 8-2 shows that return gaps and the associated benefits of diversification are low when correlations are high, but return gaps and the associated benefits of diversification are high when standard deviations are high.

The estimated return gap between the returns of two assets is

$$\text{Estimated Return Gap} = 2\sigma\sqrt{\frac{(1-\rho)}{2}},$$

where σ is the average of the standard deviations of the returns of the two investments, and ρ is the correlation between the returns of the two investments.

Investors who consider diversification should ask, "By how much will I lag or lead a diversified portfolio if I fail to diversify?" Return gaps answer this question. Compare three investors considering portfolios composed of US and international stocks. One invests his entire portfolio in US stocks, another invests it all in international stocks, and the third diversifies her portfolio between the two in equal proportions.

Imagine that we are at December 31, 2007, contemplating the yet unknown 2008 returns. We find, at the end of 2008, that the return of US stocks was a 37 percent loss and the return on international stocks was a 45 percent loss. The return gap in 2008 was 8 percentage points, as

Table 8-2 ESTIMATED ANNUAL RETURN GAPS
BETWEEN RETURNS OF TWO INVESTMENTS WITH VARYING
COMBINATIONS OF CORRELATION AND STANDARD
DEVIATION

	Standard Deviation		
Correlation	10.00 percent	15.00 percent	20.00 percent
0.99	1.41 percent	2.12 percent	2.83 percent
0.9	4.47 percent	6.71 percent	8.94 percent
0.8	6.32 percent	9.49 percent	12.65 percent
0.5	10.00 percent	15.00 percent	20.00 percent
0	14.14 percent	21.21 percent	28.28 percent

Note: The standard deviation is the average of the standard deviations of the returns of the two investments.

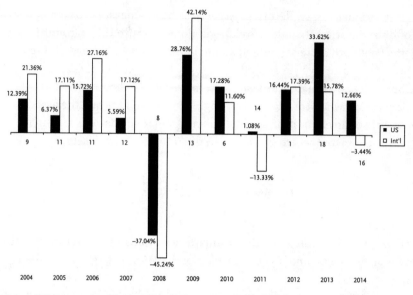

Figure 8-5 Return Gaps between US and international stocks during 2004 through 2014.
MSCI US Broad Market GR USD for US Stocks and MSCI ACWI Ex USA GR USD for international stocks.

in Figure 8-5. Investors who concentrated their portfolios entirely in US stocks are at the top of the gap. Investors who concentrated their portfolios entirely in international stocks are at the bottom of the gap, and investors who diversified their portfolios equally between the US and international stocks are inside the gap, with a 41 percent loss. A 41 percent loss is a terrible loss, but not as terrible as a 45 percent loss.

The benefits of diversification are all about falling into the gap. Diversified investors give up the hope of having their entire portfolio at the top of the gap but they gain the freedom from fear of having their entire portfolio at the bottom of the gap. The top of the gap does not necessarily provide a positive return—the entire gap can be in the region of losses. Diversification does not eliminate the possibility of losses; it only mitigates it. Only the risk-free rate eliminates the possibility of losses, and that rate is low.

ASSESSING WANTS AND CORRECTING ERRORS WITH INVESTOR QUESTIONNAIRES

Investors and financial advisers have a wide choice of questionnaires under headings such as risk questionnaire, investor questionnaire, and investment policy questionnaire. Most assess the conflicting wants for high expected returns and low risk, and guide investors toward appropriate portfolios. Sometimes risk aversion takes the form of variance aversion, whereby variance is represented by "fluctuations in value." One questionnaire probes variance aversion by the level of agreement with the following statement: "Generally, I prefer investments with little or no fluctuation in value, and I'm willing to accept the lower return associated with these investments." Investors who strongly agree with this statement are deemed to have high variance aversion, tilting recommendations toward low-variance portfolios containing high allocations to low-variance bonds and cash, and low allocations to high-variance stocks.

Risk aversion takes the form of loss aversion in other questions. One questionnaire displays a chart that shows 1-year loss and 1-year gain on three different hypothetical investments of $10,000. The questionnaire then asks, "Given the potential gain and loss in any 1 year, I would invest my money in. . . ." The choices range from a 50-50 chance for a $164 loss or a $593 gain to a 50-50 chance for a $3,639 loss or a $4,229 gain. But stakes matter, and loss-aversion increases as stakes increase.[29] Many who are willing to wager $10,000 on a 50-50 chances for a $3,639 loss or a $4,229 gain might not be willing to wager $100,000 or a $10 million portfolio on proportionally higher gains and losses.

Economist Robert Barsky and his coauthors wrote that the "principal requirement for a question aimed at measuring risk aversion is that it must involve gambles over lifetime income." They added that "experiments in the existing literature typically involve stakes that have little impact on lifetime resources."[30] To address this problem, Barsky and his coauthors asked people to consider large stakes—income each year throughout life. They offered a 50-50 chance to double lifetime income or cut it by some proportion, such as one-fifth. This question is intrinsically calibrated to people's lifetime resources, whether their annual income is $10,000 or $1 million.

Another question probes loss capacity. It states, "When making a long-term investment, I plan to hold the investment for. . . ." It offers answers ranging from one or two years to nine, ten, or more years. Older people are likely to have most of their wealth in the form of investment portfolios rather than in the form of human capital, as they have fewer years of employment ahead of them. Older investors are deemed to have lower loss capacity in their investment portfolios, tilting recommendations toward higher allocations to bonds and cash that can impose smaller losses over short horizons than do stocks.

Questionnaires often assess wants beyond high expected returns and low risk, whether measured as variance aversion or loss aversion. Wants for maximization are wants for winning. A survey of American men and women assessed wants for maximization by levels of agreement with the following statement: "I always want to have the best. Second best is not good enough for me."[31] Men have greater wants for maximization than do women, and the young have greater such wants than do the old. Great wants for maximization are associated with high declared loss tolerance, suggesting the need to examine whether high declared loss tolerance is anything more than an artifact of great wants for maximization.

Another question asks, "How much confidence do you have in your ability to make good financial decisions?" This is a question about confidence, or overconfidence, not about willingness to tolerate variance or losses. High correlations between overconfidence and loss tolerance might indicate that overconfident investors are more loss tolerant. But overconfidence is distinct from loss tolerance. Indeed, the same survey of American men and women found that people who are overconfident also state that they have high loss tolerance, suggesting the need to examine whether high declared loss tolerance is anything more than an artifact of overconfidence.

Think of the following pair of questions asked in the survey of American men and women.

> Some people believe that success in picking stocks that earn higher-than-average returns is mostly due to skill. Other people believe that success in picking stocks that earn higher-than-average returns is mostly due to luck. Please indicate your belief.
> Some people believe that they can pick stocks that would earn higher-than-average returns. Other people believe that they are unable to do so. Please indicate your belief.

Answers show that men tend to believe that success in picking stocks that earn higher-than-average returns is mostly due to skill, whereas women tend to believe that it is mostly due to luck. Answers show that 57.3 percent of men and 49.6 percent of women believe that success is mostly due to skill. Other investors believe that success is mostly due to luck or are neutral.[32]

Men are also more likely than women to commit overconfidence errors, in the form of overplacement. But there is no general propensity for overplacement. Answers show that 41.9 percent of men and 32.3 percent of women believe they can pick stocks that would earn higher-than-average returns. Other investors believe that they cannot pick such stocks or are neutral.

Maximization seeking is associated with regret aversion. As decision-making scholar Gergana Nenkov and her coauthors wrote, "[T]he potential for regret is ever present because maximizers are always asking themselves if the outcome they chose is the best and are always experiencing lingering doubt that they could have made a better choice."[33] The same survey of American men and women assessed regret aversion by levels of agreement with the following statement: "Whenever I make a choice, I try to get information about how the other alternatives turned out and feel bad if another alternative has done better than the alternative I have chosen." High maximization seeking is associated with high regret aversion, but regret aversion is not associated with loss aversion. This disparity indicates that regret aversion is distinct from loss aversion even though the two are often conflated.

A question aimed at assessing risk aversion asked investors whether they are willing to buy a stock they have previously sold at a loss. "Suppose that 5 years ago you bought shares in a highly regarded company. The same year the company experienced a severe decline in sales due to poor management. The price of the shares dropped drastically and you sold at a substantial loss. The company has been restructured under new management and most experts now expect the shares to produce better than average returns. Given your bad past experience with this company would you buy shares now?" Possible answers range from definitely yes to definitely no. This question, however, is about regret aversion rather than risk aversion. Indeed, investors are reluctant to buy stocks they have previously sold at a loss, because they want to avoid regret.[34]

Johann Klaassen designs client questionnaires for advisers affiliated with First Affirmative Financial Network, a group specializing in socially responsible investing. He said,

> We start by asking clients about their attitudes toward risk, because our primary obligation is to see that our clients' financial goals are satisfied. Our secondary obligation is to see that their social or ethical goals are satisfied. . . . We follow a rather traditional pie-chart approach to asset allocation and then, within asset categories, we try to select investments that are consistent with the client's values.

One set of questions is about risk. For example, which of the following best describes your general feelings about the volatility, stability, and growth of your investment? Possible answers are

1. I am more concerned with the risk of significant downward fluctuations in the value of this account than with maximizing returns
2. I am comfortable with balanced, consistent returns if the risk of significant fluctuations could be limited
3. I want to emphasize long-term growth of this portfolio but am willing to accept somewhat lower returns to achieve some protection against significant downward fluctuations in value
4. I want maximum growth and, therefore, am willing to accept the likelihood of significant periodic downward fluctuations in the value of this portfolio

Another set of questions is about social values: How inclined are you to seek out or avoid companies with a history of the following practices and policies? Possible choices are Seek, Neutral, Avoid, and Hold for Advocacy. One example relates to abortion policy: "in support of abortion rights" or "against abortion rights." Another relates to prohibition of use of animals: "in development and testing of medicines and medical technologies," "in development and testing of consumer products," or "for meat, fur, or leather."[35]

A portion of an investor questionnaire by Loring Ward, an investment company, is designed to educate investors about global diversification, guide them to overcome cognitive and emotional errors, and elicit their wants.

First comes education about global diversification:

> Over time, international markets and asset classes within those markets have not always moved in unison with the U.S. market. The graph below shows periods when U.S. stocks have outperformed international stocks and periods when international stocks have outperformed U.S. stocks. Historically, investing a portion of a portfolio in international stocks and bonds has demonstrated the potential to reduce volatility.

The text is accompanied by a graph, similar to Figure 8-6, showing that the returns of US stocks were higher than those of international stocks in some periods and lower in other periods.

Next comes elicitation of wants:

"Which statement best reflects your view on international investing?"

- I am very comfortable with international investments
- I am comfortable with international investments
- I am somewhat comfortable with international investments
- I am somewhat uneasy with international investments
- I am uneasy with international investments

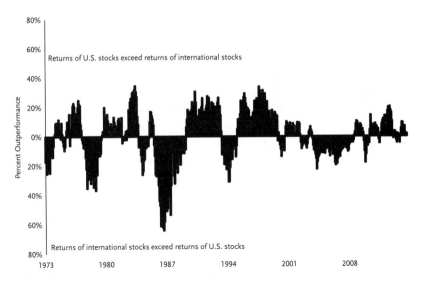

Figure 8-6 Return gaps between US and international stocks during 1972 through 2014.
Rolling 12-month differences between the returns of the S&P 500 Index and the returns of the MSCI EAFE (Europe, Australasia, and Far East) Index.

Investors who are "uneasy with international investments" are advised to allocate to international stocks 20 percent of their overall stock allocation. Investors who are "very comfortable with international investments" are advised to allocate to international stocks 60 percent of their overall stock allocation. Investors who express intermediate comfort with international investments are advised to allocate intermediate percentages of their overall stock allocation.

PORTFOLIO CHOICES ON A BEHAVIORAL-WANTS FRONTIER WHEN WANTS ARE LIMITED TO HIGH EXPECTED WEALTH AND LOW RISK

Mean-variance portfolio theory prescribes portfolios to investors who seek high expected wealth but are averse to high risk, measured as variance of portfolio wealth. We refer to the risk aversion of mean-variance investors as *variance aversion*.

Consider first behavioral-wants portfolios of normal investors whose wants are limited to the utilitarian benefits of high expected wealth and low risk. Risk is measured by probability of shortfall from aspired or target wealth, such as a shortfall from $1 million in target retirement wealth. We refer to this risk aversion as *shortfall aversion*. Probability of shortfall can be replaced by expected shortfall or the product of probability shortfall and expected shortfall.

Normal investors do not seek high variance for its own sake. Rather, high variance is payment for low probability of shortfalls from aspirations. Portfolios assessed as high risk by mean-variance investors because of high variance are assessed as low risk by normal investors when such portfolios offer low probabilities of shortfall from target wealth. *Shortfall aversion* sometimes corresponds to *variance seeking*, but normal investors are motivated by shortfall aversion and do not perceive *variance seeking* as *risk seeking*.

Mean-variance investors who have nothing but $20 do not buy a lottery ticket offering a 0.001 percent probability to win a $1 million prize. This decision is because the negative 50 percent expected return of the ticket coupled with the very high variance of its possible payouts—$1 million or $0—makes the ticket inferior to a sure $20 with a zero variance enjoyed by investors who refrain from buying lottery tickets.

Normal investors, however, might buy this ticket and similar lottery tickets if all they have is $20 and their target wealth is $1 million. The $20 ticket offers a slim 0.001 percent probability of avoiding a shortfall from $1 million in target wealth, but a $20 diversified portfolio of stocks and bonds offers an even slimmer chance.

There is affinity between behavioral portfolio theory and liability directed investing. The target wealth of a pension fund is its liability to its beneficiaries, and the target wealth of an individual is her "liability to herself." Yet pension funds are different from individuals. The liabilities of pension funds are specified by law or contracts, whereas individuals can change their target wealth—liabilities to themselves—as often and as much as they wish.

There is also affinity between measures of risk in behavioral portfolio theory and measures of downside risk such as value at risk (VaR). But whereas risk in VaR is about losses relative to current wealth, risk in behavioral portfolio theory is about losses relative to target wealth. Investing in a lottery ticket involves high risk when measured by VaR as the ticket entails a high probability of losing the entire investment, but it involves relatively low risk for investors with little wealth and high target wealth that can be reached only by winning the lottery.

Variations in behavioral-wants frontiers correspond to variations in target wealth relative to current wealth. Consider an investor with $100,000 of current wealth and $130,000, a high target wealth, by the terminal date, a year from today. The investor can form portfolios composed of one of two stocks, L (Lottery) and M (Moderate), or combinations of the two. L (Lottery) is a lottery-like stock, with a negative 10 percent expected return and a high 80 percent standard deviation of returns. M (Moderate) is a stock with a positive 20 percent expected return and a low 12 percent standard deviation of returns. The correlation between the returns of L (Lottery) and M (Moderate) is zero.

The expected wealth of an investor who invests her entire $100,000 current wealth in L (Lottery) is $90,000, presented in Figure 8-7, but the 80 percent standard deviation, amounting to $72,000, implies that she has approximately a two-thirds probability to find that her wealth at her terminal date is between $162,000, 80 percent higher than $90,000, and $18,000, 80 percent lower than $90,000.

The expected wealth of an investor who invests her entire $100,000 current wealth in M (Moderate) is $120,000, presented in Figure 8-7, but the 12 percent standard deviation of returns, amounting to $14,400, implies that she has an approximately two-thirds probability to find that her wealth at her terminal date is between $134,400, 12 percent higher than $120,000, and $105,600, 12 percent lower than $120,000.

The mean-variance frontier, presented in Figure 8-8, extends from a portfolio composed entirely of M (Moderate) to portfolio LST (Lowest) with the lowest standard deviation of terminal wealth. Portfolio LST (Lowest) is composed of approximately 96.15 percent M (Moderate) and 3.85 percent

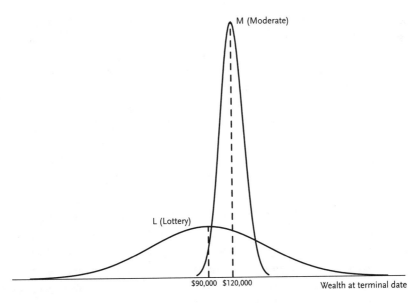

Figure 8-7 The distribution of wealth at the terminal date if $100,000 is invested fully in stock M (Moderate) or stock L (Lottery)

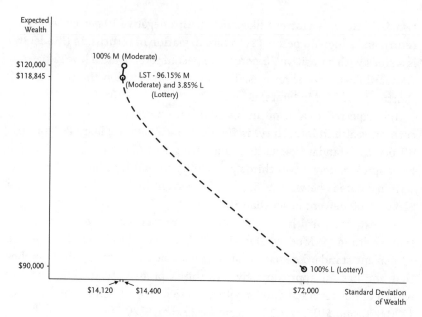

Figure 8-8 Mean-variance frontier with stocks M (Moderate), L (Lottery), and Portfolio LST (Lowest). A 100 percent M (Moderate) portfolio is on the mean-variance frontier, but a 100 percent L (Lottery) portfolio is not.

L (Lottery).[36] The expected terminal wealth of portfolio LST (Lowest) is $118,845, and its standard deviation is $14,120.[37]

Mean-variance investors who are extremely averse to standard deviation of their wealth choose the portfolio with the lowest standard deviation. Mean-variance investors who are indifferent to standard deviation of wealth choose the portfolio with the highest expected wealth, regardless of its standard deviation. Mean-variance investors who are somewhat averse to standard deviation of wealth sacrifice some expected wealth for a lower standard deviation. But no mean-variance investor is willing to sacrifice expected wealth for a *higher* standard deviation of wealth.

Mean-variance investors who are extremely averse to standard deviation of their wealth choose to invest their $100,000 in portfolio LST (Lowest) with the lowest standard deviation of wealth, $14,120. They combine 3.85 percent of their $100,000 in L (Lottery) with 96.15 percent in M (Moderate). Mean-variance investors who are indifferent to standard deviation of wealth choose to invest their $100,000 solely in portfolio M (Moderate) with the highest expected wealth, $120,000, and as standard deviation of wealth of $14,400. And mean-variance investors, who are somewhat averse to standard deviation of wealth or very averse, divide their $100,000 between M (Moderate) and L (Lottery) along the mean-variance frontier, sacrificing some expected wealth for a lower variance of terminal wealth. But no mean-variance investor chooses a portfolio composed solely of L (Lottery), because it is dominated by other portfolios, including the one composed solely of M (Moderate), with a $120,000 expected wealth, higher than the $90,000 expected wealth with L (Lottery), and a $14,400 standard deviation of wealth, lower than the $72,000 of L (Lottery).

A portfolio composed solely of L (Lottery), however, is on a behavioral-wants frontier, presented in Figure 8-9, because it provides the lowest probability of shortfall from the $130,000 terminal wealth. The probability of shortfall with a portfolio composed solely of L (Lottery) is 71.07 percent, whereas the probability of shortfall with every other portfolio is higher. For example, the probability of shortfall from the $130,000 terminal wealth with a portfolio composed solely of M (Moderate) is 75.63 percent, and the probability of shortfall from the $130,000 terminal wealth with a portfolio divided equally between L (Lottery) and M (Moderate) is 75.21 percent.[38]

Investors with low target wealth relative to their current wealth might find that a portfolio composed solely of L (Lottery) is not on the behavioral-wants frontier, presented in Figure 8-10. Consider an investor with a target wealth of $100,000, a low terminal wealth relative to his current $100,000 wealth. A portfolio composed solely of L (Lottery) is not on the behavioral-wants frontier, because it is dominated by other portfolios,

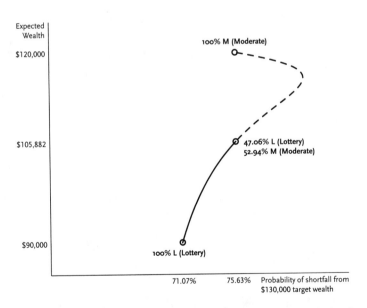

Figure 8-9 Behavioral-wants frontier when target wealth, $130,000, is high relative to $100,000 current wealth. A 100 percent L (Lottery) portfolio is on the behavioral-wants frontier, and so is a 100 percent M (Moderate) portfolio.

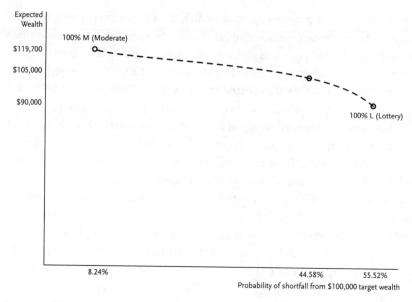

Figure 8-10 Behavioral-wants frontier when target wealth, $100,000, is low relative to $100,000 current wealth. A 100 percent L (Lottery) portfolio is not on the behavioral-wants frontier. Only a 100 percent M (Moderate) is on the behavioral-wants frontier.

including the one composed entirely of M (Moderate). The probability of shortfall from a $100,000 target wealth with a portfolio composed solely of L (Lottery) is 55.52 percent, whereas that probability is only 8.24 percent with a portfolio composed solely of M (Moderate), yet the $120,000 expected terminal wealth with M (Moderate) is higher than the $90,000 with L (Lottery).

BEHAVIORAL-WANTS PORTFOLIOS AS PYRAMIDS OF WANTS AND ASSOCIATED GOALS

A central feature in behavioral portfolio theory rests on the observation that investors view their portfolios as sets of distinct mental-account layers in a portfolio pyramid, as depicted in Figure 8-11. Each mental account corresponds to a particular want, associated goal, and their utilitarian, expressive, and emotional benefits. An optimal behavioral-wants portfolio is one that effectively balances wants while avoiding cognitive and emotional errors.

One mental account might correspond to wants for "downside protection" whose utilitarian benefits include protection from consumption constrained by poverty, and whose expressive and emotional benefits include

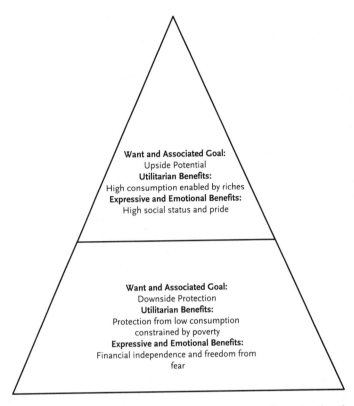

Figure 8-11 Behavioral-wants portfolios as pyramids of wants and associated goals

financial independence and freedom from fear of poverty. Another might correspond to wants for "upside potential" whose utilitarian benefits include consumption and accumulation of assets enabled by riches, and whose expressive and emotional benefits include high social status and pride.

The target wealth in the downside-protection mental account is relatively low, whereas the target wealth in the upside-potential mental account is relatively high. Investors might be variance averse in the downside-protection mental account, while variance seeking in the upside-potential one. Yet investors are risk averse in both mental accounts, when risk aversion is shortfall aversion. They are averse to shortfalls from target wealth in each mental account.

Investors can begin the process of constructing behavioral portfolios by dividing their portfolio as a whole into mental accounts of wants and associated goals. Consider again the investor with $100,000 of current wealth and an ambitious $130,000 target wealth and the investor with $100,000 of current wealth and a modest $100,000 target wealth. Combine them into one investor with $200,000 of current wealth in two mental accounts, an upside-potential mental account with $100,000 of current wealth and $130,000 target wealth and a downside-protection mental account with $100,000 of current wealth and $100,000 of target wealth. As before, the investor can form portfolios composed solely of two stocks, L (Lottery) and M (Moderate).

An optimal portfolio for this investor consists of an undiversified upside-potential mental account consisting mostly or entirely of L (Lottery), as in Figure 8-9, and a diversified downside-protection mental account consisting mostly or entirely of M (Moderate), as in Figure 8-10. More generally, the downside-protection mental account is likely composed of a diversified set of stocks, bonds, and similar investments, and the upside-potential mental account is likely composed of an undiversified handful of stocks and similar investments. Indeed, the pyramid structure of behavioral portfolios is reflected in "core and satellite" and "risk budget" portfolios composed of a well-diversified core layer geared to downside protection, and a less diversified satellite layer geared to upside potential.

Portfolios as layered pyramids of mental accounts have been with us for many years. A 1929 article recommended insurance for the foundational mental-account layer of a portfolio pyramid, geared to satisfy wants for extreme downside protection, and a cash reserve in a savings bank in the mental-account layer above that. When these mental-account layers have been filled, investors are advised to buy safe bonds and guaranteed mortgages on real estate. The next mental-account layer can be composed of preferred stocks that promise higher returns than guaranteed mortgages, and the top mental-account layers, geared to satisfy wants for extreme upside potential, consist of common stocks that promise returns exceeding those of preferred stocks.[39]

One might argue that while portfolios are described as pyramids of mental accounts, consistent with behavioral portfolio theory, investors assess portfolios as a whole, consistent with mean-variance portfolio theory. But such an argument is not supported by evidence. Consider, for example, a question in a questionnaire used by an investment company to prescribe portfolios to investors.

If you could increase your chances of improving your returns by taking more risk, would you

1. be willing to take *a lot more risk* with *all your money?*
2. be willing to take *a lot more risk* with *some of your money?*
3. be willing to take *a little more risk* with *all your money?*
4. be willing to take *a little more risk* with *some of your money?*
5. be unlikely to take much more risk?

Answers 1 and 3 make sense within the mean-variance framework. In that framework, only the risk of the portfolio as a whole—*all your money*—matters. But answers 2 and 4 make no sense within the mean-variance framework. This discrepancy is because answers 2 and 4 segment the portfolio into mental accounts where investors are willing to take *a lot more risk* or *a little more risk* with *some* of their money. Investors in mean-variance portfolio theory have a single attitude toward risk, measured as variance of the returns of the portfolio as a whole, not many attitudes, one for each mental account. In contrast, investors in behavioral portfolio theory have many attitudes toward risk, measured by shortfall from target wealth in each mental account. Investors might be willing to accept high shortfall risk in their upside-potential mental account, but only little shortfall-risk in their downside-protection mental account.

Note also that a choice of answer 2, Be willing to take *a lot more risk* with *some of your money*, very likely adds to the risk of the portfolio as a whole an increment similar to the increment added by a choice of answer 3, Be willing to take *a little more risk* with *all your money*. Yet surveys of investors and investment professionals consistently show a marked preference for answer 2, consistent with the observation that investors consider their portfolios as layered pyramids and are willing to add a lot more risk to the upper layer, geared to satisfy wants for upside potential, but less willing to add even a little more risk to the lower layer, geared to satisfy wants for downside potential.

The mental-accounting pyramid structure of behavioral portfolios offers a solution to the diversification puzzle. This is the puzzle of typical investors who depart from the prescriptions of mean-variance portfolio theory by diversifying a portion of their portfolios, such as in mutual funds, and keeping another portion in an undiversified handful of individual stocks or commodities. A review of more than 40,000 stock accounts at a brokerage firm revealed that the average number of individual stocks in portfolios was 4 and the median number was 3.[40] Another review of 14 million households revealed that their typical portfolios included one to five individual stocks.[41] These portfolios are not optimal mean-variance portfolios, because they offer expected returns no higher than the expected returns of widely diversified portfolios, yet impose higher variance of returns.

Investors who place great importance on upside-potential mental accounts do not neglect downside-protection ones. Investors might well be holding one to five individual stocks in the upside potential layers of their portfolios, while holding widely diversified mutual funds in the downside-protection layers of their portfolios, along with safe pensions and Social Security benefits. Indeed, investors often construct their portfolios as if they filled downside-protection mental accounts first before they moved on to fill upside potential ones. Many gamblers have substantial downside-protection mental accounts as they gamble with money in the upside potential mental account.[42] Gamblers are more likely to have their future secured by Social Security and pension plans than non-gamblers, and gamblers own more assets.

We see the pyramid structure of behavioral portfolios in differences between younger and older investors. Compare choices in the contexts of *job* and *investment portfolio*.[43] The *job* question says, suppose that you are the only income earner in the family, and you have a good job guaranteed to give your current family income during your lifetime. Now you are given an opportunity to take a new and equally good job. The new job has a 50-50 chance to increase by 50 percent your standard of living during your lifetime. However, the new job also has a 50-50 chance to reduce by X percent your standard of living during your lifetime. What is the maximum X percent reduction in standard of living you are willing to accept?

The *investment portfolio* question says, suppose that you are given an opportunity to replace your current investment portfolio with a new portfolio. The new portfolio has a 50-50 chance to increase by 50 percent your standard of living during your lifetime. Yet the new portfolio also has a 50-50 chance to reduce by X percent your standard of living during your lifetime. What is the maximum X percent reduction in standard of living you are willing to accept?

The distinction between job and investment portfolio is important because income from jobs offers downside protection for younger people during their working years, while investment portfolios offer them mostly upside potential during those years. Investment portfolios might consist primarily of stocks, even just a handful of stocks, reflecting relatively low loss aversion. But as people age and retire, income from jobs decreases in importance and money from investment portfolios becomes the bedrock of downside protection. The investment portfolios of older people might include higher proportions of bonds, reflecting high loss aversion. Yet the upside-potential layer of the investment portfolios of older people is not empty. Indeed, it might consist of a handful of stocks and frequent purchases of lottery tickets.

Evidence indicates that younger people indeed have higher loss aversion in jobs than in investment portfolios, whereas older people have higher loss aversion in investment portfolios than in jobs. On average, people in the 18–24 age group are willing to accept a 14.08 percent loss in their standard of living in the context of investment portfolios for a 50-50 chance of a 50 percent gain, but they are willing to accept only a 12.07 percent loss in standard of living in the context of jobs for the same chance of a gain. In contrast, people in the 55 and older age group are willing to accept only

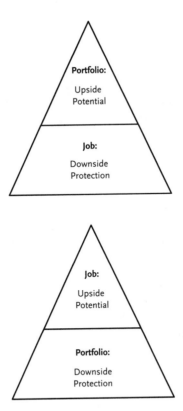

Figure 8-12 The roles of jobs and portfolios among younger and older people.

a 10.65 percent loss in the context of investment portfolios but an 11.54 percent loss in the context of jobs, illustrated in Figure 8-12.[44]

MEAN-VARIANCE PORTFOLIOS WITH MENTAL ACCOUNTS

Harry Markowitz joined Sanjiv Das, Jonathan Scheid, and Meir Statman in the development of a mental-accounting portfolio framework that combines the mental-accounting structure of behavioral portfolio theory with mean-variance optimization.[45]

Consider a 50-year-old investor with a $1 million portfolio. She divides her portfolio into three mental accounts of wants and associated goals, specified as target wealth at target dates. She places $800,000 in a mental account dedicated to retirement spending, with a $1,917,247 target wealth goal, implying a 6 percent annualized return during the 15 years until the target date. She places $150,000 in a mental account dedicated to education expenses, with an $188,957 target wealth goal, implying an 8 percent annualized return during the three years until the target date. And she places $50,000 in a mental account dedicated to bequest money, with an $850,003 target wealth goal, implying a 12 percent annualized return during the 25 years till the target date. Each mental account, as depicted in Figure 8-13, is optimized by the mean-variance procedure, where risk is measured by the standard deviation of returns.

Our investor faces three investments: a bond mutual fund with a 2 percent expected annual return and a 5 percent standard deviation of returns; a conservative stock mutual fund with an 8 percent expected annual return and a 20 percent standard deviation of returns; and an aggressive stock mutual fund with a 15 percent expected annual return and a 40 percent standard deviation of returns. The correlations between the bond fund and each of the two stock funds are zero. The correlation between the returns of the two stock funds is 0.25.

The investor calculates optimal mean-variance portfolios for each of the three mental accounts and the portfolio as a whole, displayed in Table 8-3. The annualized standard deviation of the returns of the retirement mental account

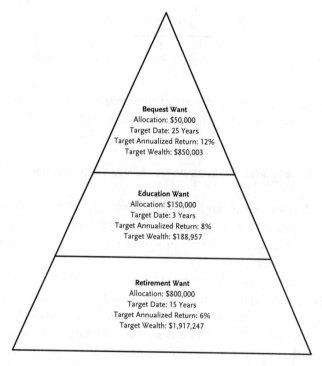

Figure 8-13 Behavioral-wants portfolio with three wants—retirement, education, and bequest.

Table 8-3 MENTAL ACCOUNTS OF WANTS AND THE PORTFOLIO AS A WHOLE

Mental Accounts of Wants	Allocation to Mental Account	Target Date	Target Annualized Return	Target Wealth at the Target Date
Bequest Want	$50,000	25 years	12.00 percent	$850,003
Education Want	$150,000	3 years	8.00 percent	$188,957
Retirement Want	$800,000	15 years	6.00 percent	$1,917,247

	Retirement Want	Education Want	Bequest Want	Portfolio as a Whole
Allocations	$800,000	$150,000	$50,000	$1,000,000
Bond Fund	52.51 percent	29.40 percent	–16.80 percent	45.58 percent
Conservative Stock Fund	31.06 percent	45.40 percent	74.06 percent	35.36 percent
Aggressive Stock Fund	16.43 percent	25.20 percent	42.74 percent	19.06 percent
Total	100 percent	100 percent	100 percent	100 percent
Expected Return	6.00 percent	8.00 percent	12.00 percent	6.60 percent
Std. Deviation	10.45 percent	15.23 percent	25.28 percent	11.85 percent

is the lowest at 10.45 percent, followed by the 15.23 percent of the education mental account and the 25.28 percent of the bequest mental account. The 6.60 percent expected return of the portfolio as a whole is a weighted average of the returns of the portfolios of the three mental accounts, but the 11.85 percent standard deviation of the portfolio as a whole is lower than the weighted average of the standard deviations of the three mental accounts.

The proportion allocated to the bond fund is highest in the retirement mental account, lower in the education mental account, and lowest in the bequest mental account. Arranging the portfolio as a set of the three mental accounts does not imply that we need three "real" bond accounts, one for the bond fund in the retirement mental account, another for the bond fund in the education mental account, and a third for the bond fund in the bequest mental account. Instead, we have one real bond account and three "virtual" bond accounts listing the allocation in the bond fund of each mental account. Investors can observe portfolios in two formats, an actual account format for the portfolio as a whole and a virtual account format for each of the mental accounts.

All the mental accounts and the portfolio as a whole are on the behavioral-wants frontier. Mental accounts and the portfolio as a whole are on the mean-variance frontier when there are no constraints on allocation, such as a preclusion of short or leveraged positions, as in

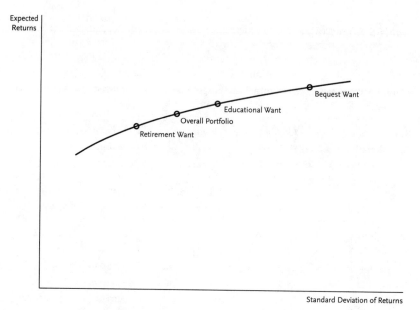

Figure 8-14 Mental accounts and the overall portfolio are on both the behavioral-wants frontier and the mean-variance frontier.

Figure 8-14. Mental accounts may be somewhat below the mean-variance frontier when such constraints are imposed. Yet such instances are rare in usual practice because few investors hold portfolio as a whole with short or leveraged positions.

The presentation of the portfolio as a whole, with the sum of the three mental accounts, has an advantage over a sole presentation of the portfolio as a whole. The mental-accounts presentation speaks the language of normal investors. Investors want to reach their goals, not only have portfolios on the mean-variance frontier. Wants-based mental accounts let investors articulate each want and associated goal, the target wealth at the target date, and the attitude toward risk, measured by standard deviation, in the mental account of each want and associated goal.

BEHAVIORAL PORTFOLIO THEORY IN PRACTICE

Central features of behavioral portfolio theory, reflected in portfolio practice, include investors' wants and associated goals, portfolios as pyramids of mental accounts of wants and associated goals, risk as shortfalls from wants and associated goals, and avoidance of cognitive and emotional errors on the way to satisfying wants and reaching associated goals. Good portfolio practice also includes features shared by both standard and behavioral portfolio theory, such as diversification, low costs, and simplicity.

Advising programs such as by MoneyGuidePro, Wealthcare, and Brunel Associates are examples of practice that incorporates features of behavioral portfolio theory. So are programs by financial services companies such as Schwab, Fidelity, and Vanguard, and advisers working at financial services companies or independently.

MoneyGuidePro

MoneyGuidePro notes that clients' financial goals are not mere expenses—they are hopes and dreams. MoneyGuidePro begins with these goals—education goals for ourselves and our children and grandchildren, pre-retirement goals, like renovating a kitchen, and retirement goals beyond day-to-day living expenses, like a new home, and bequests to family and charities. Each goal is rated by importance on a scale where 8 to 10 corresponds to "needs," 4 to 7 corresponds to "wants," and 1 to 3 corresponds to "wishes." Plan feasibility is assessed by simulation. Figure 8-15 presents an example of financial goals.

Data collection becomes a conversation about investors' wants and goals. "Financial planning does not have to be like a session in the dentist's chair," writes MoneyGuidePro, "it can actually be fun." Here is an example

Importance	Goal Description	Amount
Needs		
10	Retirement – Living Expense Nick Martha Both Retired (2021–2046) Martha Alone Retired (2047–2049)	65/2021 65/2021 $120,000 $90,000
Wants		
7	Travel in Retirement When both are retired Recurring every year for a total of 10 times	$10,000
7	529 Contributions for Grandkids In 2015 Recurring every year for a total of five times	$15,000
Wishes		
3	Bequest to University End of Nick's Plan	$50,000

Figure 8-15 MoneyGuidePro example of financial goals.

by Harold Evensky, a financial adviser and author who contributed to MoneyGuidePro's development and is using it in his advising practice.

Nick and Martha are a fifty-eight-year-old couple with two adult children and three grandchildren. Evensky divided their retirement goals into basic living expenses, categorized as a need, and travel, categorized as a want. Contributions over the next five years to their grandchildren's education savings accounts is another want, and a bequest to Nick's alma mater is a wish.

The initial plan places Nick and Martha in the middle of the "Confidence Zone," with a simulated 81 percent probability of no shortfalls from their goals. The initial plan does so by eliminating the bequest goal, making modest reductions in the other goal amounts, and maximizing Social Security benefits. Evensky noted that it is important for advisers to help clients see potential trade-offs among goals as they reflect on their wants and resources. Since Nick and Martha both work at jobs they enjoy, they decided to delay their retirement by one year and maintain their travel and education goals and their bequest goal.

Indeed, clients' ability to evaluate trade-offs between wants and consider scenarios that resonate with them is at the heart of planning. Nick, whose father needed nursing care in old age, explores the effect of three years of nursing care when he reaches 80. It turns out that the cost of nursing care would very likely leave intact all their goals with the exception of the bequest goal, which might have to be reduced or eliminated, as presented in Figure 8-16.

Wealthcare

The advising process of Wealthcare distinguishes clients' wants and associated "ideal goals" from their "acceptable goals." One example presents Tom and Katie, both 58 years old with a 19-year-old son and a $395,000 combined income. They want to travel more, support their son through graduate studies, and afford sufficient retirement spending. Their current assets consist of $1,300,000 in taxable investments, $800,000 in Tom's retirement savings account and $300,000 in Katie's.

The ideal retirement age for both Tom and Katie is 58 and the acceptable retirement age is 65. Their ideal annual income is $175,000 and the acceptable level is $160,000, their ideal risk tolerance is zero and their acceptable tolerance is a 15 percent annual loss, their ideal education goal for their son is a graduate degree, but an undergraduate degree is acceptable.

A stress test and financial plan, depicted in Figure 8-17, uses simulation to evaluate wants and associated goals, assets, and investment allocations.

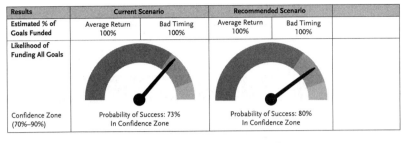

Results	Current Scenario		Recommended Scenario		
Estimated % of Goals Funded	Average Return 100%	Bad Timing 100%	Average Return 100%	Bad Timing 100%	
Likelihood of Funding All Goals					
Confidence Zone (70%–90%)	Probability of Success: 73% In Confidence Zone		Probability of Success: 80% In Confidence Zone		

	Current Scenario	What If Scenario 2	Changes in Value
Retirement			
Nick	65 in 2021	66 in 2022	1 year later
Martha	65 in 2021	66 in 2022	1 year later
Goals			
Total Spending for Life of Plan	$3,615,000	$3,495,000	Decreased 3%

Recommended Scenario – Likelihood of Reaching Goals		
Needs Only	Needs and Wants Only	Needs, Wants, and Wishes
Probability of Success: 81% In Confidence Zone	Probability of Success: 78% In Confidence Zone	Probability of Success: 77% In Confidence Zone

Figure 8-16 MoneyGuidePro example of financial plan

The confidence level is 83 percent if a goal is met or exceeded in 83 percent of simulations, implying a shortfall probability no higher than 17 percent. Wealthcare considers a plan in the "Confidence Zone" if its confidence level is higher than 75 percent but lower than 90 percent. A plan with a higher than 90 percent confidence level is deemed overfunded, implying that investors sacrifice opportunities for higher goals or lower risk, whereas a plan with lower than 75 percent confidence level is deemed underfunded, calling for adjustments.

Russ Thornton, a financial adviser using Wealthcare's program, described meeting two of his clients in June 2009, not long after the stock market hit bottom. The clients were hard-working, middle-class people in their late 50s with two adult children and three grandchildren. The husband was a former policeman now working in the private sector and his wife was an executive assistant. They earned good incomes, lived within their means, and saved a lot. Thornton guided the couple as they balanced their wants and associated ideal and acceptable goals.

How does STRESS TESTING work?

Central to the Wealthcare system is the COMFORT ZONE® Confidence Calculation

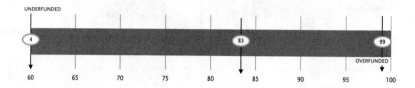

> This analysis simultaneously evaluates your goals, your investment allocation, and your assets to determine how confident you can be that your goals will be exceeded.
> The Wealthcare system subjects your goals and investment strategy to this sophisticated "stress testing" process, which simulates *1000* market environments, both good and bad. Your Confidence or Comfort is the percentage of the 1000 that exceed your goals.
> For example, if you exceeded your goals in 830 *of 1000* tests your confidence is 83%.

Example Recommendation

	IDEAL	RECOMMENDED	ACCEPTABLE
Retirement Age	58	62 - Tom	65
	58	62 - Katie	65
Retirement Income	$175,000	$175,000	$160,000
Risk Tolerance	NO RISK	−7% Annual Downside	−15% Annual Downside
Estate	$2,000,000	$500,000	$100,000
Education	MBA	MBA	Undergrad
Savings	−$15,000	$10,000	+$10,000
Jamaica Trips	$25,000	$25,000	$10,000
Comfort Level	4%	83%	99%

Figure 8-17 Example of Wealthcare stress test and financial plan

Updating their information in preparation for the June 2009 meeting, Thornton discovered that through disciplined savings they were now able to satisfy all of their wants and associated goals at their ideal levels. It was time to think of new wants and associated goals. Thornton drew an annual travel budget that would satisfy his clients' wants for an annual family vacation paid by the clients. Next, the wife confided that she would love to retire one or even two years earlier so she could spend more time with her mother while they were both still in good health.

Reviewing the clients' new wants and ideal goals relative to their financial resources, Thornton found that they could not satisfy every want and associated goal, but they were able to plan for the wife to retire a couple of years earlier than previously planned, something they wanted as their highest-priority goal. They were also able to satisfy their wants for lower investment risk and partially satisfy their want for an annual family vacation.[46]

Brunel Associates

Jean Brunel, a financial adviser to very wealthy families and author of *Goals-Based Wealth Management*, employs a method he calls "forward sequencing."[47] The first sequence focuses on wants and associated goals, ranking them as "needs," "wants," "wishes," and "dreams." People are not likely to distinguish an 80 percent probability of reaching a goal from a 90 percent probability, but they are likely to distinguish something they need from something they merely want, and something they wish they had from something they dream they will have. Advisers eliciting this information are better able than clients to attach probabilities to needs, wants, wishes, and dreams. A client might say, "I should be able to satisfy all my needs, most of my wants, and a few of my wishes. I am sure to die with some unsatisfied dreams, as dying with all dreams satisfied implies not dreaming big enough."

Some circumstances are to be avoided. Brunel's sequence for these circumstances includes "nightmares," "fears," "worries," and "concerns." A client might say, "I am pretty sure I can avoid most nightmares, many of my fears, and a few of my worries. Dying without concerns, however, implies I wasn't concerned about the nightmares, fears, and worries of my family, friends, and the wider community."

The process of sequencing goals to reach and circumstances to avoid transforms advisers from experts at investment management or estate planning to competent and caring professionals, good at eliciting clients' wants and associated goals and helping clients satisfy them. Brunel employs three series of decisions—two general and one customized. The general decisions are about market forecasts and management of portfolios. The customized decision is about the portfolio tailored to fit a specific client's wants and associated goals, target dates, cash flow patterns, and probabilities of surplus and shortfall.

A financial plan for a family with $50 million of total wealth illustrates Brunel's process. The family maintains its lifestyle with $1,000,000 of spending each year, and agrees that annual inflation would average 3 percent in the foreseeable future, except that it would be only be 2 percent during the coming five years.

The family wants a 95 percent probability of meeting its annual lifestyle spending during the coming five years, implying no higher than a 5 percent probability of shortfall. It wants an 80 percent probability of meeting its annual lifestyle spending during the 25 years after that, corresponding to the couple's life expectancy, as they are both 55 years old. Upon further discussion, the family notes that $10 million of their wealth is set aside in grantor trusts for their four children. They also indicate that they have $5 million in recently set generation-skipping trusts. The family would like to set up a family foundation in 10 years, and have set $10 million as the initial size. They also indicated that they want to keep $3 million in cash or near cash, as what they call "pillow money," even if it makes little financial sense.

The family prefers to invest any surplus assets in an equal mix of growth and capital preservation—earmarked for distribution to future generations and to charity in proportions yet to be specified. Finally, $10 million of the family's total assets are in retirement accounts that cannot be tapped for expenses for at least 15 to 20 years.

Brunel creates a "family of goals-based accounts," ranging in risk and expected returns. The pillow money account consists of cash and near cash. The grantor trusts accounts consist of growth investments, and so on. The portfolio as a whole is the sum of these accounts. The accounts and the portfolio as a whole are assessed periodically, adjusted for changes in market values and changes in family wants and associated goals.

Mutual Fund Companies

Financial services companies, such as Schwab, Vanguard, and Fidelity, offer model portfolios. They, like MoneyGuidePro, Wealthcare, and Brunel Associates, rely on perceptions of investor wants as they advise investors and construct their portfolios. Wants for familiarity and convention, reflected in home bias, are one example. The total market value—market capitalization—of all US stocks typically amounts to approximately half of the total market value of all stocks in the world, leaving the other half to international stocks.[48] Investors whose wants do not include familiarity and convention might allocate to international stocks half of the allocation to all stocks. Yet model portfolios of financial services companies typically allocate to international stocks only one-quarter of the allocation to all stocks. Similarly, mutual fund companies satisfy wants for social responsibility by offering socially responsible funds, and satisfy wants for high social status by offering hedge funds and other "alternative" funds.

Model portfolios by financial services companies are remarkably similar. For example, the "moderately conservative" model portfolio by Schwab allocates 40 percent to stocks and 60 percent to bonds and cash, equal to the allocations in the "balanced" Vanguard portfolio. The Fidelity "balanced" portfolio is not much different, 50 percent to stocks and 50 percent to bonds and cash. The proportion allocated to international stocks among all stocks is 25 percent, similar to the proportion in Fidelity portfolios.

Consider the Schwab "moderate" portfolio consisting of a total of 60 percent in stocks and 40 percent in bonds and cash, presented in Table 8-4. Among stocks, 15 percent is allocated to international stocks, 35 percent to large-capitalization stocks, and 10 percent to small-capitalization stocks. The expected return of the Schwab moderate portfolio is 10.34 percent. This is based on mean-variance parameters estimates from annual returns during the 40 years between 1972 and 2011, but general conclusions would not differ if other estimates are used. The standard deviation of the portfolio is 11.73 percent. The optimized mean-variance portfolio analogous to the Schwab moderate portfolio is the portfolio with the highest expected return and a standard deviation that does not exceed 11.73 percent. The expected return of this optimized mean-variance portfolio is 11.00 percent, not much higher than the 10.34 percent expected return of the Schwab moderate portfolio, but the allocations in the optimized portfolio are very different.

Differences are especially striking as we note that allocations in the optimized portfolio are already constrained to exclude short positions.

Table 8-4 SCHWAB MODEL PORTFOLIO AND OPTIMIZED MEAN-VARIANCE PORTFOLIO

	Moderate Portfolio		
	Schwab Portfolio	Optimized Mean-Variance Portfolio	Difference
Large-Capitalization Stocks	35%	0%	35%
Small-Capitalization Stocks	10%	40%	−30%
International Stocks	15%	5%	10%
Bonds	35%	55%	−20%
Cash	5%	0%	5%
Total	100%	100%	
Expected Annual Return of the Portfolio	10.34%	11.00%	−0.66%
Standard Deviation of the Annual Return of the Portfolio	11.73	11.73	0.00

Optimized mean-variance portfolios are calculated by using annual returns during 1972–2011. Large-capitalization stocks are represented by the S&P 500 Index. Small-capitalization stocks are represented by the CRSP 6-10 Index. International stocks are represented by the MSCI EAFE Index. Bonds are represented by five-year US Treasury notes during the period 1972–1975 and the Barclays Capital US Aggregate Bond Index during the period 1976–2011. Cash is represented by one-month US Treasury bills.

For example, the allocation to large-capitalization stocks in the optimized portfolio is zero, whereas in the Schwab moderate portfolio it is 35 percent. The allocation to small-capitalization stocks in the optimized portfolio is 40 percent, whereas in the Schwab moderate portfolios it is 10 percent. Evidently, allocations in model portfolios are chosen because they are more palatable to investors, satisfying their wants.

STRATEGIC AND TACTICAL ASSET ALLOCATION

Asset allocation is strategic in portfolios prescribed by MoneyGuide Pro, Wealthcare, Brunel Associates, mutual funds, and most financial advisers. *Strategic asset allocation* consists of allocations to asset classes that fit investors best, such as 60 percent to stocks, 30 percent to bonds, and 10 percent to cash. Strategic asset allocation may change over time as people's circumstances change, such as by marriage, children, aging, or retirement.

Tactical asset allocation consists of temporary shifts of asset allocations away from strategic allocations, such as increasing to 70 percent the allocation to stocks and decreasing to 20 percent the allocation to bonds. It is an attempt to increase portfolio returns beyond the returns of strategic asset allocation by identifying and exploiting temporary divergences of asset-class prices from their values.

Security selection consists of selection of particular securities from all securities in an asset class. It is an attempt to increase portfolio returns beyond the returns of strategic asset allocation by identifying and selecting securities that promise higher returns than others in their asset class, such as selecting shares of General Motors and deleting shares of Ford.

Money manager Gary Brinson and his coauthors studied the performance of 91 large US pension plans and found that variation in strategic asset allocation explains on average 93.6 percent of variation in the total returns of portfolios. The remainder of variation in total returns is explained by variation in tactical asset allocation and security selection.[49]

This finding is commonly interpreted as evidence that strategic asset allocation is more important than tactical asset allocation or security selection. This interpretation is misleading, however, because explaining *variation* of returns is different from explaining *magnitude* of returns and their signs, positive or negative. The percentage that tells us about magnitude of returns is negative 1.1 percentage points. Brinson and his coauthors found that tactical asset allocation and security selection *detracted* 1.1 percentage points on average from portfolio returns that would have been obtained with strategic asset allocation alone.

Strategic asset allocation is important, and so can potentially be tactical asset allocation and security selection, but they are important in different ways. Tailoring good strategic asset allocation is like tailoring a well-fitting suit. Weaving good tactical asset allocation and security selection is like weaving the suit's fabric at high quality and low cost. Both are important but in different ways. High-quality fabric woven at low cost provides little comfort when it drapes a size 40 body in a size 46 suit.

Strategic asset allocation is part of *management of investors*, focusing on the examination of wants, associated goals, and financial resources, followed by diagnosis of deficiencies, and completed by guidance to avoid cognitive and emotional errors on the way to wants and associated goals. Tactical asset allocation and security selection, however, are parts of *management of investments*, focusing on increasing returns without increasing risk. Strategic allocation involves movements *on* the frontier, such as from portfolio A to portfolio B on frontier 1 in Figure 8-18, whereas tactical asset allocation and security selection involve movements *of* the frontier, such as from portfolio A on frontier 1 to portfolio C on the higher frontier 2.[50] Investors engaging in tactical asset allocation and security selection aim to move the frontier higher, but all too often they move it lower.

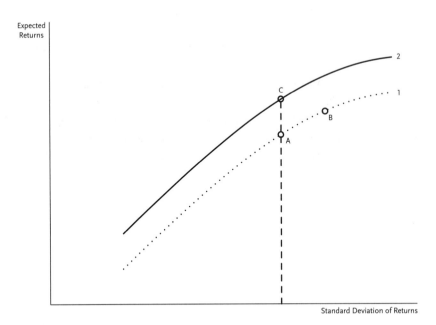

Figure 8-18 Strategic asset allocation, tactical asset allocation, and security selection— Movements *on* the frontier, such as from portfolio A to portfolio B on frontier 1, and movements *of* the frontier, such as from portfolio A on frontier 1 to portfolio C on the higher frontier 2

CONCLUSION

Mean-variance portfolio theory prescribes portfolios on *mean-variance frontiers* to investors whose wants extend no further than the utilitarian benefits of high expected returns and low risk, measured by the variance of portfolio returns or their standard deviation.

Behavioral portfolio theory prescribes portfolios on *behavioral-wants frontiers* to investors whose wants extend beyond utilitarian benefits, yet avoid cognitive and emotional errors. Examples of portfolios on the behavioral-wants frontier include those that provide the expressive and emotional benefits of promoting social responsibility, exhibiting patriotism, enjoying pride, and avoiding regret.

A central feature in behavioral portfolio theory rests on the observation that investors view their portfolios as sets of distinct mental-account layers in a portfolio pyramid. Each mental account corresponds to a particular want, associated goal, and their utilitarian, expressive, and emotional benefits. An optimal behavioral-wants portfolio is one that balances wants while avoiding cognitive and emotional errors.

In practice, frontiers and chosen portfolios, whether mean-variance frontier or behavioral-wants frontiers, do not come solely from estimates of parameters placed in an optimizer. Frontiers are clarifying concepts more than formulaic applications; they clarify trade-offs between expected returns and risk, whether measured as standard deviation as in mean-variance portfolio theory, or as shortfall from target wealth, as in behavioral portfolio theory. And they clarify trade-offs between wants, whether for social responsibility or social status. We should not be fooled by the elegance and apparent precision of the mean-variance optimizer. Application of mean-variance theory is much less formulaic than commonly perceived and much more attuned to investors' wants, described in behavioral portfolio theory.

CHAPTER 9

Behavioral Life Cycle of Saving and Spending

Portfolio theory is about the *production* of portfolios by combining investments such as stocks and bonds. Life-cycle theory, complementing portfolio theory, is about *accumulation* of assets into portfolios—converting cash into investments—and *decumulation* from them—converting investments into cash. We accumulate mostly by saving during the working years of our life cycle and decumulate by spending during our nonworking years such as when at school and in retirement.

Standard life-cycle theory is the theory of standard finance, and behavioral life-cycle theory is the theory of behavioral finance. Economists Franco Modigliani and Richard Brumberg described standard life-cycle theory in 1954[1] and Milton Friedman offered a similar "permanent income hypothesis" in 1957.[2] Hersh Shefrin and Richard Thaler laid the foundation of behavioral life-cycle theory in 1988.[3]

Standard life-cycle theory says that our sole reason for saving is spending. The ideal outcome is a simultaneous last breath of life and last dollar of spending. We want "smoothed" spending during our life cycle. More precisely, we want smoothed marginal utility of consumption and leisure during our life cycle.

We begin by estimating explicitly or implicitly our life-cycle wealth—the present value of our current income, current capital, and future income. We follow this value by choosing a saving and spending path for smoothed spending during all the years of our life cycle. The theory predicts that we spend "permanent income" each year, an amount that exhausts our life-cycle wealth during our life cycle, even as our current income, current capital, and future income fluctuate from year to year.

Behavioral life-cycle theory says that our reasons for saving consist of wants for the full range of utilitarian, expressive, and emotional benefits of wealth. These benefits come from spending on necessities such as food and shelter, discretionary items such as recreation and travel, and luxuries such as expensive cars and jewelry. It says, moreover, that mere wealth *owning*, rather than spending, also yields expressive and emotional benefits. Indeed, some spending might induce expressive and emotional costs. Think about a person who paid $100 for dinner and leaves with regret and a sense that he had been played for a fool, because he could have made a better meal at home for a fraction of that price.

A segment of the television program *60 Minutes* featured Leona and Harry Helmsley, owners of the Helmsley Palace Hotel and 200 other New York buildings. Leona described the expressive and emotional benefits they derive from their wealth as they stand on a hotel balcony overlooking New York's Central Park. Harry points at buildings and says, "I'm taking inventory. I own this, I own this, and that one, and that one."[4]

The Helmsleys displayed what has come to be called the "consumption gap" because they could have sold their buildings and spent the proceeds. Yet they never had any intention of selling their buildings and closing their consumption gap. Instead, they derived expressive and emotional benefits from mere ownership.

What is true for the Helmsleys and fellow billionaires is also true for many people of more modest means. Indeed, consumption gaps are evident even among people with median financial assets.[5] This attitude is puzzling within standard life-cycle theory. Michael Kitces, a financial adviser and commentator, noted in a blog, "In [standard life-cycle] theory, the whole point of saving and investing for retirement is that upon reaching retirement, it's time to spend down the money and enjoy it. In practice, a growing base of research finds that for most of their retirement, retirees are just continuing the growth of their pre-retirement portfolios, suggesting a 'consumption gap' between what retirees could and should spend versus what they actually do."[6]

Kitces offered his solution to the puzzle: "Accumulating continued growth throughout the early years of retirement is actually the normal, prudent course of action for anyone who anticipates living a long time, fears the potential impact of future inflation, and therefore recognizes the need for the retirement portfolio to grow in the early years to defend against the uncertainties of a long retirement future." This solution surely does not apply to the Helmsleys. Indeed, it does not apply to many of the people Kitces describes, retirees whose pre-retirement portfolios continue to grow. One retiree wrote thus in response to Kitces's blog:

I always find it fascinating the way the financial business approaches these incredibly human topics with charts and 2nd grade math. I mean really, think about the concept of spending your last dollar on the day you die. Utterly ridiculous . . .

I save aggressively, and enjoy watching my wealth accumulate . . . I enjoy even more the power it gives me to assist (where necessary) the lives of my loved ones or the social issues that move me. These pleasures trump the joy that can be derived from merely spending, and they are pleasures that are worth saving for . . .

I bought in early to the idea of saving for a "retirement of consumption," perhaps without really thinking much about it. Along the way, while saving for that mirage, I became frugal. Changing now would be traumatic for me.

It's not that I don't enjoy a steak dinner with wine. . . . It's just that I can make myself one with premium organic ingredients, for much less than the $100 Ruth's Chris [steakhouse] version. . . . My point here is that I deny myself nothing . . . but my average daily food costs are probably shockingly low compared to what I "should" spend on food. . . .

This man and similar retirees likely have high Personal Saving Orientation (PSO), an indicator of people's consistent and sustainable saving activities, reflecting personal habits that are incorporated into their lifestyle. Personal Saving Orientation is measured by answers to questions about day-to-day actions and saving lifestyles.

Day-to-day actions consistent with high PSO are indicated in agreement with statements such as "putting money into personal savings is a habit for me," "I keep a careful watch over my spending on a daily basis," and "I do not spend money thoughtlessly. I would rather save it for a rainy day."

Saving styles consistent with high PSO are indicated in agreement with statements such as "I usually save money without having a specific goal in mind," "Saving money on a regular basis should be an important part of one's life," and "Saving money is like a lifestyle, you have to keep at it."[7]

Still, not all people accumulate median wealth. And even those of us who want to match spending to "permanent income" find it difficult because we find it difficult to estimate our life-cycle wealth, longevity, and future spending needs, such as for medical expenses. These factors leave us exposed to running out of money before running out of life or running out of life before running out of money. We must muster self-control if we are to accumulate sufficient but not excessive retirement savings during our working years, and we must muster it again if we are to refrain from spending our savings too fast or too slowly during our working years and in retirement.

Behavioral life-cycle theory says that we reconcile conflicts between our wants for spending and saving by framing, mental accounting, and self-control rules. Whereas standard life-cycle theory predicts that we regard current income, current capital, and future income as mere components of life-cycle wealth, behavioral life-cycle theory predicts that we regard them as distinct. Current income includes current wages, current interest, and dividends from bonds and stocks, among other investments. Current capital includes the current value of our portfolio of bonds, stocks, and other investments, and the present value of future income that includes future wages, future interest and dividends, and future income from other investments.

We frame current income, current capital, and future income into separate mental accounts and set self-control rules that restrict dips into other than designated mental accounts. This framing includes, for example, restrictions against dipping into our children's education mental account for today's vacation spending. Standard life-cycle theory, in contrast, says

---

Box 9-1 STANDARD AND BEHAVIORAL LIFE-CYCLE THEORIES

Standard Life-Cycle Theory	Behavioral Life-Cycle Theory
1. People want to "smooth" spending during their entire life cycle, and resolve easily conflicts between wants for spending and wants for saving.	1. People want more than to "smooth" spending during their entire life cycle. They want the full range of utilitarian, expressive, and emotional benefits of wealth, including the expressive and emotional benefits of owning wealth without spending it. Moreover, even people who want to "smooth" spending during their entire life cycle find it difficult to resolve conflicts between wants for spending and wants for saving.
2. People need no tools and no help in resolving conflicts between wants.	2. People reconcile the conflict between wants by devices such as framing, mental accounting, and self-control rules that restrict dips into other than designated mental accounts. Public policy helps reconcile conflicts between wants with programs such as Social Security, and it helps overcome cognitive and emotional errors by laws and regulations such as fiduciary regulations.

that we have no use for framing, mental accounting, or self-control rules for resolving conflicts between wants for savings for tomorrow and spending it all today.

THE SPENDING-SOURCES AND SPENDING-USES PYRAMIDS

Behavioral life-cycle theory includes "spending-sources" and "spending-uses" pyramids, depicted in Figure 9-1a and Figure 9-1b. They are similar to the portfolio pyramids described in Chapter 8, "Behavioral Portfolios." The layers of spending-sources pyramids are arranged from those tapped first to those tapped last. The layers of spending-uses pyramids are arranged from those with higher spending priority to those with lower priority.

The bottom layer of the spending-sources pyramid consists of a broad category of "income," including employment income, dividends and interest, Social Security benefits, and payments from defined-benefit pension plans. Above it is a layer of "dips into regular capital," consisting of proceeds from the sale of stocks and bonds, among other investments, including those in 401(k), individual retirement account (IRA), and other defined-contribution retirement saving accounts. Above them is a layer of "dips into bequest capital," consisting of proceeds from the sale of investments intended as bequests. Houses are the most common form of bequest capital. Above them is a layer of support from family, friends, government agencies, and charities, for those who have little or nothing in the lower layers of the pyramid.

The bottom layer of spending-uses pyramids consists of spending on necessities, such as food, shelter, and support of minor children. For some, the layer also includes support of needy adult children, elderly parents, and disabled siblings. For others, these spending uses belong in the higher discretionary layer that also includes recreation, travel, gifts to grandchildren, and minor charitable contributions. For some, savings belong in the bottom layer of necessities, whereas for others savings belong in the higher discretionary layer. Above these layers is a layer of luxury and status goods, such as expensive cars, jewelry, major charitable contributions, and bequests.

Evidence is consistent with a reluctance to dip into bequest capital. Housing equity is the principal asset of a large fraction of older Americans, second only to Social Security and, for some, employer-provided pensions. Yet, on average, homes are not sold to support non-housing consumption as people age.[8] Moreover, homeowners are reluctant to enter into reverse-mortgage contracts that pay homeowners while they continue to live in

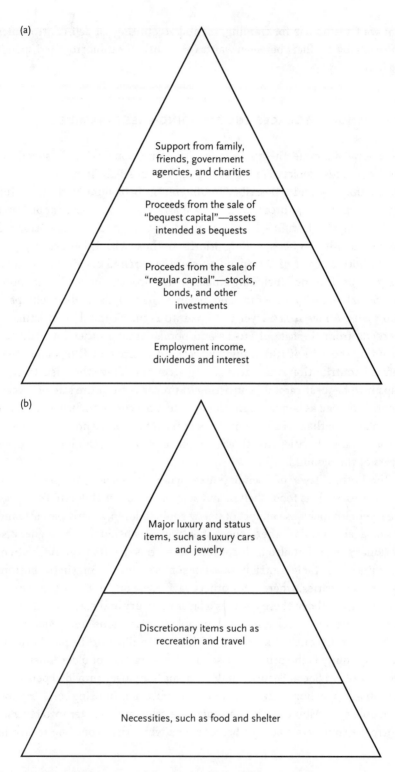

Figure 9-1 Spending-sources and spending-uses pyramids

their homes. Only 2 percent of homeowners eligible for reverse-mortgage contracts enter into them.[9]

Evidence is also consistent with a reluctance to dip into regular capital. In a study, people barely touched their 401(k), IRA, and other defined-contribution retirement accounts in their early retirement years, let alone depleted these accounts. Among people ages 60 to 69, only 7 percent of people with defined-contribution retirement accounts took annual distributions exceeding 10 percent of their balances, and only 18 percent made any withdrawals in a typical year. Moreover, withdrawal rates were low between the actual time of people's retirement and age 70½, when required minimum distributions from defined-contribution retirement accounts must begin. Proportions of assets withdrawn from defined-contribution retirement accounts remained small even after age 70½. The proportion withdrawn averages 1 percent to 2 percent between ages 60 and 69, rising to about 5 percent at age 70½, fluctuating around that level through age 85. Indeed, balances in defined-contribution retirement accounts continue to grow among people older than 70½ who are still employed.[10]

Discussions about spending sources and uses commonly assume, implicitly or explicitly, that parents offer no material support to adult children, and children offer no material support to elderly parents. Analyses accompanying such discussions proceed to calculate sustainable spending of individuals or couples who support only themselves. Yet this assumption is unfounded—witness the term "sandwich generation," describing parents supporting both their children and their elderly parents. Having elderly dependents decreases the probability of college savings and stockholdings by twice as much as poor personal health.[11]

Average transfers from older family members to the younger generation are large enough to be considered major spending items. Parents, at least one of whom was between the ages of 50 and 64, transferred to children an annual average $8,350. The corresponding average was $4,787 when at least one parent was 85 or older. Cash transfers from younger family members to older ones are smaller, but cash transfers understate total material support the young provide to the old, because much of that support is in kind, such as in caring for elderly parents who remain in their own homes or move into their children's homes.[12]

Underestimation of material support from young to old is evident in the Supplemental Security Income program. The program provides guaranteed income for the elderly, yet participation among qualified people is just over 50 percent. Transfers from children are far larger among eligible nonparticipants than indicated by the 50 percent figure, suggesting that family assistance may offset the need for public assistance.[13]

Nearly six in ten low-income families received help from family or friends, including help in finding a job, paying bills, and providing food, shelter, and child care. The poor are also aided by charitable organizations in job searches, education, skill development, literacy, housing assistance, emergency cash, temporary food assistance, and health care.[14]

Children provide greater support to parents in collectivistic countries such as China than in individualistic countries such as the United States. Parents in collectivistic countries expect that support. Matchmaking Chinese parents distort the choice of the spouses of their children because they are willing to substitute love between the couple for money that can support parents. Parent matchmaking is associated with lower marital harmony between the couple, more submissive wives, and a stronger belief that sons should support parents in old age.[15]

Poor families, like wealthy ones, crave a social identity reflecting financial responsibility and self-sufficiency. Families are reluctant to ask for assistance when they are faced with economic hardship because asking undermines this identity. Debt payments are less acute than rent or grocery payments and, therefore, receive lower priority in monthly budgets. Poor families prioritize payments of particular debts that affirm self-sufficient or upwardly mobile identities, but they reject or ignore debts they view as unfair or unjust. These coping strategies regularly trap poor families in costly cycles of indebtedness and hinder social mobility.[16]

Some spending is motivated by wants for social status, as less affluent families attempt to "keep up with the Joneses." Middle- and upper-middle income families take on more housing-related debt and have higher debt-to-income ratios in places where top incomes are high.[17] Competition for social status is dampened, however, when friends and neighbors reduce their status-motivated spending. Consumption of luxuries, such as jewelry and travel, declined in recessions not only among people with diminished incomes and wealth but also among those with intact incomes and wealth.[18] Neighbors of people experiencing bankruptcy reduced their spending at a rate equivalent to a 7 percent decline in monthly income.[19]

SELF-CONTROL

Self-control is rarely easy to muster, and some fail to muster it at all.[20] Wants for spending it all today overwhelm wants for saving for tomorrow when self-control is weak. National Football League (NFL) players enjoy very large income spikes that amount to substantial life-cycle wealth even if lasting only a few years. That wealth can provide substantial smoothed life-cycle spending, but wants for spending it all today overwhelm wants for saving for tomorrow. Bankruptcy filings of NFL players begin soon after the end of their careers and continue at substantial rates through at least the following 12 years. Moreover, having played for a long time and been well-paid does not provide much protection against bankruptcy. Bankruptcy rates are not affected by players' total earnings or career length.[21]

People hampered by weak self-control and associated lack of planning skills suffer financial distress. Moreover, differences in self-control affect the incidence of financial distress more than differences in education or financial literacy.[22] Wants for spending on luxury goods join weak self-control in undermining savings and increasing financial distress. Defaults are common among people who spent large portions of their incomes on luxuries.[23]

We are better at identifying deficient self-control in others than in ourselves. A classroom survey reveals that students believe that they would turn in assignments earlier than classmates. In a laboratory experiment, people were asked to predict their own future behavior and the average behavior of others. People displayed virtually no awareness of their own self-control deficiencies, but anticipated self-control deficiencies in others.[24]

Poverty undermines self-control, breeding scarcity and narrowing slack. Scarcity and narrow slack overload people's cognitive and emotional resources and hamper savings, job performance, and decision-making. Poverty is regularly exploited. The most profitable American credit card consumers are those on the verge of bankruptcy.[25]

People who exhaust their credit card limits, indicating narrow slack, do not reduce their demand for credit even when interest rates are increased by as much as 3 percentage points.[26] People residing in low-income zip codes refinanced mortgages and increased spending substantially when home prices rose before the 2008 financial crisis, while people in high-income zip codes did not.[27] Subprime lenders advertised expensive mortgages, misleading borrowers into inferior mortgage choices. Indeed, advertising was most effective when targeted at the uninformed, who tend to be less educated, members of minorities, and poor.[28]

Financial products are more complex now than in the past. This complexity is especially evident in structured products, such as indexed annuities, offered to individual investors. Complexity confuses investors, misleading them into products that benefit providers at their expense. Indeed, the complexity of financial products offered to uninformed investors is especially high.[29]

Some people are savers by nature, having high PSO and likely to reach financial security and wealth beyond it, while others are not. Conscientiousness is the Big Five personality trait most closely associated with self-control and is high among people adequately prepared for retirement, while neuroticism, another Big Five personality trait, is low. Both spending and wealth increase with conscientiousness, but wealth increases faster, indicating that more conscientious people save more.[30]

Self-control can be bolstered by commitment. Clients of a Philippine bank in one experiment were randomly assigned to one of three groups. The first received an offer to open a commitment account accessible only to them and unavailable until a pre-specified goal was reached. The offer included the option to keep a locked box into which cash could be deposited but whose only key is kept by the bank. The second group received one-on-one education about the importance of saving for a goal, and the third was the control group.

Clients who accepted commitment accounts increased their savings by 81 percent during the following year, relative to a control group. Moreover, clients with self-control difficulties were the ones most likely to prefer commitment accounts. A follow-up survey and bank data show continuing saving behavior two and a half years later, especially among women who had relatively little decision-making power before they had the commitment accounts, and a shift toward female-oriented durable goods purchased in the household.[31]

Conscientiousness and self-control can be excessive, however, as when they direct people to borrow at high interest rates while maintaining savings accounts earning low interest. People are likely to borrow at high interest rates in emergencies rather than dip into their savings when they believe that spending savings is what irresponsible people do.[32]

We see the conflict between wants for spending and saving in romantic relations and marriage. Tightwads are hampered by excessive self-control. They spend less than they would ideally like. Spendthrifts are hampered by insufficient self-control. They spend more than they would ideally like. Tightwads often marry spendthrifts, a rare instance where opposites attract.[33] Yet marriages of opposites tend to be unstable, as different habits of spending and saving cause friction.[34] Couples in stable marriages have similar credit scores, indicating similar wants for spending and saving.[35]

Spenders are preferred to savers in romantic settings if they are perceived as possessing ample financial resources. Yet savers are preferred if spending is perceived as depleting financial resources. An experiment demonstrated that people distinguish savers from spenders by a mere glance, without communication. Additional experiments showed that savers are perceived as possessing greater self-control, increasing their romantic appeal. The romantic appeal of savers is enhanced further by the perception of physical attractiveness because savers are expected to take better care of their bodies. Still, not everything favors savers, because self-control stands in the way of fun.[36]

The 2015 swearing-in of Justin Trudeau as Canada's prime minister was attended by his mother, Margaret Trudeau, and rekindled memories of her life and marriage to Pierre Trudeau, Justin's father and the most famous former Canadian prime minister. An article in the *New York Times* noted that while Pierre Trudeau "was wealthy thanks to his father's success in the gas station business, Mrs. Trudeau soon discovered that her husband was an exceptional tightwad." They had three children before their marriage crumbled. "Partying with the Rolling Stones, watching the scene at Studio 54 with Andy Warhol and being tutored in photography by Richard Avedon made Mrs. Trudeau . . . global tabloid fodder," beyond spending.[37]

EVIDENCE ABOUT STANDARD AND BEHAVIORAL LIFE-CYCLE THEORIES

The most compelling evidence in favor of behavior life-cycle theory might well be the vast financial advising industry helping people plan and implement spending and saving throughout their life cycles. Government saving and spending plans such as Social Security and corporate saving and spending plans such as defined-benefit pension plans and defined-contribution retirement saving plans are further evidence favoring behavioral life-cycle theory. There is no need for such industry and such plans in the world of standard life-cycle theory where people do the planning and implementation easily on their own. Other evidence involves distinctions between capital and income, manifestations of cognitive and emotional shortcuts and errors, and differences between financial liquidity and mental liquidity.

Capital and Income

A question separating standard life-cycle theory from behavioral life-cycle theory asks whether we distinguish capital from income as we make spending choices. Standard life-cycle theory predicts that we do not, because dollars of capital are indistinguishable from dollars of income in the total of our life-cycle wealth. Behavioral life-cycle theory predicts, however, that we do make the distinction, ready to spend income but reluctant to dip into capital and spend its proceeds.[38]

Evidence is consistent with behavioral life-cycle theory. American investors are more likely to spend dividends than sell shares and spend their proceeds.[39] And Finnish investors spend almost all dividends but rarely dip into capital.[40] Indeed, some investors even distinguish their capital contributions, such as the prices they paid for shares of stock, from capital gains accrued to those shares over time. Such investors find it easier to spend capital gains than capital contributions.

Two related behavioral life-cycle hypotheses predict that older people prefer stocks with high dividend yields more than younger people and that people with lower labor income prefer stocks with higher dividend yields more than people with higher labor income. This trend exists because older people and those with lower labor income are more likely to rely on their portfolios for spending. The two hypotheses are supported by a study of more than 60,000 families, indicating that older investors with lower labor income hold stocks with higher dividend yields than younger investors with higher labor income.[41] Moreover, older investors with lower labor income dip into capital opaquely such as by buying stocks before ex-dividend days, so as to collect dividends for their mental income accounts.

Managed payout mutual funds offer a controlled and transparent way to dip into capital and convert it to income. Investors in such funds receive periodic payments of pre-specified percentages, such as 4 percent, of the balances in their accounts. These payments combine interest and dividends with transparent dips into capital gains and possibly original capital contributions.

"Dividend capture" funds are different, however, in doing their dips opaquely, buying stocks before ex-dividend days and selling them afterward. One such fund, Alpine Accelerating Dividend Fund, writes that it helps investors seeking a "monthly income stream with long-term capital appreciation potential, and above average equity yield potential."[42] The dividend capture strategy does not increase total returns. Indeed, the strategy *reduces* total returns and increases investors' tax burden even as it more than doubles the dividend yield.[43]

Some investors dip into capital by buying high-yield bonds—low-credit-rated bonds also known as junk bonds. Defaults are more common among such bonds than among high-credit-rated bonds, and defaults are, in effect, dips into capital. Seeking greater yields in speculative investments can lead to even greater dips into capital, often disastrous ones. These investments include private loans to young companies like television production firms and shares in bundles of commercial real estate properties. In one case,

Mary Beck and her husband paid $470,000 for part ownership of a fleet of luxury cars. Ms. Beck was persuaded because the investment offered a higher interest rate than alternatives. "We knew that 12 percent wasn't realistic, but 7 percent seemed realistic," Ms. Beck said. "To us, it was a very conservative way to ensure that we'd increase our savings." The venture went bankrupt in 2012. Ms. Beck and her husband have been reconfiguring their retirement and are planning to work longer.[44]

Hindsight, Regret, Financial Liquidity, and Mental Liquidity

Standard life-cycle theory is consistent with investors who convert capital into cash just in time for spending. It is also consistent with considerations of financial liquidity, where financially liquid investments are cashed before illiquid ones. Investments are financially liquid when they can be cashed quickly at prices equal to their current market values. Yet standard life-cycle theory is inconsistent with holdings of substantial amounts of cash for spending needs when considerations of utilitarian benefits direct people to hold stocks and bonds, but not cash. Behavioral life-cycle theory, however, is consistent with such holdings.

No-load stock and bond mutual funds, common in investors' portfolios, possess financial liquidity, since investors can cash them at no cost at the end of each trading day at prices equal to current market values. But even such funds lack "mental liquidity." Investments possess mental liquidity when investors can cash them without exposing themselves to the cognitive errors of hindsight and the emotional costs of regret.

Investors who choose to cash shares of a stock fund today carry responsibility for a choice that might inflict losses if stock prices increase tomorrow. Tomorrow's hindsight would mislead them into thinking that they had known in foresight that stock prices would increase. The utilitarian costs of lost money are accompanied by the emotional costs of regret.

Advice by financial advisers, consistent with behavioral life-cycle theory, is to hold three to five years' worth of spending needs in cash and replenish that cash according to a strict schedule such as at the end of each quarter. The rationale for this advice is similar to the rationale for dollar-cost averaging, described in Chapter 7, "Behavioral Finance Puzzles." A strict schedule of conversion from stocks and bonds to cash reduces responsibility and alleviates potential for regret.[45] Moreover, investors are likely to be acutely aware of the prices of stocks sold yesterday, perceiving losses clearly if stock prices increase today, whereas they are not likely to be as aware of prices of stocks sold three or five years ago, obscuring those losses.

PRESCRIPTIONS OF STANDARD AND BEHAVIORAL LIFE-CYCLE THEORIES

Both standard and behavioral life-cycle theories are *descriptive*. They describe how we arrange our spending and saving during our life-cycles. Behavioral life-cycle theory also offers prescriptions, but standard life-cycle theory does not. This difference is because standard-life cycle theory is built on the premise that people need no prescriptions or other help in arranging their spending and saving during their life cycles. Nevertheless, some prescriptions of behavioral life-cycle theory conform to standard life-cycle theory. The Social Security system is one example.

The Social Security system eliminates the need to estimate life-cycle wealth and calculate smoothed spending for people relying solely on it because contributions from wages are mandatory, made automatically during working years, and smoothed inflation-adjusted monthly payments are made automatically during retirement.

The Social Security system also eliminates the need to estimate longevity among people relying solely on it, because Social Security payments continue for as long as people and their eligible dependents live. And the system makes it unnecessary to exercise self-control, as it reconciles the conflicting wants for spending and saving not only during working years but also in retirement. The system does not allow substitution of lump-sum payments for monthly payments or borrowing from future payments.

Defined-benefit pension plans, prevalent years ago and still available to some today, are another prescription of behavioral life-cycle theory that conforms to standard life-cycle theory. Employers and employees contribute into pension funds during working years and employees and their eligible dependents receive monthly pension payments in retirement. Some defined-benefit pension plans do, however, allow substitution of lump-sum payments for monthly payments and borrowing from future payments, tempting those with insufficient self-control.

The potential consequences of temptations coupled with insufficient self-control are even more severe in defined-contribution retirement saving plans that have by now taken the place of defined-benefit pension plans as the primary tools in bridging the gap between Social Security payments and adequate retirement income. People with defined-contribution retirement savings must manage their spending and saving during their working years and in retirement to mitigate uncertain longevity while facing uncertain inflation and investment returns. This is a difficult challenge for financial experts and more so for ordinary people who may not even be aware of the tasks and challenges they face.

Annuities and the Annuity Puzzle

Purchases of annuities are consistent with standard life-cycle theory. Annuities facilitate smoothing of spending and eliminate longevity risk by converting life-cycle wealth, such as $100,000, into permanent income, such as $500 each month for life. Annuities mitigate longevity risk even if only portions of savings are annuitized at retirement. People with conservative portfolios and no pension or annuity incomes expose themselves to a 67.4 percent probability of running out of money during a 30-year time horizon when their annual inflation-adjusted withdrawal rate is 4.5 percent. The corresponding probability of running out of money is only 18.7 percent when half the portfolio is annuitized.[46] Yet people are reluctant to annuitize, a reluctance we know as the "annuity puzzle."

Behavioral impediments to annuitization include aversion to transparent dips into capital. People dip into their capital account when they buy an annuity, converting capital into income. Money illusion is another behavioral impediment, making a lump sum of $100,000 seem larger than its equivalent as a $500 monthly annuity payment.[47]

Availability errors deter people from annuitizing further because images of outliving life expectancy are not as readily available to people as images of many kinds of death that might befall them soon after they sign an annuity contract, including being run over by a bus as they walk from their insurance broker's office to their parked car.[48] Availability errors interact with regret aversion, as people contemplate the possibility that their heirs would receive only pennies of their annuity dollars when death comes soon after buying an annuity.

Last, and perhaps most important, annuities emit a "smell of death," reminding people that they relinquish hope of riches. Contrary to the prediction of standard life-cycle theory, people's wants include not only downside protection, satisfied by smoothed permanent income, but also upside potential, hoping to see their $100,000 portfolio mushroom somehow into a $10 million portfolio they can spend, bequeath, or merely hoard, enjoying the social status and pride that accompany riches.

Saving and Sustainable Spending

One prescription of behavioral life-cycle theory, consistent with standard life-cycle theory, facilitates estimation of future income from savings balances, even if not converting them into annuities. The Department of Labor proposed regulations requiring providers of defined-contribution retirement saving accounts to send participants periodic estimates of lifetime monthly income corresponding to their account balances. The Department noted that "managing finances in order to provide income for life for oneself and one's spouse is a tremendously difficult but important task. The rule under consideration by the Department would provide participants with information that the Department believes will ease the burden of this task." It goes on to note that "participants may have difficulty envisioning the lifetime monthly income that can be generated from an account balance."[49] A statement would specify, for example, that the current account balance of a person is $125,000 and her projected account balance at retirement is $557,534. This projection corresponds to a monthly payment of $2,788 in retirement when no payments are made to dependents, and specific lower monthly payments if payments are made to dependents.

Income in retirement need not replace full income during working years. An 80 percent replacement ratio is sufficient to maintain one's standard of living, according to the Center for Retirement Research at Boston College. This lower amount is because retired people no longer need to save for retirement or pay work expenses. They are also likely to pay lower taxes and be free of mortgage debt. The Center prescribes that people who begin saving at age 25 should save 12 percent of their income if they plan to retire at age 67. People who begin saving at age 35 should save 18 percent of their income.[50]

Measures of necessary savings before retirement and economic readiness for retirement vary greatly, however, and conclusions vary with them. Moreover, readiness for retirement varies by gender, marital status, and education. Economists Michael Hurd and Susann Rohwedder noted that target retirement-income replacement ratios, such as 80 percent, fail to address a number of issues relevant to economic readiness for retirement.[51]

First, just one-third of full-time workers follow traditional retirement paths characterized by a sharp transition between full-time employment and no employment at all. Late-in-life employment trajectories of the other two-thirds involve continued full-time or part-time employment, unemployment, disability, and "un-retirement" in which retirement is reversed by employment. For them, it is not obvious when to stop measuring income as pre-retirement and when to start measuring it as post-retirement. The situation becomes substantially more complicated when one is assessing retirement readiness of couples with two earners.

Second, and more important, retirement income is commonly measured as Social Security payments plus defined-benefit pension payments. Annuity payments are sometimes added. Yet people can finance consumption out of savings, including defined-contribution retirement savings, and most savings are not annuitized. Financing consumption out of savings is recorded as drawdown of capital rather than as financing from income.

Other issues involve the observation that resources do not have to last indefinitely. Older people in developed countries reduce their spending substantially starting at about age seventy and accelerating afterwards, even when ample financial resources are available. Older people spend less, in large part, because physical limitations make them less able to spend, such as on travel, and because they are less inclined to spend for personal reasons, such as following the death of a spouse.[52]

Hurd and Rohwedder's consumption-based measure of economic readiness incorporates the complexities of modern post-retirement income streams and their consequences. This is a measure of whether a household has, with high probability, the resources to finance a trajectory of spending from shortly following retirement until death, in the case of a single person, or until death of the surviving spouse, in the case of a couple.

One definition of adequate retirement readiness is a 95–100 percent chance of dying with positive wealth after reducing consumption by 10 percent. By that measure, 63.6 percent of single males with less than high-school education are adequately ready, but only 29.0 percent of single females with less than high-school education are equally ready. At the other end, 86.5 percent of married males with college and graduate school education are adequately ready, and so are 90.2 percent of married females with college and graduate school education.

What are good prescriptions for sustainable withdrawal rates from savings balances in retirement? An early prescription derived from simulations of returns and withdrawals during a 30-year period specifies a 4 percent annual withdrawal rate for a 65-year-old couple with a 30-year retirement span.[53] A more recent prescription calls for an initial 2.1 percent annual withdrawal rate if the retirement span extends to 30 years and 1.49 percent if it extends to 40 years.[54]

Required minimum distributions (RMDs) are government-mandated withdrawal rates from defined-contribution retirement savings accounts, starting at age 70½. RMD rates are based on actuarial estimates of life expectancy. The annual RMD rate at age 70½ is 3.65 percent, increasing to 5.35 percent at age 80, 8.77 percent at age 90, and 15.87 percent at age 100.[55]

RMD rules have not been enacted as prescriptions for sustainable withdrawal rates. Instead, they were enacted so tax-deferred retirement savings accounts do not turn into tax shelters of infinite duration. But RMD withdrawal rates can be seen as prescriptions to be applied also to savings not subject to RMD rules. Prescribed withdrawal rates can be supplemented by prescribed tax-efficient sequencing of withdrawals.[56]

The life expectancy of a 70-year-old man is 15.4 years, according to the Social Security calculator.[57] Consider such a man with $500,000 of savings and also $100,000 in home equity and perhaps other assets he hopes to leave as a bequest while keeping the option of drawing from them if circumstances necessitate. These circumstances include living beyond age 86, somewhat longer than his 85.4 life expectancy.

Suppose that he withdraws from his $500,000 each year by the table of RMD, whether any of his savings are actually subject to the RMD rules or not.[58] The RMD table does not fully correspond to life expectancy tables, but it assumes, as sad reality and life expectancy tables do, that life expectancy diminishes with age. The RMD rate is 3.65 percent at age 70, as if life expectancy at this age were 27.4 years rather than 15.4 years.

Assume, conservatively, that the balance of the man's savings grows at a rate no higher than the rate of inflation, so amounts in the following are in inflation-adjusted dollars. He withdraws 3.65 percent of his $500,000 savings balance at age 70, amounting to $18,248. His spending resources, however, very likely exceed that amount because he also very likely collects Social Security benefits, and possibly employment income and pension payments from a defined-benefit pension plan.

He withdraws 3.77 percent of his savings balance the following year, when he is 71, amounting to $18,179, and so on. He withdraws 7.09 percent of his savings balance at age 86, his last year by the life-expectancy table, amounting to $15,695, leaving him a $205,611 savings balance at the end of that year.

The withdrawal amount at age 86 is approximately 14 percent lower than at age 70, hardly a substantial decline. Moreover, he leave a bequest of $305,611, the sum of the $205,611 savings balance and the $100,000 reserve. He can avoid the decline from $18,248 by continuing to withdraw that amount each year through his 86th year, leaving him $189,781 savings balance at the end of that year.

Next, suppose that he is fortunate enough to live beyond age 86. The average life expectancy at age 86 is 5.8 years, to age 92. He wishes to keep his annual withdrawal at $18,248. The man does not exhaust his $500,000 by age 92. Indeed, he does not exhaust it until age 97. Now he begins withdrawing from his $100,000 home equity, perhaps by a reverse mortgage, following the bumper sticker "I'm spending my children's inheritance."

These numbers, good as they are, paint a picture that is still excessively bleak, as the man's savings are likely to grow at a rate exceeding inflation. Moreover, many choose to spend less than RMD rates. This choice is evident in the effect of the 2009 one-time suspension of the RMD rules on withdrawals by members of TIAA, a large financial services company.

Roughly one-third of those subject to the RMD rules suspended withdrawals in 2009.[59]

People might choose to spend more or less than is sustainable by their objective circumstances. Younger people tend to underestimate their life expectancy, while older people tend to overestimate it. For example, 28-year-old males have a 99.4 percent objective probability of surviving beyond five years, but the subjective probability they assign to survival is only 92.8 percent. In contrast, 68-year-old males with a 71.4 percent objective probability of living to 78 assign to survival an exaggerated 82.4 percent probability. These subjective probabilities might incline the young to save too little and the old to spend too little.[60]

Disasters can decrease estimates of life expectancy and increase spending. China's Sichuan province was struck severely by an earthquake in 2008. People closer to the epicenter saved less, spent more lavishly on alcohol and cigarettes, and played majiang, a gambling game, more often.[61]

Financial Literacy, Comprehension, and Behavior

Financial literacy can be a key prescription of behavioral life-cycle theory, but only if it yields financial comprehension and promotes behavior demonstrating financial comprehension. One set of questions measuring financial literacy has been dubbed the "Big Three."[62]

1. Suppose you had $100 in a savings account and the interest rate was 2 percent per year. After 5 years, how much do you think you would have in the account if you left the money to grow: more than $102, exactly $102, or less than $102?
2. Imagine that the interest rate on your savings account was 1 percent per year and inflation was 2 percent per year. After 1 year, would you be able to buy more than, exactly the same as, or less than today with the money in this account?
3. Do you think that the following statement is true or false? "Buying a single company stock usually provides a safer return than a stock mutual fund."

Answers to the Big Three questions indicate that financial literacy is widely lacking. Only half of Americans older than fifty correctly answered the first two questions and only one-third correctly answered all three. Answers of people in some countries were more accurate than those of Americans, but financial literacy is lacking even in rich countries with well-developed financial markets, such as Canada, Germany, Japan, and Australia.[63] Financial literacy is especially lacking among women, minorities, the poor, and those without college degrees.

The Big Three questions are about financial literacy, but financial literacy is different from financial comprehension, and both are different from financial behavior demonstrating comprehension. A debate exists about the effectiveness of financial literacy education in fostering behavior demonstrating financial comprehension.[64] One report assessing many studies concluded that efforts at improving financial literacy do little to improve financial behavior.[65] But another report assessing many studies came to a more positive conclusion about the effectiveness of financial literacy.[66]

A question probing financial comprehension might ask, "Do you think that people who save much when young accumulate more savings in time for retirement than do people who save little?" It is doubtful that many would fail to answer this question correctly even if they fail to answer correctly the first of the Big Three questions, probing literacy about the facts of exponential growth of savings. A person who saves much when young accumulates much in time for retirement whether she is literate about the facts of exponential growth or not. But a person who is literate about the facts of exponential growth still accumulates little in time for retirement if he saves little when young.

Other questions probing financial comprehension include, "Do you think that a person who invests in widely diversified low-cost index mutual funds that aim to match the market is likely to accumulate more money in time for retirement than a person who invests in less diversified and higher-cost active mutual funds that aim to beat the market?" And, "Do you think that a person who buys a handful of stocks and trades them frequently is likely to accumulate more money in time for retirement than a person who buys and holds widely diversified low-cost index mutual funds?"

Probes into financial behavior demonstrating comprehension call for examination of people's savings and investment activities. Do they save regularly? Do they shun high-cost active mutual funds in favor of low-cost index funds? Do they buy and hold low-cost index mutual funds or buy a handful of stocks and trade them frequently?

One piece of evidence pointing to gaps between financial literacy, financial comprehension, and behavior demonstrating financial comprehension is the finding that men in all countries are more financially literate, on average, than women, better at answering the Big Three questions. Yet men, on average, are also more overconfident than women and they trade investments more frequently. Some frequent traders are aware of the utilitarian costs of trading but trade nevertheless because they derive expressive and emotional benefits from trading. Frequent trading among others indicates lack of financial comprehension and financial behavior demonstrating comprehension.[67]

Another piece of evidence pointing in the same direction comes from Personal Saving Orientation, an indicator of consistent and sustainable saving activities. The authors who developed it concluded that "simply teaching factual knowledge about how personal finance works as is done in conventional financial literacy programs may not be enough; it may be necessary to teach people habits that encourage consistent saving and ways to create and maintain a saving-oriented lifestyle."[68]

Employers can improve the financial behavior of their employees even without improving their financial literacy. Employers and employee roles in retirement savings have changed drastically as employers move away from defined-benefit pension plans to defined-contribution retirement saving plans. In 1975, 74 percent of all participants in private sector retirement plans were enrolled in defined-benefit pension plans, but only 6 percent were enrolled in such plans by 2012.[69]

Employees in defined-benefit pension plans do not choose their amounts of savings and do not decide how to invest them. These choices are left to employers. Employees are assured of monthly pension checks throughout their retirement, backed by the Pension Benefit Guaranty Corporation, the government entity that insures private-sector pension plans. In contrast, employees in defined-contribution retirement saving plans choose the amounts of their savings and how to invest them.

The menus of investments offered in defined-contribution retirement saving plans vary greatly from company to company. These menus act as implicit advisers, guiding employees both to good choices or poor ones. "Choice overload" hampers good choices in menus offering too many investment options. A 2004 study of employee participation rates across many defined-contribution retirement saving plans found that an increase of ten funds in a plan was associated with a 1.5 percent to 2 percent decrease in rate of employee participation. Employee participation peaked at 75 percent when only two funds were offered but declined to 60 percent when 59 funds were offered.[70]

A more recent study examined the effects of streamlining a defined-contribution retirement savings plan at a large institution. Streamlining was accomplished by deleting nearly half of the offered funds and arranging the rest in four simplified groups. The study estimated that, on average, employees are likely to gain more than $9,400 during a 20-year period, and reduce their investment risk.[71]

Employees with assets in funds deleted from the menu at that institution were allowed to shift their assets and future contributions to any other fund on the menu. The assets of employees who did not shift their assets out of deleted funds were automatically transferred to age-appropriate target date funds. Alternatively, employees could shift assets in deleted funds into a self-directed brokerage account with access to not only the deleted funds, but also to thousands of other mutual funds. Only 9 percent of employees elected the self-directed brokerage account, taking only 0.4 percent of assets.

Financial advisers can also improve the financial behavior of their client even without improving their financial literacy. Online advisers, sometimes called "Robo advisers," are an innovation in advising, competing or cooperating with live advisers in guiding investors. Financial Engines was an early online adviser, and Betterment, Wealthfront, Personal Capital, and Future Advisor are more recent ones.

"It's a new retirement out there," writes Financial Engines on its website.[72] "We've moved from a world of pension plans to a landscape that includes 401(k)s, IRAs, Social Security, and more. And now you're expected to keep track and manage it all. We'll help you become more informed to better understand your options and make decisions that could mean more for your retirement."

Financial Engines offers advice based on investors' circumstances, their retirement plans, their goals, and their risk preferences. Online Advice, one of Financial Engines' services, provides fund recommendations and personalized forecasts of accumulated savings at retirement, and lets investors explore the impact of different contribution amounts, risk levels, and goals on accumulated savings. Professional Management, another Financial Engines service, lets investors delegate their retirement savings to financial advisers who construct portfolios that protect retirement savings and provide monthly income for life.

"The Betterment portfolio," says the Betterment website, "is designed to achieve optimal returns at every level of risk. Through diversification, automated rebalancing, better behavior, and lower fees, Betterment customers can expect 4.30 percent higher returns than a typical do-it-yourself investor."[73]

The Wealthfront website says, "Set it and forget it—our software manages your investment account for you 24/7, around the clock. We'll do all the work so that you can focus on the other things that really matter to you. . . . We provide investment management at a fraction of the cost of traditional investment managers. . . . We manage your account with taxes in mind because minimizing your taxes is a key part of maximizing your long-term investment returns."[74]

STANDARD AND BEHAVIORAL LIFE-CYCLE THEORIES IN PUBLIC POLICY

Differences between standard and behavioral life-cycle theories have important implications for public policy prescriptions. There is no role for public policy in standard life-cycle theory whereby people free of cognitive and emotional errors estimate their life-cycle wealth, save accordingly, and spend their permanent income. But there is a role for public policy in behavioral life-cycle theory, protecting us from cognitive and emotional errors and from wants, such as spending it all now, that might overwhelm "shoulds," such as saving for retirement.

Public policy prescriptions for spending and saving range from libertarianism to libertarian paternalism and paternalism. Libertarians advocate *hands-off* policies, granting people freedom to save and spend as they wish, whether saving much when young and spending much when old, or saving little when young and spending little when old. Libertarian prescriptions conform to standard life-cycle theory for people who arrange their spending and saving so as to enjoy smoothed permanent income throughout their life cycle.

Libertarian paternalists advocate policies that *nudge* people toward saving when young, and toward judicious spending when old. Paternalists go further, advocating mandates that *shove* people into saving when young and judicious spending when old. Both conform to behavioral life-cycle theory whereby people are hampered in spending and saving by conflicts between wants for spending and saving, and by cognitive and emotional errors. See Box 9.2 for a summary of public policy prescriptions.

Public policy prescriptions and the role of government are evident in all of investing, saving, and spending. These roles includes direct government provisions, such as Social Security, and indirect government provisions,

---

Box 9.2 LIBERTARIANISM, LIBERTARIAN PATERNALISM, AND PATERNALISM IN SAVING AND SPENDING POLICIES

Libertarians advocate *hands-off* policies, granting people freedom to save and spend as they wish.

Libertarian paternalists advocate policies that *nudge* people toward saving when young, and toward judicious spending when old.

Paternalists advocate mandates that *shove* people into saving when young and judicious spending when old.

such as laws and regulations that defer taxes on defined-contribution retirement savings accounts and require minimum distributions from these accounts when reaching age 70½.

Social Security is paternalistic by design. Its mandatory paternalistic nature overcomes insufficient self-control by shoving people into saving, limiting today's spending to what is left after Social Security contributions have been deducted. The paternalistic nature of Social Security is also evident in its prohibition of lump-sum payments in place of monthly payments.

Defined-benefit pension plans are also paternalistic, as they are mandatory for employees in companies and government entities that provide them. But most corporate pension plans permit lump-sum payments at retirement, tempting retirees with insufficient self-control. Combined corporate and government paternalism is evident in the Pension Benefit Guarantee Corporation, which insures workers who might lose corporate pension benefits if their pension funds default.

Protection of investors from their own cognitive and emotional errors underlies many financial regulations. Margin regulations limit leverage. Stock buyers cannot borrow more than 50 percent of the value of their stock purchases. The paternalistic nature of margin regulations is reflected in a passage from the general analysis of the Senate version of the bill underlying the Securities Exchange Act of 1934. "Margin transactions involve speculation in securities with borrowed money. . . . Many thoughtful persons have taken the view that the only way to correct the evils attendant upon stock market speculation is to abolish margin trading altogether. A Federal judge furnished this committee with instances from his long experience on the bench, indicating that a large proportion of business failures, embezzlements and even suicides in recent years were directly attributable to losses incurred in speculative transactions."[75]

Suitability regulations are also paternalistic, designed to counter cognitive and emotional errors. These regulations require that brokers recommend securities to customers only if the brokers have reasonable grounds for believing that their recommendations are suitable for their customers' financial situation and needs.

Legal scholar Robert Mundheim described the difference between libertarian and paternalistic notions in the context of suitability, writing that "imposition of any suitability doctrine has a revolutionary flavor, because it shifts the responsibility for making inappropriate investment decisions from the customer to the broker-dealer. It does so in what seems to me the correct belief that disclosure requirements and practices alone have not been wholly effective in protecting the investor—including protecting him from his own greed."[76].

Suitability standards are paternalistic, but they set a low paternalism bar. For example, they allow a broker to recommend to an investor a high-cost mutual fund paying him high commissions over an identical low-cost fund paying him low commissions, as long as both funds are suitable for that investor. Fiduciary standards set a higher paternalism bar, requiring brokers to place the interests of investors ahead of their own. They do not allow a broker to recommend a high-cost mutual fund over an identical low-cost fund. In 2016 the Department of Labor imposed fiduciary standards on brokers and advisers when they recommend investments designated for retirement. "The marketing material that I see from many firms is we put our customers first," said Thomas E. Perez, the Secretary of Labor. "This is no longer a marketing slogan. It's the law."[77]

The difference between suitability and fiduciary standards is evident in the decline of the price of shares of American Equity Investment Life, a large issuer of fixed indexed annuities, when it became clear that sellers of its annuities would have to adhere to fiduciary standards. Kerry Pechter, editor of *Retirement Income Journal*, quoted John Matovina, the CEO of American Equity Investment Life: "The unexpected change regarding Fiduciary Investment Advisers in the final Department of Labor (DOL) rule and the related Best Interest Contract Exemption has cast a cloud over our future growth rate." Pechter added, "Not coincidentally, this is the type of product whose sale to middle-income senior citizens with large IRAs that the DOL aims to blunt. Agents would find it hard to rationalize the acceptance of such rich compensation under the new DOL rule, which requires sellers to ignore personal reward when recommending products to clients."[78]

The most prominent libertarian-paternalistic nudge in the context of savings is automatic enrollment into defined-contribution retirement saving plans such as 401(k), discussed by economist Richard Thaler and legal scholar Cass Sunstein in their book, *Nudge*. Making enrollment in companies' retirement saving plans the default choice is a nudge that counters the tendency to procrastinate in saving and place wants for spending over wants for saving.[79]

Congress incorporated nudges into the Pension Protection Act of 2006, and corporations apply nudges as they implement the Act. The Act authorizes corporations to establish programs for automatic enrollment of employees into defined-contribution retirement saving plans at specified contribution levels and increase these levels automatically over time.

Automatic enrollment into defined-contribution retirement saving plans increases the proportion of employees who enroll. Enrollment of new employees in one plan increased from 37 percent to 86 percent following the introduction of automatic enrollment. A substantial proportion of employees stayed, however, at the automatic default contribution of 3 percent a year later, despite a 50 percent employer match on contributions up to 6 percent of salary. Employees seem anchored to the default contribution level, considering it a contribution level recommended by the company.[80] Increasing the contribution default rate to 6 percent did not decrease participation, although default rates higher than 6 percent were accompanied by decreases.[81]

Automatic enrollment has proven especially effective among millennials, people born between the early 1980s and early 2000s. Vanguard, an investment company, found that more than six of ten millennial participants in defined-contribution retirement saving plans have been subjected to automatic enrollment in 2013, compared with four of ten early baby boomers. Millennials' income and job prospects have been reduced by the Great Recession but they are saving more because of automatic enrollment. Millennials are also twice as likely to use professionally managed allocations, including target-date funds, than early boomers. Half of the millennials held a single target-date fund at the end of 2013.[82]

Nevertheless, choice defaults fail in some circumstances, such as where default options do not match people's preferences. Less obviously, they fail when they reduce perceived choice autonomy, leading some to switch away from default options even when they match their preferences. Designing default options that retain higher perceived choice autonomy can help align people's choices with their preferences.[83]

Nudges go beyond automatic enrollment and some are ingenious. Americans were nudged into saving when they saw images of themselves as they would look when old.[84] South Africans were nudged into saving by a television soap opera. One group was assigned to watch a soap opera with financial messages, whereas the other group was assigned to watch a similar program without such messages. The financial storyline of the first soap opera showed a leading character borrowing excessively, ending up in financial distress, and seeking help. People assigned to watch that soap opera were afterwards more likely to pay low interest rates when borrowing and less likely to engage in gambling.[85]

Automatic contributions are more effective at promoting retirement savings than are tax subsidies. Tax subsidies have little effect on total savings in Denmark—each $1 of tax subsidy increases total savings by 1 cent. In contrast, policies that require no employee action—such as automatic employer contributions to retirement accounts—increased total savings substantially. Approximately 85 percent of employees are passive savers whose ranks include those least prepared for retirement. The 15 percent active savers who responded to tax subsidies did so primarily by shifting savings across accounts rather than by reducing spending.[86]

Further evidence indicates that tax considerations matter little in promoting retirement savings. Roth 401(k) contributions are not tax-deductible in the contribution year, but withdrawals in retirement are untaxed. Traditional 401(k) contributions are tax-deductible in the contribution year, but both principal and earnings of traditional 401(k)s are taxed upon withdrawal. A study of eleven companies that added a Roth contribution option to their traditional 401(k) plan between 2006 and 2010 reveals no difference in total 401(k) contribution rates between employees hired before the Roth introduction and afterwards. It implies that take-home pay declines and future retirement spending increases among those who choose the Roth introduction, possibly the outcome of employee confusion about and neglect of the tax properties of Roth accounts, or the outcome of "partition dependence," a mental shortcut whereby a fixed amount is allocated to a 401(k), regardless of whether it is traditional or Roth.[87]

Still, some people resist nudges, exercising their right to opt out of defined-contribution retirement saving plans that are voluntary. And some who enroll extract "liquidity" from their accounts by borrowing or withdrawing money from them long before retirement even when discouraged by taxes and penalties. Some withdrawals are necessary, such as for purchasing a house, or made necessary by bouts of unemployment. But other withdrawals are less necessary.

A multinational comparison of liquidity provisions of defined-contribution retirement saving plans indicates that all, with the sole exception of the United States, have made their systems overwhelmingly illiquid before contributors reach 55. Liquidity in the United States generates significant pre-retirement "leakage": for every $1 contributed to the defined-contribution accounts of savers under age 55 (not counting rollovers), 40 cents simultaneously flows out of the defined-contribution system (not counting loans or rollovers).

Early withdrawals are prohibited in Germany, Singapore, and the United Kingdom. Only disabled or terminally ill people may withdraw early. Singapore, however, allows withdrawals from defined-contribution balances for medical expenses, home purchases (which must be repaid with interest if the home is sold), and education (which must be repaid with interest in 12 years). Withdrawals are prohibited in Canada under normal circumstances, but are allowed if income is very low, below approximately US$32,400 in the following 12 months. Withdrawals in Australia are prohibited as long as members of a household remain employed, no matter how low income falls.

In the United States, however, even at a normal level of income, workers can roll over balances from a previous employer's defined-contribution account plan into an IRA and then liquidate these balances with a maximum 10 percent penalty.[88] Moreover, not all American companies offer retirement saving plans and not all that offer them encourage retirement savings by matching employee contributions. Indeed, many companies offering defined-benefit pension plans chose to "freeze" them, reducing payroll by approximately 3.5 percent by ceasing contributions.[89]

State governments have recently stepped into the savings breach with plans such as the Illinois Secure Choice Savings Program. The program requires employers who do not offer retirement saving plans to automatically place 3 percent of a worker's paycheck into a Roth IRA retirement savings account, unless an employee opts out.

The federal government has also stepped in recently with its plan for the "myRA" (My Retirement Account). In his 2014 State of the Union address, President Obama announced myRA as "a new way for working Americans to start their own retirement savings." Accounts will earn interest at the rate available to federal employees for their retirement accounts. Key features of the myRA program include automatic contributions from paychecks with no minimum, overcoming the traditional IRA $1,000 minimum. Contributions can be withdrawn tax free, and earnings can be withdrawn tax free after five years if savers are older than 59½.[90]

Mandatory defined-contribution retirement saving plans are paternalistic shoves into saving, going beyond libertarian-paternalistic nudges. They complement the shoves of Social Security and substitute for the shoves of increasingly rare defined-benefit pension plans. Mandatory defined-contribution retirement saving plans exist in a number of countries; Australia is prominent among them. Australian employers are mandated to contribute a specified percentage of employee earnings into employees' retirement savings accounts. This percentage is scheduled to increase gradually to 12 percent by 2019–2020. Employees can contribute voluntarily beyond the mandatory amount. Tax provisions encourage people to withdraw their money gradually after age 60, rather than in a lump sum.

Defined-contribution retirement saving plans at US universities and some other not-for-profit institutions are not formally mandatory but they resemble mandatory plans. Employers make contributions without imposing requirements that employees make contributions but also without granting to employees rights to substitute higher salary for employer contributions. Employer contributions average 10.1 percent at private universities and 9.5 percent at public ones. Some universities shove further, mandating contributions by employees, averaging approximately 5 percent, for a total of approximately 15 percent.[91]

We note that the switch from paternalistic defined-benefit pension plans to libertarian defined-contribution retirement saving plans did not come about by comparison of the merits of libertarianism and paternalism. Instead, it came by happenstance, offering an out to corporations whose defined-benefit pension assets are woefully short of liabilities. The Revenue Act of 1978 included a provision, section 401(k), specifying that deferred income would not be taxed. The law firm serving Hughes Aircraft Company noticed this provision and recommended that the company incorporate it into its savings plan, creating the first of what we know now as defined-contribution retirement savings plans. Other companies followed, replacing old after-tax savings plans with the new before-tax 401(k) plans, and adding 401(k) options to profit-sharing and stock bonus plans. Within two years, nearly half of all large companies were offering 401(k) plans or considering them. By now, defined-contribution retirement saving plans have overtaken defined-benefit pension plans, exposing both advantages and disadvantages of the switch from paternalism to libertarianism.[92]

RETIREMENT INCOME FOR THE WEALTHY, MIDDLE INCOME, AND POOR

Discussions about public policies that are best at promoting adequate life-cycle spending and saving, whether libertarian hands-offs, libertarian-paternalistic nudges, or paternalistic shoves, are unfocused when we fail to distinguish people by wealth, income, and personal characteristics, especially self-control.

We can focus discussions about life-cycle spending and saving policies by distinguishing among four income groups: the *wealthy, the steady middle, the precarious middle, and the poor.* The *wealthy*, even if less wealthy than the Helmsleys. earn more than adequate incomes during their working years, and their accumulated savings are large enough to assure retirement worries extending no further than estate taxes and status competitions with their wealthier neighbors. The *steady middle*, like the retiree quoted earlier in this chapter who wrote "I save aggressively,"[93] earn adequate incomes steadily throughout their working years and save enough for adequate retirement spending. The *poor* earn inadequate income throughout their working years, rendering them unable to save much for adequate retirement spending. The *precarious middle* consists of two segments, *low earners* and *high spenders*. Low earners strive to save from low earnings during their working years but their meager savings place them precariously close to poverty and inadequate retirement spending. High spenders, like bankrupt NFL players, spend their adequate incomes during their working years, failing to save enough for adequate retirement spending.

Retirement spending solutions often address the problems of one group with no mention of the others. Many address longevity risk, offering solutions such as annuities. Annuities, however, offer nothing to the wealthy, who face no longevity risk because their accumulated savings vastly exceed their spending rates, even if lavish. And an annuity solution mocks the precarious middle and the poor, whose meager savings make buying an annuity impractical or impossible.

Social Security is described as a source of retirement spending equally available to the rich, middle income, and poor. Social Security benefits are indeed progressive, such that those who have contributed little during their working years receive more relative to their contributions than those who have contributed much. Yet the monthly Social Security benefits received by the poor tend to be small. A Gallup poll reveals that many Americans underestimate their likely reliance on Social Security benefits. Among non-retirees, 33 percent expect that Social Security would be a major source of retirement income. But 57 percent of retirees go on to report that Social Security is a major source of retirement income.[94]

The savings-to-spending ratios of the steady middle are high, muting fears of longevity risk. One steady middle wrote in a Vanguard blog post, "I worked after school and weekends as a kid. I also worked summer vacations. Then after the army, I worked for an electric company in Ohio for 40 years with rarely any holidays off. . . . Then I retired at 61 and feel that if I don't start living now, I will run out of time."[95]

Savings-to-spending ratios are low among the high-spending segment of the precarious middle. Tom Palome, a 77-year-old man, is one such case. Palome earned a salary in the low six figures during some years but saved little of it. He is now working as a $10-an-hour food demonstrator at Sam's Club and a short-order cook at a golf club grill for slightly more than minimum wage. Palome receives Social Security benefits and a small pension from his last corporate job but has no defined-contribution savings or other savings.[96]

People in the high-spending segment of the precarious middle lack self-control and patience, evident among families who received federal stimulus payments that were distributed randomly across weeks. Patterns of spending vary among families, and the propensity to spend is highly related to impatience. Arrival of money caused high spending among families who "live for today," families who have not made financial plans in the last two years, and families not using coupons or deals when making purchases.[97]

Another writer on the Vanguard blog belongs to the low-earning segment of the precarious middle. "We lived below our means, saved and invested, had no debt and yet, here we are. [Our] income is 30 percent less than we and our planner 'expected.' Health insurance and medical costs take $15K annually. My parents' generation did so much better. . . ."

Shenita Simon is one of the poor, presented in a PBS *NewsHour* program about efforts to raise the minimum wage. Simon is struggling to make a living in New York City on an $8-an-hour fast-food wage with no benefits, no vacation days, no sick days, and no personal days. She supports a husband who has recently lost his job, as well as supporting a mother, brother, and three children. The children get three meals a day, said Simon. "And [the only way] my children get three meals a day is because their school provides two meals out of those three meals. If I was to [pay for] three meals a day for my children, we wouldn't make it. We would be homeless. We would be starving, one [way] or the other."[98]

The lines that separate the wealthy, middle income, and poor are not precise, because people's subjective assessments of financial security can be at odds with objective assessments. A comparison of objective and subjective financial security in retirement among American families with full-time workers between the ages of 35 and 60 shows that 58 percent suffer objective financial insecurity and 54 percent perceive subjective financial insecurity, but subjective perceptions and objective assessments are in conformity only among 52 percent of families. Specifically, among families suffering objective financial insecurity, those headed by a person with less than a high school degree have higher rates of unrealistic optimism than those headed by a person with a college degree. Surprisingly, however, people using the services of financial advisers tend to be less realistic than those not using them, and people with defined-benefit pensions tend to be less realistic than those not having them. This disparity might be because people who use the services of financial advisers assume that advisers assure financial security and people with defined-benefit pensions assume that pensions assure financial security.[99]

Another writer on the Vanguard blog illustrates the difference between subjective and objective assessments of financial security: "My husband is 81 years old [and] has been taking RMD [required minimum distribution payment] for years. We [save] this distribution each year. I will take my first RMD in 2010 due to [the] grace period in 2009. I will [save] this money as we can live without it to meet our needs."

Objective assessment places this Vanguard writer in the stable-middle group, perhaps even in the wealthy group, as she and her husband have sufficient income beyond the RMD payment, enabling them to save their

RMD payment rather than spend it. Yet she assesses herself subjectively as a member of the precarious-middle group. She continued, "Economy dictates scaling down as best we can to conserve for future years. We are okay financially at this point but are frightened by what the future may bring. So life in retirement isn't what it is cracked up to be. Can't chance taking a vacation when the dollars spent may be needed to keep us solvent with ability to pay income taxes and property taxes."

Objective financial fragility is common among the precarious middle and the poor. Almost half of Americans reported that they are incapable of obtaining $2,000 in 30 days to deal with an ordinary financial shock, such as a major car repair. Financial fragility is especially severe among those with low educational attainment, families with children, those who suffered large wealth losses, and those who are unemployed. But a sizable fraction of seemingly middle-class Americans are financially fragile.[100]

Attempts to nudge the poor into greater savings are likely to fail because the poor have few resources available for saving. A series of field experiments focused on saving rates in a federally funded program for low-income families—the Individual Development Account (IDA) program. The experiments examined whether savings can be increased by four nudges: holding savers accountable for making deposits by phone calls before and after deposit deadlines; increasing the frequency of deposits from monthly to biweekly; a lottery-based incentive structure; and an increase in the ratio of savings match by the program from $2 for every $1 saved by a person to $4 for every $1, when half of the savings goal was reached.

None of the four interventions brought the desired increase in savings. The authors concluded that poverty, rather than insufficient self-control or other cognitive or emotional errors, is the primary barrier to saving. Poor people invest much time and energy in making ends meet, leaving less time and energy for other goals. Follow-up interviews with savers bolster that conclusion. For example, people said that telephone calls "could be overwhelming when you are busy, almost like a bill collector;" "were like telemarketing calls. I knew I had to save, so I just hung up on the calls," and "[calls] were annoying. Any call that calls you when you don't expect it and you don't know what it is. . . . I got calls when I was talking to an employer and I thought it was another potential employer or something."[101]

A mandatory defined-contribution savings plan would do much for the precarious middle, especially their high-spending segment, by replacing weak self-control with strong outside control. But mandatory defined-contribution savings plans would be insufficient for the poor, who have little or nothing to save from. Financial security solutions for the poor and precarious middle would require additional measures. A non-contributory pension program in Mexico involves cash transfers to rural adults older than seventy. The program leads to higher spending levels and better mental health.[102]

CONCLUSION

Standard life-cycle theory is the theory of standard finance, centered on the hypothesis that people want smooth spending during their entire life-cycle and do so easily, balancing spending and saving from life-cycle wealth. Behavioral life-cycle theory is the theory of behavioral finance centered on the hypothesis that even people who want smooth spending during their entire life cycle find it difficult to avoid cognitive and emotional errors and balance wants for spending now and wants for saving for tomorrow.

Behavioral life-cycle theory says that we reconcile the conflict between our wants by devices such as framing, mental accounting, and self-control rules that prohibit dips into other than designated mental accounts. In contrast, standard life-cycle theory says that we have no need for framing, mental accounting, or self-control rules for resolving such conflicts. Evidence favors behavioral life-cycle theory.

Informed public policy follows the nudge and shove prescriptions of behavioral life-cycle theory better than it follows the hands-off prescriptions of standard life-cycle theory. Defined-contribution retirement savings accounts are supplemented with nudges into retirement savings, such as by automatic enrollment, and Social Security is a much needed shove into retirement savings for many people.

CHAPTER 10
Behavioral Asset Pricing

Useful asset pricing models associate expected returns of investment assets, such as stocks and bonds, with factors or characteristics, such as risk and liquidity. These models allow us to estimate expected returns once we know the factors or characteristics and their associations with expected returns. In that, investment asset pricing models are like pricing models of meals, cars, movies, and virtually every other product and service.

The characteristics of meal pricing models reflect diners' wants for the full range of meal benefits—utilitarian, expressive, and emotional. The utilitarian benefits of meals include nutrition, the expressive benefits include prestige and display of discerning taste, and the emotional benefits include enjoyment of taste and aesthetics. The nutrition in fast food meals might equal that of Michelin-star restaurants, but the prestige and aesthetics of Michelin-star meals exceed those of fast food meals. We are not surprised to learn that prices of Michelin-star meals exceed fast food prices.

Behavioral asset pricing theory, which I outlined in an article in 1999,[1] draws on economist Kelvin Lancaster's 1966 article "New Approach to Consumer Theory."[2] Lancaster turned his focus away from products, such as meals, to their characteristics, including utilitarian nutrition but also expressive and emotional aesthetics and social connections. We derive benefits from a meal, he wrote, as it "possesses nutritional characteristics but it also possesses aesthetic characteristics, and different meals will possess these characteristics in different relative proportions." The same characteristic, such as esthetics, may be included in many products "so that goods which are apparently unrelated in certain of their characteristics may be related in others." Roses do not substitute for chocolates by utilitarian nutrition but they substitute for chocolates by expressive gratitude and emotional affection.

Utilitarian benefits in investment asset pricing models include low-risk and high-liquidity. Expressive and emotional benefits include the virtue of acquiring and holding socially responsible mutual funds, the prestige of hedge funds, and the thrill of trading. Wants for investments with high utilitarian, expressive, and emotional benefits are likely to be associated with high prices and low expected returns.

The returns of low-risk stocks can be expected to be lower than those of high-risk stocks if investors are willing to accept lower expected returns for the utilitarian, expressive, and emotional benefits of lower risk. The returns of low-risk stocks can, however, be expected to be *higher* than those of high-risk stocks if investors are willing to accept lower expected returns for the emotional benefits of *hope* of attaining high returns with high-risk stocks, as they are willing to accept lower expected returns for the hope of winning a lottery.

The returns of stocks of virtuous companies can be expected to be lower than those of shunned companies if investors are willing to accept lower expected returns for the expressive benefits of shunning stocks of tobacco and other maligned companies. And the returns of investors who trade frequently can be expected to be lower than those of investors who trade rarely, if the former are willing to accept lower expected returns for the emotional thrills of frequent trading.

Meal pricing models reflect not only diners' wants for utilitarian, expressive, and emotional benefits but also diners' cognitive and emotional errors. Diners' words and functional MRI brain scans reveal that they perceive identical wines as more pleasant when told that their prices are high rather than low.[3]

Cognitive errors reflected in investment asset pricing include underestimation of intangible capital such as high employee morale that costs much in high employee wages and perks today but enhances future profits by more than its cost. Emotional errors reflected in investment asset pricing include affect that misleads investors into favoring stocks of admired companies exuding positive affect over stocks of spurned companies exuding negative affect, even when the expected returns of admired companies' stocks are lower than the expected returns of spurned companies' stocks.

We can present the association between the characteristics of a meal and its expected price in a meal pricing model as follows:

The expected price of a meal is a function of

1. wants for utilitarian benefits such as high nutrition and great convenience
2. wants for expressive and emotional benefits such as great prestige and pleasing esthetics

3. cognitive and emotional errors such as inferring wine quality from its price

Similarly, using stocks as an example of investment assets, we can present the association between the expected return of a stock and the characteristics that determine it in an asset pricing model as follows:

The expected return of a stock is a function of

1. wants for utilitarian benefits such as low risk and high liquidity
2. wants for expressive and emotional benefits such as the virtue of socially responsible funds, the prestige in hedge funds, and the thrill of stock trading
3. cognitive and emotional errors such as a belief that stocks of admired companies are likely to yield higher returns than stocks of spurned companies, and that frequent trading is likely to yield higher returns than rarer trading

ARBITRAGE IN MEAL MARKETS AND INVESTMENT MARKETS

Some diners and some investors are "normal-ignorant," succumbing to cognitive and emotional errors. Others are "normal-knowledgeable," having learned to overcome their cognitive and emotional errors but sometimes willing to sacrifice utilitarian benefits for expressive and emotional ones. Yet others are rational, immune to cognitive and emotional errors and caring only about utilitarian benefits. Rational and knowledgeable diners can potentially eliminate by arbitrage the effects of ignorant diners on meal prices, and rational and knowledgeable investors can potentially eliminate by arbitrage the effects of ignorant investors on investment asset prices.

Consider arbitrage in meal markets. Rational and knowledgeable diners can earn money by producing restaurant directories, such as the Zagat Survey, or by creating Internet sites, such as Yelp, that rate restaurants and their meals. Such media steer diners away from restaurants whose meal prices exceed meal quality into restaurants whose meal prices are short of meal quality, pressing the first group of restaurants to reduce prices and inducing the second group to raise them, eliminating gaps between prices and quality.

Now consider arbitrage in investment markets. Imagine normal investors who are willing to sacrifice the utilitarian benefits of the high expected returns of stocks of tobacco companies so as to avoid their expressive and emotional costs. The shunning of tobacco stocks by a group of investors decreases the demand for them, pressing down their prices and pushing up their expected returns. The higher expected returns attract rational investors who buy tobacco shares, potentially eliminating the effect on expected returns of investors who shun such stocks. Knowledgeable investors with no preference against stocks of tobacco companies might join rational investors or even do the arbitrage work on their own.

As we consider arbitrage and the likelihood that it would eliminate the effects of normal investors on expected returns, we note that most arbitrage opportunities are risky rather than risk free, such as where one buys an asset and simultaneously sells it at a higher price. It is optimal for investors to increase their holdings of tobacco stocks if they are absolutely certain that their tomorrow's returns would be higher than those of other stocks, but investors can rarely be absolutely certain about tomorrow's returns or even longer-period returns. As investors increase the proportion allocated to tobacco stocks, they reduce diversification in their portfolios, thereby increasing their portfolios' risk. This limits the willingness of rational and knowledgeable investors to allocate high proportions of their portfolios to tobacco stocks, thereby limiting their effect on prices and expected returns. Transaction costs and other impediments hamper arbitrage even when it is risk free. Therefore, prices and expected returns in markets with hampered arbitrage are likely to reflect wants for expressive and emotional benefits in addition to wants for utilitarian benefits, and prices and expected returns are also likely to reflect cognitive and emotional errors.

The prices of closed-end funds and exchange-traded funds are examples of the effects of hampered arbitrage. Closed-end funds are portfolios of securities such as stocks or bonds. They differ from open-end funds we know as mutual funds. Investors who want to redeem shares of mutual funds submit their redemption requests to their fund companies and receive from them payments equal to the net asset value of shares of these funds at the end of the trading day. In contrast, investors who want to redeem shares of closed-end funds do not submit redemption requests to their funds and do not receive payments from them. Instead, they sell their shares of closed-end funds in the stock market at any time during a trading day as they would sell shares of other companies, including those whose shares are in closed-end funds, whether Alphabet (Google) or General Motors.

The prices of closed-end fund shares would be identical to the net asset values of the shares they contain in markets with no arbitrage costs. In such markets, rational and knowledgeable investors would buy shares of closed-end funds and simultaneously sell shares of companies whose shares are in those funds if the prices of shares of closed-end funds were lower than their net asset values. Buying and selling would exert pressure on prices, pressing up the prices of shares of these funds and pressing down the prices of the shares of companies in these funds until differences between prices of shares of closed-end funds and their net asset values disappeared. Instead, we find that prices of shares of many such funds deviate greatly from their net asset values. Deviations of prices from net asset values indicate the presence of arbitrage costs. Indeed, deviations are greater when arbitrage costs are higher.[4]

THEORETICAL AND EMPIRICAL ASSET PRICING MODELS

Asset pricing models can be categorized as theoretical or empirical in character. Construction of theoretical models begins with theoretical rationales for investor wants for utilitarian, expressive, and emotional benefits and investor cognitive and emotional errors. Construction proceeds with examination of empirical evidence about associations between investment asset returns and factors or characteristics reflecting wants and cognitive and emotional errors. For example, we can begin with the theoretical rationale that investors prefer investments with low risk over ones with high risk and proceed with an examination of the empirical evidence about that association, assessing whether low-risk investments yield lower realized returns over long periods than the high-risk ones.

Construction of empirical asset pricing models begins with empirical evidence about associations between asset returns and factors or characteristics, such as evidence that low-risk investments yield lower or higher returns on average than high-risk investments. Construction proceeds with an examination of possible theoretical rationales for the associations.

A central difference between standard and behavioral asset pricing models, whether theoretical or empirical, is in the theoretical rationales for these associations. Theoretical rationales in standard asset pricing models account only for wants for utilitarian benefits, whereas theoretical rationales in behavioral asset pricing models also account for wants for expressive and emotional benefits and the occurrence of cognitive and emotional errors. See Box 10-1 for a side-by-side comparison.

THE THEORETICAL CAPITAL ASSET PRICING MODEL

The first investment asset pricing model of standard finance, introduced by William Sharpe, is the theoretical capital asset pricing model (CAPM), where the risk of an investment asset determines its expected return.[5,6] The CAPM is built on Markowitz's mean-variance portfolio theory.[7] That theory begins with the assumption that investors choose portfolios by expected returns and risk alone. It follows with the assumption that investors seek high expected returns but are averse to risk, measured by the standard deviation of returns. This return seeking and risk aversion leads investors to portfolios on the mean-variance frontier, offering the highest expected return for each level of standard deviation. Investors choose portfolios that are best for them by their personal trade-off between expected returns and standard deviations.

The CAPM adds two crucial assumptions to those of mean-variance portfolio theory. First is the assumption of *agreement*, whereby all investors agree on the joint distribution of the returns of all investment assets. For example, all investors have identical estimates of the expected return of Alphabet (Google) shares, their standard deviation of returns, and the correlation between their returns and the returns of every other investment asset. Second is the assumption of *borrowing and lending*, whereby investors can borrow and lend unlimited amounts at a common risk-free rate and are not averse to doing so.

Investors choose portfolios from those on the Capital Market Line, presented in Figure 10-1. The Capital Market Line is tangent to the mean-variance frontier at the market portfolio M. Investors' portfolios feature "two-fund separation," combining the market portfolio, common to all investors, with borrowing and lending according to each investor's trade-off between expected returns and standard deviations.[8]

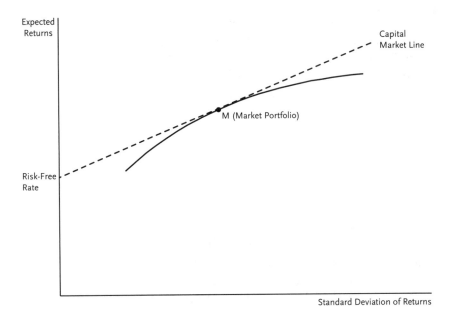

Figure 10-1 The Capital Market Line.

The market portfolio is the portfolio of all investment assets in the world—stocks, bonds, real estate, commodities, privately held companies, and even human capital embedded in each of us. The weight or proportion of each investment asset in the market portfolio is equal to its total market value relative to the total market value of all investment assets. For example, in Eqn. 10.1, if the total market value of Alphabet (Google)'s shares amounts to 0.01 percent of the total value of all investment assets in the world, the proportion of Alphabet (Google)'s stock in the market portfolio is 0.01 percent.

The CAPM equation for the expected return of Alphabet (Google)'s stock is

$$E(R_G) = R_f + \beta_G[E(R_M) - R_f], \qquad \text{Eqn. 10.1}$$

where

$E(R_G)$ is the expected return of Alphabet (Google)'s stock

$E(R_M)$ is the expected return of the market portfolio

R_f is the risk-free rate

β_G is Alphabet (Google) stock's market-factor beta

$[E(R_M) - R_f]$ is the "expected market-factor return" or "market-risk premium" or "equity premium"

The market-factor beta of an investment is its market-factor coefficient. That market-factor beta is the measure of the risk of that investment according to the CAPM. In Eqn. 10-2, the market-factor beta of Alphabet (Google)'s stock depends on the correlation between its returns and those of the market portfolio as well as on the ratio of the standard deviation of its returns to that of the market portfolio:

$$\beta_G = \rho_{GM} \frac{\sigma_G}{\sigma_M},$$

Eqn. 10-2

where

β_G is Alphabet (Google) stock's market-factor beta
ρ_{GM} is the correlation between the returns of Alphabet (Google)'s stock and the returns of the market portfolio
σ_G is the standard deviation of the returns of Alphabet (Google)'s stock
σ_M is the standard deviation of the returns of the market portfolio

The true market portfolio is prohibitively difficult to calculate. We resort to proxies of the market portfolio, such as a broad index of the US stock market, and proxies of the risk-free investment asset, such as US Treasury bills or bonds. Estimates of the expected market-factor return we know as the "equity premium" are usually based on realized returns over long periods. The realized equity premium in the United States is 6.6 percent, measured as the difference between the mean annualized returns of the S&P 500 Index and Treasury bills during more than eight decades. More reliable estimates, based on returns from 17 countries during a 106-year interval, suggest that investors can expect an annualized equity premium of 3 to 3.5 percent.[9]

Excess returns, also known as "alpha," are returns exceeding those expected according to an asset pricing model. We estimate the excess returns of Alphabet (Google)'s stock as well as its factor betas by a regression equation (Eqn. 10-3), usually with monthly realized returns, by a specific asset pricing model, such as the CAPM.

$$R_G - R_f = \alpha_G + \beta_G[R_M - R_f],$$

Eqn. 3

where

R_G is the realized return of Alphabet (Google)'s stock
R_M is the realized return of the market portfolio
α_G is the excess return of Alphabet (Google)'s stock (i.e., its alpha)
β_G is the beta of Alphabet (Google)'s stock

The theoretical rationale for the role of the beta of the market factor in the CAPM is the role of risk in determining expected returns, especially the risk of doing badly in bad times. The estimated 0.96 beta of Alphabet (Google)'s stock implies that in bad times, when the market portfolio loses 1 percent of its value, Alphabet (Google)'s stock is expected to lose only 0.96 percent of its value, making it somewhat less risky than the market portfolio. A stock with a market-factor beta of 1.50 is expected to lose 1.50 percent of its value when the market portfolio loses 1 percent of its value, making it more risky than the market portfolio. As William Sharpe wrote, "The empirical record may indicate that markets are more complex than posited in the simple CAPM. But it seems highly unlikely that expected returns are unrelated to the risks of doing badly in bad times."[10]

THE EMPIRICAL THREE-FACTOR ASSET PRICING MODEL

The CAPM predicts that differences between the expected returns of any two investment assets come only from differences between their market-factor betas. Yet much empirical evidence about realized returns does not conform to that prediction, showing excess returns when measured by the CAPM. A 1977 study found that stocks with low ratios of price per share to earnings per share had higher subsequent realized returns than predicted by the CAPM[11] and a 1981 study found similar results for stocks with small capitalizations—small total market value of their shares.[12] A 1985 study found that stocks with low ratios of price per share to book value per share had higher subsequent realized returns than predicted by the CAPM;[13] a 1989 study found similar results for stocks with low Tobin Q, the ratio of the total market value of all the securities of a company, reflecting both tangible assets such as equipment and intangible assets, such as patents, to the replacement value of the company's tangible assets.[14]

"Anomalies" is the term we use to describe deviations of realized returns from returns expected by an asset pricing model, such as the CAPM. The realized returns we refer to in the discussion of anomalies are not realized returns of a single stock during a single year. Instead, they are realized returns of groups of stocks, such as the group of small-capitalization stocks during periods extending into many decades. The returns of the group of small-capitalization stocks during many decades are an anomaly because they are higher than expected by the CAPM. The same is true for stocks with low ratios of price per share to earnings per share, stocks with low ratios of price per share to book-value per share, and stocks with low Tobin Q.

The empirical challenges to the CAPM, reflected in these anomalies, persuaded economists Eugene Fama and Kenneth French to introduce their three-factor model in 1992.[15] The three-factor model is an empirical model that begins with the known empirical associations between returns of stocks and the small-large and value-growth factors and proceeds to argue that the theoretical rationale for the association is the role of the small-large and value-growth-factor betas in measuring risk better than the market-factor beta.

The market factor is commonly measured as the difference between the return of an index of all stocks and the return of Treasury bills. The small-large factor is measured as the difference between the returns of indexes of small-capitalization and large-capitalization stocks. The value-growth factor is measured as the difference between the returns of indexes of value stocks and growth stocks. Value stocks are those with high ratios of book value per share to price per share, commonly referred to as high book-to-market ratios. Growth stocks are those with low ratios of book value per share to price per share, commonly referred to as low book-to-market ratios. In the three-factor asset pricing model, the expected return of an asset is a function of

1. risk related to the market factor
2. risk related to the small-large factor
3. risk related the value-growth factor

Consider the Barrier fund, formerly known as the Vice fund. It is a mutual fund "designed with the goal of delivering better risk-adjusted returns than the S&P 500 Index by investing in stocks within industries that have significant barriers to entry." The chosen industries are ones generally shunned by socially responsible investors, including tobacco, alcoholic beverages, gaming, and defense/aerospace.[16]

The expected monthly return of the Barrier fund, according to the CAPM and based on monthly returns from September 2002 through March 2012, can be written as

The expected return of the Barrier fund =
Risk-free rate + 0.84 [expected market-factor return]

The expected monthly return of the Barrier fund by the three-factor model based on monthly returns during the same period is written as

The expected return of the Barrier fund =
   risk-free rate
   + 0.82 [expected market-factor return]
   + 0.05 [expected small-large-factor return]
   − 0.05 [expected value-growth-factor return]

The positive 0.05 small-large-factor beta implies that the expected return of the Barrier fund tends to be high when the returns of small-capitalization stocks exceed the returns of large-capitalization stocks. The negative 0.05 value-growth-factor beta implies that the expected return of the Barrier fund tends to be low when the returns of value stocks exceed the returns of growth stocks. The 0.82 market-factor beta in the three-factor model is slightly different from the 0.84 market-factor beta of the Barrier fund in the CAPM, because of effects of the addition of the small-large and value-growth factors to the market factor in the three-factor model.

EMPIRICAL EVIDENCE AND THEORETICAL RATIONALES

Eugene Fama introduced the three-factor model along with Kenneth French, but he is not content with it or with the general state of asset pricing models. In a 2008 interview, Fama said, "There's been a ton of work done on asset pricing, risk, measurement of risk, and measurement of the relation between expected return and risk, but it hasn't been all that satisfying. For example, if we knew more, the Fama-French three-factor model would not have had such a large impact because it's a pure empirical asset pricing model. We concocted that model to cover what we observed. It's used among academics; it's used everywhere. That's a comment on the fact that more formal theories developed to explain risk and return just haven't worked that well. An empirically generated theory such as the Fama-French model seems to do better than the theoretically constructed paradigms."[17]

Concoction of asset pricing models to cover what we observe is the current norm in asset pricing models. Researchers are busy "factor mining." One study counted 315 factors associated with returns at statistically significant levels, and noted that this number very likely underestimates the population of factors.[18] It recommended stricter criteria for establishing statistically significant associations between factors and returns so as to account for the possibility that the associations reflect nothing more than factor mining. Yet strong empirical associations between factors and returns cannot substitute for theoretical rationales.

Still, Fama is overly harsh in denigrating the three-factor model as "concocted . . . to cover what we observed." Admittedly, it is pleasing to have theory placed first, such as the CAPM, offering testable hypotheses followed by empirical evidence that supports them. It is especially pleasing to have a theory such as the CAPM that offers unexpected hypotheses whereby underlying theoretical rationales become obvious only once the theory has been presented. We were surprised by the hypothesis that the market-factor beta is the measure of risk of an investment asset rather than, say, the standard deviation of its returns. Yet theoretical models are not superior to empirical ones once theoretical rationales for empirical associations have been identified. Theoretical rationales for the workings of penicillin and X-rays were identified only after empirical evidence about their effects was evident.

Consider once again a meal pricing model. Theoretical rationales exist for associations between meal prices and characteristics such as the prices of the ingredients, the restaurant's ambience, and the skill of the chef at combining ingredients into meals that please the senses. But what can be the rationale for a strong empirical association between high meal prices and high number of luxury cars per capita in the neighborhood? It might be the role of luxury cars per capita as a proxy for income per capita and an association between income and willingness to pay high prices for meals. Or perhaps it is that people with a taste for luxury cars also have a taste for luxury meals. We can possibly find tests that would point to one rationale or another as the more plausible one. Meanwhile, we might choose to include a measure of luxury cars per capita in the meal pricing model while we explore its theoretical rationale.

Turning to investment asset pricing models, consider the decades-long puzzling and seemingly perverse empirical association between returns, market-factor beta, and the variance of returns. Stocks with high variance of returns and high market-factor betas in US markets have yielded substantially *lower* returns than stocks with low variance of returns and low market-factor betas. One possible theoretical rationale for the perverse association combines common individual investors' preference for risk, the kind reflected in the demand for lottery tickets, and common institutional investors' mandates that discourage arbitrage activity that would have pressed lower the returns to stocks with low market-factor betas and pushed higher the returns of stocks with high market-factor betas. This rationale is consistent with the observation that the seemingly perverse association between returns and variance of returns and market-factor betas has strengthened as institutional investors have become more prominent.[19]

A debate exists about the rationale for the profitability, or "quality," premium, illustrating further general debates about standard vis-à-vis behavioral rationales for asset pricing factors and characteristics. A number of studies found that stocks of highly profitable companies have yielded above-average returns. Economist Robert Novy-Marx found that stocks of companies with high ratios of gross profit to book value of total assets have yielded above-average returns.[20] Economist Ray Ball and his coauthors found an even stronger association between operating profitability and stock returns.[21]

The rationale underlying the profitability premium might be standard or behavioral. The standard rationale is that profitable companies are riskier, and the higher returns of their stocks are compensation for higher risk. A behavioral rationale is that cognitive errors mislead some investors into underestimating the true value of profitable companies and high trading costs limit arbitrage that could have eliminated the profitability premium. Indeed, security analysts systematically underestimate the future returns of stocks of companies with high profitability.[22]

Ball and his coauthors argued that they can distinguish the standard from the behavioral rationale by the persistence of above-average returns of stocks of profitable companies. They found that above-average returns persist over long periods and argued that it points toward a standard risk-based rationale because, in their view, the effects of cognitive errors and limited arbitrage on returns are likely to persist only during short periods. Yet cognitive errors and limited arbitrage might well persist over long periods, undermining Ball and his coauthors' argument.

FLEETING AND SUSTAINED FACTORS IN ASSET PRICING MODELS

Associations between factors and returns in standard and behavioral asset pricing models range in duration from fleeting to sustained. A factor has a place in a sustained asset pricing model if its rationale reflects sustained wants for utilitarian, expressive, and emotional benefits or the incurring of sustained cognitive and emotional errors. This, for example, is the case in which the expected return of risky stocks is likely to exceed that of less risky bonds even if knowledge of the differential in expected returns is widely available.

A fleeting association is eliminated by arbitrage in a period as short as a day. Traders at the Chicago Board of Trade, like most traders, prefer not to realize losses, consistent with the disposition effect. Evidence indicates that traders who incur losses in the morning try to break even in the afternoon by taking extra risk. Their trades affect prices but other traders quickly eliminate that effect by arbitrage.[23]

Economists David McLean and Jeffrey Pontiff explored the duration of eighty-two factors associated with returns. Their list includes levels of stock prices, maximum daily return during a month, and the better known small-large, value-growth, and momentum factors. They observed returns during three distinct periods: the sample period of the study identifying the factor, the period following the sample period but preceding publication of a study, and the period following publication.[24]

If the association between a factor and future returns disappears subsequent to the sample period with no evidence of arbitrage, we can conclude that no real association actually existed and the found association reflects nothing more than chance. If the association disappears with evidence of arbitrage, we can conclude that the association was real yet short lived or fleeting, reflecting wants or cognitive and emotional errors of some investors, but eliminated by the arbitrage actions of other investors. If the association does not disappear with evidence of arbitrage we can conclude that the association is sustained, reflecting wants or cognitive and emotional errors of some investors that were not eliminated by the arbitrage actions of other investors.

McLean and Pontiff observed that excess returns associated with a factor commonly decline once information about the association has been published in working papers. Excess returns decline further once working papers have made their way into journals. The authors also observed direct evidence of arbitrage such as in increased trading volume and short sales. The arbitrage process is slower and less effective where arbitrage is costly, such as among small capitalization and illiquid stocks.

STANDARD AND BEHAVIORAL RATIONALES

Empirical evidence indicates that the small-large and value-growth factors have been associated with subsequent stock returns. But what theoretical rationales underlie this association? And are the likely rationales standard or behavioral? We use the factors of small-large and value-growth as examples in a more general examination of five hypotheses about theoretical rationales that might underlie empirical associations. The first two can be characterized as standard, whereas the last three can be characterized as behavioral.

1. Data-Mining Hypothesis: The empirical associations between stock returns and the small-large and value-growth factors are due to "data mining." Data mining involves examination of associations between returns and factors among a virtually infinite number of possible factors. Many strong associations are likely to be found, but these associations appeared by chance in the past and are not likely to appear in the future.

2. Risk Hypothesis: The empirical associations are due to the role of the small-large and value-growth factors as indicators of risk. Specifically, the risk of stocks of small and value companies is higher than the risk of stocks of large and growth companies.

3. Cognitive-Errors Hypothesis: The empirical associations are due to cognitive errors, such as representativeness, where investors extrapolate high past sales, earnings, and other measures into the future, making a company representative of companies with high future sales and earnings and making its stock representative of stocks that are likely to yield high future returns.

4. Emotional-Errors Hypothesis: The empirical associations are due to emotional errors, such as misleading affect. Admired companies exude positive affect, whereas spurned companies exude negative affect. Large and growth companies tend to be admired, whereas small and value companies tend to be spurned. Positive affect generates a positive halo over large and growth companies, pushing up the prices of their stocks and pressing down their expected returns. Negative affect generates a negative halo over small and value companies, pressing down stock prices and pushing up their expected returns.

5. Wants for Expressive- and Emotional-Benefits Hypothesis: The empirical associations are due to wants for the higher expressive and emotional benefits delivered by stocks of large and growth companies rather than the lower expressive and emotional benefits delivered by stocks of small and value companies.

The Data-Mining Hypothesis

The data-mining hypothesis is the claim that the positive excess returns of stocks of small and value companies, when measured by the CAPM, and the negative excess returns of stocks of large and growth companies, are due to data mining among an almost infinite number of company and stock characteristics, including "small" and "value" but also dividend yield, research and development expenditures, highest stock price during the preceding fifty-two weeks, and more. Fischer Black wrote that "it is difficult to overcome the problem of data mining because data on realized returns are limited and noisy," adding, "I don't know how to begin designing tests that escape the data-mining trap."[25]

We can escape the data-mining trap, however, by examining investors' *expectations of returns* in addition to examining *realized returns*.[26] Consider book-to-market ratios, differentiating value companies with high ratios from growth companies with low ratios. We know that empirical evidence indicates a strong association between book-to-market ratios and subsequent realized returns. If the association between *expectations* of returns and book-to-market ratios is weak, then we have reason to suspect that the association between book-to-market ratios and *realized* returns is due to data mining. This suspicion is because a weak association between investors' expectations of returns and book-to-market ratios tells us that investors do not incorporate book-to-market ratios into their expectations of returns explicitly, knowing the book-to-market ratios of companies, or implicitly, knowing only the names of companies that turn out to have particular book-to-market ratios. If, however, there is a strong association between investors' expectations of returns and book-to-market ratios or names of companies that turn out to have particular book-to-market ratios, then we should reject the data-mining hypothesis.

Think of a survey in which investors are given only names of companies and their industries and asked for their expectations of the future returns of these companies' stocks. This, in essence, is one part of the *Fortune* surveys of company reputations conducted annually since 1983. *Fortune* asks senior executives, directors, and security analysts to rate companies in their industries on eight attributes: (1) quality of management; (2) quality of products or services; (3) innovativeness; (4) long-term investment value; (5) financial soundness; (6) ability to attract, develop, and keep talented people; (7) responsibility to the community and the environment; and (8) wise use of corporate assets.

The attribute of long-term investment value is a proxy for expectations of the returns of companies' stocks.[27] A regression of expectations of stock returns on book-to-market ratios, market capitalizations, and market-factor betas shows statistically significant associations between expectations of stock returns and book-to-market ratios and market capitalizations. This regression is inconsistent with the data-mining hypothesis that predicts weak associations.

Building blocks of Behavioral Finance

Expectations of stock returns = 3.47* − 0.54* (book-to-market ratio)
+ 0.31* (market capitalization) − 0.05 (market-factor beta)
* Statistically significant at the 0.01 level or better

The Risk Hypothesis

If expectations about returns conform to the CAPM, we should find a statistically significant association between expectations of returns and market-factor betas, but no statistically significant associations between expectations of returns and book-to-market ratios and market capitalization. This, however, is not what we find. Instead, as noted above, we find no statistically significant association between expectations of returns and market-factor betas, and statistically significant associations between expectations of returns and book-to-market ratios and market capitalization. Therefore, if differences in expectations of returns are due to differences in risk, that risk is not indicated by market-factor beta, as in the CAPM.

Eugene Fama and Kenneth French conjectured that high book-to-market ratios and low market capitalizations in the three-factor model indicate high risk (see n15). If that conjecture is true, we should find that expectations of returns are high for value stocks with high book-to-market ratios and low for stocks with large market capitalizations. Yet we find that expectations of returns are *low* for stocks with high book-to-market ratios and *high* for stocks with large market capitalizations. Therefore, if differences in expectations of returns are due to differences in risk, that risk is not indicated by high book-to-market ratios or small market capitalization, as in the three-factor model.

The risk indicated by small market capitalizations and high book-to-market ratios in the three-factor model might be the risk of financial distress associated with the likelihood of bankruptcy. Financial soundness, one of the company attributes in the *Fortune* surveys, can be interpreted as a measure of financial distress, whereby low financial soundness corresponds to high financial distress. If investors expect high returns from stocks with shaky financial soundness, we should find that long-term investment value is high among stock of companies with low financial soundness. Instead, we find that long-term investment value is *low* among stocks of companies with low financial soundness. This result is contrary to the conjecture that investors expect higher returns from stocks of financially distressed companies. Further evidence inconsistent with the financial distress conjecture is the finding that stocks of financially distressed companies provided *lower* returns, even though they had much higher standard deviations and market-factor betas than stocks of companies that are not as distressed.[28]

The Cognitive-Errors Hypothesis

The cognitive-errors hypothesis is the claim that the empirical association between returns and book-to-market ratios and market capitalizations is due to cognitive errors, specifically an erroneous belief that stocks with low book-to-market ratios and large market capitalizations yield higher expected returns than stocks with high book-to-market ratios and small market capitalizations.

Economists Josef Lakonishok, Andrei Shleifer, and Robert Vishny found that stocks of value companies, whose price-to-book and price-to-earnings ratios are low, yielded higher returns than stocks of growth, or "glamour," companies whose ratios are high.[29] The authors also found that glamour stocks yielded higher past stock returns and had higher rates of growth in sales and earnings than value stocks. Lakonishok and his coauthors hypothesized that investors err by extrapolating high past returns and rates of growth of sales and earnings into high subsequent returns and rates of growth in sales and earnings. This extrapolation misleads investors to believe that stocks of glamour companies will yield higher subsequent returns than stocks of value companies, whereas empirical evidence indicates that stocks of value companies yielded subsequent higher returns.

Tobin's Q resembles a market-to-book ratio but it is broader. It is the ratio of the total market value of all the securities of a company to the replacement value of its assets. Michael Solt and Meir Statman hypothesized that cognitive errors mislead investors to identify stocks with high Tobin's Q, large market capitalizations, and high price-to-earnings ratios as stocks that are likely to yield high future returns, whereas evidence shows that on average such stocks yielded *low* returns.[30]

The findings of Lakonishok and his coauthors and Solt and Statman are consistent with the cognitive-errors hypothesis. Yet Lakonishok and his coauthors offered no evidence that investors actually extrapolate past returns and rates of growth in sales and earnings into subsequent returns and rates of growth in sales and earnings. And Solt and Statman offered no evidence that investors actually consider Tobin's Q, market capitalizations, or price-to-earnings ratios as associated with subsequent stock returns.

The cognitive-errors hypothesis in this case is better called the characteristics hypothesis because it claims that investors consider but misinterpret characteristics, such as observing the characteristic of high past growth of earnings and misinterpreting it as an indication of high subsequent growth of earnings, accompanied by high stock returns.

To examine the characteristics hypothesis, consider an experiment in which high-net-worth investors completed a questionnaire that provided only characteristics of companies and their stocks, not their names or industries. Table 10-1 is a truncated version of the questionnaire.[31] The three characteristics are price-to-book ratio, market capitalization, and past stock returns. The last characteristic is associated with the momentum factor. Price-to-book ratio was used rather than its book-to-price inverse because it is more familiar to investors.

Characteristics were classified into one of three categories: high, average, and low. There are twenty-seven possible combinations of the three characteristics. The instruction to investors said, "Look at the characteristics of each company and quickly rate the feeling associated with it on a scale ranging from bad to good. Don't spend time thinking about the rating. Just go with your quick, intuitive feeling." The definitions of the characteristics were given below the instructions.

Characteristics
Price-to-book is the ratio of the stock price to its book value
Market capitalization is the total value of all the stock of the company
Past stock return is the stock return during the previous year

The characteristics score of each combination of the three characteristics is the mean score assigned to it by investors. For example, the score assigned to the combination of low price to book, high market capitalization, and average past returns was 5.67 out of a minimum of zero and a

Table 10-1 QUESTIONNAIRE IN WHICH SURVEYED INVESTORS HAD ONLY THE CHARACTERISTICS OF COMPANIES

Company	Price-to-Book	Market Capitalization	Past Stock Return	Bad									Good
Company 1	Low	High	Average	1	2	3	4	5	6	7	8	9	10
Company 2	Average	Low	High	1	2	3	4	5	6	7	8	9	10
Company 3	Average	High	Low	1	2	3	4	5	6	7	8	9	10
Company 4	High	Low	High	1	2	3	4	5	6	7	8	9	10

maximum of 10. Next, each stock was classified as a member of one of the three categories by each characteristic, "high" if it was among the top 70 of the 210 companies by that characteristic, "average" if it was among the middle 70, and "low" if it was among the bottom 70. Cisco was in the "high" category by each of the three characteristics, so it was assigned a 6.78 score of stocks with high price-to-book ratio, large market capitalization, and high past returns. Accenture was in the "high" category by price-to-book ratio and past stock returns but in the "average" category by market capitalization, so it was assigned a 6.33 score of stocks with high price-to-book ratio and past returns but average market capitalization.

If investors consider characteristics as they estimate future returns, such as by extrapolating past returns, we would find that high characteristics scores correspond to high *Fortune* ratings on long-term investment value. But this is not what we find. The coefficient of a regression of *Fortune* ratings on characteristics scores is positive, but it is far from statistical significance:

> Expectations of stock returns = 5.93 + 0.06 (characteristic score)
> This rating indicates weak support, at best, for the cognitive-errors hypothesis.

The Emotional-Errors Hypothesis

The emotional-errors hypothesis is the claim that the empirical association between stock returns, book-to-market ratios, and market capitalizations is due to emotional errors, specifically those caused by misleading affect.

We admire a company or spurn it when we hear its name, whether Alphabet (Google) or General Motors, before we consider its book-to-market ratio or market capitalization. Companies and their stocks, like meals, cars, and houses, exude affect. We regularly attribute to each a specific quality of "goodness" or "badness," a feeling that occurs rapidly and automatically, often unconsciously, to something we are evaluating.[32]

The emotional-errors hypothesis here refers to the claim that affect creates halos over companies and their stocks, misleading investors into the belief that stocks of companies with positive affect yield higher returns and impose lower risk than stocks of companies with negative affect. One prediction of the emotional-errors hypothesis is that positive affect is associated in the eyes of investors with high long-term investment value. We can test this prediction by examining the association between affect elicited by company names and their *Fortune* ratings on long-term investment value.

A group of high-net-worth investors were asked to complete a questionnaire listing only the names of 210 companies from the *Fortune* survey, their industries, and a 10-point affect scale ranging from bad to good. Table 10-2 is a truncated version of the questionnaire.[33] The instructions said, "Look at the name of the company and its industry and quickly rate the feeling associated with it on a scale ranging from bad to good. Don't spend time thinking about the rating. Just go with your quick, intuitive feeling." The affect score of a company is the mean score by the surveyed investors.

It turned out that companies whose names elicit positive affect tend to elicit expectations of high stock returns, as measured by *Fortune* ratings of long-term investment value.

This is consistent with the emotional errors hypothesis.
Expectations of stock returns = 2.13 + 0.6* (Affect score)
* Statistically significant at the 0.01 level or better

The emotional-errors hypothesis also predicts that *names* of companies and the images they bring to investors' minds are what elicit misleading affect, rather than company characteristics.

Consider an experiment in which a group of high-net-worth investors were given the names of companies, their industries, and the three characteristics. The score of a stock is the mean score assigned to it by the surveyed investors. The questionnaire said, "Look at the name, industry, and

Table 10-2 QUESTIONNAIRE IN WHICH SURVEYED INVESTORS HAD ONLY THE NAMES OF COMPANIES AND THEIR INDUSTRIES

Company	Industry	Bad									Good	Never Heard of the Company
Apache	Crude oil	1	2	3	4	5	6	7	8	9	10	O
Sara Lee	Food	1	2	3	4	5	6	7	8	9	10	O
Cardinal Health	Health care	1	2	3	4	5	6	7	8	9	10	O
Procter & Gamble	Household	1	2	3	4	5	6	7	8	9	10	O

characteristics of each company and quickly rate the feeling associated with it on a scale ranging from bad to good. Don't spend time thinking about the rating. Just go with your quick, intuitive feeling." The definitions of the characteristics were given below the instruction.

The 0.18 R-Squared between *Fortune* ratings on long-term investment value and scores based on company names, industries, and characteristics is only slightly higher than the 0.17 R-Squared between *Fortune* ratings and scores based only on company names and industries, showing that characteristics alone had almost no influence on investors' assessments. This finding indicates that the data support the emotional-errors hypothesis more than the characteristics version of the cognitive-errors hypothesis.

A second prediction of the emotional-errors hypothesis is that the halo of affect leads investors to expect that stocks of companies with positive affect would not only yield high returns, but also impose *low* risk. In another experiment, two groups of high-net-worth investors were given the names and industries of the 210 companies. One group of investors was asked to rate the future *return* of each stock, while the other group was asked to rate the *risk* of each stock. The risk and return scores of stocks are the mean ratings assigned to them by the investors. The instructions to investors who received the return questionnaire said, "Look at the name of the company and its industry and quickly rate the future return of its stock on a scale ranging from 1-'low' to 10-'high.' Don't spend time thinking about the rating. Just go with your quick, intuitive feeling." The instruction to investors who received the risk questionnaire was identical, but where the term "risk" replaced "future returns." The future returns and risk scores of a company are the mean scores by the surveyed investors.[34]

The risk hypothesis predicts that expectations of high future returns are accompanied by assessments of high risk. Yet it turned out that expectations of high future returns are accompanied by assessment of *low* risk.

> This, too, is consistent with the emotional errors hypothesis.
> Expected-return score = 8.4 − 0.4* (Risk score)
> * Statistically significant at the 0.01 level or better

There is also a link between return scores, risk scores, and *Fortune* ratings on long-term investment value. High *Fortune* ratings on long-term investment value are associated with high future return scores. The coefficient of the future return scores is positive and statistically significant.

Expectations of stock returns = 2.7 + 0.6* (Expected-return score)
* Statistically significant at the 0.01 level or better

Similarly, high *Fortune* ratings on long-term investment value are associated with low risk scores. The coefficient of the risk scores is negative and statistically significant.

Expectations of stock returns = 8.0 − 0.3* (Risk score)
* Statistically significant at the 0.01 level or better

Other studies provide further support for the emotional errors hypothesis.[35] Two groups looked at a list of thirty countries. One group was asked for its expectations of the future return of the stock index of each country, whereas the other was asked for its assessment of the risk of the stock index of each country. The risk hypothesis predicts that expectations of high returns would be accompanied by assessments of high risk, but this is not what was found. Instead, countries where future returns were expected to be high were also countries where the risk of stocks was assessed as low. Similar evidence comes from experiments with students and investment professionals.[36]

Stocks rated A−, A, or A+ by S&P's tend to be stocks with low book-to-market ratios and large market capitalizations, characteristics associated with low future returns. Such stocks, however, tend to appeal to investors, very likely because of an association of A ratings with excellence. Indeed, investors are misled to prefer Class A shares of companies' stock over Class B shares, even though Class B shares are superior, having all the benefits of Class A shares in addition to greater voting rights.[37]

LeRoy Gross did not commit this emotional error in his manual for stockbrokers. Instead, he advised brokers to exploit it.[38] "When selecting a stock to attempt to merchandise in a big way to many people, one of my essential requirements is that the stock be rated A−, A, or A+ by Standard & Poor's. These ratings are based on an assessment of a company's financial strength. The quality rating has no bearing whatsoever on the direction the price may take in the future."

Gross explained the rationale for his advice: "Investors who lose money on high quality issues frequently direct their anger more toward the market than toward the broker who recommended the stock. Investors who lose on low quality issues tend to direct their anger toward the broker, and they may seek redress through court action."

The Wants for Expressive- and Emotional-Benefits Hypothesis

The wants hypothesis is the claim that the empirical association between stock returns, book-to-market ratios, and market capitalizations is due to investors' wants for the expressive and emotional benefits of stocks of large-growth companies—companies with large market capitalizations and low book-to-market ratios.

Wants are not always easy to distinguish from errors, because some wants are implicit rather than explicit. Wants are implicit when we are reluctant to admit them to others or even to ourselves. Admitting our want for socially responsible investing is easy and therefore likely explicit. Admitting our want for high social status is difficult and therefore likely implicit.

Investors might be enticed into preferring large-growth stocks over small-value stocks by cognitive errors, believing that the former offer higher expected returns than the latter, or they might want, explicitly or implicitly, the expressive and emotional benefits of stocks of admired companies, stocks that tend to be large-growth stocks, sacrificing the utilitarian benefits of the higher returns of the stocks of spurned companies, stocks that tend to be small-value stocks.

In sum, the evidence favors the emotional-errors and wants hypotheses over the data-mining, risk, and cognitive-errors hypotheses in explaining the empirical association between stock returns, book-to-market ratios, and market capitalizations.

Standard and Behavioral Asset Pricing Rationales

Empirical findings are often consistent with more than one theoretical interpretation and more than one possible rationale. Possible rationales underlying the momentum factor are one example. Momentum refers to the empirical finding that stocks that yielded returns higher than peers' during 6-month to 12-month periods tend to continue to yield returns higher than peers' in the following months, and stocks that yielded lower returns tend to continue to yield lower ones. Momentum is evident in 212 years of U.S. stock returns (1801–2012), and it is also evident outside the United States[39]

Standard rationales might underlie momentum. Company assets and growth opportunities change in predictable ways as a consequence of optimal investment choices. This trend imparts predictability to changes in companies' systematic risk, explaining the prevalence of momentum.[40]

Also, company-specific risks can generate momentum. Business risks at market and company-specific levels affect companies' investment decisions, and companies have some ability to forecast company-specific risks, such as those due to changes in demand or technology innovations. When companies adjust their operations by their forecast company risks, they impose on their investors company-specific risk in addition to market risk. These two risks jointly create a nonlinear risk premium, which simultaneously explains momentum and the three factors of market, small-large, and value-growth.[41]

Alternatively, behavioral rationales might underlie momentum. The disposition effect, reflected in the tendency to hold onto losing stocks, creates underreaction of prices to new information, leading to momentum. Consider news, such as encouraging results of a test of a cancer drug that increases by 20 percent the intrinsic value of the stock of its company. The price of the stock would increase instantaneously by 20 percent in a market in which all investors are rational. Imagine, however, a market in which some investors are normal, evident in reluctance to realize losses. Imagine further that some of them bought the stock at prices exceeding the price that prevailed before the encouraging test results were announced.

As the price of the stock increases toward the 20 percent increase in intrinsic value it reaches levels equal to prices paid by some investors. Those investors might rush to sell the stock, now that they can break even and close the mental account on the stock without realizing a loss. In turn, selling presses down the stock price, retarding its increase toward the 20 percent increase in intrinsic value. What should have been an instantaneous 20 percent price increase might take weeks and perhaps months of gradual increase to 20 percent, a gradual increase we know as momentum. Empirical evidence based on mutual fund data is consistent with this process.[42]

Another behavioral rationale for momentum draws on the "frog in the pan" observation that investors are less attentive to information when it arrives gradually in small bits than to the same information when it arrives instantaneously in one large lump. Continuous information induces momentum as stock prices change gradually.[43]

Rationales for momentum vary in their predictions about its profitability in various settings. A behavioral rationale based on investor overconfidence predicts lower-momentum profits in markets with more sophisticated investors. A standard rationale based on information availability predicts lower-momentum profits in markets with smaller differences in information availability among investors. A standard rationale based on institutional structures predicts lower-momentum profits in markets with lower conflicts of interest between money managers and investors who delegate investment management to money managers.

Analysis of the 19th-century stock market in imperial Russia offers a test of these predictions. There was no delegated investment management during the period, and a regulatory change in 1893 reduced differences in information availability. It turns out that the momentum effect in Russia during the period surrounding 1893 is similar in magnitude to that in modern markets and stronger during the post-1893 period than the pre-1893 period, consistent with the behavioral overconfidence rationale of momentum.[44]

The Early Behavioral Asset Pricing Model

The early behavioral asset pricing model introduced by Hersh Shefrin and Meir Statman in 1994 was spurred by the same challenges to the CAPM that spurred Eugene Fama and Kenneth French to introduce the three-factor model. These challenges include a weak association between realized stock returns and market-factor betas, and strong associations between realized stock returns and market capitalization, and book-to-market ratios.[45]

Cognitive errors do play roles in the model but not emotional errors or wants for expressive and emotional benefits. The cognitive errors in the model are representativeness errors reflected in the tendency to form expectations of future returns by extrapolating past returns or expecting their reversals. Susceptibility to the cognitive errors of representativeness is described in Chapter 3, "Cognitive Shortcuts and Errors."

The model describes investment asset prices as the outcome of struggles over the "steering wheel" of prices by two kinds of traders as drivers, "information drivers" and "noise drivers." Information drivers are rational drivers, free of cognitive errors, whereas noise drivers are normal drivers susceptible to cognitive errors.

Prices of securities equal their intrinsic values in markets in which all drivers are information drivers. Moreover, in such markets the market portfolio is on the mean-variance frontier. But prices can deviate from intrinsic values in markets in which some drivers are noise drivers who steer prices in directions corresponding to their cognitive errors. In such markets the market portfolio is no longer on the mean-variance frontier. Portfolios on the mean-variance frontier are instead tilted toward small and value stocks. Specifically, the proportions allocated to small and value stocks in portfolios on the mean-variance frontier exceed their proportions in the market portfolio. Conversely, the proportions allocated to large and growth stocks are short of their proportions in the market portfolio.

It is becoming increasingly evident that investors' expectations of returns matter in steering prices. Economists Nicholas Barberis, Robin Greenwood, Lawrence Jin, and Andrei Shleifer offered X-CAPM as an asset pricing model that incorporates investors' expectations of returns. Their model, like that of Shefrin and Statman, shows the interaction between non-extrapolating rational investors and normal extrapolating investors.[46]

Specifically, good news that increases intrinsic values, such as surprisingly high earnings, prompts increased stock prices. Extrapolators expect further increases, buying stocks and pushing prices higher than intrinsic values would warrant. Non-extrapolators understand the effects of extrapolators' trades and correctly expect low future prices, but are unable or unwilling to engage fully in arbitrage that would press stock prices down all the way to intrinsic values. Prices inflated by extrapolators are eventually deflated as the effect of the good news fades, bad news arrives, and extrapolators sell stocks.

Behavioral asset pricing models must, however, account for more than investors' cognitive errors. Emotions, mood, and affect matter as well, in the form of emotional errors or emotional benefits and costs. For example, losses in soccer, cricket, rugby, and basketball games impart negative mood that infects stock movements. A loss in the soccer World Cup elimination stage led, on average, to a negative 0.49 percent excess return the following day.[47]

The effects of emotion, mood, and affect on stock prices are also evident in the observation that stocks tend to yield especially high returns in the month of the Cultural New Year. Examination of stocks in ten major countries that celebrate four distinct Cultural New Year holidays on days other than January 1 concluded that the evidence is most consistent with the hypothesis that investors' uplifted mood in celebrating the holidays leads to bullish sentiment that elevates stock prices. Average monthly stock return is one to three percentage points higher during the Cultural New Year months than during other non-January months. Further, stocks with substantial individual investor clienteles yielded significantly higher returns than did other stocks.[48] Moreover, behavioral asset pricing models must account for investors' wants for expressive and emotional benefits, beyond utilitarian benefits.

BEHAVIORAL ASSET PRICING MODELS

Behavioral asset pricing models, like standard asset pricing models, are factors or characteristics models that begin with theoretical rationales for factors and characteristics or strive to identify theoretical rationales for factors and characteristics found empirically. But behavioral asset pricing models and standard asset pricing models differ in the breadth of theoretical rationales. Theoretical rationales in behavioral asset pricing models encompass wants for utilitarian, expressive, and emotional benefits and the presence of cognitive and emotional errors, whereas theoretical rationales in the standard asset pricing models are limited to wants for utilitarian benefits among investors free of cognitive and emotional errors.

We can illustrate behavioral asset pricing models by adding two social-responsibility factors to the four-factor asset pricing model with market, small-large, value-growth, and momentum factors. The first factor, reflecting cognitive errors, is a "top-bottom" factor, consisting of the difference between the returns of stocks of companies ranked high and low on five social responsibility criteria. They are community (e.g., generous giving, support for housing), diversity (e.g., promotion of women and minorities, outstanding family benefits), employee relations (e.g., strong union relations, cash profit sharing), environment (e.g., pollution prevention, recycling), and products (e.g., product quality and safety, provision of products for the economically disadvantaged).

The second factor, reflecting wants for expressive and emotional benefits, is an "accepted-shunned" factor, consisting of the difference between the returns of stocks of companies commonly accepted by socially responsible investors and the returns of company stocks commonly shunned by them. Shunned stocks, again, include stocks of companies in the alcohol, tobacco, gambling, firearms, military, and nuclear industries.[49]

Underestimation of the value of intangible capital such as that embodied in good employee and community relations is a cognitive error very likely to be committed because the cost of intangible capital is immediately evident in lower current earnings, whereas its benefits are less evident and lie in the future.[50] We know that stocks of companies that ranked high overall on the five social responsibility criteria yielded high returns and argue that cognitive errors in estimation of intangible capital underlie these returns and the top-bottom factor.[51]

The association between climate change and stock prices is a case in point. Climate change seems remote and intangible and therefore possibly underestimated by investors. One study focused on drought, the most damaging natural disaster for crops and food-company cash flows. It found that a prolonged drought in a country, measured by the Palmer Drought Severity Index, forecasts poor stock returns for food companies in that country. The authors wrote that their findings raise concerns of underestimation of climate risks and called for disclosure of corporate exposure to such risks.[52]

Investments in stock of companies in the alcohol, tobacco, gambling, firearms, military, and nuclear industries impose expressive and emotional costs on socially responsible investors, as those industries violate social norms.[53] A study of the relative returns of stocks of shunned and accepted companies revealed that stocks of shunned companies yielded higher returns than those of accepted companies, consistent with the argument that wants for avoiding these expressive and emotional costs of holding shunned stocks is the rationale underlying the accepted-shunned factor in a behavioral asset pricing model.[54]

Many investors are aware of trade-offs between wants, and some are willing to trade utilitarian expected returns for the expressive and emotional benefits of avoiding stocks of shunned companies. A financial manager of the Church of the Brethren said that church members ask regularly whether they are sacrificing returns by excluding stocks of shunned companies. So do representatives of congregations that have received donations and bequests. Representatives may agree with excluding stocks of shunned companies from a personal standpoint, but as fiduciaries they must consider trade-offs between investment returns and adherence to the values of the church.[55]

The social responsibility factors are constructed with MSCI-ESG (Morgan Stanley Capital International-Environmental, Social and Governance) data. The staff of MSCI-ESG analyzes information relevant to strengths of companies and concerns about them in each criterion of social responsibility: community, diversity, employee relations, environment, and products. It assigns a score of 1 when a company demonstrates strength on an indicator on the list of criteria (e.g., charitable giving) and zero if it does not. Similarly, it assigns a score of 1 when a company's record raises concern on an indicator on the list (e.g., investment controversies) and zero otherwise.

The construction of the two social responsibility factors begins by calculating for each company, as of the end of each year, its top-bottom and accepted-shunned scores. These scores are matched with monthly stock returns in the subsequent 12 months. The "top" portfolio is a portfolio of stocks of companies rated in the top third by the five social responsibility criteria. The "bottom" portfolio is a portfolio of stocks of companies rated in the bottom third by the five social responsibility criteria. The top-bottom factor is the difference between the monthly returns of the two portfolios.

Similarly, the "accepted" portfolio is a portfolio of stocks of accepted companies and the "shunned" portfolio is a portfolio of stocks of shunned companies. The accepted-shunned factor is the difference between the monthly returns of the two portfolios. The two social responsibility factors are added as factors five and six to the four-factor asset pricing model that includes the factors of market, small-large, value-growth, and momentum.

Table 10-3 COMPARISON OF THE BARRIER FUND TO THE VANGUARD 500 FUND BY A SIX-FACTOR MODEL

	Barrier Fund	Vanguard 500 Fund
Alpha (annualized)	1.48 percent	−0.68 percent
Beta of market factor	0.87	0.98
Beta of small-large factor	0.15	−0.16
Beta of value-growth factor	−0.11	0.01
Beta of momentum factor	0.11	0.00
Beta of top-bottom factor	−0.05	0.03
Beta of accepted-shunned factor	−0.40	0.01

Table 10-3 presents a side-by-side comparison of the Barrier Fund and the Vanguard 500 Fund by the six-factor model that includes the two added social responsibility factors.[56] The negative 0.40 accepted-shunned-factor beta of the Barrier Fund indicates that it tilts away from stocks of accepted companies, consistent with its preference for stocks of shunned ones. There is no such preference in the Vanguard 500 fund, evident in its negligible 0.01 accepted-shunned-factor beta. The negative 0.05 top-bottom-factor beta of the Barrier fund indicates that it tilts away from stocks of top companies but the difference between that factor beta and the corresponding 0.03 factor beta of the Vanguard 500 fund is not nearly as great as the difference between the accepted-shunned-factor betas.

Barrier's market-factor beta is lower than that of the Vanguard 500, indicating that its return moves up or down less than the return of the Vanguard 500 when the return of the stock market moves up or down. The positive Barrier's small-large-factor beta indicates that it tilts toward small stocks, whereas Vanguard 500's negative small-large-factor beta indicates that it tilts toward large stocks. The positive Barrier's momentum-factor beta indicates that it tilts toward momentum stocks, whereas the near-zero Vanguard 500's momentum-factor beta indicates no tilt.

The positive excess returns—alpha—of Barrier indicates that its realized return exceeds the return that could be expected by the six-factor model, whereas the negative excess returns of Vanguard 500 indicates that its realized return falls short of the return that could be expected according to the six-factor model.

The four-factor model introduced by economists Robert Stambaugh and Yu Yuan offers another illustration of behavioral asset pricing models.[57] They noted that studies identified many anomalies, whereby realized returns are higher or lower than expected by the three-factor model. Behavioral rationales very likely underlie many of these anomalies.

Stambaugh and Yuan constructed two factors based on eleven prominent anomalies they described as sentiment driven, including those associated with net stock issues, net operating assets, asset growth, momentum, and gross profitability. They combined them with the market factor and a small-large factor into a four-factor model.

Stambaugh and Yuan found that their four-factor model, with two sentiment factors in addition to the market and small-large factors, explains the set of eleven anomalies better than alternative models. They noted that factor models can be useful whether expected returns reflect standard risk rationale or behavioral sentiment rationale. Standard and behavioral rationales might well jointly underlie factors and characteristics in asset pricing models.

Factors and Characteristics in Asset Pricing Models

Factor asset pricing models are easy to estimate. A factor model of mutual fund returns requires no more than the returns of the funds and the returns of the factors to estimate the betas of factors. But the betas of factors in factor models might be biased measures of characteristics. Characteristics asset pricing models are an alternative to factors asset pricing models, replacing factors such as accepted-shunned with company and stock characteristics, such as whether a company is accepted or shunned.

Think of gambling casinos in Las Vegas, belonging to the group of shunned companies. The sign of their accepted-shunned betas is likely negative because their returns tend to be high when the returns of shunned companies are high relative to the returns of accepted companies. Now think of a supermarket located close to these gambling casinos. Its returns are likely high when the returns of casinos are high because casino customers are also likely to be supermarket customers. The proximity to casinos might impart to the supermarket a negative accepted-shunned-factor beta, similar to that of casinos, implying that the supermarket belongs to the group of shunned companies. Yet its characteristics might well be those of an accepted company.

Characteristics models, however, are more difficult to estimate than factor models. Measuring the characteristics of a stock mutual fund requires that we "open" the fund and measure the characteristics of each of its stocks. Consider opening a stock mutual fund. Each stock held by the fund in a given quarter is graded on each of the five social responsibility criteria as top, bottom, or middle. For example, a stock earns a positive 1 on employee relations if its company is among the top third of companies by employee relations, a negative 1 if its company is among the bottom third, and a grade of zero if its company is among the middle third. Each stock is graded similarly on the four other criteria: community relations, environmental protection, diversity, and products. The maximum top-bottom characteristic grade of a stock is a positive 5, if it is graded 1 on each of the five criteria, and the minimum grade of a stock is a negative 5. The top-bottom characteristic grade of a mutual fund is an average of the top-bottom characteristic grades of its stocks.

The accepted-shunned characteristic grade of a mutual fund is calculated similarly. A stock is graded a positive 1 if its company is in the accepted group and a negative 1 if its company is in the shunned group of tobacco, military, gambling, and similar industries. The accepted-shunned characteristic grade of a fund is the average of the grades of the stocks it contains.

Factor betas correspond to characteristics grades at times. The Parnassus Workplace fund had a relatively high top-bottom characteristic grade and a corresponding high top-bottom-factor beta. LKCM Aquinas Small Cap fund had a negative top-bottom characteristic grade and a corresponding negative top-bottom-factor beta.

At other times, however, factors do not correspond to characteristics. The factor model yields a negative accepted-shunned-factor beta for the Barrier fund and a small positive accepted-shunned-factor beta for the Vanguard 500 fund. This finding implies that the holdings of the Barrier fund, but not those of the Vanguard 500 fund, tilt away from stocks of accepted companies. There is a conforming negative accepted-shunned characteristic grade for the Barrier fund and a conforming positive accepted-shunned characteristic grade for the Vanguard 500 fund. Yet while the factor models of the Barrier fund and the Vanguard 500 fund show similar top-bottom-factor betas, their top-bottom characteristics grades are very different, much lower at the Barrier fund than at the Vanguard 500.

"SMART BETA" AND ASSET PRICING MODELS

The portfolio in the market factor of the CAPM is the market portfolio. This is the market-capitalization weighted portfolio of all assets in which the weight of each asset equals the proportion of its market capitalization relative to the total market capitalization of all assets. According to the CAPM, the market-capitalization weighted market portfolio not only lies on the mean-variance frontier but also provides the best combinations of expected returns and standard deviations when combined with borrowing and lending. Indeed, the same market portfolio is the portfolio in the market factor of all factor models.

But what if the market portfolio lies below the mean-variance frontier? What if portfolios that lie on the mean-variance frontier are tilted toward small and value stocks such that their proportions in mean-variance efficient portfolios exceed their proportions in the market portfolio? What if portfolios on the mean-variance efficient frontier are tilted in additional directions associated with excess returns, such as toward momentum, causing further departures from proportions in the market portfolio?

"Smart beta" portfolios are portfolios in which the proportions of assets depart from their proportions in the market portfolio, aiming at higher ratios of expected returns to standard deviations than provided by that portfolio.[58] A portfolio tilting toward small and value stocks is a smart-beta portfolio, as it assigns greater proportions to small and value stocks than their proportions in the market portfolio. So is a portfolio tilting toward small and value stocks and also toward momentum stocks and other stock characteristics associated with positive excess returns.

We can see smart-beta portfolios and indexes as reflections of behavioral asset pricing models in which differences between expected returns of portfolios depend not only on differences in their market-factor betas but also on differences in betas of other factors. They include the small-large factor, value-growth factor, momentum factor, top-bottom factor, accepted-shunned factor, and other factors that distinguish portfolios with high expected returns from portfolios with low expected returns.

AQR, a large investment company, settled on four factors in its smart-beta portfolios, in addition to the market factor. They are the value factor, reflecting the tendency of relatively "cheap" assets to outperform relatively "expensive" ones; the momentum factor, reflecting the tendency of assets' recent relative performance to continue in the near future; the carry factor, reflecting the tendency of higher-yielding assets to provide higher returns than lower-yielding assets; and the defensive factor, reflecting the tendency of lower-risk and higher-quality assets to generate higher risk-adjusted returns.[59]

CONCLUSION

Behavioral asset pricing models, like standard asset pricing models, are factors or characteristics models that begin with theoretical rationales for factors and characteristics or strive to identify theoretical rationales for factors and characteristics found empirically. Behavioral asset pricing models and standard asset pricing models differ in the breadth of theoretical rationales.

Theoretical rationales in behavioral asset pricing models encompass wants for utilitarian, expressive, and emotional benefits and the presence of cognitive and emotional errors, whereas theoretical rationales in the standard asset pricing model are limited to wants for utilitarian benefits.

Both behavioral and standard asset pricing models are in effect works in progress in finance, manifested in two ways. First, the list of factors is expanding as the one-factor model consisting of the market factor alone was expanded into the three-factor model consisting of the market, small-large, and value-growth factors, later expanded further to include the momentum factor. Second, the identification of the theoretical rationales for factors is incomplete. The theoretical rationale for the small-large and value-growth factors might be wants for the utilitarian benefits of low risk, fitting within standard asset pricing models, or wants for utilitarian, expressive, and emotional benefits and the concurring cognitive and emotional errors, fitting within behavioral asset pricing models.

In practice, evolving factor-based behavioral asset pricing models look very much like evolving factor-based standard asset pricing models. For example, we can classify the three-factor asset pricing model as a standard asset pricing model if we conclude that wants for the utilitarian benefits of low risk are the rationale for the small-large and value-growth factors, or we can classify the same three-factor model as a behavioral asset pricing model if we conclude that wants and cognitive and emotional errors are the rationale for the same factors. We can pit the behavioral asset model against the standard asset pricing model if we conclude that rationales for factors are more likely behavioral or more likely standard.

We must also know more if we are to distinguish wants for utilitarian benefits from wants for expressive and emotional benefits and from cognitive and emotional errors. Yet distinctions between choices motivated by particular wants and errors are more important conceptually than practically. Errors can be as persistent as wants—investors motivated to trade by cognitive and emotional errors affect asset prices no differently from how other investors do when they are motivated by wants for utilitarian benefits or wants for expressive and emotional benefits.

How many factors would behavioral asset pricing models contain? A long list of factors would make models comprehensive but also cumbersome. A short list would make them less cumbersome but also less comprehensive. Behavioral asset pricing models are evolving over time, as we weigh the trade-offs between the benefits of comprehensive models and their drawbacks. And behavioral asset pricing models are also evolving over time as empirical evidence and theory favor the addition of some factors and the deletion of others.

CHAPTER 11

Behavioral Efficient Markets

The decision of the Nobel Prize committee to award the 2013 Nobel Prize in economics to Eugene Fama and Robert Shiller puzzled many. "If you've been wondering whether it's possible to regularly beat the stock market averages," wrote Steven Rattner, a Wall Street financier and commentator, "you didn't get any guidance from the Nobel Prize committee this year."[1]

Rattner placed Shiller in one corner, claiming that he "argues that markets are often irrational and therefore beatable." He placed Fama in the opposite corner, describing him as "the father of the view that markets are efficient," whose "followers believe that investors who try to beat the averages will inevitably fail."

The efficient-market hypothesis is central to standard finance, and many believe that behavioral finance refutes it. Indeed, many believe that refutation of the efficient-market hypothesis is the most important contribution of behavioral finance. Yet discussions are unfocused when they fail to distinguish between two versions of efficient markets and their corresponding efficient market hypotheses, the *price-equals-value market hypothesis* and the *hard-to-beat market hypothesis*. And discussions are lacking when they fail to explain why so many investors believe that markets are easy to beat.

Behavioral finance provides evidence contradicting the *price-equals-value market hypothesis* but its evidence is generally consistent with the *hard-to-beat market hypothesis*. Behavioral finance also explains why so many investors believe that markets are easy to beat when, in truth, they are hard to beat.

Price-equals-value markets are markets where investment prices always equal their intrinsic values and the price-equals-value market hypothesis is the claim that investment prices always equal their intrinsic values. Hard-to-beat markets are markets where some investors are able to beat the market, earning consistent excess returns, but most are unable to do so. Excess returns generally correspond to above-average returns. More precisely, they are returns in excess of returns that can be expected according to a correct asset pricing model.

Price-equals-value markets are impossible to beat because excess returns come from exploiting gaps between prices and intrinsic values, gaps absent in price-equals-value markets. But hard-to-beat markets are not necessarily price-equals-value markets. It might be that prices deviate greatly from intrinsic values, taking them far from price-equals-value efficiency, but deviations are hard to identify in time or difficult to exploit for excess returns. In other words, markets may be crazy, but this realization does not make you a psychiatrist.

The rational investors of standard finance know that markets are hard to beat, but many of the normal investors described in behavioral finance believe that markets are easy to beat. In truth, most investors who attempt to beat the market are beaten by it. Such investors are misled by cognitive and emotional errors or are willing to sacrifice returns and their utilitarian benefits for the expressive benefits of the image of being "active" rather than "passive" investors, and the emotional benefits of hope of beating the market.

Economist Kenneth French estimated that active investors—investors who try to beat the market—would have saved an annual 0.67 percent of the aggregate value of their investments, on average, if they had refrained from attempts to beat the market and chosen passive match-the-market low-cost index funds. That percentage amounted to more than $100 billion in 2006 alone.[2] The estimate of potential savings by John Bogle, founder of the Vanguard Group, is even higher.[3]

"Why do active investors continue to play a negative-sum game?" asked French. He drew his answers from behavioral finance. One part of the answer is ignorance. Many investors are unaware that the returns of active investors are, on average, lower than those of passive investors.

Another part is purposeful or inadvertent exploitation of investors' cognitive and emotional errors by financial companies and the financial press. Exploitation of availability errors is common. A small handful of financial companies promote passive funds over active funds, but the general message from financial companies is that beating the market with active funds is easy. This message is reinforced by the financial press, which makes available stories about stocks whose prices diverge from values and money managers who beat the market by exploiting these divergences.

Exploitation of traders' overconfidence errors is also common. Overconfidence leads to excessive trading. Moreover, traders who are overconfident in their above-average ability to beat the market are unlikely to be discouraged by the knowledge that the returns of frequent traders are, on average, lower than those of buy-and-hold passive investors.

Yet another part is wants for expressive and emotional benefits. Some investors are willing to sacrifice the utilitarian benefits of higher expected returns for the expressive and emotional benefits that accompany beating the market. Others sacrifice the utilitarian benefits of low cost and diversification of passive mutual funds for the expressive and emotional benefits of having their own separate accounts.

Intrinsic Values

John Burr Williams illustrated intrinsic values in a ditty he included in his otherwise very serious 1938 book, *The Theory of Investment Value*.[4] Williams placed a stock side by side with a cow and a hen.

A cow for her milk,
A hen for her eggs,
And a stock, by heck, for her dividends.

The intrinsic value of a cow is the present value of the expected net proceeds from its milk during its life and its meat afterwards. Rational farmers care about no more than these net proceeds and are unwilling to pay for a cow any more than its intrinsic value. In a price-equals-value cow market, the price of a cow always equals its intrinsic value. Similarly, the intrinsic value of a stock is the present value of its expected dividends during its life, and rational investors care about no more than that. In a price-equals-value stock market, the price of a stock always equals its intrinsic value.

The intrinsic value of a stock is determined by expected dividends during a company's life, including the expected dividend received at the end of its life, whether it is zero if it goes bankrupt or billions if another company buys it. Dividends are received in installments over many years. The time value of money relates to the observation that money to be received in the future, even if sure money, is less valuable than money received today. We discount future expected dividends to account for the stock's required return, determined by a correct asset pricing model. That model accounts for utilitarian benefits and costs such as the cost of risk, as well as expressive and emotional costs and benefits. We also know the required return as the expected return and as the cost of equity. The intrinsic value of a stock is the sum of the expected dividends during a company's expected life, discounted to account for the stock's required return. Rational investors refuse to buy stocks at prices exceeding intrinsic values.

Price-Equals-Value Markets and Hard-to-Beat Markets

Rattner, who described himself as "someone whose professional life centers on evaluating investment managers," placed himself in Shiller's corner because he has "met many investors who have consistently outperformed the market," including Warren Buffett (see n1).

Warren Buffett illustrated the distinction between price-equals-value markets and hard-to-beat markets and the confusion that arises when they are lumped into efficient markets. Buffett was considering buying bonds of Citizens Insurance, established by the state of Florida and backed by state taxes to cover hurricane damage. Berkshire Hathaway, his company, received three bids from sellers of Citizens Insurance bonds, one at a price that would yield 11.33 percent, one at 9.87 percent, and one at 6.00 percent. "It's the same bond, the same time, the same dealer. And a big issue," said Buffett. "This is not some little anomaly, as they like to say in academic circles every time they find something that disagrees with their [efficient market] theory."[5]

Buffett referred to "efficient market," but the term price-equals-value market would have been more precise. The story of the Citizens Insurance bonds is, as Buffett noted, an anomaly, contradicting the claim that the market for these bonds is a price-equals-value market. The intrinsic value of each Citizens Insurance bond is identical to the intrinsic value of every other Citizens Insurance bond, since all of them are identical in every feature. The fact that the bonds were selling at different prices contradicts the claim that the market for these bonds is a price-equals-value market, since three different prices cannot all equal one intrinsic value. Two of the prices, and perhaps all three, must diverge from intrinsic value.

Hard-to-beat markets, however, are distinct from price-equals-value markets. Whereas prices always equal intrinsic values in price-equals-value markets, prices sometimes deviate from intrinsic values in hard-to-beat markets. A market is hard to beat if most investors find it hard to earn consistent excess returns.

Buffett cautioned investors not to jump too fast from evidence that markets are not price-equals-value markets to the conclusion that markets are not hard-to-beat markets. When asked, "What advice would you give to someone who is not a professional investor?" Buffett said, "Well, if they're not going to be an active investor—and very few should try that—then they should just stay with index funds. Any low-cost index fund. . . . They're not going to be able to pick the right price and the right time."

On January 1, 2008, Buffett on one side placed roughly $320,000 on a bet that the Admiral Shares' class of the Vanguard 500, a mutual fund tracking the S&P 500 Index, would outperform a portfolio of hedge funds over the following 10 years. On the other side was Protégé Partners, LLC, a hedge fund company, whose people placed an identical amount on a bet that the hedge funds they have chosen would beat the Vanguard 500 fund. All the money was placed in a zero-coupon bond that would grow to $1 million by December 31, 2017, and go to charity, to Absolute Returns for Kids if Protégé won, and to Girls Inc. if Buffett did.

Protégé argued that "funds of [hedge] funds with the ability to sort the wheat from the chaff will earn returns that amply compensate for the extra layer of fees their clients pay," and noted that the Paulson & Co. hedge fund is among its investments. John Paulson made billions in profits for his company by selling short investments linked to subprime mortgages. But Buffett said, "A lot of very smart people set out to do better than average in investment markets. Call them active [beat-the-market] investors. Their opposites, passive [index] investors, will by definition do about average." But investors in hedge funds are unlikely to overcome their costs. "Investors, on average and over time," concluded Buffett, "will do better with a low-cost index fund than with a group of [hedge] funds."[6]

By the end of 2014, seven years into the bet's 10 years, the return of the Vanguard 500 fund was 63.5 percent, whereas the return of Protégé's hedge funds of funds was 19.6 percent. Protégé's Ted Seides said, "The odds now are that we'll need to see a severe market contraction for our side of the ledger to stage an epic comeback."[7] The odds of Protégé improved somewhat as its funds gained 1.70 percent in 2015, whereas the Vanguard 500 fund gained only 1.36 percent. Yet the 10-year odds still favor the Vanguard 500 fund.[8]

Palm Pilot's spin-off from its parent 3Com Corporation illustrates further the distinction between price-equals-value markets and hard-to-beat markets. The spin-off occurred at the height of the Internet boom in early 2000.[9] Initially, only 5 percent of Palm Pilot shares were sold to investors. The other 95 percent remained with 3Com. Enthusiasm for the shares of Palm Pilot was so great and their price shot up so high that the total value of the 95 percent of Palm Pilot shares still owned by 3Com greatly exceeded the total value of 3Com shares, implying the absurd conclusion that the rest of 3Com's business had negative value. The more likely conclusion is that the price of 3Com shares was far below their intrinsic value, or that the price of Palm Pilot shares was far above their intrinsic value, or both.

The prices of Palm Pilot and 3Com shares were not consistent with the price-equals-value hypothesis, yet they were consistent with the hard-to-beat market hypothesis because investors could not execute arbitrage to beat the market and, in the process, eliminate gaps between prices and intrinsic values.

Arbitrage would have been executed by selling short Palm Pilot shares, whose price was higher than intrinsic value, and simultaneously buying 3Com shares, whose price was lower than intrinsic value. Yet arbitrage could not be executed, because selling short shares of Palm Pilot required borrowing them from investors who own them, and there were not enough shares of Palm Pilot available for borrowing, as almost all were owned by 3Com. Eventually, the price of Palm Pilot shares declined toward its intrinsic value as 3Com sold more of them.

Investors might not care much about whether markets are price-equals-value markets if all they want is to beat the market. But everyone should care about whether markets are price-equals-value markets because such markets are crucial for proper allocation of the economy's resources, be these labor or capital. Proper allocation of the economy's resources benefits everyone.

Think of a stock market in which the $100 price per share of a software company exceeds its $60 intrinsic value. Managers of this company choose to sell 10,000 shares at $100 each for a total of $1 million and use the proceeds to expand their operations, buying equipment and hiring employees. They would have forgone expanding their operations if the sale of the 10,000 shares had fetched only $600,000.

Now think of a biotechnology company whose $60 price per share is short of its $100 intrinsic value. Managers of this company choose to forgo expanding their operations, as the sale of 10,000 shares would have yielded only $600,000, whereas they would have chosen to expand their operations if the price per share had been $100, fetching $1 million.

This is a case in which resources are not allocated properly. Resources in the form of equipment and employees are allocated to the software company, whereas they would have done more good for us as a whole if they had been allocated to the biotechnology company.

The Price-Equals-Value Market Hypothesis

The price-equals-value market hypothesis is the claim that the prices of all investments equal their intrinsic values at all times. Testing the hypothesis directly is difficult because estimating the intrinsic value of investments is difficult. This problem leads to the common but usually implicit replacement of the price-equals-value market hypothesis with the hard-to-beat market hypothesis in discussions of the efficient market hypothesis, and the implicit assumption that the two hypotheses are the same. Yet again, the two are different. Price-equals-value markets are impossible to beat, but hard-to-beat markets are not necessarily price-equals-value markets.

The price-equals-value market hypothesis implies as a corollary the *change-price-equals-change-value* market hypothesis, whereby *changes* in prices equal *changes* in intrinsic values. This hypothesis is easier to test. The story of the *Titanic* illustrates a change-price-equals-change-value market hypothesis and is generally consistent with it. The *Titanic* left Southampton, England, on its way to New York on April 10, 1912, and collided with a giant iceberg on the night of April 14. By the morning of April 15, the ship and 1,503 of its 2,207 passengers lay at the bottom of the Atlantic Ocean. The *Titanic* was owned by the IMM Corporation, whose shares were traded on the New York Stock Exchange. How did the intrinsic value of IMM change as the *Titanic* sank? And how did its stock price change when the news arrived?

The *Titanic*, built for $7,500,000, was insured by Lloyd's for $5,000,000. So the net loss of intrinsic value from its sinking was $2,500,000 if we assume that no further losses occurred, such as loss of future business. If the market for IMM's stock were change-price-equals-change-value market, the price of all IMM's shares would have declined by a total of $2,500,000 soon after the *Titanic* news arrived. It turns out the price of all IMM's shares declined by a total of $2,604,500 during April 15 and 16, the two days following the

Titanic disaster. The change in price was somewhat higher than the change in intrinsic value but the two are close enough to support the claim that the market for IMM's shares was a change-price-equals-change-value market.[10]

The stories of aviation disasters also illustrate the change-price-equals-change-value market hypothesis but are generally inconsistent with it. The average decline in intrinsic value of companies following an aviation disaster is no more than $1 billion, but the average decline in stock prices corresponds to a loss of more than $60 billion.[11]

Economist Ray Fair found instances in which large changes in the level of the S&P 500 Index occurred with no events likely associated with changes in intrinsic value, inconsistent with the change-price-equals-change-value market hypothesis. He wrote, "The results ... suggest that stock price determination is complicated. Many large price changes correspond to no obvious events, and so many large changes appear to have no easy explanation. Also, of the hundreds of fairly similar announcements that have taken place between 1982 and 1999, only a few have led to large price changes.... And it does not appear easy to explain why some do and some do not."[12]

Economist Richard Roll also found evidence inconsistent with the change-price-equals-change-value market hypothesis.[13] He calculated R-squared, the proportion of the variation of the returns of stocks that is accounted for by news about changes in their intrinsic values, and concluded that the average R-squared is only 0.35 when monthly returns are used, and only 0.20 when daily returns are used. The R-squared would have been 1.00 if only news about changes in intrinsic values caused changes in stock prices. More recent work by economist Jacob Boudoukh and his coauthors indicates that news accounts for more of the variation in stock prices than found by Roll, providing greater support for the change-price-equals-change-value market hypothesis.[14] Whereas Roll used newspaper reports to identify news, Boudoukh and his coauthors used advanced textual analysis that made it possible to identify news by type and tone. Once news has been correctly identified in this manner, there is evidence of a stronger, but hardly perfect, relation between news and stock price changes.

Robert Shiller provided evidence inconsistent with the change-price-equals-change-value market hypothesis early on, in articles published in 1979 and 1981.[15] He found greater changes in bond and stock prices than can be expected by considering only changes in intrinsic values and argued that differences are best explained by investor psychology. He wrote that changing perceptions and tastes affect the selection of stocks and bonds as they affect the selection of food, clothing, health, and politics. Several early studies cast doubt on Shiller's empirical tests but his conclusions have stood the test of time.

The Forms of the Hard-to-Beat Market Hypothesis

The three forms of the hard-to-beat market hypothesis (Box 11-2) are the exclusively available-information, the narrowly available-information, and the widely available-information forms. The exclusively available-information form is the claim that not even investors with exclusively available information can beat the market. The narrowly available-information form accepts that investors with exclusively available information can beat the market but claims that investors with no more than narrowly available information cannot beat it. The widely available-information form accepts that investors with exclusively or narrowly available information can beat the market but claims that investors with no more than widely available information cannot.

Exclusively available information is information available to only one person, such as a company CEO. Narrowly available information is information available to only a few, such as the group of top executives of a company, analysts following the company, and readers of publications directed at narrow professional audiences. *Nature* magazine is one example, directed at research scientists. Widely available information includes, for example, information published in major newspapers directed at wide audiences, such as *The New York Times*. Gradations of information can be made finer, such as distinguishing narrowly available information from very narrowly available information.

Box 11-2 THE THREE FORMS OF THE HARD-TO-BEAT
MARKET HYPOTHESIS

1. The exclusively available-information form of the hard-to-beat market hypothesis is the claim that not even investors with exclusively available information can beat the market.
2. The narrowly available-information form of the hard-to-beat market hypothesis accepts that investors with exclusively available information can beat the market but claims that investors with no more than narrowly available information cannot beat it.
3. The widely available-information form of the hard-to-beat market hypothesis accepts that investors with exclusively or narrowly available information can beat the market but claims that investors with no more than widely available information cannot.

Eugene Fama divided the efficient market hypothesis into three forms, strong, semi-strong, and weak. The strong form is the claim that not even investors with private information can beat the market. The semi-strong form accepts that investors with private information can beat the market, but claims that investors with no more than public information cannot. The weak form is a claim that investors with no more than a subset of public information—past stock prices and volume of trading—cannot beat the market.[16]

Fama went on to describe an efficient market as one "in which prices always 'fully reflect' available information." "Available information," however, is an ambiguous term, and so are the terms "public information" and "private information." Publication in *Nature* makes information publicly available, and so does publication on the front page of *The New York Times*. Yet publication on the front page of the *Times* makes information widely available, whereas publication in *Nature* or even on an inside page of the *Times* makes it only narrowly available. Information known to only one person is private information and so is information known to only a few, but the first is exclusively available information, whereas the second is narrowly available information.

The three forms of the hard-to-beat market hypothesis are similar to Fama's three forms in some ways, but different in others. Consider the case of EntreMed (ENMD), a biotechnology company, explored by economists Gur Huberman and Tomer Regev.[17] The Sunday, May 3, 1998, edition of *The New York Times* reported on its front page a breakthrough in cancer research and mentioned ENMD, a company with licensing rights to the breakthrough.[18] The price of ENMD's shares increased substantially following that report, yet the substance of the information had been published in *Nature* more than five months earlier.[19] Moreover, the substance of the information had also been published in the *Times* itself in November 1997, although on an inside page, rather than on the front page, as in May 1998.[20]

Huberman and Regev interpreted their finding as inconsistent with a semi-strong efficient market, because the price of ENMD's shares changed following the front page *New York Times* report in May 1998, in the absence of new information. The information in *Nature* was public information in 1997 and so was the same information on an inside page of the *Times* in 1997 and on the front page of the *Times* in May 1998. The "new-news content of the *Times* story [in May 1998] was nil," they wrote. Yet the information in *Nature* and on the inside page of the *Times* was narrowly available, whereas the May 1998 front page publication in the *Times* made it widely available.

The fact that ENMD's stock price did not increase in the months following the May 1998 publication in the *Times*, beyond its immediate increase following the publication, is consistent with the widely available-information form of the hard-to-beat market hypothesis. Readers of the *Times* were unable to beat the market by buying ENMD shares at the low price prevailing before the May 1998 date of the front page *Times* publication, and sell them at a higher price following that date. But the fact that the price of ENMD shares increased when its information was made widely available on the May 1998 front page of the *Times* is inconsistent with the narrowly available-information form of the hard-to-beat market hypothesis. Readers of the ENMD story in *Nature* or in the inside page of the *Times* who bought shares in 1997, when information was narrowly available, did beat the market, gaining as the stock's price increased when the information became widely available in May 1998, on the front page of the *Times*.

WHO BEATS A HARD-TO-BEAT MARKET?

Hard-to-beat markets are not impossible to beat. Investors with exclusively available information find it easy to beat the market, and investors with narrowly available information find it hard but not impossible to beat the market. Yet, on average, investors with nothing more than widely available information find it impossible to beat the market. Such investors are beaten by the market more often than they beat it. Indeed, investors with exclusively available and narrowly available information gain their market-beating returns by emptying the pockets of investors who attempt to beat the market with widely available information alone.

Evidence that investors with exclusively available information beat the market is inconsistent with the exclusively available-information form of the beat-the-market hypothesis, and the strong form of the efficient market hypothesis. Evidence indicates that corporate executives beat the market with exclusively and narrowly available information. Executives earn excess returns as they buy shares of their own companies before prices increase and sell them before prices decrease. Moreover, executives such as chairmen of boards with access to exclusively or very narrowly available information are able to beat the market by wider margins than lower-ranked executives with access to information that is not as narrowly available.[21] Insiders earned excess returns of about 35 percent over 21 days on average, and those closer to the original source earned higher excess returns.[22]

The use of some exclusively and narrowly available information in trading is illegal, prohibited by insider trading regulations. Matthew Martoma of the SAC Capital hedge fund was convicted of using inside information to avoid losses exceeding $276 million.[23] A jury concluded that Martoma received inside information from neurologist Sidney Gilman that showed that a drug under development by Elan and Wyeth failed to halt the progression of Alzheimer's disease. SAC beat the market by selling shares it owned in the two companies and selling short additional shares before a public announcement made the information widely available.

Insiders have long exhibited an ability to win the trading race against outsiders. "Opportunistic" trades by insiders are likely motivated by exclusively or narrowly available information, whereas "routine" trades are not. The most opportunistic insiders are local, nonexecutive insiders in geographically concentrated, poorly governed companies. They earn almost 10 percentage points of annual excess returns because they prevail in trading against outsiders.[24]

Jerrold Rosenbaum, founder of retailer Body Central Corporation and Beth Angelo, his daughter, are opportunistic insiders. They sold a combined $2.9 million of Body Central stock on May 1, May 2, and early on May 3, 2012. Later on May 3 the company cut its 2012 earnings estimate and the stock plunged 48.5 percent.[25]

Insiders are required to file their trades with the Securities and Exchange Commission (SEC). These filings illustrate further the process by which narrowly available information becomes more widely available. SEC disclosure of filings expands information availability beyond a narrow group of insiders, but the information is still narrowly available, as digging out insiders' trading information from SEC files requires greater effort than getting it from a newspaper. Dissemination of information from SEC files by the media increases the availability of the information, and investors who have gained that information while it was narrowly available beat the market when the information becomes widely available.[26]

Money managers beat the market by digging out exclusively or narrowly available information. Managers at Viking Global Investors and Karsch Capital Management dug out narrowly available information about the evolving Affordable Care Act (Obamacare) in meetings with senators whose support for the Act was crucial. Viking and Karsch managers learned that the law would not include a government-run insurance plan and proceeded to buy shares of health insurance companies whose profits would have been hurt by a government-run insurance plan. They beat the market when the information became widely available.[27]

Money managers also dig out narrowly available information in private meetings with corporate executives. Executives of publicly traded companies spend considerable time in meeting privately with money managers, despite regulations prohibiting disclosure of material nonpublic information in private meetings. Executives share narrowly available information that helps money managers make more informed trading decisions and beat the market.[28]

"Insider trading is widely viewed as commonplace on China's domestic bourses," wrote the *Financial Times*, in 2014.[29] Interviews with Chinese regulatory officials are consistent with this view. One official said that "insider trading is not only extensive, but also ingrained. . . ." Another said, "Insider trading is not a taboo subject. It is very hard to outperform in the market and survive if you do not engage in something illegal such as insider trading. Many people do not trade shares unless they have inside information. We simply have no choice in such an environment. . . ."[30]

Chinese insiders share their narrowly available inside information with mutual fund managers who proceed to beat the market.[31] Institutional investors trading on the Shanghai Stock Exchange also beat the market with narrowly available information.[32]

Connections, such as those formed while people are attending elite schools, also are conduits for narrowly available information. A study of money managers connected to initial public offering (IPO) underwriters reveals that they beat the market, but only in months when connected underwriters conduct IPOs, suggesting that connections rather than elite school education underlie their beat-the-market returns. Further, connected funds benefit from favorable IPO allocations, especially of significantly underpriced IPOs in hot markets.[33]

Hedge fund managers are prominent among money managers possessing narrowly available information. Two large brokerage firms settled allegations of disclosing such information to favored hedge funds before making it widely available. Favored hedge funds used that narrowly available information to beat the market by an annualized excess return of 9.96 percent for information about upgrades of stocks and avoid an annualized excess loss of 11.28 percent for information about downgrades. In contrast, excess returns on other stocks traded by the hedge funds were not significantly different from zero.[34]

Hedge fund managers also gain beat-the-market advantages from connections to lobbyists. Lobbyists have access to narrowly available information about ongoing or impending government actions because they routinely exchange information with legislators and many are themselves former legislators. By hiring lobbyists, hedge fund managers gain access to that information.

Before 2012, trading by hedge funds on narrowly available information obtained from within Congress did not violate insider trading laws. The Stop Trading on Congressional Knowledge (STOCK) Act, signed into law in

April 2012, imposes a duty of trust and confidence on government officials, thus exposing hedge funds to potential insider trading liability.

Analysis of stock holdings by hedge funds and lobbyist connections from 1999 through 2012 shows that hedge funds gained substantial excess returns on their political holdings when they were connected to lobbyists. Excess returns decreased significantly after the STOCK Act became effective.[35]

Analysts employed by brokerage firms regularly tip institutional clients with narrowly available information before making it widely available. Institutional clients beat the market as they "buy the rumor and sell the fact." Amateur investors, mostly individual investors, are unlikely to be tipped off. They buy or sell only once information has been made widely available, failing to beat the market.[36]

Hedge funds hide narrowly available information that gives them beat-the-market advantages. Confidential holdings are holdings that are disclosed with a significant delay. Indeed, hiding narrowly available information is the dominant motive for confidentiality. Stocks in such holdings are disproportionately associated with information-sensitive events such as mergers and acquisitions. Moreover, confidential holdings yield beat-the-market returns up to the typical confidential period of twelve months, suggesting the presence of valuable narrowly available information.[37]

Some traders possessing exclusively or narrowly available information are especially clever at camouflaging their information by trading through accounts of children. Also, some parents are very successful at picking stocks for their children's accounts. Moreover, parents tend to channel their best trades through their children's accounts, especially when they trade just before major earnings announcements, large price changes, and takeover announcements.[38]

Traders possessing exclusively or narrowly available information also enhance their ability to beat the market by trading strategically. They use stealth by dividing large batches of shares into smaller batches that they trade gradually over time.[39] This way, they forestall bites into their potential profits by fellow traders who would be alerted by observing trades of large batches.

Traders with exclusively or narrowly available information have always employed stealth, as in the market for English securities in the Netherlands during the 1770s and 1780s. This pattern is evident in changes in prices of English securities in Amsterdam between the arrival dates of sailing boats that transmitted information from London. The speed of price changes in Amsterdam crucially depended on how long traders with exclusively or narrowly available information expected it would take for their information to become widely available.[40]

Today's traders need not wait for arrival of boats for information, but the old pattern holds in an episode during which the SEC, by error, disseminated securities filings to a small group of private investors before releasing them to the general public. Still, it took minutes—not seconds—for informed traders to incorporate this narrowly available information into stock prices through their trades.[41]

Possession of exclusively and narrowly available information is not limited to investment professionals. Some amateur investors possess such information. Active amateur investors in Sweden's Premium Pension outperformed passive investors, and funds chosen by active investors outperformed funds they discarded.[42]

Amateur investors who submit their stock picks to the "CAPS" website run by the Motley Fool company have also beaten the market. Success was mostly driven by recommendations to sell short. Recommendations to buy produced only average returns.[43] The finding that short selling is likely motivated by exclusively or narrowly available information is reinforced in the finding that short selling is generally followed by low stock returns.[44]

More evidence, however, points to beat-the-market failures by amateur investors, suggesting that they possess nothing more than widely available information. On average, American investors who traded frequently earned as much as 7 percentage points less than buy-and-hold investors.[45] The losses of Swedish frequent traders amounted on average to almost 4 percent of their total financial wealth each year.[46] The returns of Taiwanese day traders varied greatly. Top day traders gained 0.38 percent daily after-fees, whereas bottom day traders lost 0.29 percent. Fewer than 1 percent of day traders, however, earned consistent excess returns.[47]

Many investors trade at the Borsa Istanbul, the stock exchange in Istanbul, Turkey, and the turnover of shares there is among the highest in the world. Yet few traders are fully successful. The returns of almost three quarters of traders trailed the returns of investors who did not trade. Those who traded the most trailed by most. Men traded more than women, younger people traded more than older ones, and young men trailed the most, befitting earlier findings that young men are the most overconfident among traders.[48]

Bull markets inflate investors' confidence and bear markets deflate it. Chinese amateur investors displayed greater overconfidence in bull markets than in bear markets, evident in more frequent trading in bull markets. Stocks bought by amateurs in bull markets yielded lower returns than stocks they sold, making them double losers. Deflated confidence benefits amateurs as they trade less in bear markets.[49]

Frequent traders trail further behind buy-and-hold investors because they tend to buy high and sell low, reversing the trading maxim of buy low and sell high. Frequent traders in 19 major international stock markets trailed buy-and-hold investors by an annual average 1.5 percentage points.[50] Investors who switched among mutual funds frequently trailed buy-and-hold mutual fund investors by an annual 0.84 percentage points when switching among US stock funds, 1.24 percentage points when switching among international stock funds, and 2.05 percentage points when switching among taxable bond funds.[51]

Technical analysts, often called chartists, attempt to beat the market by predicting future prices from widely available charts of past prices, such as charts of moving-average prices. Many German amateur investors employ charts of moving average prices as they trade. Trading activity increases by 30 percent when moving-average rules signal profitable trades, but such trades produce no excess returns.[52]

Some amateur investors have access to narrowly available information about local companies, giving them a potential trading edge. Examination of Twitter posts from amateur investors relating to American companies revealed that, on average, investors are prone to pick stocks that yield negative excess returns, but local investors do better. The local advantage is concentrated in companies without public news coverage and companies with high information asymmetry, indicating that the local advantage results from local investors' access to narrowly available and exclusive information.[53] Another study indicated, however, that the folk wisdom of "invest in what you know" yielded few benefits. Amateurs prefer local stocks but these stocks did not yield excess returns.[54]

People mimic peers' behavior because they want to maintain their status by "keeping up with the Joneses" or because they learn from their peers by observation. People begin investing in the stock market when their neighbors do, and buy stocks their neighbors buy. A study of stockholding of people sharing a workplace found that social interaction leads them to converge to the "social norm." People who allocate to stocks less than their coworkers tend to increase their allocations, while those who allocate more to stocks tend to decrease their allocations. Moreover, people with lower stock returns than their coworkers in the prior quarter tend to increase their stock allocations, while those who have better returns than their coworkers do not reduce their stock allocations.[55]

Social interactions can potentially improve investment performance, but they do not always do. A drastic reform in the Israeli capital market shifted the power to choose investments from employers to employees. In the first year following the reform, 7 percent of the employees switched out of the funds they had, but switches did not improve investment performance. Switching was strongly affected by coworkers from the same ethnic group and nonprofessional colleagues.[56]

Social interactions can also potentially improve investment performance of investment clubs by reducing risk through diversification, yet many investment clubs form undiversified ones. The portfolios of clubs consist of substantially fewer stocks when they seek consensus decisions. Moreover, the number of stocks in portfolios decreases when clubs follow decision processes that hamper diversification.[57]

WHY DO INVESTORS WITH ONLY WIDELY AVAILABLE INFORMATION TRY TO BEAT THE MARKET? THE ROLES OF WANTS AND ERRORS

Think of a stock-market game as a tennis game. You profit by $100 if you do not play. You profit by $150 if you play and win, and by $50 if you play and lose. Would you play if all you want is to avoid below-average profits?

Match-the-market investors choose not to play. Instead, they buy and hold low-cost diversified stock-market index mutual funds to match the market, collecting their $100 average profit. Beat-the-market investors, however, choose to play, buying an undiversified handful of stocks, trading them frequently, and collecting $150 if they win or $50 if they lose.

Divide beat-the-market players into two kinds, amateurs possessing nothing but widely available information, and professionals possessing exclusively or narrowly available information, and imagine that there are an equal number of each. Professionals win half the games when facing professionals on the other side of the metaphorical net, collecting $100 on average in each game. Professionals always win when facing amateurs, collecting $150 in each game, for an overall $125 average.

Amateurs win half the games when facing amateurs, collecting $100 on average in each game. They lose all games when facing professionals, collecting $50 in each game, for an overall $75 average.

Why do so many amateurs with nothing more than widely available information exert themselves to play beat-the-market games when their average $75 profit is below the $100 profit that match-the-market index investors collect by merely sitting on the sidelines? Why do so many amateurs trade when they are more likely to be beaten by professionals than beat them? Knowledgeable investors with nothing more than widely available information refuse to trade, depriving investors with exclusively or narrowly available information of opportunities to trade and beat them. Why, then, is there so much trading? This is the trading puzzle.

Fischer Black described the trading puzzle in "Noise," his American Finance Association Presidential Address. He wrote, "A person with information or insights about individual firms will want to trade, but will realize that only another person with information or insights will take the other side of the trade. Taking the other side's information into account, is it still worth trading? From the point of view of someone who knows what both the traders know, one side or the other must be making a mistake. If the one who is making a mistake declines to trade, there will be no trading on information."[58]

Black distinguished "information traders" from "noise traders." We can think of information traders as those with exclusively or narrowly available information who are willing to trade and those with only widely available information who refrain from trading. We can think of noise traders as those who are willing to trade despite having nothing more than widely available information.

Noise trading, wrote Black, is the key to solving the trading puzzle. "People who trade on noise are willing to trade even though from an objective point of view they would be better off not trading." Some noise traders are motivated to trade by ignorance about their cognitive and emotional errors. "Perhaps they think the noise they are trading on is information," wrote Black. Other noise traders are motivated to trade by wants. "Or perhaps they just like to trade."

Some beat-the-market investors are do-it-yourself investors, choosing investments they hope would beat the market. Others engage investment professionals who attempt to beat the market, such as with "active" mutual funds or hedge funds. In contrast, match-the-market investors buy and hold "passive" low-cost diversified index funds. Index fund managers charge fees as low as an annual 0.05 percent, whereas beat-the-market managers charge higher fees.

Investors holding beat-the-market funds fail to beat the market even when fund managers beat the market if managers charge fees equal to or exceeding the excess returns they generate. Economists Jonathan Berk and Jules van Binsbergen found that beat-the-market mutual fund managers generated an average annual $3.2 million of excess returns per fund. Yet they also found that managers took the entire $3.2 million as fees, delivering to investors in their funds returns equal, on average, to match-the-market index fund returns.[59]

This finding poses a question. Investors in match-the-market index funds earn returns equal to average market returns. According to Berk and van Binsbergen, so do, on average, investors in beat-the-market funds. Whose returns, then, lag average market returns? Berk and van Binsbergen concluded that those are mostly do-it-yourself beat-the-market investors, such as those who buy handfuls of stocks and trade them frequently.

Others concluded, however, that beat-the-market fund managers extract some of their fees from their own investors, delivering to them average returns lower than index fund returns. Economist Burton Malkiel, famed author of *Random Walk down Wall Street*, wrote that "managed funds are regularly outperformed by broad index funds, with equivalent risk."[60] And Eugene Fama and Kenneth French found that "the high costs of active management show up intact as lower returns to investors."[61]

Early studies of the performance of hedge funds concluded that their investors beat the market even after fees were accounted for, delivering to their investors, on average, 3 to 5 annualized percentage points of excess returns.[62] More recent studies concluded, however, that the ability of hedge funds to deliver excess returns to their investors waned over time. One found that hedge funds earned higher gross returns than mutual funds, but these higher returns vanished on their way to their investors, consumed by hedge funds' fees.[63] Another found only limited and sporadic evidence that funds investing in collections of hedge funds beat the market.[64] And yet another found that hedge fund managers failed to beat the market even before their fees are accounted for, and hedge fund investors did poorly especially because they tend to join the funds after periods of high returns. Returns of hedge fund investors were lower than the returns of the S&P 500 index, and were only marginally higher than the risk-free rate.[65]

Tom Toles, a cartoonist at the *Washington Post*, drew well the state of affairs in a four-panel cartoon featuring a hedge fund manager.

The reason I make a billion a year is I'm smarter than everybody.
True, my fund didn't deliver for the investors this year, but I still got a billion dollar bonus.
How does it prove I'm smarter than everybody?
Pretty obvious.[66]

Professors of finance possess useful financial-facts knowledge but they are not likely to possess exclusively or narrowly available information. These professors know the benefits of diversification, the drawbacks of heavy trading, and the difficulty of beating the market. But some professors lack critical human-behavior knowledge about cognitive and emotional errors, and some have wants that extend beyond utilitarian benefits.

The beliefs of most finance professors do reflect financial-facts knowledge. Most of them believe that markets are not price-equals-values markets, so security prices sometimes deviate from intrinsic values. But they also believe that investors lacking exclusively or narrowly available information will very likely fail to beat the market. The investments of finance professors are generally consistent with their beliefs, as two-thirds of them are match-the-market index investors, a proportion much higher than the proportion of match-the-market investors among all in that category. Yet not all finance professors are match-the-market investors, as some succumb to cognitive and emotional errors and some pursue wants for the expressive and emotional benefits of beat-the-market investing, beyond the utilitarian benefits of high expected returns and low risk.[67]

Framing errors are one critical kind of cognitive error. The consequences of faulty framing are evident in trading around the time of CEO interviews on CNBC.[68] Knowledgeable investors who consider buying shares of companies touted by CEOs know that they are not alone in watching the interviews. They also know that they are the slow runners in the trading race if they lack exclusively or narrowly available information. Therefore, they refrain from trading. Many investors ignorant of such information nevertheless trade. Investors who buy stocks soon after CEO interviews typically lose, buying at high prices that soon fall below their pre-interview levels. Moreover, interviews that draw much attention also draw much short selling, suggesting that investors possessing human-behavior and financial-facts knowledge and perhaps exclusively or narrowly available information knowledge anticipate the behavior of investors lacking such knowledge and win the trading race against them.

The consequences of faulty framing are also evident in trading by spammers, who post false information. Fast spammers win their trading race against their slow victims with exaggerated target-price projections combined with ostensibly credible information quoted from previously issued company press releases. Trading volume following such spam emails is high, and so are spammers' profits.[69]

Deficient financial-facts and human-behavior knowledge obscures trading disadvantages. These disadvantages are especially large in opaque markets such as foreign exchange and bond markets. Bonds regularly pass through series of dealers before they are sold to investors. Bond prices rise as dealers add markups before selling them to investors.[70] Mary Jo White, former chairman of the Securities and Exchange Commission, presented in 2014 a plan to make bond prices more transparent. The *Wall Street Journal* wrote that "the effort comes amid a broader push by Ms. White to erode some of the trading advantages enjoyed by certain large traders that aren't available to most rank-and-file investors."[71]

A 2014 Bloomberg article reported that salesmen at brokerage firms overcharged unsophisticated currency customers.[72] When salespeople received orders to buy currencies from such customers, often by email, they would buy them and wait to see if currency prices changed during the day. If currency prices changed, they would charge the higher prices. Experienced foreign-exchange customers call in their orders and insist on staying on the phone while the orders are placed so they can hear the price at which they are executed.

Trading disadvantages trip up investors even in markets considered transparent, such as stock markets. Some brokerage firms route their clients' trading orders to exchanges paying them larger rebates even when such routing disadvantages their clients.[73] Testifying before a Senate committee in 2014, an executive of a brokerage firm admitted that the firm received $80 million the year before from such rebates.[74]

Deficient financial-facts and human-behavior knowledge is evident even in choices among identical index funds. All S&P 500 index funds are identical, as all track the S&P 500 Index, yet they bring different returns to investors because some impose higher fees than others. Investors, even intelligent ones, are susceptible to faulty framing, ranking S&P 500 index funds by historical returns rather than by fees. University undergraduate and graduate students as well as staff members received information about historical returns and fees of S&P 500 index funds. Not all funds seemed to have equal investment success, because their returns varied by the dates when they were introduced and the dates when their prospectuses were published.

Knowledgeable investors frame S&P 500 index funds by fees and choose the one with the lowest fees. Ignorant investors, however, frame the same funds by historical returns. Nine out of 10 staff and undergraduate students chose funds with high fees, and so did eight out of 10 graduate students. In an experiment, staff and students chose funds with the highest historical returns, apparently ignorant that historical returns variation came only from variations in prospectus dates. Moreover, staff ranked fees as the fifth most important factor in their choice of funds, out of 11 factors, and students ranked it eighth. Staff chose funds whose annual fees exceeded the minimum fee by more than 2 percentage points on average, and students chose funds whose fees exceeded the minimum fee by more than 1 percentage point.[75]

Not all investors commit framing errors, however. Investors with only widely available information who refrain from trading may commit no framing errors. But some who avoid framing errors trade nevertheless, because they commit the overplacement variety of overconfidence errors. They know that the tennis player on the other side of the net might be number-one-placed Novak Djokovic and the trader on the other side of the trading net might be an insider employing narrowly available information, but are overconfident in their skill at beating them. I never played against Djokovic, they say, so my chance of winning must be 50-50. A survey of amateur traders, noted earlier, reveals that 62 percent expected to beat the market during the following 12 months and 29 percent expected to match the market. The survey does not say whether the remaining 9 percent expected to lag the market or merely demurred from answering the question.[76]

Traders are also susceptible to availability errors. Undiversified investors who trade frequently are likely to earn extreme returns, high or low, relative to diversified investors who trade infrequently. Undiversified frequent traders with high returns are more likely to make their success known on social networks than those with low returns. Availability errors mislead fellow investors into the erroneous belief that undiversification and frequent trading yield high returns because the combination of undiversification, frequent trading, and high returns is more readily available to memory than the more common but less available combination of undiversification, frequent trading, and low returns.[77]

The media tend to highlight money managers with high returns, making such returns available to memory and tripping investors into availability errors. The high returns of the private equity of Yale University's endowment are a case in point. The advantages of Yale, however, including special access and low fees, are rare among investors. The average returns of private equity are no higher than those of publicly traded stocks.[78]

Traders commit representativeness errors when forming expectations about returns. In particular, they focus on "representativeness information" in the form of their own recent returns, neglecting to examine "base-rate information," in the form of the average returns of all investors over long time periods. Moreover, overconfident investors who also commit representativeness errors change their expectations abruptly as stock prices change, supplying them with reasons to trade.[79] Traders also commit representativeness errors when using technical analysis, inferring future stock prices from what seem like representative patterns in past stock prices. Records of Dutch traders reveal that technical analysis subtracted more than 7 percentage points from their annual returns.[80]

Representativeness errors are also reflected in a tendency to see patterns in random series and attribute random success to skill. In a study, amateur day traders in foreign exchange markets who had gained during one week increased dramatically their trading in the following weeks. Yet past gains did not predict future gains. The effects are more pronounced among novice traders, consistent with more intense but erroneous "learning" in early trading periods.[81]

Representativeness errors lead to herding when people assign much weight to representativeness information about investment success they receive from friends and neighbors but overlook broader base-rate information about investment success. Herding is evident in the US housing boom and bust before and during the 2008 crisis. Many novice investors in the housing market were "infected" by others in their own neighborhoods and performed poorly.[82] Herding is also evident in Ponzi schemes. Typical Ponzi schemes involve sums that are much smaller than those of the highly publicized schemes by Bernard Madoff and Allen Stanford. A study of 376 Ponzi schemes prosecuted by the SEC revealed that their average life was about four years and their median investment per investor was approximately $87,800. Ponzi schemes tend to target the elderly and are especially intense where affinity links are present and where perpetrators provide financial incentives to third parties to recruit victims into the scheme.[83]

Another study of a large Ponzi scheme illustrated the way investment ideas spread epidemically through social contagion. Investors could join the scheme only by personal invitation from an existing member, and the scheme spread by inviter-invitee relationships. The social network structure differs significantly from randomly formed networks and explains why word-of-mouth information can spread rapidly even if the average investor does not share it with many others.[84]

Shared social identities between victims and perpetrators tilt the composition of investors toward a socially homogeneous and fraud-tolerant group. This trend is evident among clients of the largest stockbroker in Kenya's Nairobi Securities Exchange, expelled after defrauding one-quarter of its 100,000 clients. Members of the stockbroker's ethnic group were more likely to remain as clients than members of other ethnic groups.[85]

High past returns lead to emotional errors, as they imbue investors with a positive mood and imbue investments with positive affect. Brokerage records and matching monthly surveys show that high past returns are associated with increased return expectations combined with decreased risk perception and risk aversion.[86] Stock-market declines, however, induce fear and negative mood and color investments with negative affect, misleading investors into expectations of low returns combined with high risk. Analysis of Gallup/UBS surveys and Michigan Surveys of Consumer Attitudes reveal that investors who believe that the economy will do poorly expect low returns along with high risk. This finding is difficult to reconcile with the standard finance view that expected returns increase to compensate investors for increased risks.[87]

Investment professionals are not immune to cognitive and emotional errors and wants beyond high returns and low risk, inducing them into failing attempts to beat the market. Cognitive and emotional errors are evident in the work of committees of investment professionals. Group polarization is one error, where groups tend to render more extreme decisions than individuals. Most committees polarize toward conservative decisions. More than 77 percent agreed that "my committee tends to make more conservative decisions than I would make working alone," rather than "my committee tends to make riskier decisions than I would make working alone."

Overconfidence in the form of overplacement is common among investment committee members, of whom 83 percent claimed in an analysis that the collective knowledge in their committee is above average and 61 percent claimed that their committees seldom make mistakes. Overconfidence leads not only to high turnover of managers hired and fired but also to confirmation errors whereby committee members seek confirming evidence for the committee's views. Nearly four in 10 admitted that their committees commit confirmation errors.[88]

Investment professionals who act as plan sponsors, such as in pension plans, regularly engage consultants to help them beat the market by hiring good money managers and firing poor ones. Evidence, however, casts doubt on the ability of consultants to improve performance. Plan sponsors hire investment managers who delivered large excess returns in the recent past, but such managers do not actually deliver future excess returns. If plan sponsors had kept fired investment managers, their returns would have been no different from those delivered by newly hired ones.[89]

Still, investment professionals are generally more aware of cognitive and emotional errors than amateur investors, and they are better at overcoming them. Investment professionals holding stocks of companies targeted for takeovers are reluctant to sell them in takeover attempts if selling implies the realization of losses.[90] This reluctance implies that investment professionals, like amateur ones, are susceptible to the disposition effect, inducing them to realize gains but not losses. But investment professionals are better than amateur ones at overcoming the disposition effect.[91] Similarly, experienced investment professionals are aware of the limitations of their investment skills, countering their limitations by increasing their holdings of mutual funds following poor performance of their personal portfolios.[92]

Wants affect behavior even in the absence of cognitive and emotional errors. Many amateur investors and some investment professionals choose to play beat-the-market games because such games, like tennis, satisfy wants for expressive and emotional benefits—it is fun to play against Djokovic even if we lose. A survey of Dutch investors indicates that they care about the expressive and emotional benefits of investing more than they care about utilitarian benefits. They agreed with the statement "I invest because I like to analyze problems, look for new constructions, and learn" and the statement "I invest because it is a nice free-time activity" more than they agreed with the statement "I invest because I want to safeguard my retirement."[93] Other surveys indicate that German investors who enjoyed investing traded twice as much as other investors,[94] and a quarter of American investors buy stocks as a hobby or because it is something they like to do.[95]

A Fidelity survey found that 78 percent of traders trade for reasons beyond profits; 54 percent enjoy "the thrill of the hunt," 53 percent enjoy learning new investment skills, and more than half enjoy engaging in social activities, sharing news of their investing wins and losses with friends and family—yet tending to share news of wins more often than losses. "This research confirms the obvious satisfaction traders receive when generating cash from their activities, but it also highlights their desire to learn new skills and to share, teach, and mentor others," said James C. Burton, president of Fidelity's retail brokerage business.[96]

MONEY MANAGERS CATER TO INVESTORS' WANTS AND EXPLOIT THEIR COGNITIVE AND EMOTIONAL ERRORS

Managers of beat-the-market funds satisfy their investors' wants for the utilitarian benefits of high returns and the expressive and emotional benefits of playing the beat-the-market game and winning. Other beat-the-market managers exploit investors' wants and their cognitive and emotional errors.

Managers of "behavioral funds" identify common wants and cognitive and emotional errors of investors and attempt to exploit them for the benefit of their own investors. For instance, they identify wants for convention and attempt to exploit these by investing unconventionally, such as in stocks of companies shunned by most investors. One study examined sixteen mutual funds that identified themselves as behavioral or have been identified by the media as such. Some of these funds earned excess returns for their investors, but not all. On average, the funds failed to earn excess returns for their investors.[97]

Holding period returns reported by mutual funds, such as for the most recent three or five years, depend on both the most recent return observation added to the calculation and the oldest return observation dropped from the calculation. Dropping negative oldest returns gives the false impression of improved fund returns. Investors misled by false impressions chase illusory returns by investing more money in such funds. Fund managers take advantage of the predictable nature of investors' reactions to dropping the negative oldest returns, timing advertising campaigns to promote false impressions of improved fund returns. The managers also use this opportunity to raise fees.[98]

Names frame funds, indicating investment styles, whether growth or value, large capitalization or small. Investors looking for growth funds are not likely to examine funds whose names contain the word value. Mutual fund managers change their funds' names, such as by deleting the word "value" or adding the word "growth," to take advantage of hot investment styles. Investors react by investing more money into funds that changed their names, yet name changes do not increase returns. The increase in money flowing into funds with name changes but no investment style changes is similar to the increase in money flows into funds whose names match their styles. The similarity in flows suggests that investors are indeed fooled by name changes.[99]

Advertising makes mutual funds more available to memory and increases the amounts invested in them. Advertising mutual fund families attract more investors, and advertising also slows redemptions from poorly performing funds.[100] Fund companies exploit availability errors further by advertising the returns of their best performing funds with no hint of the returns of their other funds.

Mutual fund managers also exploit availability errors by "window dressing," changing the composition of their portfolios to increase their appeal when disclosed to investors. Managers who perform poorly are more likely to window dress near quarter ends, buying stocks whose prices rose during the quarter and selling stocks whose prices declined. Funds engaged in this tactic in one quarter performed poorly in the following quarter. Further, funds that charge higher fees engage in more window dressing.[101]

Window dressing among hedge fund managers takes the form of misreporting stock positions. Hedge fund managers employ misreporting strategically to smooth their reported returns and push otherwise small negative returns above zero. Misreporting is more pronounced among managers who report their performance to commercial hedge fund databases and misreporting increases after managers start reporting.[102]

Fund managers can increase the wealth of their investors with profitable investment strategies that increase the returns of their funds. Yet they decrease their own wealth when such investment strategies reduce the amounts of money in their funds. One potentially profitable trading strategy calls for mutual fund managers to act as contrarians, investing in stocks with negative affect that investors find unattractive. Evidence indicates, however, that some mutual fund managers deliberately invest in stocks with positive affect that investors find attractive, yet yield lower returns. Greater amounts of money flowing into funds with attractive stocks more than offset lesser amounts of money withdrawn from funds because of lower returns.[103] Hedge fund companies act similarly by launching multiple funds, drawing on their successful flagship funds. These hedge fund companies charge higher fees on their newly launched funds and set more onerous redemption terms yet attract greater inflows and generate higher fees.[104]

Fund managers are rewarded greatly when their funds are among the top performing funds, as money flows into top funds. Penalties for landing at the bottom, however, are smaller in magnitude than rewards for placing at the top, and penalties for landing in the middle are not much smaller than penalties for landing at the bottom. This asymmetry between rewards and penalties leads fund managers to increase the risk of their funds in mid-year if they find themselves in the middle or bottom of the list. Middling funds in the first half of the year tend to be more volatile in the second half, as their managers gamble in hope of reaching the top. Conversely, top funds in the first half of the year tend to be less volatile in the second half, as their managers try to maintain their top positions.[105]

Lagging returns pose career risks to mutual fund managers. Investment losses pose extra career risks. Career concerns motivate mutual fund managers to herd into stocks that analysts upgrade, so as not to lag, and especially out of stocks they downgrade, so as not to lose. The influence of analyst revisions on herding is stronger among managers with greater career concerns, and is more pronounced for downgrades.[106]

Net inflows into mutual funds that outperform their benchmarks in down markets are lower than for funds that outperform in up markets. Similarly, net outflows out of mutual funds that underperform their benchmark in down markets are lower than for funds that underperform in up markets. This trend is likely because investors base their investment decisions on the sign and magnitude of fund returns, rather than on fund returns relative to benchmark returns. Managers respond to investors' behavior by turning their funds into "closet index funds" in down markets, moving their portfolios closer to benchmark portfolios so as not to lag them, and turning away from closet indexing in up markets.[107]

Funds-of-mutual-funds are mutual funds that invest in stand-alone funds. Managers of funds-of-funds buy stocks that managers of stand-alone funds want to sell and sell stocks that managers of stand-alone funds want to buy. This degrades the returns of funds-of-mutual-funds but enhances the returns of stand-alone funds, as they absorb inflows of money without having to buy stocks at high prices, and withstand outflows without having to sell stocks at low prices.[108]

Wants and cognitive and emotional errors make even professional investors prey for money managers. "Bunched trades" are trades of the same stock, on the same day, in the same direction, whether buying or selling, for more than one client. Favored clients received higher prices when they sold and paid lower prices when they bought.[109]

A survey of investment consultants and chief investment officers of large Australian pension funds revealed that both groups are captive to a pervasive bias toward beat-the-market money management, reinforced by a competitive environment and supported by a mix of behavioral, agency, organizational, and cultural factors.[110]

Investors do learn to overcome their errors, even if slowly. As the adaptive market hypothesis notes, amateurs make mistakes but they learn and adjust, and competition among money managers fosters adaptation and innovation. Beat-the-market funds charge lower fees and generate higher excess returns when they face competitive pressure from low-cost index funds.[111]

We see pushback of investors against beat-the-market money managers in the decision of the California Public Employees' Retirement System (CalPERS), the largest US pension fund, to unwind its entire $4 billion hedge fund investment.[112] Ted Eliopoulos, interim chief investment officer at CalPERS, said that hedge funds did not merit a role in the CalPERS portfolio, because of their complexity and high cost.

Other investors also push back against beat-the-market money managers by pouring money into low-cost index funds, such as Vanguard's. John Aravosis, a self-employed writer in Washington, DC, moved his individual retirement account into Vanguard's index funds when he found that he was paying nearly half his yearly savings in fees to his longtime broker. The pension fund of Montgomery County, Pennsylvania, moved most of its $470 million into Vanguard's index funds after its officials spoke with John Bogle, Vanguard's founder. Josh Shapiro, chairman of the Montgomery County Board of Commissioners, said he frequently speaks with other pension funds interested in moving to index funds.[113]

MAKING THE MARKET HARD TO BEAT BY BEATING IT

We face what seems like a paradox: Investors who believe that the hard-to-beat market hypothesis is *false* can make the hard-to-beat market hypothesis come *true*. Indeed, they can even make the price-equals-value market hypothesis come true. Markets can be *neither* hard-to-beat *nor* price-equals-value if all investors believe that markets *are already* hard to beat and price equals value. Markets can be moved closer to hard-to-beat and price-equals-value status by investors who believe not only that markets are not in the price-equals-value category but also that the investors can beat them. Indeed, absence of attempts to beat the market, such as by widespread holdings of index funds, can increase gaps between prices and values, as that absence reduces incentives to acquire information about gaps and trade to exploit these gaps for higher returns.[114]

Imagine inferring intrinsic values as inferring the particular model of a car in a mosaic. Each of two investors has an incomplete mosaic, where some tiles are missing, illustrated in 11-1a, Figure 11-1b, and Figure 11-1c. The incomplete mosaic of each investor makes it difficult to infer the particular model. The aggregate mosaic, however, makes inference easier, even if not perfect.

Now think of a series of intrinsic values of a security over time as a series of mosaics. Investors dig out tiles of exclusively and narrowly available information and fit them into empty spaces in a mosaic that includes tiles of widely available information and perhaps some tiles of exclusively and narrowly available information. Investors infer that their overall mosaic, even if incomplete, shows intrinsic values higher or lower than prices, and proceed to buy investments whose prices are lower than inferred intrinsic values, and sell investments whose prices are higher than the inferred intrinsic ones.

No single investor has all the information tiles necessary for complete mosaics and their corresponding estimates of intrinsic values. The genius of the market, presumed by the price-equals-value market hypothesis, is its ability to aggregate investors' information tiles and partial mosaics into complete mosaics, such that in the end prices equal intrinsic values.

Economists Andrew Lo and Craig MacKinlay used an engine metaphor to describe the process by which mosaics are aggregated and prices move closer to intrinsic values.[115] Gaps between prices and intrinsic values indicate that markets are not in the price-equals-value category, but these gaps are the "oil that lubricates" the process by which traders narrow gaps as they strive to beat the market. Traders motivated by potential excess returns that come with beating the market buy stocks whose prices are lower than their intrinsic value. Their buying actions push prices higher, closer to intrinsic values. And traders are similarly motivated to sell stocks whose prices are higher than their intrinsic value. Their selling actions press prices lower, closer to intrinsic values. This process is also central in Andrew Lo's adaptive markets hypothesis by which the dynamics of adaptation determine not only the efficiency of markets but also the waxing

(a) Mosaic of Investor 1

(b) Mosaic of Investor 2

(c) Aggregate mosaic of 1 and 2

Figure 11-1 Mosaics of Investor 1, Investor 2, and the aggregate mosaic of Investors 1 and 2.

and waning of financial institutions, investment products, and, ultimately, institutional and individual fortunes.[116]

John Paulson's hedge fund gained $15 billion in a bet against subprime mortgage securities before the 2008 financial crisis. Later he described his process of digging out exclusively and narrowly available information tiles and combining them with widely available information tiles in a mosaic of subprime mortgage securities. First was the tile, dug out from his personal experience during years of living in New York, that real estate prices do not always go up. Instead, they often bubble up only to deflate later. "New York periodically goes through a real estate crisis," as it did in the 1970s, early 1980s, and early 1990s. "I didn't subscribe to the school that real estate only goes up."[117]

Paulson dug out additional exclusively and narrowly available information tiles when he researched the subprime market and was astounded by the low standards set for borrowers. He compared these low standards to the high ones he had to satisfy when he bought his own home. "When I purchased my home, it was [by] very strict underwriting standards. I had to provide two pay stubs, two years' tax returns, three months of bank statements, all sorts of credit card information. All of a sudden I saw these lowest quality mortgages with basically no underwriting standards at all." Paulson added, "When you get to a private guy who doesn't care, he may just fill it in, state an income, and say 'yes we check' when they didn't. That's when you got the really bad quality stuff."

Some evidence indicates that markets are indeed good at aggregating mosaics to levels of clarity corresponding to the aggregate information tiles of all investors. One part of that evidence comes from announcements of the Israeli Consumer Price Index (CPI) in the early 1980s. Each of us very likely sees today a portion of the aggregate mosaic that makes up the CPI number that will be unveiled by the Central Bureau of Statistics next month. Each sees some clear tiles, perhaps tiles showing the price of milk or automobiles. Each can infer whether the CPI number in the aggregate mosaic to be unveiled would be high or low. And each can trade on that inference, selling bonds if we infer that inflation is higher than reflected in the current prices of bonds, or buying them if we conclude that inflation is lower than reflected in the current prices of bonds. If the bond market aggregates our tiles perfectly we should find that bond prices do not change at all when the CPI number is unveiled, because they portray perfectly the aggregate CPI mosaic before the Bureau unveils it.

It turned out that bond prices changed little when the Bureau unveiled the CPI numbers, consistent with the price-equals-value market hypothesis that the market is indeed good at aggregating information tiles into mosaics whose clarity reflects all available information.[118] Another early study reached similar conclusions. Announcements of changes in bond ratings by rating agencies exerted little effect on bond prices, implying that the bond market is good at aggregating information tiles into clear mosaics before the rating agencies aggregate them in their ratings.[119]

A more recent study of changes in bond ratings indicates, however, that markets are poor at aggregating information tiles into mosaics whose clarity corresponds to the aggregate of the information tiles of all investors. The study found that stocks of companies whose ratings increased had higher subsequent returns than those of companies whose bond ratings decreased, implying that not all available information is aggregated in current prices.[120] Another study found that stock prices are poor at aggregating information tiles that are geographically dispersed. Specifically, future earnings and cash flows of companies can be predicted from past earnings and cash flows of other companies in related geographical regions, also implying that not all available information is aggregated in current prices.[121]

Still, trading motivated by exclusively and narrowly available information can move prices closer to intrinsic values. Evidence indicates that increased ownership of stocks by hedge funds likely to possess such information leads to narrowing gaps between prices and intrinsic values.[122] The contributions of hedge funds to narrowing gaps are greater than those of other types of institutional investors, such as mutual funds or banks that are less likely to possess exclusively and narrowly available information. Nevertheless, extreme gaps between prices and intrinsic values can occur in stocks held by hedge funds, as occurred in the last quarter of 2008 during the financial crisis. Gaps were most pronounced among hedge funds using leverage and among those connected to Lehman Brothers that went bankrupt at that time.

Consider the lessons of Figure 11-2. On the horizontal axis we have a measure of the aggregate efforts to beat the market by digging out exclusively and narrowly available information and assembling mosaics of intrinsic values. On the vertical axis we have an index of price-equals-value market efficiency, measured by the average width of gaps between prices and intrinsic values. A 100-index number corresponds to a market with no gaps between prices and values.

No one is digging out information tiles in markets where all believe that all prices are already equal to intrinsic values, so markets would not be of the price-equals-value category. Think of yesterday's $80 price of shares of an oil company, equal to yesterday's intrinsic value, and imagine that it announced today the discovery of a major new oil field. Its intrinsic value moves to $120, reflecting higher future dividends when oil is pumped from the new field. If everyone believes that the market for shares of this

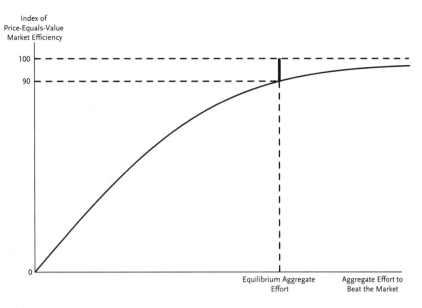

Figure 11-2 Equilibrium aggregate effort to beat the market and level of price-equal-value efficiency.

company is already a price-equals-value market, no one has the incentive to dig out information tiles about the new oil field, let alone try to beat the market by buying for $80 shares worth $120.

Now some traders are likely to notice when the market is not a price-equals-value market and they can beat it easily, digging out information tiles buried no more deeply than newspaper pages or computer screens. The price of shares rises above $80 as more traders compete to buy shares with $120's worth of intrinsic value, narrowing the gap between the price and intrinsic value, pushing the price closer to the intrinsic value and making the market more difficult to beat.

The cost of digging out information tiles and trading impedes price-equals-value markets. We cannot expect markets to be 100-index price-equals-value, because traders' expected profits from efforts at beating such markets do not cover their costs, including not only traders' digging and trading costs but also traders' forgone income in alternative occupations, such as accounting or engineering.[123] These costs can be substantial. This is evident in a 2013 *Wall Street Journal* story about Genscape, a company whose helicopters provide narrowly available information about the contents of oil tanks by infrared reconnaissance images before the US government makes public similar information. Traders pay an annual $90,000 for Genscape's private reports.[124]

Think of a market in which all traders are rational or normal-knowledge-able, of the kind who care only about returns and their utilitarian benefits. Traders who are skilled at digging out exclusively and narrowly available information beat the market, earning returns equal to or exceeding their costs. Traders who are not as skilled quit when they fail to earn such returns. In the end, markets converge to somewhat less than 100-index price-equals-value status, perhaps to 90-index price-equals-value markets, leaving gaps between prices and values that are wide enough to let skilled traders beat the market by magnitudes that are at least equal to their costs.

Uncertainty poses an impediment to price-equals-value markets beyond costs. Uncertainty about estimates of intrinsic values and the timing of convergence of prices to intrinsic values limits the amounts that rational and normal-knowledgeable traders are willing to bet on their estimates of gaps between prices and intrinsic values. In turn, smaller bets retard convergence between the two. Paulson inferred from his pre-2008 information mosaic that the market for subprime mortgages was not a price-equals-value market. But he could not have been entirely certain that his inference was correct. He surely could not have known that prices would fall to his estimates of intrinsic values soon, before he ran out of funds or fortitude. Indeed, Paulson endured losses during the early months. Peers thought that he was likely to lose his bet against subprime mortgage securities. "Most of them, when we did express our viewpoints, thought we were inexperienced novices in the mortgage market. We were very, very much in the minority. If I said a thousand-to-one, we were the one. Even friends of ours thought we were so wrong, they felt sorry for us."[125] Moreover, some markets lack securities that allow investors to place bets. Indeed, Paulson wanted to bet against subprime mortgage securities earlier than he did but was delayed by the absence of securities facilitating such bets.

Gaps between prices and intrinsic values are larger in some markets than in others, implying lower price-equals-value market efficiency. This discrepancy can be because the costs of digging out information tiles and trading are higher in some markets than in others, as are the corresponding uncertainties. For example, the costs of digging out information tiles and trading, and the levels of uncertainty are higher in markets of small-capitalization stocks and markets of developing-countries stocks than in those of large capitalization and developed countries. This trend is illustrated in Figure 11-3.

Some infer that lower price-equals-value market efficiency implies lower hard-to-beat market efficiency, making markets of small-capitalization and developing-countries stocks easier to beat than markets of large-capitalization and developed-countries stocks. Yet this conclusion is unwarranted

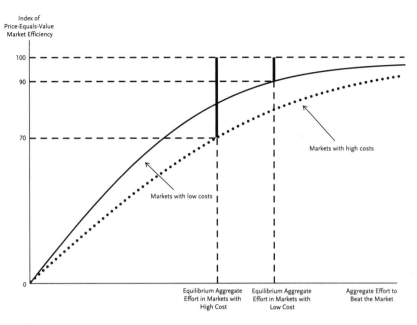

Figure 11-3 Equilibrium aggregate effort to beat the market and levels of price-equal-value efficiency in markets with high costs and low costs.

for two reasons. First, the costs of digging out information and trading can be higher in markets with lower price-equals-value efficiency, negating the benefits of exploiting larger gaps between prices and intrinsic values in such markets. Indeed, larger gaps between prices and intrinsic values in such markets are likely *a consequence* of greater costs of digging out information tiles and trading. Second, the market-sum rule holds equally in all markets. Index investors in small-capitalization and developing-countries' stock markets earn market returns. If some investors beat the market, earning higher than market returns, other investors must be beaten by the market, earning lower than market returns.

As Fischer Black noted, trading by noise traders—normal-ignorant traders—underlies the solution to the trading puzzle, as there is no trading in markets where all participants are rational information traders. The good news is that noise traders makes trading possible, and high trading volume lets us observe investments' prices frequently. The bad news is that noise traders also introduce noise into prices as they trade, swayed by cognitive and emotional errors and wants for expressive and emotional benefits. That noise drives markets away from price-equals-value by increasing gaps between prices and intrinsic values. Black wrote that the prices of investments in markets where noise traders operate "reflects both the information that information traders trade on and the noise that noise traders

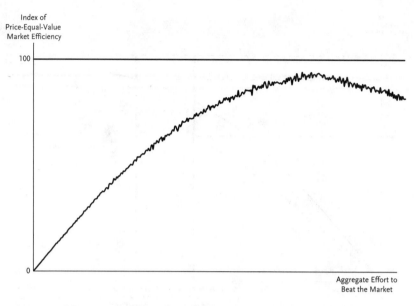

Index of
Price-Equal-Value
Market Efficiency

Aggregate Effort to
Beat the Market

Figure 11-4 Aggregate effort to beat the market and levels of price-equal-value efficiency in markets in which noise traders join information traders.

trade on."[126] Figure 11-4 shows increases in gaps between prices and intrinsic values as noise traders join information traders.

Black's conjecture implies that high trading volume might indicate trading by noise traders who *impede* price-equals-value markets, rather than trading by information traders who *promote* price-equals-value markets. Evidence consistent with Black's conjecture comes from the finding that prices of investments with high trading volumes moved *more slowly* toward their intrinsic values than prices of investments with low volumes.[127] This evidence is especially compelling because it comes from the TradeSports exchange, where many professional traders from Chicago, London, and New York routinely wager thousands of dollars in sports and financial markets.

Noise traders can move stock and bond prices powerfully. For example, stocks in pension funds account for 30 percent of stocks available for trading in Chile. Pension investors regularly switch their entire pension account balances between funds holding mostly stocks and those holding mostly bonds in attempts to "time the market." These frequent switches are coordinated across investors by a popular investment advisory company. Pension funds often face redemption requests amounting to 10 percent of their stocks and 20 percent of their bonds within a few days. This coordinated noise trading has led to increases and decreases of almost 2.5 percent in stock prices and more than 0.30 percent in the prices of bonds, which trade in a more liquid market than the stock market.[128]

The power of noise traders to move prices is also evident in price movements following resurfaced old news, such as the September 2008 resurfaced news about the 2002 bankruptcy of United Airlines' parent company. Noise traders apparently believed that this old news was new, and United Airlines' stock price dropped by 76 percent within a few minutes before the NASDAQ stock exchange halted trading. The price rebounded after the news had been identified as old, but was still 11.2 percent lower at the end of the day.[129]

At times, traders deliberately push prices away from intrinsic values, hampering price-equals-value efficiency. Some hedge funds manipulate stock prices at critical reporting dates. Prices of stocks held in large quantities by hedge funds increase on the last day of the quarter and decrease on the following day. Analysis of volume of trading and buy-and-sell order imbalances during these days provides further evidence consistent with manipulation, as the pattern of price movements is more clearly evident among funds with stronger incentives to improve their ranking relative to their peers.[130]

BUBBLES IN RATIONAL AND HARD-TO-BEAT MARKETS

"Positive" bubbles exist when prices exceed intrinsic values, and "negative" bubbles exist when prices are short of intrinsic values. Bubbles cannot exist in price-equals-value markets because bubbles imply deviations of prices from intrinsic values. Bubbles, however, can persist in hard-to-beat markets if investors are unable to time the market, identifying bubbles in time and exploiting them for beating the market. This inability can be because digging out exclusively and narrowly available information is difficult, trading is costly, and actions based on imprecise estimates of intrinsic values can bring losses. Investors who know that their estimates of intrinsic values are imprecise are deterred from investing much in attempts to exploit bubbles, as they contemplate losses if their estimates are wrong.

Investors can suffer losses even if they are right to conclude that bubbles exist. Gaps between prices and intrinsic values can widen over months, even years, before they narrow. Investors might not have sufficient funds or fortitude to sustain their investments during extended periods when their intrinsic value estimates are right, yet prices continue to be wrong. As they say, markets can be crazy longer than investors can stay solvent.

Witness the debacle of the hedge fund Long Term Capital Management, whose managers were good at exploiting gaps between prices of pairs of similar investments with similar intrinsic values, selling the security whose price exceeds intrinsic value and buying the security whose price is short of intrinsic value. They reaped profits when gaps between prices and intrinsic values narrowed. The 1998 Russian financial crisis, however, widened gaps and Long Term Capital Management went bankrupt before gaps narrowed.

Moreover, investors might find that inflating bubbles and riding them by buying investments whose prices exceed intrinsic values is more profitable than deflating bubbles by selling such investments. Hedge funds did well as they bought dot-com securities in the late 1990s, riding the bubble as it inflated, and successfully dismounted later, selling such securities as the bubble started to deflate.[131]

The quest for utilitarian, expressive, and emotional benefits can inflate bubbles. The quest for such benefits is central in a bubble model in which status-seeking investors are motivated to "keep up with the Joneses," inflating bubbles as they buy investments bought by their Joneses peers so as not to fall behind if the investments of the Joneses turn out well.[132]

The quest for utilitarian, expressive, and emotional benefits underlies another bubble model centered on herding money managers. High professional reputation brings not only high utilitarian income but also the expressive and emotional benefits of high status. Money managers are driven to join investment herds because damage to their professional reputation is greatest when they run alone behind the herd.[133] This attitude is immortalized in the words of Citigroup's CEO Chuck Prince in the time leading to the 2008 financial crisis: "But as long as the music is playing, you've got to get up and dance."[134] This attitude is also reflected in the late 1990s actions of money managers specializing in value stocks when the performance of growth stocks, especially dot-com stocks, left them far behind. Some value managers quit or were fired, and others herded into growth stocks.

Indeed, professional investors often inflate bubbles more than amateur investors. Korean amateur investors in one case acted as aggressive contrarians by selling large-capitalization stocks whose prices increased, while foreign and domestic institutional investors bought these stocks, further inflating the bubble.[135]

Investors misled by cognitive errors can inflate bubbles. The cognitive errors of representativeness and confirmation are at the center of feedback-trading models of bubbles. The arrival of good news such as about fast economic growth prompts investors to buy investments, pushing up their prices. Further price increases follow as representativeness errors mislead investors into excessive extrapolation of prices, and confirmation errors mislead them into searching for information confirming their optimistic views and neglecting disconfirming data. News media amplified representativeness and confirmation errors during the dot-com period and afterward, with positive stories about dot-com stocks as the bubble inflated and negative stories once the bubble had deflated.[136]

Sentiment, bullish or bearish, is likely to exert its greatest effect on stocks of companies with small capitalization that are young, unprofitable, highly volatile, paying no dividends, or in financial distress. Such stocks are disproportionately sensitive to broad waves of investor sentiment for two reasons. First, estimating the intrinsic values of such stocks is especially difficult, magnifying the effects of cognitive and emotional errors and making valuation mistakes more likely. Second, arbitrage that would have possibly countered valuation mistakes is hampered because it is especially costly.[137]

Market structures such as restrictions on short selling exacerbate the effects of cognitive errors in bubbles. Prices exceed intrinsic values, reflecting the bullish sentiment of optimistic investors, when restrictions on short selling prevent traders with pessimistic views from exerting a countervailing force. This approach is reflected in a "castles in the air" model in which prices rise above intrinsic values as investors pay inflated prices for investments today, expecting to sell them at even more inflated prices tomorrow.[138] The model predicts that prices will exceed intrinsic values by greater margins when dispersion of views, optimistic and pessimistic, is greater. The finding that prices of stocks with high dispersions of earnings' forecasts are especially high relative to intrinsic values is consistent with this prediction.[139]

The bubble effects of sentiment are reflected in IPO waves, in which optimistic investors build their hopes into "castles in the air" and pay prices exceeding intrinsic values for stocks of new companies with low profit margins perceived as having large future growth opportunities. IPOs of stocks of companies with low gross profit margins were overvalued relative to IPOs of companies with high gross margins, underperforming by about 12 percent per year during the subsequent four-year period. Indeed, the average return on IPOs of companies with low gross profit margins was below the risk-free return.[140]

Emotional errors can underlie bubbles where positive affect of stocks and excessive hope mislead investors into a belief that stocks offer both high expected returns and low risk, or where negative affect of stocks and excessive fear mislead them into thinking that stocks offer both low expected returns and high risk.

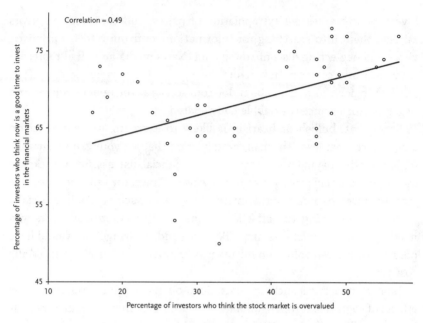

Figure 11-5 Investors think that times when the stock market is overvalued are good times to invest in financial markets (June 1998–July 2002).

A Gallup survey asked investors if they believed that the market is over-valued or undervalued and whether they thought that now is a good time to invest in the financial markets. Figure 11-5 shows that months when large proportions of investors believed that the stock market is *overvalued* were also months when they thought that now is a *good* time to invest in the financial markets.

CAN INVESTORS FORESEE BUBBLES AND EXPLOIT THEM?

A rejection of the price-equals-value market hypothesis does not nec-essarily imply the demise of the hard-to-beat market hypothesis. Knowledge that bubbles exist does not necessarily imply that investors can identify them as they occur and exploit them for excess returns. "The U.S. market may be in an incipient bubble," said economist Paul Samuelson in March 1999, but economists "have no theory of how long a bubble will last."[141]

Robert Shiller argued that investors can foresee bubbles, at least when bubbles are extreme. In 2013, soon after winning the Nobel Prize in eco-nomics, he said to an NPR *Planet Money* interviewer, "You can have a fairly high degree of confidence. That's what I felt in the stock market in late 1990s. [When] I wrote the first edition of my book, 'Irrational Exuberance,' ... I told my publisher, Princeton, 'Please get this out! Because I want this book out before the crash, not after.' And then again I felt that in the 2000s with the housing bubble."

But Eugene Fama, a fellow recipient of the 2013 Nobel Prize, disagrees. He said to the same interviewer, "The word 'bubble' drives me nuts, frankly, because I don't think there's anything in the statistical evidence that says anybody can reliably predict when prices go down. So if you interpret the word 'bubble' to mean I can predict when prices are going to go down, you can't do it."[142]

Confirmation errors induce us to focus on bubbles—booms followed by crashes—because they are memorable. We remember well the crash following the boom of the late 1990s and the 2008 crash following the boom of the mid-2000s. But this focus can mislead us into the conclusion that booms are always followed by crashes. Economist William Goetzmann examined the frequency of booms and crashes in the returns of world stock markets since the beginning of the 20th century. It may help understand his findings by noting that one definition of boom is a 100 percent real price increase in one calendar year, and a definition of a crash is a 50 percent real price decline in one calendar year. The frequency of a boom in any calendar year was 2.13 percent and the frequency of a crash was 2.21 percent. The frequency of a crash following a boom was 4.17 percent, almost double the 2.21 percent overall frequency of a crash. But the frequency of a boom following a boom was 8.33 percent, almost four times the 2.13 percent overall frequency of a boom. Other definitions of booms and crashes yield similar results. "In simple terms," wrote Goetzmann, "bubbles are booms that went bad. Not all booms are bad."[143]

Hindsight and confirmation errors mislead us into speaking about bubble periods as if everyone were irrationally exuberant, expecting prices to continue on their way up. But it is never so. There are always bullish investors *and* bearish ones, making it easy to be misled by hindsight and confirmation errors to investors who turned out to be right.

Many investors were bullish on December 31, 1999, when Yahoo's stock price was at $216.35, close to its $237.50 peak. One bullish investor responded to the doubts of a bearish one on Yahoo's message board: "You have no imagination. Do you really think Yahoo and [its] business model in 2015 will be anything like it is now? The whole idea of your comparison is based on the flawed assumption that Yahoo will be much like it is now. What people see is that Yahoo is becoming the Internet brand and whatever the Internet becomes, Yahoo will be at the center of it as long as they take the right steps. Information/communication/media/entertainment will all flow through Yahoo if they play their cards right. The sky is the limit."[144]

Not all posters on message boards were bullish in late 1999, and outright bulls were countered by outright bears. On December 26, 1999, as Home Depot's share price was nearing its peak, an investor posted the following: "There is more to investing than buying, it is called selling. Heard the saying, bulls make money, bears make money, pigs like [you] get slaughtered."[145] A day earlier, another investor supported his or her bearishness with facts gleaned from experience as a Home Depot department manager: "Granted [Home Depot] will double stores in 3 or 4 years but will or should the market cap double from here . . . , or are we entering a market bubble where a customer wants a 10 percent discount on a $5 tool but thinks nothing of paying $100 for a stock share that will net 5 percent?"[146]

Many investors who were not outright bears in late 1999 were wary, anticipating the pop of a bubble but hoping to ride it a little longer. One investor posted on Amazon's board on December 8, 1999, "A needed correction will occur after [Amazon] tests the 100/105 level. Still long . . . , until signs of true financial collapse emerge."[147] Other investors decided it was time to dismount what they perceived as a bubble. On December 4, 1999, an investor posted on Amazon's board, "First time I shorted a stock was yesterday. . . . I believe in the Internet sector and believe in their potential. . . . However, I think that a big correction is coming."[148]

We must be mindful of hindsight and confirmation errors as we assess prediction abilities. Consider the case of economist Nouriel Roubini, who is known for his accurate prediction of the housing and stock-market crashes in 2008. A proper assessment of his prediction ability, however, requires examination of all his predictions and their realizations. Yet hindsight and confirmation errors get in the way, obscuring disconfirming evidence. On March 9, 2009, when the S&P 500 Index was at 677, its very bottom, Roubini said in a Bloomberg interview, "My main scenario is that it's highly likely it goes to 600 or below." A level of "500 is less likely, but there is some possibility you get there."[149]

Hindsight and confirmation errors are also evident in the failure to consider the poor prediction records of Wall Street market strategists. On December 20, 2007, BusinessWeek published the predictions of strategists of the level of the S&P 500 Index at the end of 2008. We know now, in hindsight, that the S&P was more than 38 percent lower at the close of 2008 than at its beginning. One strategist predicted a 22 percent increase in 2008 and recommended an all-stock portfolio. Another predicted a 16 percent increase and singled out AIG's stock as a good investment. Yet another predicted a 15 percent increase and recommended stocks of financial institutions. AIG would have gone bankrupt in 2008 if not for a government bailout, and stocks of financial institutions were hit especially hard. The most pessimistic prediction was of an 8 percent decline in the S&P 500 Index, still far from its subsequent decline.[150]

The practice of securitization led to lax screening of subprime borrowers during 2004–2006, but mid-level managers in securitized finance had no foresight about the housing bubble and looming crisis, evident in their personal home transactions. Indeed, some groups of securitization managers were particularly aggressive in buying houses during the period.[151]

Corporate insiders of financial companies had no better insight into the impending crisis than mid-level managers in securitized finance. Institutional investors and financial analysts had some foresight in this period, preferring non-financial stocks over financial stocks. But corporate insiders of financial companies appear to have had no foresight. Net purchases of stocks of financial companies by managers of financial companies exceeded those of managers of non-financial companies over the entire 2006–2008 period.[152]

Some economists, most notably John Campbell and Robert Shiller, have argued that high price-to-earnings ratios and low dividend yields alert us to the presence of bubbles.[153] But others, including economists Amit Goyal and Ivo Welch, concluded otherwise.[154] Consider Figure 11-6 showing Shiller's cyclically adjusted price-to-earnings ratio (CAPE ratio) in the months of

Figure 11-6 Monthly cyclically adjusted price-to-earnings (P/E) ratio (CAPE ratio) in 1926–2015.

1926–2015. Earnings in the CAPE ratio are average inflation-adjusted earnings of S&P 500 Index companies during the previous 10 years.

The ups and downs of the CAPE ratio might indicate inflation of bubbles and their deflation, inconsistent with the price-equals-value market hypothesis. Or they might point to the operation of a price-equals-value market, in which changes in prices correspond to changes in intrinsic values.

Consider, too, the association between CAPE ratios in the Decembers of years and annualized S&P 500 Index returns during the subsequent 10 years (Figure 11-7). The regression line shows a distinct negative slope, with a 0.71 correlation, indicating that high CAPE ratios in those Decembers are generally followed by low returns in the subsequent 10 years. This negative slope seemingly contradicts both the price-equals-value and the hard-to-beat market hypotheses. Yet the dispersion around the regression line is high, indicating that high CAPE ratios are sometimes followed by high returns rather than low returns.

We can explore the usefulness of the CAPE ratio for beating the market by examining, as in Figure 11-8, the success of trading rules that guide us to switch from stocks to Treasury bills when the CAPE ratio is high and back to stocks when it is low. But what is a high CAPE? Is it a CAPE ratio exceeding the median CAPE? Is it a CAPE ratio exceeding 25?

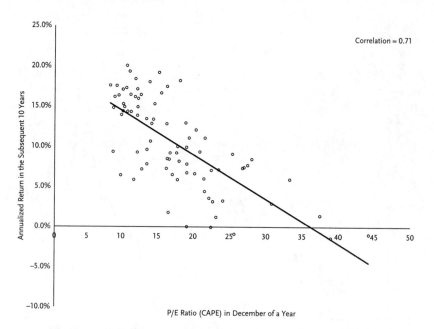

Figure 11-7 P/E ratio (CAPE) in December of a year and annualized S&P 500 Index returns in the subsequent 10 years.

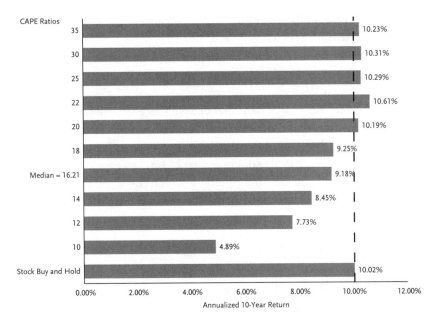

CAPE Ratios

35	10.23%
30	10.31%
25	10.29%
22	10.61%
20	10.19%
18	9.25%
Median = 16.21	9.18%
14	8.45%
12	7.73%
10	4.89%
Stock Buy and Hold	10.02%

Annualized 10-Year Return

Figure 11-8 Returns associated with trading rules based on CAPE ratios.

Buying and holding the S&P 500 Index continuously during 1926–2015 would have yielded an annualized 10.02 percent return. The median CAPE ratio in Decembers of these years was 16.21. Consider a trading rule whereby we switch from stocks to Treasury bills at the beginning of January of a year if the CAPE ratio in December of the preceding year is above that median. We hold Treasury bills during the year, and switch back to stocks at the beginning of January of the following year if the CAPE ratio in the preceding December falls below the median. We keep our Treasury bills if the CAPE ratio in the preceding December remains above the median. This trading rule would have yielded less, an annualized 9.18 percent.

Next consider a trading rule whereby the "switching CAPE ratio" is 18, such that we switch from stocks into Treasury bills if the CAPE ratio exceeds 18 and switch back into stocks if it falls below 18. That trading rule would have yielded an annualized 9.21 percent, still lower than the annualized 10.02 percent buy-and-hold stock return. Setting the switching CAPE ratio higher, such as 22, would have yielded an annualized 10.61 percent, exceeding the buy-and-hold stock return. Even higher switching CAPE ratios would have also yielded more than the buy-and-hold stock return, although short of the 10.61 percent annualized return when the switching CAPE ratio is set at 22. For example, the annualized return when the switching CAPE ratio is set at 25 is 10.29 percent, and it is 10.23 percent when the switching CAPE ratio is set at 35.

Shiller is well aware that the CAPE ratio is far from a sure market timing device, as he discussed in the NPR interview (see n137).

> INTERVIEWER: Fama says he would believe there were bubbles if you could predict 10 of them in a row.
> SHILLER: Yeah, but I don't live that long. You know, these big bubbles are rare events that play out over years. They can go a long time.
> INTERVIEWER: If you lived long enough, do you think you could make good on Gene Fama's request that you predict 10 bubbles in a row?
> SHILLER: If I lived long enough, yeah.
> INTERVIEWER: You do think you could?
> SHILLER: Uh. I think so. Yeah. I'm not the most self-confident person.

For several reasons, well-calibrated confidence should deter most investors from attempting to identify and exploit bubbles. First, finding trading rules that provide a return advantage by identifying and exploiting bubbles is easier in hindsight than in foresight, and the wrong trading rule might bring losses rather than gains. Second, the expected annual return advantage of trading rules that succeed at identifying exploiting bubbles is fairly small and might not occur during periods extending to decades. Third, the periods when an investor holds Treasury bills might extend into years, while the stock market roars ahead—think of the late 1990s. Investors can easily lose their nerve and switch from Treasury bills to stocks, as in late 1999, just in time for the crash that followed.

THE JOINT HYPOTHESIS: MARKET EFFICIENCY, ASSET PRICING, AND "SMART BETA"

The efficient market hypothesis, whether in the version of price-equals-value market hypothesis or hard-to-beat market hypothesis, cannot be tested on its own. As Eugene Fama noted, the hypothesis must be tested jointly with an asset pricing model, such as the CAPM or the three-factor model.[155] Excess returns of small-capitalization and value stocks when measured by the CAPM might indicate that the market is not efficient. Or they might indicate that the CAPM is a faulty model of expected returns.

To understand the nature of the joint hypothesis, imagine shopping for a bag of sugar at your local grocery store. Each bag on the store's shelf says that it weighs 5 pounds and its price is $3.60. You place a bag on a scale next to the shelf and the scale's needle points to 5 pounds. You place another bag on the scale and its needle points to 6 pounds.

One possibility is that market for sugar bags is not a price-equals-value one. If the value of a 5-pound bag is equal to its $3.60 price, then the value of a 6-pound bag cannot be equal to its $3.60 price; there must be a gap between the price and the value of the first bag, the second bag, or both bags. Moreover, the market is not a hard-to-beat one. You can easily buy the 6-pound bag for the price of a 5-pound bag, gaining a 1-pound "excess return." The 1-pound excess return is an "anomaly," indicating that the market is not efficient, exemplifying neither price-equals-value nor hard-to-beat conditions.

The other possibility is that, in truth, both bags weigh 5 pounds. In this case the market for sugar bags is efficient, conforming to both price-equals-value and a hard-to-beat, but the scale is faulty, sometimes pointing to 5 pounds and sometimes to 6 pounds when a 5-pound bag is placed on it. A faulty scale is analogous to a faulty asset pricing model.

The problem of jointly testing market efficiency and asset pricing models dooms us to attempts to determine two variables with only one equation. We can overcome the joint hypothesis problem by assuming one variable and determining the other. We can assume that markets are efficient and determine an asset pricing model. Or we can assume an asset pricing model and determine whether markets are efficient.

Standard finance proponents were happy with the CAPM as its asset pricing model as long as it served to show that markets are efficient-hard to beat, and perhaps also reflective of price equals value. But they abandoned the CAPM in favor of the three-factor model when the CAPM seemed to indicate that markets are not efficient. In a 2008 interview, Fama said, "At the peak of euphoria in research on finance in the early 1970s . . . the CAPM looked rather good, and market efficiency looked rather good. However, then things on the asset pricing side started to fall apart. . . . It turned out that the CAPM never really worked. We had just never looked at it carefully enough."

The three-factor model has been replaced by the four-factor model when it failed to account for excess returns associated with the momentum factor. In turn, the four-factor model is being replaced by factor models that account for excess returns when measured by the four-factor model. They include models that account for excess returns related to earnings surprises, idiosyncratic volatility, financial distress, net stock issues, composite issuance, investment and profitability, and many others.[156]

The three-factor asset pricing model and subsequent empirical asset pricing models represent, in effect, a choice to overcome the joint hypothesis problem by assuming that markets are efficient and using this assumption to determine good asset pricing models—models that extinguish excess returns. This is a reasonable choice in investment asset markets as it is in other markets, whether for watches, cars, or restaurant meals.

When we observe variation in price per calorie between a fancy restaurant and a modest one, we do not rush to conclude that the market for restaurant meals is not efficient. Instead, we begin with an explicit or implicit assumption that the market for restaurant meals is efficient and proceed to infer what makes up the restaurant-meals pricing model. Did we remember to add a taste factor into the model? Did we add an esthetics factor? Did we add a prestige factor?

Discussions about "smart beta" reflect the joint hypothesis. Smart-beta strategies center on portfolios whose allocations do not correspond to market capitalizations. The proportion allocated to a particular value stock might be 0.5 percent in a portfolio in which allocations are made by relative market capitalization of stocks. But the proportion allocated to this value stock might be 2 percent in a smart-beta portfolio in which allocations to value stocks exceed allocations by their relative market capitalization. We can regard excess returns of smart-beta strategies as evidence that investment markets are not efficient. Or we can view smart-beta strategies as representations of asset pricing models, ones that account for the market factor, the small-large and value-growth factors, and other factors of asset pricing models.

A discussion about smart betas in an *Institutional Investors Journal* webcast illustrates the joint hypothesis. The discussion featured analysts Andrew Ang of BlackRock, Clifford Asness of AQR, and Jennifer Bender of State Street Global Investors. Bender presented smart-beta strategies as reflections of asset pricing models rather than reflections of markets that are not efficient. She said, "For smart beta, the end investor makes a decision to have exposure to certain factors he believes will persist over the long term, and he implements that view in a passive, transparent, rules-based way. This is very different from, say, a traditional quantitative manager who would use factors, but employ them dynamically and in a discretionary way to generate [market-beating] alpha." Bender added that much of excess returns attributed to beating inefficient markets is better attributed to asset pricing models. "[I]n much empirical research, quite a bit of active returns can be explained by very simple rules-based factor portfolios. And that does present a challenge to active investing overall!"[157]

CONCLUSION

Discussions about market efficiency in finance are unfocused when they fail to distinguish between the *price-equals-value market hypothesis* and the *hard-to-beat market hypothesis*. And discussions are further lacking when they fail to explain why so many investors believe that markets are easy to beat when, in truth, they are hard to beat. Behavioral finance contributes positively to these discussions by making the distinction between the price-equals-value market hypothesis and the hard-to-beat market hypothesis and by explaining why so many investors believe that markets are easy to beat when, in truth, that is hard to do.

Behavioral finance concludes that markets are not price-equals-value markets but they are quite hard to beat by investors lacking exclusively or narrowly available information. And behavioral finance elucidates the cognitive and emotional errors that mislead investors with nothing but widely available information into the belief that markets are easy to beat.

The decision of the Nobel Prize committee to award the prize to both Eugene Fama and Robert Shiller provides good guidance on Steven Rattner's question of "whether it's possible to regularly beat the stock market averages." The Nobel Prize committee said, in effect, that Warren Buffett and others who possess exclusively and narrowly available information can beat the market consistently, but ordinary investors possessing only widely available information cannot.

In the end, Rattner reached the same conclusion, recommending that nonexpert investors choose low-cost index funds. "That's where the nonexpert should park his money," he wrote. "As the commercials say, when it comes to active investing, don't try this at home."[158]

CHAPTER 12

Lessons of Behavioral Finance

Some years ago I was on a bus with fellow academics on our way to a conference dinner. I tried to persuade a seatmate I had just met that we want more than utilitarian benefits when we choose a car. We also want expressive and emotional benefits. My seatmate disagreed, insisting that he chooses cars by utilitarian benefits alone. His colleague, sitting behind us, chuckled. It turned out that my seatmate was a fan of expensive sports cars, quite willing to trade utilitarian low price for expressive prestige and emotional thrills.

My seatmate is not alone in blindness to his wants. We all need mirrors to see ourselves as we truly are. I hope you see yourself in this book and learn to identify your wants, correct your errors, and improve your financial behavior.

Behavioral finance teaches financial lessons to all—financial amateurs and professionals alike. Indeed, financial professionals distinguish themselves from financial amateurs by knowledge of the lessons of finance. Amateurs encounter financial questions in their roles as savers, consumers, and investors. Financial professionals encounter them in roles such as investment managers, corporate managers, and financial advisers.

The lessons of behavioral finance guide us to know our wants. They teach us about financial facts and human behavior, including making cognitive and emotional shortcuts and errors. And they guide us to balance our wants and correct cognitive and emotional errors on the way to satisfying our wants.

These lessons draw on what we know about us—normal people— including our wants, cognition, and emotions. And they draw on the roles of these factors in behavioral portfolio theory, behavioral life-cycle theory, behavioral asset pricing theory, and behavioral market efficiency.

LESSON 1: KNOW YOUR WANTS

We want three kinds of benefits—utilitarian, expressive, and emotional—from all products and services, including financial products and services. Utilitarian benefits answer this question: What does something do for me and my pocketbook? Expressive benefits answer this question: What does something say about me to others and to me? Emotional benefits answer this question: How does something make me feel?

Our wants regarding automobiles include the utilitarian benefits of safety, as by a Volvo; the expressive benefits of high social status, as by a Rolls Royce; and the emotional benefits of exhilaration, as by a Ferrari. Our investment wants include the utilitarian benefits of safety, as by an insured bank deposit; the expressive benefits of high social status, as by a hedge fund; and the emotional benefits of exhilaration, as by a successful initial public offering.

Ferrari, the auto maker, conducted the initial public offering of its shares in late 2015. The offering price was set high and shot up higher on the offering day. Sergio Marchionne, the CEO of Fiat Chrysler Automobiles, which owns Ferrari, did not pitch Ferrari's shares as those of an auto maker. Instead, he pitched them as emblems of high social status, like Birkin handbags made by Hermès or cashmere sweaters made by Brunello Cucinelli, the Italian luxury apparel company.[1]

The utilitarian benefits of Birkin handbags that cost many thousands of dollars and Cucinelli cashmere sweaters that cost a few thousand are no greater than the utilitarian benefits of no-name handbags that cost $200 and no-name sweaters that cost $100. All handbags carry our stuff, and all sweaters keep us warm. But Birkin handbags and Cucinelli sweaters satisfy certain expressive and emotional wants that no-name handbags and sweaters cannot satisfy.

The utilitarian benefits of a Ferrari automobile in the six-figure range are no greater than those of a Toyota automobile costing five figures. Both take you from home to work and back. Indeed, the utilitarian benefits of Ferraris are lower than those of Toyotas and their utilitarian costs are higher because Ferraris consume more gasoline, cost more to insure, and are more likely to catch the eyes of highway patrolmen dispensing speeding tickets. But Ferraris satisfy expressive and emotional wants that Toyotas cannot satisfy. An eighty year old in a Toyota is old, but an eighty year old in a Ferrari feels young.

The utilitarian benefits of hedge funds are no higher than those of index funds. Indeed, the utilitarian benefits of hedge funds are likely lower because their returns to investors are lower and their fees higher. But hedge funds offer investors the expressive and emotional benefits of high social status because they are available only to the wealthy, whereas index funds are available to almost all. Similarly, the utilitarian benefits of shares sold at initial public offerings are no greater than those of shares of established companies. Indeed, the utilitarian benefits of IPO shares are likely lower because their returns are likely lower. But shares sold at initial public offerings offer emotional benefits of hope and exhilaration that established companies' shares cannot match.

LESSON 2: KNOW FINANCIAL FACTS

Knowledge of behavioral asset pricing models is one example of financial-facts knowledge. A behavioral pricing model of automobiles decomposes their prices by features, costs, and benefits, whether utilitarian, expressive, or emotional. A basic Toyota Camry LE costs $22,970. An auto-dimming rearview mirror adds $329 to that price, a garage door transmitter adds $329, and a power moon roof adds a further $915.

A behavioral asset pricing model of investments similarly decomposes their expected returns into their features, costs, and benefits, whether utilitarian, expressive, or emotional. A typical low-risk stock might have a 6 percent expected return. The feature of higher risk adds utilitarian costs, compensated by an added 2 percentage points to the expected return. The feature of admiration, as toward Apple, Alphabet (Google), or Facebook, adds expressive and emotional benefits to their stocks, penalized by a subtracted 1 percentage point. The feature of "sin," as in tobacco, adds expressive and emotional costs to tobacco company stocks, compensated by an added 1.5 percentage points.

Knowledge of the two versions of efficient markets, those of price-equals-value efficient markets and hard to-beat ones, is another part of financial-facts knowledge. Price-equals-value market efficiency in automobile markets implies that the value of a power moon roof equals its $915 price. Hard-to-beat market efficiency implies that while it is possible to find and buy a power moon roof for less than $915, doing so is hard, requiring effort such as Internet searches and negotiations with dealers.

Price-equals-value in investment markets implies that the value of the expressive and emotional benefits of avoiding stocks of sin companies equals its 1.5-percentage-point subtraction from expected returns. Hard-to-beat market efficiency implies that it is possible to construct a portfolio that excludes stocks of sin companies without subtracting 1.5 percentage points of expected returns, but doing so again is hard, requiring effort such as digging out exclusively or narrowly available information.

Financial amateurs and professionals often speak as if the mere observation of markets that are not price-equals-value efficient implies that they are also not hard to beat. Many fail, however, to distinguish between those two versions of efficient markets, and many fail to know the market-sum nature of investment markets.

Think of stocks as ingredients of a stew, some with fat returns and some with lean. Now think of a stock market as a giant well-mixed pot of stew that contains all stocks. Index investors dip their ladles into the stew and fill them with fat and lean elements in proportions equal to those in the pot. Beat-the-market investors strive to fill their ladles with higher proportions of fat than those in the pot. But it is impossible for all beat-the-market investors to succeed because the pot game is a pot-sum game and the market game is a market-sum game. If the ladles of some beat-the-market investors contain higher proportions of fat returns than the proportion in the market pot, the ladles of other beat-the-market investors must contain lower proportions of fat returns than the proportions overall.

Evidence indicates that investment markets are not price-equals-value efficient but are hard-to-beat efficient. The lesson for professionals is to attempt to beat the market by digging out exclusively or narrowly available information. They should know, however, that their attempts at beating the market are costly and often fail. The lesson to amateurs is to refrain from attempts at beating the market, choosing low-cost index funds instead. They too should know that attempts at beating the market on their own are costly and most often fail, and their attempts at beating the market by hiring beat-the-market professionals are also likely to fail because fees charged by beat-the-market professionals are higher than fees of low-cost index funds.

Knowledge of the benefits and costs of diversification is another example of financial-facts knowledge. An undiversified portfolio consisting of a few stocks can deliver the utilitarian, expressive, and emotional benefits of great riches, but it can also impose the costs of deep poverty. A diversified portfolio, in contrast, is likely to deliver the benefits of modest riches or impose the costs of mild poverty.

The benefits and costs of diversification are evident in a November 18, 2015, email from Motif, an online brokerage that offers undiversified thematic portfolios consisting of no more than 30 stocks. The gain of the Buy-the-Dip theme during the month ending that day was 10.7 percent, the gain of the Onward-Online-Ads theme was 9.5 percent, and the gain of China-Internet was 8.6 percent.

But not all themes delivered gains. The loss of the Precious-Metals theme during the month was –18.7 percent, the loss of the Dr. Copper theme was –16.3 percent, and the loss of the For-Profit-Colleges theme was –12.1 percent.

VTI, an exchange traded fund diversified among thousands of stocks, gained 2.2 percent during the month, much less than the 10.7 percent gain of the Buy-the-Dip, but much better than the –18.7 percent loss of the Precious-Metals theme. We should consider balancing potential gains and losses through diversification.

LESSON 3: KNOW HUMAN BEHAVIOR

Cognitive and emotional shortcuts lead us on the right path most of the times but can also mislead us into errors. Human-behavior knowledge helps us distinguish shortcuts from errors. The cognitive shortcuts and errors of representativeness are one example. We use representativeness shortcuts correctly when we assess an email offer by Ms. Neomi Surugaba to share $20 million. Representative information indicates that it is a good deal. We would receive $4 million from an account left in an African country by this relative of a corrupt official for nothing more than our bank information. We reject Ms. Surugaba's offer because we properly consider not only representativeness information but also base-rate information. That information tells us that, on average, deals such as those offered by Ms. Surugaba are scams yielding losses rather than gains.

Representativeness shortcuts turn into representativeness errors when we consider representativeness information but fail to consider base-rate information. Listen to a commercial by a commodities broker.

MAN: I really need to diversify.
WOMAN: Stocks aren't the only game in town. I tried commodities.
MAN: What do I know about pork bellies?
WOMAN: Well, trade what you know. You know about gold, right? Crude oil? . . . With commodities you don't have to worry about stuff like PE ratios or CEO scandals. . . . It's a pure price play.
MAN: Interesting . . .
ANNOUNCER: Commodities are everywhere; what are you trading?[2]

Representativeness information about gold and crude oil indicates that they are easy to analyze and offer good opportunities to beat the market, unlike stocks, which are difficult to analyze. But base-rate information indicates that gold and crude oil markets are no easier to beat than stock markets, because all investment markets are market-sum markets. Some investors are bound to lose in the gold and oil games, earning below-market returns. Losers are likely amateur investors like the people in the commercial whose information about gold and crude oil is widely available, extending little beyond what is printed in newspapers and seen on television. Winners are likely professional investors employing exclusively and narrowly available information. And the commodities broker is a sure winner, collecting commissions from both losers and winners.

The emotional shortcuts and errors of affect are another example. Affect is the faint whisper of emotion or mood. We use affect shortcuts correctly when we continue to watch a movie if we find its story line appealing and its characters attractive, and we use them correctly when we terminate consideration of buying an automobile if we find it ugly.

Affect shortcuts lead us correctly, but affect errors mislead us. Investments, like automobiles and movies, exude affect, beautiful or ugly, attractive or repulsive. "Dot-com" names exuded positive affect during the dot-com boom of the late 1990s. Companies boosted their stocks' prices by jettisoning mundane names, such as Computer Literacy Inc., and adopting dot-com names, such as a FatBrain.com. Dot-com names conveyed negative affect in the dot-com bust of the early 2000s, and companies boosted their stocks' prices by jettisoning dot-com names.[3]

LESSON 4: KNOW TRADE-OFFS AMONG WANTS AND BALANCE THEM

Automobile buyers balance their wants when choosing a Toyota or a Ferrari. They might assess the utilitarian benefits of a Toyota higher than those of a Ferrari, but they value its expressive and emotional benefits lower. Assessments of costs and benefits vary from person to person, however, and so does balance between wants. Some people derive substantial expressive and emotional benefits from a Ferrari, in high social status and exhilaration, but other people do not. Indeed, some are embarrassed to drive a Ferrari but proud to drive a Toyota. Moreover, some who want the expressive and emotional benefits of a Ferrari are nevertheless willing to trade them for the utilitarian benefits of a Toyota. The same is true when one is choosing investments, such as shares of Toyota or Ferrari.

One buyer of Ferrari shares balances his wants of the expressive and emotional benefits of a Ferrari automobile with the consolation of his wants in Ferrari shares. "I will never own a Ferrari [automobile], but I can own the stock!" But another potential buyer is unwilling to trade the utilitarian benefits of high stock returns for the expressive and emotional benefits of Ferrari shares, knowing that high P/E ratios of shares might bring low future returns. "P/E of 36? No thanks."

Should you choose silver or white as the color of your next automobile? The intuitive System 1 and associated cognitive or emotional shortcuts are adequate for a choice when the consequences of the wrong choice are small and assessment by the reflective System 2 would not improve choice. The expressive and emotional benefits of driving a car with a pleasing color are likely large relative to utilitarian costs.

Should you choose a Ferrari or Toyota as your next automobile? The intuitive System 1 and its associated cognitive or emotional shortcuts are not adequate for this choice, because the consequences of the wrong choice are large. Consideration of expressive and emotional benefits might draw you closer to a Ferrari than to a Toyota, but you are wise to engage the reflective System 2 before you choose. Did you reflect on differences in safety and the cost of insurance? Did you take test drives long enough to determine differences in comfort, handling, and noise? Did you read *Consumer Reports'* comparison of the two cars and its recommendations?

Behavioral portfolio theory guides us to portfolios on the behavioral-wants frontier of investments as it might guide us to automobiles on the behavioral-wants frontier of automobiles. In each case, behavioral portfolio theory prescribes choices that balance our wants best. The behavioral-wants frontier of investments reflects trade-offs between those such as high expected returns, low risk, great social responsibility, and high social status. But each portfolio on the behavioral-wants frontier provides the highest expected return for each level of risk, social responsibility, and social status.

Behavioral life-cycle theory guides us toward saving and spending during our life cycles. The theory acknowledges conflicting wants, such as buying a Ferrari today or securing retirement income 40 years in the future, and prescribes tools for balancing spending and saving. These include personal tools such as self-control and public-policy tools such as nudging people into retirement savings plans or mandating retirement savings plans, as Social Security is mandated.

CONCLUSION

Behavioral finance is finance for normal people, like you and me. We do not go out of our way to be ignorant, and we do not go out of our way to commit cognitive and emotional errors. Instead, we do so on our way to the utilitarian, expressive, and emotional benefits we want, such as hope for riches and freedom from the fear of poverty, nurturing our children and families, being true to our values, gaining high social status, and playing games and winning.

This book offers behavioral finance as a unified structure that incorporates parts of standard finance, replaces others, and includes bridges between theory, evidence, and practice. The rational people of standard finance are easier to place into elegant models than the normal people of behavioral finance, but it is models that must conform to people, not the other way around. As Albert Einstein is reputed to have said, "If you're out to describe the truth, leave elegance to the tailors." Normal people are more complex than rational ones, yet normal people are who we are—often normal-ignorant, sometime normal-foolish, but always able to become normal-knowledgeable and increase the ratio of smart to foolish behavior.

NOTES

INTRODUCTION

1. Sheelah Kolhatkar, "Paulson Forgoes Prognostication as Greatest Trade Sequel Flops," *Bloomberg*, June 28, 2012, http://www.bloomberg.com/news/2012-06-28/paulson-forgoes-prognostication-as-greatest-trade-sequel-flops.html.
2. Merton Miller and Franco Modigliani, "Dividend Policy, Growth, and the Valuation of Shares," *Journal of Business* 34 (1961): 411–433.
3. Eugene F. Fama, "The Behavior of Stock-Market Prices," *Journal of Business* 38 (1965): 34–105.
4. Harry Markowitz, "Portfolio Selection," *Journal of Finance* 7 (1952): 77–91.
5. Harry Markowitz, *Portfolio Selection: Efficient Diversification of Investments* (New York: John Wiley & Sons, 1959).
6. William Sharpe, "Capital Asset Prices: A Theory of Market Equilibrium under Conditions of Risk," *Journal of Finance* 19 (1964): 425–442.
7. Hersh Shefrin and Meir Statman, "Explaining Investor Preference for Cash Dividends," *Journal of Financial Economics* 13 (1984): 253–282.
8. Merton Miller, "Behavioral Rationality in Finance: The Case of Dividends," *Journal of Business* 59 (1986): 451–468.

CHAPTER 1

1. Miller and Modigliani, "Dividend Policy," p. 412; see n2 in the Introduction. All other quotes in this chapter without alternative attribution are from Miller and Modigliani, "Dividend Policy."
2. Keith E. Stanovich, and Richard F. West, "Individual Differences in Reasoning: Implications for the Rationality Debate?" *Behavioral and Brain Sciences* 23, no. 5 (2000): 645–665; Daniel Kahneman, *Thinking, Fast and Slow* (New York: Farrar, Straus and Giroux, 2011).
3. Shane Frederick, "Cognitive Reflection and Decision Making," *Journal of Economic Perspectives* 19 (2005): 25–42.
4. System 1 would have led more of us to the correct answer to an equivalent question, "If it takes 9 women 9 months to give birth to 9 babies, how long would it take 100 women to give birth to 100 babies?"
5. Richard P. Larrick, Richard E. Nisbett, and James N. Morgan, "Who Uses the Normative Rules of Choice," in *Rules for Reasoning*, ed. Richard E. Nisbett (Hillsdale, NJ: Lawrence Erlbaum, 1993), 277–294.

6. Geert Bekaert, Kenton Hoyem, Wei-Yin Hu, and Enrichetta Ravina, "Who Is Internationally Diversified? Evidence from 296 401(k) Plans" (April 21, 2015), available at SSRN: http://ssrn.com/abstract=2417976.

7. Paola Sapienza and Luigi Zingales, "Economic Experts versus Average Americans," *American Economic Review* 103 (2013): 636–642.

8. Kenneth Fisher and Meir Statman, "Investor Sentiment and Stock Returns," *Financial Analysts Journal* 56 (2000): 16–23.

9. Sumit Agarwal, Richard J. Rosen, and Vincent W. Yao, "Why Do Borrowers Make Mortgage Refinancing Mistakes?" (March 18, 2015). Forthcoming, *Management Science*, available at SSRN: https://ssrn.com/abstract=2446753 or http://dx.doi .org/10.2139/ssrn.2446753.

10. FINRA Foundation, "Americans' Financial Capability Growing Stronger, but not for All Groups: FINRA Foundation Study," July 12, 2016, https://www.finra .org/newsroom/2016/americans-financial-capability-growing-stronger-not-all- groups-finra-foundation-study.

CHAPTER 2

1. Meir Statman, *What Investors Really Want* (New York: McGraw-Hill, 2011).

2. Frank Scott and Aaron Yelowitz, "Pricing Anomalies in the Market for Diamonds: Evidence of Conformist Behavior," *Economic Inquiry* 48, no. 2 (April 2010): 353–368, available at SSRN: http://ssrn.com/abstract=1578523.

3. Daniel Grosshans and Stefan Zeisberger, "All's Well That Ends Well? On the Importance of How Returns Are Achieved" (July 4, 2016), available at SSRN: http://ssrn.com/abstract=2579636 or http://dx.doi.org/10.2139/ ssrn.2579636.

4. Sanford E. DeVoe and Julian House, "Time, Money and Happiness: How Does Putting a Price on Time Affect Our Ability to Smell the Roses?" *Journal of Experimental Social Psychology* 48 (2012): 466–474.

5. E*TRADE Group, "E*TRADE Launches Provocative Brand Advertising Campaign Designed to Capture the New Spirit of Investors Who Are Taking Charge of Their Financial Lives," *PRNewswire* (April 12, 1999), http://www.prnewswire .com/news-releases/etrade-launches-provocative-brand-advertising-campaign- designed-to-capture-the-new-spirit-of-investors-who-are-taking-charge-of- their-financial-lives-73955882.html.

6. Advertisement in *Money* (December 2009): 33.

7. Jack S. Ellenberger, Ellen P. Mahar, and Law Librarians' Society of Washington, D.C., *Legislative History of the Securities Act of 1933 and Securities Exchange Act of 1934* (South Hackensack, NJ: Published for the Law Librarians' Society of Washington, D.C., by F. B. Rothman, 1973).

8. David A. Moss, *When All Else Fails: Government as the Ultimate Risk Manager* (Cambridge, MA: Harvard University Press, 2002).

9. Advertisement in *Literary Digest* (December 28, 1929): 45.

10. Advertisement in *Money* (May 2007): 52.

11. Thomas F. Juster and John Laitner, "New Evidence on Altruism: A Study of TIAA-CREF Retirees," *American Economic Review* 86, no. 4 (September 1996): 893–908. Wojciech Kopczuk and Joseph Lupton, "To Leave or Not to Leave: The Distribution of Bequest Motives," *Review of Economic Studies* 74, no. 1 (2007): 207–235.

12. Richard A. Settersten, "Becoming Adult: Meanings and Markers for Young Americans," in *Coming of Age in America*, eds. Patrick Carr and Maria Kefalas,

March 2006, http://health.oregonstate.edu/sites/health.oregonstate.edu/files/faculty-staff/profilepubs/settersten_et_al-becoming_adult-emerging_trends.pdf.

13. Karen Ross and Robert Schoeni, "Material Assistance from Families during the Transition to Adulthood," in *On the Frontier of Adulthood: Theory, Research, and Public Policy*, ed. Richard A. Settersten Jr., Frank F. Furstenberg Jr., and Ruben G. Rumbaut (Chicago: University of Chicago Press, 2005), 243–286, 396–416.

14. Angel Jennings, "Nest Eggs Emptying, not the Nests." *New York Times,* July 14, 2007: B1.

15. "Get Rich Quick: A Runaway Dream," *Christian Science Monitor,* http://www.csmonitor.com/2000/0426/p15s2.html.

16. Peter Millman, "The Day Trader," audiovideo interview by Vincent Laforet, *New York* magazine, YouTube video, 1:57, January 27, 2009, https://www.youtube.com/watch?v=XruhYQW6unA.

17. Ben Steverman, "Motif Investing: How to Invest around a Theme," *Bloomberg.com*, October 8, 2015, http://www.bloomberg.com/news/articles/2015-10-08/motif-investing-how-to-invest-around-a-theme.

18. Bjorn Eraker and Mark J. Ready, "Do Investors Overpay for Stocks with Lottery-Like Payoffs? An Examination of the Returns on OTC Stocks," *Journal of Financial Economics* 115, no. 3 (March 2015): 486–504.

19. Charlene C. Wu, Peter Bossaerts, and Brian Knutson, "The Affective Impact of Financial Skewness on Neural Activity and Choice," *PLoS ONE* 6, no. 2 (February 15, 2011), available at SSRN: http://ssrn.com/abstract=1762399.

20. Chip Heath and Amos Tversky, "Preferences and Beliefs: Ambiguity and Competence in Choice under Uncertainty," *Journal of Risk and Uncertainty* 4 (1991): 5–28.

21. John R. Graham, Campbell R. Harvey, and Hai Huang, "Investor Competence, Trading Frequency, and Home Bias," *Management Science* 55 (2009): 1094–1106.

22. Advertisement in *Kiplinger's*, September 2006: 29.

23. Meir Statman, "Quiet Conversations: The Expressive Nature of Socially Responsible Investors," *Journal of Financial Planning* (2008): 40–46.

24. "UPDATE 1-Calpers to Divest Stake in 2 Makers of Guns, Ammunition," *Reuters,* February 19, 2013, http://www.reuters.com/article/financial-calpers-gunmakers-idUSL1N0BJ9OZ20130219.

25. Andrew Ross Sorkin, "Gun Shares Have Done Well, but Divestment Push Grows," *New York Times,* December 8, 2015: B1.

26. Martin Brown, Jan Schmitz, and Christian Zehnder, "Social Norms and Strategic Default," University of St. Gallen, School of Finance Research Paper No. 2016/08 (March 7, 2016), available at SSRN: http://ssrn.com/abstract=2743278.

27. Advertisement in *New York Times Magazine*, October 5, 2003: 129.

28. Heather Moore and Bryan Young, "Letter to the Editor," *Economist*, January 13, 2007: 16.

29. Daniel Miller, "Film Entrepreneur Draws Mixed Reviews," *Los Angeles Times*, August 12, 2014, http://www.latimes.com/entertainment/envelope/cotown/la-et-ct-bradley-media-society-20140812-story.html#page=1.

30. Christophe Spaenjers, "The Long-Term Returns to Durable Assets," HEC Paris Research Paper No. FIN-2016-1143 (March 11, 2016), available at SSRN: http://ssrn.com/abstract=2746356.

31. Mike Isaac, "For Start-Ups, How Many Angels Is Too Many?" *New York Times*, July 6, 2015, http://www.nytimes.com/2015/07/07/technology/for-start-ups-how-many-angels-is-too-many.html?ref=business.

32. Sarah Max, "A Global Academy's Crash Course Makes Angels out of Investors," *New York Times,* November 12, 2015, http://www.nytimes.com/2015/11/13/business/dealbook/a-global-academys-crash-course-makes-angels-out-of-investors.html.

33. Ernst G. Maug, Alexandra Niessen-Ruenzi, and Evgenia Zhivotova, "Pride and Promotion: Why Some Firms Pay Their CEOs Less," September 5, 2014. https://niessen.bwl.uni-mannheim.de/fileadmin/files/niessen/files/Papers/Pride_and_Prestige_NieRueMauZhi.pdf.

34. Judd Bagley, "Schwab Investing Pep-Talk Ad 2002," YouTube video, February 1, 2010, https://www.youtube.com/watch?v=24sTGLxNNKs

35. Hersh Shefrin and Meir Statman, "Ethics, Fairness, and Efficiency in Financial Markets," *Financial Analysts Journal* 49 (1993): 21–29.

36. *United States v. O'Hagan* 117 S. CT. 2199, 138 L.ED. 2D 724 (1997), available at http://www.law.cornell.edu/supct/search/display.html?terms=securities&url=/supct/html/96-842.ZS.html.

37. Chao Jiang, "Legal Expertise and Insider Trading" (April 2015), available at SSRN: http://ssrn.com/abstract=2658969.

38. Steven Kaplan, "Executive Compensation and Corporate Governance in the U.S.: Perceptions, Facts and Challenges," *Journal of Applied Corporate Finance* 25 (2013): 8–25.

39. Kelly Shue and Richard R. Townsend, "Growth through Rigidity: An Explanation of the Rise of CEO Pay," *Journal of Financial Economics,* forthcoming (December 8, 2015), available at SSRN: http://ssrn.com/abstract=2424860.

40. Camelia M. Kuhnen and Alexandra Niessen, "Public Opinion and Executive Compensation," *Management Science* 58 (2012): 1249–1272.

41. Gilberto R. Loureiro, Anil K. Makhija, and Dan Zhang, "The Ruse of a One-Dollar CEO Salary" (January 10, 2014). Charles A. Dice Center Working Paper No. 2011-7; Fisher College of Business Working Paper No. 2011-03-007. Available at SSRN: https://ssrn.com/abstract=1571823 or http://dx.doi.org/10.2139/ssrn.1571823.

42. Jeffery L. Yablon, "Avoidance, Evasion, and Planning." In *As Certain as Death—Quotations about Taxes,* Tax Analysts, 2010: 223–259. http://www.taxanalysts.com/www/freefiles.nsf/Files/Yablon2010_9_Avoidance.pdf/$file/Yablon2010_9_Avoidance.pd

43. Abigail B. Sussman and Christopher Y. Olivola, "Axe the Tax: Taxes Are Disliked More Than Equivalent Costs," *Journal of Marketing Research* 48 (November 2011): 91–101.

44. Marukku Kaustia, Knüpfer Samuli, and Torstila Sami, Stock Ownership and Political Behavior: Evidence from Demutualizations (December 12, 2013). SAFE Working Paper No. 2. Available at SSRN: https://ssrn.com/abstract=2209645 or http://dx.doi.org/10.2139/ssrn.2209645.

45. Gerardo Perez Cavazos and Andreya Marie Silvas, "Tax-Minded Executives and Corporate Tax Strategies: Evidence from the 2013 Tax Hikes" (November 15, 2014), available at SSRN: http://ssrn.com/abstract=2529509 or http://dx.doi.org/10.2139/ssrn.2529509.

46. Iftekhar Hasan, Chun Keung (Stan) Hoi, Qiang Wu, and Hao Zhang, "Beauty Is in the Eye of the Beholder: The Effect of Corporate Tax Avoidance on the Cost of Bank Loans," *Journal of Financial Economics* 113, no. 1 (July 2014): 109–130.

47. Laura Saunders, "Inside Swiss Banks' Tax-Cheating Machinery," *Wall Street Journal*, October 22, 2015, http://www.wsj.com/articles/inside-swiss-banks-tax-cheating-machinery-1445506381.

48. Risto Moisio, Eric J. Arnould, and James Gentry, "Productive Consumption in the Class-Mediated Construction of Domestic Masculinity: Do-It-Yourself (DIY) Home Improvement in Men's Identity Work," *Journal of Consumer Research* 40 (2013): 203–222.

49. Alain Cohn, Ernst Fehr, and Michel André Maréchal, "Business Culture and Dishonesty in the Banking Industry," *Nature* 516 (2014): 86–89.

50. "Raise Your Children to Rely on Them: Asian Culture and Finances," *Make Love, not Debt: A Relationship Finance Blog,* http://www.makelovenotdebt.com/2007/05/raise_your_children_to_rely_on_them_asian_culture_and_finances.php.

51. "Status Symbols around the World," InterNations GmbH, https://www.internations.org/about-internations.

52. Harrison Hong, Wenxi Jiang, and Bin Zhao, "Trading for Status," *Review of Financial Studies* 27, no. 11 (2014): 3171–3212.

53. Irena Hutton, Danling Jiang, and Alok Kumar, "Political Values, Culture, and Corporate Litigation," *Management Science* 61, no. 12 (April 17, 2015): 2905–2925.

54. Lieven Baele, Moazzam Farooq, and Steven Ongena, "Of Religion and Redemption: Evidence from Default on Islamic Loans," CEPR Discussion Paper No. DP8504 (August 2011), available at SSRN: http://ssrn.com/abstract=1908552.

55. Leonardo Bursztyn, Stefano Fiorin, Daniel Gottlieb, and Martin Kanz, "Moral Incentives: Experimental Evidence from Repayments of an Islamic Credit Card," NBER Working Paper No. w21611 (October 2015), available at SSRN: http://ssrn.com/abstract=2669800.

56. Kristin Hussey, "After Ruling, Paul Smith's College Won't Get Weills' $20 Million Renaming Gift," *New York Times,* October 22, 2015, http://www.nytimes.com/2015/10/23/nyregion/weills-20-million-renaming-gift-to-paul-smiths-college-is-withdrawn.html?_r=0.

57. Erik Holm, "Ackman v. Berkshire: Whose Holdings Are More Immoral?" *Wall Street Journal,* November 11, 2015, http://blogs.wsj.com/moneybeat/2015/11/11/ackman-fires-back-at-munger-says-coke-has-damaged-society.

58. Dragana Cvijanovic and Christophe Spaenjers, "Real Estate as a Luxury Good: Non-Resident Demand and Property Prices in Paris," January 7, 2015, HEC Paris Research Paper No. FIN-2015-1073, available at SSRN: http://ssrn.com/abstract=2546689 or http://dx.doi.org/10.2139/ssrn.2546689.

59. Sumit Agarwal, Crocker Herbert Liu, Walter N. Torous, and Vincent W. Yao, "Financial Decision Making When Buying and Owning a Home" (September 18, 2014), available at SSRN: http://ssrn.com/abstract=2498111or http://dx.doi.org/10.2139/ssrn.2498111.

60. Alexander L. Brown and Joanna N. Lahey, "Small Victories: Creating Intrinsic Motivation in Savings and Debt Reduction," *Journal of Marketing Research* 52, no. 6 (December 2015): 768–783.

61. Daniel Read and Barbara Van Leeuwen, "Predicting Hunger: The Effects of Appetite and Delay on Choice," *Organizational Behavior and Human Decision Processes* 76, no. 2 (November 1998): 189–205.

62. Bryan Bollinger, Phillip Leslie, and Alan Sorensen, "Calorie Posting in Chain Restaurants," *American Economic Journal: Economic Policy* 3 (2011): 91–128.

63. Brian Wansink and Pierre Chandon, "Can 'Low-Fat' Nutrition Labels Lead to Obesity?" *Journal of Marketing Research* 43, no. 4 (November 2006): 605–617.

64. Pierre Chandon and Brian Wansink, "The Biasing Health Halos of Fast Food Restaurant Health Claims: Lower Calorie Estimates and Higher Side-Dish Consumption Intentions," *Journal of Consumer Research* 34, no. 3 (2007): 301–314.

65. Robert J. Shiller, "Owning a Home Isn't Always a Virtue," *New York Times,* July 13, 2013, http://www.nytimes.com/2013/07/14/business/owning-a-home-isnt-always-a-virtue.html?_r=0.

66. Andrew Ross Sorkin, "Gun Shares Have Done Well, but Divestment Push Grows." *New York Times,* December 8, 2015: B1.

67. Vanessa C. Burbano, "Social Responsibility Messages and Worker Wage Requirements: Field Experimental Evidence from Online Labor Marketplaces," *Organization Science* 27, no. 4 (June 30, 2016): 1010–1028.

68. Dirk Jenter and Katharina Lewellen, "CEO Preferences and Acquisitions," *Journal of Finance* 70, no. 6 (December 2015): 2813–2852.

69. Konrad Raff and Linus Siming, "Knighthoods, Damehoods, and CEO Behaviour," *Journal of Corporate Finance,* forthcoming (June 29, 2015), available at SSRN: http://ssrn.com/abstract=2420066.

70. Nerissa C. Brown, Kelsey D. Wei, and Russ Wermers, "Analyst Recommendations, Mutual Fund Herding, and Overreaction in Stock Prices," *Management Science* 60, no. 1 (March 2013): 1–20.

71. "The Generation Gap," *SEI Private Wealth Management,*" 2011, https://www.seic .com/Wealth/SEI_The-Generation-Gap_Scorpio.pdf

CHAPTER 3

1. "Asics Running Commercial," Mightzozo, YouTube video, September 4, 2009, https://www.youtube.com/watch?v=D-ie_aFsfb8.

2. Shimon Kogan, Thomas Gilbert, Lars A. Lochstoer, and Ataman Ozyildirim, "Investor Inattention and the Market Impact of Summary Statistics," *Management Science* 58, no. 2 (February 2012): 336–350.

3. Abigail B. Sussman and Adam L. Alter, "The Exception Is the Rule: Underestimating and Overspending on Exceptional Expenses," *Journal of Consumer Research* 39 (2012): 800–814.

4. Alok Gangaramany, "Dustin Hoffman's Mental Accounting," YouTube video, April 7, 2013, https://www.youtube.com/watch?v=t96LNX6tk0U.

5. Justine S. Hastings and Jesse M. Shapiro, "Mental Accounting and Consumer Choice: Evidence from Commodity Price Shocks," NBER Working Paper No. w18248 (July 2012), available at SSRN: http://ssrn.com/abstract=2114874.

6. Luc Christiaensen and Lei Pan, "On the Fungibility of Spending and Earnings: Evidence from Rural China and Tanzania" (December 1, 2012). World Bank Policy Research Working Paper No. 6298, available at SSRN: https://ssrn.com/ abstract=2194779.

7. Hans K. Hvide and Jae Ho Lee, "Does Source of Income Affect Risk and Intertemporal Choices?" (February 25, 2016), available at SSRN: http://ssrn .com/abstract=2648604 or http://dx.doi.org/10.2139/ssrn.2648604.

8. "The Bunkers and Inflation (Part 4)" was the fourth episode of the fifth season, and the 89th overall episode, of *All in the Family.* The Season 4 episode first aired on CBS-TV on October 5, 1974. The final installment of a four-episode story arc was written by Don Nicholl, Michael Ross, and Bernie West, the episode was directed by H. Wesley Kenney.

9. Thomas Alexander Stephens and Jean-Robert Tyran, "'At Least I Didn't Lose Money': Nominal Loss Aversion Shapes Evaluations of Housing Transactions," (October 12, 2012). University of Copenhagen Department of Economics Discussion Paper No. 12-14, available at SSRN: https://ssrn.com/ abstract=2162415 or http://dx.doi.org/10.2139/ssrn.2162415.

10. Baruch Fischhoff, "Debiasing," in *Judgment under Uncertainty: Shortcuts and Biases,* ed. Daniel Kahneman, Paul Slovic, and Amos Tversky, 422–444 (Cambridge UK: Cambridge University Press, 1982).

11. Bruno Biais and Martin Weber, "Hindsight Bias, Risk Perception and Investment Performance," *Management Science* 55, no. 6 (June 2009): 1018–1029, available at SSRN: http://ssrn.com/abstract=1209774.

12. E. S. Browning, Steven Rusolillo, and Jessica E. Vascellaro, "Apple Now Biggest-Ever U.S. Company," *Wall Street Journal,* August 20, 2012, accessed December 22, 2015, http://www.wsj.com/articles/SB10000872396390443855804577601773524745182.

13. These quotes and those in the following paragraph were posted on the http://finance.yahoo.com message boards on the dates given. The webpages are now no longer available.

14. Bin Gu, JaeHong Park, Prabhudev Konana, Alok Kumar, and Rajagopal Raghunathan, "Information Valuation and Confirmation Bias in Virtual Communities: Evidence from Stock Message Boards," *Information Systems Research* 24, no. 4 (November 2013): 1050–1067.

15. Vicki Bogan and David Just, "What Drives Merger Decision Making Behavior? Don't Seek, Don't Find, and Don't Change Your Mind," *Journal of Economic Behavior and Organization* 72, no. 3 (2009): 930–943.

16. Michael E. Solt and Meir Statman, "How Useful Is the Sentiment Index?" *Financial Analysts Journal* 44, no. 5 (September–October 1988): 45–55.

17. Phoebe C. Ellsworth and Barbara O'Brien, "Prosecutorial Blind Spots: Features of the Adversarial Criminal Justice System That Promote Confirmation Bias," Society of Experimental Social Psychology, Annual Conference Paper (October 2009), Portland, ME.

18. Drew Westen, Pavel S. Blagov, Keith Harenski, Clint Kilts, and Stephan Hamann, "Neural Bases of Motivated Reasoning: An fMRI Study of Emotional Constraints on Partisan Political Judgment in the 2004 U.S. Presidential Election," *Journal of Cognitive Neuroscience* 18 (2006): 1947–1958.

19. Jessica Y. Y. Kwong and Ellick K. F. Wong, "Is 7300m Equal to 7.3km? Same Semantics but Different Anchoring Effects," *Organizational Behavior and Human Decision Processes* 82 (July 2000): 314–333.

20. Amos Tversky and Daniel Kahneman, "Judgment under Uncertainty: Heuristics and Biases," *Science* 185 (1974): 1124–1131.

21. Roger G. Clarke and Meir Statman, "The DJIA Crossed 652,230," *Journal of Portfolio Management* 26, no. 2 (Winter 2000): 89–92.

22. Sean D. Campbell and Steven A. Sharpe, "Anchoring Bias in Consensus Forecasts and Its Effect on Market Prices," Finance and Economics Discussion Series Divisions of Research & Statistics and Monetary Affairs, Federal Reserve Board, Washington, D.C. (2007).

23. Thomas J. George and Chuan-Yang Hwang, "The 52-Week High and Momentum Investing," *Journal of Finance* 59 (2004): 2145–2176.

24. Fengfei Li, Chen Lin, and Tse-Chun Lin, "Does Anchoring Heuristic Affect Analyst Recommendation Revisions?" (July 1, 2015), available at SSRN: http://ssrn.com/abstract=2517238 or http://dx.doi.org/10.2139/ssrn.2517238.

25. Eeva Alho, Markku Kaustia, and Vesa Puttonen, "How Much Does Expertise Reduce Behavioral Biases? The Case of Anchoring Effects in Stock Return Estimates," *Financial Management* 37, no. 3 (Autumn 2008): 391–411, available at SSRN: http://ssrn.com/abstract=1066641.

26. Anna Dodonova and Yuri Khoroshilov, "Anchoring and Transaction Utility: Evidence from On-line Auctions," *Applied Economics Letters* 11 (2004): 307–310, available at SSRN: http://ssrn.com/abstract=870445.

27. Zur Shapira and Itzhak Venezia, "On the Preference for Full-Coverage Policies: Why Do People Buy Too Much Insurance?" *Journal of Economic Psychology* 29, no. 5 (2008): 747–761.

28. Nassim Nicholas Taleb, *The Black Swan: The Impact of the Highly Improbable* (New York: Random House, 2007).

29. Amos Tversky and Daniel Kahneman, "Judgment under Uncertainty: Heuristics and Biases," *Science* 185 (1974): 1124–1131.

30. James B. Stewart, "The Narrative Frays for Theranos and Elizabeth Holmes," *New York Times*, October 29, 2015, http://www.nytimes.com/2015/10/30/business/the-narrative-frays-for-theranos-and-elizabeth-holmes.html?_r=0.

31. Jaideep Sengupta and Dengfeng Yan, "The Influence of Base Rate and Case Information on Health-Risk Perceptions: A Unified Model of Self-Positivity and Self-Negativity," *Journal of Consumer Research* 39, no. 5 (February 2013): 931–946.

32. Vyacheslav Mikhed and Michael Vogan, "Out of Sight, Out of Mind: Consumer Reaction to News on Data Breaches and Identity Theft," FRB of Philadelphia Working Paper No. 15-42 (November 16, 2015), available at SSRN: http://ssrn.com/abstract=2691902.

33. Claus Bjorn Galbo-Jörgensen, Sigrid Suetens, and Jean-Robert Tyran, "Predicting Lotto Numbers: A Natural Experiment on the Gambler's Fallacy and the Hot Hand Fallacy," *Journal of the European Economic Association* (2015).

34. Rogier J. D. Potter van Loon, Martijn J. Van den Assem, Dennie Van Dolder, and Tong V. Wang, "Number Preferences in Lotteries" (November 1, 2015), available at SSRN: http://ssrn.com/abstract=2657776 or http://dx.doi.org/10.2139/ssrn.2657776.

35. "UBS Index of Investor Optimism," Gallup Organization, December 2007.

36. Sanjiv R. Das and Priya Raghubir, "The Long and Short of It: Why Are Stocks with Shorter Runs Preferred?" *Journal of Consumer Research* 36 (2010): 964–982.

37. Daniel L. Chen, Tobias J. Moskowitz, and Kelly Shue, "Decision-Making under the Gambler's Fallacy: Evidence from Asylum Judges, Loan Officers, and Baseball Umpires," Chicago Booth Research Paper No. 15-27 (November 4, 2014), available at SSRN: http://ssrn.com/abstract=2635524 or http://dx.doi.org/10.2139/ssrn.2635524.

38. William Brock, Josef Lakonishok, and Blake LeBaron, "Simple Technical Trading Rules and the Stochastic Properties of Stock Returns," *Journal of Finance* 47, no. 5 (1992): 1731–1764.

39. Jiali Fang, Ben Jacobsen, and Yafeng Qin, "Predictability of the Simple Technical Trading Rules: An Out-of-Sample Test," *Review of Financial Economics* 23, no. 1 (2014): 30–45.

40. Arvid O. I. Hoffmann and Thomas Post, "Self-Attribution Bias in Consumer Financial Decision-Making: How Investment Returns Affect Individuals' Belief in Skill," *Journal of Behavioral and Experimental Economics* 52 (May 23, 2014): 23–28, available at SSRN: http://ssrn.com/abstract=2367230 or http://dx.doi.org/10.2139/ssrn.2367230.

41. Walt Bogdanich and Jacqueline Williams, "For Addicts, Fantasy Sites Can Lead to Ruinous Path," *New York Times,* November 22, 2015, http://www.nytimes

.com/2015/11/23/sports/fantasy-sports-addiction-gambling-draftkings-fanduel.html.

42. Kahneman, *Thinking, Fast and Slow.*

43. Stefano DellaVigna and Ethan Kaplan, "The Fox News Effect: Media Bias and Voting," *Quarterly Journal of Economics* 122, no. 3 (2007): 1187–1234.

44. Brad M. Barber and Terrance Odean, "All That Glitters: The Effect of Attention and News on the Buying Behavior of Individual and Institutional Investors," *Review of Financial Studies* 21 (2008): 785–818.

45. Hans K. Hvide and Per Ostberg, "Stock Investments at Work" (February 2014). CEPR Discussion Paper No. DP9837, available at SSRN: https://ssrn.com/abstract=2444838.

46. Weiyu Kuo, Tse-Chun Lin, and Jing Zhao, "Cognitive Limitation and Investment Performance: Evidence from Limit Order Clustering," *Review of Financial Studies* 28, no. 3 (February 2014): 838–875.

47. Alexander Hillert and Heiko Jacobs, "The Power of Primacy: Alphabetic Bias, Investor Recognition, and Market Outcomes" (October 2014), available at SSRN: http://ssrn.com/abstract=2390015.

48. David H. Solomon, Eugene F. Soltes, and Denis Sosyura, "Winners in the Spotlight: Media Coverage of Fund Holdings as a Driver of Flows," *Journal of Financial Economics* 113, no. 1 (July 2014): 53–72.

49. Jonathan J. Koehler and Molly Mercer, "Selection Neglect in Mutual Fund Advertisements," *Management Science* 55 (2009): 1107–1121.

50. Paul J. Healy and Don A. Moore, "The Trouble with Overconfidence," *Psychological Review* 115, no. 2 (2008): 502–517.

51. Cameron Anderson, Sebastien Brion, Don A. Moore, and Jessica A. Kennedy, "A Status-Enhancement Account of Overconfidence," *Journal of Personality and Social Psychology* 103 (2012): 718–735.

52. Jessica A. Kennedy, Cameron Anderson, and Don A. Moore, "When Overconfidence Is Revealed to Others: Testing the Status-Enhancement Theory of Overconfidence," *Organizational Behavior and Human Decision Processes* 122 (2013): 266–279.

53. Ido Erev, Thomas S. Wallsten, and David V. Budescu, "Simultaneous Over- and Underconfidence: The Role of Error in Judgment Processes," *Psychological Review* 101, no. 3 (July 1994): 519–527.

54. Healy and Moore, "The Trouble with Overconfidence."

55. Ola Svenson, "Are We All Less Risky and More Skillful Than Our Fellow Drivers?" *Acta Psychologica* 47, no. 2 (1981): 143–148.

56. Justin Kruger, "Lake Wobegon Be Gone! The 'Below-Average Effect' and the Egocentric Nature of Comparative Ability Judgments," *Journal of Personality and Social Psychology* 77, no. 2 (1999): 221–232.

57. Neil D. Weinstein, "Unrealistic Optimism about Future Life Events," *Journal of Personality and Social Psychology* 39 (1980): 806–820.

58. Justin Kruger and Jeremy Burrus, "Egocentrism and Focalism in Unrealistic Optimism (and Pessimism)," *Journal of Experimental Social Psychology* 40 (2004): 332–340.

59. Itzhak Ben-David, John R. Graham, and Campbell R. Harvey, "Managerial Miscalibration," *Quarterly Journal of Economics* 128, no. 4 (2013): 1547–1584.

60. Gilles Hilary and Charles Hsu, "Endogenous Overconfidence in Managerial Forecasts," *Journal of Accounting and Economics* 51 (2011): 300–313.

61. Catherine M. Schrand and Sarah Zechman, "Executive overconfidence and the slippery slope to financial misreporting," *Journal of Accounting and Economics* 53 (2012): 311–329.

62. Ulrike Malmendier and Geoffrey Tate, "CEO Overconfidence and Corporate Investment," *Journal of Finance* 60, no. 6 (December 2005): 2661–2700.

63. Albert E. Mannes and Don A. Moore, "A Behavioral Demonstration of Overconfidence in Judgment," *Psychological Science* 24, no. 7 (2013): 1190–1197.

64. Christoph Merkle, "Financial Overconfidence over Time: Foresight, Hindsight, and Insight of Investors," AFA 2013 San Diego Meetings Paper; EFA 2012 Copenhagen Meetings Paper (August 31, 2013), available at SSRN: http://ssrn .com/abstract=2001513.

65. "Fidelity® Poll Showcases Active Investors' Confidence," *FMR LLC*, May 16, 2012, http://www.businesswire.com/news/home/20120516005964/en/Fidelity®-Poll-Showcases-Active-Investors'-Confidence#.VaJxbflViko.

66. Michal Herzenstein, Sharon Horsky, and Steven S. Posavac, "Living with Terrorism or Withdrawing in Terror: Perceived Control and Consumer Avoidance," *Journal of Consumer Behaviour* 14 (2015): 228–236, available at SSRN: http://ssrn.com/abstract=2663516

67. Mark Fenton-O'Creevy, Nigel Nicholson, Emma Soane, and Paul Willman, "Trading on Illusions: Unrealistic Perceptions of Control and Trading Performance," *Journal of Occupational and Organizational Psychology* 76 (2003): 53–68.

68. Lysann Damisch, Thomas Mussweiler, and Barbara Stoberock, "Keep Your Fingers Crossed! How Superstition Improves Performance," *Psychological Science* 21 (2007): 1014–1020.

69. Deborah A. Cobb-Clark, Sonja C. Kassenboehmer, and Mathias Sinning, "Locus of Control and Savings," *Journal of Banking and Finance* 73 (2016): 113–130.

CHAPTER 4

1. Justin S. Feinstein, Ralph Adolphs, Antonio Damasio, and Daniel Tranel, "The Human Amygdala and the Induction and Experience of Fear," *Current Biology* 21, no. 1 (January 2011): 34–38.

2. Antonio Damasio, *Descartes' Error: Emotion, Reason, and the Human Brain* (New York: HarperCollins, 1994). See also Shiv Baba, George Loewenstein, Antoine Bechara, Hanna Damasio, and Antonio R. Damasio, "Investment Behavior and the Negative Side of Emotion," *Psychological Science* 16, no. 6 (2005): 435–439.

3. Maria Popova, "Charles Darwin's List of the Pros and Cons of Marriage," *Brain Pickings*, August 14, 2012, https://www.brainpickings.org/index.php/2012/08/14/darwin-list-pros-and-cons-of-marriage.

4. Paul Ekman, "Are There Basic Emotions?" *Psychological Review* 99 (1992): 550–553.

5. Seunghee Han, Jennifer S. Lerner, and Dacher Keltner, "Feelings and Consumer Decision Making: Extending the Appraisal-Tendency Framework," *Journal of Consumer Psychology* 17, no. 3 (2007): 184–187.

6. Craig A. Smith and Phoebe C. Ellsworth, "Patterns of Cognitive Appraisal in Emotion," *Journal of Personality & Social Psychology* 48, no. 4 (1985): 813–838.

7. Lea Dunn and Joandrea Hoegg, "The Impact of Fear on Emotional Brand Attachment," *Journal of Consumer Research* 41, no. 1 (June 2014): 152–168.

8. Joseph Engelberg and Christopher A. Parsons, "Worrying about the Stock Market: Evidence from Hospital Admissions," *Journal of Finance* 71 (2016): 1227–1250.

9. Anita Ratcliffe and Karl Taylor, "Who Cares about Stock Market Booms and Busts? Evidence from Data on Mental Health," *Oxford Economic Papers*, 67, no. 3 (2015): 826–845.

10. William N. Goetzmann, Dasol Kim, and Robert J. Shiller, "Crash Beliefs from Investor Surveys" (March 19, 2016), available at SSRN: http://ssrn.com/abstract=2750638 or http://dx.doi.org/10.2139/ssrn.2750638.

11. Alain Cohn, Jan Engelmann, Ernst Fehr, and Michel André Maréchal, "Evidence for Countercyclical Risk Aversion: An Experiment with Financial Professionals," *American Economic Review* 105, no. 2 (2015): 860–885.

12. Lieven Baele, Geert Bekaert, Koen Inghelbrecht, and Min Wei, "Flights to Safety," NBER Working Paper No. w19095 (May 2013).

13. Joe Light, "Retirement Investors Flock Back to Stocks," *Wall Street Journal,* May 1, 2014, http://www.wsj.com/articles/SB10001424052702303948104579535840428373528.

14. Arvid O. I. Hoffmann and Thomas Post, "(forthcoming) How Return and Risk Experiences Shape Investor Beliefs and Preferences." *Accounting and Finance.*

15. Chan Jean Lee and Eduardo B. Andrade, "Fear, Social Projection, and Financial Decision Making," *Journal of Marketing Research* 48, no. SPL (November 2011): S121–S129.

16. Luigi Guiso, Paola Sapienza, and Luigi Zingales, "Time Varying Risk Aversion," NBER Working Paper No. 19284 (August 2013). Journal of Financial Economics (forthcoming).

17. Nikolai Roussanov and Pavel Savor, "Marriage and Managers' Attitudes to Risk," *Management Science* 60 (2014): 2496–2508.

18. Rachel A. J. Pownall, Meir Statman, and Kees G. Koedijk, "Aspirations for Income: Status, Competitiveness and Risk Attitudes," Working Paper, Tilburg University (June 8, 2016).

19. Jennifer S. Lerner, Deborah A. Small, and George Loewenstein, "Heart Strings and Purse Strings: Carryover Effects of Emotions on Economic Decisions," *Psychological Science* 15, no. 5 (2004): 337–341.

20. Tao Shu, Johan Sulaeman, and P. Eric Yeung, "Does Sadness Influence Investor Behavior? Evidence from Bereaved Fund Managers" (August 2015), available at SSRN: http://ssrn.com/abstract=2658815 or http://dx.doi.org/10.2139/ssrn.2658815.

21. John Ifcher and Homa Zarghamee, "Happiness and Time Preference: The Effect of Positive Affect in a Random-Assignment Experiment," *American Economic Review* 101 (2011): 3109–3129.

22. Seunghee Han, Jennifer Lerner, and Richard J. Zeckhauser, "The Disgust-Promotes-Disposal Effect," *Journal of Risk and Uncertainty* 44, no. 2 (2012): 101–113.

23. Elisa Gambetti and Fiorella Giusberti, "The Effect of Anger and Anxiety Traits on Investment Decisions," *Journal of Economic Psychology* 33 (2012): 1059–1069.

24. Maia J. Young, Larissa Z. Tiedens, Heajung Jung, and Ming-Hong Tsai, "Mad Enough to See the Other Side: Anger and the Search for Disconfirming Information," *Cognition & Emotion* 25 (2011): 10–21.

25. Dacher Keltner and Jennifer S. Lerner, "Fear, Anger, and Risk," *Journal of Personality and Social Psychology* 81, no. 1 (2001): 146–159.

26. Paul Litvak, Jennifer Lerner, Larissa Tiedens, and Katherine Shonk, "Fuel in the Fire: How Anger Impacts Judgment and Decision-Making," in *International Handbook of Anger*, ed. Michael Potegal, Gerhard Stemmler, and Charles Spielberger (New York: Springer, 2010), 287–310.

27. Jean-François Coget, Christophe Haag, and Donald E. Gibson, "Anger and Fear in Decision-Making: The Case of Film Directors on Set," *European Management Journal* 29, no. 6 (2011): 476–490.

28. Jeremy A. Yip, and Martin Schweinsberg, "Infuriating Impasses: Expressing Anger Increases Negotiation Impasses" (April 22, 2016), available at SSRN: http://ssrn.com/abstract=2628940.

29. Associated Press, "Obama Signs New Rules for Credit Cards into Law," NBCnews.com, May 22, 2009. http://www.nbcnews.com/id/30884011/ns/business-personal_finance/t/obama-signs-new-rules-credit-cards-law/#.WDWaufkrKM8.

30. Michael Lewis, *Flash Boys: A Wall Street Revolt* (New York: W. W. Norton, 2014).

31. Susan B. Shimanoff, "Commonly Named Emotions in Everyday Conversations," *Perceptual and Motor Skills* 58 (April 1984): 514.

32. Michal Ann Strahilevitz, Terrance Odean, and Brad M. Barber, "Once Burned, Twice Shy: How Naive Learning, Counterfactuals, and Regret Affect the Repurchase of Stocks Previously Sold," *Journal of Marketing Research* 48 (Special Issue 2011): S102–S120.

33. Douglas MacMillan, "Facebook's Missing Millionaires," *Bloomberg Business Week*, March 8, 2012, http://www.businessweek.com/articles/2012-03-08/facebooks-missing-millionaires.

34. Gael Fashingbauer Cooper, "'Bachelorette' Missing out on Facebook Millions," *TODAY.com*. February 23, 2012, http://www.today.com/popculture/bachelorette-missing-out-facebook-millions-176682.

35. Jessica Y. Y. Kwong and Kin Fai Ellick Wong, "Reducing and Exaggerating Escalation of Commitment by Option Partitioning," *Journal of Applied Psychology* 99, no. 4 (July 2014): 697–712.

36. Marcel Zeelenberg, Jane Beattie, Joop Van Der Pligt, and Nanne K. De Vries, "Consequences of Regret Aversion: Effects of Expected Feedback on Risky Decision Making," *Organizational Behavior and Human Decision Processes* 65, no. 2 (February 1996): 148–158.

37. René Richard, Joop Van Der Pligt, and Nanne De Vries, "Anticipated Regret and Time Perspective: Changing Sexual Risk-Taking Behavior," *Journal of Behavioral Decision Making* 9 (1996): 185–199.

38. John Ameriks, Andrew Caplin, John Leahy, and Tom Tyler, "Measuring Self-Control," *American Economic Review* 97 (2007): 966–972.

39. Brian Knutson, George Loewenstein, Drazen Prelec, Scott Rick, and G. Elliott Wimmer, "Neural Predictors of Purchases," *Neuron* 53 (January 2007): 147–156.

40. Walter Mischel and Yuichi Shoda, "A Cognitive-Affective System Theory of Personality: Reconceptualizing Situations, Dispositions, Dynamics, and Invariance in Personality Structure," *Psychological Review* 102, no. 2 (1995): 246–268.

41. Ayelet Fishbach and James Shah, "Self Control in Action: Implicit Dispositions toward Goals and away from Temptations," *Journal of Personality and Social Psychology* 90, no. 5 (2006): 820–832.

42. B. J. Casey et al., "Behavioral and Neural Correlates of Delay of Gratification 40 Years Later," *Proceedings of the National Academy of Sciences of the United States of America* 108, no. 36 (2011): 14998–15003.

43. Henrik Cronqvist and Stephan Siegel, "The Origins of Savings Behavior," *Journal of Political Economy* 123 (2015): 123–169.

44. Jan-Emmanuel De Neve and James H. Fowler, "Credit Card Borrowing and the Monoamine Oxidase A (MAOA) Gene," *Journal of Economic Behavior and Organization* 107, Part B (November 2014): 428–439.

45. Warren K. Bickel, Kris Kirby, and Nancy M. Petry, "Heroin Addicts Have Higher Discount Rates for Delayed Rewards Than Non-Drug-Using Controls," *Journal of Experimental Psychology* 128, no. 1 (1999): 78–87.

46. Angela Duckworth and David Weir, "Personality and Response to the Financial Crisis" (December 1, 2011). Michigan Retirement Research Center Research Paper No. WP 2011-260, available at SSRN: https://ssrn.com/abstract=2006595 or http://dx.doi.org/10.2139/ssrn.2006595.

47. Arndt R. Reichert, Boris Augurzky, and Harald Tauchmann, "Self-Perceived Job Insecurity and the Demand for Medical Rehabilitation: Does Fear of Unemployment Reduce Health Care Utilization?" *Health Economics* 24 (January 2015): 8–25.

48. Edward M. Saunders, "Stock Prices and Wall Street Weather," *American Economic Review* 83, no. 5 (1993): 1337–1345.

49. David Hirshleifer and Tyler Shumway, "Good Day Sunshine: Stock Returns and the Weather," *Journal of Finance* 58, no. 3 (2003): 1009–1032.

50. William N. Goetzmann, Dasol Kim, Alok Kumar, and Qin (Emma) Wang, "Weather-Induced Mood, Institutional Investors, and Stock Returns" (September 8, 2014), available at SSRN: https://ssrn.com/abstract=2323852 or http://dx.doi.org/10.2139/ssrn.2323852.

51. Doron Kliger, Yaron Raviv, Joshua G. Rosett, Thomas Bayer, and John Page, "Auction Prices and the Weather: New Evidence from Old Masters," (August 26, 2010). Available at SSRN: https://ssrn.com/abstract=1666550 or http://dx.doi.org/10.2139/ssrn.1666550.

52. Lisa A. Kramer and J. Mark Weber, "This Is Your Portfolio on Winter: Seasonal Affective Disorder and Risk Aversion in Financial Decision Making," *Social Psychological and Personality Science* (2011): 193–199.

53. Mark J. Kamstra, Lisa A. Kramer, and Maurice D. Levi, "Winter Blues: A Sad Stock Market Cycle," *American Economic Review* 93 (2003): 324–343.

54. Mark J. Kamstra, Lisa A. Kramer, Maurice D. Levi, and Russ Wermers, "Seasonal Asset Allocation: Evidence from Mutual Fund Flows," Journal of Financial and Quantitative Analysis (forthcoming) 25th Australasian Finance and Banking Conference 2012 Paper (August 12, 2014), available at SSRN: http://ssrn.com/abstract=1907904.

55. Markku Kaustia and Elias Henrikki Rantapuska, "Does Mood Affect Trading Behavior?" *Journal of Financial Markets* 29 (June 2016): 1–26.

56. Andrew R. Grant, Petko S. Kalev, Avanidhar Subrahmanyam, and P. Joakim Westerholm, "Stressors and Financial Market Trading: The Case of Marital Separation" (June 2, 2014). FIRN Research Paper, available at SSRN: https://ssrn.com/abstract=2445073 or http://dx.doi.org/10.2139/ssrn.2445073.

57. Sumit Agarwal, Ran Duchin, and Denis Sosyura, "In Mood for a Loan: The Causal Effect of Sentiment on Credit Origination," (November 1, 2012). Available at SSRN: https://ssrn.com/abstract=2141030 or http://dx.doi.org/10.2139/ssrn.2141030.

58. Yueran Ma, "Bank CEO Optimism and the Financial Crisis," (September 3, 2015). Available at SSRN: https://ssrn.com/abstract=2392683 or http://dx.doi.org/10.2139/ssrn.2392683.

59. Constantinos Antoniou, Alok Kumar, and Anastasios Maligkris, "The Affect Heuristic and Analysts' Earnings Forecasts" (December 10, 2015), available at SSRN: http://ssrn.com/abstract=2702051 or http://dx.doi.org/10.2139/ssrn.2702051.

60. Stuart Wolpert, "UCLA Psychologists Discover a Gene's Link to Optimism, Self-Esteem," *UCLA Newsroom,* September 13, 2011, http://newsroom.ucla.edu/releases/ucla-life-scientists-discover-215259.

61. Manju Puri and David T. Robinson, "Optimism and Economic Choice," *Journal of Financial Economics* 86 (2007): 71–99.

62. Vidhi Chhaochharia, George M. Korniotis, and Alok Kumar, "Prozac for Depressed States? Effect of Mood on Local Economic Recessions," *SSRN Electronic Journal* (April 30, 2011), available at SSRN: http://ssrn.com/abstract=1814083 or http://dx.doi.org/10.2139/ssrn.1814083.

63. Elizabeth R. Tenney, Jennifer M. Logg, and Don A. Moore, "(Too) Optimistic about Optimism: The Belief That Optimism Improves Performance," *Journal of Personality and Social Psychology* 108, no. 3 (March 2015): 377–399.

64. Ari Hyytinen and Hanna Putkuri, "Household Optimism and Borrowing" (May 8, 2012). Bank of Finland Research Discussion Paper No. 21/2012, available at SSRN: https://ssrn.com/abstract=2101025 or http://dx.doi.org/10.2139/ssrn.2101025.

65. Emily Oster, E. Ray Dorsey, and Ira Shoulson, "Limited Life Expectancy, Human Capital and Health Investments," *American Economic Review* 103 (2013): 1977–2002.

66. A. W. Marshall and William Meckling, "Predictability of the Costs, Time, and Success of Development," in *The Rate and Direction of Inventive Activity: Economic and Social Factors*, ed. National Bureau of Economic Research (Princeton: Princeton University Press, 1962), 461–476.

67. Bent Flyvbjerg, "How Optimism Bias and Strategic Misrepresentation in Early Project Development Undermine Implementation," *Concept Report*, no. 17 (2007): 41–45.

68. Edwin Mansfield, John Rapoport, Jerome Schnee, Samuel Wagner, and Michael Hamburger, *Research and Innovation in the Modern Corporation* (New York: W. W. Norton, 1971): 157–185.

69. Daniel Kahneman and Dan Lovallo, "Delusions of Success: How Optimism Undermines Executives' Decisions," *Harvard Business Review* (2003), https://hbr.org/2003/07/delusions-of-success-how-optimism-undermines-executives-decisions.

70. Jihae Shin and Katherine L. Milkman, "How Backup Plans Can Harm Goal Pursuit: The Unexpected Downside of Being Prepared for Failure" (December 15, 2014), available at SSRN: http://ssrn.com/abstract=2538889 or http://dx.doi.org/10.2139/ssrn.2538889.

71. Robert B. Zajonc, "Feeling and Thinking: Preferences Need No Inferences," *American Psychologist* 35 (1980): 151–175.

72. Anne Barnard and Karam Shoumali, "Image of Drowned Syrian, Aylan Kurdi, 3, Brings Migrant Crisis into Focus," *New York Times,* September 3, 2015, http://www.nytimes.com/2015/09/04/world/europe/syria-boy-drowning.html?_r=0.

73. Deborah A. Small, George Loewenstein, and Paul Slovic, "Sympathy and Callousness: The Impact of Deliberative Thought on Donations to Identifiable

and Statistical Victims," *Organizational Behavior and Human Decision Processes* 102 (2007): 143–153.

74. Camelia M. Kuhnen and Brian Knutson, "The Influence of Affect on Beliefs, Preferences, and Financial Decisions," *Journal of Financial and Quantitative Analysis* 46, no. 3 (June 2011): 605–626.

75. Sumit Agarwal, Jia He, Haoming Liu, Ivan P. L. Png, Tien Foo Sing, and Wei-Kang Wong, "Superstition and Asset Markets: Evidence from Singapore Housing" (March 27, 2014), available at SSRN: http://ssrn.com/abstract=2416832.

76. David Hirshleifer, Ming Jian, and Huai Zhang, "Superstition and Financial Decision Making," Asian Finance Association (AsianFA) 2015 Conference Paper (September 15, 2014), available at SSRN: http://ssrn.com/abstract=1460522.

77. James S. Ang, Ansley Chua, and Danling Jiang, "Is A Better Than B? How Affect Influences the Marketing and Pricing of Financial Securities," *Financial Analysts Journal* 66, no. 5 (September–October 2010): 40–54.

78. Marianne Bertrand, Dean Karlan, Sendhil Mullainathan, Eldar Shafir, and Jonathan Zinman, "What's Advertising Content Worth? Evidence from a Consumer Credit Marketing Field Experiment," *Quarterly Journal of Economics* 125 (February 2010): 263–305.

79. Enrichetta Ravina, "Love and Loans: The Effect of Beauty and Personal Characteristics in Credit Markets" (November 22, 2012), available at SSRN: https://ssrn.com/abstract=1101647 or http://dx.doi.org/10.2139/ssrn.1101647.

80. Meir Statman, Kenneth L. Fisher, and Deniz Anginer, "Affect in a Behavioral Asset Pricing Model," *Financial Analysts Journal* 64, no. 2 (March–April 2008): 20–29.

81. Paul Slovic, Baruch Fischhoff, and Sarah Lichtenstein, "Facts versus Fears: Understanding Perceived Risk," in *Judgment under Uncertainty: Heuristics and Biases,* ed. Daniel Kahneman, Paul Slovic, and Amos Tversky (Cambridge: Cambridge University Press, 1982), 463–489.

82. Paul Slovic, Melissa Finucane, Ellen Peters, and Donald G. MacGregor, "The Affect Heuristic," in *Heuristics and Biases: The Psychology of Intuitive Judgment,* ed. Thomas Gilovich, Dale Griffin, and Daniel Kahneman (New York: Cambridge University Press, 2002), 397–420.

83. Daniel Kahneman and Shane Frederick, "Representativeness Revisited," in *Heuristics and Biases: The Psychology of Intuitive Judgment,* ed. Thomas Gilovich, Dale Griffin, and Daniel Kahneman (New York, Cambridge University Press, 2002), 49–81.

CHAPTER 5

1. John Y. Campbell, Tarun Ramadorai, and Benjamin Ranish, "Getting Better: Learning to Invest in an Emerging Stock Market," (December 1, 2014), available at SSRN: https://ssrn.com/abstract=2176222 or http://dx.doi.org/10.2139/ssrn.2176222.

2. Daniel Kahneman and Gary Klein, "Conditions for Intuitive Expertise: A Failure to Disagree," *American Psychologist* 64, no. 6 (September 2009): 515–526.

3. Bart J. Bronnenberg, Jean-Pierre Dubé, Matthew Gentzkow, and Jesse M. Shapiro, "Do Pharmacists Buy Bayer? Informed Shoppers and the Brand Premium," *Quarterly Journal of Economics* 130 (2015): 1669–1726.

4. James S. Doran, David R. Peterson, and Colby Wright, "Confidence, Opinions of Market Efficiency, and Investment Behavior of Finance Professors," *Journal of Financial Markets* 13, no. 1 (2010): 174–195.

5. Hugh H. Kim, Raimond Maurer, and Olivia S. Mitchell, "Time Is Money: Rational Life Cycle Inertia and the Delegation of Investment Management?" *Journal of Financial Economics* 121, no. 2 (August 2016): 427–447.

6. Maximilian D. Schmeiser and Jeanne M. Hogarth, "Good Advice, Good Outcomes? How Financial Advice-Seeking Relates to Self-Perceived Financial Well-Being" (May 7, 2013), available at SSRN: http://ssrn.com/abstract=2261707.

7. Marc M. Kramer, "Financial Advice and Individual Investor Portfolio Performance," *Financial Management* (2012): 395–428.

8. Marc Kramer and Robert Lensink, "The Impact of Financial Advisors on the Stock Portfolios of Retail Investors," *SSRN Journal SSRN Electronic Journal*, available at SSRN: http://ssrn.com/abstract=2021883 or http://dx.doi.org/10.2139/ssrn.2021883.

9. Gjergji Cici, Alexander Kempf, and Christoph Sorhage, "Do Financial Advisors Provide Tangible Benefits for Investors? Evidence from Tax-Motivated Mutual Fund Flows" (July 2015). EFA 2014 Lugano Meetings Paper, available at SSRN: https://ssrn.com/abstract=2177401 or http://dx.doi.org/10.2139/ssrn.2177401.

10. J. Michael Collins and Maximilian D. Schmeiser, "Estimating the Effects of Foreclosure Counseling for Troubled Borrowers," (July 19, 2010), available at SSRN: https://ssrn.com/abstract=1645339 or http://dx.doi.org/10.2139/ssrn.1645339.

11. Daniel Fernandes, John G. Lynch Jr., and Richard G. Netemeyer, "Financial Literacy, Financial Education, and Downstream Financial Behaviors," *Management Science* 60, no. 8 (2014): 1861–1883.

12. Victor Stango and Jonathan Zinman, "Limited and Varying Consumer Attention: Evidence from Shocks to the Salience of Bank Overdraft Fees." *Review of Financial Studies*, 27, no. 4 (2014): 990–1030.

13. Sule Alan, Mehmet Cemalcilar, Dean S. Karlan, and Jonathan Zinman, "Unshrouding Effects on Demand for a Costly Add-On: Evidence from Bank Overdrafts in Turkey," NBER Working Paper No. w20956 (February 2015), available at SSRN: http://ssrn.com/abstract=2565629.

14. Henrik Cronqvist and Stephan Siegel, "Why Do Individuals Exhibit Investment Biases?" *SSRN Journal SSRN Electronic Journal* (May 22, 2012), available at SSRN: http://ssrn.com/abstract=2009094 or http://dx.doi.org/10.2139/ssrn.2009094.

15. Mark Grinblatt, Matti Keloharju, and Juhani T. Linnainmaa, "IQ, Trading Behavior, and Performance," *Journal of Financial Economics* 104 (2012): 339–362.

16. Keith E. Stanovich and Richard F. West, "On the Relative Independence of Thinking Biases and Cognitive Ability," *Journal of Personality and Social Psychology* 94, no. 4 (2008): 672–695.

17. Emily Pronin, Daniel Y. Lin, and Lee Ross, "The Bias Blind Spot: Perceptions of Bias in Self versus Others," *Personality and Social Psychology Bulletin* 28, no. 3 (March 2002): 369–381.

18. Samuel D. Bond, Kurt A. Carlson, and Ralph L. Keeney, "Improving the Generation of Decision Objectives," *Decision Analysis* 7, no. 3 (2010): 238–255.

19. Gretchen B. Chapman and Eric J. Johnson, "Incorporating the Irrelevant: Anchors in Judgments of Belief and Value," in *Heuristics and Biases: The Psychology of Intuitive Judgment*, ed. T. Gilovich, D. W. Griffin, and D. Kahneman (New York: Cambridge University Press), 120–138.

20. Yan Zhang, Ye Li, and Ting Zhu, "How Multiple Anchors Affect Judgment: Evidence from the Lab and EBay," (November 25, 2014). Columbia Business School Research Paper No. 14-62. Available at SSRN: https://ssrn.com/abstract=2530690 or http://dx.doi.org/10.2139/ssrn.2530690.

21. John Gathergood and Joerg Weber, "Self-Control, Financial Literacy and the Co-Holding Puzzle," *Journal of Economic Behavior and Organization* 107 (2014): 455–469.

22. Edward J. Russo and Paul J. H. Schoemaker, "Overconfidence." In Teece, David and Mie Augier (eds.), *Palgrave Encyclopedia of Strategic Management*, forthcoming (DOI: 10.1057/9781137294678.0505).

23. Katherine L. Milkman, John W. Payne, and Jack B. Soll, "A User's Guide to Debiasing," in *Wiley-Blackwell Handbook of Judgment and Decision Making*, ed. Gideon Keren and George Wu (Chichester, UK: John Wiley & Sons, 2015).

24. Stefan M. Herzog and Ralph Hertwig, "The Wisdom of Many in One Mind: Improving Individual Judgments with Dialectical Bootstrapping," *Psychological Science* 20 (2009): 231–237.

25. F. Douglas Foster and Geoff Warren, "Interviews with Institutional Investors: The How and Why of Active Investing," *Journal of Behavioral Finance* 17 (2016): 60–84.

26. Alan J. Marcus, "The Magellan Fund and Market Efficiency," *Journal of Portfolio Management* 17, no. 1 (Fall 1990): 85–88.

27. Peter C. Wason, "On the Failure to Eliminate Hypotheses in a Conceptual Task," *Quarterly Journal of Experimental Psychology* 12 (1960): 129–140.

28. Leda Cosmides, "The Logic of Social Exchange: Has Natural Selection Shaped How Humans Reason? Studies with Wason Selection Task," *Cognition* 31 (1989): 187–276.

29. Gerd Gigerenzer and Klaus Hug, "Domain-Specific Reasoning: Social Contracts, Cheating and Perspective Change," *Cognition* 43 (1992): 127–171.

30. Hillel J. Einhorn and Robin M. Hogarth, "Confidence in Judgment: Persistence of the Illusion of Validity." *Psychological Review* 85, no. 5 (September 1978): 395–416; Joshua Klayman and Young-Won Ha, "Confirmation, Disconfirmation, and Information in Hypothesis Testing," *Psychological Review* 94 (1987): 211–228.

31. Michael Lewis, *Moneyball: The Art of Winning an Unfair Game* (New York: W. W. Norton, 2014).

32. Eben Otuteye and Mohammad Siddiquee, "Overcoming Cognitive Biases: A Heuristic for Making Value Investing Decisions," *Journal of Behavioral Finance* 16, no. 2 (April 2015): 140–149.

33. Berkeley J. Dietvorst, Joseph P. Simmons, and Cade Massey, "Algorithm Aversion: People Erroneously Avoid Algorithms after Seeing Them Err," *Journal of Experimental Psychology: General* 144, no. 1 (February 2015): 114–126.

34. Daniel Kahneman, Jack L. Knetsch, and Richard H. Thaler, "Experimental Tests of the Endowment Effect and the Coase Theorem," *Journal of Political Economy* 98 (1990): 1325–1348.

35. Maya Bar-Hillel and Efrat Neter, "Why Are People Reluctant to Exchange Lottery Tickets?" *Journal of Personality and Social Psychology* 70, no. 1 (1996): 17–27.

36. Peter Sokol-Hessner, Ming Hsu, Nina G. Curley, Mauricio R. Delgado, Colin F. Camerer, and Elizabeth A. Phelps, "Thinking like a Trader Selectively Reduces Individuals' Loss Aversion," *Proceedings of the National Academy of Sciences of the United States of America* 106, no. 13 (2009): 5035–5040.

37. Dilip Soman and Amar Cheema, "Earmarking and Partitioning: Increasing Saving by Low-Income Households," *Journal of Marketing Research* 48 (2011): S14–S22.

38. Hal E. Hershfield, Daniel G. Goldstein, William F. Sharpe, Jesse Fox, Leo Yeykelis, Laura L. Carstensen, and Jeremy N. Bailenson, "Increasing Saving Behavior through Age-Progressed Renderings of the Future Self," *Journal of Marketing Research* 48 (2011): S23–S37.

39. Kelly L. Haws, William O. Bearden, and Gergana Y. Nenkov, "Consumer Spending Self Control Effectiveness and Outcome Elaboration Prompts," *Journal of the Academy of Marketing Science* 40, no. 5 (2012): 695–710.

40. Nava Ashraf, Dean Karlan, and Wesley Yin, "Tying Odysseus to the Mast: Evidence from a Commitment Savings Product in the Philippines," *Quarterly Journal of Economics* 121, no. 2 (2006): 635–672.

41. Dan Ariely and Klaus Wertenbroch, "Procrastination, Deadlines, and Performance: Self-Control by Precommitment," *Psychological Science* 13, no. 3 (2002): 219–224.

42. Scott D. Halpern, David A. Asch, and Kevin G. Volpp, "Commitment Contracts as a Way to Health," *British Medical Journal* 344, no. 1 (2012): e522–e522.

43. Xavier Gine, Dean Karlan, and Jonathan Zinman, "Put Your Money Where Your Butt Is: A Commitment Contract for Smoking Cessation," *American Economic Journal: Applied Economics* 2 (October 2010): 213–235.

44. Katherine L. Milkman, Julia A. Minson, and Kevin G. M. Volpp, "Holding the Hunger Games Hostage at the Gym: An Evaluation of Temptation Bundling," *Management Science* 60 (2013): 283–299.

45. J. Anthony Cookson, "When Saving Is Gambling." Finance Down Under 2015: Building on the Best from the Cellars of Finance Paper (January 27, 2016), available at SSRN: http://ssrn.com/abstract=2517126 or http://dx.doi.org/10.2139/ssrn.2517126.

46. Ran Kivetz and Itamar Simonson, "Self-Control for the Righteous: Toward a Theory of Precommitment to Indulgence," *Journal of Consumer Research* 29 (September 2002): 199–217.

47. Katherine L. Milkman, John W. Payne, and Jack B. Soll, "A User's Guide to Debiasing." In *Wiley-Blackwell Handbook of Judgment and Decision Making*, ed. Gideon Keren and George Wu (Chichester, UK: John Wiley & Sons, 2015).

48. Shawn Allen Cole, Martin Kanz, and Leora F. Klapper, "Incentivizing Calculated Risk-Taking: Evidence from an Experiment with Commercial Bank Loan Officers," *Journal of Finance* 70, no. 2 (April 2015): 537–575.

49. Zhuoqiong (Charlie) Chen and Tobias Gesche, "Persistent Bias in Advice-Giving," University of Zurich, Department of Economics, Working Paper No. 228 (June 1, 2016), available at SSRN: http://ssrn.com/abstract=2787825.

50. Kremena Bachmann and Thorsten Hens, "Investment Competence and Advice Seeking," *Journal of Behavioral and Experimental Finance* 6 (2015): 27–41.

51. Utpal Bhattacharya, Andreas Hackethal, Simon Kaesler, Benjamin Loos, and Steffen Meyer, "Is Unbiased Financial Advice to Retail Investors Sufficient? Review of Financial Studies, 25 (2012): 975–1032.

52. Henriette Prast, Federica Teppa, and Anouk Smits, "Is Information Overrated? Evidence from the Pension Domain," Netspar Discussion Paper No. 12/2012-050 (December 2012).

53. Sendhil Mullainathan, Eldar Shafir, and Anuj K. Shah, "Some Consequences of Having Too Little," *Science* 338, no. 6107 (November 2012): 682–685.

54. Shai Danziger, Jonathan Levav, and Liora Avnaim-Pesso, "Extraneous Factors in Judicial Decisions," *Proceedings of the National Academy of Science of the United States of America* 108 (2011): 6889–6892.

55. Marc A. Rodwin, "Commentary: The Politics of Evidence-Based Medicine," Agency for Healthcare Research and Quality, April 2001. http://www.ahrq.gov/research/findings/evidence-based-reports/jhppl/rodwin.html.

56. "Medical Merchandising: The Same Old Crap, Repackaged," *Angry Orthopod,* June 22, 2011, http://angryorthopod.com/2011/06/medical-merchandising-the-same-old-crap-repackaged.

57. Xavier Gabaix and David Laibson, "Shrouded Attributes, Consumer Myopia, and Information Suppression in Competitive Markets," *Quarterly Journal of Economics* 121, no. 2 (2006): 505–540.

58. Victor Stango and Jonathan Zinman, "Fuzzy Math, Disclosure Regulation and Credit Market Outcomes: Evidence from Truth in Lending Reform," *SSRN Electronic Journal* (June 2009), available at SSRN: http://ssrn.com/abstract=1081635 or http://dx.doi.org/10.2139/ssrn.1081635.

59. Fabian Duarte and Justine S. Hastings, "Fettered Consumers and Sophisticated Firms: Evidence from Mexico's Privatized Social Security Market," NBER Working Paper No. 18582 (December 2012).

60. Jaimie W. Lien and Jia Yuan, "Selling to Biased Believers: Strategies of Online Lottery Ticket Vendors," *Economic Inquiry* 53, no 3 (July 2015): 1506–1521.

61. Jonathan J. Koehler and Molly Mercer, "Selection Neglect in Mutual Fund Advertisements," *Management Science* 55 (2009): 1107–1121.

62. Sendhil Mullainathan, Markus Noeth, and Antoinette Schoar, "The Market for Financial Advice: An Audit Study," NBER Working Paper No. W17929 (March 2012).

63. Santosh Anagol, Shawn Allen Cole, and Shayak Sarkar, "Bad Advice: Explaining the Persistence of Whole Life Insurance," *SSRN Electronic Journal* (February 8, 2011), available at SSRN: http://ssrn.com/abstract=1786624 or http://dx.doi.org/10.2139/ssrn.1786624.

64. Stephen Foerster, Juhani Linnainmaa, Brian Melzer, and Alessandro Previtero, "Retail Financial Advice: Does One Size Fit All?" *Journal of Finance,* forthcoming, Chicago Booth Research Paper No. 14-38 Fama-Miller Working Paper (July 2, 2015).

65. Sumit Agarwal, Gene Amromin, Itzhak Ben-David, and Douglas D. Evanoff, "Loan Product Steering in Mortgage Markets" (August 1, 2016), Charles A. Dice Center Working Paper No. 2016-18; Fisher College of Business Working Paper No. 2016-03-18, available at SSRN: https://ssrn.com/abstract=2841312 or http://dx.doi.org/10.2139/ssrn.2841312.

66. Stefano DellaVigna and Ulrike Malmendier, "Paying Not to Go to the Gym," *American Economic Review* 96 (2006): 694–719.

67. Hong Ru and Antoinette Schoar, "Do Credit Card Companies Screen for Behavioral Biases?" (June 13, 2016), available at SSRN: http://ssrn.com/abstract=2795030.

68. Sumit Agarwal, Souphala Chomsisengphet, Neale Mahoney, and Johannes Stroebel, "Regulating Consumer Financial Products: Evidence from Credit Cards," *Quarterly Journal of Economics* 130 (2015): 111–164.

69. Hal E. Hershfield and Neal J. Roese, "Dual Payoff Scenario Warnings on Credit Card Statements Elicit Suboptimal Payoff Decisions," *Journal of Consumer Psychology* 25 (2015): 15–27.

70. John Beshears, James J. Choi, David Laibson, Brigitte C. Madrian, and Katherine L. Milkman, "The Effect of Providing Peer Information on Retirement Savings Decisions," *Journal of Finance* 70 (2015): 1161–1201.

71. Craig R. M. McKenzie and Michael J. Liersch, "Misunderstanding Savings Growth: Implications for Retirement Savings Behavior," *Journal of Marketing Research* 48 (Special Issue 2011): S1–S13.

72. Eric Eisenstein and Stephen Hoch, "Intuitive Compounding: Framing, Temporal Perspective, and Expertise," Working Paper. December 2005. http://eric-eisenstein.com/papers/Eisenstein&Hoch-Compounding.pdf.

73. Eric A. Posner and E. Glen Weyl, "An FDA for Financial Innovation: Applying the Insurable Interest Doctrine to 21st Century Financial Markets," *Northwestern University Law Review* 107 (2013): 1307–1358.

CHAPTER 6

1. Daniel Kahneman and Angus Deaton, "High Income Improves Evaluation of Life but not Emotional Well-Being," *Proceedings of the National Academy of Sciences of the United States of America* 107 (2010): 16489–16493.

2. Daniel Bernoulli, "Exposition of a New Theory on the Measurement of Risk," *Econometrica* 22 (1954): 23–36 (original work published 1738).

3. Daniel Kahneman and Amos Tversky, "Prospect Theory: An Analysis of Decisions under Risk," *Econometrica* 47 (1979): 313–327

4. Merton Miller and Franco Modigliani, "Dividend Policy, Growth, and the Valuation of Shares." *Journal of Business* 34 (1961): 411–433.

5. Carrie Pan and Meir Statman, "Questionnaires of Risk Tolerance, Regret, Overconfidence, and Other Investor Propensities," *Journal of Investment Consulting* 13 (2012): 54–63.

6. Eric J. Allen, Patricia M. Dechow, Devin G. Pope, and George Wu, "Reference-Dependent Preferences: Evidence from Marathon Runners," *Management Science*, http://www.nber.org/papers/w20343.

7. Teck Ho, Ivan P. L. Png, and Sadat Reza, "Sunk Cost Fallacy in Driving the World's Costliest Cars," *SSRN Electronic Journal* (January 22, 2014), available at SSRN: http://ssrn.com/abstract=2254483 or http://dx.doi.org/10.2139/ssrn.2254483.

8. Mark Lattman and Andrew Ross Sorkin, "Figure in Insider Case Sought to Quit Goldman," *New York Times*, March 13, 2011, http://dealbook.nytimes.com/2011/03/13/associate-in-insider-case-sought-to-quit-goldman/?_r=0.

9. Anita Raghavan, "Rajat Gupta's Lust for Zeros," *New York Times,* May 17, 2013, http://www.nytimes.com/2013/05/19/magazine/rajat-guptas-lust-for-zeros.html?pagewanted=all&_r=0.

10. Andrew Eric Clark, Claudia Senik, and Katsunori Yamada, "The Joneses in Japan: Income Comparisons and Financial Satisfaction," ISER Discussion Paper No. 866.

11. Sumit Agarwal, Vyacheslav Mikhed, and Barry Scholnick, "Does Inequality Cause Financial Distress? Evidence from Lottery Winners and Neighboring

Bankruptcies," FRB of Philadelphia Working Paper No. 16-4 (February 11, 2016), available at SSRN: http://ssrn.com/abstract=2731562.

12. Milton Friedman and Leonard J. Savage, "The Utility Analysis of Choices Involving Risk," *Journal of Political Economy* LVI (August 1948): 279–304.

13. Harry Markowitz, "The Utility of Wealth," *Journal of Political Economy* LX, no. 2 (1952): 151–158.

14. Daniel Kahneman and Amos Tversky, "Prospect Theory: An Analysis of Decisions under Risk," *Econometrica* 47, no. 2 (1979): 263–292.

15. Kahneman, *Thinking, Fast and Slow*.

16. Christopher K. Hsee and Yuval Rottenstreich, "Money, Kisses, and Electric Shocks: An Affective Psychology of Risk," *Psychological Science* 12, no. 3 (2001): 185–190.

17. William N. Goetzmann, Dasol Kim, and Robert J. Shiller, Crash Beliefs from Investor Surveys (March 19, 2016). Available at SSRN: https://ssrn.com/abstract=2750638 or http://dx.doi.org/10.2139/ssrn.2750638.

CHAPTER 7

1. Miller and Modigliani, "Dividend Policy."

2. Fischer Black, "The Dividend Puzzle," *Journal of Portfolio Management* 2 (1976): 5–8.

3. Shefrin and Statman, "Explaining Investor Preference."

4. Miller and Modigliani, "Dividend Policy," p. 414.

5. Shefrin and Statman, "Explaining Investor Preference."

6. Alon Brav, John R. Graham, Campbell R. Harvey and Roni Michaely, "The Effect of the May 2003 Dividend Tax Cut on Corporate Dividend Policy: Empirical and Survey Evidence," *National Tax Journal* 61 (2008): 381–396.

7. http://www.economist.com/node/348586.

8. Black, "The Dividend Puzzle," p. 5.

9. Ravi Dhar and Ning Zhu, "Up Close and Personal: Investor Sophistication and the Disposition Effect," *Management Science* 52, no. 5 (May 2006): 726–740; Zur Shapira and Yitzhak Venezia, "Patterns of Behavior of Professionally Managed and Independent Investors," *Journal of Banking and Finance* 25, no. 8 (August 2001): 1573–1587; Mark Grinblatt and Matti Keloharju, "What Makes Investors Trade?" *Journal of Finance* 56, no. 2 (2001): 589–616; Andrew Jackson, "The Aggregate Behaviour of Individual Investors" (July 29, 2003), available at SSRN: http://papers.ssrn.com/s013/papers.cfm?abstract_id=536942; Cristiana C. Leal, Manuel J. Rocha Armada, and Joao Duque, "Are All Individual Investors Equally Prone to the Disposition Effect All the Time? New Evidence from a Small Market," *Frontiers in Finance and Economics*, 7, no. 2 (October 2010): 38–68; Lei Feng and Mark Seasholes, "Do Investor Sophistication and Trading Experience Eliminate Behavioral Biases in Financial Markets?" *Review of Finance* 9 (2005): 305–351.

10. Ryan Garvey, Anthony Murphy, and Fei Wu, "Do Losses Linger? Evidence from Proprietary Stock Traders," *Journal of Portfolio Management* 33 (2007): 75–83.

11. Shefrin and Statman, "Explaining Investor Preference."

12. W. Howard T. Snyder, "How to Take a Loss and Like It," *Financial Analysts Journal* 13, no. 2 (May 1957): 115–116.

13. Cary Frydman and Colin Camerer, "Neural Evidence of Regret and Its Implications for Investor Behavior," *Review of Financial Studies*. First published online February 26, 2016.

14. Leroy Gross, *The Art of Selling Intangibles: How to Make your Million ($) by Investing Other People's Money* (New York: New York Institute of Finance, 1982).

15. Gilles Grolleau, Martin G. Kocher, and Angela Sutan, "Cheating and Loss Aversion: Do People Lie More to Avoid a Loss?" *Management Science*, http://dx.doi.org/10.1287/mnsc.2015.2313.

16. Gross, *The Art of Selling Intangibles*, p. 150.

17. Barbara Summers and Darren Duxbury, "Decision-Dependent Emotions and Behavioral Anomalies," *Organizational Behavior and Human Decision Processes*, 118, no. 2 (July 2012): 226–238.

18. Tom Chang, David H. Solomon, and Mark M. Westerfield, "Looking for Someone to Blame: Delegation, Cognitive Dissonance, and the Disposition Effect," *Journal of Finance* 71, no. 1 (February 2016): 267–302.

19. Cary Frydman, Samuel M. Hartzmark, and David H. Solomon, "Rolling Mental Accounts" (August 26, 2015), available at SSRN: http://ssrn.com/abstract=2653929 or http://dx.doi.org/10.2139/ssrn.2653929.

20. Jaakko Aspara and Arvid O. I. Hoffmann, "Selling Losers and Keeping Winners: How (Savings) Goal Dynamics Predict a Reversal of the Disposition Effect," *Marketing Letters* 26, no. 2 (June 2015): 201–211.

21. Diana Falsetta and Richard A. White, "The Impact of Income Tax Withholding Position and Stock Position on the Sale of Stock," *Journal of the American Taxation Association* 27, no. 1 (2005): 1–23.

22. Daniel Richards, Janette Rutterford, Devendra Kodwani, and Mark Fenton-O'Creevy, "Stock Market Investors' Use of Stop Losses and the Disposition Effect," *European Journal of Finance*, http://dx.doi.org/10.1080/1351847X.2015.1048375. Available at SSRN: https://ssrn.com/abstract=2612898.

23. Cary Frydman and Antonio Rangel, "Debiasing the Disposition Effect by Reducing the Saliency of Information about a Stock's Purchase Price," *Journal of Economic Behavior & Organization* 107 (2014): 541–552; Alasdair Brown and Fuyu Yang, "Salience and the Disposition Effect: Evidence from the Introduction of 'Cash-Outs' in Betting Markets" (October 2, 2015), available at SSRN: http://ssrn.com/abstract=2668618 or http://dx.doi.org/10.2139/ssrn.2668618.

24. Nicholas Barberis and Wei Xiong, "Realization Utility," *Journal of Financial Economics* 104 (2012): 251–271.

25. Cary Frydman, Nicholas Barberis, Colin Camerer, Peter Bossaerts, and Antonio Rangel, "Using Neural Data to Test a Theory of Investor Behavior: An Application to Realization Utility," *Journal of Finance* 69 (2014): 907–946.

26. Ira Glick, "A Social Psychological Study of Futures Trading," PhD diss., University of Chicago, 1957.

27. Sonny Kleinfield, *The Traders* (New York: Holt, Rinehart and Winston, 1983).

28. Gjergji Cici, "The Relation of the Disposition Effect to Mutual Fund Trades and Performance" (December 7, 2010), available at SSRN: https://ssrn.com/abstract=645841 or http://dx.doi.org/10.2139/ssrn.645841.

29. Kleinfield, *The Traders*.

30. Melvyn Teo and Paul G. J. O'Connell, "Prospect Theory and Institutional Investors," (October 2003), available at SSRN: https://ssrn.com/abstract=457741 or http://dx.doi.org/10.2139/ssrn.457741

31. Raymond Da Silva Rosa, Huong Minh To, and Terry S. Walter, "Evidence Contrary to the Disposition Effect amongst UK Managed Funds" (February

2005), available at SSRN: https://ssrn.com/abstract=676342 or http://dx.doi.org/10.2139/ssrn.676342.

32. Itzhak Ben-David and David Hirshleifer, "Are Investors Really Reluctant to Realize Their Losses? Trading Responses to Past Returns and the Disposition Effect," *Review of Financial Studies* 25, no. 8 (2012): 2485–2532.

33. Nachum Sicherman, George Loewenstein, Duane J. Seppi, and Stephen P. Utkus, "Financial Attention" (July 29, 2015), available at SSRN: http://ssrn.com/abstract=2339287 or http://dx.doi.org/10.2139/ssrn.2339287.

34. Robert G. Cooper, Scott J. Edgett, and Elko J. Kleinschmidt, *Portfolio Management for New Products* (Reading, MA: Addison-Wesley, 1998).

35. Christine A. Russell, "Problems in Ending a Project: Theory and Case Study," term paper, Santa Clara University (November 1983).

36. Uwe E. Reinhardt, "Break-Even Analysis for Lockheed's Tri Star: An Application of Financial Theory," *Journal of Finance* 28, no. 4 (September 1973): 821–838.

37. Barry M. Staw, "Knee-Deep in the Big Muddy: A Study of Escalating Commitment to a Chosen Course of Action," *Organizational Behavior and Human Performance* (June 1976): 27–44.

38. Roberto L. Pedace and Janet Kiholm Smith, "Loss Aversion and Managerial Decisions: Evidence from Major League Baseball," *Economic Inquiry* 51, no. 2 (April 2013): 1475–1488.

39. Yihui Pan, Tracy Yue Wang, and Michael Weisbach, "CEO Investment Cycles," *Review of Financial Studies*, http://rfs.oxfordjournals.org/content/29/11/2955.

40. George M. Constantinides, "A Note on the Suboptimality of Dollar-Cost Averaging as an Investment Policy," *Journal of Financial and Quantitative Analysis* 14, no. 2 (June 1979): 443–450.

41. Michael Rozeff, "Lump-Sum Investing versus Dollar-Averaging," *Journal of Portfolio Management* 20 (Winter 1994): 45–50.

42. CRSP 1-10 Universe from 1926 to 2014. Data. http://www.crsp.com/products/documentation/crsp-cap-based-portfolios-0.

43. Paul Samuelson, "Risk and Uncertainty: A Fallacy of Large Numbers," *Scientia* 57, no. 6 (April–May 1963): 1–6; Samuelson, "Lifetime Portfolio Selection by Dynamic Stochastic Programming." *Review of Economics and Statistics* 51, no. 3 (August 1969): 247–257; Samuelson, "The Long-Term Case for Equities: And How It Can Be Oversold." *Journal of Portfolio Management* 21, no. 1 (Fall 1994): 15–24.

44. Kenneth L. Fisher and Meir Statman, "A Behavioral Framework for Time Diversification," *Financial Analysts Journal* 55 (1999): 88–97.

45. "Starting with Dollar Cost Averaging," *AAII: The American Association of Individual Investors*, http://www.aaii.com/investing/article/starting-with-dollar-cost-averaging

46. J. Fred Weston, "Some Theoretical Aspects of Formula Timing Plans," *Journal of Business*, 22, no. 4 (October 1949): 249–270.

47. William F. Sharpe, *Investments* (Englewood Cliff, NJ: Prentice-Hall, 1981).

48. Jerome B. Cohen, Edward D. Zinbarg, and Arthur Zeikel, *Investment Analysis and Portfolio Management* (Homewood, IL: R. D. Irwin, 1977).

49. Jeremy J. Siegel and Richard H. Thaler, "Anomalies: The Equity Premium Puzzle," *Journal of Economic Perspectives* 11 (1997): 191–200.

50. Shlomo Benartzi and Richard Thaler, "Myopic Loss Aversion and the Equity Premium Puzzle," *Quarterly Journal of Economics* 110 (1995): 73–92; Shlomo

Benartzi and Richard Thaler, "Risk Aversion or Myopia? Choices in Repeated Gambles and Retirement Investments," *Management Science* 45 (1999): 364–381

51. Data. CRSP 1-10 Universe and Five-Year U.S. Treasuries from 1926 to 2014.
52. John Beshears, James J. Choi, David Laibson, and Brigitte C. Madrian, "Does Aggregated Returns Disclosure Increase Portfolio Risk-Taking?" *Review of Financial Studies,* forthcoming.
53. Gábor Kézdi and Robert J. Willis, "Household Stock Market Beliefs and Learning," NBER Working Paper No. 17614 (2011).
54. James K. Glassman and Kevin A. Hassett, "Dow 36000 Revisited," *Wall Street Journal,* August 1, 2002, ttp://online.wsj.com/news/articles/SB10281598615871 25680#printMode.
55. George M. Cohen, P. de Fontenay, Gordon L. Gould, Martin C. Sirera and Zvi Bodie, "Long-Run Risk in Stocks," *Financial Analysts Journal* 52 (1996), no. 5: 72–76.
56. Samuelson, "Long-Term Case for Equities."
57. Jeff Opdyke and Aparajita Saha-Bubn, "How to React to Latest Move from Fed." *Wall Street Journal,* March 28, 2005: D1.
58. Jane Bryant Quinn, "Weighing the Pros and Cons of Buying Bonds vs. Bond Funds," *San Jose Mercury News,* August 5, 1996.
59. Vanessa O'Connell, "Zero-Coupon Bonds Offer Safety Net with a Bounce," *Wall Street Journal,* May 29, 1996: C1

CHAPTER 8

1. Markowitz, *Portfolio Selection.*
2. Hersh Shefrin and Meir Statman, "Behavioral Portfolio Theory," *Journal of Financial and Quantitative Analysis* 35 (2000): 127–151. Hersh Shefrin and Meir Statman, Research proposal funded by the National Science Foundation, grant NSF SES-8709237 (1987).
3. Harry M. Markowitz, "The Early History of Portfolio Theory: 1600–1960," *Financial Analysts Journal* 55 (1999): 5–16.
4. Markowitz, *Portfolio Selection*; Harry M. Markowitz, "Individual versus Institutional Investing," *Financial Services Review* 1, no. 1 (1991): 1–8.
5. Harry M. Markowitz, "Consumption, Investment and Insurance in the Game of Life," *Journal of Investment Management* 13, no. 3 (2015): 5–23.
6. George J. Stigler, "The Cost of Subsistence," *Journal of Farm Economics* 27 (1945): 303–314.
7. Meir Statman, "Socially Responsible Investors and Their Advisors," *Journal of Investment Consulting* 9 (2008): 14–25.
8. "Millionaires Don't Think Monolithically: Spectrem," *Retirement Income Journal/ Adviser* (June 14, 2012), http://retirementincomejournal.com/issue/rij-advisor/ article/millionaires-dont-think-monolithically.
9. Christopher Geczy, David Levin, and Robert Stambaugh, "Investing in Socially Responsible Mutual Funds," Working Paper, Wharton (October 2005).
10. Under the assumption that expected returns are determined by the four-factor asset pricing model.
11. Statman, *What Investors Really Want.*
12. Jonathan Haidt, "When and Why Nationalism Beats Globalism," *American Interest,* July 10, 2016. http://www.the-american-interest.com/2016/07/10/ when-and-why-nationalism-beats-globalism.
13. Adair Morse and Sophie Shive, "Patriotism in Your Portfolio," *Journal of Financial Markets* 14 (2011): 411–440.

14. David Atkin, "The Caloric Costs of Culture: Evidence from Indian Migrants," *American Economic Review* 106 (2016): 1144–1181.

15. Alok Kumar, Alexandra Niessen-Ruenzi, and Oliver G. Spalt, "What Is in a Name? Mutual Fund Flows When Managers Have Foreign Sounding Names," *Review of Financial Studies* 28 (2015): 2281–2321; Gur Huberman, "Familiarity Breeds Investment," *Review of Financial Studies* 14, no. 3 (2001): 659–680.

16. Roger Lowenstein, "97 Moral: Drop Global-Investing Bunk," *Wall Street Journal*, December 18, 1997: C1.

17. Gross, *Art of Selling Intangibles*.

18. Richard Roll, "A Mean/Variance Analysis of Tracking Error," *Journal of Portfolio Management* 18 (1992): 13–22.

19. Roger G. Clarke, Scott Krase, and Meir Statman, "Tracking Errors, Regret and Tactical Asset Allocation," *Journal of Portfolio Management* 20 (1994): 16–24.

20. Richard C. Green and Burton Hollifield, "When Will Mean-Variance Efficient Portfolios Be Well Diversified?" *Journal of Finance* 47 (1992): 1785–1809.

21. Harry Markowitz, "Portfolio Theory: As I Still See It," *Annual Review of Financial Economics* 2 (2010): 1–23

22. Nicola Fuchs-Schundeln and Michael Haliassos, "Does Product Familiarity Matter for Participation?" (May 19, 2015), available at SSRN: https://ssrn.com/abstract=2384746 or http://dx.doi.org/10.2139/ssrn.2384746.

23. Mor Haziza and Avner Kalay, "Broker Rebates and Investor Sophistication" (September 9, 2014), available at SSRN: http://ssrn.com/abstract=2493693 or http://dx.doi.org/10.2139/ssrn.2493693.

24. Camelia M. Kuhnen and Andrei C. Miu, "Socioeconomic Status and Learning from Financial Information," NBER Working Paper No. w21214 (May 2015), available at SSRN: http://ssrn.com/abstract=2612769.

25. Nicholas Reinholtz, Philip M. Fernbach, and Bart De Langhe, "Do People Understand the Benefit of Diversification?" (January 20, 2016), available at SSRN: http://ssrn.com/abstract=2719144 or http://dx.doi.org/10.2139/ssrn.2719144.

26. Yoram Kroll, Haim Levy, and Amnon Rapoport, "Experimental Tests of the Separation Theorem and the Asset Pricing Model," *American Economic Review* 78 (1988): 500–518.

27. Lisa Holton, "Is Markowitz Wrong? Market Turmoil Fuels Nontraditional Approaches to Managing Investment Risk," *Journal of Financial Planning* 22 (January 2009): 20–26.

28. Meir Statman and Jonathan Scheid, "Correlation, Return Gaps, and the Benefits of Diversification," *Journal of Portfolio Management* 34 (2008): 132–139.

29. Charles A. Holt and Susan K. Laury, "Risk Aversion and Incentive Effects," *American Economic Review* 92 (2002): 1644–1655.

30. Robert B. Barsky, F. Thomas Juster, Miles S. Kimball, and Matthew D. Shapiro, "Preference Parameters and Behavioral Heterogeneity: An Experimental Approach in the Health and Retirement Study," *Quarterly Journal of Economics* 112, no. 2 (May 1997): 537–579.

31. Pan and Statman, "Questionnaires of Risk Tolerance."

32. Calculation from raw data of Pan and Statman, "Questionnaires of Risk Tolerance."

33. Gergana Y. Nenkov, Maureen Morrin, Andrew Ward, Barry Schwartz, and John Hulland, "A Short Form of the Maximization Scale: Factor Structure, Reliability and Validity Studies," *Judgment and Decision Making* 3, no. 5 (June 2008): 371–388.

34. Strahilevitz et al., "Once Burned, Twice Shy."
35. Statman, "Socially Responsible Investors."
36. Proportion in Moderate = variance of Lottery / (variance of Lottery + variance of Moderate)
    72,000**2 / (72,000**2 + 14,400**2) = 0.9615
37. Expected wealth is 0.9615 • $120,000 + 0.0385 • ($90,000) = $118,845
    Variance of wealth is 0.9615**2 • 14,400**2 + .0385**2 • 72,000**2 = 199,383,984 as variance and 14,120 as standard deviation.
38. The Z score of exceeding the $130,000 target wealth with Lottery is (130,000–90,000)/72,000 = 0.556. Using the table of the normal distribution, we find that the probability of exceeding $130,000 with (L) Lottery is 28.93%, implying that the probability of shortfall from the $130,000 target wealth is 71.07%.
    The Z score of exceeding the $130,000 target wealth with (M) Moderate is (130,000–120,000)/14,400 = 0.694. Using the table of the normal distribution, we find that the probability of exceeding $130,000 with Moderate stock is 24.37%, implying that the probability of shortfall from the $130,000 target wealth is 75.63%, a probability higher than the 71.07% probability of shortfall with (L) Lottery.
39. "No Royal Road for the Small Investor," *Literary Digest* 103, no. 11 (December 14, 1929): 52–55.
40. William N. Goetzmann and Alok Kumar, "Equity Portfolio Diversification," *Review of Finance* 12 (2008): 433–463.
41. Valery Polkovnichenko, "Household Portfolio Diversification: A Case for Rank-Dependent Preferences," *Review of Financial Studies* 18 (2005): 1467–1501.
42. US Commission on the Review of the National Policy Toward Gambling, "Gambling in America: Final Report of the Commission on the Review of the National Policy Toward Gambling," Washington, DC: Commission on the Review of the National Policy Toward Gambling, 1976.
43. Pan and Statman, "Questionnaires of Risk Tolerance."
44. Pan and Statman, "Questionnaires of Risk Tolerance."
45. Sanjiv Das, Harry Markowitz, Jonathan Scheid, and Meir Statman, "Portfolios for Investors Who Want to Reach Their Goals While Staying on the Mean–Variance Efficient Frontier," *Journal of Wealth Management* 14 (2011): 25–31; Sanjiv Das, Harry Markowitz, Jonathan Scheid, and Meir Statman, "Portfolio Optimization with Mental Accounts," *Journal of Financial and Quantitative Analysis* 45 (2010): 311–334.
46. Russ Thornton, "The Levers to Financial Freedom," *Advisor Perspectives,* September 1, 2009, http://www.advisorperspectives.com/newsletters09/pdfs/The_Levers_to_Financial_Freedom.pdf.
47. Jean L. P. Brunel, *Goals-Based Wealth Management: An Integrated and Practical Approach to Changing the Structure of Advisory Practices*, Wiley Finance Series (Hoboken, NJ: Wiley, 2015).
48. "Top 20 Nations Listed by Stock Market Cap (in Billions)," August 25, 2013, https://blogs.law.harvard.edu/willbanks/2013/08/25/top-20-nations-listed-by-company-market-cap/.
49. Gary Brinson, Randolph Hood, and Gilbert Beebower, "Determinants of Portfolio Performance," *Financial Analysts Journal* (July–August 1986): 39–44; Gary Brinson, Brian Singer, and Gilbert Beebower, "Determinants of Portfolio Performance II: An Update," *Financial Analysts Journal* 47, no. 3 (1991): 40–48.

50. Meir Statman, "The 93.6% Question of Financial Advisors," *Journal of Investing* 9, no. 1 (Spring 2000): 16–20.

CHAPTER 9

1. Franco Modigliani and Richard Brumberg, "Utility Analysis and the Consumption Function: An Interpretation of Cross-Section Data," in *Post Keynesian Economics,* ed. K. Kurihara (New Brunswick, NJ: Rutgers University Press, 1954), 388–436.
2. Milton Friedman, *A Theory of the Consumption Function* (Princeton, NJ: Princeton University Press, 1957).
3. Hersh M. Shefrin and Richard H. Thaler, "The Behavioral Life-Cycle Hypothesis." *Economic Inquiry* 26 (1988): 609–643.
4. http://www.cbsnews.com/videos/queen-of-the-palace-2/
   JANUARY 27, 1985, 1:00 PM | She is rich, powerful, and notoriously pushy. Leona Helmsley, married to real estate baron Harry Helmsley, is known as much for her attitude as for her chain of hotels. Mike Wallace interviews the businesswoman who rules her empire with a jeweled fist.
5. Chris Browning, Tao Guo, Yuanshan Cheng, and Michael S. Finke, "Spending in Retirement: Determining the Consumption Gap," *Journal of Financial Planning* 29 (2016): 42–53.
6. Michael Kitces, "Why Most Retirees Will Never Draw Down Their Retirement Portfolio," https://www.kitces.com/blog/consumption-gap-in-retirement-why-most-retirees-will-never-spend-down-their-portfolio/.
7. Utpal Dholakia, Leona Tam, Sunyee Yoon, and Nancy Wong, "The Ant and the Grasshopper: Understanding Personal Saving Orientation of Consumers," *Journal of Consumer Research* 43 (2016): 134–155.
8. Steven F. Venti and David A. Wise, "Aging and Housing Equity: Another Look," in *Perspectives on the Economics of Aging,* ed. D. A. Wise (Chicago: University of Chicago Press, 2004), 127–180.
9. Thomas Davidoff, "Reverse Mortgage Demographics and Collateral Performance" (February 25, 2014), available at SSRN: http://ssrn.com/abstract=2399942 or http://dx.doi.org/10.2139/ssrn.2399942.
10. James M. Poterba, Steven F. Venti, and David A. Wise, "The Drawdown of Personal Retirement Assets," NBER Working Paper 16675 (January 2011).
11. Vicki L. Bogan, "Household Asset Allocation, Offspring Education, and the Sandwich Generation" (October 10, 2014), available at SSRN: http://ssrn.com/abstract=2508486 or http://dx.doi.org/10.2139/ssrn.2508486.
12. Sudipto Banerjee, "Intra-Family Cash Transfers in Older American Households," EBRI Issue Brief, Number 415 (June 1, 2015), available at SSRN: http://ssrn.com/abstract=2620835.
13. Kathleen M. McGarry and Robert F. Schoeni, "Understanding Participation in SSI," Michigan Retirement Research Center Working Paper WP 2015–319 (January 2015), available at SSRN:http://ssrn.com/abstract=2599541 or http://dx.doi.org/10.2139/ssrn.2599541.
14. Scott W. Allard, Sandra Danziger, and Maria Wathen, "Receipt of Public Benefits and Private Support among Low-Income Households with Children after the Great Recession," National Poverty Center, Policy Brief #31 (April 2012).
15. Fali Huang, Ginger Zhe Jin, and Lixin Colin Xu, "Love, Money, and Old Age Support: Does Parental Matchmaking Matter? (February 22, 2015), available

at SSRN: http://ssrn.com/abstract=2568471 or http://dx.doi.org/10.2139/ssrn.2568471.

16. Laura Tach and Sara Sternberg Greene, "'Robbing Peter to Pay Paul': Economic and Cultural Explanations for How Lower-Income Families Manage Debt," *Social Problems* 61, no. 1 (2014): 1–21, available at SSRN: http://ssrn.com/abstract=2514963.

17. Jeffrey P. Thompson, "Do Rising Top Incomes Lead to Increased Borrowing in the Rest of the Distribution?" FEDS Working Paper No. 2016-046 (May 2, 2016), available at SSRN: http://ssrn.com/abstract=2783607 or http://dx.doi.org/10.17016/FEDS.2016.046.

18. Wagner Kamakura and Rex Yuxing Du, "How Economic Contractions and Expansions Affect Expenditure Patterns," *Journal of Consumer Research* 39 (2012): 229–247.

19. Sumit Agarwal, Wenlan Qian, and Xin Zou, "Thy Neighbor's Misfortune: Peer Effect on Consumption" (May 17, 2016), available at SSRN: http://ssrn.com/abstract=2780764 or http://dx.doi.org/10.2139/ssrn.2780764.

20. Stephen G. Dimmock, Roy Kouwenberg, Olivia S. Mitchell, and Kim Peijnenburg, "Ambiguity Aversion and Household Portfolio Choice Puzzles: Empirical Evidence," *Journal of Financial Economics* 119, no. 3 (March 2016): 559–577.

21. Kyle Carlson, Joshua Kim, Annamaria Lusardi, and Colin Camerer, "Bankruptcy Rates among NFL Players with Short-Lived Income Spikes," *American Economic Review* 105, no. 5 (2015): 381–384.

22. Yvonne McCarthy, "Behavioural Characteristics and Financial Distress," ECB Working Paper No. 1303 (February 14, 2011), available at SSRN: http://ssrn.com/abstract=1761570.

23. Annette Vissing-Jorgensen, "Consumer Credit: Learning Your Customer's Default Risk from What (S)He Buys" (April 13, 2011), available at SSRN: http://ssrn.com/abstract=2023238.

24. Anastassia Fedyk, "Asymmetric Naivete: Beliefs about Self-Control" (February 22, 2016), available at SSRN: http://ssrn.com/abstract=2727499 or http://dx.doi.org/10.2139/ssrn.2727499.

25. Andrea Freeman, "Payback: A Structural Analysis of the Credit Card Problem," *Arizona Law Review* 55, no. 151 (March 2013), available at SSRN: http://ssrn.com/abstract=2231738.

26. Sule Alan, Ruxandra Dumitrescu, and Gyongyi Loranth, "Subprime Consumer Credit Demand: Evidence from a Lender's Pricing Experiment," *Review of Financial Studies* 26, no. 9 (2013): 2353–2374.

27. Atif Mian and Amir Sufi, "House Price Gains and U.S. Household Spending from 2002 to 2006," National Bureau of Economic Research Working Paper Series No. 20152 (May 2014), http://www.nber.org/papers/w20152.

28. Umit G. Gurun, Gregor Matvos, and Amit Seru, "Advertising Expensive Mortgages," *Journal of Finance* 71, no. 5 (October 2016): 2371–2416.

29. Claire Celerier and Boris Vallee, "What Drives Financial Innovation? A Look into the European Retail Structured Products Market," Paris December 2012 Finance Meeting EUROFIDAI-AFFI Paper (July 2013).

30. Michael D. Hurd, Angela Duckworth, Susann Rohwedder, and David R. Weir, "Personality Traits and Economic Preparation for Retirement" (September 1, 2012), available at SSRN: http://ssrn.com/abstract=2239766.

31. Ashraf et al., "Tying Odysseus to the Mast."

32. Abigail B. Sussman and Rourke L. O'Brien, "Knowing When to Spend: Unintended Financial Consequences of Earmarking to Encourage Savings," *Journal of Marketing Research* 53, no. 5 (October 2016): 790–803.

33. Scott I. Rick, Deborah A. Small, and Eli J. Finkel, "Fatal (Fiscal) Attraction: Spendthrifts and Tightwads in Marriage," *Journal of Marketing Research* 48 (April 2011): 228–237.

34. Paul R. Amato and Stacy J. Rogers, "A Longitudinal Study of Marital Problems and Subsequent Divorce," *Journal of Marriage and the Family* 59 (August 1997): 612–624.

35. Jane Dokko, Geng Li, and Jessica Hayes, "Credit Scores and Committed Relationships," FEDS Working Paper No. 2015-081 (August 29, 2015), available at SSRN: http://ssrn.com/abstract=2667158 or http://dx.doi.org/10.2139/ssrn.2667158.

36. Jenny G. Olson and Scott Rick, "A Penny Saved Is a Partner Earned: The Romantic Appeal of Savers" (June 27, 2014), available at SSRN: http://ssrn.com/abstract=2281344 or http://dx.doi.org/10.2139/ssrn.2281344.

37. Ian Austen, "The Quiet Comeback of Margaret Trudeau," *New York Times*, November 7, 2015, http://www.nytimes.com/2015/11/08/fashion/margaret-trudeau-canada-comeback.html?_r=0.

38. Shefrin and Statman, "Explaining Investor Preference."

39. Malcolm Baker, Stefan Nagel, and Jeffrey Wurgler, "The Effect of Dividends on Consumption," *Brookings Papers on Economic Activity* (1: 2007): 231–276.

40. Markku Kaustia and Elias Rantapuska, "Rational and Behavioral Motives to Trade: Evidence from Reinvestment of Dividends and Tender Offer Proceeds," *Journal of Banking and Finance* 36, no. 8 (2012): 2366–2378.

41. John R. Graham and Alok Kumar, "Do Dividend Clienteles Exist? Evidence on Dividend Preferences of Retail Investors," *Journal of Finance* 61 (2006): 1305–1336.

42. "Alpine Rising Dividend Fund," *Alpine Woods Capital Investors, LLC,* http://www.alpinefunds.com/default.asp?P=856340&S=857564.

43. Lawrence Harris, Samuel M. Hartzmark, and David H. Solomon, "Juicing the Dividend Yield: Mutual Funds and the Demand for Dividends," *Journal of Financial Economics* 116, no. 3 (June 2015): 433–451.

44. Nathaniel Popper, "Speculative Bets Prove Risky as Savers Chase Payoff," *New York Times*, February 10, 2013, http://www.nytimes.com/2013/02/11/business/wave-of-investor-fraud-extends-to-ordinary-retirement-savers.html?_r=0&adxnnl=1&pagewanted=all&adxnnlx=1424012902-LhBhSRA5hBsYdSN/vezaCA.

45. Alexander Muermann, Olivia S. Mitchell, and Jaqueline Volkman, "Regret, Portfolio Choice, and Guarantees in Defined Contribution Schemes," *Insurance: Mathematics and Economics* 39 (2006): 219–229.

46. John Ameriks, Robert Veres, and Mark J. Warshawsky, "Making Retirement Income Last a Lifetime," *Journal of Financial Planning* 14, no. 12 (December 2001): 60–76.

47. Daniel G. Goldstein, Hal E. Hershfield, and Shlomo Benartzi, "The Illusion of Wealth and Its Reversal" *Journal of Marketing Research* 53 (2016): 804–813.

48. Wei-Yin Hu and Jason S. Scott, "Behavioral Obstacles in the Annuity Market," *Financial Analysts Journal* 63, no. 6 (2007): 71–82.

49. Mark J. Warshawsky, "Illustrating Retirement Income for Defined Contribution Plan Participants: A Critical Analysis of the Department of Labor Proposal," *Journal of Retirement* 3 (2015): 12–26.

50. Alicia H. Munnell, Francesca Golub-Sass, and Anthony Webb, "How Much to Save for a Secure Retirement," *Center for Research at Boston College* (November 2011): 11–13.

51. Michael D. Hurd and Susann Rohwedder, " Measuring Economic Preparation for Retirement: Income versus Consumption" (September 2015), available at SSRN: http://ssrn.com/abstract=2712684 or http://dx.doi.org/10.2139/ssrn.2712684.

52. Fred M. Vettese, "How Spending Declines with Age, and the Implications for Workplace Pension Plans," C. D. Howe Institute e-brief 238 (June 16, 2016), available at SSRN: http://ssrn.com/abstract=2799376.

53. W. P. Bengen, "Determining Withdrawal Rates Using Historical Data," *Journal of Financial Planning* 7, no. 4 (October 1994): 171–180.

54. Wade D. Pfau and Wade Dokken, "Rethinking Retirement: Sustainable Withdrawal Rates for New Retirees in 2015," *WealthVest* (2015).

55. "IRA Required Minimum Distribution Worksheet," Internal Revenue Service, https://www.irs.gov/pub/irs-tege/uniform_rmd_wksht.pdf.

56. Kirsten A. Cook, William Meyer, and William Reichenstein, "Tax-Efficient Withdrawal Strategies," *Financial Analysts Journal* 71 (2015): 91–107.

57. https://www.ssa.gov/OACT/population/longevity.html.

58. https://www.irs.gov/pub/irs-tege/uniform_rmd_wksht.pdf.

59. Jeffrey R. Brown, James M. Poterba, and David P. Richardson, "Do Required Minimum Distributions Matter? The Effect of the 2009 Holiday on Retirement Plan Distributions," *Journal of Public Economics*, available online August 14, 2016, http://www.nber.org/papers/w20464.

60. Rawley Heimer, Kristian Ove R. Myrseth, and Raphael Schoenle, "Yolo: Mortality Beliefs and Household Finance Puzzles," Netspar Discussion Paper No. 11/2015-070 (November 2, 2015), available at SSRN: http://ssrn.com/abstract=2749543 or http://dx.doi.org/10.2139/ssrn.2749543.

61. Mateusz J. Filipski, Ling Jin, Xiaobo Zhang, and Kevin Z. Chen, "Living Like There's No Tomorrow: Saving and Spending Following the Sichuan Earthquake," IFPRI Discussion Paper 1461 (September 18, 2015), available at SSRN: http://ssrn.com/abstract=2685305.

62. Olivia S. Mitchell and Annamaria Lusardi, "Financial Literacy and Planning: Implications for Retirement Wellbeing," in *Financial Literacy: Implications for Retirement Security and the Financial Marketplace,* ed. O. S. Mitchell and Annamaria Lusardi (Oxford: Oxford University Press, 2011), 17–39.

63. Olivia S. Mitchell and Annamaria Lusardi, "Financial Literacy and Economic Outcomes: Evidence and Policy Implications," *Journal of Retirement* 3 (2015): 107–114.

64. Annamaria Lusardi and Olivia S. Mitchell, "The Economic Importance of Financial Literacy: Theory and Evidence," *Journal of Economic Literature* 52, no. 1 (2014).

65. Fernandes et al., "Financial Literacy."

66. Margaret Miller, Julia Reichelstein, Christian Salas, and Bilal Zia, "Can You Help Someone Become Financially Capable? A Meta-Analysis of the Literature," World Bank Policy Research Working Paper 6745 (2014), http://documents.worldbank

.org/curated/en/297931468327387954/Can-you-help-someone-become-financially-capable-a-meta-analysis-of-the-literature.

67. Olivia S. Mitchell and Annamaria Lusardi, "Financial Literacy and Economic Outcomes: Evidence and Policy Implications," *Journal of Retirement* 3 (2015): 107–114.

68. Dholakia et al., "Ant and the Grasshopper."

69. "Private Pension Plan Bulletin Historical Tables and Graphs," Employee Benefits Security Administration (September 2014), US Department of Labor, http://www.dol.gov/ebsa/pdf/historicaltables.pdf.

70. Sheena Iyengar, Wei Jiang, and Gur Huberman, "How Much Choice Is Too Much? Contributions to 401(k) Retirement Plans," in *Pension Design and Structure: New Lessons from Behavioral Finance,* ed. O. S. Mitchell and S. P. Utkus (New York: Oxford University Press, 2004), 83–95.

71. Donald B. Keim and Olivia S. Mitchell, "Simplifying Choices in Defined Contribution Retirement Plan Design," NBER Working Paper No. w21854 (January 2016), available at SSRN: http://ssrn.com/abstract=2713579.

72. "Financial Engines: For Individuals," *Financial Engines Inc.*, https://corp.financialengines.com/individuals/.

73. "Betterment: Investing Made Better," *Betterment LLC,* https://www.betterment.com/.

74. "Investment Management, Online Financial Advisor," Wealthfront, https://www.wealthfront.com/.

75. Roberta S. Karmel, "The Investment Banker and the Credit Regulations," *New York University Law Review* 45 (1970): 59–88.

76. Robert H. Mundheim, "Professional Responsibilities of Broker-Dealers: The Suitability Doctrine," *Duke Law Journal* 3 (Summer 1965): 445–480.

77. Tara Siegel Bernard, "Customers First to Become the Law in Retirement Investing," *New York Times,* April 6, 2016.

78. Kerry Pechter, "First Sign of Blood from DOL Fiduciary Rule," *Retirement Income Journal* (April 29, 2016).

79. Richard H. Thaler and Cass R. Sunstein, *Nudge: Improving Decisions about Health, Wealth, and Happiness* (New Haven, CT: Yale University Press, 2008).

80. Brigitte C. Madrian and Dennis F. Shea, "The Power of Suggestion: Inertia in 401(k) Participation and Savings Behavior," *Quarterly Journal of Economics* 116 (2001): 1149–1187.

81. James J. Choi, David Laibson, Brigitte C. Madrian, and Andrew Metrick, "Defined Contribution Pensions: Plan Rules, Participant Decisions, and the Path of Least Resistance," *Tax Policy and the Economy* 16 (2002): 67–114.

82. Jean A. Young, "The Auto Savings Generation: Steering Millennials to Better Retirement Outcomes," *Vanguard Research* (October 2014), https://institutional.vanguard.com/iam/pdf/GENERP.pdf?cbdForceDomain=false.

83. Jon M. Jachimowicz, Shannon Duncan, and Elke U. Weber, "Default-Switching: The Hidden Cost of Defaults" (February 3, 2016), available at SSRN: http://ssrn.com/abstract=2727301 or http://dx.doi.org/10.2139/ssrn.2727301.

84. Hershfield et al., "Increasing Saving Behavior."

85. Gunhild Berg and Bilal Zia, "Harnessing Emotional Connections to Improve Financial Decisions: Evaluating the Impact of Financial Education in Mainstream Media," *Journal of the European Economic Association,*

forthcoming, http://www.bloomberg.com/news/articles/2015-01-15/fighting-poverty-and-hiv-with-soap-operas.

86. Raj Chetty, John Friedman, Soren Leth-Petersen, Torben Nielsen, and Tore Olsen, "Active vs. Passive Decisions and Crowdout in Retirement Savings Accounts: Evidence from Denmark," *Quarterly Journal of Economics* 129, no. 3 (2014): 1141–1219.

87. John L. Beshears, James J. Choi, David Laibson, and Brigitte C. Madrian, "Does Front-Loading Taxation Increase Savings? Evidence from Roth 401(k) Introductions," NBER Working Paper No. w20738 (December 2014), available at SSRN: http://ssrn.com/abstract=2538324.

88. John Beshears, James J. Choi, Joshua Hurwitz, David Laibson, and Brigitte C. Madrian, "Liquidity in Retirement Savings Systems: An International Comparison," *American Economic Review* 105 (2015): 420–425.

89. Joshua D. Rauh, Irina Stefanescu, and Stephen P. Zeldes, "Cost Saving and the Freezing of Corporate Pension Plans," Columbia Business School Research Paper No. 16-4; Stanford University Graduate School of Business Research Paper No. 16-4 (December 3, 2015), available at SSRN: http://ssrn.com/abstract=2706448 or http://dx.doi.org/10.2139/ssrn.2706448.

90. "MyRA: My Retirement Account," US Department of the Treasury (March 1, 2016), http://www.treasury.gov/initiatives/myra/Pages/default.aspx.

91. John T. Ragnoni, "Defining Excellence: A Report on Retirement Readiness in the Not-for-Profit Higher Education Industry," *Fidelity Perspectives* (Winter 2012).

92. "History of 401(k) Plans: An Update," Employee Benefit Research Institute (February 2005), http://www.ebri.org/pdf/publications/facts/0205fact.a.pdf.

93. Kitces, "Why Most Retirees Will Never Draw Down Their Retirement Portfolio."

94. Dennis Jacobe, "More Nonretirees Expect to Rely on Social Security," Gallup Organization, April 30, 2012, http://www.gallup.com/poll/154277/nonretirees-expect-rely-social-security.aspx.

95. John Ameriks, "When to Start Spending Your Retirement Savings," *Vanguard Blog* (May 5, 2010), available at http://www.vanguardblog.com/2010.05.05/when-to-start-spending.html.

96. Carol Hymowitz, "Why $100,000 Salary May Yield Retirement Flipping Burgers," *Bloomberg* (September 23, 2013), http://www.bloomberg.com/news/2013-09-23/why-100-000-salary-may-yield-retirement-flipping-burgers.html.

97. Jonathan A. Parker, "Why Don't Households Smooth Consumption? Evidence from a 25 Million Dollar Experiment," NBER Working Paper No. w21369 (July 2015), available at SSRN: http://ssrn.com/abstract=2633325.

98. "One NYC Family's Struggle to Survive on a Fast Food Salary," audio blog post, Public Broadcasting Service (November 4, 2013), http://www.pbs.org/newshour/bb/nation-july-dec13-minimumwage_11-04/.

99. Kyoung Tae Kim and Sherman D'Hanna, "Do U.S. Households Perceive Their Retirement Preparedness Realistically?" *Financial Services Review* 24 (February 15, 2015): 139–155, available at SSRN: http://ssrn.com/abstract=2565268.

100. Annamaria Lusardi, Daniel Schneider, and Peter Tufano, "Financially Fragile Households: Evidence and Implications," Netspar Discussion Paper No. 03/2011-013 (March 7, 2011), available at SSRN: http://ssrn.com/abstract=1809708.

101. Caezilia Loibl, Lauren Eden Jones, Emily Haisley, and George Loewenstein, "Testing Strategies to Increase Saving and Retention in Individual Development

Account Programs" (February 20, 2016), available at SSRN: http://ssrn.com/abstract=2735625 or http://dx.doi.org/10.2139/ssrn.2735625.

102. Sebastian Galiani, Paul J. Gertler, and Rosangela Bando, "Non-Contributory Pensions," *Labour Economics* 38 (2016): 47–58.

CHAPTER 10

1. Meir Statman, "Behavioral Finance: Past Battles and Future Engagements," *Financial Analysts Journal* 55 (1999): 18–27.

2. Kelvin J. Lancaster, "A New Approach to Consumer Theory," *Journal of Political Economy* 74 (April 1966): 132–157.

3. Hilke Plassmann, John O'Doherty, Baba Shiv, and Antonio Rangel, "Marketing Actions Can Modulate Neural Representations of Experienced Pleasantness," *Proceedings of the National Academy of Sciences of the United States of America* 105 (2008): 1050–1054.

4. Jeffrey Pontiff, "Costly Arbitrage: Evidence from Closed-End Funds," *Quarterly Journal of Economics* 111 (1996): 1135–1151.

5. Sharpe, "Capital Asset Prices."

6. John Lintner, "The Valuation of Risk Assets and The Selection of Risky Investments in Stock Portfolios and Capital Budgets," *Review of Economics and Statistics* 47 (1965): 13–37.

7. Markowitz, "Portfolio Selection."

8. James Tobin, "Liquidity Preference as Behavior toward Risk," *Review of Economic Studies* 25 (1958): 65–86.

9. Elroy Dimson, Paul Marsh and Mike Staunton, "The Worldwide Equity Premium: A Smaller Puzzle," in *Handbook of the Equity Risk Premium,* ed. Rajnish Mehra (Amsterdam: Elsevier, 2008): 468–514.

10. William Sharpe, *Investors and Markets* (Princeton, NJ: Princeton University Press, 2007)

11. Sanjoy Basu, "Investment Performance of Common Stocks in Relation to Their Price-Earnings Ratios: A Test of the Efficient Market Hypothesis," *Journal of Finance* 32 (1977): 663–682.

12. Rolf W. Banz, "The Relationship between Return and Market Value of Common Stocks," *Journal of Financial Economics* 9 (1981): 3–18.

13. Barr Rosenberg, Kenneth Reid, and Ronald Lanstein, "Persuasive Evidence of Market Inefficiency," *Journal of Portfolio Management* 11 (1985): 9–17.

14. Michael E. Solt and Meir Statman, "Good Companies, Bad Stocks," *Journal of Portfolio Management* 15 (1989): 39–44.

15. Eugene Fama and Kenneth French, "The Cross-Section of Expected Stock Returns," *Journal of Finance* 47 (1992): 427–465.

16. "Barrier Funds," USAMutual, March 31, 2015, http://www.usamutuals.com/i/u/6149817/f/Fact_Sheet_-_Barrier_Fund-2015-Q1.pdf.

17. Eugene Fama, "Ideas That Changed the Theory and Practice of Investing: A Conversation with Eugene F. Fama," *Journal of Investment Consulting* 9 (2008): 6–14.

18. Campbell R. Harvey, Yan Liu, and Heqing Zhu, ". . . And the Cross-Section of Expected Returns," *Review of Financial Studies* 29, no. 1 (2016): 5–68.

19. Malcolm P. Baker, Jeffrey Wurgler, and Brendan Bradley, "A Behavioral Finance Explanation for the Success of Low Volatility Portfolios," NYU Working Paper No. 2451/29537 (January 2010), available at SSRN: http://ssrn.com/abstract=2284643.

20. Robert Novy-Marx, "The Other Side of Value: The Gross Profitability Premium," *Journal of Financial Economics* 108 (2013): 1–28.

21. Ray Ball, Joseph J. Gerakos, Juhani T. Linnainmaa, and Valeri V. Nikolaev, "Deflating Profitability," *Journal of Financial Economics* 117 (2015): 225–248.

22. Jean-Philippe Bouchaud, Ciliberti Stefano, Augustin Landier, Guillaume Simon, and David Thesmar, "The Excess Returns of 'Quality' Stocks: A Behavioral Anomaly," HEC Paris Research Paper No. FIN-2016–1134 (January 15, 2016), available at SSRN: http://ssrn.com/abstract=2717447 or http://dx.doi.org/10.2139/ssrn.2717447.

23. Joshua D. Coval and Tyler Shumway, "Do Behavioral Biases Affect Prices?" *Journal of Finance* 60 (2005): 1–34.

24. R. David McLean and Jeffrey Pontiff, "Does Academic Research Destroy Stock Return Predictability?" *Journal of Finance* 71 (2016): 5–32.

25. Fischer Black, "Beta and Return," *Journal of Portfolio Management* 20, no. 1 (Fall 1993): 8–18.

26. Hersh Shefrin and Meir Statman, "The Style of Investment Expectation," in *Handbook of Equity Style Management*, ed. T. Daniel Coggin and Frank J. Fabozzi (New York: Wiley, 2003), 195–218.

27. Clark, Martire and Bartolomeo, a marketing and opinion research firm that conducted the *Fortune* surveys, stated that this attribute stands for expectations of the future return of the company's stock.

28. John Campbell, Jens Hilscher, and Jan Szilagyi, "In Search of Distress Risk," *Journal of Finance* 63, no. 6 (2008): 2899–2939.

29. Josef Lakonishok, Andrei Shleifer, and Robert W. Vishny, "Contrarian Investment, Extrapolation, and Risk," *Journal of Finance* 49 (1994): 1541–1578.

30. Michael E. Solt and Meir Statman, "Good Companies, Bad Stocks," *Journal of Portfolio Management* 15 (1989): 39–44.

31. Meir Statman, "Investor Sentiment, Stock Characteristics, and Returns," *Journal of Portfolio Management* 37 (2011): 54–61.

32. Slovic et al., "The Affect Heuristic."

33. Meir Statman, "Investor Sentiment, Stock Characteristics, and Returns," *Journal of Portfolio Management* 37 (2011): 54–61.

34. Meir Statman, Kenneth Fisher, and Deniz Anginer, "Affect in a Behavioral Asset Pricing Model," *Financial Analysts Journal* 64 (2008): 20–29.

35. Yoav Ganzach, "Judging Risk and Return of Financial Assets," *Organizational Behavior and Human Decision Processes* 83 (2000): 353–370.

36. Hersh Shefrin, *A Behavioral Approach to Asset Pricing* (Burlington, MA: Elsevier Academic Press, 2005).

37. Ang et al., "Is A Better than B?"

38. Gross, *Art of Selling Intangibles.*

39. Christopher Geczy and Mikhail Samonov, "212 Years of Price Momentum (The World's Longest Backtest: 1801–2012)" (August 1, 2013), available at SSRN: http://ssrn.com/abstract=2292544.

40. Jonathan B. Berk, Richard C. Green, and Vasant Naik, "Optimal Investment, Growth Options, and Security Returns," *Journal of Finance* 54 (1999): 1553–1607.

41. Hong Zhang, "Dynamic Beta, Time-Varying Risk Premium, and Momentum," Yale ICF Working Paper No. 04-26 (2004).

42. Andrea Frazzini, "The Disposition Effect and Under-Reaction to News," *Journal of Finance* 61 (2006): 2017–2046.

43. Zhi Da, Umit G. Gurun, and Mitch Warachka, "Frog in the Pan: Continuous Information and Momentum," *Review of Financial Studies* 27 (2014): 3389–3440.

44. William N. Goetzmann and Simon Huang, "Momentum in Imperial Russia," NBER Working Paper No. w21700 (November 2015), available at SSRN: http://ssrn.com/abstract=2687848.

45. Hersh Shefrin and Meir Statman, "Behavioral Capital Asset Pricing Theory," *Journal of Financial and Quantitative Analysis* 29 (1994): 323–349.

46. Nicholas Barberis, Robin Greenwood, Lawrence Jin, and Andrei Shleifer, "X-CAPM: An Extrapolative Capital Asset Pricing Model," *Journal of Financial Economics* 115 (2015): 1–24.

47. Alex Edmans, Diego Garcia, and Oyvind Norli, "Sports Sentiment and Stock Returns," *Journal of Finance* 62 (2007): 1967–1998.

48. Kelley Bergsma and Danling Jiang, "Cultural New Year Holidays and Stock Returns around the World," *Financial Management* 45, no. 1 (Spring 2016): 3–35.

49. Harrison Hong and Marcin Kacperczyk, "The Price of Sin: The Effects of Social Norms on Markets," *Journal of Financial Economics* 93 (2009): 15–36; Meir Statman and Denys Glushkov, "The Wages of Social Responsibility," *Financial Analysts Journal* 65 (2009): 33–64.

50. Alex Edmans, "Does the Stock Market Fully Value Intangibles? Employee Satisfaction and Equity Prices," *Journal of Financial Economics* 101 (2011): 621–640.

51. Alexander Kempf and Peer Osthoff, "SRI Funds: Nomen Est Omen," *Journal of Business Finance and Accounting* 35 (2008): 1276–1294; Statman and Glushkov, "Wages of Social Responsibility."

52. Harrison G. Hong, Frank Weikai Li, and Jiangmin Xu, "Climate Risks and Market Efficiency" (May 7, 2016), available at SSRN: http://ssrn.com/abstract=2776962 or http://dx.doi.org/10.2139/ssrn.2776962.

53. Hong and Kacperczyk, "Price of Sin."

54. Statman and Glushkov, "Wages of Social Responsibility."

55. Meir Statman, "Quiet Conversations: The Expressive Nature of Socially Responsible Investors," *Journal of Financial Planning* 21, no. 2 (February 2008): 40–46.

56. Meir Statman and Denys Glushkov, "Classifying and Measuring the Performance of Socially Responsible Funds," *Journal of Portfolio Management* 42, no. 2 (Winter 2016): 140–151.

57. Robert F. Stambaugh and Yu Yuan, "Mispricing Factors" (July 4, 2015), available at SSRN: http://ssrn.com/abstract=2626701 or http://dx.doi.org/10.2139/ssrn.2626701.

58. More precisely, higher Sharpe ratio, the difference between expected returns and the risk-free rate divided by the standard deviation of that difference.

59. Ronen Israel and Thomas Maloney, "Understanding Style Premia," *Journal of Investing* 23 (2014): 15–22.

CHAPTER 11

1. Steven Rattner, "Who's Right on the Stock Market?" *New York Times*, November 15, 2013: A29, http://www.nytimes.com/2013/11/15/opinion/rattner-whos-right-on-the-stock-market.html.

2. Kenneth French, "The Cost of Active Investing," *Journal of Finance* 63, no. 4 (2008): 1537–1573.

3. John Bogle, "A Question So Important That It Should Be Hard to Think about Anything Else," *Journal of Portfolio Management* 34 (Winter 2008): 95–102.

4. John Burr Williams, *The Theory of Investment Value* (Burlington, VT: Fraser Publishing Company, 1938).

5. Nicholas Varchaver, "What Warren Thinks . . ." *Fortune,* April 14, 2008, http://money.cnn.com/galleries/2008/fortune/0804/gallery.buffett.fortune/index.html.

6. Carol J. Loomis, "Buffett's Big Bet," *Fortune* (June 23, 2008): 45–51.

7. Loomis, Carol J., "Warren Buffett Adds to His Lead in $1 Million Hedge-Fund Bet," *Fortune* (February 3, 2015), http://fortune.com/2015/02/03/berkshires-buffett-adds-to-his-lead-in-1-million-bet-with-hedge-fund.

8. Carol J. Loomis, "Warren Buffett Loses a Bit of Ground in His 'Million-Dollar Bet,'" *Fortune* (February 16, 2016), http://fortune.com/author/carol-j-loomis/.

9. Burton G. Malkiel, "The Efficient Market Hypothesis and Its Critics," *Journal of Economic Perspectives* 17, no. 1 (Winter 2003): 59–82.

10. Arun Khanna, "The *Titanic:* The Untold Economic Story," *Financial Analysts Journal* 54 (1998): 16–17.

11. Guy Kaplanski and Haim Levy, "Sentiment and Stock Prices: The Case of Aviation Disasters," *Journal of Financial Economics* 95 (2010): 174–201.

12. Ray Fair, "Events That Shook the Market," *Journal of Business* 75 (2002): 713–731.

13. Richard Roll, "R^2," *Journal of Finance* 43 (1988): 541–566.

14. Jacob Boudoukh, Ronen Feldman, Shimon Kogan, and Matthew Richardson, "Which News Moves Stock Prices: A Textual Analysis," Working paper, University of Pennsylvania, Wharton (October 14, 2013).

15. Robert Shiller, "The Volatility of Long-Term Interest Rates and Expectations Models of the Term Structure," *Journal of Political Economy* 87 (1979): 1190–1219; Robert Shiller, "Do Stock Prices Move Too Much to Be Justified by Subsequent Changes in Dividends?" *American Economic Review* 71, no. 3 (June 1981): 421–436.

16. Eugene Fama, "Efficient Capital Markets: II," *Journal of Finance* 46 (1991): 1575–1617.

17. Gur Huberman and Tomer Regev, "Contagious Speculation and a Cure for Cancer: A Nonevent That Made Stock Prices Soar," *Journal of Finance* 56 (2001): 387–396.

18. Gina Kolata, "Hope in the Lab: A Special Report; A Cautious Awe Greets Drugs That Eradicate Tumors in Mice," *New York Times* (May 3, 1998), 1:1.

19. Thomas Boehm, Judah Folkman, Timothy Browder, and Michael S. O'Reilly, "Antiangio Genic Therapy of Experimental Cancer Does Not Induce Acquired Drug Resistance," *Nature* 390 (1997): 404–407.

20. Nicholas Wade, "Tests on Mice Block Defense by Cancer," *New York Times* (November 27, 1997): A28.

21. Nejat H. Seyhun, "Insiders' Profits, Cost of Trading, and Market Efficiency," *Journal of Financial Economics* 16 (1985): 189–212.

22. Kenneth R. Ahern, "Information Networks: Evidence from Illegal Insider Trading Tips" (February 5, 2015), available at SSRN: http://ssrn.com/abstract=2511068.

23. Nathan Vardi, "Mathew Martoma Sentenced to Nine Years for Insider Trading," *Forbes* (September 8, 2014), http://www.forbes.com/sites/nathanvardi/2014/09/08/mathew-martoma-sentenced-to-nine-years-for-insider-trading/print.

24. Lauren Cohen, Christopher Malloy, and Lukasz Pomorski, "Decoding Inside Information," *Journal of Finance* 67, no. 3 (June 2012): 1009–1043.

25. Rob Barry and Susan Pulliam, "Executives' Good Luck in Trading Own Stock," *Wall Street Journal,* November 27, 2012, http://online.wsj.com/news/articles/SB10000872396390444100404577641463717344178.

26. Jonathan L. Rogers, Douglas J. Skinner, and Sarah L. C. Zechman, "The Role of the Media in Disseminating Insider-Trading Activity," *Review of Accounting Studies* 21, no. 3 (September 2016): 711–739.

27. Brody Mullins and Susan Pulliam, "Inside Capitol, Investor Access Yields Rich Tips," *Wall Street Journal* (December 20, 2011), http://www.wsj.com/news/articles/SB10001424052970204844504577100260349084878.

28. David H. Solomon and Eugene F. Soltes, "What Are We Meeting For? The Consequences of Private Meetings with Investors," *Journal of Law and Economics* 58, no. 2 (May 2015): 325–355.

29. Gabriel Wildau, "China Takes on 'Rat Traders' in Stock Market Probe," *Financial Times* (July 7, 2014).

30. (Robin) Hui Huang, "An Empirical Study of the Incidence of Insider Trading in China" (May 12, 2007), available at SSRN: https://ssrn.com/abstract=993341 or http://dx.doi.org/10.2139/ssrn.993341.

31. Yeguang Chi, "Performance Evaluation of Chinese Actively Managed Stock Mutual Funds," Chicago Booth Research Paper No. 13-55; Fama-Miller Working Paper (May 2013), available at SSRN: http://ssrn.com/abstract=2268773.

32. James J. Choi, Li Jin, and Hongjun Yan, "Informed Trading and Expected Returns" (January 22, 2016), available at SSRN: https://ssrn.com/abstract=2193733 or http://dx.doi.org/10.2139/ssrn.2193733

33. Chuan-Yang Hwang, Sheridan Titman, and Yuxi Wang, "Is It Who You Know or What You Know? Evidence from IPO Allocations and Mutual Fund Performance" (August 20, 2015). Asian Finance Association (AsianFA) 2016 Conference, available at SSRN: https://ssrn.com/abstract=2648732 or http://dx.doi.org/10.2139/ssrn.2648732.

34. April Klein, Anthony Saunders, and Yu T. F. Wong, "Do Hedge Funds Trade on Private Information? Evidence from Upcoming Changes in Analysts' Stock Recommendations" (April 7, 2014), available at SSRN: http://ssrn.com/abstract=2421801.

35. Meng Gao and Jiekun Huang, "Capitalizing on Capitol Hill: Informed Trading by Hedge Fund Managers," AFA 2012 Chicago Meetings Paper; Fifth Singapore International Conference on Finance 2011 (June 4, 2015), available at SSRN: http://ssrn.com/abstract=1707181.

36. Ohad Kadan, Roni Michaely, and Pamela C. Moulton, "Speculating on Private Information: Buy the Rumor, Sell the News" (March 10, 2015), available at SSRN: http://ssrn.com/abstract=2427282 or http://dx.doi.org/10.2139/ssrn.2427282.

37. Vikas Agarwal, Wei Jiang, Yuehua Tang, and Baozhong Yang, "Uncovering Hedge Fund Skill from the Portfolio Holdings They Hide," *Journal of Finance* 68 (2013): 739–783.

38. Henk Berkman, Paul D. Koch, and P. Joakim Westerholm, "Informed Trading through the Accounts of Children," *Journal of Finance* 69 (2014): 363–404.

39. Albert S. Kyle, "Continuous Auctions and Insider Trading," *Econometrica* 53 (1985): 1335–1355.

40. Peter Koudijs, "Those Who Know Most': Insider Trading in 18th C. Amsterdam," *Journal of Political Economy* 126 (2015): 1356–1409.

41. Robert J. Jackson, Wei Jiang, and Joshua Mitts, "How Quickly Do Markets Learn? Private Information Dissemination in a Natural Experiment," Columbia Business School Research Paper No. 15-6 (April 2015), available at SSRN: http://ssrn.com/abstract=2544128.

42. Magnus Dahlquist, Jose V. Martinez, and Paul Söderlind, "Individual Investor Activity and Performance," University of St. Gallen, School of Finance Research Paper No. 2014/8 (March 2015), available at SSRN: http://ssrn.com/abstract=2432930.

43. Christopher Avery, Judith A. Chevalier, and Richard J. Zeckhauser, "The 'CAPS' Prediction System and Stock Market Returns," *Review of Finance* 20, no. 4 (2016): 1363–1381.

44. Eric K. Kelley and Paul C. Tetlock, "Retail Short Selling and Stock Prices," Columbia Business School Research Paper No. 13-70 (November 2013).

45. Brad M. Barber and Terrance Odean, "Trading Is Hazardous to Your Wealth: The Common Stock Investment Performance of Individual Investors," *Journal of Finance* 55 (2000): 773–806.

46. Anders Anderson, "Trading and Under-Diversification," *Review of Finance* 17, no. 5 (2013): 1699–1741.

47. Brad M. Barber, Yi-Tsung Lee, Yu-Jane Liu, and Terrance Odean, "The Cross-Section of Speculator Skill: Evidence from Day Trading," *Journal of Financial Markets* 18 (2014): 1–24.

48. Orhan Erdem, Evren Arık, and Serkan Yüksel, "Trading Puzzle, Puzzling Trade" (April 3, 2013), available at SSRN: http://ssrn.com/abstract=2244186.

49. Zhen Shi and Na Wang, "Don't Confuse Brains with a Bull Market: Attribution Bias, Overconfidence, and Trading Behavior of Individual Investors," EFA 2010 Frankfurt Meetings Paper (August 12, 2013), available at SSRN: http://ssrn.com/abstract=1979208.

50. Ilia Dichev, "What Are Stock Investors' Actual Historical Returns? Evidence from Dollar-Weighted Returns," *American Economic Review* 97 (2007): 386–402.

51. Christine Benz, "The Error-Proof Portfolio: OK, People—What Have We Learned? The Bull Market Is Entering Its Fifth Year, but How Have Investors Done Since the Market Recovered?" *Morningstar* (October 28, 2013), http://news.morningstar.com/articlenet/article.aspx?id=616424.

52. Thomas Etheber, Andreas Hackethal, and Steffen Meyer, "Trading on Noise: Moving Average Trading Heuristics and Private Investors" (November 7, 2014), available at SSRN: http://ssrn.com/abstract=2520346.

53. Robert C. Giannini, Paul J. Irvine, and Tao Shu, "Do Local Investors Know More? A Direct Examination of Individual Investors' Information Set," Asian Finance Association (AsFA) 2013 Conference Paper (March 31, 2015), available at SSRN: http://ssrn.com/abstract=1866267.

54. Mark S. Seasholes and Ning Zhu, "Investing in What You Know: The Case of Individual Investors and Local Stocks," *Journal of Investment Management* 11 (2013): 20–30.

55. Timothy (Jun) Lu, "Social Interaction Effects and Individual Portfolio Choice: Evidence from 401(k) Pension Plan Investors," *SSRN Electronic Journal* (August 2011), available at SSRN: http://ssrn.com/abstract=1921431 or http://dx.doi.org/10.2139/ssrn.1921431.

56. Yevgeny Mugerman, Orly Sade, and Moses Shayo, "Long Term Savings Decisions: Inertia, Peer Effects and Ethnicity," *Journal of Economic Behavior and Organization* 106 (2014): 235–253.

57. Markus Glaser, Florian Haagen, and Torsten Walther, "Preference Aggregation in Investment Clubs an Explanation for Underdiversification?" *SSRN Electronic Journal* (April 2014), available at SSRN: http://ssrn.com/abstract=2424661 or http://dx.doi.org/10.2139/ssrn.2424661.

58. Fischer Black, "Noise," *Journal of Finance* 41 (1986): 529–543.

59. Jonathan B. Berk and Jules H. Van Binsbergen, "Measuring Managerial Skill in the Mutual Fund Industry," *Journal of Financial Economics* 118, no. 1 (October 2015): 1–20.

60. Burton G. Malkiel, "The Efficient Market Hypothesis and Its Critics," *Journal of Economic Perspectives* 17, no. 1 (Winter 2003): 59–82.

61. Eugene F. Fama and Kenneth R. French, "Luck versus Skill in the Cross-Section of Mutual Fund Returns," *Journal of Finance* 65, no. 5 (October 2010): 1915–1947.

62. Roger G. Ibbotson, Peng Chen, and Kevin X. Zhu, "The ABCs of Hedge Funds: Alphas, Betas, and Costs," *Financial Analysts Journal* 67 (2011): 15–25; Doron Avramov, Robert Kosowski, Narayan Y. Naik, and Melvyn Teo, "Hedge Funds, Managerial Skill, and Macroeconomic Variables," *Journal of Financial Economics* 99 (2011): 672–692; Stephen J. Brown, William N. Goetzmann, and Roger G. Ibbotson, "Offshore Hedge Funds: Survival and Performance, 1989–95," *Journal of Business* 72 (1999): 91–117.

63. Carl Ackermann, Richard McEnally, and David Ravenscraft, "The Performance of Hedge Funds: Risk, Return, and Incentives," *Journal of Finance* 54 (1999): 833–874.

64. William Fung, David A. Hsieh, Narayan Y. Naik, and Tarun Ramadorai, "Hedge Funds: Performance, Risk, and Capital Formation," *Journal of Finance* 63 (2008): 1777–1803.

65. Ilia Dichev and Gwen Yu, "Higher Risk, Lower Returns: What Hedge Fund Investors Really Earn," *Journal of Financial Economics* 100 (2011): 248–263.

66. Cited in Meir Statman, "How Your Emotions Get in the Way of Smart Investing," *Wall Street Journal* (June 15, 2015).

67. Doran et al., "Confidence, Opinions of Market Efficiency."

68. Y. Han (Andy) Kim and Felix Meschke. "CEO Interviews on CNBC," *Fifth Singapore International Conference on Finance 2011* (August 11, 2014), available at SSRN: http://ssrn.com/abstract=1745085.

69. Karen K. Nelson, Richard A. Price, and Brian Rountree, "Are Individual Investors Influenced by the Optimism and Credibility of Stock Spam Recommendations," *Journal of Business Finance & Accounting* 49, nos. 9–10 (November 2013): 1155–1183.

70. Paul Schultz, "The Market for New Issues of Municipal Bonds: The Roles of Transparency and Limited Access to Retail Investors," *Journal of Financial Economics* 106 (2012): 492–512.

71. William Alden, "S.E.C.'s Mary Jo White Seeks to Shine Light into Opaque Bond Markets," *DealBook—New York Times*, June 20, 2014, http://dealbook.nytimes.com/2014/06/20/s-e-c-chief-seeks-to-enhance-disclosure-in-bond-markets/.

72. Keri Geiger, Liam Vaughan, and Julia Verlaine, "Currency Probe Widens as U.S. Said to Target Markups," *Bloomberg Business*, June 18, 2014, http://www.bloomberg.com/news/2014-06-19/currency-probe-widens-as-u-s-said-to-target-markups.html.

73. Robert H. Battalio, Shane A. Corwin, and Robert H. Jennings, "Can Brokers Have It All? On the Relation between Make-Take Fees and Limit Order Execution Quality" (March 31, 2015), available at SSRN: http://ssrn.com/abstract=2367462.

74. William Alden, "At Senate Hearing, Brokerage Firms Called Out for Conflicts," *DealBook—New York Times*, June 17, 2014, http://dealbook.nytimes.com/2014/

06/17/trader-who-called-markets-rigged-tempers-his-critique/?module=Search &mabReward=relbias%3Aw.

75. James J. Choi, David Laibson, and Brigitte C. Madrian, "Why Does the Law of One Price Fail? An Experiment on Index Mutual Funds," *Review of Financial Studies* 23, no. 4 (2009): 1405–1432.

76. "Experienced Traders Bullish about the S&P 500® Index and Optimistic about Stocks; Low Interest Rates Drive Investments in Dividend-Paying Stocks," *Business Wire* (May 16, 2012), http://www.businesswire.com/news/home/20120516005964/en/Fidelity%C2%AE-Poll-Showcases-Active-Investors%E2%80%99-Confidence#.VYW_wvlViko.

77. Bing Han and David Hirshleifer, "Self-Enhancing Transmission Bias and Active Investing" (May 2015), available at SSRN: https://ssrn.com/abstract=2032697 or http://dx.doi.org/10.2139/ssrn.2032697. Rawley Heimer and David Simon, "Facebook Finance: How Social Interaction Propagates Active Investing," Working Paper 1522, Federal Reserve Bank of Cleveland, 2015 Rawley Z. Heimer, "Friends do let friends buy stocks actively," *Journal of Economic Behavior and Organization*, 107, Part B, November (2014): 527–540

78. Ludovic Phalippou, "Why Is the Evidence on Private Equity Performance So Confusing?" (June 14, 2011), available at SSRN: http://ssrn.com/abstract=1864503.

79. Arvid O. I. Hoffmann and Thomas Post, "Self-Attribution Bias in Consumer Financial Decision-Making: How Investment Returns Affect Individuals' Belief in Skill," *Journal of Behavioral and Experimental Economics* 52 (May 23, 2014): 23–28, available at SSRN: http://ssrn.com/abstract=2367230 or http://dx.doi.org/10.2139/ssrn.2367230.

80. Arvid O. I. Hoffmann and Hersh Shefrin, "Technical Analysis and Individual Investors," *Journal of Economic Behavior and Organization* 107 (February 2014): 487–511, available at SSRN: http://ssrn.com/abstract=2401230.

81. Itzhak Ben-David, Justin Birru, and Viktor Prokopenya, "Uninformative Feedback and Risk Taking: Evidence from Retail Forex Trading," NBER Working Paper No. w22146 (April 2016), available at SSRN: http://ssrn.com/abstract=2762097.

82. Patrick J. Bayer, Kyle Mangum, and James W. Roberts, "Speculative Fever: Investor Contagion in the Housing Bubble," NBER Working Paper No. w22065 (March 2016), available at SSRN: http://ssrn.com/abstract=2743064.

83. Stephen Deason, Shivaram Rajgopal, and Gregory B. Waymire, "Who Gets Swindled in Ponzi Schemes?" (March 28, 2015), available at SSRN: http://ssrn.com/abstract=2586490 or http://dx.doi.org/10.2139/ssrn.2586490.

84. Ville Rantala, "How Do Investment Ideas Spread through Social Interaction? Evidence from a Ponzi Scheme," 6th Miami Behavioral Finance Conference Paper (November 18, 2015), available at SSRN: http://ssrn.com/abstract=2579847 or http://dx.doi.org/10.2139/ssrn.2579847.

85. Christopher B. Yenkey, "Distrust and Market Participation: Social Relations as a Moderator of Organizational Misconduct" (January 3, 2016), available at SSRN: http://ssrn.com/abstract=2566000 or http://dx.doi.org/10.2139/ssrn.2566000.

86. Hoffmann and Post, "How Return and Risk Experiences Shape Investor Beliefs and Preferences."

87. Gene Amromin and Steven A. Sharpe, "From the Horse's Mouth: Economic Conditions and Investor Expectations of Risk and Return," *Management Science* 60 (2013): 845–866.

88. Karin Peterson LaBarge, "What Matters Most, an Analysis of Investment Committee Hire/Fire Decisions," Vanguard Group (September 2010).

89. Amit Goyal and Sunil Wahal, "The Selection and Termination of Investment Management Firms by Plan Sponsors," *Journal of Finance* 63, no. 4 (August 2008): 1805–1847; Tim Jenkinson, Howard Jones, and Jose V. Martinez, "Picking Winners? Investment Consultants' Recommendations of Fund Managers," *Journal of Finance* (October 2015), available at SSRN: http://ssrn.com/abstract=2327042.

90. Pengfei Ye, "Does the Disposition Effect Matter in Corporate Takeovers? Evidence from Institutional Investors of Target Companies," *Journal of Financial and Quantitative Analysis* 49 (2014): 221–248.

91. Sankar De, Naveen R. Gondhi, and Subrata Sarkar, "Behavioral Biases, Investor Performance, and Wealth Transfers between Investor Groups" (November 15, 2011), available at SSRN: http://ssrn.com/abstract=2022992.

92. Andriy Bodnaruk and Andrei Simonov, "Do Financial Experts Make Better Investment Decisions?" *Journal of Financial Intermediation* 24, no. 4 (October 2015): 514–536.

93. Arvid O. I. Hoffmann, "Individual Investors' Needs and the Investment Professional: Lessons from Marketing," *Journal of Investment Consulting* 8, no. 2 (2007): 80–91.

94. Daniel Dorn and Paul Sengmueller, "Trading as Entertainment?" *Management Science* 55, no. 4 (2009): 591–603.

95. Ravi Dhar and William N. Goetzmann, "Bubble Investors: What Were They Thinking?" (August 17, 2006), Yale ICF Working Paper No. 06-22, available at SSRN: https://ssrn.com/abstract=683366.

96. "Fidelity® Research Reveals Traders' Motivations beyond Investment Gains," *Benzinga*, January 27, 2012, http://www.benzinga.com/pressreleases/12/01/b2292810/fidelity-research-reveals-traders-motivations-beyond-investment-gains#ixzz3ddLr5wIi.

97. Colby Wright, Prithviraj Banerjee, and Vaneesha R. Boney, "Behavioral Finance: Are the Disciples Profiting from the Doctrine?" *Journal of Investing* 17, no. 4 (Winter 2008): 82–90.

98. Blake Phillips, Kantura Pukthuanthong and P. Raghavendra Rau, "Past Performance May Be an Illusion: Performance, Flows, and Fees in Mutual Funds," *Critical Finance Review* 5 (2016): 351–398.

99. Michael J. Cooper, Huseyin Gulen, and Raghavendra Rau, "Changing Names with Style: Mutual Fund Name Changes and Their Effects on Fund Flows," *Journal of Finance* 60, no. 6 (2005): 2825–2858.

100. Steven T. Gallaher, Ron Kaniel, and Laura T. Starks, "Advertising and Mutual Funds: From Families to Individual Funds," CEPR Discussion Paper No. DP10329 (January 2015), available at SSRN: http://ssrn.com/abstract=2554403.

101. Vikas Agarwal, Gerald D. Gay, and Leng Ling, "Window Dressing in Mutual Funds," *Review of Financial Studies* 27 (2014): 3133–3170.

102. Gjergji Cici, Alexander Kempf, and Alexander Puetz, "The Valuation of Hedge Funds' Equity Positions," AFA 2012 Chicago Meetings Paper (May 16, 2013), available at SSRN: http://ssrn.com/abstract=1664461.

103. Massimo Massa and Vijay N. Yadav, "Investor Sentiment and Mutual Fund Strategies," *Journal of Financial and Quantitative Analysis* 50, no. 4 (2015): 699–727.

104. William Fung, David A. Hsieh, Narayan Y. Naik, and Melvyn Teo, "Growing the Asset Management Franchise: Evidence from Hedge Fund Firms" (July 21, 2015), available at SSRN: http://ssrn.com/abstract=2542476. or http://dx.doi.org/10.2139/ssrn.2542476.

105. Ying Li and Hossein B. Kazemi, "Do Hedge Funds Conduct Mid-Year Risk Shifting?" (March 11, 2011), available at SSRN: http://ssrn.com/abstract=1787004.

106. Brown et al., "Analyst Recommendations."

107. Aron A. Gottesman, Matthew R. Morey, and Menahem Rosenberg, "Outperformance, Underperformance and Mutual Fund Flows in Up and Down Markets," *SSRN Electronic Journal* (Jaunary 5, 2013), available at SSRN: http://ssrn.com/abstract=2197570 or http://dx.doi.org/10.2139/ssrn.2197570.

108. Utpal Bhattacharya, Jung Hoon Lee, and Veronika K. Pool, "Conflicting Family Values in Mutual Fund Families," *Journal of Finance* 68, no. 1 (February 2013): 173–200.

109. Azi Ben-Rephael and Ryan D. Israelsen, "Are Some Clients More Equal Than Others? Evidence of Price Allocation by Delegated Portfolio Managers," *SSRN Electronic Journal* (November 13, 2013), available at SSRN: http://ssrn.com/abstract=2333786 or http://dx.doi.org/10.2139/ssrn.2333786.

110. Ron Bird, Jack Gray, and Massimo Scotti, "Why Do Investors Favor Active Management to the Extent They Do?," *Rotman International Journal of Pension Management* 6, no. 2 (2013), available at SSRN: https://ssrn.com/abstract=2330352 or http://dx.doi.org/10.2139/ssrn.2330352.

111. Martijn Cremers, Miguel A. Ferreira, Pedro P. Matos, and Laura T. Starks, "Indexing and Active Fund Management: International Evidence," *Journal of Financial Economics* 120, no. 3 (June 2016): 539–560.

112. Dan Fitzpatrick, "Calpers to Exit Hedge Funds," *Wall Street Journal*, September 15, 2014, http://www.wsj.com/articles/calpers-to-exit-hedge-funds-1410821083.

113. Kirsten Grind, "Vanguard Sets Record Funds Inflow," *Wall Street Journal*, January 4, 2015, http://www.wsj.com/articles/vanguard-sets-record-funds-inflow-1420430643.

114. Nan Qin and Vijay Singal, "Indexing and Stock Price Efficiency," *SSRN Electronic Journal* (November 15, 2013), available at SSRN: http://ssrn.com/abstract=2229263 or http://dx.doi.org/10.2139/ssrn.2229263.

115. Andrew W. Lo and A. Craig MacKinlay, *A Non-Random Walk down Wall Street* (Princeton, NJ: Princeton University Press, 2002).

116. Andrew W. Lo, "The Adaptive Markets Hypothesis," *Journal of Portfolio Management* 30 (2004): 15–29.

117. Financial Crisis Inquiry Report, 2011 (Washington, DC: US Government Printing Office).

118. Gur Huberman and William Schwert, "Information Aggregation, Inflation, and the Pricing of Indexed Bonds," *Journal of Political Economy* 93 (1985): 92–114.

119. Mark Weinstein, "The Effect of a Rating Change Announcement on Bond Price," *Journal of Financial Economics* 5 (1977).

120. Ilia D. Dichev and Joseph D. Piotroski, "The Long-Run Stock Returns Following Bond Ratings Changes," *Journal of Finance* 56 (2001): 173–203.

121. Jawad M. Addoum, Aalok Kumar, and Kelvin Law, "Geographic Diffusion of Information and Stock Returns" (October 21, 2013), available at SSRN: http://ssrn.com/abstract=2343335.

122. Charles Cao, Bing Liang, Andrew W. Lo, and Lubomir Petrasek, "Hedge Fund Holdings and Stock Market Efficiency," FEDS Working Paper No. 2014-36 (May 12, 2014), available at SSRN: http://ssrn.com/abstract=2439816 or http://dx.doi.org/10.2139/ssrn.2439816.

123. Sanford Grossman and Joseph Stiglitz, "On the Impossibility of Informationally Efficient Markets," *American Economic Review* 70 (1980): 393–408.

124. Michael Rothfeld and Scott Patterson, "Traders Seek an Edge with High-Tech Snooping," *Wall Street Journal*, December 18, 2013, http://www.wsj.com/articles/SB10001424052702303497804579240182187225264.

125. Azam Ahmed, "Even Paulson's Friends Pitied His Subprime Bet," *DealBook—New York Times*, February 14, 2011, http://dealbook.nytimes.com/2011/02/14/even-paulsons-friends-pitied-his-subprime-bet/?pagemode=print.

126. Black, "Noise."

127. Paul C. Tetlock, "Liquidity and Prediction Market Efficiency" (May 1, 2008), available at SSRN: https://ssrn.com/abstract=929916 or http://dx.doi.org/10.2139/ssrn.929916.

128. Zhi Da, Borja Larrain, Clemens Sialm, and José Tessada, "Coordinated Noise Trading: Evidence from Pension Fund Reallocations" (August 31, 2015), available at SSRN: http://ssrn.com/abstract=2558773 or http://dx.doi.org/10.2139/ssrn.2558773.

129. Carlos Carvalho, Nicholas Klagge, and Emanuel Moench, "The Persistent Effects of a False News Shock," *Journal of Empirical Finance* 18, no. 4 (September 1, 2011), available at SSRN: http://ssrn.com/abstract=1946042.

130. Itzhak Ben-David, Francesco Franzoni, Augustin Landier, and Rabih Moussawi, "Do Hedge Funds Manipulate Stock Prices?" *Journal of Finance* 68 (2013): 2383–2434.

131. Markus K. Brunnermeier and Stefan Nagel, "Hedge Funds and the Technology Bubble," *Journal of Finance* 59 (2004): 2013–2040.

132. Peter M. DeMarzo, Ron Kaniel, and Ilan Kremer, "Relative Wealth Concerns and Financial Bubbles," *Review of Financial Studies* 21 (2008): 19–50.

133. David S. Scharfstein and Jeremy C. Stein, "Herd Behavior and Investment," *American Economic Review* 80 (1990): 465–479.

134. Michiyo Nakamoto and David Wighton, "Bullish Citigroup Is 'Still Dancing' to the Beat of the Buy-Out Boom," *Financial Times*, July 10, 2007, http://www.ft.com/cms/s/0/5cefc794-2e7d-11dc-821c-0000779fd2ac.html.

135. Jongmoo Jay Choi, Haim Kedar-Levy, and Sean Sehyun Yoo, "Are Individual or Institutional Investors the Agents of Bubbles?" (July 17, 2014), available at SSRN: http://ssrn.com/abstract=2023766.

136. Utpal Bhattacharya, Neal Galpin, and Rina Ray, "The Role of the Media in the Internet IPO Bubble," *Journal of Financial and Quantitative Analysis* 44 (2009): 657–682.

137. Malcolm P. Baker and Jeffrey Wurgler, "Investor Sentiment in the Stock Market," *Journal of Economic Perspectives* 21, no. 2 (Spring 2007): 129–151, available at SSRN: http://ssrn.com/abstract=983435.

138. Jose Scheinkman and Wei Xiong, "Overconfidence and Speculative Bubbles," *Journal of Political Economy* 111 (2003): 1183–1219.

139. Karl B. Diether, Christopher J. Malloy, and Anna Scherbina, "Difference of Opinion and the Cross-Section of Stock Returns," *Journal of Finance* 57 (2002): 2113–2141.

140. Zhi Da, Ravi Jagannathan, and Jianfeng Shen, "Building Castles in the Air: Evidence from Industry IPO Waves," January 23, 2013. NBER Working Paper 18555, http://www.nber.org/papers/w18555.

141. Robert McGough, "Bulls Say a Heated Market Could Get Even Warmer," *Wall Street Journal*, March 30, 1999: C1.

142. "Episode 493: What's a Bubble (Nobel Edition)," *Planet Money*, National Public Radio, November 11, 2013, http://www.npr.org/sections/money/2013/11/01/242351065/episode-493-whats-a-bubble-nobel-edition.

143. William N. Goetzmann, "Bubble Investing: Learning from History" (January 11, 2016), available at SSRN: http://ssrn.com/abstract=2784281.

144. Msg #180245, December 31, 1999, Yahoo.com.

145. Msg #19554, December 26, 1999, Yahoo.com.

146. Msg #19508, December 25, 1999, Yahoo.com.

147. Msg #90850, December 8, 1999, Amazon.com.

148. Msg #189506, December 4, 1999, Amazon.com.

149. Jeff Kearns, "Roubini Says S&P 500 May Drop to 600 as Profits Fall (Update2)," *Bloomberg*, March 9, 2009, http://www.bloomberg.com/apps/news?pid=newsarc hive&sid=a0oeKmwfkr9k.

150. "Business Week 2008 Forecasters Expect Further Gains," *Seeking Alpha*, December 21, 2007, http://seekingalpha.com/article/58150-business-week-2008-forecasters-expect-further-gains.

151. Ing-Haw Cheng, Sahil Raina, and Wei Xiong, "Wall Street and the Housing Bubble," *American Economic Review* 104 (2014): 2797–2829.

152. Paul Brockman, Biljana Nikolic, and Xuemin Sterling Yan, "Anticipating the 2007–2008 Financial Crisis: Who Knew What and When Did They Know it?" *Journal of Financial and Quantitative Analysis* 50, no. 4 (August 2015): 647–669.

153. John Y. Campbell and Robert J. Shiller, "Valuation Ratios and the Long-Run Stock Market Outlook," *Journal of Portfolio Management* (Winter 1998): 11–26.

154. Amit Goyal and Ivo Welch, "Predicting the Equity Premium with Dividend Ratios," *Management Science* 49 (2003): 639–654.

155. Fama, "Efficient Capital Markets: II."

156. Kewei Hou, Chen Xue, and Lu Zhang, "Digesting Anomalies: An Investment Approach," *Review of Financial Studies* 28, no. 3 (2015): 650–705.

157. Cathy Scott, "Practical Applications of Alpha, Beta & the Blend," *Smart Beta Special Issue* 3 (2015): 1–7, http://www.iijournals.com/doi/pdfplus/10.3905/pa.2015.3.sb.003.

158. Steven Rattner, "Who's Right on the Stock Market?" *New York Times*, November 15, 2013: A29, http://www.nytimes.com/2013/11/15/opinion/rattner-whos-right-on-the-stock-market.html.

CHAPTER 12

1. Corrie Driebusch and Eric Sylvers, "Ferrari IPO Prices at Top of Range," *Wall Street Journal*, October 20, 2015, http://www.wsj.com/articles/ferrari-ipo-prices-at-high-end-of-range-1445375676?alg=y.

2. http://www.businessinsider.com/heres-why-precious-metals-are-the-next-big-risky-investments-2011-5.

3. Michael J. Cooper, Orlin Dimitrov, and P. Raghavendra Rau, "A Rose.com by Any Other Name," *Journal of Finance* 56, no. 6 (December 2001): 2371–2388; Michael J. Cooper, Ajay Khorana, Igor Osobov, Ajay Patel, and Rau Raghavendra, "Managerial Actions in Response to a Market Downturn: Valuation Effects of Name Changes in the Dot.com Decline," *Journal of Corporate Finance* 11 (2005): 319–335.

REFERENCES

AAII: The American Association of Individual Investors. "Starting with Dollar Cost Averaging." http://www.aaii.com/investing/article/starting-with-dollar-cost-averaging.

Ackermann, Carl, Richard McEnally, and David Ravenscraft. "The Performance of Hedge Funds: Risk, Return, and Incentives." *Journal of Finance* 54 (1999): 833–874.

Addoum, Jawad M., Alok Kumar, and Kelvin Law. "Geographic Diffusion of Information and Stock Returns" (October 21, 2013). Available at SSRN: http://ssrn.com/abstract=2343335.

Agarwal, Sumit, Gene Amromin, Itzhak Ben-David, and Douglas D. Evanoff, "Loan Product Steering in Mortgage Markets" (August 1, 2016). Charles A. Dice Center Working Paper No. 2016-18; Fisher College of Business Working Paper No. 2016-03-18. Available at SSRN: https://ssrn.com/abstract=2841312 or http://dx.doi.org/10.2139/ssrn.2841312.

Agarwal, Sumit, Souphala Chomsisengphet, Neale Mahoney, and Johannes Stroebel. "Regulating Consumer Financial Products: Evidence from Credit Cards." *Quarterly Journal of Economics* 130 (2015): 111–164.

Agarwal, Sumit, Ran Duchin, and Denis Sosyura. "In Mood for a Loan: The Causal Effect of Sentiment on Credit Origination." (November 1, 2012). Available at SSRN: https://ssrn.com/abstract=2141030 or http://dx.doi.org/10.2139/ssrn.2141030.

Agarwal, Sumit, Jia He, Haoming Liu, Ivan P. L. Png, Tien Foo Sing, and Wei-Kang Wong. "Superstition and Asset Markets: Evidence from Singapore Housing" (March 27, 2014). Available at SSRN: http://ssrn.com/abstract=2416832.

Agarwal, Sumit, Crocker Herbert Liu, Walter N. Torous, and Vincent W. Yao. "Financial Decision Making When Buying and Owning a Home" (September 18, 2014). Available at SSRN: http://ssrn.com/abstract=2498111 or http://dx.doi.org/10.2139/ssrn.2498111.

Agarwal, Sumit, Vyacheslav Mikhed, and Barry Scholnick. "Does Inequality Cause Financial Distress? Evidence from Lottery Winners and Neighboring Bankruptcies." FRB of Philadelphia Working Paper No. 16-4 (February 11, 2016). Available at SSRN: http://ssrn.com/abstract=2731562.

Agarwal, Sumit, Wenlan Qian, and Xin Zou. "Thy Neighbor's Misfortune: Peer Effect on Consumption" (May 17, 2016). Available at SSRN: http://ssrn.com/abstract=2780764 or http://dx.doi.org/10.2139/ssrn.2780764.

Agarwal, Sumit, Richard J. Rosen, and Vincent W. Yao, "Why Do Borrowers Make Mortgage Refinancing Mistakes?" (March 18, 2015). Forthcoming, *Management Science*, available at SSRN: https://ssrn.com/abstract=2446753 or http://dx.doi.org/10.2139/ssrn.2446753.

Agarwal, Vikas, Gerald D. Gay, and Leng Ling. "Window Dressing in Mutual Funds." *Review of Financial Studies* 27 (2014): 3133–3170.

Agarwal, Vikas, Wei Jiang, Yuehua Tang, and Baozhong Yang. "Uncovering Hedge Fund Skill from the Portfolio Holdings They Hide." *Journal of Finance* 68 (2013): 739–783.

Ahern, Kenneth R. "Information Networks: Evidence from Illegal Insider Trading Tips" (February 5, 2015). Available at SSRN: http://ssrn.com/abstract=2511068.

Ahmed, Azam. "Even Paulson's Friends Pitied His Subprime Bet." *DealBook—The New York Times*, February 14, 2011. http://dealbook.nytimes.com/2011/02/14/even-paulsons-friends-pitied-his-subprime-bet/?pagemode=print.

Alan, Sule, Mehmet Cemalcilar, Dean S. Karlan, and Jonathan Zinman. "Unshrouding Effects on Demand for a Costly Add-On: Evidence from Bank Overdrafts in Turkey." NBER Working Paper No. w20956 (February 2015). Available at SSRN: http://ssrn.com/abstract=2565629.

Alan, Sule, Ruxandra Dumitrescu, and Gyongyi Loranth. "Subprime Consumer Credit Demand: Evidence from a Lender's Pricing Experiment." *Review of Financial Studies* 26 (2013): 2353–2374.

Alden, William. "At Senate Hearing, Brokerage Firms Called Out for Conflicts." *DealBook—New York Times*, June 17, 2014. http://dealbook.nytimes.com/2014/06/17/trader-who-called-markets-rigged-tempers-his-critique/?module=Search&mabReward=relbias%3Aw.

Alden, William. "S.E.C.'s Mary Jo White Seeks to Shine Light into Opaque Bond Markets." *DealBook—The New York Times*, June 20, 2014. http://dealbook.nytimes.com/2014/06/20/s-e-c-chief-seeks-to-enhance-disclosure-in-bond-markets/.

Alho, Eeva, Markku Kaustia, and Vesa Puttonen. "How Much Does Expertise Reduce Behavioral Biases? The Case of Anchoring Effects in Stock Return Estimates." *Financial Management* 37, no. 3 (Autumn 2008): 391–411. Available at SSRN: http://ssrn.com/abstract=1066641.

Allard, Scott W., Sandra Danziger, and Maria Wathen. "Receipt of Public Benefits and Private Support among Low-Income Households with Children after the Great Recession." National Poverty Center, Policy Brief #31 (April 2012).

Allen, Eric J., Patricia M. Dechow, Devin G. Pope, and George Wu. "Reference-Dependent Preferences: Evidence from Marathon Runners." *Management Science*, http://www.nber.org/papers/w20343.

Alpine Woods Capital Investors. "Alpine Rising Dividend Fund." http://www.alpinefunds.com/default.asp?P=856340&S=857564.

Amato, Paul R., and Stacy J. Rogers. "A Longitudinal Study of Marital Problems and Subsequent Divorce." *Journal of Marriage and the Family* 59 (August 1997): 612–624.

Ameriks, John. "When to Start Spending Your Retirement Savings." *Vanguard Blog* (May 5, 2010). Available at http://www.vanguardblog.com/2010.05.05/when-to-start-spending.html.

Ameriks, John, Andrew Caplin, John Leahy, and Tom Tyler. "Measuring Self-Control." *American Economic Review* 97 (2007): 966–972.

Ameriks, John, Robert Veres, and Mark J. Warshawsky. "Making Retirement Income Last a Lifetime." *Journal of Financial Planning* 14, no. 12 (December 2001): 60–76.

Amromin, Gene, and Steven A. Sharpe. "From the Horse's Mouth: Economic Conditions and Investor Expectations of Risk and Return." *Management Science* 60 (2013): 845–866.

Analog, Santosh, Shawn Allen Cole, and Shayak Sarkar. "Bad Advice: Explaining the Persistence of Whole Life Insurance" (February 8, 2011). Available at SSRN: http://ssrn.com/abstract=1786624 or http://dx.doi.org/10.2139/ssrn.1786624.

Anderson, Anders. "Trading and Under-Diversification." *Review of Finance* 17, no. 5 (2013): 1699–1741.

Anderson, Cameron, Sebastien Brion, Don A. Moore, and Jessica A. Kennedy. "A Status-Enhancement Account of Overconfidence." *Journal of Personality and Social Psychology* 103 (2012): 718–735.

Ang, James S., Ansley Chua, and Danling Jiang. "Is A Better Than B? How Affect Influences the Marketing and Pricing of Financial Securities." *Financial Analysts Journal* 66, no. 5 (September–October 2010): 40–54.

Angry Orthopod. "Medical Merchandising: The Same Old Crap, Repackaged." June 22, 2011. http://angryorthopod.com/2011/06/medical-merchandising-the-same-old-crap-repackaged.

Anon. "Top 20 Nations Listed by Stock Market Cap (in Billions)." August 25, 2013. https://blogs.law.harvard.edu/willbanks/2013/08/25/top-20-nations-listed-by-company-market-cap/.

Antoniou, Constantinos, Alok Kumar, and Anastasios Maligkris. "The Affect Heuristic and Analysts' Earnings Forecasts" (December 10, 2015). Available at SSRN: http://ssrn.com/abstract=2702051 or http://dx.doi.org/10.2139/ssrn.2702051.

Ariely, Dan, and Klaus Wertenbroch. "Procrastination, Deadlines, and Performance: Self-Control by Precommitment." *Psychological Science* 13, no. 3 (2002): 219–224.

Ashraf, Nava, Dean Karlan, and Wesley Yin. "Tying Odysseus to the Mast: Evidence from a Commitment Savings Product in the Philippines." *Quarterly Journal of Economics* 121, no. 2 (2006): 635–672.

Aspara, Jaakko, and Arvid O. I. Hoffmann. "Selling Losers and Keeping Winners: How (Savings) Goal Dynamics Predict a Reversal of the Disposition Effect." *Marketing Letters* 26, no. 2 (June 2015): 201–211.

Associated Press, "Obama Signs New Rules for Credit Cards into Law." NBCnews.com, May 22, 2009. http://www.nbcnews.com/id/30884011/ns/business-personal_finance/t/obama-signs-new-rules-credit-cards-law/#.WDWaufkrKM8.

Atkin, David. "The Caloric Costs of Culture: Evidence from Indian Migrants." *American Economic Review* 106 (2016): 1144–1181.

Austen, Ian. "The Quiet Comeback of Margaret Trudeau." *New York Times,* November 7, 2015. http://www.nytimes.com/2015/11/08/fashion/margaret-trudeau-canada-comeback.html?_r=0.

Avery, Christopher, Judith A. Chevalier, and Richard J. Zeckhauser. "The 'CAPS' Prediction System and Stock Market Returns." *Review of Finance* 20, no. 4 (2016): 1363–1381.

Avramov, Doron, Robert Kosowski, Narayan Y. Naik, and Melvyn Teo. "Hedge Funds, Managerial Skill, and Macroeconomic Variables." *Journal of Financial Economics* 99 (2011): 672–692.

Bachmann, Kremena, and Thorsten Hens. "Investment Competence and Advice Seeking." *Journal of Behavioral and Experimental Finance* 6 (2015): 27–41.

Baele, Lieven, Geert Bekaert, Koen Inghelbrecht, and Min Wei. "Flights to Safety." NBER Working Paper No. w19095 (May 2013).

Baele, Lieven, Moazzam Farooq, and Steven Ongena. "Of Religion and Redemption: Evidence from Default on Islamic Loans." CEPR Discussion Paper No. DP8504 (August 2011). Available at SSRN: http://ssrn.com/abstract=1908552.

Bagley, Judd. "Schwab Investing Pep-Talk Ad 2002." YouTube video. February 1, 2010. https://www.youtube.com/watch?v=24sTGLxNNKs.

Baker, Malcolm P., and Jeffrey Wurgler. "Investor Sentiment in the Stock Market." *Journal of Economic Perspectives* 21, no. 2 (Spring 2007): 129–151. Available at SSRN: http://ssrn.com/abstract=983435.

Baker, Malcolm P., Jeffrey Wurgler, and Brendan Bradley. "A Behavioral Finance Explanation for the Success of Low-Volatility Portfolios." NYU Working Paper No. 2451/29537 (January 2010). Available at SSRN: http://ssrn.com/abstract=2284643.

Baker, Malcolm, Stefan Nagel, and Jeffrey Wurgler. "The Effect of Dividends on Consumption." *Brookings Papers on Economic Activity* 1 (2007): 231–276.

Ball, Ray, Joseph Gerakos, Juhani T. Linnainmaa and Valeri V. Nikolaev. "Deflating Probability." *Journal of Financial Economics* 117, no. 2 (2015): 225–248.

Banerjee, Sudipto. "Intra-Family Cash Transfers in Older American Households." *EBRI Issue Brief Number 415* (June 2015). Available at SSRN: http://ssrn.com/abstract=2620835.

Banz, Rolf W. "The Relationship between Return and Market Value of Common Stocks." *Journal of Financial Economics* 9 (1981): 3–18.

Barber, Brad M., and Terrance Odean. "All That Glitters: The Effect of Attention and News on the Buying Behavior of Individual and Institutional Investors." *Review of Financial Studies* 21 (2008): 785–818.

Barber, Brad M., and Terrance Odean. "Trading Is Hazardous to Your Wealth: The Common Stock Investment Performance of Individual Investors." *Journal of Finance* 55 (2000): 773–806.

Barber, Brad M., Yi-Tsung Lee, Yu-Jane Liu, and Terrance Odean. "The Cross-Section of Speculator Skill: Evidence from Day Trading." *Journal of Financial Markets* 18 (2014): 1–24.

Barberis, Nicholas, Robin Greenwood, Lawrence Jin, and Andrei Shleifer. "X-CAPM: An Extrapolative Capital Asset Pricing Model." *Journal of Financial Economics* 115 (2015): 1–24.

Barberis, Nicholas, and Wei Xiong. "Realization Utility." *Journal of Financial Economics* 104 (2012): 251–271.

Bar-Hillel, Maya, and Efrat Neter. "Why Are People Reluctant to Exchange Lottery Tickets?" *Journal of Personality and Social Psychology* 70, no. 1 (1996): 17–27.

Barnard, Anne, and Karam Shoumali. "Image of Drowned Syrian, Aylan Kurdi, 3, Brings Migrant Crisis into Focus." *New York Times*, September 3, 2015. http://www.nytimes.com/2015/09/04/world/europe/syria-boy-drowning.html?_r=0.

Barry, Rob, and Susan Pulliam. "Executives' Good Luck in Trading Own Stock." *Wall Street Journal*, November 27, 2012. http://online.wsj.com/news/articles/SB10000872396390444100404577641463717344178.

Barsky, Robert B., F. Thomas Juster, Miles S. Kimball, and Matthew D. Shapiro. "Preference Parameters and Behavioral Heterogeneity: An Experimental

Approach in the Health and Retirement Study." *Quarterly Journal of Economics* 112, no. 2 (May 1997): 537–579.

Basu, Sanjoy. "Investment Performance of Common Stocks in Relation to Their Price-Earnings Ratios: A Test of the Efficient Market Hypothesis." *Journal of Finance* 32 (1977): 663–682.

Battalio, Robert H., Shane A. Corwin, and Robert H. Jennings. "Can Brokers Have It All? On the Relation between Make-Take Fees and Limit Order Execution Quality" (March 31, 2015). Available at SSRN: http://ssrn.com/abstract=2367462.

Bayer, Patrick J., Kyle Mangum, and James W. Roberts. "Speculative Fever: Investor Contagion in the Housing Bubble." NBER Working Paper No. w22065 (March 2016). Available at SSRN: http://ssrn.com/abstract=2743064.

Bekaert, Geert, Kenton Hoyem, Wei-Yin Hu, and Enrichetta Ravina. "Who Is Internationally Diversified? Evidence from 296 401(k) Plans" (April 21, 2015). Available at SSRN: http://ssrn.com/abstract=2417976.

Benartzi, Shlomo, and Richard Thaler. "Myopic Loss Aversion and the Equity Premium Puzzle." *Quarterly Journal of Economics* 110 (1995): 73–92.

Benartzi, Shlomo, and Richard Thaler. "Risk Aversion or Myopia? Choices in Repeated Gambles and Retirement Investments." *Management Science* 45 (1999): 364–381.

Ben-David, Itzhak, Justin Birru, and Viktor Prokopenya. "Uninformative Feedback and Risk Taking: Evidence from Retail Forex Trading." NBER Working Paper No. w22146 (April 2016). Available at SSRN: http://ssrn.com/abstract=2762097.

Ben-David, Itzhak, Francesco Franzoni, Augustin Landier, and Rabih Moussawi. "Do Hedge Funds Manipulate Stock Prices?" *Journal of Finance* 68 (2013): 2383–2434.

Ben-David, Itzhak, John R. Graham, and Campbell R. Harvey. "Managerial Miscalibration." *Quarterly Journal of Economics* 128, no. 4 (2013): 1547–1584.

Ben-David, Itzhak, and David Hirshleifer. "Are Investors Really Reluctant to Realize Their Losses? Trading Responses to Past Returns and the Disposition Effect." *Review of Financial Studies* 25, no. 8 (2012): 2485–2532.

Bengen, W. P. "Determining Withdrawal Rates Using Historical Data." *Journal of Financial Planning* 7, no. 4 (October 1994): 171–180.

Ben-Rephael, Azi, and Ryan D. Israelsen. "Are Some Clients More Equal than Others? Evidence of Price Allocation by Delegated Portfolio Managers." *SSRN Electronic Journal* (November 13, 2013). Available at SSRN: http://ssrn.com/abstract=2333786 or http://dx.doi.org/10.2139/ssrn.2333786.

Benz, Christine. "The Error-Proof Portfolio: OK, People—What Have We Learned? The Bull Market Is Entering Its Fifth Year, But How Have Investors Done Since the Market Recovered?" Morningstar (October 28, 2013). http://news.morningstar.com/articlenet/article.aspx?id=616424.

Benzinga. "Fidelity® Research Reveals Traders' Motivations beyond Investment Gains." January 27, 2012. http://www.benzinga.com/pressreleases/12/01/b2292810/fidelity-research-reveals-traders-motivations-beyond-investment-gains#ixzz3ddLr5wIi.

Berg, Gunhild, and Bilal Zia. "Harnessing Emotional Connections to Improve Financial Decisions: Evaluating the Impact of Financial Education in Mainstream Media." https://papers.ssrn.com/sol3/papers.cfm?abstract_id=2248477.

Bergsma, Kelley, and Danling Jiang. "Cultural New Year Holidays and Stock Returns around the World." *Financial Management* 45, no. 1 (Spring 2016): 3–35.

Berk, Jonathan B., Richard C. Green, and Vasant Naik. "Optimal Investment, Growth Options, and Security Returns." *Journal of Finance* 54 (1999): 1553–1607.

Berk, Jonathan B., and Jules H. Van Binsbergen. "Measuring Managerial Skill in the Mutual Fund Industry." *Journal of Financial Economics* 118, no. 1 (October 2015): 1–20.

Berkman, Henk, Paul D. Koch, and P. Joakim Westerholm. "Informed Trading through the Accounts of Children." *Journal of Finance* 69 (2014): 363–404.

Bernard, Tara Siegel. "Customers First to Become the Law in Retirement Investing." *New York Times*, April 6, 2016.

Bernoulli, Daniel. "Exposition of a New Theory on the Measurement of Risk." *Econometrica* 22 (1954): 23–36. (Original work published 1738.)

Bertrand, Marianne, Dean Karlan, Sendhil Mullainathan, Eldar Shafir, and Jonathan Zinman. "What's Advertising Content Worth? Evidence from a Consumer Credit Marketing Field Experiment." *Quarterly Journal of Economics* 125 (February 2010): 263–305.

Beshears, John, James J. Choi, Joshua Hurwitz, David Laibson, and Brigitte C. Madrian. "Liquidity in Retirement Savings Systems: An International Comparison." *American Economic Review* 105 (2015): 420–425.

Beshears, John, James J. Choi, David Laibson, and Brigitte C. Madrian. "Does Aggregated Returns Disclosure Increase Portfolio Risk-Taking?" NBER Working Paper No. 16868 (March 2011).

Beshears, John L., James J. Choi, David Laibson, and Brigitte C. Madrian. "Does Front-Loading Taxation Increase Savings? Evidence from Roth 401(k) Introductions." NBER Working Paper No. w20738 (December 2014). Available at SSRN: http://ssrn.com/abstract=2538324.

Beshears, John, James J. Choi, David Laibson, Brigitte C. Madrian, and Katherine L. Milkman. "The Effect of Providing Peer Information on Retirement Savings Decisions." *Journal of Finance* 70 (2015): 1120–1161.

Betterment LLC. "Betterment: Investing Made Better." https://www.betterment.com/.

Bhattacharya, Utpal, Neal Galpin, and Rina Ray. "The Role of the Media in the Internet IPO Bubble." *Journal of Financial and Quantitative Analysis* 44 (2009): 657–682.

Bhattacharya, Utpal, Andreas Hackethal, Simon Kaesler, Benjamin Loos, and Steffen Meyer. "Is Unbiased Financial Advice to Retail Investors Sufficient? Answers from a Large Field Study." *Review of Financial Studies* 25 (2012): 975–1032.

Bhattacharya, Utpal, Jung Hoon Lee, and Veronika K. Pool. "Conflicting Family Values in Mutual Fund Families." *Journal of Finance* 68, no. 1 (February 2013): 173–200.

Biais, Bruno, and Martin Weber. "Hindsight Bias, Risk Perception and Investment Performance." *Management Science* 55, no. 6 (June 2009): 1018–1029. Available at SSRN: http://ssrn.com/abstract=1209774.

Bickel, Warren K., Kris Kirby, and Nancy M. Petry. "Heroin Addicts Have Higher Discount Rates for Delayed Rewards than Non-Drug-Using Controls." *Journal of Experimental Psychology* 128, no. 1 (1999): 78–87.

Bird, Ron, Jack Gray, and Massimo Scotti, "Why Do Investors Favor Active Management . . . To the Extent They Do?" *Rotman International Journal of*

Pension Management 6, no. 2 (2013), available at SSRN: https://ssrn.com/abstract=2330352 or http://dx.doi.org/10.2139/ssrn.2330352.

Black, Fischer. "Beta and Return." *Journal of Portfolio Management* 20, no. 1 (Fall 1993): 8–18.

Black, Fischer. "The Dividend Puzzle." *Journal of Portfolio Management* 2 (1976): 5–8.

Black, Fischer. "Noise." *Journal of Finance* 41 (1986): 529–543.

Bodnaruk, Andriy, and Andrei Simonov. "Do Financial Experts Make Better Investment Decisions?" *Journal of Financial Intermediation* 24, no. 4 (October 2015): 514–536.

Boehm, Thomas, Judah Folkman, Timothy Browder, and Michael S. O'Reilly. "Antiangio-Genic Therapy of Experimental Cancer Does Not Induce Acquired Drug Resistance." *Nature* 390 (1997): 404–407.

Bogan, Vicki L. "Household Asset Allocation, Offspring Education, and the Sandwich Generation" (October 10, 2014). Available at SSRN: http://ssrn.com/abstract=2508486 or http://dx.doi.org/10.2139/ssrn.2508486

Bogan, Vicki, and David Just. "What Drives Merger Decision Making Behavior? Don't Seek, Don't Find, and Don't Change Your Mind." *Journal of Economic Behavior and Organization* 72, no. 3 (2009): 930–943.

Bogdanich, Walt, and Jacqueline Williams. "For Addicts, Fantasy Sites Can Lead to Ruinous Path." *New York Times*, November 22, 2015. http://www.nytimes.com/2015/11/23/sports/fantasy-sports-addiction-gambling-draftkings-fanduel.html.

Bogle, John. "A Question So Important That It Should Be Hard to Think about Anything Else." *Journal of Portfolio Management* 34 (Winter 2008): 95–102.

Bollinger, Bryan, Phillip Leslie, and Alan Sorensen. "Calorie Posting in Chain Restaurants." *American Economic Journal: Economic Policy* 3 (2011): 91–128.

Bond, Samuel D., Kurt A. Carlson, and Ralph L. Keeney. "Improving the Generation of Decision Objectives." *Decision Analysis* 7, no. 3 (2010): 238–255.

Bouchaud, Jean-Philippe, Ciliberti Stefano, Augustin Landier, Guillaume Simon, and David Thesmar. "The Excess Returns of 'Quality' Stocks: A Behavioral Anomaly." HEC Paris Research Paper No. FIN-2016-1134 (January 15, 2016). Available at SSRN: http://ssrn.com/abstract=2717447 or http://dx.doi.org/10.2139/ssrn.2717447.

Boudoukh, Jacob, Ronen Feldman, Shimon Kogan, and Matthew Richardson. "Which News Moves Stock Prices: A Textual Analysis." Working paper, University of Pennsylvania, Wharton (October 14, 2013).

Brav, Alon, John R. Graham, Campbell R. Harvey, and Roni Michaely. "The Effect of the May 2003 Dividend Tax Cut on Corporate Dividend Policy: Empirical and Survey Evidence." *National Tax Journal* 61 (2008): 381–396.

Brinson, Gary, Randolph Hood, and Gilbert Beebower. "Determinants of Portfolio Performance." *Financial Analysts Journal* (July–August 1986): 39–44.

Brinson, Gary, Brian Singer, and Gilbert Beebower. "Determinants of Portfolio Performance II: An Update." *Financial Analysts Journal* 47, no. 3 (1991): 40–48.

Brock, William, Josef Lakonishok, and Blake LeBaron. "Simple Technical Trading Rules and the Stochastic Properties of Stock Returns." *Journal of Finance* 47, no. 5 (1992): 1731–1764.

Brockman, Paul, Biljana Nikolic, and Xuemin Sterling Yan. "Anticipating the 2007–2008 Financial Crisis: Who Knew What and When Did They Know It?" *Journal of Financial and Quantitative Analysis* 50, no. 4 (August 2015): 647–669.

Bronnenberg, Bart J., Jean-Pierre Dubé, Matthew Gentzkow, and Jesse M. Shapiro. "Do Pharmacists Buy Bayer? Informed Shoppers and the Brand Premium." *Quarterly Journal of Economics* 130 (2015): 1669–1726.

Brown, Alasdair, and Fuyu Yang. "Salience and the Disposition Effect: Evidence from the Introduction of 'Cash-Outs' in Betting Markets" (October 2, 2015). Available at SSRN: http://ssrn.com/abstract=2668618 or http://dx.doi.org/10.2139/ssrn.2668618.

Brown, Alexander L., and Joanna N. Lahey. "Small Victories: Creating Intrinsic Motivation in Savings and Debt Reduction." National Bureau of Economic Research Working Paper Series No. 20125 (2014).

Brown, Jeffrey R., James M. Poterba, and David P. Richardson. "Do Required Minimum Distributions Matter? The Effect of the 2009 Holiday on Retirement Plan Distributions." *Journal of Public Economics*, available online August 14, 2016, http://www.nber.org/papers/w20464.

Brown, Martin, Jan Schmitz, and Christian Zehnder. "Social Norms and Strategic Default." University of St. Gallen, School of Finance Research Paper No. 2016/08 (March 7, 2016). Available at SSRN: http://ssrn.com/abstract=2743278 or http://dx.doi.org/10.2139/ssrn.2743278.

Brown, Nerissa C., Kelsey D. Wei, and Russ Wermers. "Analyst Recommendations, Mutual Fund Herding, and Overreaction in Stock Prices." *Management Science* 60, no. 1 (September 2013): 1–20.

Brown, Stephen J., William N. Goetzmann, and Roger G. Ibbotson. "Offshore Hedge Funds: Survival and Performance, 1989–95." *Journal of Business* 72 (1999): 91–117.

Browning, Chris, Tao Guo, Yuanshan Cheng, and Michael S. Finke. "Spending in Retirement: Determining the Consumption Gap." *Journal of Financial Planning* 29 (2016): 42–53.

Browning, E. S., Steven Rusolillo, and Jessica E. Vascellaro. "Apple Now Biggest-Ever U.S. Company." *Wall Street Journal*, August 20, 2012. Accessed December 22, 2015. http://www.wsj.com/articles/SB100008723963904438558045776017735247445182.

Brunel, Jean L. P. *Goals-Based Wealth Management: An Integrated and Practical Approach to Changing the Structure of Advisory Practices.* Wiley Finance Series. Hoboken, NJ: Wiley, 2015.

Brunnermeier, Markus K., and Stefan Nagel. "Hedge Funds and the Technology Bubble." *Journal of Finance* 59 (2004): 2013–2040.

Burbano, Vanessa C. "Social Responsibility Messages and Worker Wage Requirements: Field Experimental Evidence from Online Labor Marketplaces." *Organization Science* 27, no. 4 (June 30, 2016): 1010–1028.

Bursztyn, Leonardo, Stefano Fiorin, Daniel Gottlieb, and Martin Kanz. "Moral Incentives: Experimental Evidence from Repayments of an Islamic Credit Card." NBER Working Paper No. w21611 (October 2015). Available at SSRN: http://ssrn.com/abstract=2669800.

Business Wire. "Experienced Traders Bullish about the S&P 500® Index and Optimistic about Stocks; Low Interest Rates Drive Investments in Dividend-Paying Stocks," May 16, 2012. http://www.businesswire.com/news/home/20120516005964/en/Fidelity%C2%AE-Poll-Showcases-Active-Investors%E2%80%99-Confidence#.VYW_wvlViko.

Campbell, John, Jens Hilscher, and Jan Szilagyi. "In Search of Distress Risk." *Journal of Finance* 63, no. 6 (2008): 2899–2939.

Campbell, John Y., Tarun Ramadorai, and Benjamin Ranish. "Getting Better or Feeling Better? How Equity Investors Respond to Investment Experiences" (December 1, 2014), available at SSRN: https://ssrn.com/abstract=2176222 or http://dx.doi.org/10.2139/ssrn.2176222.

Campbell, John Y., and Robert J. Shiller. "Valuation Ratios and the Long-Run Stock Market Outlook." *Journal of Portfolio Management* (Winter 1998): 11–26.

Campbell, Sean D., and Steven A. Sharpe. "Anchoring Bias in Consensus Forecasts and Its Effect on Market Prices." Finance and Economics Discussion Series. Divisions of Research & Statistics and Monetary Affairs, Federal Reserve Board, Washington, DC, 2007.

Cao, Charles, Bing Liang, Andrew W. Lo, and Lubomir Petrasek. "Hedge Fund Holdings and Stock Market Efficiency." FEDS Working Paper No. 2014-36 (May 12, 2014). Available at SSRN: http://ssrn.com/abstract=2439816 or http://dx.doi.org/10.2139/ssrn.2439816.

Carlson, Kyle, Joshua Kim, Annamaria Lusardi, and Colin Camerer. "Bankruptcy Rates among NFL Players with Short-Lived Income Spikes." *American Economic Review* 105, no. 5 (2015): 381–384.

Carvalho, Carlos, Nicholas Klagge, and Emanuel Moench. "The Persistent Effects of a False News Shock." *Journal of Empirical Finance* 18, no. 4 (September 1, 2011). Available at SSRN: http://ssrn.com/abstract=1946042.

Casey, B. J., et al., "Behavioral and Neural Correlates of Delay of Gratification 40 Years Later," *Proceedings of the National Academy of Sciences of the United States of America* 108, no. 36 (2011): 14998–15003.

Cavazos, Gerardo Perez, and Andreya Marie Silvas. "Tax-Minded Executives and Corporate Tax Strategies: Evidence from the 2013 Tax Hikes" (November 15, 2014). Available at SSRN: http://ssrn.com/abstract=2529509 or http://dx.doi.org/10.2139/ssrn.2529509.

Celerier, Claire, and Boris Vallee. "What Drives Financial Innovation? A Look into the European Retail Structured Products Market." Finance Meeting EUROFIDAI-AFFI Paper, Paris, December 2012 (July 2013).

Cerqueira Leal, Cristiana, Manuel J. Rocha Armada, and Joao C. Duque. "Are All Individual Investors Equally Prone to the Disposition Effect All The Time? New Evidence from a Small Market," *Frontiers in Finance and Economics* 7, no. 2 (October 2010): 38–68.

Chandon, Pierre, and Brian Wansink. "The Biasing Health Halos of Fast Food Restaurant Health Claims: Lower Calorie Estimates and Higher Side-Dish Consumption Intentions." *Journal of Consumer Research* 34, no. 3 (2007): 301–314.

Chang, Tom, David H. Solomon, and Mark M. Westerfield. "Looking for Someone to Blame: Delegation, Cognitive Dissonance, and the Disposition Effect." *Journal of Finance* 71, no. 1 (February 2016): 267–302.

Chapman, Gretchen B., and Eric J. Johnson. "Incorporating the Irrelevant: Anchors in Judgments of Belief and Value." In *Heuristics and Biases: The Psychology of Intuitive Judgment*, ed. T. Gilovich, D. W. Griffin, and D. Kahneman, 120–138. New York: Cambridge University Press, 2002.

Chen, Daniel L., Tobias J. Moskowitz, and Kelly Shue. "Decision-Making under the Gambler's Fallacy: Evidence from Asylum Judges, Loan Officers, and Baseball Umpires." Chicago Booth Research Paper No. 15-27 (November 4, 2014). Available at SSRN: http://ssrn.com/abstract=2635524 or http://dx.doi.org/10.2139/ssrn.2635524.

Chen, Zhuoqiong (Charlie), and Tobias Gesche. "Persistent Bias in Advice-Giving." University of Zurich, Department of Economics, Working Paper No. 228 (June 1, 2016). Available at SSRN: http://ssrn.com/abstract=2787825.

Cheng, Ing-Haw, Sahil Raina, and Wei Xiong. "Wall Street and the Housing Bubble." *American Economic Review* 104 (2014): 2797–2829.

Chetty, Raj, John Friedman, Soren Leth-Petersen, Torben Nielsen, and Tore Olsen. "Active vs. Passive Decisions and Crowdout in Retirement Savings Accounts: Evidence from Denmark." *Quarterly Journal of Economics* 129, no. 3 (2014): 1141–1219.

Chhaochharia, Vidhi, George M. Korniotis, and Alok Kumar. "Prozac for Depressed States? Effect of Mood on Local Economic Recessions." *SSRN Electronic Journal* (April 30, 2011). Available at SSRN: http://ssrn.com/abstract=1814083 or http://dx.doi.org/10.2139/ssrn.1814083.

Chi, Yeguang. "Performance Evaluation of Chinese Actively Managed Stock Mutual Funds." Chicago Booth Research Paper No. 13-55; Fama-Miller Working Paper (May 2013). Available at SSRN: http://ssrn.com/abstract=2268773.

Choi, James J., Li Jin, and Hongjun Yan. "Informed Trading and Expected Returns" (January 22, 2016). Available at SSRN: https://ssrn.com/abstract=2193733 or http://dx.doi.org/10.2139/ssrn.2193733.

Choi, James J., David Laibson, and Brigitte C. Madrian. "Why Does the Law of One Price Fail? An Experiment on Index Mutual Funds." *Review of Financial Studies* 23, no. 4 (2009): 1405–1432.

Choi, James J., David Laibson, Brigitte C. Madrian, and Andrew Metrick. "Defined Contribution Pensions: Plan Rules, Participant Decisions, and the Path of Least Resistance." *Tax Policy and the Economy* 16 (2002): 67–114.

Choi, Jongmoo Jay, Haim Kedar-Levy, and Sean Sehyun Yoo. "Are Individual or Institutional Investors the Agents of Bubbles? " (July 17, 2014). Available at SSRN: http://ssrn.com/abstract=2023766.

Christiaensen, Luc, and Lei Pan. "On the Fungibility of Spending and Earnings: Evidence from Rural China and Tanzania" (December 1, 2012). World Bank Policy Research Working Paper No. 6298. Available at SSRN: https://ssrn.com/abstract=2194779.

Christian Science Monitor. "Get Rich Quick: A Runaway Dream." Accessed August 13, 2016. http://www.csmonitor.com/2000/0426/p15s2.html.

Cici, Gjergji. "The Relation of the Disposition Effect to Mutual Fund Trades and Performance" (December 7, 2010), available at SSRN: https://ssrn.com/abstract=645841 or http://dx.doi.org/10.2139/ssrn.645841.

Cici, Gjergji, Alexander Kempf, and Alexander Puetz. "The Valuation of Hedge Funds' Equity Positions." AFA 2012 Chicago Meetings Paper (May 16, 2013). Available at SSRN: http://ssrn.com/abstract=1664461.

Cici, Gjergji, Alexander Kempf, and Christoph Sorhage. "Do Financial Advisors Provide Tangible Benefits for Investors? Evidence from Tax-Motivated Mutual Fund Flows" (July 2015). EFA 2014 Lugano Meetings Paper. Available at SSRN: https://ssrn.com/abstract=2177401 or http://dx.doi.org/10.2139/ssrn.2177401.

Clark, Andrew, Claudia Senik, and Katsunori Yamada. "The Joneses in Japan: Income Comparisons and Financial Satisfaction" (March 14, 2013). ISER Discussion Paper No. 866. Available at SSRN: https://ssrn.com/abstract=2233223 or http://dx.doi.org/10.2139/ssrn.2233223.

Clarke, Roger G., Scott Krase, and Meir Statman. "Tracking Errors, Regret and Tactical Asset Allocation." *Journal of Portfolio Management* 20 (1994): 16–24.

Clarke, Roger G., and Meir Statman. "The DJIA Crossed 652,230." *Journal of Portfolio Management* 26, no. 2 (Winter 2000): 89–92.

Cobb-Clark, Deborah A., Sonja C. Kassenboehmer, and Mathias Sinning. "Locus of Control and Savings." *Journal of Banking and Finance* 73 (2016): 113–130.

Coget, Jean-François, Christophe Haag, and Donald E. Gibson. "Anger and Fear in Decision-Making: The Case of Film Directors on Set." *European Management Journal* 29, no. 6 (2011): 476–490.

Cohen, George M., P. de Fontenay, Gordon L. Gould, Martin C. Sirera, and Zvi Bodie. "Long-Run Risk in Stocks." *Financial Analysts Journal* 52, no. 5 (1996), 72–76.

Cohen, Jerome B., Edward D. Zinbarg, and Arthur Zeikel. *Investment Analysis and Portfolio Management*. Homewood, IL: R. D. Irwin, 1977.

Cohen, Lauren, Christopher Malloy, and Lukasz Pomorski. "Decoding Inside Information." *Journal of Finance* 67, no. 3 (June 2012): 1009–1043.

Cohn, Alain, Jan Engelmann, Ernst Fehr, and Michel André Maréchal. "Evidence for Countercyclical Risk Aversion: An Experiment with Financial Professionals." *American Economic Review* 105, no. 2 (2015): 860–885.

Cohn, Alain, Ernst Fehr, and Michel André Maréchal. "Business Culture and Dishonesty in the Banking Industry." *Nature* 516 (2014): 86–89.

Cole, Shawn Allen, Martin Kanz, and Leora F. Klapper. "Incentivizing Calculated Risk-Taking: Evidence from an Experiment with Commercial Bank Loan Officers." *Journal of Finance* 70, no. 2 (April 2015): 537–575.

Collins, J. Michael, and Maximilian D. Schmeiser. "Estimating the Effects of Foreclosure Counseling for Troubled Borrowers" (July 19, 2010), available at SSRN: https://ssrn.com/abstract=1645339 or http://dx.doi.org/10.2139/ssrn.1645339.

Constantinides, George M. "A Note on the Suboptimality of Dollar-Cost Averaging as an Investment Policy." *Journal of Financial and Quantitative Analysis* 14, no. 2 (June 1979): 443–450.

Cook, Kirsten A., William Meyer, and William Reichenstein. "Tax-Efficient Withdrawal Strategies." *Financial Analysts Journal* 71 (2015): 91–107.

Cookson, J. Anthony. "When Saving Is Gambling." Finance Down Under 2015: Building on the Best from the Cellars of Finance Paper (January 27, 2016). Available at SSRN: http://ssrn.com/abstract=2517126 or http://dx.doi.org/10.2139/ssrn.2517126.

Cooper, Gael Fashingbauer. "'Bachelorette' Missing out on Facebook Millions." *TODAY.com*. February 23, 2012. http://www.today.com/popculture/bachelorette-missing-out-facebook-millions-176682.

Cooper, Michael J., Orlin Dimitrov, and P. Raghavendra Rau. "A Rose.com by Any Other Name." *Journal of Finance* 56, no. 6 (December 2001): 2371–2388.

Cooper, Michael J., Huseyin Gulen, and Raghavendra Rau. "Changing Names with Style: Mutual Fund Name Changes and Their Effects on Fund Flows." *Journal of Finance* 60, no. 6 (2005): 2825–2858.

Cooper, Michael J., Ajay Khorana, Igor Osobov, Ajay Patel, and Rau Raghavendra. "Managerial Actions in Response to a Market Downturn: Valuation Effects of Name Changes in the Dot.com Decline." *Journal of Corporate Finance* 11 (2005): 319–335.

Cooper, Robert G., Scott J. Edgett, and Elko J. Kleinschmidt. *Portfolio Management for New Products*. Reading, MA: Addison-Wesley, 1998.

Cosmides, Leda. "The Logic of Social Exchange: Has Natural Selection Shaped How Humans Reason? Studies with Wason Selection Task." *Cognition* 31 (1989): 187–276.

Coval, Joshua D., and Tyler Shumway. "Do Behavioral Biases Affect Prices?" *Journal of Finance* 60 (2005): 1–34.

Cremers, Martijn, Miguel A. Ferreira, Pedro P. Matos, and Laura T. Starks. "Indexing and Active Fund Management: International Evidence." *Journal of Financial Economics* 120, no. 3 (June 2016): 539–560.

Cronqvist, Henrik, and Stephan Siegel. "The Origins of Savings Behavior." *Journal of Political Economy* 123 (2015): 123–169.

Cronqvist, Henrik, and Stephan Siegel. "Why Do Individuals Exhibit Investment Biases?" *SSRN Electronic Journal* (May 22, 2012). Available at SSRN: http://ssrn.com/abstract=2009094 or http://dx.doi.org/10.2139/ssrn.2009094.

Cvijanovic, Dragana, and Christophe Spaenjers. "Real Estate as a Luxury Good: Non-Resident Demand and Property Prices in Paris" (January 7, 2015). HEC Paris Research Paper No. FIN-2015-1073. Available at SSRN: http://ssrn.com/abstract=2546689 or http://dx.doi.org/10.2139/ssrn.2546689.

Da, Zhi, Borja Larrain, Clemens Sialm, and José Tessada. "Coordinated Noise Trading: Evidence from Pension Fund Reallocations" (August 31, 2015). Available at SSRN: http://ssrn.com/abstract=2558773 or http://dx.doi.org/10.2139/ssrn.2558773.

Da, Zhi, Umit G. Gurun, and Mitch Warachka. "Frog in the Pan: Continuous Information and Momentum." *Review of Financial Studies* 27 (2014): 3389–3440.

Da, Zhi, Ravi Jagannathan, and Jianfeng Shen. "Building Castles in the Air: Evidence from Industry IPO Waves" (November 2012). NBER Working Paper No. w18555. Available at SSRN: https://ssrn.com/abstract=2179393.

Dahlquist, Magnus, Jose V. Martinez, and Paul Söderlind. "Individual Investor Activity and Performance." University of St. Gallen, School of Finance Research Paper No. 2014/8 (March 2015). Available at SSRN: http://ssrn.com/abstract=2432930.

Damasio, Antonio R. *Descartes' Error: Emotion, Reason, and the Human Brain.* New York: HarperCollins, 1994.

Damisch, Lysann, Thomas Mussweiler, and Barbara Stoberock. "Keep Your Fingers Crossed! How Superstition Improves Performance." *Psychological Science* 21 (2007): 1014–1020.

Danziger, Shai, Jonathan Levav, and Liora Avnaim-Pesso. "Extraneous Factors in Judicial Decisions." *Proceedings of the National Academy of Science of the United States of America* 108 (2011): 6889–6892.

Das, Sanjiv, Harry Markowitz, Jonathan Scheid, and Meir Statman. "Portfolio Optimization with Mental Accounts." *Journal of Financial and Quantitative Analysis* 45 (2010): 311–334.

Das, Sanjiv, Harry Markowitz, Jonathan Scheid, and Meir Statman. "Portfolios for Investors Who Want to Reach Their Goals While Staying on the Mean–Variance Efficient Frontier." *Journal of Wealth Management* 14 (2011): 25–31.

Das, Sanjiv R., and Priya Raghubir. "The Long and Short of It: Why Are Stocks with Shorter Runs Preferred?" *Journal of Consumer Research* 36 (2010): 964–982.

Davidoff, Thomas. "Reverse Mortgage Demographics and Collateral Performance" (February 25, 2014). Available at SSRN: http://ssrn.com/abstract=2399942 or http://dx.doi.org/10.2139/ssrn.2399942.

De, Sankar, Naveen R. Gondhi, and Subrata Sarkar. "Behavioral Biases, Investor Performance, and Wealth Transfers between Investor Groups" (November 15, 2011). Available at SSRN: http://ssrn.com/abstract=2022992.

Deason, Stephen, Shivaram Rajgopal, and Gregory B. Waymire. "Who Gets Swindled in Ponzi Schemes?" (March 28, 2015). Available at SSRN: http://ssrn.com/abstract=2586490 or http://dx.doi.org/10.2139/ssrn.2586490.

DellaVigna, Stefano, and Ethan Kaplan. "The Fox News Effect: Media Bias and Voting." *Quarterly Journal of Economics* 122, no. 3 (2007): 1187–1234.

DellaVigna, Stefano, and Ulrike Malmendier. "Paying Not to Go to the Gym." *American Economic Review* 96 (2006): 694–719.

DeMarzo, Peter M., Ron Kaniel, and Ilan Kremer. "Relative Wealth Concerns and Financial Bubbles." *Review of Financial Studies* 21 (2008): 19–50.

De Neve, Jan-Emmanuel, and James H. Fowler. "Credit Card Borrowing and the Monoamine Oxidase A (MAOA) Gene." *Journal of Economic Behavior and Organization* 107, Part B (November 2014): 428–439.

DeVoe, Sanford E., and Julian House. "Time, Money and Happiness: How Does Putting a Price on Time Affect our Ability to Smell the Roses?" *Journal of Experimental Social Psychology* 48 (2012): 466–474.

Dhar, Ravi, William N. Goetzmann, "Bubble Investors: What Were They Thinking?" (August 17, 2006). Yale ICF Working Paper No. 06-22. Available at SSRN: https://ssrn.com/abstract=683366.

Dhar, Ravi, and Ning Zhu. "Up Close and Personal: Investor Sophistication and the Disposition Effect." *Management Science* 52, no. 5 (May 2006): 726–740.

Dholakia, Utpal, Leona Tam, Sunyee Yoon, and Nancy Wong. "The Ant and the Grasshopper: Understanding Personal Saving Orientation of Consumers." *Journal of Consumer Research* 43 (2016): 134–155.

Dichev, Ilia D., and Joseph D. Piotroski. "The Long-Run Stock Returns Following Bond Ratings Changes." *Journal of Finance* 56 (2001): 173–203.

Dichev, Ilia. "What Are Stock Investors' Actual Historical Returns? Evidence from Dollar-Weighted Returns." *American Economic Review* 97 (2007): 386–402.

Dichev, Ilia, and Gwen Yu. "Higher Risk, Lower Returns: What Hedge Fund Investors Really Earn." *Journal of Financial Economics* 100 (2011): 248–263.

Diether, Karl B., Christopher J. Malloy, and Anna Scherbina. "Difference of Opinion and the Cross-Section of Stock Returns." *Journal of Finance* 57 (2002): 2113–2141.

Dietvorst, Berkeley J., Joseph P. Simmons, and Cade Massey. "Algorithm Aversion: People Erroneously Avoid Algorithms after Seeing Them Err." *Journal of Experimental Psychology: General* 144, no. 1 (February 2015): 114–126.

Dimmock, Stephen G., Roy Kouwenberg, Olivia S. Mitchell, and Kim Peijnenburg. "Ambiguity Aversion and Household Portfolio Choice Puzzles: Empirical Evidence." *Journal of Financial Economics* 119, no. 3 (March 2016): 559–577.

Dimson, Elroy, Paul Marsh, and Mike Staunton. "The Worldwide Equity Premium: A Smaller Puzzle," in *Handbook of the Equity Risk Premium*, ed. Rajnish Mehra, 468–514. Amsterdam: Elsevier, 2008.

Dodonova, Anna, and Yuri Khoroshilov. "Anchoring and Transaction Utility: Evidence from On-Line Auctions." *Applied Economics Letters* 11 (2004): 307–310. Available at SSRN: http://ssrn.com/abstract=870445.

Dokko, Jane, Geng Li, and Jessica Hayes. "Credit Scores and Committed Relationships." FEDS Working Paper No. 2015-081 (August 29, 2015). Available at SSRN: http://ssrn.com/abstract=2667158 or http://dx.doi.org/10.2139/ssrn.2667158.

Doran, James S., David R. Peterson, and Colby Wright. "Confidence, Opinions of Market Efficiency, and Investment Behavior of Finance Professors." *Journal of Financial Markets* 13, no. 1 (February 2010): 174–195.

Dorn, Daniel, and Paul Sengmueller. "Trading as Entertainment?" *Management Science* 55, no. 4 (2009): 591–603.

Driebusch, Corrie, and Eric Sylvers. "Ferrari IPO Prices at Top of Range." *Wall Street Journal*, October 20, 2015. http://www.wsj.com/articles/ferrari-ipo-prices-at-high-end-of-range-1445375676?alg=y.

Duarte, Fabian, and Justine S. Hastings. "Fettered Consumers and Sophisticated Firms: Evidence from Mexico's Privatized Social Security Market." NBER Working Paper No. 18582 (December 2012).

Duckworth, Angela, and David Weir. "Personality and Response to the Financial Crisis" (December 1, 2011). Michigan Retirement Research Center Research Paper No. WP 2011-260. Available at SSRN: https://ssrn.com/abstract=2006595 or http://dx.doi.org/10.2139/ssrn.2006595.

Dunn, Lea, and Joandrea Hoegg. "The Impact of Fear on Emotional Brand Attachment." *Journal of Consumer Research* 41, no. 1 (June 2014): 152–168.

Edmans, Alex. "Does the Stock Market Fully Value Intangibles? Employee Satisfaction and Equity Prices." *Journal of Financial Economics* 101 (2011): 621–640.

Edmans, Alex, Diego Garcia, and Oyvind Norli. "Sports Sentiment and Stock Returns." *Journal of Finance* 62 (2007): 1967–1998.

Einhorn, Hillel J., and Robin M. Hogarth. "Confidence in Judgment: Persistence of the Illusion of Validity." *Psychological Review* 85, no. 5 (September 1978): 395–416.

Eisenstein, Eric, and Stephen Hoch. "Intuitive Compounding: Framing, Temporal Perspective, and Expertise." Working Paper. December 2005. http://eric-eisenstein.com/papers/Eisenstein&Hoch-Compounding.pdf.

Ekman, Paul. "Are There Basic Emotions?" *Psychological Review* 99 (1992): 550–553.

Ellenberger, Jack S., Ellen P. Mahar, and Law Librarians' Society of Washington, D.C. *Legislative History of the Securities Act of 1933 and Securities Exchange Act of 1934.* South Hackensack, NJ: Published for the Law Librarians' Society of Washington, DC, by F. B. Rothman, 1973.

Ellsworth, Phoebe C., and Barbara O'Brien. "Prosecutorial Blind Spots: Features of the Adversarial Criminal Justice System That Promote Confirmation Bias." Society of Experimental Social Psychology, Annual Conference (October 2009), Portland, ME.

Employee Benefit Research Institute. "History of 401(k) Plans: An Update" (February 2005). http://www.ebri.org/pdf/publications/facts/0205fact.a.pdf.

Engelberg, Joseph, and Christopher A. Parsons. "Worrying about the Stock Market: Evidence from Hospital Admissions." *Journal of Finance* 71 (2016): 1227–1250.

Eraker, Bjorn, and Mark J. Ready. ""Do Investors Overpay for Stocks with Lottery-Like Payoffs? An Examination of the Returns on OTC Stocks." *Journal of Financial Economics* 115, no. 3 (March 2015): 486–504.

Erdem, Orhan, Evren Arık, and Serkan Yüksel. "Trading Puzzle, Puzzling Trade" (April 3, 2013). Available at SSRN: http://ssrn.com/abstract=2244186.

Erev, Ido, Thomas S. Wallsten, and David V. Budescu. "Simultaneous Over- and Underconfidence: The Role of Error in Judgment Processes." *Psychological Review* 101, no. 3 (July 1994): 519–527.

Etheber, Thomas, Andreas Hackethal, and Steffen Meyer. "Trading on Noise: Moving Average Trading Heuristics and Private Investors" (November 7, 2014). Available at SSRN: http://ssrn.com/abstract=2520346.

Fair, Ray. "Events That Shook the Market." *Journal of Business* 75 (2002): 713–731.

Falsetta, Diana, and Richard A. White. "The Impact of Income Tax Withholding Position and Stock Position on the Sale of Stock." *Journal of the American Taxation Association* 27, no. 1 (2005): 1–23.

Fama, Eugene F. "Efficient Capital Markets: II." *Journal of Finance* 46 (1991): 1575–1617.

Fama, Eugene F. "The Behavior of Stock-Market Prices." *Journal of Business* 38 (1965): 34–105.

Fama, Eugene. "Ideas That Changed the Theory and Practice of Investing: A Conversation with Eugene F. Fama." *Journal of Investment Consulting* 9 (2008): 6–14.

Fama, Eugene, and Kenneth French. "The Cross-Section of Expected Stock Returns." *Journal of Finance* 47 (1992): 427–465.

Fama, Eugene F., and Kenneth R. French. "Luck versus Skill in the Cross-Section of Mutual Fund Returns." *Journal of Finance* 65, no. 5 (October 2010): 1915–1947.

Fang, Jiali, Ben Jacobsen, and Yafeng Qin. "Predictability of the Simple Technical Trading Rules: An Out-of-Sample Test." *Review of Financial Economics* 23, no. 1 (2014): 30–45.

Fedyk, Anastassia. "Asymmetric Naivete: Beliefs about Self-Control" (February 22, 2016). Available at SSRN: http://ssrn.com/abstract=2727499 or http://dx.doi .org/10.2139/ssrn.2727499.

Feinstein, Justin S., Ralph Adolphs, Antonio Damasio, and Daniel Tranel. "The Human Amygdala and the Induction and Experience of Fear." *Current Biology* 21, no. 1 (January 2011): 34–38.

Feng, Lei, and Mark Seasholes. "Do Investor Sophistication and Trading Experience Eliminate Behavioral Biases in Financial Markets?" *Review of Finance* 9 (2005): 305–351.

Fenton-O'Creevy, Mark, Nigel Nicholson, Emma Soane, and Paul Willman. "Trading on Illusions: Unrealistic Perceptions of Control and Trading Performance." *Journal of Occupational and Organizational Psychology* 76 (2003): 53–68.

Fernandes, Daniel, John G. Lynch Jr., and Richard G. Netemeyer. "Financial Literacy, Financial Education, and Downstream Financial Behaviors." *Management Science* 60, no. 8 (2014): 1861–1883.

Filipski, Mateusz J., Ling Jin, Xiaobo Zhang, and Kevin Z. Chen. "Living Like There's No Tomorrow: Saving and Spending Following the Sichuan Earthquake." IFPRI Discussion Paper 1461 (September 18, 2015). Available at SSRN: http://ssrn .com/abstract=2685305.

Financial Crisis Inquiry Report, 2011. Washington, DC: US Government Printing Office.

Financial Engines, Inc. "Financial Engines: For Individuals." https://corp .financialengines.com/individuals/.

FINRA Foundation. "Americans' Financial Capability Growing Stronger, but Not for All Groups: FINRA Foundation Study," July 12, 2016. https://www.finra.org/ newsroom/2016/americans-financial-capability-growing-stronger-not-all-groups-finra-foundation-study.

Fishbach, Ayelet, and James Shah. "Self-Control in Action: Implicit Dispositions toward Goals and away from Temptations." *Journal of Personality and Social Psychology* 90, no. 5 (2006): 820–832.

Fischhoff, Baruch. "Debiasing." In *Judgment under Uncertainty: Shortcuts and Biases* ed. Daniel Kahneman, Paul Slovic, and Amos Tversky, 422–444. Cambridge, UK: Cambridge University Press, 1982.

Fisher, Kenneth L., and Meir Statman. "A Behavioral Framework for Time Diversification." *Financial Analysts Journal* 55 (1999): 88–97.

Fisher, Kenneth, and Meir Statman. "Investor Sentiment and Stock Returns." *Financial Analysts Journal* 56 (2000): 16–23.

Fitzpatrick, Dan. "Calpers to Exit Hedge Funds." *Wall Street Journal,* September 15, 2014. http://www.wsj.com/articles/calpers-to-exit-hedge-funds-1410821083.

Flyvbjerg, Bent. "How Optimism Bias and Strategic Misrepresentation in Early Project Development Undermine Implementation." *Concept Report,* no. 17 (2007): 41–45.

FMR LLC. "Fidelity® Poll Showcases Active Investors' Confidence." May 16, 2012. http://www.businesswire.com/news/home/20120516005964/en/Fidelity®-Poll-Showcases-Active-Investors'-Confidence#.VaJxbflViko.

Foerster, Stephen, Juhani Linnainmaa, Brian Melzer, and Alessandro Previtero. "Retail Financial Advice: Does One Size Fit All?" *Journal of Finance,* forthcoming.

Foster, F. Douglas, and Geoff Warren. "Interviews with Institutional Investors: The How and Why of Active Investing." *Journal of Behavioral Finance* 17 (2016): 60–84.

Frazzini, Andrea. "The Disposition Effect and Under-Reaction to News." *Journal of Finance* 61 (2006): 2017–2046.

Frederick, Shane. "Cognitive Reflection and Decision Making." *Journal of Economic Perspectives* 19 (2005): 25–42.

Freeman, Andrea. "Payback: A Structural Analysis of the Credit Card Problem." *Arizona Law Review* 55, no. 151 (March 2013). Available at SSRN: http://ssrn.com/abstract=2231738.

French, Kenneth. "The Cost of Active Investing." *Journal of Finance* 63, no. 4 (2008): 1537–1573.

Friedman, Milton, and Leonard J. Savage. "The Utility Analysis of Choices Involving Risk." *Journal of Political Economy* LVI (August 1948): 279–304.

Friedman, Milton. *A Theory of the Consumption Function.* Princeton, NJ: Princeton University Press, 1957.

Frydman, Cary, Nicholas Barberis, Colin Camerer, Peter Bossaerts, and Antonio Rangel. "Using Neural Data to Test a Theory of Investor Behavior: An Application to Realization Utility." *Journal of Finance* 69 (2014): 907–946.

Frydman, Cary, and Colin Camerer. "Neural Evidence of Regret and Its Implications for Investor Behavior." *Review of Financial Studies,* http://rfs.oxfordjournals.org/content/29/11/3108.

Frydman, Cary, Samuel M. Hartzmark, and David H. Solomon. "Rolling Mental Accounts" (August 26, 2015). Available at SSRN: http://ssrn.com/abstract=2653929 or http://dx.doi.org/10.2139/ssrn.2653929.

Frydman, Cary, and Antonio Rangel. "Debiasing the Disposition Effect by Reducing the Saliency of Information about a Stock's Purchase Price." *Journal of Economic Behavior & Organization* 107 (2014): 541–552.

Fuchs-Schundeln, Nicola, and Michael Haliassos. "Does Product Familiarity Matter for Participation?" (May 19, 2015). Available at SSRN: https://ssrn.com/abstract=2384746 or http://dx.doi.org/10.2139/ssrn.2384746.

Fung, William, David A. Hsieh, Narayan Y. Naik, and Melvyn Teo. "Growing the Asset Management Franchise: Evidence from Hedge Fund Firms" (July 21, 2015). Available at SSRN: http://ssrn.com/abstract=2542476 or http://dx.doi.org/10.2139/ssrn.2542476.

Fung, William, David A. Hsieh, Narayan Y. Naik, and Tarun Ramadorai. "Hedge Funds: Performance, Risk, and Capital Formation." *Journal of Finance* 63 (2008): 1777–1803.

Gabaix, Xavier, and David Laibson. "Shrouded Attributes, Consumer Myopia, and Information Suppression in Competitive Markets." *Quarterly Journal of Economics* 121, no. 2 (2006): 505–540.

Galiani, Sebastian, Paul J. Gertler, and Rosangela Bando. "Non-Contributory Pensions." NBER Working Paper No. w19775 (January 2014). Available at SSRN: http://ssrn.com/abstract=2374552.

Gallaher, Steven T., Ron Kaniel, and Laura T. Starks. "Advertising and Mutual Funds: From Families to Individual Funds." CEPR Discussion Paper No. DP10329 (January 2015). Available at SSRN: http://ssrn.com/abstract=2554403.

Gallup Organization. "UBS Index of Investor Optimism." December 2007.

Gallup Organization. "UBS/PaineWebber Index of Investor Optimism." September 2001.

Gambetti, Elisa, and Fiorella Giusberti. "The Effect of Anger and Anxiety Traits on Investment Decisions." *Journal of Economic Psychology* 33 (2012): 1059–1069.

Gangaramany, Alok. "Dustin Hoffman's Mental Accounting." *YouTube* video. April 7, 2013. https://www.youtube.com/watch?v=t96LNX6tk0U.

Ganzach, Yoav. "Judging Risk and Return of Financial Assets." *Organizational Behavior and Human Decision Processes* 83 (2000): 353–370.

Gao, Meng, and Jiekun Huang. "Capitalizing on Capitol Hill: Informed Trading by Hedge Fund Managers." Fifth Singapore International Conference on Finance 2011 ; AFA 2012 Chicago Meetings Paper; Fifth Singapore International Conference on Finance 2011; *Journal of Financial Economics* (JFE), forthcoming (November 10, 2015). Available at SSRN: https://ssrn.com/abstract=1707181 or http://dx.doi.org/10.2139/ssrn.1707181.

Garvey, Ryan, Anthony Murphy, and Fei Wu. "Do Losses Linger? Evidence from Proprietary Stock Traders." *Journal of Portfolio Management* 33 (2007): 75–83.

Gathergood, John, and Joerg Weber. "Self-Control, Financial Literacy and the Co-Holding Puzzle." *Journal of Economic Behavior and Organization* 107 (2014): 455–469.

Geczy, Christopher, David Levin, and Robert Stambaugh. "Investing in Socially Responsible Mutual Funds." Working Paper, Wharton (October 2005).

Geczy, Christopher, and Mikhail Samonov. "212 Years of Price Momentum (The World's Longest Backtest: 1801–2012)" (August 1, 2013). Available at SSRN: http://ssrn.com/abstract=2292544.

Geiger, Keri, Liam Vaughan, and Julia Verlaine. "Currency Probe Widens as U.S. Said to Target Markups." *Bloomberg.* June 18, 2014. http://www.bloomberg.com/news/articles/2014-06-19/currency-probe-widens-as-u-s-said-to-target-markups.

George, Thomas J., and Chuan-Yang Hwang. "The 52-Week High and Momentum Investing." *Journal of Finance* 59 (2004): 2145–2176.

Giannini, Robert C., Paul J. Irvine, and Tao Shu. "Do Local Investors Know More? A Direct Examination of Individual Investors' Information Set." Asian Finance Association (AsFA) 2013 Conference (March 31, 2015). Available at SSRN: http://ssrn.com/abstract=1866267.

Gigerenzer, Gerd, and Klaus Hug. "Domain-Specific Reasoning: Social Contracts, Cheating and Perspective Change." *Cognition* 43 (1992): 127–171.

Gine, Xavier, Dean Karlan, and Jonathan Zinman. "Put Your Money Where Your Butt Is: A Commitment Contract for Smoking Cessation." *American Economic Journal: Applied Economics* 2 (October 2010): 213–235.

Glaser, Markus, Florian Haagen, and Torsten Walther. "Preference Aggregation in Investment Clubs an Explanation for Underdiversification?" *SSRN Electronic Journal* (April 2014). Available at SSRN: http://ssrn.com/abstract=2424661 or http://dx.doi.org/10.2139/ssrn.2424661.

Glassman, James K., and Kevin A. Hassett. "Dow 36000 Revisited." *Wall Street Journal,* August 1, 2002. Available at http://online.wsj.com/news/articles/SB10 28159861587125680#printMode.

Glick, Ira. "A Social Psychological Study of Futures Trading." PhD diss., University of Chicago, 1957.

Goetzmann, William N. "Bubble Investing: Learning from History" (January 11, 2016). Available at SSRN: https://ssrn.com/abstract=2784281 or http://dx.doi .org/10.2139/ssrn.2784281.

Goetzmann, William N., and Simon Huang. "Momentum in Imperial Russia." NBER Working Paper No. w21700 (November 2015). Available at SSRN: http://ssrn .com/abstract=2687848.

Goetzmann, William N., Dasol Kim, Alok Kumar, and Qin (Emma) Wang. "Weather-Induced Mood, Institutional Investors, and Stock Returns" (September 8, 2014). Available at SSRN: https://ssrn.com/abstract=2323852 or http://dx.doi .org/10.2139/ssrn.2323852.

Goetzmann, William N., Dasol Kim, and Robert J. Shiller. "Crash Beliefs from Investor Surveys" (March 19, 2016). Available at SSRN: http://ssrn.com/ abstract=2750638 or http://dx.doi.org/10.2139/ssrn.2750638.

Goetzmann, William N., and Alok Kumar. "Equity Portfolio Diversification." *Review of Finance* 12 (2008): 433–463.

Goldstein, Daniel G., Hal E. Hershfield, and Shlomo Benartzi. "The Illusion of Wealth and Its Reversal" *Journal of Marketing Research* 53 (2016): 804–813.

Gottesman, Aron A., Matthew R. Morey, and Menahem Rosenberg. "Outperformance, Underperformance and Mutual Fund Flows in Up and Down Markets." *SSRN Journal SSRN Electronic Journal* (Jaunary 5, 2013). Available at SSRN: http:// ssrn.com/abstract=2197570 or http://dx.doi.org/10.2139/ssrn.2197570.

Goyal, Amit, and Sunil Wahal. "The Selection and Termination of Investment Management Firms by Plan Sponsors." *Journal of Finance* 63, no. 4 (August 2008): 1805–1847.

Goyal, Amit, and Ivo Welch. "Predicting the Equity Premium with Dividend Ratios." *Management Science* 49 (2003): 639–654.

Graham, John R., Campbell R. Harvey, and Hai Huang. "Investor Competence, Trading Frequency, and Home Bias." *Management Science* 55 (2009): 1094–1106.

Graham, John R., and Alok Kumar. "Do Dividend Clienteles Exist? Evidence on Dividend Preferences of Retail Investors." *Journal of Finance* 61 (2006): 1305–1336.

Grant, Andrew R., Petko S. Kalev, Avanidhar Subrahmanyam, and P. Joakim Westerholm. "Stressors and Financial Market Trading: The Case of Marital Separation" (June 2, 2014). FIRN Research Paper. Available at SSRN: https://ssrn.com/abstract=2445073 or http://dx.doi.org/10.2139/ssrn.2445073.

Green, Richard C., and Burton Hollifield. "When Will Mean-Variance Efficient Portfolios Be Well Diversified?" *Journal of Finance* 47 (1992): 1785–1809.

Grinblatt, Mark, and Matti Keloharju. "What Makes Investors Trade?" *Journal of Finance* 56, no. 2 (2001): 589–616.

Grinblatt, Mark, Matti Keloharju, and Juhani T. Linnainmaa. "IQ, Trading Behavior, and Performance." *Journal of Financial Economics* 104 (2012): 339–362.

Grind, Kirsten. "Vanguard Sets Record Funds Inflow." *Wall Street Journal*, January 4, 2015. Available at http://www.wsj.com/articles/vanguard-sets-record-funds-inflow-1420430643.

Grolleau, Gilles, Martin G. Kocher, and Angela Sutan. "Cheating and Loss Aversion: Do People Lie More to Avoid a Loss?" *Management Science*, Available at http://dx.doi.org/10.1287/mnsc.2015.2313.

Gross, Leroy. *The Art of Selling Intangibles: How to Make Your Million ($) by Investing Other People's Money*. New York: New York Institute of Finance, 1982.

Grossman, Sanford, and Joseph Stiglitz. "On the Impossibility of Informationally Efficient Markets." *American Economic Review* 70 (1980): 393–408.

Grosshans, Daniel, and Stefan Zeisberger. "All's Well That Ends Well? On the Importance of How Returns Are Achieved" (July 4, 2016). Available at SSRN: http://ssrn.com/abstract=2579636 or http://dx.doi.org/10.2139/ssrn.2579636.

Gu, Bin, JaeHong Park, Prabhudev Konana, Alok Kumar, and Rajagopal Raghunathan. "Information Valuation and Confirmation Bias in Virtual Communities: Evidence from Stock Message Boards." *Information Systems Research* 24, no. 4 (November 2013): 1050–1067.

Guiso, Luigi, Paola Sapienza, and Luigi Zingales. "Time Varying Risk Aversion." NBER Working Paper No. 19284 (August 2013). *Journal of Financial Economics* (forthcoming).

Gurun, Umit G., Gregor Matvos, and Amit Seru. "Advertising Expensive Mortgages." *Journal of Finance* 71, no. 5 (October 2016): 2371–2416.

Haidt, Jonathan. "When and Why Nationalism Beats Globalism." *American Interest*, July 10, 2016. http://www.the-american-interest.com/2016/07/10/when-and-why-nationalism-beats-globalism/.

Halpern, Scott D., David A. Asch, and Kevin G. Volpp. "Commitment Contracts as a Way to Health." *British Medical Journal* 344, no. 1 (2012): 344:e522.

Han, Seunghee, Jennifer S. Lerner, and Dacher Keltner. "Feelings and Consumer Decision Making: Extending the Appraisal-Tendency Framework." *Journal of Consumer Psychology* 17, no. 3 (2007): 184–187.

Han, Seunghee, Jennifer Lerner, and Richard J. Zeckhauser. "The Disgust-Promotes-Disposal Effect." *Journal of Risk and Uncertainty* 44, no. 2 (2012): 101–113.

Harris, Lawrence, Samuel M. Hartzmark, and David H. Solomon. "Juicing the Dividend Yield: Mutual Funds and the Demand for Dividends." *Journal of Financial Economics* 116, no. 3 (June 2015): 433–451.

Harvey, Campbell R., Yan Liu, and Heqing Zhu. ". . . And the Cross-Section of Expected Returns." *Review of Financial Studies* 29, no. 1 (2016): 5–68.

Hasan, Iftekhar, Chun Keung (Stan) Hoi, Qiang Wu, and Hao Zhang. "Beauty Is in the Eye of the Beholder: The Effect of Corporate Tax Avoidance on the Cost of Bank Loans." *Journal of Financial Economics* 113, no. 1 (July 2014), 109–130.

Hastings, Justine S., and Jesse M. Shapiro. "Mental Accounting and Consumer Choice: Evidence from Commodity Price Shocks." *NBER Working Paper No. w18248* (July 2012). Available at SSRN: http://ssrn.com/abstract=2114874.

Haws, Kelly L., William O. Bearden, and Gergana Y. Nenkov. "Consumer Spending, Self-Control Effectiveness, and Outcome Elaboration Prompts." *Journal of the Academy of Marketing Science* 40, no. 5 (2012): 695–710.

Haziza, Mor, and Avner Kalay. "Broker Rebates and Investor Sophistication" (September 9, 2014). Available at SSRN: http://ssrn.com/abstract=2493693 or http://dx.doi.org/10.2139/ssrn.2493693.

Healy, Paul J., and Don A. Moore. "The Trouble with Overconfidence." *Psychological Review* 115, no. 2 (2008): 502–517.

Heath, Chip, and Amos Tversky. "Preferences and Beliefs: Ambiguity and Competence in Choice under Uncertainty." *Journal of Risk and Uncertainty* 4 (1991): 5–28.

Heimer, Rawley, Kristian Ove R. Myrseth, and Raphael Schoenle. "Yolo: Mortality Beliefs and Household Finance Puzzles." Netspar Discussion Paper No. 11/2015-070 (November 2, 2015). Available at SSRN: http://ssrn.com/abstract=2749543 or http://dx.doi.org/10.2139/ssrn.2749543.

Heimer, Rawley, and David Simon, "Facebook Finance: How Social Interaction Propagates Active Investing," Working Paper 1522, Federal Reserve Bank of Cleveland, 2015

Heimer, Rawley Z., "Friends do let friends buy stocks actively," *Journal of Economic Behavior and Organization*, 107, Part B, November (2014): 527–540

Hershfield, Hal E., Daniel G. Goldstein, William F. Sharpe, Jesse Fox, Leo Yeykelis, Laura L. Carstensen, and Jeremy N. Bailenson. "Increasing Saving Behavior through Age-Progressed Renderings of the Future Self." *Journal of Marketing Research* 48, no. SPL (November 2011): S23–S37.

Hershfield, Hal E., and Neal J. Roese. "Dual Payoff Scenario Warnings on Credit Card Statements Elicit Suboptimal Payoff Decisions." *Journal of Consumer Psychology* 25 (2015): 15–27.

Herzenstein, Michal, Sharon Horsky, and Steven S. Posavac. "Living with Terrorism or Withdrawing in Terror: Perceived Control and Consumer Avoidance." *Journal of Consumer Behaviour* 14 (2015): 228–236. Available at SSRN: http://ssrn.com/abstract=2663516.

Herzog, Stefan M., and Ralph Hertwig. "The Wisdom of Many in One Mind: Improving Individual Judgments with Dialectical Bootstrapping." *Psychological Science* 20 (2009): 231–237.

Hilary, Gilles, and Charles Hsu. "Endogenous Overconfidence in Managerial Forecasts." *Journal of Accounting and Economics* 51 (2011): 300–313.

Hillert, Alexander, and Heiko Jacobs. "The Power of Primacy: Alphabetic Bias, Investor Recognition, and Market Outcomes" (October 2014). Available at SSRN: http://ssrn.com/abstract=2390015.

Han, Bing, and David A. Hirshleifer. "Self-Enhancing Transmission Bias and Active Investing" (May 2015). Available at SSRN: https://ssrn.com/abstract=2032697 or http://dx.doi.org/10.2139/ssrn.2032697.

Hirshleifer, David, Ming Jian, and Huai Zhang. "Superstition and Financial Decision Making." Asian Finance Association (AsianFA) 2015 Conference

Paper (September 15, 2014). Available at SSRN: http://ssrn.com/abstract=1460522.

Hirshleifer, David, and Tyler Shumway. "Good Day Sunshine: Stock Returns and the Weather." *Journal of Finance* 58, no. 3 (2003): 1009–1032.

Ho, Teck, Ivan P. L. Png, and Sadat Reza. "Sunk Cost Fallacy in Driving the World's Costliest Cars." *SSRN Electronic Journal* (January 22, 2014). Available at SSRN: http://ssrn.com/abstract=2254483 or http://dx.doi.org/10.2139/ssrn.2254483.

Hoffmann, Arvid O. I. "Individual Investors' Needs and the Investment Professional: Lessons from Marketing." *Journal of Investment Consulting* 8, no. 2 (2007): 80–91.

Hoffmann, Arvid O. I., and Thomas Post. "Self-Attribution Bias in Consumer Financial Decision-Making: How Investment Returns Affect Individuals' Belief in Skill." *Journal of Behavioral and Experimental Economics* 52 (May 23, 2014): 23–28. Available at SSRN: http://ssrn.com/abstract=2367230 or http://dx.doi.org/10.2139/ssrn.2367230.

Hoffmann, Arvid O. I., and Thomas Post. "How return and risk experiences shape investor beliefs and preferences," forthcoming in *Accounting and Finance*.

Hoffmann, Arvid O. I., and Hersh Shefrin. "Technical Analysis and Individual Investors." *Journal of Economic Behavior and Organization* 107 (November 2014): 487–511. Available at SSRN: http://ssrn.com/abstract=2401230.

Hogarth, Jeanne M., and Maximilian D. Schmeiser. "Good Advice, Good Outcomes? How Financial Advice-Seeking Relates to Self-Perceived Financial Well-Being. (May 7, 2013). Available at SSRN: http://ssrn.com/abstract=2261707.

Holm, Erik. "Ackman v. Berkshire: Whose Holdings Are More Immoral?" *Wall Street Journal*, November 11, 2015. http://blogs.wsj.com/moneybeat/2015/11/11/ackman-fires-back-at-munger-says-coke-has-damaged-society/.

Holt, Charles A., and Susan K. Laury. "Risk Aversion and Incentive Effects." *American Economic Review* 92 (2002): 1644–1655.

Holton, Lisa. "Is Markowitz Wrong? Market Turmoil Fuels Nontraditional Approaches to Managing Investment Risk." *Journal of Financial Planning* 22 (January 2009): 20–26.

Hong, Harrison G., Wenxi Jiang, Na Wang, and Bin Zhao. "Trading for Status," *Review of Financial Studies* 27, no. 11 (2014): 3171–3212.

Hong, Harrison, and Marcin Kacperczyk. "The Price of Sin: The Effects of Social Norms on Markets." *Journal of Financial Economics* 93 (2009): 15–36.

Hong, Harrison G., Frank Weikai Li, and Jiangmin Xu. "Climate Risks and Market Efficiency" (May 7, 2016). Available at SSRN: http://ssrn.com/abstract=2776962 or http://dx.doi.org/10.2139/ssrn.2776962.

Hou, Kewei, Chen Xue, and Lu Zhang. "Digesting Anomalies: An Investment Approach." *Review of Financial Studies* 28, no. 3 (2015): 650–705.

Hsee, Christopher K., and Yuval Rottenstreich. "Money, Kisses, and Electric Shocks: An Affective Psychology of Risk." *Psychological Science* 12, no. 3 (2001): 185–190.

Hu, Wei-Yin, and Jason S. Scott. "Behavioral Obstacles in the Annuity Market." *Financial Analysts Journal* 63, no. 6 (2007): 71–82.

Huang, Fali, Ginger Zhe Jin, and Lixin Colin Xu. "Love, Money, and Old Age Support: Does Parental Matchmaking Matter?" (February 22, 2015). Available at SSRN: http://ssrn.com/abstract=2568471 or http://dx.doi.org/10.2139/ssrn.2568471.

Huang, (Robin) Hui. "An Empirical Study of the Incidence of Insider Trading in China" (May 12, 2007). Available at SSRN: https://ssrn.com/abstract=993341 or http://dx.doi.org/10.2139/ssrn.993341.

Huberman, Gur. "Familiarity Breeds Investment." *Review of Financial Studies*, 14, no. 3 (2001): 659–680.

Huberman, Gur, and Tomer Regev. "Contagious Speculation and a Cure for Cancer: A Nonevent That Made Stock Prices Soar." *Journal of Finance* 56 (2001): 387–396.

Huberman, Gur, and William Schwert. "Information Aggregation, Inflation, and the Pricing of Indexed Bonds." *Journal of Political Economy* 93 (1985): 92–114.

Hurd, Michael D., Angela Duckworth, Susann Rohwedder, and David R. Weir. "Personality Traits and Economic Preparation for Retirement." September 1, 2012. Available at SSRN: http://ssrn.com/abstract=2239766.

Hurd, Michael D., and Susann Rohwedder. "Measuring Economic Preparation for Retirement: Income versus Consumption" (September 2015). Available at SSRN: http://ssrn.com/abstract=2712684 or http://dx.doi.org/10.2139/ssrn.2712684.

Hussey, Kristin. "After Ruling, Paul Smith's College Won't Get Weills' $20 Million Renaming Gift." *New York Times*, October 22, 2015. http://www.nytimes.com/2015/10/23/nyregion/weills-20-million-renaming-gift-to-paul-smiths-college-is-withdrawn.html?_r=0.

Hutton, Irena, Danling Jiang, and Alok Kumar. "Political Values, Culture, and Corporate Litigation." *Management Science* 61, no. 12 (April 17, 2015): 2905–2925.

Hvide, Hans K., and Jae Ho Lee. "Does Source of Income Affect Risk and Intertemporal Choices?" (February 25, 2016). Available at SSRN: http://ssrn.com/abstract=2648604 or http://dx.doi.org/10.2139/ssrn.2648604.

Hvide, Hans K. and Per Östberg. "Stock Investments at Work" (February 2014). CEPR Discussion Paper No. DP9837. Available at SSRN: https://ssrn.com/abstract=2444838.

Hwang, Chuan-Yang, Sheridan Titman, and Yuxi Wang. "Is It Who You Know or What You Know? Evidence from IPO Allocations and Mutual Fund Performance" (August 20, 2015). Asian Finance Association (AsianFA) 2016 Conference. Available at SSRN: https://ssrn.com/abstract=2648732 or http://dx.doi.org/10.2139/ssrn.2648732.

Hymowitz, Carol. "Why $100,000 Salary May Yield Retirement Flipping Burgers." *Bloomberg* (September 23, 2013). http://www.bloomberg.com/news/2013-09-23/why-100-000-salary-may-yield-retirement-flipping-burgers.html.

Hyytinen, Ari, and Hanna Putkuri. "Household Optimism and Borrowing" (May 8, 2012). Bank of Finland Research Discussion Paper No. 21/2012. Available at SSRN: https://ssrn.com/abstract=2101025 or http://dx.doi.org/10.2139/ssrn.2101025.

Ibbotson, Roger G., Peng Chen, and Kevin X. Zhu. "The ABCs of Hedge Funds: Alphas, Betas, and Costs." *Financial Analysts Journal* 67 (2011): 15–25.

Ifcher, John, and Homa Zarghamee. "Happiness and Time Preference: The Effect of Positive Affect in a Random-Assignment Experiment." *American Economic Review* 101 (2011): 3109–3129.

Internal Revenue Service. "IRA Required Minimum Distribution Worksheet." https://www.irs.gov/pub/irs-tege/uniform_rmd_wksht.pdf

InterNations GmbH. "Status Symbols around the World." https://www.internations .org/about-internations/.

Isaac, Mike. "For Start-Ups, How Many Angels Is Too Many?" *New York Times,* July 6, 2015. http://www.nytimes.com/2015/07/07/technology/for-start-ups-how-many-angels-is-too-many.html?ref=business.

Israel, Ronen, and Thomas Maloney. "Understanding Style Premia." *Journal of Investing* 23 (2014): 15–22.

Iyengar, Sheena, Wei Jiang, and Gur Huberman. "How Much Choice Is Too Much?: Contributions to 401(k) Retirement Plans." In *Pension Design and Structure: New Lessons from Behavioral Finance,* ed. O. S. Mitchell and S. P. Utkus, 83–95. New York: Oxford University Press, 2004.

Jachimowicz, Jon M., Shannon Duncan, and Elke U. Weber. "Default-Switching: The Hidden Cost of Defaults" (February 3, 2016). Available at SSRN: http://ssrn .com/abstract=2727301 or http://dx.doi.org/10.2139/ssrn.2727301.

Jackson, Andrew. "The Aggregate Behaviour of Individual Investors" (July 29, 2003) Available at SSRN: http://papers.ssrn.com/s013/papers.cfm?abstract_ id=536942.

Jackson, Robert J., Wei Jiang, and Joshua Mitts. "How Quickly Do Markets Learn? Private Information Dissemination in a Natural Experiment." Columbia Business School Research Paper No. 15-6 (April 2015). Available at SSRN: http://ssrn.com/abstract=2544128.

Jacobe, Dennis. "More Nonretirees Expect to Rely on Social Security." Gallup Organization. April 30, 2012. http://www.gallup.com/poll/154277/ nonretirees-expect-rely-social-security.aspx.

Jenkinson, Tim, Howard Jones, and Jose V. Martinez. "Picking Winners? Investment Consultants' Recommendations of Fund Managers." *Journal of Finance* (October 2015). Available at SSRN: http://ssrn.com/abstract=2327042.

Jennings, Angel. "Nest Eggs Emptying, not the Nests." *New York Times,* July 14, 2007, B1.

Jenter, Dirk, and Katharina Lewellen. "CEO Preferences and Acquisitions." *Journal of Finance* 70, no. 6 (December 2015): 2813–2852.

Jiang, Chao. "Legal Expertise and Insider Trading" (April 2015). Available at SSRN: http://ssrn.com/abstract=2658969.

Juster, Thomas F., and John Laitner. "New Evidence on Altruism: A Study of TIAA-CREF Retirees." *American Economic Review* 86, no. 4 (September 1996): 893–908.

Kadan, Ohad, Roni Michaely, and Pamela C. Moulton. "Speculating on Private Information: Buy the Rumor, Sell the News" (March 10, 2015). Available at SSRN: http://ssrn.com/abstract=2427282 or http://dx.doi.org/10.2139/ ssrn.2427282.

Kahneman, Daniel. *Thinking, Fast and Slow.* New York: Farrar, Straus and Giroux, 2011.

Kahneman, Daniel, and Angus Deaton. "High Income Improves Evaluation of Life but not Emotional Well-Being." *Proceedings of the National Academy of Sciences of the United States of America* 107 (2010): 16489–16493.

Kahneman, Daniel, and Shane Frederick. "Representativeness Revisited." In *Heuristics and Biases: The Psychology of Intuitive Judgment,* ed. Thomas Gilovich, Dale Griffin, and Daniel Kahneman, 49–81. New York: Cambridge University Press, 2002.

Kahneman, Daniel, and Gary Klein. "Conditions for Intuitive Expertise: A Failure to Disagree." *American Psychologist* 64, no. 6 (September 2009): 515–526.

Kahneman, Daniel, Jack L. Knetsch, and Richard H. Thaler. "Experimental Tests of the Endowment Effect and the Coase Theorem." *Journal of Political Economy* 98 (1990): 1325–1348.

Kahneman, Daniel, and Dan Lovallo. "Delusions of Success: How Optimism Undermines Executives' Decisions." *Harvard Business Review* (2003). https://hbr.org/2003/07/delusions-of-success-how-optimism-undermines-executives-decisions.

Kahneman, Daniel, and Amos Tversky. "An Analysis of Decision under Risk." *Econometrica* 47, no. 2 (1979): 263–292.

Kahneman, Daniel, and Amos Tversky. "Prospect Theory: An Analysis of Decisions under Risk." *Econometrica* 47 (1979): 313–327.

Kamakura, Wagner, and Rex Yuxing Du. "How Economic Contractions and Expansions Affect Expenditure Patterns." *Journal of Consumer Research* 39 (2012): 229–247.

Kamstra, Mark J., Lisa A. Kramer, and Maurice D. Levi. "Winter Blues: A Sad Stock Market Cycle." *American Economic Review* 93 (2003): 324–343.

Kamstra, Mark J., Lisa A. Kramer, Maurice D. Levi, and Russ Wermers. "Seasonal Asset Allocation: Evidence from Mutual Fund Flows." *Journal of Financial and Quantitative Analysis* (forthcoming). 25th Australasian Finance and Banking Conference 2012 paper (August 12, 2014). Available at SSRN: http://ssrn.com/abstract=1907904.

Kaplan, Steven. "Executive Compensation and Corporate Governance in the U.S.: Perceptions, Facts and Challenges." *Journal of Applied Corporate Finance* 25 (2013): 8–25.

Kaplanski, Guy, and Haim Levy. "Sentiment and Stock Prices: The Case of Aviation Disasters." *Journal of Financial Economics* 95 (2010): 174–201.

Karmel, Roberta S. "The Investment Banker and the Credit Regulations." *New York University Law Review* 45 (1970): 59–88.

Kaustia, Markku, and Elias Henrikki Rantapuska. "Does Mood Affect Trading Behavior?" *Journal of Financial Markets* 29 (June 2016): 1–26.

Kaustia, Markku, and Elias Rantapuska. "Rational and Behavioral Motives to Trade: Evidence from Reinvestment of Dividends and Tender Offer Proceeds." *Journal of Banking and Finance* 36, no. 8 (2012): 2366–2378.

Kaustia, Markku, Samuli Knüpfer, and Sami Torstila, Stock Ownership and Political Behavior: Evidence from Demutualizations (December 12, 2013). SAFE Working Paper No. 2. Available at SSRN: https://ssrn.com/abstract=2209645 or http://dx.doi.org/10.2139/ssrn.2209645.

Kearns, Jeff. "Roubini Says S&P 500 May Drop to 600 as Profits Fall (Update2)." *Bloomberg*, March 9, 2009. http://www.bloomberg.com/apps/news?pid=newsarchive&sid=a0oeKmwfkr9k.

Keim, Donald B., and Olivia S. Mitchell. "Simplifying Choices in Defined Contribution Retirement Plan Design." NBER Working Paper No. w21854 (January 2016). Available at SSRN: http://ssrn.com/abstract=2713579.

Kelley, Eric K., and Paul C. Tetlock. "Retail Short Selling and Stock Prices." Columbia Business School Research Paper No. 13-70 (November 2013).

Keltner, Dacher, and Jennifer S. Lerner. "Fear, Anger, and Risk." *Journal of Personality and Social Psychology* 81, no. 1 (2001): 146–159.

Kempf, Alexander, and Peer Osthoff. "SRI Funds: Nomen Est Omen." *Journal of Business Finance and Accounting* 35 (2008): 1276–1294.

Kennedy, Jessica A., Cameron Anderson, and Don A. Moore. "When Overconfidence Is Revealed to Others: Testing the Status-Enhancement Theory of Overconfidence." *Organizational Behavior and Human Decision Processes* 122 (2013): 266–279.

Kézdi, Gábor, and Robert J. Willis. "Household Stock Market Beliefs and Learning." NBER Working Paper No. 17614 (November 2011).

Khanna, Arun. "The Titanic: The Untold Economic Story." *Financial Analysts Journal* 54 (1998): 16–17.

Kim, Hugh H., Raimond Maurer, and Olivia S. Mitchell. "Time Is Money: Rational Life Cycle Inertia and the Delegation of Investment Management?" *Journal of Financial Economics* 121, no. 2 (August 2016): 427–447.

Kim, Kyoung Tae, and Sherman D'Hanna. "Do U.S. Households Perceive Their Retirement Preparedness Realistically?" *Financial Services Review* 24 (February 15, 2015): 139–155. Available at SSRN: http://ssrn.com/abstract=2565268.

Kim, Y. Han (Andy), and Felix Meschke. "CEO Interviews on CNBC." Fifth Singapore International Conference on Finance 2011 (August 11, 2014). Available at SSRN: http://ssrn.com/abstract=1745085.

Kiplinger's. Advertisement. September 2006, 29.

Kitces, Michael. "Why Most Retirees Never Spend Their Retirement Assets." *Kitces .com* (July 6, 2016). https://www.kitces.com/blog/consumption-gap-in-retirement-why-most-retirees-will-never-spend-down-their-portfolio/.

Kivetz, Ran, and Itamar Simonson. "Self-Control for the Righteous: Toward a Theory of Precommitment to Indulgence." *Journal of Consumer Research* 29 (September 2002): 199–217.

Klayman, Joshua, and Young-Won Ha. "Confirmation, Disconfirmation, and Information in Hypothesis Testing." *Psychological Review* 94 (1987): 211–228.

Klein, April, Anthony Saunders, and Yu T. F. Wong. "Do Hedge Funds Trade on Private Information? Evidence from Upcoming Changes in Analysts' Stock Recommendations" (April 7, 2014). Available at SSRN: http://ssrn.com/abstract=2421801.

Kleinfield, Sonny. *The Traders.* New York: Holt, Rinehart and Winston, 1983.

Kliger, Doron, Yaron Raviv, Joshua G. Rosett, Thomas Bayer, and John Page. "Auction Prices and the Weather: New Evidence from Old Masters." (August 26, 2010). Available at SSRN: https://ssrn.com/abstract=1666550 or http://dx.doi.org/10.2139/ssrn.1666550.

Koehler, Jonathan J., and Molly Mercer. "Selection Neglect in Mutual Fund Advertisements." *Management Science* 55 (2009): 1107–1121.

Kolata, Gina. "Hope in the Lab: A Special Report; A Cautious Awe Greets Drugs That Eradicate Tumors in Mice." *New York Times* (May 3, 1998): 1:1.

Knutson, Brian, George Loewenstein, Drazen Prelec, Scott Rick, and G. Elliott Wimmer. "Neural Predictors of Purchases." *Neuron* 53 (January 2007): 147–156.

Koehler, Jonathan J., and Molly Mercer. "Selection Neglect in Mutual Fund Advertisements." *Management Science* 55 (2009): 1107–1121.

Kogan, Shimon, Thomas Gilbert, Lars A. Lochstoer, and Ataman Ozyildirim. "Investor Inattention and the Market Impact of Summary Statistics." *Management Science* 58, no. 2 (February 2012): 336–350.

Kolhatkar, Sheelah. "Paulson Forgoes Prognostication as Greatest Trade Sequel Flops." *Bloomberg*, June 28, 2012. http://www.bloomberg.com/news/

2012-06-28/paulson-forgoes-prognostication-as-greatest-trade-sequel-flops. html.

Kopczuk, Wojciech, and Joseph Lupton. "To Leave or Not to Leave: The Distribution of Bequest Motives." *Review of Economic Studies* 74, no. 1 (2007): 207–235.

Koudijs, Peter. "'Those Who Know Most': Insider Trading in 18th C. Amsterdam." *Journal of Political Economy* 126 (2015): 1356–1409.

Kramer, Lisa A., and J. Mark Weber. "This Is Your Portfolio on Winter: Seasonal Affective Disorder and Risk Aversion in Financial Decision Making." *Social Psychological and Personality Science* (2011): 193–199.

Kramer, Marc M. "Financial Advice and Individual Investor Portfolio Performance." *Financial Management* (2012): 395–428.

Kramer, Marc, and Robert Lensink. "The Impact of Financial Advisors on the Stock Portfolios of Retail Investors." *SSRN Electronic Journal*. Available at SSRN: http://ssrn.com/abstract=2021883 or http://dx.doi.org/10.2139/ssrn.2021883.

Kroll, Yoram, Haim Levy, and Amnon Rapoport. "Experimental Tests of the Separation Theorem and the Asset Pricing Model." *America Economic Review* 78 (1988): 500–518.

Kruger, Justin. "Lake Wobegon Be Gone! The 'Below-Average Effect' and the Egocentric Nature of Comparative Ability Judgments." *Journal of Personality and Social Psychology* 77, no. 2 (1999): 221–232.

Kruger, Justin, and Jeremy Burrus. "Egocentrism and Focalism in Unrealistic Optimism (and Pessimism)." *Journal of Experimental Social Psychology* 40 (2004): 332–340.

Kuhnen, Camelia M., and Brian Knutson. "The Influence of Affect on Beliefs, Preferences, and Financial Decisions." *Journal of Financial and Quantitative Analysis* 46, no. 3 (June 2011): 605–626.

Kuhnen, Camelia M., and Andrei C. Miu. "Socioeconomic Status and Learning from Financial Information." NBER Working Paper No. w21214 (May 2015). Available at SSRN: http://ssrn.com/abstract=2612769.

Kuhnen, Camelia M., and Alexandra Niessen. "Public Opinion and Executive Compensation." *Management Science* 58 (2012): 1249–1272.

Kumar, Alok, Alexandra Niessen-Ruenzi, and Oliver G. Spalt. "What Is in a Name? Mutual Fund Flows When Managers Have Foreign-Sounding Names." *Review of Financial Studies* 28 (2015): 2281–2321.

Kuo, Weiyu, Tse-Chun Lin, and Jing Zhao. "Cognitive Limitation and Investment Performance: Evidence from Limit Order Clustering." *Review of Financial Studies* 28, no. 3 (February 2014): 838–875.

Kwong, Jessica Y. Y., and Ellick K. F. Wong. "Is 7300m Equal to 7.3km? Same Semantics but Different Anchoring Effects." *Organizational Behavior and Human Decision Processes* 82 (July 2000): 314–333.

Kwong, Jessica Y. Y., and Kin Fai Ellick Wong. "Reducing and Exaggerating Escalation of Commitment by Option Partitioning." *Journal of Applied Psychology* 99, no. 4 (July 2014): 697–712.

Kyle, Albert S. "Continuous Auctions and Insider Trading." *Econometrica* 53 (1985): 1335–1355.

LaBarge, Karin Peterson. "What Matters Most: An Analysis of Investment Committee Hire/Fire Decisions." Vanguard Group (September 2010).

Lakonishok, Josef, Andrei Shleifer, and Robert W. Vishny. "Contrarian Investment, Extrapolation, and Risk." *Journal of Finance* 49 (1994): 1541–1578.

Lancaster, Kelvin J. "A New Approach to Consumer Theory." *Journal of Political Economy* 74 (April 1966): 132–157.

Larrick, Richard P., Richard E. Nisbett, and James N. Morgan. "Who Uses the Normative Rules of Choice." In *Rules for Reasoning*, ed. Richard. E. Nisbett, 277–294. Hillsdale, NJ: Lawrence Erlbaum Associates, 1993.

Lattman, Mark, and Andrew Ross Sorkin. "Figure in Insider Case Sought to Quit Goldman." *New York Times*, March 13, 2011. http://dealbook.nytimes.com/2011/03/13/associate-in-insider-case-sought-to-quit-goldman/?_r=0.

Cerqueira Leal, Cristiana, Manuel J. Rocha Armada and Joao C. Duque. "Are All Individual Investors Equally Prone to the Disposition Effect All The Time? New Evidence from a Small Market," *Frontiers in Finance and Economics* 7, no. 2 (October 2010): 38-68.

Lee, Chan Jean, and Eduardo B. Andrade. "Fear, Social Projection, and Financial Decision Making." *Journal of Marketing Research* 48, no. SPL (November 2011): S121–S129.

Litvak, Paul, Jennifer Lerner, Larissa Tiedens, and Katherine Shonk, "Fuel in the Fire: How Anger Impacts Judgment and Decision-Making." In *International Handbook of Anger*, ed. Michael Potegal, Gerhard Stemmler, and Charles Spielberger, 287–310. New York: Springer, 2010.

Lerner, Jennifer S., Deborah A. Small, and George Loewenstein. "Heart Strings and Purse Strings: Carryover Effects of Emotions on Economic Decisions." *Psychological Science* 15, no. 5 (2004): 337–341.

Lewis, Michael. *Flash Boys: A Wall Street Revolt*. W. W. Norton, 2014.

Lewis, Michael. *Moneyball: The Art of Winning an Unfair Game*. New York: W. W. Norton, 2014.

Li, Fengfei, Chen Lin, and Tse-Chun Lin. "Does Anchoring Heuristic Affect Analyst Recommendation Revisions?" (July 1, 2015). Available at SSRN: http://ssrn.com/abstract=2517238 or http://dx.doi.org/10.2139/ssrn.2517238.

Li, Ying, and Hossein B. Kazemi. "Do Hedge Funds Conduct Mid-Year Risk Shifting?" (March 11, 2011). Available at SSRN: http://ssrn.com/abstract=1787004.

Lien, Jaimie W., and Jia Yuan. "Selling to Biased Believers: Strategies of Online Lottery Ticket Vendors." *Economic Inquiry* 53, no. 3 (July 2015): 1506–1521. Available at SSRN: http://ssrn.com/abstract=2605234 or http://dx.doi.org/10.1111/ecin.12198.

Light, Joe. "Retirement Investors Flock Back to Stocks." *Wall Street Journal,* May 1, 2014. http://www.wsj.com/articles/SB10001424052702303948104579535840428373528.

Lintner, John. "The Valuation of Risk Assets and the Selection of Risky Investments in Stock Portfolios and Capital Budgets." *Review of Economics and Statistics* 47 (1965): 13–37.

Literary Digest. Advertisement. December 28, 1929, 45.

Literary Digest. "No Royal Road for the Small Investor." Vol. 103, no. 11 (December 14, 1929): 52–55.

Lo, Andrew W. "The Adaptive Markets Hypothesis." *Journal of Portfolio Management* 30 (2004): 15–29.

Lo, Andrew W., and A. Craig MacKinlay. *A Non-Random Walk down Wall Street*. Princeton, NJ: Princeton University Press, 2002

Loibl, Caezilia, Lauren Eden Jones, Emily Haisley, and George Loewenstein. "Testing Strategies to Increase Saving and Retention in Individual Development

Account Programs" (February 20, 2016). Available at SSRN: http://ssrn.com/abstract=2735625 or http://dx.doi.org/10.2139/ssrn.2735625.

Loomis, Carol J. "Buffett's Big Bet," *Fortune* (June 23, 2008): 45–51.

Loomis, Carol J. "Warren Buffett Adds to His Lead in $1 Million Hedge-Fund Bet." *Fortune* (February 3, 2015). http://fortune.com/2015/02/03/berkshires-buffett-adds-to-his-lead-in-1-million-bet-with-hedge-fund/.

Loomis, Carol J. "Warren Buffett Loses a Bit of Ground in His 'Million-Dollar Bet.'" *Fortune* (February 16, 2016). http://fortune.com/author/carol-j-loomis/.

Loureiro, Gilberto R., Anil K. Makhija, and Dan Zhang. "The Ruse of a One-Dollar CEO Salary" (January 10, 2014). Charles A. Dice Center Working Paper No. 2011-7; Fisher College of Business Working Paper No. 2011-03-007. Available at SSRN: https://ssrn.com/abstract=1571823 or http://dx.doi.org/10.2139/ssrn.1571823.

Lowenstein, Roger. "97 Moral: Drop Global-Investing Bunk." *Wall Street Journal*, December 18, 1997: C1.

Lu, Timothy (Jun). "Social Interaction Effects and Individual Portfolio Choice: Evidence from 401(k) Pension Plan Investors." *SSRN Electronic Journal* (August 2011). Available at SSRN: http://ssrn.com/abstract=1921431 or http://dx.doi.org/10.2139/ssrn.1921431.

Lusardi, Annamaria, and Olivia S. Mitchell. "The Economic Importance of Financial Literacy: Theory and Evidence." *Journal of Economic Literature* 52, no. 1 (2014).

Lusardi, Annamaria, Daniel Schneider, and Peter Tufano. "Financially Fragile Households: Evidence and Implications." Netspar Discussion Paper No. 03/2011-013 (March 7, 2011). Available at SSRN: http://ssrn.com/abstract=1809708.

Ma, Yueran. "Bank CEO Optimism and the Financial Crisis" (September 3, 2015). Available at SSRN: https://ssrn.com/abstract=2392683 or http://dx.doi.org/10.2139/ssrn.2392683.

MacMillan, Douglas. "Facebook's Missing Millionaires." *Bloomberg Business Week*, March 8, 2012. http://www.businessweek.com/articles/2012-03-08/facebooks-missing-millionaires.

Madrian, Brigitte C., and Dennis F. Shea. "The Power of Suggestion: Inertia in 401(k) Participation and Savings Behavior." *Quarterly Journal of Economics* 116 (2001): 1149–1187.

Malkiel, Burton G. "The Efficient Market Hypothesis and Its Critics." *Journal of Economic Perspectives* 17, no. 1 (Winter 2003): 59–82.

Malmendier, Ulrike, and Geoffrey Tate. "CEO Overconfidence and Corporate Investment." *Journal of Finance* 60, no. 6 (December 2005): 2661–2700.

Make Love, not Debt: A Relationship Finance Blog. "Raise Your Children to Rely on Them: Asian Culture and Finances." http://www.makelovenotdebt.com/2007/05/raise_your_children_to_rely_on_them_asian_culture_and_finances.php.

Mannes, Albert E., and Don A. Moore. "A Behavioral Demonstration of Overconfidence in Judgment." *Psychological Science* 24, no. 7 (2013): 1190–1197.

Mansfield, Edwin, John Rapoport, Jerome Schnee, Samuel Wagner, and Michael Hamburger. *Research and Innovation in the Modern Corporation.* New York: W. W. Norton, 1971. 157–185.

Marcus, Alan J. "The Magellan Fund and Market Efficiency." *Journal of Portfolio Management* 17, no. 1 (Fall 1990): 85–88.

Markowitz, Harry M. "Consumption, Investment and Insurance in the Game of Life." *Journal of Investment Management* 13, no. 3 (2015): 5–23.

Markowitz, Harry M. "The Early History of Portfolio Theory: 1600–1960." *Financial Analysts Journal* 55 (1999): 5–16.

Markowitz, Harry M. "Individual Versus Institutional Investing." *Financial Services Review* 1, no. 1 (1991): 1–8.

Markowitz, Harry. "Portfolio Selection." *Journal of Finance* 7 (1952): 77–91.

Markowitz, Harry. *Portfolio Selection: Efficient Diversification of Investments.* New York: John Wiley & Sons, 1959.

Markowitz, Harry. "Portfolio Theory: As I Still See It." *Annual Review of Financial Economics* 2 (2010): 1–23.

Markowitz, Harry. "The Utility of Wealth." *Journal of Political Economy* LX, no. 2 (1952): 151–158.

Marshall, A. W., and William Meckling. "Predictability of the Costs, Time, and Success of Development." In *The Rate and Direction of Inventive Activity: Economic and Social Factors*, ed. National Bureau of Economic Research (Princeton: Princeton University Press, 1962): 461–476.

Massa, Massimo, and Vijay N. Yadav. "Investor Sentiment and Mutual Fund Strategies," *Journal of Financial and Quantitative Analysis* 50, no. 4 (2015): 699–727.

Maug, Ernst G., Alexandra Niessen-Ruenzi, and Evgenia Zhivotova. "Pride and Promotion: Why Some Firms Pay Their CEOs Less" (September 5, 2014). Available at https://niessen.bwl.uni-mannheim.de/fileadmin/files/niessen/files/Papers/Pride_and_Prestige_NieRueMauZhi.pdf.

Max, Sarah. "A Global Academy's Crash Course Makes Angels out of Investors." *New York Times.* November 12, 2015. http://www.nytimes.com/2015/11/13/business/dealbook/a-global-academys-crash-course-makes-angels-out-of-investors.html.

McCarthy, Yvonne. "Behavioural Characteristics and Financial Distress." ECB Working Paper No. 1303 (February 14, 2011). Available at SSRN: http://ssrn.com/abstract=1761570.

McGarry, Kathleen M., and Robert F. Schoeni. "Understanding Participation in SSI." *Michigan Retirement Research Center Working Paper WP 2015-319* (January 2015). Available at SSRN: http://ssrn.com/abstract=2599541 or http://dx.doi.org/10.2139/ssrn.2599541.

McGough, Robert. "Bulls Say a Heated Market Could Get Even Warmer." *Wall Street Journal,* March 30, 1999: C1.

McKenzie, Craig R. M., and Michael J. Liersch. "Misunderstanding Savings Growth: Implications for Retirement Savings Behavior." *Journal of Marketing Research* 48 (Special Issue 2011): S1–S13.

McLean, R. David, and Jeffrey Pontiff. "Does Academic Research Destroy Stock Return Predictability?" *Journal of Finance* 71 (2016): 5–32.

Merkle, Christoph. "Financial Overconfidence over Time: Foresight, Hindsight, and Insight of Investors." AFA 2013 San Diego Meetings Paper; EFA 2012 Copenhagen Meetings Paper (August 31, 2013). Available at SSRN: http://ssrn.com/abstract=2001513.

Mian, Atif, and Amir Sufi. "House Price Gains and U.S. Household Spending from 2002 to 2006." National Bureau of Economic Research Working Paper Series No. 20152 (May 2014). Available at http://www.nber.org/papers/w20152.

Mightzozo. "Asics Running Commercial." YouTube video. September 4, 2009. https://www.youtube.com/watch?v=D-ie_aFsfb8.

Mikhed, Vyacheslav, and Michael Vogan. "Out of Sight, out of Mind: Consumer Reaction to News on Data Breaches and Identity Theft." FRB of Philadelphia Working Paper No. 15-42 (November 16, 2015). Available at SSRN: http://ssrn.com/abstract=2691902.

Milkman, Katherine L., Julia A. Minson, and Kevin G. M. Volpp. "Holding the Hunger Games Hostage at the Gym: An Evaluation of Temptation Bundling." *Management Science* 60 (2013): 283–299.

Milkman, Katherine L., John W. Payne, and Jack B. Soll. "A User's Guide to Debiasing." In *Wiley-Blackwell Handbook of Judgment and Decision Making*, ed. Gideon Keren and George Wu. Chichester, UK: John Wiley & Sons, 2015.

Miller, Daniel. "Film Entrepreneur Draws Mixed Reviews." *Los Angeles Times*, August 12, 2014. http://www.latimes.com/entertainment/envelope/cotown/la-et-ct-bradley-media-society-20140812-story.html#page=1.

Miller, Margaret, Julia Reichelstein, Christian Salas, and Bilal Zia. "Can You Help Someone Become Financially Capable? A Meta-Analysis of the Literature." Policy Research working paper no. WPS 6745. Washington, DC: World Bank Group, 2014. Available at http://documents.worldbank.org/curated/en/297931468327387954/Can-you-help-someone-become-financially-capable-a-meta-analysis-of-the-literature.

Miller, Merton. "Behavioral Rationality in Finance: The Case of Dividends." *Journal of Business* 59 (1986): 451–468.

Miller, Merton, and Franco Modigliani. "Dividend Policy, Growth, and the Valuation of Shares." *Journal of Business* 34 (1961): 411–433.

Millman, Peter, "The Day Trader," audiovideo interview by Vincent Laforet, *New York* magazine, YouTube video, 1:57, January 27, 2009, https://www.youtube.com/watch?v=XruhYQW6unA.

Mischel, Walter, and Yuichi Shoda. "A Cognitive-Affective System Theory of Personality: Reconceptualizing Situations, Dispositions, Dynamics, and Invariance in Personality Structure." *Psychological Review* 102, no. 2 (1995): 246–268.

Mitchel, Olivia S., and Annamaria Lusardi. "Financial Literacy and Economic Outcomes: Evidence and Policy Implications." *Journal of Retirement* 3 (2015): 107–114.

Mitchel, Olivia S., and Annamaria Lusardi. "Financial Literacy and Planning: Implications for Retirement Wellbeing." In *Financial Literacy: Implications for Retirement Security and the Financial Marketplace*, ed. O. S. Mitchell and Annamaria Lusardi, 17–39 (Oxford: Oxford University Press, 2011).

Modigliani, Franco, and Richard Brumberg. "Utility Analysis and the Consumption Function: An Interpretation of Cross-Section Data." In *Post Keynesian Economics*, ed. K. Kurihara, 388–436. Brunswick, NJ: Rutgers University Press, 1954.

Moisio, Risto, Eric J. Arnould, and James Gentry. "Productive Consumption in the Class-Mediated Construction of Domestic Masculinity: Do-It-Yourself (DIY) Home Improvement in Men's Identity Work." *Journal of Consumer Research* 40 (2013): 203–222.

Money. Advertisement. May 2007, 52.

Money. Advertisement. December 2009, 33.

Moore, Heather, and Bryan Young. "Letter to the Editor." *Economist.* January 13, 2007, 16.

Morse, Adair, and Sophie Shive. "Patriotism in Your Portfolio." *Journal of Financial Markets* 14 (2011): 411–440.

Moss, David A. *When All Else Fails: Government as the Ultimate Risk Manager.* Cambridge, MA: Harvard University Press, 2002.

Muermann, Alexander, Olivia S. Mitchell, and Jaqueline Volkman. "Regret, Portfolio Choice, and Guarantees in Defined Contribution Schemes." *Insurance: Mathematics and Economics* 39 (2006): 219–229.

Mugerman, Yevgeny, Orly Sade, and Moses Shayo. "Long-Term Savings Decisions: Inertia, Peer Effects and Ethnicity." *Journal of Economic Behavior and Organization* 106 (2014): 235–253.

Mullainathan, Sendhil, Markus Noeth, and Antoinette Schoar. "The Market for Financial Advice: An Audit Study." NBER Working Paper No. W17929 (March 2012).

Mullainathan, Sendhil, Eldar Shafir, and Anuj K. Shah. "Some Consequences of Having Too Little." *Science* 338, no. 6107 (November 2012): 682–685.

Mullins, Brody, and Susan Pulliam. "Inside Capitol, Investor Access Yields Rich Tips." *Wall Street Journal* (December 20, 2011). http://www.wsj.com/news/articles/SB10001424052970204844504577100260349084878.

Mundheim, Robert H. "Professional Responsibilities of Broker-Dealers: The Suitability Doctrine." *Duke Law Journal* 3 (Summer 1965): 445–480.

Munnell, Alicia H., Francesca Golub-Sass, and Anthony Webb. "How Much to Save for a Secure Retirement." *Center for Research at Boston College* 11–13 (November 2011): 1–11.

Nakamoto, Michiyo, and David Wighton. "Bullish Citigroup Is 'Still Dancing' to the Beat of the Buy-out Boom." *Financial Times*, July 10, 2007. http://www.ft.com/cms/s/0/5cefc794-2e7d-11dc-821c-0000779fd2ac.html.

Nelson, Karen K., Richard A. Price, and Brian Rountree. "Are Individual Investors Influenced by the Optimism and Credibility of Stock Spam Recommendations?" *Journal of Business Finance & Accounting* 49, nos. 9–10 (November 2013): 1155–1183.

Nenkov, Gergana Y., Maureen Morrin, Andrew Ward, Barry Schwartz, and John Hulland. "A Short Form of the Maximization Scale: Factor Structure, Reliability and Validity Studies." *Judgment and Decision Making* 3, no. 5 (June 2008): 371–388.

Novy-Marx, Robert. "The Other Side of Value: The Gross Profitability Premium." *Journal of Financial Economics* 108 (2013): 1–28.

National Public Radio. "Episode 493: What's a Bubble (Nobel Edition)." *Planet Money.* November 11, 2013. http://www.npr.org/sections/money/2013/11/01/242351065/episode-493-whats-a-bubble-nobel-edition.

O'Connell, Vanessa. "Zero-Coupon Bonds Offer Safety Net with a Bounce." *Wall Street Journal,* May 29, 1996: C1.

Olson, Jenny G., and Scott Rick. "A Penny Saved Is a Partner Earned: The Romantic Appeal of Savers" (June 27, 2014). Available at SSRN: http://ssrn.com/abstract=2281344 or http://dx.doi.org/10.2139/ssrn.2281344.

Opdyke, Jeff, and Aparajita Saha-Bubn. "How to React to Latest Move from Fed." *Wall Street Journal,* March 28, 2005: D1.

Oster, Emily, E. Ray Dorsey, and Ira Shoulson. "Limited Life Expectancy, Human Capital and Health Investments." *American Economic Review* 103 (2013): 1977–2002.

Otuteye, Eben, and Mohammad Siddiquee. "Overcoming Cognitive Biases: A Heuristic for Making Value Investing Decisions." *Journal of Behavioral Finance* 16, no. 2 (April 2015): 140–149.

Pan, Carrie, and Meir Statman. "Questionnaires of Risk Tolerance, Regret, Overconfidence, and Other Investor Propensities." *Journal of Investment Consulting* 13 (2012): 54–63.

Pan, Yihui, Tracy Yue Wang, and Michael Weisbach. "CEO Investment Cycles." *Review of Financial Studies*, http://rfs.oxfordjournals.org/content/29/11/2955.

Parker, Jonathan A. "Why Don't Households Smooth Consumption? Evidence from a 25 Million Dollar Experiment." NBER Working Paper No. w21369 (July 2015). Available at SSRN: http://ssrn.com/abstract=2633325.

Pechter, Kerry. "First Sign of Blood from DOL Fiduciary Rule." *Retirement Income Journal* (April 29, 2016).

Pedace, Roberto L., and Janet Kiholm Smith. "Loss Aversion and Managerial Decisions: Evidence from Major League Baseball." *Economic Inquiry* 51, no. 2 (April 2013): 1475–1488.

Pfau, Wade D., and Wade Dokken. "Rethinking Retirement: Sustainable Withdrawal Rates for New Retirees in 2015." *WealthVest* (2015): 1–14. http://www.fa-mag .com/userfiles/stories/whitepapers/2015/WealthVest_Sept_2015_ Whitepaper/12040-Pfau-Sustainable-Withdrawal-Rates-Whitepaper-.pdf.

Phalippou, Ludovic. "Why Is the Evidence on Private Equity Performance So Confusing?" (June 14, 2011). Available at SSRN: http://ssrn.com/abstract=1864503.

Phillips, Blake, Kantura Pukthuanthong and P. Raghavendra Rau, "Past Performance May Be an Illusion: Performance, Flows, and Fees in Mutual Funds," *Critical Finance Review* 5 (2016): 351–398.

Plassmann, Hilke, John O'Doherty, Baba Shiv, and Antonio Rangel. "Marketing Actions Can Modulate Neural Representations of Experienced Pleasantness." *Proceedings of the National Academy of Sciences of the United States of America* 105 (2008): 1050–1054.

Polkovnichenko, Valery. "Household Portfolio Diversification: A Case for Rank-Dependent Preferences." *Review of Financial Studies* 18 (2005): 1467–1501.

Pontiff, Jeffrey. "Costly Arbitrage: Evidence from Closed-End Funds." *Quarterly Journal of Economics* 111 (1996): 1135–1151.

Popova, Maria. "Charles Darwin's List of the Pros and Cons of Marriage." *Brain Pickings*. August 14, 2012. https://www.brainpickings.org/index.php/2012/08/ 14/darwin-list-pros-and-cons-of-marriage.

Popper, Nathaniel. "Speculative Bets Prove Risky as Savers Chase Payoff." *New York Times,* February 10, 2013. http://www.nytimes.com/2013/02/11/business/ wave-of-investor-fraud-extends-to-ordinary-retirement-savers.html?_r=0 &adxnnl=1&pagewanted=all&adxnnlx=1424012902-LhBhSRA5hBsYdSN/ vezaCA.

Posner, Eric A., and E. Glen Weyl. "An FDA for Financial Innovation: Applying the Insurable Interest Doctrine to 21st-Century Financial Markets." *Northwestern University Law Review* 107 (2013): 1307–1358.

Poterba, James M., Steven F. Venti, and David A. Wise. "The Drawdown of Personal Retirement Assets." NBER Working Paper 16675 (January 2011).

Potter van Loon, Rogier J. D., Martijn J. Van den Assem, Dennie Van Dolder, and Tong V. Wang. "Number Preferences in Lotteries" (November 1, 2015). Available at SSRN: http://ssrn.com/abstract=2657776 or http://dx.doi.org/ 10.2139/ssrn.2657776.

Pownall, Rachel A. J., Meir Statman, and Kees C. G. Koedijk. "Aspirations, Well-Being, Risk-Aversion and Loss-Aversion." Working Paper, Tilburg University (June 8, 2016).

Prast, Henriette, Federica Teppa, and Anouk Smits. "Is Information Overrated? Evidence from the Pension Domain." Netspar Discussion Paper No. 12/2012-050 (December 2012).

PRNewswire. "E*TRADE Launches Provocative Brand Advertising Campaign Designed to Capture the New Spirit of Investors Who Are Taking Charge of Their Financial Lives." April 12, 1999. http://www.prnewswire.com/news-releases/etrade-launches-provocative-brand-advertising-campaign-designed-to-capture-the-new-spirit-of-investors-who-are-taking-charge-of-their-financial-lives-73955882.html.

Pronin, Emily, Daniel Y. Lin, and Lee Ross. "The Bias Blind Spot: Perceptions of Bias in Self versus Others." *Personality and Social Psychology Bulletin* 28, no. 3 (March 2002): 369–381.

Public Broadcasting Service. "One NYC Family's Struggle to Survive on a Fast Food Salary." Audio blog post, November 4, 2013, http://www.pbs.org/newshour/bb/nation-july-dec13-minimumwage_11-04/.

Puri, Manju, and David T. Robinson. "Optimism and Economic Choice." *Journal of Financial Economics* 86 (2007): 71–99.

Qin, Nan, and Vijay Singal. "Indexing and Stock Price Efficiency." *SSRN Electronic Journal* (November 15, 2013). Available at SSRN: http://ssrn.com/abstract=2229263 or http://dx.doi.org/10.2139/ssrn.2229263.

Quinn, Jane Bryant. "Weighing the Pros and Cons of Buying Bonds vs. Bond Funds." *San Jose Mercury News,* August 5, 1996.

Raff, Konrad, and Linus Siming. "Knighthoods, Damehoods, and CEO Behaviour." *Journal of Corporate Finance,* forthcoming. Available online October 11, 2016. Available at SSRN: http://ssrn.com/abstract=2420066.

Raghavan, Anita. "Rajat Gupta's Lust for Zeros." *New York Times,* May 17, 2013. http://www.nytimes.com/2013/05/19/magazine/rajat-guptas-lust-for-zeros.html?pagewanted=all&_r=0.

Ragnoni, John T. "Defining Excellence: A Report on Retirement Readiness in the Not-for-Profit Higher Education Industry." *Fidelity Perspectives* (Winter 2012).

Rantala, Ville. "How Do Investment Ideas Spread through Social Interaction? Evidence from a Ponzi Scheme." 6th Miami Behavioral Finance Conference (November 18, 2015). Available at SSRN: http://ssrn.com/abstract=2579847 or http://dx.doi.org/10.2139/ssrn.2579847.

Ratcliffe, Anita, and Karl Taylor. "Who Cares about Stock Market Booms and Busts? Evidence from Data on Mental Health." *Oxford Economic Papers* 67, no. 3 (2015): 826–845.

Rattner, Steven. "Who's Right on the Stock Market?" *New York Times,* November 15, 2013: A29. http://www.nytimes.com/2013/11/15/opinion/rattner-whos-right-on-the-stock-market.html.

Rauh, Joshua D., Irina Stefanescu, and Stephen P. Zeldes. "Cost Saving and the Freezing of Corporate Pension Plans." Columbia Business School Research Paper No. 16-4; Stanford University Graduate School of Business Research Paper No. 16-4 (December 3, 2015). Available at SSRN: http://ssrn.com/abstract=2706448 or http://dx.doi.org/10.2139/ssrn.2706448.

Ravina, Enrichetta, "Love and Loans: The Effect of Beauty and Personal Characteristics in Credit Markets" (November 22, 2012). Available at

SSRN: https://ssrn.com/abstract=1101647 or http://dx.doi.org/10.2139/ssrn.1101647.

Read, Daniel, and Barbara Van Leeuwen. "Predicting Hunger: The Effects of Appetite and Delay on Choice." *Organizational Behavior and Human Decision Processes* 76, no. 2 (November 1998): 189–205.

Reichert, Arndt R., Boris Augurzky, and Harald Tauchmann. "Self-Perceived Job Insecurity and the Demand for Medical Rehabilitation: Does Fear of Unemployment Reduce Health Care Utilization?" *Health Economics* 24 (January 2015): 8–25.

Reinhardt, Uwe E. "Break-Even Analysis for Lockheed's Tri Star: An Application of Financial Theory." *Journal of Finance* 28, no. 4 (September 1973): 821–838.

Reinholtz, Nicholas, Philip M. Fernbach, and Bart De Langhe. "Do People Understand the Benefit of Diversification?" (January 20, 2016). Available at SSRN: http://ssrn.com/abstract=2719144 or http://dx.doi.org/10.2139/ssrn.2719144.

Retirement Income Journal/Adviser. "Millionaires Don't Think Monolithically: Spectrem" (June 14, 2012). http://retirementincomejournal.com/issue/rij-advisor/article/millionaires-dont-think-monolithically.

Reuters. "UPDATE 1-Calpers to Divest Stake in 2 Makers of Guns, Ammunition." February 19, 2013. http://www.reuters.com/article/financial-calpers-gunmakers-idUSL1N0BJ9OZ20130219.

Richard, René, Joop Van Der Pligt, and Nanne De Vries. "Anticipated Regret and Time Perspective: Changing Sexual Risk-Taking Behavior." *Journal of Behavioral Decision Making* 9 (1996): 185–199.

Richards, Daniel, Janette Rutterford, Devendra Kodwani, and Mark Fenton-O'Creevy. "Stock Market Investors' Use of Stop Losses and the Disposition Effect." *European Journal of Finance*, http://dx.doi.org/10.1080/1351847X.2015.1048375. Available at SSRN: https://ssrn.com/abstract=2612898.

Rick, Scott I., Deborah A. Small, and Eli J. Finkel. "Fatal (Fiscal) Attraction: Spendthrifts and Tightwads in Marriage." *Journal of Marketing Research* 48 (April 2011): 228–237.

Rodwin, Marc A. "Commentary: The Politics of Evidence-Based Medicine." *Agency for Healthcare Research and Quality* (April 2001). http://www.ahrq.gov/research/findings/evidence-based-reports/jhppl/rodwin.html.

Rogers, Jonathan L., Douglas J. Skinner, and Sarah L. C. Zechman. "The Role of the Media in Disseminating Insider-Trading Activity." *Review of Accounting Studies* 21, no. 3 (September 2016): 711–739.

Roll, Richard. "A Mean/Variance Analysis of Tracking Error." *Journal of Portfolio Management* 18 (1992): 13–22.

Roll, Richard. "R^2." *Journal of Finance* 43 (1988): 541–566.

Rosa, Raymond da Silva, Huong Minh To, and Terry S. Walter. "Evidence Contrary to the Disposition Effect amongst UK Managed Funds" (February 2005). Available at SSRN: https://ssrn.com/abstract=676342 or http://dx.doi.org/10.2139/ssrn.676342.

Rosenberg, Barr, Kenneth Reid, and Ronald Lanstein. "Persuasive Evidence of Market Inefficiency." *Journal of Portfolio Management* 11 (1985): 9–17.

Ross, Karen, and Robert Schoeni. "Material Assistance from Families during the Transition to Adulthood." In *On the Frontier of Adulthood: Theory, Research, and Public Policy*, ed. Richard A. Settersten Jr., Frank F. Furstenberg Jr., and Ruben G. Rumbaut, 243–286, 396–416. Chicago: University of Chicago Press, 2005.

Rothfeld, Michael, and Scott Patterson. "Traders Seek an Edge with High-Tech Snooping." *Wall Street Journal*, December 18, 2013. http://www.wsj.com/articles/SB10001424052702303497804579240182187225264.

Roussanov, Nikolai, and Pavel Savor. "Marriage and Managers' Attitudes to Risk," *Management Science* 60 (2014): 2496–2508.

Rozeff Michael. "Lump-Sum Investing versus Dollar-Averaging." *Journal of Portfolio Management* 20 (Winter 1994): 45–50.

Ru, Hong, and Antoinette Schoar. "Do Credit Card Companies Screen for Behavioral Biases?" (June 13, 2016). Available at SSRN: http://ssrn.com/abstract=2795030.

Russell, Christine A. "Problems in Ending a Project: Theory and Case Study." Term paper, Santa Clara University (November 1983).

Russo, Edward J., and Paul J. H Schoemaker. "Overconfidence." In David Teece and Mie Augier (eds.), *Palgrave Encyclopedia of Strategic Management*, forthcoming. Available at DOI: 10.1057/9781137294678.0505.

Samuelson, Paul. "Lifetime Portfolio Selection by Dynamic Stochastic Programming." *Review of Economics and Statistics* 51, no. 3 (August 1969): 247–257.

Samuelson, Paul. "The Long-Term Case for Equities: And How It Can Be Oversold." *Journal of Portfolio Management* 21, no. 1 (Fall 1994): 15–24.

Samuelson, Paul. "Risk and Uncertainty: A Fallacy of Large Numbers." *Scientia* 57, no. 6 (April–May 1963): 1–6.

Sapienza, Paola, and Luigi Zingales. "Economic Experts versus Average Americans." *American Economic Review* 103 (2013): 636–642.

Saunders, Edward M. "Stock Prices and Wall Street Weather." *American Economic Review* 83, no. 5 (1993): 1337–1345.

Saunders, Laura. "Inside Swiss Banks' Tax-Cheating Machinery." *Wall Street Journal*, October 22, 2015. http://www.wsj.com/articles/inside-swiss-banks-tax-cheating-machinery-1445506381.

Scharfstein, David S., and Jeremy C. Stein. "Herd Behavior and Investment." *American Economic Review* 80 (1990): 465–479.

Scheinkman, Jose, and Wei Xiong. "Overconfidence and Speculative Bubbles." *Journal of Political Economy* 111 (2003): 1183–1219.

Schmeiser, Maximilian D., and Jeanne M. Hogarth. "Good Advice, Good Outcomes? How Financial Advice-Seeking Relates to Self-Perceived Financial Well-Being" (May 7, 2013). Available at SSRN: https://ssrn.com/abstract=2261707 or http://dx.doi.org/10.2139/ssrn.2261707.

Schrand, Catherine M., and Sarah L. C. Zechman. "Executive Overconfidence and the Slippery Slope to Financial Misreporting." *Journal of Accounting and Economics* 53 (2012): 311–329.

Schultz, Paul. "The Market for New Issues of Municipal Bonds: The Roles of Transparency and Limited Access to Retail Investors." *Journal of Financial Economics* 106 (2012): 492–512.

Scott, Cathy. "Practical Applications of Alpha, Beta & the Blend." *Smart Beta Special Issue* 3, no. sb (2015): 1–7. Available at http://www.iijournals.com/doi/pdfplus/10.3905/pa.2015.3.sb.003.

Scott, Frank, and Aaron Yelowitz. "Pricing Anomalies in the Market for Diamonds: Evidence of Conformist Behavior." *Economic Inquiry* 48, no. 2 (April 2010): 353–368. Available at SSRN: http://ssrn.com/abstract=1578523.

SEI Private Wealth Management. "The Generation Gap" (2011): 1–4. Available at https://www.seic.com/Wealth/SEI_The-Generation-Gap_Scorpio.pdf.

Seasholes, Mark S., and Ning Zhu. "Investing in What You Know: The Case of Individual Investors and Local Stocks." *Journal of Investment Management* 11 (2013): 20–30.

Seeking Alpha. "Business Week 2008 Forecasters Expect Further Gains." December 21, 2007. Available at http://seekingalpha.com/article/58150-business-week-2008-forecasters-expect-further-gains.

Sengupta, Jaideep, and Dengfeng Yan. "The Influence of Base Rate and Case Information on Health-Risk Perceptions: A Unified Model of Self-Positivity and Self-Negativity." *Journal of Consumer Research* 39, no. 5 (February 2013): 931–946.

Richard A. Settersten. "Becoming Adult: Meanings and Markers for Young Americans." In *Coming of Age in America,* eds. Patrick Carr and Maria Kefalas, March 2006, http://health.oregonstate.edu/sites/health.oregonstate.edu/files/faculty-staff/profilepubs/settersten_et_al-becoming_adult-emerging_trends.pdf.

Seyhun, Nejat H. "Insiders' Profits, Cost of Trading, and Market Efficiency." *Journal of Financial Economics* 16 (1985): 189–212.

Shapira, Zur, and Yitzhak Venezia. "Patterns of Behavior of Professionally Managed and Independent Investors." *Journal of Banking and Finance* 25, no. 8 (August 2001): 1573–1587.

Shapira, Zur, and Itzhak Venezia. "On the Preference for Full-Coverage Policies: Why Do People Buy Too Much Insurance?" *Journal of Economic Psychology* 29, no. 5 (2008): 747–761.

Sharpe, William. "Capital Asset Prices: A Theory of Market Equilibrium under Conditions of Risk." *Journal of Finance* 19 (1964): 425–442.

Sharpe, William F. *Investments.* Englewood Cliff, NJ: Prentice-Hall, 1981.

Sharpe, William. *Investors and Markets.* Princeton, NJ: Princeton University Press, 2007.

Shefrin, Hersh. "A Behavioral Approach to Asset Pricing." Burlington, MA: Elsevier Academic Press, 2005.

Shefrin, Hersh, and Meir Statman. "Behavioral Capital Asset Pricing Theory." *Journal of Financial and Quantitative Analysis* 29 (1994): 323–349.

Shefrin, Hersh, and Meir Statman. "Behavioral Portfolio Theory." *Journal of Financial and Quantitative Analysis* 35 (2000): 127–151.

Shefrin, Hersh, and Meir Statman, Research proposal funded by the National Science Foundation, Grant NSF SES-8709239 (1987).

Shefrin, Hersh, and Meir Statman. "Ethics, Fairness, and Efficiency in Financial Markets." *Financial Analysts Journal* 49 (1993): 21–29.

Shefrin, Hersh, and Meir Statman. "Explaining Investor Preference for Cash Dividends." *Journal of Financial Economics* 13 (1984): 253–282.

Shefrin, Hersh, and Meir Statman. "The Style of Investment Expectation." In *Handbook of Equity Style Management,* ed. T. Daniel Coggin and Frank J. Fabozzi, 195–218. New York: Wiley, 2003.

Shefrin, Hersh M., and Richard H. Thaler. "The Behavioral Life-Cycle Hypothesis." *Economic Inquiry* 26 (1988): 609–643.

Shi, Zhen, and Na Wang. "Don't Confuse Brains with a Bull Market: Attribution Bias, Overconfidence, and Trading Behavior of Individual Investors." EFA 2010 Frankfurt Meetings Paper (August 12, 2013). Available at SSRN: http://ssrn.com/abstract=1979208.

Shiller, Robert. "Do Stock Prices Move Too Much to Be Justified by Subsequent Changes in Dividends?" *American Economic Review* 71, no. 3 (June 1981): 421–436.

Shiller, Robert J. "Owning a Home Isn't Always a Virtue." *New York Times,* July 13, 2013. http://www.nytimes.com/2013/07/14/business/owning-a-home-isnt-always-a-virtue.html?_r=0.

Shiller, Robert. "The Volatility of Long-Term Interest Rates and Expectations Models of the Term Structure." *Journal of Political Economy* 87 (1979): 1190–1219.

Shimanoff, Susan B. "Commonly Named Emotions in Everyday Conversations." *Perceptual and Motor Skills* 58 (April 1984): 514.

Shin, Jihae, and Katherine L. Milkman. "How Backup Plans Can Harm Goal Pursuit: The Unexpected Downside of Being Prepared for Failure" (December 15, 2014). Available at SSRN: http://ssrn.com/abstract=2538889 or http://dx.doi.org/10.2139/ssrn.2538889.

Shiv, Baba, George Loewenstein, Antoine Bechara, Hanna Damasio, and Antonio R. Damasio. "Investment Behavior and the Negative Side of Emotion." *Psychological Science* 16, no. 6 (2005): 435–439.

Shu, Tao, Johan Sulaeman, and P. Eric Yeung. "Does Sadness Influence Investor Behavior? Evidence from Bereaved Fund Managers" (August 2015). Available at SSRN: http://ssrn.com/abstract=2658815 or http://dx.doi.org/10.2139/ssrn.2658815.

Shue, Kelly, and Richard R. Townsend. "Growth through Rigidity: An Explanation for the Rise in CEO Pay" (December 8, 2015). *Journal of Financial Economics* (JFE), forthcoming. Available at SSRN: https://ssrn.com/abstract=2424860 or http://dx.doi.org/10.2139/ssrn.2424860.

Sicherman, Nachum, George Loewenstein, Duane J. Seppi, and Stephen P. Utkus. "Financial Attention" (July 29, 2015). Available at SSRN: http://ssrn.com/abstract=2339287 or http://dx.doi.org/10.2139/ssrn.2339287.

Siegel, Jeremy J., and Richard H. Thaler. "Anomalies: The Equity Premium Puzzle." *Journal of Economic Perspectives* 11 (1997): 191–200.

Slovic, Paul, Melissa Finucane, Ellen Peters, and Donald G. MacGregor. "The Affect Heuristic." In *Heuristics and Biases: The Psychology of Intuitive Judgment,* ed. T. Gilovich, D. Griffin, and D. Kahneman, 397–420. New York: Cambridge University Press, 2002.

Slovic, Paul, Baruch Fischhoff, and Sarah Lichtenstein. "Facts versus Fears: Understanding Perceived Risk." In *Judgment under Uncertainty: Heuristics and Biases,* ed. Daniel Kahneman, Paul Slovic, and Amos Tversky, 463–489. Cambridge, UK: Cambridge University Press, 1982.

Small, Deborah A., George Loewenstein, and Paul Slovic. "Sympathy and Callousness: The Impact of Deliberative Thought on Donations to Identifiable and Statistical Victims." *Organizational Behavior and Human Decision Processes* 102 (2007): 143–153.

Smith, Craig A., and Phoebe C. Ellsworth. "Patterns of Cognitive Appraisal in Emotion." *Journal of Personality & Social Psychology* 48, no. 4 (1985): 813–838.

Snyder, W. Howard T. "How to Take a Loss and Like It." *Financial Analysts Journal* 13, no. 2 (May 1957): 115–116.

Sokol-Hessner, Peter, Ming Hsu, Nina G. Curley, Mauricio R. Delgado, Colin F. Camerer, and Elizabeth A. Phelps. "Thinking Like a Trader Selectively Reduces Individuals' Loss Aversion." *Proceedings of the National Academy of Sciences of the United States of America* 106, no. 13 (2009): 5035–5040.

Solomon, David H., and Eugene F. Soltes. "What Are We Meeting For? The Consequences of Private Meetings with Investors." *Journal of Law and Economics* 58, no. 2 (May 2015): 325–355.

Solomon, David H., Eugene F. Soltes, and Denis Sosyura. "Winners in the Spotlight: Media Coverage of Fund Holdings as a Driver of Flows." *Journal of Financial Economics* 113, no. 1 (July 2014): 53–72.

Solt, Michael E., and Meir Statman. "Good Companies, Bad Stocks." *Journal of Portfolio Management* 15 (1989): 39–44.

Solt, Michael E., and Meir Statman. "How Useful Is the Sentiment Index?" *Financial Analysts Journal* 44, no. 5 (September–October 1988): 45–55.

Soman, Dilip, and Amar Cheema. "Earmarking and Partitioning: Increasing Saving by Low-Income Households." *Journal of Marketing Research* 48 (2011): S14–S22.

Sorkin, Andrew Ross. "Gun Shares Have Done Well, but Divestment Push Grows." *New York Times,* December 8, 2015: B1.

Spaenjers, Christophe. "The Long-Term Returns to Durable Assets." HEC Paris Research Paper No. FIN-2016-1143. March 11, 2016. Available at SSRN: http://ssrn.com/abstract=2746356.

Stambaugh, Robert F., and Yu Yuan. "Mispricing Factors" (July 4, 2015). Available at SSRN: http://ssrn.com/abstract=2626701 or http://dx.doi.org/10.2139/ssrn.2626701.

Stango, Victor, and Jonathan Zinman. "Fuzzy Math, Disclosure Regulation and Credit Market Outcomes: Evidence from Truth in Lending Reform." *SSRN Electronic Journal* (June 2009). Available at SSRN: http://ssrn.com/abstract=1081635 or http://dx.doi.org/10.2139/ssrn.1081635.

Stango, Victor, and Jonathan Zinman. "Limited and Varying Consumer Attention: Evidence from Shocks to the Salience of Bank Overdraft Fees." *Review of Financial Studies* 27, no. 4 (2014): 990–1030.

Stanovich, Keith E., and Richard F. West. "Individual Differences in Reasoning: Implications for the Rationality Debate?" *Behavioral and Brain Sciences* 23, no. 5 (2000): 645–665.

Stanovich, Keith E., and Richard F. West. "On the Relative Independence of Thinking Biases and Cognitive Ability." *Journal of Personality and Social Psychology* 94, no. 4 (2008): 672–695.

Statman, Meir. "Behavioral Finance: Past Battles and Future Engagements." *Financial Analysts Journal* 55 (1999): 18–27.

Statman, Meir. "How Your Emotions Get in the Way of Smart Investing," *Wall Street Journal* (June 15, 2015).

Statman, Meir. "Investor Sentiment, Stock Characteristics, and Returns." *Journal of Portfolio Management* 37 (2011): 54–61.

Statman, Meir. "The 93.6% Question of Financial Advisors." *Journal of Investing* 9, no. 1 (Spring 2000): 16–20.

Statman, Meir. "Quiet Conversations: The Expressive Nature of Socially Responsible Investors." *Journal of Financial Planning* (2008): 40–46.

Statman, Meir. "Socially Responsible Investors and Their Advisors." *Journal of Investment Consulting* 9 (2008): 14–25.

Statman, Meir. "What Do Investors Want?" *Journal of Portfolio Management*, 30th Anniversary Issue (2004): 153–161.

Statman, Meir. *What Investors Really Want.* New York: McGraw-Hill, 2011.

Statman, Meir, Kenneth L. Fisher, and Deniz Anginer. "Affect in a Behavioral Asset Pricing Model." *Financial Analysts Journal* 64, no. 2 (March–April 2008): 20–29.

Statman, Meir, and Denys Glushkov. "Classifying and Measuring the Performance of Socially Responsible Funds." *Journal of Portfolio Management* 42, no. 2 (Winter 2016): 140–151.

Statman, Meir, and Denys Glushkov. "The Wages of Social Responsibility." *Financial Analysts Journal* 65 (2009): 33–64.

Statman, Meir, and Jonathan Scheid. "Correlation, Return Gaps, and the Benefits of Diversification." *Journal of Portfolio Management* 34 (2008): 132–139.

Staw, Barry M. "Knee-Deep in the Big Muddy: A Study of Escalating Commitment to a Chosen Course of Action." *Organizational Behavior and Human Performance* (June 1976): 27–44.

Stephens, Thomas Alexander, and Jean-Robert Tyran. "'At Least I Didn't Lose Money': Nominal Loss Aversion Shapes Evaluations of Housing Transactions" (October 12, 2012). University of Copenhagen Department of Economics Discussion Paper No. 12-14. Available at SSRN: https://ssrn.com/abstract=2162415 or http://dx.doi.org/10.2139/ssrn.2162415.

Steverman, Ben. "Motif Investing: How to Invest around a Theme." *Bloomberg.com*, October 8, 2015. http://www.bloomberg.com/news/articles/2015-10-08/motif-investing-how-to-invest-around-a-theme.

Stewart, James B. "The Narrative Frays for Theranos and Elizabeth Holmes." *New York Times*, October 29, 2015. http://www.nytimes.com/2015/10/30/business/the-narrative-frays-for-theranos-and-elizabeth-holmes.html?_r=0.

Stigler, George J. "The Cost of Subsistence." *Journal of Farm Economics* 27 (1945): 303–314.

Strahilevitz, Michal Ann, Terrance Odean, and Brad M. Barber. "Once Burned, Twice Shy: How Naive Learning, Counterfactuals, and Regret Affect the Repurchase of Stocks Previously Sold." *Journal of Marketing Research* 48 (Special Issue 2011): S102–S120.

Suetens, Sigrid, Claus Bjorn Galbo-Jörgensen, and Jean-Robert Tyran. "Predicting Lotto Numbers: A Natural Experiment on the Gambler's Fallacy and the Hot Hand Fallacy." *Journal of the European Economic Association* 14, no. 3 (2016): 584–607.

Summers, Barbara, and Darren Duxbury. "Decision-Dependent Emotions and Behavioral Anomalies." *Organizational Behavior and Human Decision Processes* 118, no. 2 (July 2012): 226–238.

Sussman, Abigail B., and Adam L. Alter. "The Exception Is the Rule: Underestimating and Overspending on Exceptional Expenses." *Journal of Consumer Research* 39 (2012): 800–814.

Sussman, Abigail B., and Rourke L. O'Brien. "Knowing When to Spend: Unintended Financial Consequences of Earmarking to Encourage Savings." *Journal of Marketing Research* 53, no. 5 (October 2016): 790–803.

Sussman, Abigail B., and Christopher Y. Olivola. "Axe the Tax: Taxes Are Disliked More Than Equivalent Costs." *Journal of Marketing Research* 48 (November 2011): 91–101.

Svenson, Ola. "Are We All Less Risky and More Skillful Than Our Fellow Drivers?" *Acta Psychologica* 47, no. 2 (1981): 143–148.

Tach, Laura, and Sara Sternberg Greene. "'Robbing Peter to Pay Paul': Economic and Cultural Explanations for How Lower-Income Families Manage Debt." *Social Problems* 61, no. 1 (2014): 1–21.

Taleb, Nassim Nicholas. *The Black Swan: The Impact of the Highly Improbable*. New York: Random House, 2007.

Tenney, Elizabeth R., Jennifer M. Logg, and Don A. Moore. "(Too) Optimistic about Optimism: The Belief That Optimism Improves Performance." *Journal of Personality and Social Psychology* 108, no. 3 (March 2015): 377–399.

Teo, Melvyn, and Paul G. J. O'Connell. "Prospect Theory and Institutional Investors" (October 2003). Available at SSRN: https://ssrn.com/abstract=457741 or http://dx.doi.org/10.2139/ssrn.457741.

Tetlock, Paul C. "Liquidity and Prediction Market Efficiency" (May 1, 2008). Available at SSRN: https://ssrn.com/abstract=929916 or http://dx.doi.org/10.2139/ssrn.929916.

Thaler, Richard H., and Cass R. Sunstein. *Nudge: Improving Decisions about Health, Wealth, and Happiness.* New Haven, CT: Yale University Press, 2008.

Thompson, Jeffrey P. "Do Rising Top Incomes Lead to Increased Borrowing in the Rest of the Distribution?" FEDS Working Paper No. 2016-046 (May 2, 2016). Available at SSRN: http://ssrn.com/abstract=2783607 or http://dx.doi.org/10.17016/FEDS.2016.046.

Thornton, Russ. "The Levers to Financial Freedom." *Advisor Perspectives*, September 1, 2009. http://www.advisorperspectives.com/newsletters09/pdfs/The_Levers_to_Financial_Freedom.pdf.

Tobin, James. "Liquidity Preference as Behavior toward Risk." *Review of Economic Studies* 25 (1958): 65–86.

Tversky, Amos, and Daniel Kahneman. "Judgment under Uncertainty: Heuristics and Biases." *Science* 185 (1974): 1124–1131.

USAMutual. "Barrier Funds." March 31, 2015. http://www.usamutuals.com/i/u/6149817/f/Fact_Sheet_-_Barrier_Fund-2015-Q1.pdf

US Commission on the Review of the National Policy toward Gambling. "Gambling in America: Final Report of the Commission on the Review of the National Policy Toward Gambling." Washington, DC: Commission on the Review of the National Policy toward Gambling, 1976.

US Department of Labor. "Private Pension Plan Bulletin Historical Tables and Graphs." Employee Benefits Security Administration (September 2014). http://www.dol.gov/ebsa/pdf/historicaltables.pdf.

US Department of the Treasury. "MyRA—My Retirement Account." March 01, 2016. http://www.treasury.gov/initiatives/myra/Pages/default.aspx.

Varchaver, Nicholas. "What Warren Thinks . . ." *Fortune,* April 14, 2008. Available at http://money.cnn.com/galleries/2008/fortune/0804/gallery.buffett.fortune/index.html.

Vardi, Nathan. "Mathew Martoma Sentenced to Nine Years for Insider Trading." *Forbes,* September 8, 2014. Available at http://www.forbes.com/sites/nathanvardi/2014/09/08/mathew-martoma-sentenced-to-nine-years-for-insider-trading/print/

Venti, Steven F., and David A. Wise. "Aging and Housing Equity: Another Look." NBER Working Paper No. w8608 (November 2001).

Venti, Steven F., and David A. Wise. "Aging and Housing Equity: Another Look." In *Perspectives on the Economics of Aging,* ed. David A. Wise, 127–180. Chicago: University of Chicago Press, 2004.

Vettese, Fred M. "How Spending Declines with Age, and the Implications for Workplace Pension Plans." C. D. Howe Institute e-brief 238 (June 16, 2016). Available at SSRN: http://ssrn.com/abstract=2799376.

Vissing-Jorgensen, Annette. "Consumer Credit: Learning Your Customer's Default Risk from What (S)He Buys" (April 13, 2011). Available at SSRN: http://ssrn.com/abstract=2023238.

Wade, Nicholas. "Tests on Mice Block Defense by Cancer." *New York Times* (November 27, 1997): A28.

Wansink, Brian, and Pierre Chandon. "Can 'Low-Fat' Nutrition Labels Lead to Obesity?" *Journal of Marketing Research* 43, no. 4 (November 2006): 605–617.

Warshawsky, Mark J. "Illustrating Retirement Income for Defined Contribution Plan Participants: A Critical Analysis of the Department of Labor Proposal." *Journal of Retirement* 3 (2015): 12–26.

Wason, Peter C. "On the Failure to Eliminate Hypotheses in a Conceptual Task." *Quarterly Journal of Experimental Psychology* 12 (1960): 129–140.

Wealthfront. "Investment Management, Online Financial Advisor." https://www.wealthfront.com/.

Weinstein, Mark. "The Effect of a Rating Change Announcement on Bond Price." *Journal of Financial Economics* 5, no. 3 (1977): 271–442.

Weinstein, Neil D. "Unrealistic Optimism about Future Life Events." *Journal of Personality and Social Psychology* 39 (1980): 806–820.

Westen, Drew, Pavel S. Blagov, Keith Harenski, Clint Kilts, and Stephan Hamann. "Neural Bases of Motivated Reasoning: An fMRI Study of Emotional Constraints on Partisan Political Judgment in the 2004 U.S. Presidential Election." *Journal of Cognitive Neuroscience* 18 (2006): 1947–1958.

Weston, J. Fred. "Some Theoretical Aspects of Formula Timing Plans." *Journal of Business* 22, no. 4 (October 1949): 249–270.

Wildau, Gabriel. "China Takes on 'Rat Traders' in Stock Market Probe." *Financial Times* (July 7, 2014).

Williams, John Burr. *The Theory of Investment Value.* Burlington, VT: Fraser Publishing Company, 1938.

Wolpert, Stuart. "UCLA Psychologists Discover a Gene's Link to Optimism, Self-Esteem." *UCLA Newsroom*, September 13, 2011. http://newsroom.ucla.edu/releases/ucla-life-scientists-discover-215259.

Wright, Colby, Prithviraj Banerjee, and Vaneesha R. Boney. "Behavioral Finance: Are the Disciples Profiting from the Doctrine?" *Journal of Investing* 17, no. 4 (Winter 2008): 82–90.

Wu, Charlene C., Peter Bossaerts, and Brian Knutson. "The Affective Impact of Financial Skewness on Neural Activity and Choice." *PLoS ONE* 6, no. 2 (February 15, 2011). Available at SSRN: http://ssrn.com/abstract=1762399.

Yablon, Jeffery L. "Avoidance, Evasion, and Planning." In *As Certain as Death—Quotations about Taxes*, Tax Analysts, 2010: 223–259. http://www.taxanalysts.com/www/freefiles.nsf/Files/Yablon2010_9_Avoidance.pdf/$file/Yablon2010_9_Avoidance.pdf.

Ye, Pengfei. "Does the Disposition Effect Matter in Corporate Takeovers? Evidence from Institutional Investors of Target Companies." *Journal of Financial and Quantitative Analysis* 49 (2014): 221–248.

Yenkey, Christopher B. "Distrust and Market Participation: Social Relations as a Moderator of Organizational Misconduct" (January 3, 2016). Available at SSRN: http://ssrn.com/abstract=2566000 or http://dx.doi.org/10.2139/ssrn.2566000.

Yip, Jeremy A., and Martin Schweinsberg. "Infuriating Impasses: Expressing Anger Increases Negotiation Impasses" (April 22, 2016). Available at SSRN: http://ssrn.com/abstract=2628940.

Young, Jean A. "The Auto Savings Generation: Steering Millennials to Better Retirement Outcomes." *Vanguard Research* (October 2014). https://institutional.vanguard.com/iam/pdf/GENERP.pdf?cbdForceDomain=false.

Young, Maia J., Larissa Z. Tiedens, Heajung Jung, and Ming-Hong Tsai. "Mad Enough to See the Other Side: Anger and the Search for Disconfirming Information." *Cognition & Emotion* 25 (2011): 10–21.

Zajonc, Robert B. "Feeling and Thinking: Preferences Need No Inferences." *American Psychologist* 35 (1980): 151–175.

Zeelenberg, Marcel, Jane Beattie, Joop Van Der Pligt, and Nanne K. De Vries. "Consequences of Regret Aversion: Effects of Expected Feedback on Risky Decision Making." *Organizational Behavior and Human Decision Processes* 65, no. 2 (February 1996): 148–158.

Zhang, Hong. "Dynamic Beta, Time-Varying Risk Premium, and Momentum" (July 2004). Yale ICF Working Paper No. 04-26. Available at SSRN: https://ssrn.com/abstract=571006.

Zhang, Yan, Ye Li, and Ting Zhu. "How Multiple Anchors Affect Judgment: Evidence from the Lab and eBay" (November 25, 2014). Columbia Business School Research Paper No. 14-62. Available at SSRN: https://ssrn.com/abstract=2530690 or http://dx.doi.org/10.2139/ssrn.2530690.

AUTHOR INDEX

SUBJECT INDEX

empirical, 257, 261, 263–64,
    286, 333–34
factor, 260–65, 278, 280–86, 332–34
factor-based behavioral, 286
factor-based standard, 286
four-factor, 280–82, 333
theoretical rationales, 257, 263,
    279–80, 285–86
three-factor, 261–63, 278, 283,
    286, 332–33
assets, 25, 108, 129, 146–47, 153, 189,
    201, 204, 210, 214, 219–20,
    224–25, 236, 240, 247, 253, 255,
    258–59, 261, 265, 268, 270,
    276, 283–85
  intangible, 261
  tangible, 261
association, 40, 45, 49, 85–86, 104,
    117–18, 159, 253–55, 257,
    262–70, 272–73, 275–76, 278,
    280, 304, 330
  empirical, 257, 262–64, 266–68, 270,
    272, 276
  fleeting, 265–66
  perverse, 264
  reliable, 49
  strong, 85, 263–64, 267–68, 278
  weak, 268, 272, 278
assumption, 225, 258, 293, 327, 334
  implicit, 293, 334
asylum, 55
asymmetry, 302, 313
Atlantic Ocean, 293
attentional activity, 73
attraction, 153, 169
attractiveness, 81, 96, 229
  physical, 229
attributes, 268–69
auction, 23, 42, 84
  art, 84
audio novels, 105
auditors, 109–10
Australia, 15, 26, 144, 238, 245–46
Australian, 246, 314
auto-dimming rearview mirror, 339
auto maker, 338
automatic
  employer contributions, 244
  enrollment, 243–44, 251
  reinvestment, 139

automatic action, 147
automobile, 84, 338–39, 342–43
  buyers, 342
  markets, 339
automobiles, 317, 338–39, 342–43
autonomy, 107, 244
availability, 13, 36, 39, 58–59, 69, 90,
    94–95, 101, 106, 109, 114, 139,
    233, 277–78, 288, 298, 308, 312
average cost, 86–87, 159–60, 162
  overruns, 86–87
average-down, 153
average income, 97
averse, 22, 89, 124–25, 127, 129, 176,
    195, 198, 201, 258
  loss, 124–25
aversion, 22, 74, 76, 78, 80, 84, 102,
    119–27, 130–34, 141, 152–53,
    159, 164–66, 168, 171, 176, 183,
    191, 193, 195–96, 201, 204, 233,
    258, 309
  ambiguity, 22
  regret, 80, 119, 131, 133, 152–53, 168,
    193, 233
award, 131, 287, 335

Bachelorette, 81
badness, 272
bags, 333
  5-pound, 333
  6-pound, 333
  sugar, 333
balances, 24, 33, 41, 97, 111, 153, 171,
    200, 218, 225, 230, 233–35,
    245–46, 322, 342
  credit card, 41, 97, 111
  defined-contribution, 225,
    233, 245–46
  spending, 225, 233, 245
ball, 67, 82, 265
  cotton, 82
Balloon Analog Risk task, 79
balloon explosions, 79
balloons, 79
balloon task, 79
bank advertisement, 19
bankers, 29, 46
banking, 24
bankruptcy, 101, 226–27, 269, 323
  filings, 227

banks, 28, 43, 85, 107, 151, 318
central, 43
Barclays Capital US Aggregate Bond
Index, 215
Barrier Fund, 282
baseball, 55, 101, 140, 157
players, 101, 157
umpires, 55
base-rate, 52–55, 68–69, 87, 98–99,
308–9, 341
information, 52–55, 68–69, 87,
98–99, 308–9, 341
low, 54
neglect, 98
bearish, 48–49, 74, 85, 325, 327
consumer, 74
Bear Stearns, 52
beat the market, 5, 58, 66, 98, 238,
288–89, 291–92, 295–306, 308,
310–11, 314–15, 318–22,
335, 340–41
failures, 301
beat-the-market investors, 303–5, 340
do-it-yourself, 304–5
players, 303
behavior, 1–2, 4–5, 12–13, 26, 30, 33,
39–40, 47, 66, 71, 73, 80, 82–83,
93–96, 106–7, 113–14, 137, 139,
141, 143, 145, 147, 149, 151–53,
155, 157, 159, 161, 163, 165–67,
169–71, 177, 179, 181, 183,
185–87, 189, 191, 193, 195, 197,
199, 201, 203, 205, 207, 209,
211, 213, 215, 217, 221, 223, 225,
227–29, 231, 233, 235, 237–41,
243, 245, 247, 249, 251, 255, 257,
259, 261, 263, 265, 267, 269,
271, 273, 275, 277, 279, 281, 283,
285, 289, 291, 293, 295, 297,
299, 301–3, 305–7, 309–11, 313,
315, 317, 319, 321, 323, 325, 327,
329, 331, 333, 335, 337, 339,
341, 343–44
addictive, 83
consumer, 30, 186, 309
financial, 1–2, 5, 12–13, 39–40, 71,
93–95, 106, 113–14, 171–72, 186,
209–10, 212, 227, 229, 237–40,
269–70, 306–7, 337, 340

normal, 2, 4–5, 26, 113–14, 137, 180,
245–46, 255, 337, 344
physician, 107
behavioral asset pricing rationales, 276
Behavioral Efficient Markets, 287
behavioral finance, 2–5, 37, 67, 90–91,
112, 116, 135, 173, 175–76, 178,
180, 182, 184, 186, 188, 190, 192,
194, 196, 198, 200, 202, 204,
206, 208, 210, 212, 214, 216,
218–20, 222, 226, 228, 230–32,
234, 236, 238, 240, 242, 244,
246, 248, 250–51, 254, 256, 258,
260, 262, 264, 266, 268, 270,
272, 274, 276, 278, 280, 282,
284, 286–88, 290, 292, 294, 296,
298, 300, 302, 304, 306, 308,
310, 312, 314, 318, 320, 322,
324, 326, 328, 330, 332, 334–35,
337–38, 340, 342–44
lessons of, 2, 337, 343
theory of, 175, 219, 251, 326
behavioral impediments, 233
behavioral portfolios, 175, 201–4, 223
constructing, 201
behavioral portfolio theory, 3, 175–77,
181, 196, 200, 202–3, 205, 208–9,
218, 337, 343
behavioral portfolio theory in
practice, 208
behavioral-wants frontiers, 175, 180,
183, 196, 218
beliefs, 18, 49, 68, 74, 86, 88–89, 109,
152, 166, 186, 306
incorrect, 89
optimistic, 86
benefits, 1–5, 9–12, 14–15, 17–18, 20–25,
27–37, 43, 79, 89, 95, 102,
106, 109, 116, 127–32, 135–36,
139–40, 144–48, 151, 155, 158,
160–62, 166, 169, 171, 175–76,
179–84, 186–90, 195, 200–201,
203, 210, 218, 220, 222–23, 231,
236, 239, 242, 248–49, 253–58,
265, 267, 275–76, 278–81, 286,
288–90, 292, 302, 305–6, 311,
320–21, 324, 337–40, 342–43
corporate pension, 242
current, 36, 129–30, 180, 220, 231, 280